Historical Guide to
World Media Freedom

Historical Guide to World Media Freedom

A Country-by-Country Analysis

Jenifer Whitten-Woodring
University of Massachusetts Lowell

Douglas A. Van Belle
Victoria University of Wellington

Los Angeles | London | New Delhi
Singapore | Washington DC

Los Angeles | London | New Delhi
Singapore | Washington DC

FOR INFORMATION:

CQ Press
An Imprint of SAGE Publications, Inc.
2455 Teller Road
Thousand Oaks, California 91320
E-mail: order@sagepub.com

SAGE Publications Ltd.
1 Oliver's Yard
55 City Road
London EC1Y 1SP
United Kingdom

SAGE Publications India Pvt. Ltd.
B 1/I 1 Mohan Cooperative Industrial Area
Mathura Road, New Delhi 110 044
India

SAGE Publications Asia-Pacific Pte. Ltd.
3 Church Street
#10-04 Samsung Hub
Singapore 049483

Printed in the United States of America.

Library of Congress Cataloging-in-Publication Data

Whitten-Woodring, Jenifer.

Historical guide to world media freedom : a country-by-country analysis / Jenifer Whitten-Woodring, University of Massachusetts Lowell, Douglas A. Van Belle, Victoria University of Wellington.

pages cm
Includes bibliographical references and index.

ISBN 978-1-60871-765-1 (hardcover : alk. paper)

1. Freedom of the press. 2. Government and the press. 3. Mass media—Censorship. 4. Censorship. 5. Freedom of expression. I. Van Belle, Douglas A., 1965–II. Title.

PN4735.W55 2014

323.44'5—dc23   2014009490

This book is printed on acid-free paper.

Acquisitions Editor: Jim Brace-Thompson
Developmental Editor: Diana E. Axelsen
Production Editor: David C. Felts
Copy Editor: Deanna Noga
Typesetter: C&M Digitals (P) Ltd.
Proofreaders: Jeff Bryant, Sally Jaskold
Indexer: Mary Mortensen
Cover Designer: Rose Storey
Marketing Manager: Carmel Schrire

14 15 16 17 18 10 9 8 7 6 5 4 3 2 1

Contents

Preface

This book was born out of a four-inch red binder, overstuffed to the point of bursting with coding notes from our work on the update of the Global Press Freedom Data (which is available at http://faculty.uml.edu/Jenifer_whitten woodring). We were discussing coding issues over lunch, and as we flipped through that binder, using the notes on how the media environment had shifted and changed over time, in country after country, we realized that it was more than just notes. It was a collection of stories that needed to be told. Fortunately, we had no idea how complicated it would be or how long it would take to integrate the contents of the binder with the box of index cards from the original coding and turn that mess into a book. If we had known how much work it would be, we probably would not have tackled the project. This book is a qualitative companion to the Global Media Freedom Dataset, but it is much more than simply a collection of histories on the evolution of media freedom for 196 countries. Instead, it is an analytical history of media freedom that examines the concept itself, the definitions (or lack thereof) that people have used, the way the idea has been championed and challenged over time, and from that foundation, there is then the collection of information on how media freedom as a political condition has developed, evolved, and disintegrated around the world.

It may surprise many to learn that media freedom is a difficult concept to pin down and define. The biggest problem in both defining and evaluating media freedom stems from its entanglement with ideology. Many studies of news media have focused on an idealized conceptualization of journalism as a fourth estate that holds government accountable. Thus, media freedom has historically been defined by the factors that limit it or prevent it from fulfilling this function. Often, this results in an unrealistic emphasis on activist journalism. Not only does this lead to an exaggeration of minor variations among Western countries with well-established free media environments, but it also makes it a challenge to apply a consistent coding regime over time. The information on media function and practice that is emphasized in the past few decades, and in the descriptions of Western countries, is scarce in discussions of the 1950s and 1960s, and still sometimes difficult to find for many countries in Asia, Africa, South America, and Oceania. Often, the information that was available reads like a list of infractions of an undefined ideal media freedom rather than a real discussion of the political, economic, and social environment. Often, there was little information about the extent to which journalists could and did criticize government, which was our key criterion. As a result, we had to gather a great deal of general historical information for each country to evaluate, describe, and explain the shifts in the media environment over time.

This project was completed with substantial assistance and patience from our friends, family, and colleagues. We would like to thank Doug Goldenberg-Hart, formerly of CQ Press, for believing in this project when we showed him that red binder and for not giving up on us when it took years longer than expected to complete. The editorial team at SAGE/CQ Press led by Diana Axelsen and Jim Brace-Thompson deserve a special thank you for their extraordinary patience and expertise. We appreciate the support of the University of Massachusetts Lowell, especially the Department of Political Science, Dr. Fred Lewis, Dean Luis M. Falcón, and Provost Ahmed Abdelal. And we have to thank Pat James at the University of Southern California for recognizing our mutual interest in media freedom and introducing us.

This book would not have been possible if we had not been able to access the early reports gathered by the International Press Institute (IPI); thus, we are grateful to IPI Executive Director

Alison McKenzie for allowing us access to the IPI archives in Vienna, Austria; to Christiane Klint, Membership & Global Relations, for her assistance in sorting through all those years of reports; and to the IPI staff whose advocacy and assistance has helped reporters worldwide and whose monitoring of media freedom provides a valuable resource for scholars. We also appreciate Paul Losch for responding to our call for help in gathering information about the Americas and providing access to the early reports of the Inter American Press Association in the Latin American Collection at the University of Florida's Smathers Library. Thanks to historians Abby Chandler, Lisa Edwards, and Tom Maulucci for helping these political scientists locate historical resources, and the team of research assistants at the University of Southern California and the University of Massachusetts Lowell who helped with the data gathering—Kaitlin Everly, Ellen Fehr, Pamela Mizuno, Natalia Nyczak, Amanda Peterson, Brett Power, and Jai-Ayla Sutherland. And thanks especially to Salvatore Schiano who came on board during the final push to finish this book and provided invaluable research assistance when we needed it most!

Finally, we would not have been able to complete this project without the support and patience of our families, especially our spouses, Terry and Wendy; our children, Patrick, Alex, Tabitha, Jensen, and Samantha; and David, Jo, and Guy Whitten. We spent many family holidays and weekends writing about media freedom.

Jenifer Whitten-Woodring
Douglas A. Van Belle

About the Authors

Jenifer Whitten-Woodring is an assistant professor in the Department of Political Science at the University of Massachusetts Lowell. Her research focuses on the causes and effects of media freedom and the role of media in repression and dissent. Her articles have been published in *The Journal of Conflict Resolution, International Studies Quarterly,* and *Political Communication.* Prior to becoming a political scientist, Whitten-Woodring worked as a journalist in print and broadcast media and received five first place awards from the New York State Associated Press Broadcasters Association. She became particularly interested in media freedom and the relationship between media and politics when she was a journalism instructor and student newspaper adviser, first at Cedar Crest College and then at California State University at San Marcos. To pursue these research interests, she went back to school and completed her PhD in Politics and International Relations at the University of Southern California in 2010. She also has a master's degree in Radio, Television, and Film from Syracuse University's Newhouse School.

Douglas A. Van Belle is a Senior Lecturer in Media Studies at Victoria University of Wellington. He was the first person to have served as the president of both the Foreign Policy Analysis and the International Communication research sections in the International Studies Association. He has also served as the Editor-in-Chief of *International Studies Perspectives* and *Foreign Policy Analysis* and has conducted extensive research on media systems and information flows in international politics. He created the press freedom data set that precedes this study, to examine the effect of media freedom on international conflict, as exemplified by "Press Freedom and the Democratic Peace" (*Journal of Peace Research*). That initial analysis was expanded to complete *Press Freedom and Global Politics* (Praeger), which provides the foundation for the extension conducted here. Studies of popular media and political theory led to the undergraduate textbook, *A Novel Approach to Politics*, which is now in its 4th edition. Also, before returning to the analysis of media freedom with this project, he conducted a series of studies examining the relationship between information flows, disasters, and foreign aid, including *Media, Bureaucracies and Foreign Aid* (Palgrave: With Potter and Rioux).

Chapter 1

Introduction

A journalist is a grumbler, a censurer, a giver of advice, a regent of sovereigns, a tutor of nations. Four hostile newspapers are more to be feared than a thousand bayonets.

—Napoleon Bonaparte

For hundreds of years, people have assumed that news media are a powerful force against corruption, repression, and dictatorship, but only as long as media are free from government control. Media freedom is seen as critical to democracy and perhaps even a key to spreading democracy. Human rights organizations advocate for media freedom in nondemocratic countries, and Western democracies spend millions on media assistance programs aimed at encouraging the development of media freedom, providing better access to media and improving the quality of journalism in developing countries. Almost every country on the planet has some sort of constitutional guarantee of media freedom, and each of these countries also has laws that restrict media freedom. Even in countries with limited media freedom, journalists risk their lives to bring people news that is critical of government (see the picture and story about Japanese photographer Kenji Nagai who was killed while trying to document the Burmese military's brutal treatment of protesters) (Human Rights Watch 2007). Although there is great demand for media freedom, we

BOX 1.1

A DEADLY PROFESSION

September 2007, Yangon, Myanmar (also known as Burma): Japanese photographer Kenji Nagai was trying to document the Burmese military's brutal crackdown on nonviolent protesters when he was fatally shot. We see him here pleading for his life. Reuters Chief Photographer Adrees Latif won a Pulitzer Prize for this photo.

In an effort to keep the rest of the world from learning about the crackdown, the Burmese generals silenced mobile phone networks and halted Internet traffic. These measures constrained the flow of information to a mere trickle, but some news did reach the rest of the world.

Some enterprising and brave individuals found ways to get mobile phone video footage of the demonstrations and crackdown out of the country and onto the world's television screens. This provided a small window into the violence and repression.

Source: Human Rights Watch (2007).

Kenji Nagai of APF tries to take photographs as he lies injured after police and military officials fired upon and then charged at protesters in Yangon's city center, in Myanmar (Burma) on September 27, 2007. Nagai, 50, a Japanese video journalist, was shot by soldiers as they fired to disperse the crowd. Nagai later died.

Source: Reuters/Adrees Latif.

know very little about it and how it has evolved and devolved across countries and over time. With this book we seek to answer some basic questions about media freedom. How has media freedom developed and changed in different countries? How have governments sought to limit media freedom? What is the role of media freedom in democratic and nondemocratic countries? And what exactly *is* media freedom?

Defining media freedom is surprisingly difficult—so difficult that most people who defend it, study it, and measure it fail to specify what they really mean by *media freedom*. Defenders of media freedom document violations of it. For example, since 1950, the International Press Institute (www.freemedia.at) has been monitoring and interceding when governments imprison, harass, and sometimes even murder journalists, but this focus on government infringement on media freedom only tells us what prevents media freedom. It does little to explain what media freedom actually is. Freedom House (www.freedomhouse.org) provides annual press freedom scores for all available countries, but again the focus is on what constrains media freedom. Defining media freedom is a challenge that we take up in Chapter 2. For now, let's just say that media freedom has to do with whether journalists are able to function independently of the government so that they are able to safely let people know what the political leaders are doing, even if those leaders would prefer that journalists not provide this information. Because independence from government control is an important aspect of media freedom, we will sometimes refer to media freedom as *media independence*.

You may have noticed by now that we are using the term *media freedom* instead of *press freedom*. Actually, we use both terms interchangeably throughout the rest of this book. Literally, press freedom has to do with freedom of printed journalism, meaning newspapers and magazines, but most people who use the term *press freedom* are concerned about violations of journalistic freedom in other media as well. Print journalism came first (well, actually after town criers, wandering minstrels, and marathon runners—and even those early purveyors of information had to be careful about the messages they communicated, but that is going back a bit too far). Because print journalism was the first mass medium for communicating

information, it was also the first medium that those in power, especially government leaders, sought to systematically control through censorship, taxation, intimidation, imprisonment, and sometimes even murder. With the emergence of radio in early 1900s and then television in 1940s, the printed press was no longer the only game in town. From the beginning, broadcast journalists faced similar pressures and attacks as print journalists. Now, with the increased popularity of the Internet, bloggers and tweeters are facing similar threats. The Committee to Protect Journalists (www.cpj.org), an organization that tracks attacks on journalists, is now documenting a number of attacks on online journalists:

> Laws like the Computer Crime Act [in Thailand], originally presented as targeting hackers and those who commit fraud, are being applied to reporters and news websites around the world. And in many cases, from Angola to Saudi Arabia, governments are using claims of online disorder as a cover to introduce far more repressive laws that unashamedly target journalists and the right to free expression. (O'Brian 2012, para. 4)

Journalists are vulnerable to censorship regardless of the medium they use. So when we talk about *press freedom* these days, we actually mean *media freedom*, and we apply these terms to any medium used to transmit news and information.

Media freedom is part of a larger group of rights that fall under the umbrella of the right to *freedom of expression*. According to Article 19 of the Universal Declaration of Human Rights (www.un.org/en/documents/udhr):

> Everyone has the right to freedom of opinion and expression; this right includes freedom to hold opinions without interference and to seek, receive and impart information and ideas through any media and regardless of frontiers. (United Nations 1948)

Similarly, the First Amendment to the U.S. Constitution (http://www.archives.gov/exhibits/charters/constitution.html) provides a list of rights that are included under the freedom of expression:

Congress shall make no law respecting an establishment of religion, or prohibiting the free exercise thereof; or abridging the freedom of speech, or of the press; or the right of the people peaceably to assemble, and to petition the Government for a redress of grievances.

Thus, freedom of expression includes freedom of artistic expression, freedom of religious expression, freedom of speech (for everyone, not just journalists), freedom to assemble, and freedom to petition, as well as freedom of the press (these days meaning journalists using any medium).

Today, ideals and idealism reverberate through every discussion of freedom of expression and, in particular, media freedom. In an ideal world, journalists who are free to do so would provide citizens with important information about political candidates, public officials, government agencies, business leaders, and businesses, and this information would be unbiased so that people could form their own opinions. In this same ideal world, newspapers, radio stations, television stations, and online news sites would provide a voice for the voiceless and give ordinary citizens a platform to express their own ideas. And finally, these same journalists would investigate the actions and policies of political officials, government, businesses, and business leaders. Thus independent news media are expected to provide a venue for people to express their ideas and concerns about their political leaders; they also provide a forum for candidates for political offices to let people know where they stand on important issues and how they compare to their competitors. To put it simply, news media are expected to facilitate political competition. News media are also seen as providing information that is critical to the democratic process. Indeed, without this information, it would be difficult for people make informed decisions when they step into the voting booth. In short, freedom of the press and freedom of expression are seen as crucial to democracy.

In fact, some have argued that freedom of expression, and by extension freedom of the press, is more important to democracy than the right to vote because, "if citizens have the right to complain, to petition, to organize, to protest, to demonstrate, to strike, to threaten to emigrate, to shout, to publish" (Mueller 1992, 984), government will be more responsible and more responsive. In addition to providing information to help people make voting decisions, independent news media are expected to serve as *watchdogs* over government. In this view, news media are a powerful check on government, or as Irish political philosopher Edmond Burke put it, a *fourth estate*, meaning a powerful, but not officially recognized, political force. Thus advocates for press freedom claim that free media will hold government accountable, shine a spotlight on corruption, and improve human rights. "By exposing human rights abuses and giving voice to marginalised parts of the community, the media can at its best encourage the proper application of justice and stimulate debates" (Amnesty International 2006, para. 19).

Whether independent news media actually fulfill this expectation is the subject of much debate among scholars and media critics. In particular, scholars of media and politics in the United States argue that reporters rely too much on official government sources, and that this makes it difficult for news media to serve as watchdogs over government (for more on this critique, see Bennett 2009; Bennett, Lawrence, and Livingston 2007; Entman 2004; Gans 1979; Parenti 1986). Of course, these critiques are based on the idealistic notion that news media should function as watchdogs. While there is much debate about whether news media fulfill this idealized role, there seems to be a consensus—among media critics, consumers, and in particular, journalists—that this is the role that news media *should* play in society.

In fact, the idealistic view of news media and media freedom is probably the biggest challenge we faced in writing this book. Media freedom is an all but sacred cultural meme, and this normative, emotional investment in media freedom as an ideal biases every discussion of the topic, even down to our definitions of media freedom (as you will see in Chapter 2). Because there is a consensus (especially in the United States and Western Europe) that media should be free, most discussions about media freedom focus on how to spread, support, and enhance media freedom. These assumptions also create a hostile environment for questions about whether media freedom should always be spread, supported, and enhanced in all economic, social, cultural, or political contexts.

Make no mistake, independent news media are sometimes irresponsible, disreputable, and even dangerous. Consider the tabloids in the United States that publish lurid stories detailing celebrity love triangles and alien abductions. Consider the *Sun*, a top-selling British newspaper that regularly features photos of topless women. And consider the Ugandan weekly the *Rolling Stone* (pictured here) that published pictures of people it claimed were homosexual with a banner reading "Hang Them" (and no, this Ugandan paper has no connection to the American magazine). Sometimes journalists and citizens use the platform provided by news media and social media to publish material that is deliberately offensive, and the consequences can be deadly. For example, in 2006, the Danish newspaper *Jyllands-Posten* published twelve cartoons featuring the Prophet Muhammad. Depicting the image of Muhammad is considered blasphemous by many Muslims, and these cartoons were particularly provocative because they were intentionally unflattering (one portrayed Muhammad with a bomb in his turban). The cartoons sparked protests around the world, some of which turned violent. In Nigeria, more than 100 people died in riots (Polgreen 2006).

BOX 1.2

WHEN MEDIA ARE
FREE TO SPREAD HATE

October 2010, Kampala, Uganda: The weekly tabloid *Rolling Stone* published 100 pictures of people it claimed were homosexual. The paper also reported that homosexuals were raiding schools and urged readers to "Hang Them" (in a yellow banner on the front page). One of the men pictured on this front page was gay-rights activist David Kato. In January of 2011, Kato and two other activists won a lawsuit against the paper, but just weeks after this victory, Kato was bludgeoned to death with a hammer. Homosexual sex is illegal in Uganda and lawmakers have considered a bill that would impose life imprisonment or the death penalty on those found guilty of engaging in same-sex relations.

Rolling Stone **is a Ugandan newspaper that first attracted international attention in October 2010, when it published a list of the country's "100 Top Homosexuals." The inside pages of that edition featured the names, addresses, and pictures of several alleged homosexuals, some of whom, according to gay rights activists, were reportedly attacked after their involuntary outing and many have gone into hiding in fear of their lives.**

Source: Benedicte Desrus/Sipa Press/Newscom.

The idealization of media freedom is based on the assumption that independent news media will serve as watchdogs and renders taboo questions about when press freedom is problematic. Because of this idealization, many Western scholars focus on subtle nuances in the differences between countries with media freedom and magnify the slightest of shifts in the freedom of the media within these countries. While this vigilance may help maintain a higher level of press freedom, it can also lead to unrealistic expectations of what free media can or should do in these countries. Similarly, this normative focus discourages consideration of the potential for media freedom to have negative effects in nondemocratic countries.

This idealization of media freedom also constrains debates about its costs and benefits. The emotional nature of the normative arguments associated with media freedom is particularly problematic because it tends to go unnoticed or unacknowledged. For example, all too often commentators quote Thomas Jefferson on the merits of press freedom without contextualizing those quotes regarding the practical politics of the early United States and the contentious fight over the ratification of the U.S. Constitution. Similarly, even when a project is focused firmly on the practical aspects of media and politics, media freedom is always assumed to be beneficial.

For example, directors of programs aimed at improving journalism and access to journalism in developing countries seldom take into consideration the potential negative consequences of media freedom, especially the dangers posed to journalists. The idealized role of media freedom is often implicitly treated as a universal truth.

BOX 1.3

Thomas Jefferson—a founding father, the primary author of the Declaration of Independence, and the third president of the United States—is considered one of the early champions of press freedom. Some of his more famous quotes on the subject include the following:

> The basis of our government being the opinion of the people, the very first object should be to keep that right; and were it left to me to decide whether we should have a government without newspapers, or newspapers without a government, I should not hesitate a moment to prefer the latter. But I should mean that every man should receive those papers and be capable of reading them. (1787)

> When the press is free and every man able to read, all is safe. (1799)

> No government ought to be without censors; and where the press is free no one ever will. (1799)

Official presidential portrait of Thomas Jefferson.

Source: White House Historical Association.

During these years Jefferson was involved in political battles, and his statements regarding press freedom are best understood within this context. For example, the "newspapers without government" quote came during the same year as the Constitutional Convention, which pitted the Antifederalists—those who favored independent states—against those who were pushing for a stronger central (federal) government—the Federalists. Antifederalists favored rights such as press freedom because they were against a strong central government. Although he did not attend the Constitutional Convention, Jefferson's political philosophy was more in line with that of the Antifederalists.

Similarly, the quotes from 1799 came in the wake of the Alien and Sedition Acts that were signed by President John Adams in reaction to the French Revolution. In particular, the Sedition Act criminalized opposition to the government and led to the imprisonment of several newspaper editors who were critical of Adams and his administration. Jefferson, a long-time political opponent of Adams, characterized these acts as a "reign of witches" (in reference to the infamous 1692 witch trials in Salem, Massachusetts). When Jefferson defeated Adams in the election of 1800, his campaign song was "Jefferson and Liberty." The lyrics of the first verse promise that "the reign of terror now is o'er; Its gags, inquisitors and spies, Its herds of harpies are no more." During the campaign, Jefferson's party referred to Adams' administration as the "Federalist Reign of Terror" because of the powers assumed by the government through the Alien and Sedition Acts. Though we do not know for sure, it seems likely that the reference to "gags" could be the gags the Sedition Act imposed on freedom of speech and freedom of the press.

Once president, Jefferson pardoned the newspaper editors and others who had been imprisoned under the Sedition Act.

In short, while Jefferson spoke in favor of press freedom and against government censorship, he was doing so for political reasons. His quotes had more to do with politics than ideals.

If we are to truly understand the causes and effects of media freedom, we must confront the challenge presented by its status as a treasured ideal. First and foremost, that idealistic element must be acknowledged, and questions must be asked about how the norms are or might be shaping every aspect of press freedom, from definitions to advocacy to analysis. In this book, we highlight and explore points that are often overwhelmed by the idealization of the topic and propose questions that are underexplored or appear to be overlooked entirely. It is not possible to completely excise normative and cultural frameworks. In fact, the last thing we want to do is to dispute the normative and practical value of media freedom. However, to provide the solid empirical foundation for research and study, we make a conscious effort to dispassionately emphasize the pragmatic side of media freedom.

With this practical view in mind, in Chapter 2, we consider the difficulties in defining and measuring press freedom. We discuss some of the controversies and challenges in conceptualizing a threshold above which news media are able to function freely and below which they are not. We present the simple and minimal definition that we use in this book to compare the evolution and devolution of press freedom within each country from 1948 to 2012.

In Chapter 3, we present an overview of the history of media freedom, from the invention of the printing press to Twitter. Although it is beyond the scope of this book to provide a comprehensive history of media freedom, in order to put the changes within each country in context, we provide a brief recounting of the major developments. In addition to the history of media freedom, we consider why media are sometimes free, sometimes imperfectly free, and sometimes not free. Specifically, we discuss the conditions that make a country more or less likely to have free media—that is, we identify the correlates of media freedom.

Chapter 4 provides a country-by-country account of the changes and developments in media freedom from 1948 to 2012. (We start at 1948, because it marks the end of World War II and the beginning of a new organization of countries in international relations.) Beginning with Afghanistan and finishing with Zimbabwe, we provide a history for each country of how the relationship between news media and government has shifted over the years, focusing in particular on whether journalists have been and are able to criticize political leaders.

References and Further Readings

Amnesty International. 2006. *Press Freedom: Journalists in Need of Protection*. Amnesty International. Available at http://www.amnesty.org/en/news-and-updates/press-freedom-journalists-need-protection-20060305

Bennett, W. Lance. 2009. *News: The Politics of Illusion*. New York: Longman.

Bennett, W. Lance, Regina G. Lawrence, and Steven Livingston. 2007. *When the Press Fails*. Chicago and London: The University of Chicago Press.

Entman, Robert M. 2004. *Projections of Power*. Chicago: University of Chicago Press.

Gans, Herbert J. 1979. *Deciding What's News: A Study of CBS Evening News, NBC Nightly News, Newsweek and Time*. New York: Random House.

Human Rights Watch. 2007. Crackdown: Repression of the 2007 Popular Protests in Burma. Human Rights Watch.

Mueller, John. 1992. "Democracy and Ralph's Pretty Good Grocery: Elections, Equality, and the Minimal Human Being." *American Journal of Political Science* 36 (4): 983–1003.

Newspaper Association of American Foundation. 2005. *Speaking of a Free Press: 200 Years of Notable Quotations About Press Freedoms*. Arlington: Newspaper Association of America Foundation.

O'Brian, Danny. 2012. *Using Internet 'Crime' Laws, Authorities Ensnare Journalists*. Committee to Protect Journalists 2012 [cited March 18 2012]. Available at http://www.cpj.org/2012/02/attacks-on-the-press-in-2011-regulating-the-intern.php.

Parenti, Michael. 1986. *Inventing Reality: The Politics of Mass Media*. New York: St. Martin's Press.

Polgreen, Lydia. 2006. "Nigeria Counts 100 Deaths over Danish Caricatures." *The New York Times*, February 24. Section A; Column 1; p. 8.

United Nations. 1948. Universal Declaration of Human Rights. United Nations.

U.S. Constitution, Amendment 1.

Chapter 2

Defining and Measuring Media Freedom

Given the intense interest in media freedom and the extent of its advocacy around the world, it is surprisingly difficult to identify a clear and precise definition of the concept. This generates significant challenges for any attempt to assemble or use a catalog of information on the topic. At the very least, it means that both the aggregate data and the country summaries provided in this volume must be contextualized regarding definitions, or more accurately, the lack of clear definitions in the literature and how that relates to the plethora of concepts, expectations, presumptions, and often incompatible arguments that have become part of the discussion of media freedom.

In this chapter, we review existing definitions of media freedom or, rather, we review existing definitions of how media freedom is constrained, because although the conceptualization of it has changed over time, media freedom has consistently been defined by the factors that limit it rather than by what it actually is. Yet if we want to research the causes and effects of media freedom, we must be able to assess whether and to what extent media freedom exists in a particular country at a given time. In other words, we have to develop a method of measurement that is reliable (meaning that the method of measurement produces consistent, replicable results), valid (meaning that we are really measuring media freedom), and robust (meaning that the measure can withstand challenges).

We begin by investigating how definitional shortcomings have hindered data gathering efforts. A primary challenge in both defining and measuring media freedom is its ensnarement in ideals regarding the role news media should play in society. We consider the influence of ideals in data gathering efforts and provide a detailed discussion of the Freedom House Freedom of the Press data. We focus on Freedom House because, starting in 2001, this multidimensional conceptualization is most compatible with the historic data we provide in this book. Additionally, we provide an overview and critique of other indices of media freedom that have become available in recent years. We then review the necessary and sufficient conditions for media freedom and introduce the applied definition used for the Global Media Freedom Dataset, which is the foundation for the country reports in this guide. (This dataset is also available in the charts in Appendix A.) Building on this definition, we provide an overview of our coding process and an explanation of how the data were gathered.

To begin with, the language related to laws and other guarantees of press freedom is probably the least valuable information on the topic. Almost all countries have some form of constitutional or legal promise of media freedom or freedom of expression, yet these legal provisions seldom guarantee these rights in practice (Breunig 1994). In fact, these laws are often outright fiction. For example, under Colonel Muammar Muhammad al-Gaddafi, Article 13 of the Libyan Constitution guaranteed media freedom (as an extension of freedom of expression), but only to the extent that media act "within the limits of public interest and the principles of the Revolution" (Libya Constitution 1969). This caveat left open the possibility of defining anything and everything as outside those vague limits, and as a result, prior to the 2011 revolt against Gaddafi, Libya had both a legal guarantee of media freedom and media that were among the most restricted in the world (Freedom House 2010).

Although many constitutional provisions guaranteeing media freedom fail to provide it in practice, the nearly universal existence of these laws appears to reflect an international consensus that media should be free. Article 19 of the United Nations Universal Declaration of Human Rights calls for freedom of expression and specifies that this includes the right "to seek, receive and impart information and ideas through any media" without regard to national boundaries (United Nations 1948). Again, however, both the practical value and the conceptual value of such legalistic statements are at best marginal. All countries, no matter how liberal or free, acknowledge the need for exceptions to this statement for some combination of security, transactional, commercial, and personal privacy reasons. In fact, in the United States, this exception has been turned around to an almost ironic extent with the First Amendment to the Constitution, which guarantees media freedom, also being interpreted as one of the constitutional elements supporting a constitutional guarantee of secrecy in the form of a right to personal privacy. Across the developed and democratic countries that most would agree serve as stalwarts of media freedom, there are libel laws, name suppression for criminal defendants, transactional secrecy provisions that allow government to hide their part in business contract negotiations by conducting them through third parties, decency laws, national and military security exceptions, sedition, treason, responsible speech, hate speech . . . there are so many internationally accepted exceptions to the legal commitments to press freedom or freedom of expression that in any aggregate sense, the legal language of media freedom is not helpful in forming a clear definition of the concept. In spite of the long-standing international call for media freedom, there is little legal agreement regarding what constitutes media freedom.

Changes in technology and society complicate this issue further by turning media freedom into something of a moving target. In fact, not long ago, media freedom would have simply been referred to as *press freedom*, but a few decades of rapid growth in information technologies have seen the electronic dissemination of information overtake if not overwhelm the hardcopy sources that had previously made printing all

but synonymous with the mediated communication of public information. Though we will not try to predict the forms global communication technologies will take in the future, our challenge is to define media freedom in a way that is equally applicable to periods when locally printed newspapers were the only effective form of mass communication and to today's electronically interconnected world.

Further complicating matters, many if not most discussions of media freedom adopt an inverted approach to conceptualizing or addressing the concept. More often than not, media freedom is discussed, examined, or even advocated in terms of what threatens it, or what it is *not* rather than what it *is*. For example, McQuail (2000, 146–47) defines media freedom as "the right to publish without any prior censorship or license and without incurring penalties, within the limits of other legal obligations." Writing in the early years of the 20th century, historian Lucy Maynard Salmon (1923) acknowledged both the variability of the conceptualization of press freedom and the consistency of efforts to compromise it, and it is notable just how often the idea is presented as a reflection of what it is not:

> Preceded by censorship and by regulation, followed by government control and by press bureaus, publicity committees, and organized propaganda, freedom of the press seems reduced to a mere mathematical point. The conception of it has always been fluctuating, never stable. It has been limited in one country by government action, in another by vested wealth, in another by political parties; elsewhere it has been controlled by the Church, in another country by the ascendant industry, in another by chauvinism, and everywhere by authority. (280)

From John Milton's argument in his *Areopagitica* (1644) for an end to prepublication censorship to the Committee to Protect Journalists (2011) "Attacks on the Press" report, there is far more clarity about the factors that constrain media freedom or that threaten its existence than there is regarding the criteria that establish it.

While these kinds of definitions are often useful, the difficulty with taking an inverted approach to a concept is that the term can then be interpreted to include anything not explicitly excluded. This leaves a great deal of room for conceptual and argumentative confusion when similar ideas, associated concepts like democracy, or related facets of the subject are referred to by the same terms. Defining press freedom in terms of the absence of explicit government control has led to debates and discussions of media freedom that include issues such as artistic freedom of expression, pornography, government transparency, government funding of media, elite dominance of news sources, concentrations and diversity of private media ownership, the advertising of prescription medications, and even the legal definition of a financial corporation as a person.

More direct and positive efforts to corral the concept of media freedom have failed to produce better, or more useful, definitions. Siebert (1956b) divided media freedom into negative and positive rights, with the negative aspect being the rights of the press to be free from restraints (in particular, government and economic limitations) and the positive aspect being the right of the people to have access to a free press. This and other attempts to define press freedom in terms of both what it is and what it is not did little to clarify the topic; in fact, they may have created more conceptual problems than they solved.

Evidence of the difficulties that arise from trying to define what media freedom is, or what its ideal form should be, can been found in the U.S. press' rejection of the 1947 report of the Commission on Freedom of the Press. That report warned that the ability of a press to remain free depended on its fulfillment of its democratic responsibilities (Bates 1995). The Commission called for the media to provide

- a truthful, comprehensive, and intelligent account of the day's events in a context which gives them meaning;
- a forum for the exchange of comment and criticism;
- the projection of a representative picture of the constituent groups in the society;
- the presentations and clarification of the goals and values of the society; and
- full access to the day's intelligence. (Commission on Freedom of the Press 1947, pp. 17–29)

Although we will not delve into the objections that led to the rejection of this report as a framework for conceptualizing press freedom, consider the political conflicts that could arise from the normative statements—both explicit and implicit—in those five bullet points. Consider how a conservative critic of the "liberal" news establishment would react to those points. Consider how a liberal critic of the commercialization of the news media would use them. Consider too the similarity of the phrase "the presentations and clarification of the goals and values of the society" to the phrase that Gaddafi used to justify massive repression and control of Libya's media—that media freedom must take place "within the limits of public interest and the principles of the Revolution" (Libya Constitution 1969).

As an example of a more recent effort to define the free media in terms of what it is rather than what it is not, Picard (1985) envisioned the requirements for press freedom as a flight of stairs in which each lower step is a prerequisite for the next step, which in turn yields a higher level of freedom. This staircase begins with basic technology and audience accessibility, progresses to the lack of economic and government constraints and the availability of a variety of media at the middle levels, and ascends to public access, newsroom autonomy and public ownership at the top (Picard 1985).

These, as well as other efforts to build a definition of press freedom around what it does or should do, avoid some of the issues related to an inverted or negative definition. For example, they clearly situate media freedom as a political issue related to the public sphere or the communal aspects of political and social information. This separates the discussion of freedom of expression, particularly regarding the artistic, from the debate over news as the fourth estate of government and other political aspects of its role in society; however, it does very little to help generate a measurable definition, particularly one that can be applied comparatively across diverse societies with differing goals and values.

Definitions and Data Gathering

Surprisingly enough, efforts to gather and catalog data on press freedom have not helped clarify this definitional confusion. Even though the advocates of media freedom include several of the largest nongovernmental organizations (NGOs) in the world—the World Bank, the United Nations, Human Rights Watch, and Amnesty International, to name a few—not to mention government agencies in many of the developed Western democracies in the world, it is difficult to find consistent, reliable, and valid measures of media freedom, particularly historically. The data that do exist often suffer from significant issues related to these definitional shortcomings.

In the wake of World War II, a group of editors founded the International Press Institute (IPI) with aim of promoting press freedom, which the founders defined as "free access to the news, free transmission of news, free publication of newspapers and free expression of views" (International Press Institute 2011). In 1952, the IPI published its first survey of press freedom. However, even though they defined press freedom in what appears to be a positive way, the degree to which their measures are explicitly built from that definition is debatable. Their reports are largely filled with descriptions of the transgressions committed against journalists rather than any consistent, rigorous, or transparent measure of the nature of the political, social, or economic environment in which the media function. The IPI reports, however, are probably the best of the early data gathering efforts, particularly in terms of definition. At least they offer a definition.

In what was probably a reaction to McCarthyism and other cold war threats to the liberal aspects of democracies (see Hocking 1947; Chenery 1955), the late 1950s and early 1960s witnessed a brief surge in academic interest and related empirical studies of press freedom (Nixon 1960, 1965; Farace and Donohew 1965; Farace 1966). In most of this early empirical literature, an understanding of press freedom is taken as a given; no definition, no coding criteria, and no coding methods are discussed (Nixon 1960, 1965). Nixon (1960) sought to identify the conditions that might foster or prevent press freedom, and he hypothesized that literacy and distribution of wealth were important to the development and sustainment of media freedom. He categorized and compared the media in 85 countries and later (Nixon 1965) compared the results from his first study to those of an expanded study which included 117 countries.

He did in fact find that media freedom was associated with countries that had higher literacy rates and greater wealth.

These studies are typical of the period, with the simplicity of the measures and the analyses matching the best tools available at the time; what is not typical is the way the topic disappeared. There is no evolution of the empirical measures; little effort to develop more useful, refined, and measurable definitions; and no effort to apply new methods as the available computational and statistical resources advanced. It was not until Freedom House published its first annual survey in 1978 that a global measure followed up on Nixon's work. The Freedom House data led to a subsequent analysis of the changes that had occurred over this time (Weaver, Buddenbaum, and Fair 1985), but it is not until the end of the century (Van Belle 1997, 2000) that anyone assembles a historical catalog that spans the gap between the 1950s and the 1980s. Van Belle is also the first to use an explicit, albeit simple, definition of press freedom as the starting point for the development of the data and is the first to apply a transparent measurement methodology for anything prior to 1979.

From a broad view, one could argue that the lack of clear definition in the study or analysis of media freedom reflects a presumption that the term represents ideals that are so deeply shared and so completely manifested in the common knowledge that they need no definition. That is clearly the case in the early studies. Unfortunately, this is seldom a reasonable belief. Those elevating the democratic, watchdog ideal of the news media are not talking about the same thing as those who would elevate freedom of expression as the most treasured ideal, and neither is actually talking about the concept of freedom of access that Cook (1998) argues was the real focus of the debates in the United States that led to the First Amendment to the U.S. Constitution. Contrary to the idea of independence of the media from government control or influence, Cook paints an interesting picture of freedom of the press as guaranteeing that the owner of press receiving support in the form of government printing contracts could not manipulate an election or policy debate by shutting out a party or candidate. In other words, Cook suggests the original supporters of the First Amendment viewed a "free press" as one that offers access to all citizens (and all political competitors) so that their views can be heard.

Because of these different and sometimes conflicting ideals, definitional issues are far more prominent in this volume than would normally be expected for a historical guide, and readers may often need to interpret the data and the country reports provided here in terms of these challenges.

BOX 2.1

MONITORING MEDIA FREEDOM

The Inter American Press Association: Tracking Media Freedom in the Americas since 1942

Although the idea to create a permanent organization emerged in 1926 at the first Pan American Congress of Journalists, it was not until the second Congress met in 1942 that the Inter American Press Association (IAPA) was formed.[1] In 1951, the IAPA began to publish its reports, documenting developments in the press and attacks on the press with the aim of fostering "a wider knowledge and greater interchange amongst the peoples of America in support of the basic principles of a free society and individual liberty."[2] From the beginning, a central activity of the IAPA was to track media freedom, and its Committee of Freedom of the Press and Information presented reports twice a year at the General Assemblies and the midyear meetings.

The IAPA membership was made up of owners and editors of print news outlets, and the group was not politically neutral. During the 1960s, the IAPA's quest for press freedom was linked to the fight against communism and any communist sympathies in the press. This was particularly evident in the proceedings of the 1962 Annual Meeting that took place during the Cuban missile crisis:

> We deplore the use of that free press to incite to irresponsible and senseless violence to overthrow democratic governments by force. We cannot and will not, condone irresponsibility of this or any other nature. We prefer that due process of law be followed to counter such organized subversion through the printed word.[3]

Today the IAPA has about 1,400 member publications and continues to provide assessments of the state of media freedom in the Americas at its General Assemblies and midyear meetings.

In the mid-1990s, IAPA launched the Chapultepec Project, and the Declaration of Chapultepec was adopted by the Hemispheric Conference on Free Speech in Mexico City in March 1994. It featured a number of principles, the first of which is "A free press enables societies to resolve their conflicts, promote their well-being and protect their liberty. No law or act of government may limit freedom of expression or of the press, whatever the medium."[4] According to the IAPA, so far the Declaration has been ratified in twenty-four countries.

Honduran President Porfirio Lobo (R) and Gonzalo Marroquin (L) vice president of the Inter American Press Association take part in a ceremony to sign the Chapultepec declaration in Tegucigalpa on February 18, 2010. The Declaration is based on the essential precept that no law or act of government may limit freedom of expression or of the press, whatever the medium of communication.

Source: ORLANDO SIERRA/AFP/Getty Images/Newscom.

Alison Bethel McKenzie, left, executive director of the International Press Institute (IPI), presents the Free Media Pioneer award to members of Malaysia's Radio Free Sarawak including Clare Rewcastle Brown, 2nd left, during a ceremony at the IPI World Congress in Amman, Jordan, May 20, 2013. The congress honored journalists killed in Syria, including Marie Colvin and Mika Yamamoto, while Malaysia's Radio Free Sarawak was presented with the Free Media Pioneer award.

Source: REUTERS/Muhammad Hamed.

(Continued)

(Continued)

The International Press Institute: Tracking Media Freedom since 1951

The International Press Institute (IPI) was founded in 1951 by a group of thirty-four newspaper editors from fifteen countries. Motivated by concerns about the manipulation of news media to spread propaganda during World War II, the founders' goals included protecting and promoting press freedom and improving the quality of journalism.[5] In 1952, the IPI began publishing its monthly *IPI Reports* and held its first general assembly in Paris. In the 1950s, in addition to articles about violations of press freedom, the *IPI Report* featured stories about the detrimental effects of television on newspapers. Yet in 1965, the IPI resolved to allow broadcast journalists to become members. Initially, the IPI was headquartered in Zurich. In 1976, it moved to London, and in 1992, it relocated to its current headquarters in Vienna. Today the IPI has members (most of them editors and media executives) from more than 120 countries.[6] The organization continues to monitor press freedom and sends delegations on press freedom missions to facilitate the development of free and independent media.

Freedom House: Tracking Media Freedom since 1980

First Lady Eleanor Roosevelt is shown here during a radio interview for CBS on September 12, 1937. She was one of the cofounders of Freedom House and an active supporter of the formation of the United Nations.

Source: Keystone Pictures USA/ZUMAPRESS/Newscom.

Freedom House, a nongovernment organization, was founded in 1941 in New York City under the leadership of Eleanor Roosevelt and Wendell Willkie. Initially the goal was to increase support for U.S. involvement in World War II. Following the war, Freedom House's mission transitioned to "the expansion of freedom around the world and the strengthening of human rights and civil liberties" in the United States.[7] In 1980, Freedom House launched its annual Freedom of the Press Report. Today Freedom House's headquarters are in Washington, D.C., but it also maintains offices in New York City, Jordan, Kyrgyzstan, Mexico, and South Africa. In 1980, Freedom House began its series of annual reports on media freedom.

Critics of Freedom House note that the majority of its funding comes from the U.S. government, and some have claimed that this influences Freedom House's reports.[8] Yet a study comparing Freedom House's press freedom measure to that of the French nongovernment organization Reporters Sans Frontiers and the U.S.-based International Research and Exchanges Board (IREX) concluded that the ratings of the three are highly correlated.[9]

Definitions of Media Freedom, Ideals, and the Freedom House Data

The Freedom House data can be used to explore some of the empirical implications of definitions or lack thereof. Several of the points made in this section are critical, but in no way should that be taken as an indictment of the data or the organization. This is both a conceptual discussion about measurement and definitions and a necessary step in linking the historical data provided here to the current and future data provided by Freedom House.

Since 2001, Freedom House has provided a comprehensive discussion of its methodology for coding media freedom around the world. However, it is interesting to note that even

though Freedom House (2012) clearly, transparently, and robustly defines its measurement methodology, it never defines exactly what it is that all its carefully weighted indicators are capturing. Working backward from the empirical indicators makes it possible to identify what might be called a multidimensional, inductive conceptualization of media freedom that is made up of three categories of factors related to a country's media environment—legal, political, and economic—but that is far different than working from a definition to build a measurement and coding scheme to best capture a concept.

The following list of coding questions and weights is reproduced from the Freedom House 2012 annual report.[10]

A. Legal Environment (0–30 Points)

1. Does the constitution or other basic laws contain provisions designed to protect freedom of the press and of expression, and are they enforced? (0–6 points)

2. Do the penal code, security laws, or any other laws restrict reporting, and are journalists punished under these laws? (0–6 points)

3. Are there penalties for libeling officials or the state, and are they enforced? (0–3 points)

4. Is the judiciary independent, and do courts judge cases concerning the media impartially? (0–3 points)

5. Is freedom of information legislation in place, and are journalists able to make use of it? (0–2 points)

6. Can individuals or business entities legally establish and operate private media outlets without undue interference? (0–4 points)

7. Are media regulatory bodies, such as a broadcasting authority or national press or communications council, able to operate freely and independently? (0–2 points)

8. Is there freedom to become a journalist and to practice journalism, and can professional groups freely support journalists' rights and interests? (0–4 points)

B. Political Environment (0–40 Points)

1. To what extent are media outlets' news and information content determined by the government or a particular partisan interest? (0–10 points)

2. Is access to official or unofficial sources generally controlled? (0–2 points)

3. Is there official censorship? (0–4 points)

4. Do journalists practice self-censorship? (0–4 points)

5. Is media coverage robust, and does it reflect a diversity of viewpoints? (0–4 points)

6. Are both local and foreign journalists able to cover the news freely? (0–6 points)

7. Are journalists, bloggers, or media outlets subject to extralegal intimidation or physical violence by state authorities or any other actor? (0–10 points)

C. Economic Environment (0–30 Points)

1. To what extent are media owned or controlled by the government, and does this influence their diversity of views? (0–6 points)

2. Is media ownership transparent, thus allowing consumers to judge the impartiality of the news? (0–3 points)

3. Is media ownership highly concentrated, and does it influence diversity of content? (0–3 points)

4. Are there restrictions on the means of news production and distribution? (0–4 points)

5. Are there high costs associated with the establishment and operation of media outlets? (0–4 points)

6. Does the state or other actors try to control the media through allocation of advertising or subsidies? (0–3 points)

7. Do journalists, bloggers, or media outlets receive payment from private or public sources whose design is to influence their journalistic content? (0–3 points)

8. Does the overall economic situation negatively impact media outlets' financial sustainability? (0–4 points)

These Freedom House coding guidelines are applicable across countries and over time. Yet these guidelines focus on factors that constrain media freedom. They do not provide a positive definition of media freedom.

Criticisms of Freedom House Methodology

What is probably most notable about Freedom House's array of coding questions is that it sidesteps the question of definition by using at least one indicator for just about every ideal and every conceptualization of media freedom that might be offered. The transparency of their methodology since 2001 makes their data something of a gold mine, but when these data are used indiscriminately at an aggregate level, the absence of a foundation in a conceptual definition is problematic, especially when analysts use these data as an interval scale and employ techniques that compare fine levels of variation in levels of media freedom. Put simply, it is not clear that all these elements are equal. Different perspectives on media freedom might make some more important than others or might even see some factors as absolutely necessary. Other factors might represent variations in the qualities of a free or restricted media while not really altering the level at which media function in a pragmatic or practical sense.

Most of the Freedom House questions focus on journalism and the political role of the news, but the very first question, A1, adds freedom of expression to the mix by asking, "Do the constitution or other basic laws contain provisions designed to protect freedom of the press and of expression, and are they enforced?" Worse, that question is a perfect example of the methodological sin of the double-barreled question; actually, it is a quadruple-barreled question that raises four issues—(1) Are there freedom of the press laws, and, if so, (2) are they enforced? (3) Are there freedom of expression laws, and if so, (4) are they enforced?—but allows for only one answer. How do you deal with a question that asks multiple questions but allows only one answer? For example, consider Lebanon in the 1970s, which had reasonable legal protections for freedom of the press as an arena of political criticism and debate, but severe legal restrictions on artistic expressions, particularly regarding sexual content and blasphemy. A compound sentence joining two or more propositions is false when at least one of the conjuncts is false. Thus, the sentence "Lebanon has freedom of the press and Lebanon has freedom of expression" is false if either form of freedom is lacking. So, from a strictly logical point of view, if media freedom requires both of these types of freedom, Lebanon should receive no points on question A1 in the Freedom House survey. Moreover, the possibility of assigning from 0 to 6 points for the amount of press freedom suggests that the question is really "How much press freedom is there?" where there

could be none, some, or a lot. So there could be a weighting question either because of the multiple-barreled question or because of the nonbinary nature of measures of freedom. How do you assign those degrees of media freedom? Do you weight both the political freedom of the media and freedom of expression as different but equal factors and give Lebanon a three?

Question A5 (Is freedom of information legislation in place, and are journalists able to make use of it?) brings freedom of information acts into the discussion and, together with question B2 (Is access to official or unofficial sources generally controlled?), adds the internal component of the ideal of transparency to the discussion, while question B5 (Is media coverage robust, and does it reflect a diversity of viewpoints?) adds some of the external aspect of the transparency debate (see Lord and Finel 2000). *Internal transparency* refers to access to government records and processes, whereas *external transparency* refers to access to information from foreign sources. In both cases, the coding guidelines from Freedom House are vague and open to multiple interpretations.

Several questions, such as C7 (Do journalists, bloggers, or media outlets receive payment from private or public sources whose design is to influence their journalistic content?), touch on the content of the media, and these indirectly reflect another set of ideals that are most often reflected in criticisms of elite dominance of news sources and concerns over ownership concentration in the media industry. While the issue of indirect government or elite control through intimidation or economic manipulation can complicate the study of media freedom, there is again the problem with inserting an ideal into the measurement without contextualizing it with a clear definition. Consider the "or other actors" in question C6: "Do the state or other actors try to control the media through allocation of advertising or subsidies?" (Freedom House 2012). Do "other actors" include terrorist threats made to suppress "insults" to Islam? What about grassroots organizations such as anti-fur campaigners who organize advertising boycotts of channels or programs, U.S. conservatives who threatened to pressure members of Congress to review the broadcast licenses of stations that aired a TV movie about Ronald Reagan, and talk radio hosts who use the mass media to criticize what the mass media broadcasts?

These and other criticisms that could be made of the questions used in the Freedom House coding reflect the lack of a clear operational definition from which the coding rules were constructed. If the Freedom House data are used carefully, their wide-net approach to coding press freedom by capturing a variety of the ideals and conceptual perspectives on the topic, can be a valuable asset. Because of the transparency of Freedom House's coding and method, a scholar can define media freedom as desired and use that definition to select which measures to employ and what weight they will be given in an analysis.

For example, someone who equates media freedom with freedom of expression would probably want to emphasize scores from questions A1 and A3 and not use the score from question A5 about freedom of information laws. Variations in freedom of information laws have nothing to do with freedom of expression, and including them in the analysis clouds the issue when freedom of expression is the point of emphasis or even the definition of media freedom.

In contrast, those who elevate the watchdog function of the media as the key to effective media freedom would probably want to emphasize question A5 and not use the score from B5 on the diversity of voices because the diversity of voices probably doesn't have that much impact on the watchdog function. After all, the Watergate story (arguably the best example of watchdog reporting in recent U.S. history) was broken by the *Washington Post*, a newspaper that caters to political and economic elites, and usually relies on these same elites (and not diverse sources) for information. A different selection of measures and weights would be best for those who define media freedom in terms of media as an arena of political competition, or those who idealize the grassroots, bottom-up communication function of a democratic media as the key idea of media freedom.

Regardless of how a scholar defines media freedom or which ideal or set of ideals are emphasized in that definition, some of the Freedom House measures will need to be included or emphasized, and measures that are less relevant or irrelevant to that ideal or definition deemphasized or removed. Freedom House does provide the information necessary to link its measures to a specific concept of media freedom, but almost no one, including Freedom House, does this, and that is a problem.

Definitions and Other Indices of Media Freedom

In recent years, other organizations have begun tracking and measuring media freedom. These indices measure the current state of the media and do not offer comprehensive historic measures of media freedom or a definition that can be effectively applied to a historical analysis. However, they do offer interesting alternatives to the Freedom House data and the Global Media Freedom Data presented in this volume. In 2001, the International Research and Exchanges Board (IREX) released its first Media Sustainability Index, which focused originally on the post-Soviet countries, but more recently, it has included countries in Africa and Asia. The compilation of this index has been funded largely by government organizations involved in media assistance, including USAID, UNESCO, and the Canadian International Development Agency (Burgess 2010). As its title suggests, the IREX index centers on the factors that promote sustainable as well as independent media. IREX neither provides a definition of media freedom nor purports to measure media freedom. Instead, it measures what it terms "media sustainability" defined as "the ability of the media to play its vital role as the 'fourth estate,'" a focus that privileges the watchdog role of media (IREX 2011). To compile this index, IREX puts together a panel of media experts from each country and asks them to evaluate each country's media in terms of five criteria that promote "successful" media:

1. Legal and social norms protect and promote free speech and access to public information.

2. Journalism meets professional standards of quality.

3. Multiple news sources provide citizens with reliable, objective news.

4. Independent media are well-managed businesses, allowing editorial independence.

5. Supporting institutions function in the professional interests of independent media. (IREX 2011)

IREX uses a series of indicators for each of the above statements to give the country a score ranging from 0 (objective not met at all) to 4 (objective fully realized) for each statement, and then these scores are averaged to obtain the country's overall score (IREX 2011). As with Freedom House's questions, these criteria seem to require a "yes, present" or "no, absent" answer, but the 0 to 4 scoring implies that there are degrees to which each of these criteria may be present or absent. Similarly, some of these criteria are actually multiple criteria. For example, the first criterion, "Legal and social norms protect and promote free speech and access to public information," really asks whether *legal norms* protect free speech, whether they promote free speech, whether they protect access to public information, and whether they promote access to public information; and whether *social norms* protect free speech, whether they promote free speech, whether they protect access to public information, and whether they promote access to public information. Moreover the fourth criterion, "Independent media are well-managed businesses, allowing editorial independence," does not allow for the possibility that there might be well-managed (at least from a business perspective) independent media that are not editorially independent.

Reporters Without Borders is a French-based, international, nonprofit NGO that monitors attacks on press freedom and provides assistance to journalists facing legal challenges and those working in perilous environments. In 2002, Reporters Without Borders began publishing its Press Freedom Index, which ranks countries from best to worst regarding media freedom. Like Freedom House, Reporters Without Borders fails to clearly define its conceptualization of media freedom. The index is compiled using a survey that focuses on attacks against journalists, state censorship and journalists' self-censorship, government monopoly of media, and attempts to control information on the Internet (Reporters Without Borders 2011).

In spite of these differences in intent and approach, the measures of Freedom House, IREX, and Reporters Without Borders are highly correlated (Becker, Vlad, and Nusser 2007). Not surprisingly then, the criticism of all three is similar. In a report for the Center for International Media Assistance (CIMA) at the National Endowment for Democracy,[11] John Burgess (2010) (a Washington, D.C.-based reporter and editor) found that these indices are frowned on by journalists, social scientists, and diplomats:

> The most basic accusations involve bias. In its starkest form, this critique depicts the three organizations as arms of Western governments, working to advance particular foreign policy outcomes. In some capitals, Freedom House is seen as delivering the American view of the hour; MSI's close association with USAID has led to a similar characterization. Reporters Without Borders has the distinction of drawing charges from both sides of the Atlantic that its true loyalties lie on the other. (17)

In general, there is disagreement about what role media should play in promoting development, peace, and stability. According to the Western conceptualization, a free press will hold government accountable and keep citizens apprised of any government wrongdoing and corruption and thereby facilitate a better government and stronger economy; however, a competing view conceptualizes media as a key partner in government efforts to promote peace and economic development, and as such media are expected to portray government leaders and policies in a positive light and prevent unrest, regardless of the actions and policies of government (Burgess 2010). Of course, the potential for unrestrained media to spur unrest has long been used to justify censorship. This is the same argument made by Samuel Johnson in response Milton's (1644) call for an end to pre-publication censorship:

> If every dreamer of innovations may propagate his projects, there can be no settlement; if every murmurer at government may diffuse discontent, there can be no peace; and if every skeptick in theology may teach his follies, there can be no religion. (quoted in Siebert 1956a, 36)

Dissatisfaction with Freedom House, IREX, and Reporters Without Borders has led to the development of new region-specific measures of media freedom such as the African Media Barometer (Burgess 2010). While such measures

It seems reasonable to argue that policies that ensure the freedom of reporting for journalists working for government-funded news agencies could compensate for strict government restrictions on the establishment of private media outlets. After all, until quite recently, all the television channels available in most of the smaller democratic countries around the world were government owned and heavily regulated, but most organizations monitoring media freedom considered those countries to have free media environments. Similarly, at what point might the number of media outlets available compensate for heavily partisan influence over the available media outlets? And at what point might the agency of reporters as social and political actors—their willingness to take risks or challenge authority to fulfill their watchdog role—be sufficient to make efforts at intimidation or other forms of indirect control ineffective and create a functionally free press?

All those questions are questions of definition, though they may be empirical as well. Although it is almost never discussed, this is a very significant concern with the way that the Freedom House data are used. Social scientists conducting statistical analyses on the effects of media freedom tend to use the aggregate scores from Freedom House (which range from 0 to 100, where 0 is most free and 100 is least free). Anyone who uses the aggregate Freedom House measure is implicitly defining all the measured factors whether they are legal, political, or economic as equally compensatory, but is that always the case?

Related to the idea of compensatory factors are noncompensatory factors. These are elements of media freedom that are essential components; if they are lacking, no other factors can compensate for them.

Noncompensatory elements are usually defined in terms of minimum or maximum thresholds, such as a minimum height requirement for an amusement park ride. Depending on the conceptual or theoretical perspective, again a definitional issue, many of the factors measured by Freedom House could be considered noncompensatory. These are often referred to as *necessary* or *critical conditions*, things that must be there for the media to be considered free.

A third, related point is the positive side of noncompensatory factors, the sufficient condition.

A British bookplate with a 17th century engraving of John Milton. Underneath are six lines from John Dryden's "Three Poets in Three Distant Ages Born."

Source: © Victoria and Albert Museum, London, Dyce Collection.

may be more sensitive to cultural variation, by definition they do not facilitate global studies of media freedom.

Necessary and Sufficient Elements in Multifaceted Concepts

Further complicating the issue of definition are what are technically referred to as *compensatory factors* that may be acting across the different dimensions of the complex social and political context that is media freedom. Put simply, these factors compensate for a low level or absence of one characteristic by providing a high level of something else. For example, a sports team can compensate for a poor defense with a high-powered offense. When it comes to media freedom, when we consider compensatory factors, we again see definitional issues that arise in trying to measure the concept.

A sufficient condition is by itself enough to establish media freedom. If we were to take Mueller's (1992) "ability to complain" as a working definition of media freedom, then there could be literally dozens of ways that could be achieved. It doesn't matter if there is one means to complain, or a dozen, just so long as it is possible and any single factor or any combination of factors that opens a channel to air grievances is sufficient. As long as one of those channels is open, then media freedom exists, and having more channels through which those grievances might be expressed may not really make the media any more free. Similarly, some definitions might imply or explicitly require necessary conditions, such as an absence of official censorship and no matter how many other factors might be in place, they do not matter until that one necessary condition is met. It could also be that a combination of two or even several factors are necessary for a given conceptualization of media freedom and the absence of any one of them makes a country *not free*, regardless of the other factors that might signal media freedom.

Applied Definition of Global Media Freedom

In this book, we offer a definition of media freedom and use that definition to develop coding practices and procedures to produce an historical guide to global media freedom. The definition and related coding tools were originally developed by Van Belle (1997, 2000) for his analysis of global press freedom and are applied here as they were in the original work. Most of the definitional issues are relevant to both the definition itself, the translation of that definition into coding, and the data that it produces.

Van Belle (1997, 2000) defines *media freedom* as the ability to safely criticize government. Three aspects of this definition are conceptually critical. First, it is an explicitly political definition. Second, it clearly defines a necessary condition that can be brought about by a variety of sufficient conditions. Third, this specific threshold implies that many of the other key elements that are often associated with media freedom, such as freedom of expression, are also present even though it does not guarantee them. In other words, if the news media are free to criticize the government, it is highly likely, but not necessarily guaranteed, that artists will be free to depict images that may be considered offensive, such as full or partial nudity, cartoons featuring political leaders, or satirical humor related to religion.

The political focus of this definition clearly situates the resulting measure in terms of the environment in which media operate. The logic is that a public sphere of open debate over government will naturally evolve in a political environment that allows the public or political opposition to safely criticize government. Its form will differ as the physical environments of countries differ. A small country is likely to have a few centralized media organizations, while large countries or heavily populated countries will probably be able to support a greater diversity. The nature of that political public sphere will also change as technology changes, but its function will remain reasonably consistent.

This ability to safely criticize government is clearly a necessary condition for media freedom, but the medium through which that criticism is allowed really does not matter to the pragmatic, political role it plays. As long as criticism can be safely and credibly communicated to others, it does not matter whether it comes by way of highly partisan outlets, diverse outlets, mass market centralized outlets, or government-owned or privately owned media; whether it is broadcast or peer-to-peer; or whether it is electronic or print in form.

When criticism is allowed, political elites will naturally move to use that public sphere as an arena for competition for support. Consequently, as Mueller (1992) argued, most of the political dynamics we associate with democratic government, particularly leadership responsiveness, will usually exist even in the absence of elections. Similarly, the watchdog function of the news media will also exist because it is essentially the ultimate expression of a government critique. Thus, the potential for news organizations to watchdog is part of the conceptual operationalization of this definition. Focusing only on the ability of news media to criticize government allows the key areas of social differentiation between countries to be expressed in law and practice. Countries may have different laws and policies governing media freedom, such as those involving artistic and religious limitations on speech; however, so long as open political dialogue is permitted in the public sphere, they will have media freedom as defined here. This approach resolves questions such as whether Lebanon could be considered to have media freedom during the 1970s, when it had freedom of press but restrictions on freedom of expression, and it avoids the difficulties posed by hate speech laws, pornography statutes, and state religion. Because this volume focuses on media freedom defined in terms of the freedom to criticize, persons interested in those aspects of media freedom will have to supplement the information provided here.

From Concept to Measurement

There is no perfect measure for any political or social concept. There are always a variety of conceptual, theoretical, and practical compromises that must be balanced against one another in the process of gathering and encoding the information, and media freedom is no exception to that rule. In fact, in many ways it exemplifies that rule. In addition to the definitional issues, the basics of measurement and analysis create a dynamic tension between accuracy, precision, reliability, and robustness. These issues must also be reflected in both the design and application of coding procedures that engage the pragmatics of the nature of the raw data and the challenges arising from the use of human coders. Because there are so many compromises inherent in this or any other effort to code and catalogue complex social concepts, the key is providing a clear description of choices, delineations, and processes so that others know what they have and know what adjustments they need to make to address their specific research question when they use the data and descriptions in this volume.

This project uses the simple definition developed by Van Belle (1997, 2000) to produce a simple coding scheme for media freedom that covers the years 1948 to 2001. For these years, the media environments around the world are sorted into three basic categories.[12]

1—Free—Countries where criticism of government and government officials is a common and normal part of the political dialogue in the mediated public sphere.

2—Imperfectly Free—Countries where social, legal, or economic costs related to the criticism of government or government officials limits public criticism, but investigative journalism and criticism of major policy failings can and does occur.

3—Not Free—Countries where it is not possible to safely criticize government or government officials.

In the dataset, additional codes are used for identifying states that for one reason or another cannot be effectively coded.

0—No Media—Countries where there is no effective national media.

8—Missing Data—Countries where political or social disruption makes it impossible to code for the year.

9—Missing Data—Countries where media were known to exist but there is insufficient historical material to effectively code the nature of the media environment.

999—Missing Data—Countries that did not exist as independent political entities. Often occupied by foreign forces, annexed, or dissolved.

There are several questions that immediately arise and need to be addressed to inform users of the data. Why that time period? Why simple categories rather than something complex like those used by Freedom House? What do the categories mean, and how are they distinguished from one another? What is the actual measurement and coding process?

Choosing the Time Period

The first question can be answered rather quickly. The data start in 1948, because that is about as early as it is possible to reliably code a reasonably complete catalog of countries in the post–World War II global political environment. Prior to 1948, there is very little information available consistently across countries. Organizations like the International Press Institute and the Inter American Press Association did not begin to publish reports on media freedom until the 1950s. By 1948, political situations and contexts following World War II had stabilized, so it is a natural starting point. The end point, 2001, is defined by introduction of a new and far more transparent coding scheme by Freedom House. As described in the appendix, the data from the new Freedom House coding scheme can be easily and reliably translated into these categories. Thus, the data provided here fill a critical historical gap in the data and can be carried forward as far as needed for those conducting empirical analyses.

Why Use Simple Categories?

The three basic categories of the coding scheme—Free, Imperfectly Free, and Not Free—reflect the nature of the definition, the nature of the phenomena of media freedom, and the pragmatics of coding this data covering a long time period.

First, defining media freedom as the ability to criticize government safely naturally lends itself to a simple coding scheme organized around the threshold defined by that necessary condition. In theory, this should lead to a binary coding scheme. You can either criticize government or you cannot. Qualitative differences in how that criticism is allowed or prevented are unimportant, so issues such as media ownership, licensing journalists, and the legal environment matter only if they push the social and/or political context over that threshold in one direction or the other. For example, even though the BBC dominates the British television news environment, its commitment to independent and critical journalism means that Britain is effectively just as free as the United States, where there are a plethora of television news networks. Similarly, if criticism is not allowed, it does not matter if it is prevented by direct government control of the newsroom, paramilitary attacks on journalists, or indirect economic coercion through taxes or the supply of government advertising.

Unfortunately, the reality of media freedom doesn't quite match this ideal. In countries classified as not free, it does seem that there is little practical difference between different methods of restricting the media; however, where there is media freedom, one has to take into account the political agency of journalists and how that can overcome the costs journalists might face for criticizing government or government officials.

No matter how free the media environment, criticizing government carries costs. This cost can be as small and as simple as an incremental increase in the reluctance of political elites to interact with a critical journalist, it can involve significant costs including overt and intentional efforts to exert legal or economic pressure, or it can involve physical attacks on a journalist. Regardless of the nature of these costs, when they are kept low, as they are in a free media environment, they can usually be overcome by the journalist's political agency or intent to act as a participant in the political process through mechanisms such as investigative journalism. For example, a politician may refuse to grant an interview to a critical reporter, but in a free media environment, if the story is important, the reporter can minimize this cost and strike back by documenting and publishing the politician's refusal to cooperate.

As a state approaches the ideal of media freedom, the cost of criticism drops so low that it is all but insignificant, and criticism becomes so routine that it is the norm for political coverage. This condition is seen as typical in developed Western democracies; in these contexts, even minor efforts to restrict coverage that might be critical of government, such as preventing the publication of pictures of military coffins returning from a war zone, are controversial. In fact, the U.S. ban on pictures of military coffins was lifted in 2009 and replaced with a policy that allows journalists to take pictures as long as the family of the deceased agrees. In other contexts, particularly in developing countries and countries that have experienced political volatility or social unrest in the recent past, the costs of criticizing government can be high enough to impede routine criticism on minor issues. However, in these countries, the media environment can still be free enough to allow the watchdog function of the news media to expose significant government failings. When politically engaged journalists can expose serious corruption and political challengers can offer alternative policy options, the media will be able to act as a public sphere for political competition and force government to be responsive to the content of the media. The difference between a context where the costs of criticism are so low that they do not create any noticeable impediment and a context where those costs are significant enough to seriously limit the reporting of journalists is important enough to warrant a distinction in the coding. Thus, the intermediate category of Imperfectly Free is included. For most analyses, this category can and should be considered as equivalent to Free because the media are functionally free, but this distinction is valuable for investigations of the more nuanced aspects of media freedom, particularly those that focus on the causes of media freedom and transitions in the media environment.

Another reason for applying these three simple categories is that they also fit well with the observed nature of the media. There is a significant and clear gap between the (3) Not Free category and the (2) Imperfectly Free category, and the vast majority of media environments fall clearly and obviously on one side or the other of this gap. Further, as a rule of thumb, once media environments are established on one side of this gap or the other, they tend to be stable. States may persist on the border between (1) Free and (2) Imperfectly Free for several years, often as a result of an oligarchic democratic structure that limits political competition to a small elite that collectively acts to limit criticism of that structure, and distinguishing between these two categories can sometimes be a challenge; however, it is extremely unusual for states to hover at the threshold between (2) Imperfectly Free and (3) Not Free.

These simple categories are employed because it is important that the data generated are robust and comparable across the full geographical and temporal extent of the data set. Simple, clear categories that focus on a very general political aspect of the media environment can sustain the same meaning and practical effect across changing technological environments and across a wide variety of social and cultural contexts. The nature of the media environment can shift from print and radio alone to a global media commons, but criticism of a political leader or a government policy means the same thing whether in a contemporary blog or a 1950s magazine article. There may be modest differences in nuances regarding the social concept of criticizing government in different societies, but the ability to express complaints serves to disrupt elite efforts to create and sustain preference falsification[13] as an element of social control.

Finally, the simpler the categories used to classify something, the easier it is to create reliable, replicable, and robust measures. All three terms offer slightly different ways of asking how certain we can be that the code for a state during a certain year is the right code. A measure is reliable when

reapplying the process of measurement will produce the same code each time. A measure is replicable if different people applying the coding scheme will get the same measure. A measure is robust if the code remains the same even when the coding is based on different sources of raw data. As a general rule, the simpler and broader the category, the easier it is to satisfy these criteria for evaluating measurement.

The simplicity of these categories must be balanced against the usefulness or potential value of the detail within the measure. As demonstrated by the wide variety of studies conducted using Van Belle's original data set (see, for example, Whitten-Woodring 2009; Choi and James 2006), ample value can be derived from a simple measure of media freedom. However, the creation of a structured description of the historical context of media freedom in each of the 196 countries profiled in this volume represents an acknowledgment that many questions require more detail and nuance than those used to determine whether the media are free. It is expected that many will wish to supplement the data set by contextualizing the coding with details from these descriptions.

There is also the simple practical question of what level of detail is possible with the available raw data. With media freedom, this is a significant issue. For many countries in the period from 1948 to 2001, it is a challenge to find enough historical material addressing the political environment of the media to place them in these simple categories. Further, biased accounts were common, particularly during the cold war, and it is often necessary to triangulate the underlying reality from conflicting statements and claims. Nicaragua during the 1980s is a perfect example of this. U.S. sources often depicted the Sandinistas as totalitarian communists, while Latin American sources depicted them as defenders of liberty and freedom. As a result, in many ways, these simple categories are the finest detail that the available information will provide for the entire catalog of states across the full period covered.

Distinguishing Between Categories

The operationalization of the definition of media freedom so that countries can be located within the set of categories relies on what might be called a critical question method. In essence, the divide between the categories is conceptualized as the answer to a simple exemplar question that distinguishes between them.

For the crucial gap between Not Free and Imperfectly Free, the exemplar question is

> Could a domestic news organization publish or broadcast the full story of a government scandal on the scale of Watergate?

This is a surprisingly effective way to conceptualize the break between a media system than can or cannot work as a public sphere for domestic political competition. First, focusing on the idea of a major scandal reduces the tendency to increasingly inflate the significance of minor impediments or failings as the media become more and more free. You must already have a functioning free media before you can even ask questions about how the predominance of elite voices in the mainstream press or partisan news outlets affects the media's ability to function as a means of political discourse. Not until a country is near the top of the media freedom scale can something like the effects of commercialization on news content even become an issue worth discussing. This question also takes the reporter's or outlet's marginal cost-benefit calculus out of the coding. Focusing on a major scandal such as Watergate largely eliminates the question of whether it is worth the cost and reframes it in terms of the assumption that any professional journalist would consider it worth the marginal cost of upsetting political or economic powerbases.

Second, the major scandal question quickly focuses the coder on evidence regarding the ability to publish. Critical coverage in the media immediately places states on one side of this threshold, and reports such as those from the International Press Institute and the Inter American Press Association will often provide clear evidence of government actions that make it impossible for a reporter or news outlet to publish a story about such a scandal. As a result, with this question at least 95 percent of cases can be easily located as clearly on one side or the other of this critical threshold. The remaining cases then require more detailed examination of historical and contextual detail, but again, using the question as a touchstone provides the key to sorting through that detail, and, in the vast majority of cases, a clear distinction can be made. In most cases where there is still confusion over this

threshold, it is a transitory phenomena and indicative of unrest or change.

The gap between Imperfectly Free and Free is less distinct and more difficult to measure; however, it is applicable only to the cases that have already been sorted into the functionally free category by the first question. The operational question for distinguishing between Imperfectly Free and Free is

> Is the criticism of government, political leaders and economic elites sufficiently costless as to appear routine?

Again, the distinction tends to be fairly clear-cut in practice. In most countries that have been sorted into the free category, either there will be reports or other evidence of intimidation, or there will be nearly ubiquitous criticism and response of both incumbent and challenging political and social elites in the media content. The difficulty is distinguishing the often-strident expression of concerns about issues such as elite dominance of free media outlets, ownership concentration, or commercial influence from the instances where those issues are actually impeding the media's ability to function as a political arena of debate and political competition. Often, when cases were difficult to code, it was the distinction between the free and imperfectly categories that was an issue.

The Process of Measurement

A relatively simple, multistage, multicoder sorting technique was used to code the base data. This was supplemented by the retention of notes on the coding decisions. This information was then used to flesh out the descriptive profiles and indicate where, when, and to what extent there was uncertainty in the coding.

In all cases, at least two coders independently extracted raw data from historical documents, noted the significant detail in that data, and coded the country for every year of its inclusion in the database. In the majority of cases, the coders agreed on the code for a country-year and neither noted any significant uncertainty in the code they assigned, which then completed the coding for that case.[14] In the cases where the coders did not agree on the code or one of the coders indicated significant concerns about their code, the case was passed to a third coder[15] who examined the evidence identified by each of the original coders. Most of the cases with discrepant coding were a result of one or sometimes both coders finding historical accounts that the other did not find, and simply combining the raw data resolved the discrepancy. A small number of cases involved conflicting information or other difficulties that required more extended investigation by the third coder and sometimes a fourth. In those instances, the conclusions were vetted and discussed by a small group that included one or both of the principal investigators.

This multistep, multicoder process was time-consuming and occasionally arduous, but it produced a coding that is robust and allows the identification of any significant uncertainties in the data.

References and Further Readings

Bates, Stephen. 1995. *Realigning Journalism with Democracy: The Hutchins Commission, Its Times and Ours*. Washington, DC: The Annenberg Washington Program in Communications Policy Studies of Northwestern University.

Becker, Lee B., Tudor Vlad, and Nancy Nusser. 2007. "An Evaluation of Press Freedom Indicators." *International Communication Gazette*, no. 69 (5): 5–28.

Breunig, Christian. 1994. *Kommunikationsfreiheiten: Ein Internationaler Vergleich*. Universitaetsverlag Konstanz, Konstanz.

Burgess, John. 2010. *Evaluating the Evaluators*. Center for International Media Assistance, National Endowment for Democracy. Center for Global Communication Studies, Annenberg School for Communication, University of Pennsylvania.

Chenery, William Ludlow. 1955. *Freedom of the Press*. New York: Harcourt.

Choi, Seung-Whan and Patrick James. 2006. "Media Openness, Democracy and Militarized Interstate Disputes: An Empirical Analysis." *British Journal of Political Science*, no. 37: 23–46.

Commission on Freedom of the Press. 1947. *A Free and Responsible Press: A General Report on Mass Communication: Newspapers, Radio, Motion Pictures, Magazines and Books*. Chicago: The University of Chicago Press.

Committee to Protect Journalists. 2011. "Attacks on the Press. Committee to Protect Journalists 2010" [cited April 1 2011]. Available from http://www.cpj.org/attacksonthepress/.

Cook, Timothy. 1998. *Governing with the News*. Chicago: University of Chicago Press.

Farace, Vincent. 1966. "A Study of Mass Communication and National Development." *Journalism & Mass Communication Quarterly*, no. 43: 305–13.

Farace, Vincent, and Lewis Donohew. 1965. "Mass Communication in National Social Systems: A Study of 43 Variables in 115 Countries." *Journalism & Mass Communication Quarterly*, no. 42: 253–61.

Freedom House. 2010. "Freedom of the Press 2010." Available from http://www.freedomhouse.org/report/freedom-press/2010/libya.

Freedom House. 2012. "Freedom of the Press 2012: Breakthroughs and Pushback in the Middle East Freedom House 2012" [cited July 24, 2013]. Available from http://www.freedomhouse.org/report/freedom-press/freedom-press-2012.

Hocking, William. 1947. *Freedom of the Press: A Framework of Principle*. Chicago: University of Chicago Press.

International Press Institute. 2011. "History of the IPI. International Press Institute 2010" [cited April 8, 2011]. Available from http://www.freemedia.at/about-us/history/the-first-decade/.

IREX. 2011. "IREX Media Sustainability Index. International Research & Exchanges Board 2011" [cited April 22, 2011]. Available from http://www.irex.org/project/media-sustainability-index-msi.

Lord, Kristin M. and Bernard I. Finel. 2000. *Power and Conflict in the Age of Transparency*. New York: St. Martin's Press.

Libya Constitution. 1969. Available at http://unpan1.un.org/intradoc/groups/public/documents/cafrad/unpan004643.pdf.

McQuail, Denis. 2000. *McQuail's Mass Communication Theory*. London: Sage.

Milton, John. 1644 [2010]. "Areopagitica: A Speech of Mr. John Milton for the Liberty of Unlicensed Printing to the Parlament of England 1644" [cited January 14, 2010]. Available from http://www.dartmouth.edu/~milton/reading_room/areopagitica/index.shtml.

Mueller, John. 1992. "Democracy and Ralph's Pretty Good Grocery: Elections, Equality, and the Minimal Human Being." *American Journal of Political Science*, no. 36 (4): 983–1003.

Nixon, Raymon B. 1960. "Factors Related to Freedom in National Press Systems." *Journalism Quarterly*, no. 37 (1): 13–28.

Nixon, Raymond B. 1965. "Freedom in the World's Press: A Fresh Appraisal With New Data." *Journalism Quarterly*, no. 42 (1): 9–14.

Picard, Robert G. 1985. *The Press and the Decline of Democracy*. Westport, Connecticut and London, England: Greenwood Press.

Reporters Without Borders. 2011. "How the Index Was Drawn Up. Reporters Without Borders 2002" [cited April 8 2011]. Available from http://en.rsf.org/how-the-index-was-drawn-up-23-10-2002,04118.html.

Salmon, Lucy Maynard. 1923. *The Newspaper and Authority*. New York: Oxford University Press American Branch.

Siebert, Fred S. 1956a. "The Authoritarian Theory." In *Four Theories of the Press,* edited by Fred S. Siebert, Theodore Peterson, and Wilbur Schramm. Urbana: University of Illinois Press.

———. 1956b. "The Libertarian Theory." In *Four Theories of the Press,* edited by Fred S. Siebert, Theodore Peterson, and Wilbur Schramm. Urbana: University of Illinois Press.

U.S. Department of State. 2010. *2009 Human Rights Report: Libya*. U.S. Department of State.

United Nations. 1948. *Universal Declaration of Human Rights*. United Nations.

Van Belle, Douglas. 1996. "Leadership and Collective Action: The Case of Revolution." *International Studies Quarterly* no. 40: 107–32.

Van Belle, Douglas A. 1997. "Press Freedom and the Democratic Peace." *Journal of Peace Research*, no. 34 (4): 405–14.

———. 2000. *Press Freedom and Global Politics*. Westport, CT: Praeger Publishers.

Weaver, David H., Judith M. Buddenbaum, and Jo Ellen Fair. 1985. "Press Freedom, Media, and Development, 1950–1979: A Study of 134 Nations." *Journal of Communication*, no. 35 (2): 104–17.

Whitten-Woodring, Jenifer. 2009. "Watchdog or Lapdog: Media Freedom, Regime Type and Government Respect for Human Rights." *International Studies Quarterly*, no. 53: 595–625.

Notes

1. *History of the IAPA* (Miami, FL: Inter American Press Association, 2013). Available at http://www.sipiapa.org/en/sip/history-of-iapa/.

2. *Inter American Press Association Reports* (Miami, FL: Inter American Press Association Constitution, 1951) 1, no. 1: 1.

3. *XVIII Annual Meeting Santiago de Chile, October 1962* (Miami, FL: Inter American Press Association, 1963), 141.

4. *About the Declaration* (Miami, FL: Inter American Press Association, 1994). Available at http://www.sipiapa.org/en/chapultepec/about-the-declaration/.

5. *History of the IPI* (Zurich: International Press Institute, 2013). Available at http://www.freemedia.at/about-us/history/1950-1959.html.

6. Ibid.

7. *Our History* (Washington, DC: Freedom Press, 2013), para. 3. Available at http://www.freedomhouse.org/content/our-history.

8. Deigo Giannone, "Political and Ideological Aspects in the Measurement of Democracy: The Freedom House Case," *Democratization* 17, no. 1 (2010).

9. Lee B. Becker, Tudor Vlad, and Nancy Nusser, "An Evaluation of Press Freedom Indicators," *International Communication Gazette* 69, no. 5 (2007).

10. These can also be found on pages 38–39 of the report *Freedom of the Press 2012: Breakthroughs and Pushback in the Middle East*. This is available at http://www.freedomhouse.org/report/freedom-press/freedom-press-2012.
   Freedom House also has detailed reports for 2001 through 2013 and data for 1980–2013 available at http://www.freedomhouse.org/report-types/freedom-press.

11. The National Endowment for Democracy is a private, nonprofit foundation that is funded by the U.S. Congress and supports nongovernmental groups that work to strengthen democratic institutions.

12. In the original use of the Van Belle definition and coding there were four categories, but with the end of the cold war and the massive growth in information technology, distinguishing between state-operated news media and media that are controlled by other means has become something of a pointless exercise. Aside from North Korea, it is difficult to argue that any states have media run exclusively by the state as so many were during the cold war.

13. Roughly speaking, *preference falsification* refers to forcing people, usually through threats of punishment, to hide their actual opinions and publicly express expected or demanded opinions. It serves to prevent revolt by keeping people from knowing how many other people share their grievances (see Van Belle 1996).

14. A small number of these cases were double-checked by a third coder. This included anywhere a question later arose about the coding and some that were chosen at random.

15. Usually one of the principal investigators.

Chapter 3

The Historical Development and Correlates of Media Freedom

It is impossible to pinpoint the beginning of media freedom, but if we could do so, we would probably also identify the first effort to constrain it. Historically, every potential advance in media freedom has been met with attempts to rein it in. In fact, producing and delivering news has always been a perilous business. Variations on the phrase "don't shoot the messenger" appear in literature penned more than two thousand years ago. For example, back around 442 BCE, Sophocles wrote, "no man delights in the bearer of bad news."[1] So for thousands of years, people providing news and information have known that they might get into trouble when others— especially those in power—dislike what they have to say. Yet attacks on journalists, messengers, heralds, and town criers (arguably the earliest journalists) have long been considered bad form. For example, in medieval England and Scotland, heralds, who were usually employed by kings to make proclamations (formal announcements), were protected by law and to harm them was treason (MacCannell 2009). Thus, the history of efforts to control and protect news providers dates back hundreds, if not thousands, of years.

This chapter begins with an overview of important legal, political, and technological developments in the history of media freedom and concludes with an analysis of some factors that influence media freedom. Throughout history, technological advances have made it possible to produce and disseminate information faster to larger and larger groups of people. In response to these technological advances, governments have developed legal measures, some of which advance and some of which limit media

freedom. Political and cultural developments have also shaped and reshaped the environment in which media function, thereby contributing to both the evolution and devolution of media freedom.

The Legal History of Media Freedom

The earliest purveyors of news were messengers and town criers, but these first reporters were working for those who were in power. Heralds and town criers were delivering messages and news *from* conquerors, kings, and lords *to* the people. They were not monitoring and criticizing government or questioning authority; instead, they were extensions of government, and therefore, the protections extended to them were aimed at protecting them from angry masses or, in times of war, angry opponents. These early newsmen proudly flaunted their allegiance to those in political power. For example, heralds in Elizabethan England sported coats of arms as a sort of passport, which indicated that "to hurt or kill any of them in that business, is treason" (English antiquarian Arthur Agard, quoted in MacCannell 2009, xi). Thus, the first laws aimed at protecting those who provide the news were protecting those who delivered government messages.

If media or press freedom is defined negatively, in terms of the efforts to exert authoritative control of media content, then the history of media freedom begins in either 1501, with the first of the proclamations and actions of Pope Alexander VI requiring prepublication approval of all published works, or in 1535 when King

Henry VIII of England instituted severe penalties, including death, for unlicensed printing. Clearly these first efforts to exert control must have come in response to a preceding lack of control, or freedom.[2] Alternatively, when media freedom is implicitly or explicitly defined in terms of more modern notions of freedom of expression and government, either the stamp act that was one of the sparks of the U.S. Revolutionary War (1765), the First Amendment to the U.S. Constitution (1791), or perhaps poet John Milton's *Aeropagitica* (1644)[3] can be tagged as the point to start a discussion of the legal history of media freedom.

Both Pope Alexander VI's proclamation and Henry VIII's mandate for prepublication approval represent reactions of authorities to ongoing struggles to deal with the emerging social effects of the products of the Gutenberg press. At some point, the products of that press began affecting society and thus prompted reactions from church and secular governing authorities, often at a local level. Both 16th century authoritative proclamations were countered with the smuggling of printed works into the territories where the authority of the Pope or the King of England held sway. This suggests that press freedom was actually present elsewhere and these two locations represent Europe's most repressive regimes of that time. Milton's comments in *Aeropagitica* (1644) suggest the Low Countries, which would today be the Dutch provinces of Holland and Belgium, either were or became the source of much of this contraband fruit of the independent press.[4] This combination of historical tidbits suggests that there were multiple locations around Europe taking advantage of the commercial opportunities created by authoritarian rulers turning publications into valuable contraband.

The 18th-century establishment of the U.S. Bill of Rights included the First Amendment which famously states, "Congress shall make no law respecting an establishment of religion, or prohibiting the free exercise thereof, or abridging the freedom of speech, or of the press . . ." (U.S. Constitution, Amendment 1). This measure is widely seen as the first law promoting press freedom. But the first law promising press freedom was actually created in the Polish-Lithuanian Commonwealth in 1539 (Zamoyski 1987). In addition to Poland, Sweden and Denmark also passed laws ensuring the freedom of the press

long before the U.S. First Amendment was penned. However, the duration of those early experiments with media freedom was generally short. Denmark's was revoked within a year. It is also unclear if there was any real substance to them. There is little indication that any kind of publishing industry or early form of media system arose. Therefore, it could be argued that the 1791 U.S. First Amendment was the first successful, legal guarantee of media freedom.

If the United States was the first country to successfully adopt a law protecting press freedom in the 18th century, it was neither the only country nor the last country to do so. As the country reports that follow this chapter indicate, by the 21st century, nearly every country on the planet had some sort of constitutional provision for media freedom. But every country, including the United States, also had laws that limit media freedom. These include laws the prohibit libel, defamation, and hate speech, as well as laws that protect national security and national secrets.

Cultural and Political Influences on Early Media Freedom

In the process of digging through the hints and vague references in historical texts that were never really intended to be applied to the topic of media freedom, it is tempting to draw all kinds of inferences and extrapolate indications of significance from rather modest empirical foundations. For example, the historical period in which the Low Countries were a significant source for the smuggling of the contraband publications that so vexed English authorities coincided with a flourishing artistic community in the Netherlands. It is tempting to conclude that periods of surges in artistic expression could be indirect indicators of media freedom. This is particularly true if modern notions of freedom of expression are a significant aspect of the way you view the concept of media freedom. However, there is more evidence that contradicts such an inference than there is to support it. The Pope's 1501 proclamation establishing death as the punishment for unlicensed printing fell right in the heart of the Italian Renaissance, and there is no indication that this clearest and most draconian of early efforts to restrict the press had any negative affect on artistic expression. The Italian Renaissance lasted at least fifty years beyond that proclamation.

Developments in early forms of the newspaper could also be used as proxies for press freedoms. This again comes from the Dutch-speaking Low Countries of Holland and Belgium. It is a relatively common argument that the first significant appearance of press freedom occurred in Amsterdam in the early 1600s (e.g., Stephens 1988, 167), and many of the early aspects of the modern commercial news media appear to have originated with or were established by printers in Amsterdam during this period. However, the word *relatively* is almost always invoked in discussions about Dutch press freedom during this period. Also, the term *restrained* is used a great deal as it was clear that the publications were business oriented, with most of their content focusing on shipping, trade, and foreign events with a clear intent to avoid anything that might irritate local authorities. Any realistic measure would consider the press of Amsterdam during this time to be highly self-censored even though it was the freest in relative terms.

Still, as an historical example, Amsterdam during this period has some intriguing aspects. The earliest English language papers were published in Amsterdam in about 1618, providing some of the best evidence that the presses were intentionally serving an export and contraband market. Further, the business and trade orientation of the papers in Amsterdam can be anecdotally tied to the rise of the Dutch as a trading power, offering some powerful points regarding the exchange of information as part of the generation of wealth in the establishment and growth of media freedom. However, the most significant point may be the simple fact that the Dutch provinces were a flash point of religious and civil strife during the 16th and 17th centuries, including forced conversions, persecutions, and an extended civil war. The emergence of Amsterdam's limited and restrained press freedom occurred right in the middle of these eighty years of war and faded quickly when the war ended. This offers an interesting parallel to the fact that the first period that merits any mention of press freedom in England is during the civil war (1642–1651) and the reinstitution of controls on the English presses after the postwar reestablishment of central authority (Stephens 1988, 92).

Of all the points that could be inferred from any anecdotes from the earliest historical examples of press freedom or near freedom, the association with disruptions of central political authority is probably the most likely to be relevant to a considered discussion of the early roots of modern media freedom. The early years of the U.S. experience with press freedom also invokes the association of the rise of media freedom with the absence of a central authority that is capable of restricting the press (Cook 1998). Without slighting the philosophical points made by Jefferson and other American intellectual and political leaders of the time, it is possible to say that the fledgling U.S. government could not have controlled the press if it had wanted to do so. It could be that the United States took a very pragmatic course regarding press freedom.[5] Having used the press as part of the revolutionary war effort, the U.S. government had essentially trained a cadre of guerilla printers who had grown quite adept at evading British control, and the new government had nowhere near the level of resources of the British. This was essentially the point of those arguing against the First Amendment to the Constitution—that writing an explicit guarantee of the freedom of the press was pointless when the government could not control the press anyway. The only real option the framers of the U.S. Constitution had was to build a government around the fact that the press would be uncontrollable for the foreseeable future, whether they liked it or not. The result was the first truly free press.

Definition and Media Freedom History

At this point, the definition of media freedom used in this book—that news media have the ability to safely criticize government—can bring a great deal of clarity to the discussion of the early history of press freedom. In those first periods of relative press freedom in the Netherlands and England, and during the Revolutionary War years in America, it would be hard to argue that it was "safe" to criticize government using the press. It was not until the United States won its independence that it became safe to use the press as a critical part of the political discourse. Thus, the establishment of the United States provides the first clear instance of press freedom in the world.

The definition also provides insights into the type of information that was most valuable in the earlier historic instances and events that were relevant to the establishment of the first free press regime. The information that mattered was news that let citizens know that their government was behaving badly. And for the first time, this news was produced within the country. In none of the earlier instances was it ever safe to criticize those who governed the home of the press. In both the Dutch and the English examples, the news that was critical of a government was produced for export to the territory of the government being criticized; it was not produced within the territory controlled by the government or authority being criticized. In the Dutch case, all the Dutch Low Countries exported news critical of the English government to England and the protestant Dutch territories of the north exported news that was critical of the Catholic Church to the Catholic territories of the south. Propaganda and religious texts published in England were exported into the Dutch provinces, with both Catholic and Protestant publishers sending material into the provinces controlled by their opponents. That was also the case in the United States during the Revolutionary War period; the possibility of criticizing local government in the media emerged only in the aftermath of the U.S. victory.

Perhaps most important, applying this definition reduces the emphasis on the freedom of expression and artistic elements that might be emphasized when looking back from a modern perspective. In the current context, some of the most prominent recent debates over media freedom are often provoked by artistic expressions, such as those that challenge social morals. That can make it easy to overlook the fact that the entire Renaissance occurred in the context of authoritarian regimes where publishers and authors were regularly put to death.

The emphasis on safely criticizing those who govern also takes the focus off the economics of the news media and media freedom. Economics are prominent in the most comprehensive history of the news (Stephens 1988), both as a driver of the printing industry's evolution into packaging news as a commercial, often sensational product for an ever-growing audience and as one of the key purposes the news served, providing information that businesses could use for commercial decision making. Both purposes, however, can clearly be served in a restricted press

environment. It is easy to argue that these aspects are more prominent or efficient in a free press environment, but there is ample evidence that they preceded the establishment of any free press and exist outside free press regimes. The key element that makes a press free is that ability to safely criticize, and that definition clarifies a great deal.

None of that is to dismiss the value of the events and sometimes heroic sacrifices that preceded the establishment of the United States as a government built around press freedom. They are part of the prehistory and are essential parts of the evolution of that first free press regime; however, the history of press freedom starts with the establishment of that first government to recognize that it would need to find a way to function with a press that was beyond their ability to control and was going to serve as an arena of political debate, including criticism of government and those who govern.

Technological Advances: Wonders and Disappointments

Every technological advance in communication has been hailed as a harbinger of a world in which the freedom to communicate minimizes political divisions:

> This binds together by a vital cord all the nations of the earth. It is impossible that old prejudices and hostilities should longer exist, while such an instrument has been created for an exchange of thought between all nations of the earth. (Briggs and Maverick 1858, 22)

That passage could have been written in the 1990s, predicting a united world with the emergence of the Internet, but this one was penned in 1858, and Charles Briggs and Augustus Maverick were imagining a new world in the wake of the invention of the telegraph. Yet, as with the telegraph and the Internet, every new medium has prompted the development of regulations that divide countries and limit the flow of information.

Throughout history, technology has both facilitated and limited the dissemination of news. Again, if we think of journalists as people whose work is to deliver news, then the first reporters were messengers, heralds, and town criers whose voices were their medium. Consequently, their audience—the people who could actually hear their message—was limited. They had no way to reach a mass audience (say for example, an entire country). The invention of the printing press changed that.

Although most people trace the beginning of mass media to around 1440 when German goldsmith Johannes Gutenberg invented the movable printing press, wood block printing in China began hundreds of years earlier—most likely during the Sui Dynasty, which lasted from 589 CE to 618 CE (Zuzao 2010). The development of woodblock printing was driven at least in part by politics. To stabilize his empire, Emperor Wendi advocated the expansion of Buddhism, which created a need for religious documents, and a system of "feudal imperial examination" to select officials, which created a market for books on exam preparation (Zuzao 2010). Around 618 CE, the T'ang Dynasty used block printing to produce copies of official newsletters for the elite called the *tipao* (Stephens 2007). By the 11th century (during the Song dynasty), about 400 years before Gutenberg started up his press, the Chinese were using movable type to produce relatively inexpensive books.

Although the invention of movable type made book publishing possible, this technology was not used to produce widely distributed and regularly printed newspapers until the 17th century (Starr 2004). While the printing press facilitated the production of books and pamphlets, it was the development of postal systems that made it feasible to produce and disseminate news to a large audience. Of course, as mentioned above, the emergence of newspapers prompted governments to develop laws aimed at controlling both content and ownership.

Starting in the mid-1800s, waves of technological innovations transformed the communication. With each new invention, governments had to decide how to regulate the new medium. Would it be government owned and controlled, privately owned but regulated, or some sort of combination of public and private ownership and control? Different countries followed different paths, and in each case, the choices made influenced present and future media freedom.

First in the 1840s, the telegraph made it possible to transmit information instantly. This technology expanded the ability of newspapers to cover events in faraway places, and it also encouraged newspapers to form partnerships to share and minimize the costs of acquiring foreign news, resulting in the establishment of news services (Starr 2004). In the United States, Western Union secured a monopoly on telegraph services, and the Associated Press developed a similarly exclusive news service.

In the mid-1870s, the introduction of the telephone offered another means of instant communication, but it took several decades to develop telephone networks, and the costs of long distance calling remained high, while the quality of the connections remained low. Interestingly, although there were a few telephone-based news services that emerged and arguably offered the first broadcast newscasts, this idea did not catch on worldwide, and there is no indication that these services faced government censorship (for more, read about Telefon-Hirmondo in Box 3.1).

As these technologies emerged around the world, governments came up with different means of regulating them. A crucial issue was whether they should be privately or publically owned. While many countries combined their postal service, telephone, and telegraph into a single government agency, the United States retained a government post office and privately owned telegraph and telephone companies. Nevertheless, the privately owned telephone company sought regulation as a defense of its monopoly position. By emphasizing politically controlled monopoly rather than market-oriented competition, the U.S. private telephone company developed many characteristics similar to the European publically owned telephone companies and to the U.S. Post Office (Brock 2003, 2).

Thus, in the early years of electronic mass communication, the end results of public and private ownership of these media were essentially similar: a monopoly where the prices were set for consumers. For the news medium of the time, the newspaper, these technologies made it possible to gather and dispense news from around the world, but the effects of these technologies were somewhat complicated. On the one hand, telegraph news services, most notably the Associated

BOX 3.1

CALLING FOR NEWS: TELEPHONE-BASED NEWS AND ENTERTAINMENT SERVICES

Budapest, Hungary (1893): Long before the iPhone, in the late 1870s, when telephones were first developed, people recognized the potential that phones could do much more than connect people for a quick chat—they envisioned that these devices could also be used for entertainment and news. Writing for the *Ladies' Home Journal* in 1900, John Elfreth Watkins predicted that by the year 2000, wireless phones would make it possible to "telephone China quite as readily as we now talk from New York to Brooklyn" and that "Grand Opera will be telephoned to private homes, and will sound as harmonious as though enjoyed from a theatre box" (Watkins, 8).[6] While most of the early entertainment-by-phone projects were experimental in nature and short-lived, Hungarian inventor Tivadar Puskas launched a successful telephone news service in 1893 in Budapest. Although Puskas died shortly after starting *Telefon Hírmondó*, his invention endured and eventually evolved into a radio station, but continued to be available via telephone until 1944 (White 1996). W. G. Fitz-Gerald reviewed *Telefon Hírmondó* for *Scientific American* in 1907:

A *Telefon Hírmondó* stentor reading the day's news (1901).

Source: Wikimedia Commons / Denison, Thomas S. (April 1901). "The Telephone Newspaper." World's Work: 640-643. Retrieved on November 20, 2007. (Electronic copy made available by Karla Tonella of University of Iowa.)

> Far from being the fad of a moment, the "Telefon-Hirmondo" has all the attributes of a great daily journal save mere concrete type, ink and paper. It has a staff of over two-hundred people in the busy winter months, and its circulation falls only when the editor-in-chief or his "stentors" slack off a little in their ceaseless stream of eloquence, wherein are queerly mingled events fraught with the rise or fall of nations and "ads" of soap and pills! (p. 507)

While Fitz-Gerald's report on *Telefon Hírmondó* did not indicate that the news service was censored by any government agency, the editor admitted to Fitz-Gerald that the journalists practiced self-censorship. "We realize the responsibility of our position, and all our editorial staff, from editors to stentors, are most careful to tone down, alter, and omit items of news which might in any way be objectionable when delivered into the home" (Fitz-Gerald 1907, 507).

Press, increased the information that newspapers could provide to readers, but on the other hand, the monopolies these news services developed diminished the number of sources providing this information.

In 1921, President Harding told Congress that both domestic and international regulation was essential to maximize the potential of new technologies:

> Particularly desirable is the provision of ample cable and radio services at reasonable rates for the transmission of press matter, so that the American reader may receive a wide range of news and the foreign readers receive full accounts of American activities. The daily press of all countries may well be put in position to contribute to international understandings by the publication of interesting foreign news. ("President's Address to Congress on Domestic and Foreign Policies," April 12, 1921)

Radio technology from the late 1890s through World War I was used primarily for communication between and from ships, but in the 1920s, people began to use this technology to broadcast music and news. From the beginning, political leaders recognized the potential power of this new technology.

The accessibility of radio made it possible to bring news to a wider range of people. Unlike newspapers, which required that consumers be able to read, radio news required only that they be able to listen and have access to a radio. Indeed radio today is arguably the most accessible medium because radios are relatively inexpensive and, while many people cannot read, most can hear. Consequently, some governments have developed different regulations for radio. For example, India today allows private ownership of newspapers, television channels, and radio stations, but when it comes to radio, only the state-owned All India Radio is permitted to broadcast news (WAN-IFRA 2010).

As with the telegraph and the telephone, governments had to decide how to handle radio and different countries chose different paths. The United States devised a system where private companies applied to an independent regulatory commission for licenses to use publicly held airwaves—a system which has promoted commercialization. In contrast, most European governments opted for publicly owned radio stations.

> In countries where broadcasting developed as a tax-financed, public function, the analogous question of organizational selection involved the locus of broadcasting within the state. One option was to locate radio in a bureaucracy under direct political control—a system of official state broadcasting that was adopted not only by authoritarian governments but also by some democracies. Another option for radio was a quasi-independent, professionally run public corporation—an approach pioneered by Great Britain, that came to be known as public-service broadcasting. (Starr 2004, 330)

For most countries, the decision of how to handle radio paved the way for how they would handle television.

In the United States, development of television broadcasting stalled because of concerns about monopoly ownership. Countries that had in place systems of government ownership of radio were able to move more quickly to the new medium. In May 1935, Nazi Germany launched the first public television service, and in the late 1930s, the British Broadcasting Corporation provided televised news casts (Starr 2004). It was not until after World War II that television broadcasting took hold in the United States and the same companies that controlled much of the radio network, NBC and CBS, gained control of the U.S. television market. Just as radio replaced newspapers as the most popular source of news in many countries, television soon became more popular than radio in developed countries. Eighty-five percent of all U.S. households had television sets by 1960, but in less developed countries, television penetration was and still is limited (FCC 2005).

As with the telegraph, the emergence of the Internet in the 1990s was hailed as revolutionary technology and a democratizing force that would unite people across the planet and facilitate a flow of information that no government could staunch. Similarly, the evolution of cell phones to smart phones has made it possible for people in remote corners of the world to communicate and harness the power of the Internet. Yet, as with their predecessors, the Internet and mobile phones have limitations. The Internet's architecture makes it vulnerable to manipulation at different levels: at the wired level, the code level, and at the content level (Benkler 2000; Lessig 2001). At the wired level, companies or governments that provide access to the Internet—the connections between computers—can sever those connections or erect virtual borders to limit Internet activity. Similarly, mobile phone service can be cut off and personal usage can be monitored. A few cases in point: in September 2007, during the protests of the Saffron Revolution, the Burmese government shut down all Internet and mobile phone service (Human Rights Watch 2007); in January 2011, during the Arab Spring, the Egyptian government convinced almost all Internet service providers to halt Internet traffic; and in August 2011, the Bay Area Rapid Transit Authority (BART) shut down cell phone service at several stations near a scheduled Occupy protest in San Francisco. At the code level, filters can be created to block certain types of content, and labels can be used to track usage. The same labeling technology that makes the web user friendly makes it possible for Internet service providers and governments to track where people travel on the web and what information they access (Mailland 2010).

And at the content level, good old-fashioned threats and intimidation can discourage users from providing or accessing information. Journalists and citizens who post content online that displeases those in power often face harassment, intimidation, imprisonment, and physical attacks. A number of nongovernment organizations—including the Committee to Protect Journalists, Freedom House, the International Press Institute, and Reporters Without Borders—track these infractions. For example, in 2011, Ethiopian blogger Eskinder Nega criticized his government for using antiterror laws to intimidate journalists and other critics. In July 2012, Nega himself was sentenced to eighteen years behind bars on charges that his articles were inciting revolution in Ethiopia. A United Nations panel concluded that Eskinder was merely exercising his right to free speech (Rhodes 2013).

Without doubt, new technologies like smart phones, the Internet, and social media have facilitated and transformed global communication.

This was also true, however, of the telegraph, the telephone, the radio, the television, and other earlier communication revolutions, all of which dramatically increased the number and speed of communications, and dramatically lowered their costs. These communication technologies produced radical changes in human organization and interaction, and required governments to develop new strategies for regulating human affairs. But they did not displace the central role of territorial government in human governance. (Goldsmith and Wu 2008, 180)

Indeed, there seems to be a pattern of technological advances fueling bursts of change that at first revolutionize communication and increase media freedom but are in the long run reined in. Moreover, these new media can also be used by government. Consider the use of Facebook by the Bahraini government in the wake of the Pearl Roundabout Protests.

BOX 3.2

A SOCIAL MEDIA WITCH HUNT: THE CRACKDOWN ON PROTESTERS IN BAHRAIN

Manama, Bahrain (March 2011): In the wake of the revolutionary demonstrations in Tunisia and Egypt, people in Bahrain launched their own antigovernment protests and set up camp at the Pearl Roundabout, a landmark in the capital of Manama. Like their counterparts in Tunisia and Egypt, activists in Bahrain used social media, in particular Facebook and Twitter, and text messaging to mobilize protesters (Bassiouni et al. 2011). Though these protests were for the most part peaceful, in mid-March 2011, they were brutally shut down by the Bahraini military and security forces, which were reinforced by troops from Saudi Arabia (Human Rights Watch 2012).

Following the crackdown, the government then used state-controlled television, Twitter, and Facebook to launch a witch hunt for protesters (Welsh 2011). Viewers of Bahrain TV were urged to turn in those who had taken part in the protests, especially those who were famous. On a live talk show, several of Bahrain's soccer stars were phoned and chastised for their participation in the Pearl Roundabout protests. At least twenty-five sports celebrities were accused of being national traitors and arrested (Welsh 2011). On Facebook, a page titled "Together to Unmask the Shi'a Traitors" encouraged people to provide the name and workplace of anyone

Ayat Hassan Mohammed al-Qurmezi became known as the poet of the revolution after she recited poems critical of Bahrain's rulers in early 2011 at a gathering of protestors near the Pearl Roundabout in Manama. She was arrested in late March and sentenced to 12 months in jail on June 12, 2011. Following protests in Bahrain and internationally, she was released and placed on house arrest in mid-July 2011. She continues to take part in anti-government protest; she is shown here reciting a poem at a gathering on Sitra Island, Bahrain, on January 24, 2014, at which leading opposition groups demanded equal rights for all citizens, Sunni and Shiite.

Source: Mazen Mahdi/EPA/Newscom.

they knew who had taken part in the protests (Welsh 2011). Another Facebook page targeted Ayat al-Qurmezi, a twenty-year-old woman who took the stage at the protest and read her poems criticizing King Hamad and the Prime Minister. She was arrested, and after three months behind bars, her confession was aired on state television (Welsh 2011). She was sentenced to a year in prison but was released and placed under house arrest in July 2011. Upon her release, she said she had been beaten and tortured during her interrogations (Solomon and Fullerton 2011).

Journalists who were critical of the government were also targets of social media campaigns. The Bahrain Independent Commission that was formed to investigate the allegations of government abuses received a number of reports that journalists were targeted and threatened via the Facebook page "Bahrain's List of Shame" and the Twitter group named "Harghum" (Bassiouni et al. 2011). Several members of the foreign press were beaten when they tried to document the protests, and two Bahraini journalists died while in government custody (Committee to Protect Journalists 2012). In April 2011, blogger Zakariya Rashid Hassan al-Ashiri died a week after he was arrested on charges of "disseminating false news"; Karim Fakhrawi, founder of Bahrain's independent newspaper *Al-Wasat* died less than a week later after he was taken into custody on charges of fabricating news (Committee to Protect Journalists 2012).

Correlates of Modern Media Freedom

In the country reports that follow this chapter, we consider how laws that protect press freedom and laws that restrict media freedom interact with political and economic factors to shape the environment in which journalists gather and report the news. These reports describe how media freedom has evolved or devolved differently in different countries. And that raises the question of why media freedom varies across countries. Why is it that some countries have free media and others do not? Are there certain characteristics that make media freedom more or less likely? To begin to address that question, we conducted a study of 151 countries from 1951 to 2007 (these were the countries and years for which we were able to gather the most information).[7] While we would expect to find that most democracies have media freedom and most nondemocracies do not, we find that this is *usually* but *not always* the case. Some democracies lack media freedom (Colombia 2000–2005; Mauritius 1970–1975; Poland 1991–1994; Portugal 1976–1994; Thailand 1992–1997) and some nondemocracies have free or imperfectly free media (Mexico 1948–1996; Nepal 1980–1992; Tanzania 1992–2012). We found that the following factors make a country *more likely* to have media freedom:

- *Executive constraints.* Institutions that check and balance the decision-making power of the leader, such as legislatures, an independent judiciary, or, in nondemocracies, the military (Marshall, Gurr, and Jaggers 2010), will potentially foster media freedom because a free press can help keep the leader in check. If journalists are free to engage in investigative reporting and report critically about government actions, they can help monitor the leader's behavior. Additionally, members of the legislature, the judiciary, and the military can leak stories to the press.

- *Economic development.* People have basic needs that probably must be met before a free press can emerge. It is hard to imagine that people and politicians would be able to engage in anything close to a civil, nonviolent, and politically literate discourse when starvation and massive deprivation are a norm.

- *Access to mobile phones* (which in turn provide access to new media). New media, especially the Internet, are more difficult (but certainly not impossible) for government to control.

These factors make a country *less likely* to have media freedom:

- *International conflict and/or war.* National security is one of the primary justifications for limiting media freedom. Studies have shown that people are more willing to relinquish civil liberties in times of conflict.

- *Internal conflict and/or war.* As with international conflict, internal conflict threatens national security, but internal conflict is potentially a greater and more direct threat to political leaders because it is usually a direct challenge to their ability to govern.

Controlling communication and access to information is a direct means of taking control of a country. Consider the shutdown of the Internet in Egypt in January of 2011 during the Arab Spring protests. Of course, sometimes internal conflict makes it difficult for government to maintain control of media—consider the early emergence of somewhat free media in the Low Country and England in the 17th century.

- *Religious laws.* These include laws that give religious leaders and or religious institutions official powers and laws that stem from religious beliefs, such as dietary restrictions, restrictions on women, mandated religious education, and blasphemy laws (Fox 2012).[8] Governments that legislate religion are unlikely to tolerate a free press that might question that religious authority.

Interestingly, these factors seem to influence media freedom in democracies and nondemocracies in different ways. In democracies, overall wealth (as measured by the gross domestic product per capita) increases the odds that a state will have free or imperfectly free media rather than not free media. In nondemocracies, wealth does not appear to make a difference. In nondemocracies, executive constraints appear to greatly increase the chances that a country will have free or imperfectly free media. While executive constraints also increase the likelihood of media freedom in democracies, the magnitude of the effect is far greater in nondemocracies. While both international and domestic conflict appear to negatively influence media freedom in nondemocracies, only domestic conflict appears to minimize media freedom in democracies. We find some evidence that access to new media, in particular mobile phones, increases the chances of a democracy having free or imperfectly free media rather than not free media, but we do not find that access to new media makes a difference in media freedom in nondemocracies. However, new media are by definition new arrivals, which means there is a lack of information about new media.

Finally, an early scholar of press freedom, Raymond Nixon, predicted that the ability of people to read—a country's literacy rate—would increase the likelihood of press freedom (Nixon

1960, 1965). In contrast, our findings regarding the effect of literacy on media freedom were mixed. In most of our analyses, literacy did not have a significant effect, but when we looked only at democratic countries, we found that countries with a higher literacy rate were *less likely* to have free media. Because these findings are inconsistent, we remain uncertain about the effects of literacy on media freedom. Perhaps a government is more likely to control media when it has a population that has greater potential to consume media (of course, the literacy rate would only increase the accessibility of media that must be read—print and some online media). It could be that when literacy is low and access to broadcast media is limited, there is little need to constrain media. If this is the case, increased literacy or increased access to broadcast media could lead to decreased media freedom. Consider the case of Boss Tweed of New York City's Tammany Hall in the 1860s and 1870s. Tweed was not concerned about articles exposing his corrupt actions because most of his constituents could not read, but cartoons proved to be Tweed's undoing (see the cartoon and the story about Boss Tweed's fall from grace). And, as mentioned earlier, in India today, print and television news are for the most part free, but only state-run radio stations are allowed to provide news coverage, and radio is the most accessible medium for the poor and illiterate. Thus, literacy might influence media freedom, but not in the way Nixon expected.

Conclusion

Historically, media freedom has both expanded and contracted because of technological advances, but it is largely shaped by political and economic factors. From the printing press to smart phones, advances in technology initially facilitate a freer flow of communication and information, but technology can also be used to stem that flow. Where there is a political will to minimize media freedom, there is an economic, legal, or political means of doing so. A printing press will not produce a newspaper without paper or ink, a radio station cannot broadcast if its license is revoked, and journalists cannot investigate corruption if they are imprisoned or killed. In the country reports that follow, we describe how media freedom has changed from 1948 to the present in countries around the world.

BOX 3.3

CARTOONS VS. CORRUPTION: HOW CARICATURIST THOMAS NAST DREW DOWN BOSS TWEED

New York City (1868): He was not the mayor or governor, but from 1863 to 1871 William Magear Tweed ruled over the governments of New York City and state. Known as *Boss Tweed*, he rose to power in Tammany Hall, a group that had absolute power over the local Democratic Party. Tweed controlled who got jobs with the city as well as which businesses were awarded contracts and enriched himself and his supporters through a system of kickbacks. In all, Tweed and his Tammany Hall compatriots are estimated to have skimmed between $1 billion to $4 billion (in 2011 dollars) (Dunlap 2011). The Tammany Hall crew also enjoyed control over the press, largely through bribery.

In this 1886 cartoon, Thomas Nast reprised his favorite subject, Boss Tweed, eight years after Tweed's death in prison. As a diamond studded convict, Tweed's spirit of corruption still dominated New York City politics.

Source: Everett Collection/Newscom.

Eventually, though, the press helped bring Tweed down. First came the cartoons drawn by Thomas Nast for *Harper's Weekly*. In 1868, Nast launched a cartoon campaign against Tweed. In picture after picture, he depicted Tweed as a gluttonous thief. These drawings proved more effective against Tweed than negative news articles because Tweed's constituents, for the most part poor Irish immigrants, could not read. In fact, Tweed is alleged to have raged to his underlings, "Stop them damned pictures. I don't care what the papers write about me. My constituents can't read. But, damn it, they can see pictures" (Thomas Nast: Prince of Caricaturists 2012).

Then in 1871, the *New York Times*, which at the time was a Republican paper, published a series of articles documenting Tweed's corrupt acts. In particular, the *Times* obtained ledgers from a courthouse construction project that showed "penny for penny, the sums that were nominally going to fit out and furnish the courthouse, but were actually bound for the pockets of Boss Tweed and crew" (Dunlap 2011). In 1871 New York City Controller Richard B. Connolly offered *New York Times* publisher George Jones $5 million (worth about $100 million today) to stop the story from running. Jones refused.

Eventually Tweed was tried and sentenced to prison. He escaped and fled to Spain, where he was recognized due to one Nast's cartoons. He was arrested and returned to the United States, where he died in prison in 1878.

References and Further Readings

Bassiouni, Mahmoud Cherif, Nigel Rodley, Badria Al-Awadhi, Philippe Kirsch, and Mahnoush H. Arsanjani. 2011. *Report of the Bahrain Independent Commission of Inquiry*. Manama, Bahrain.

Benkler, Yochai. 2000. "From Consumers to Users: Shifting the Deeper Structures of Regulation toward Sustainable Commons and User Access." *Federal Communications Law Journal* no. 52: 561–79.

Briggs, Charles Frederick and Augustus Maverick. 1858. *The Story of the Telegraph, and a History of the Great Atlantic Cable*. New York: Rudd & Carleton.

Brock, Gerald W. 2003. *The Second Information Revolution*. Cambridge, MA: Harvard University Press.

Committee to Protect Journalists. 2012. Attacks on the Press in 2011: Bahrain. http://cpj.org/2012/02/attacks-on-the-press-in-2011-bahrain.php.

Cook, Timothy. 1998. *Governing with the News*. Chicago: The University of Chicago Press.

Dunlap, David W. 2011. "A Happy 200th to The Time's First Publisher, Whom Boss Tweed Couldn't Buy or Kill." *The New York Times*.

FCC. 2012. *History of Communications: Historical Periods in Television Technology*. Federal Communications Commission 20052012. Available from http://transition.fcc.gov/omd/history/tv/1930–1959.html.

Fitz-Gerald, W. G. 1907. "A Telephone Newspaper." *Scientific American*, June 22, 507.

Fox, Johnathan. 2012. Religion and State Codebook: Round 2 (version 5).

Goldsmith, Jack and Tim Wu. 2008. *Who Controls the Internet? Illusions of a Borderless World*. Oxford: Oxford University Press.

Hocking, William. 1947. *Freedom of the Press: A Framework of Principle*. Chicago: The University of Chicago Press.

Human Rights Watch. 2007. Crackdown: Repression of the 2007 Popular Protests in Burma. Human Rights Watch.

———. 2012. World Report 2012: Bahrain.

Lessig, Lawrence. 2001 *The Future of Ideas: The Fate of the Commons in a Connected World*. New York: Random House.

MacCannell, Daniel. 2009. *Cultures of Proclamation: The Decline and Fall of the Anglophone News Process, 1460–1642*, History and History of Art. Aberdeen: University of Aberdeen.

Mailland, Julien. 2010. "The Semantic Web and Information Flow: A Legal Framework." *North Carolina Journal of Law & Technology* 11 (2).

Marshall, Monty G., Ted Robert Gurr, and Keith Jaggers. 2010. *Polity IV Project: Political Regime Characteristics and Transitions, 1800–2009*. Edited by Center for Systemic Peace.

Milton, John. 2010. *Areopagitica: A Speech for the Liberty of Unlicensed Printing to the Parlament of England* 1644 [cited January 14, 2010]. Available from www.dartmouth.edu/~milton/reading_room/areopagitica/index.shtml.

Nixon, Raymon B. 1960. "Factors related to freedom in national press systems." *Jounalism Quarterly* 37 (1): 13–28.

Nixon, Raymond B. 1965. "Freedom in the World's Press: A Fresh Appraisal with New Data." *Journalism Quarterly* 42 (1): 9–14.

"President's Address to Congress on Domestic and Foreign Policies." 1921. *New York Times*, April 13, 1921.

Rhodes, Tom. 2013. UN Panel: Eskinder Nega jailing violates international law. *CPJ Blog Press Freedom News and View*. http://www.cpj.org/blog/2013/04/un-panel-eskinder-negas-jailing-violates-internati.php.

Sandal, Nukhet and Jenifer Whitten-Woodring. 2012. "Holding the Sacred Accountable: The Effect of Government Support for Religion on Media Freedom." In *University of Massachusetts Lowell Faculty Research Symposium*. Lowell, MA.

Solomon, Erika and Elizabeth Fullerton. 2011. *Bahrain puts protest poet under house arrest*. http://www.reuters.com/article/2011/07/14/oukwd-uk-bahrain-protests-idAFTRE76D1QD20110714?pageNumber=1&virtualBrandChannel=0.

Sophocles. 1994–2000. Antigone. In *The Internet Classics Archive*, edited by Daniel C. Stevenson: Web Atomics.

Starr, Paul. 2004. *The Creation of the Media: Political Origins of Modern Communications*. Cambridge, MA: Basic Books.

Stephens, Mitchell. 1988. *A History of News: From the Drum to the Satellite*. New York: Viking Adult.

Stephens, Mitchell. 2007. *A History of News* (Third Edition). New York: Oxford University Press.

Thomas Nast: Prince of Caricaturists. 2012. Ohio State University Library. http://cartoons.osu.edu/digital_albums/thomasnast/. U.S. Constitution, Amendment 1.

WAN-IFRA. 2010. *World Press Trends 2010*. Darmstatd-Paris-Lyon-Stockhold-Madrid-Chennai-Singapore: World Association of Newspapers and News Publishers.

Watkins, John Elfreth. 1900. "What May Happen in the Next Hundred Years." *Ladies' Home Journal*, 8.

Welsh, May Ying. 2011. *Bahrain: Shouting in the Dark*. Al Jazeera.

White, Thomas H. 2013. *United States Early Radio History*. Available from http://earlyradiohistory.us/.

Whitten-Woodring, Jenifer and Douglas Van Belle. *The Correlates of Media Freedom* (Working paper). Available at http://faculty.uml.edu/Jenifer_WhittenWoodring/index.aspx.

Zamoyski, Adam. 1987. *The Polish Way: A Thousand-Year History of the Poles and Their Culture*. New York: Hippocrene Books.

Zuzao, Lin. 2010. "One of the Great Wonders in the Library's Collections—A Case Study on Wood Blocks for Printing in the Zhejiang Library." In *The History and Cultural Heritage of Chinese Calligraphy, Printing and Library Work*, edited by Susan M. Allen, Lin Zuzao, Cheng Xiaolan, and Jan Bos. Munich: De Gruyter Saur.

Notes

1. This quote is from the play *Antigone* in which a guard bitterly complains about having to tell the king that someone defied his orders (Sophocles 1994–2000).

2. Hocking (1947) provides an example of this kind of discussion.

3. For more on Milton's argument for unlicensed printing and against pre-publication censorship see Chapter 2.

4. Dutch is an adjective here, the southern half of what is now the Netherlands and is traditionally called Holland and the northern half of what is now Belgium are ethnically Dutch provinces and cities in these regions were the locations from which these presses operated.

5. For an excellent discussion of this see Governing the News by Timothy Cook (1998).

6. For more information on the emergence of telephone and radio see the *United States Early Radio History* website created by Thomas H. White (1996). http://earlyradiohistory.us/.

7. For more information on this study see "The Correlates of Media Freedom" (Whitten-Woodring and Van Belle 2013).

8. For further reading on this see "Holding the Sacred Accountable" (Sandal and Whitten-Woodring 2012).

Chapter 4

The Evolution (and Devolution) of Media Freedom Since World War II

Introduction

This chapter features country profiles on how media freedom has evolved (or devolved) since 1948 for all 196 independent countries that were in existence at the end of 2013.[1] Here we provide some details about the information used to create these profiles.

The media freedom data from 1948 to 1994 are from the Van Belle Global Press Freedom Data. The data from 1995 to 2001 are from an update prepared for this volume. For the most part, the data from 2001 to 2012 are drawn from Freedom House's Reports on Freedom of the Press. Yet, in gathering information to provide narratives on the changes in media freedom for each country, we inevitably uncovered new information that led to some coding changes. Furthermore, our definition of media freedom has led to some (though few) differences between our codes and those of Freedom House. Generally, the historic narratives are based on a number of sources, many of which are country specific, but we have consistently relied on information from the International Press Institute, the Inter American Press Association, the Country Studies from the Federal Research Division of the Library of Congress, and the U.S. Department of State's Country Reports on Human Rights Practices.

To put each media environment in context, we provide information about the political environment. In the Year-by-Year charts, in addition to the status of the media, we note the regime type of the country for each year. For the most part we rely on data from the Center for Systemic Peace's Polity IV Project (Marshall, Gurr, Jaggers

2013). This dataset includes a measure of regime type that ranges from most autocratic (−10) to most democratic (10). We use the categories recommended by the authors of the dataset:

- countries ranging from −10 to −6 are labeled "autocracies,"
- those ranging from −5 to 5 are labeled "anocracies"—meaning they are somewhere in the middle, and
- those ranging from 6 to 10 are labeled "democracies."

In the cases where the Polity data are not available, usually smaller countries, we rely on Freedom House's Freedom of the World Dataset which rates countries on a scale of 1 (most free) to 7 (least free) and labels countries ranging from 1 to 2.5 as "democracies," those ranging from 3 to 5 as "anocracies," and those from 5.5 to 7 as "autocracies." In very few cases where both Freedom House and the Polity IV Project are not available, we have used the descriptions from the U.S. Department of State's Country Reports on Human Rights Practices. In addition to these three categories, we also indicate periods of transition using the Polity Project's transitional categories of "foreign interruption," "interregnum" (or anarchy), and "in transition."

Finally, to provide current information on the state of the news media for each country, we have relied on data from the following sources:

- The World Association of Newspapers and News Publishers' *World Press Trends*, which provides the number of paid-for daily newspapers and the total average circulation per issue.

- The International Telecommunication Union's ICT Indicators Database, which provides annual internet access data
- Freedom House's Report on Freedom of the Press, which provides detailed information about the current status of the news media including laws and practices regarding media freedom, and availability of news media
- The Committee to Protect Journalists, which tracks information on attacks on news media and violence against journalists
- Reporters Without Borders, which monitors media freedom and records attacks on journalists and news outlets
- The BBC News Country Profiles, which provide current conditions for news media as well as timelines that document important political events

The following profiles provide narratives of how the media environments have changed for all available countries, from Afghanistan to Zimbabwe from 1948 to 2012.

Reference

Marshall, Monty G., Ted Robert Gurr, and Keith Jaggers. 2013. Dataset Users' Manual *Polity IV Project: Political Regime Characteristics and Transitions, 1800–2012*. Center for Systemic Peace. Available from www.systemicpeace.org.

Note

1. We include Taiwan because it functions as an independent state even though it is not officially recognized as an independent state by the international community for political reasons. We do not include the Holy See (Vatican City) because, given its small population (estimated at 839 in 2013) and its location (within Italy), it does not function as an independent media market.

Afghanistan: 1948–2012

Afghanistan Year by Year

Year	Media	Government
1948	Not Free	Autocracy
1949	Not Free	Autocracy
1950	Not Free	Autocracy
1951	Not Free	Autocracy
1952	Not Free	Autocracy
1953	Not Free	Autocracy
1954	Not Free	Autocracy
1955	Not Free	Autocracy
1956	Not Free	Autocracy
1957	Not Free	Autocracy
1958	Not Free	Autocracy
1959	Not Free	Autocracy
1960	Not Free	Autocracy
1961	Not Free	Autocracy
1962	Not Free	Autocracy
1963	Not Free	Autocracy
1964	Not Free	Autocracy
1965	Not Free	Autocracy
1966	Not Free	Autocracy
1967	Not Free	Autocracy
1968	Not Free	Autocracy
1969	Not Free	Autocracy
1970	Not Free	Autocracy
1971	Not Free	Autocracy
1972	Not Free	Autocracy
1973	Not Free	Autocracy
1974	Not Free	Autocracy
1975	Not Free	Autocracy

(Continued)

MEDIA FREEDOM HISTORY IN A NUTSHELL

- Afghanistan's decades of war and foreign occupation have made it almost impossible for news media to function
- In the last decade independent news media have emerged, but journalists continue to face threats, attacks, and censorship to the extent that the media environment is decisively not free
- As of 2012, Afghanistan had more than 400 newspapers, more than seventy-five television stations, and about 150 radio stations (Freedom House Freedom of the Press 2013 Report)
- As of 2012, about 6 percent of Afghans had Internet access (International Telecommunication Union's 2012 ICT Indicators Database)

In Brief

Afghanistan's tumultuous history, including long periods of foreign occupation, has contributed to a dangerous and restrictive media environment. After decades of little or no news media, independent media outlets have emerged in Afghanistan, but conditions in this war-torn country remain inhospitable for journalists.

Chronology

1948–2012: Not Free

In the late 1940s and early 1950s, news media were "more or less non-existent" in Afghanistan.[1] By 1959, Afghanistan had three daily newspapers in Kabul and a dozen daily or weekly newspapers in the provinces.[2] Yet all of these publications were at least somewhat, if not entirely, dependent on Afghanistan's Press Department, which also operated Radio Kabul.[3] It was difficult for privately owned news media to

(Continued)

Year	Media	Government
1976	Not Free	Autocracy
1977	Not Free	Autocracy
1978	Not Free	Anocracy
1979	Not Free	Foreign Interruption
1980	Not Free	Foreign Interruption
1981	Not Free	Foreign Interruption
1982	Not Free	Foreign Interruption
1983	Not Free	Foreign Interruption
1984	Not Free	Foreign Interruption
1985	Not Free	Foreign Interruption
1986	Not Free	Foreign Interruption
1987	Not Free	Foreign Interruption
1988	Not Free	Foreign Interruption
1989	Not Free	Autocracy
1990	Not Free	Autocracy
1991	Not Free	Autocracy
1992	Not Free	Interregnum
1993	Not Free	Interregnum
1994	Not Free	Interregnum
1995	Not Free	Interregnum
1996	Not Free	Autocracy
1997	Not Free	Autocracy
1998	Not Free	Autocracy
1999	Not Free	Autocracy
2000	Not Free	Autocracy
2001	Not Free	Foreign Interruption
2002	Not Free	Foreign Interruption
2003	Not Free	Foreign Interruption
2004	Not Free	Foreign Interruption
2005	Not Free	Foreign Interruption
2006	Not Free	Foreign Interruption
2007	Not Free	Foreign Interruption
2008	Not Free	Foreign Interruption
2009	Not Free	Foreign Interruption
2010	Not Free	Foreign Interruption
2011	Not Free	Foreign Interruption
2012	Not Free	Foreign Interruption

survive in this hostile climate. In 1967, the International Press Institute noted that the government had closed down three independent newspapers in Kabul and that two others had closed down due to financial problems, leaving the city with two newspapers.[4]

Following the 1978 *coup d'état*, the People's Democratic Party of Afghanistan, which clearly appreciated the potential influence of news media, took steps to gain control of all government newspapers and television stations.[5] When the new communist government was threatened, the Soviet Union sent in thousands of troops, beginning the Soviet Occupation, which continued until 1989. During this period, news media were under direct government control with guidance and supervision from the Soviet Union.[6] Just a few years after the 1989 departure of the Soviet troops, civil war erupted. During this time, the few news outlets that existed were restricted. These restrictions increased when the Taliban gained control in 1996. Newspapers were closed, television was banned, and the Taliban's Voice of Sharia Law radio station was used to disseminate propaganda and prayers.[7]

Following the September 11, 2001, terrorist attacks on the United States and the Taliban's failure to hand over Osama bin Laden, the United States and its allies attacked the country and Afghanistan was once again under foreign occupation. During the occupation, independent news media began to reemerge, but these outlets faced a number of restrictions and threats from both government and warlords.[8]

Media Today

Although Afghanistan now has several hundred newspapers and magazines and a wide range of broadcast media, journalists continue to face threats, attacks, and censorship. Afghanistan has constitutional provisions for media freedom, but content that violates Islamic principles is restricted. A new media bill proposed in 2012 would increase government control of news media, but so far media freedom proponents have kept it from passing into law. Radio remains the most accessible medium, especially in rural areas. As of 2012, only about 6 percent of Afghans had Internet access, yet there are some indications that the increasing availability of mobile phones will increase both access to the Internet and news media.

Notes

1. *Government Pressures on the Press*, IPI Survey (Zurich: International Press Institute, 1955), 6.
2. Quintus C. Wilson, *Press Freedom Gains in Afghanistan*, IPI Report (Zurich: International Press Institute, November 1959).
3. Ibid.
4. *News of the World's Press: Afghanistan Down to Two Papers*, IPI Report (Zurich: International Press Institute, June 1967).
5. Peter R. Blood, *Afghanistan: A Country Study*, Library of Congress Country Studies (Washington, DC: Library of Congress, 1997). Available at http://lcweb2 .loc.gov/frd/cs/.
6. *World Press Freedom Review*, IPI Report (Zurich: International Press Institute, 1984).
7. *World Press Freedom Review*, IPI Report (Vienna: International Press Institute, 1996).
8. *Freedom of the Press* (Washington, DC: Freedom House, 2003). Available at http://freedomhouse .org/reports.

Albania: 1948–2012

Albania Year by Year

Year	Media	Government
1948	Not Free	Autocracy
1949	Not Free	Autocracy
1950	Not Free	Autocracy
1951	Not Free	Autocracy
1952	Not Free	Autocracy
1953	Not Free	Autocracy
1954	Not Free	Autocracy
1955	Not Free	Autocracy
1956	Not Free	Autocracy
1957	Not Free	Autocracy
1958	Not Free	Autocracy
1959	Not Free	Autocracy
1960	Not Free	Autocracy
1961	Not Free	Autocracy
1962	Not Free	Autocracy
1963	Not Free	Autocracy
1964	Not Free	Autocracy
1965	Not Free	Autocracy
1966	Not Free	Autocracy
1967	Not Free	Autocracy
1968	Not Free	Autocracy
1969	Not Free	Autocracy
1970	Not Free	Autocracy
1971	Not Free	Autocracy
1972	Not Free	Autocracy
1973	Not Free	Autocracy
1974	Not Free	Autocracy
1975	Not Free	Autocracy

MEDIA FREEDOM HISTORY IN A NUTSHELL

- Autocratic Soviet Bloc state with strictly controlled media from 1948 through 1989
- Authoritarian controls remained in force until 1994 with frequent short-term fluctuations in the media environment
- A two-year transition in the media environment begins in 1995
- Beginning in late 1996, there is notable, clear evidence of media criticisms of government
- Desperate economic conditions have made media in the post-communist era vulnerable to economic pressures.
- As of 2009, there were twenty-nine paid-for daily newspapers with a total average circulation of 70,000, and at least sixty-four private television stations, and forty-four private radio stations in addition to the national television and radio stations (World Association of Newspaper's 2010 World Newspaper Trends).
- As of 2012 Internet media were unrestricted, but only about 45 percent of Albanians had Internet access (International Telecommunication Union's 2012 ICT Indicators Database)

In Brief

Both Western-oriented nationalist and Soviet-oriented communist resistance forces were active during the German and Italian occupations of World War II. That resistance transitioned into civil war well before the end of the war and after the war the communists quickly won. Media control was one of the first and most jealously guarded resources of the socialist regime. Albania benefitted greatly from communist rule, seeing decades of rapid economic growth, albeit from an incredibly low base situation that had been created by disastrous failures in democratic and monarchical leadership after World War I and

Year	Media	Government
1976	Not Free	Autocracy
1977	Not Free	Autocracy
1978	Not Free	Autocracy
1979	Not Free	Autocracy
1980	Not Free	Autocracy
1981	Not Free	Autocracy
1982	Not Free	Autocracy
1983	Not Free	Autocracy
1984	Not Free	Autocracy
1985	Not Free	Autocracy
1986	Not Free	Autocracy
1987	Not Free	Autocracy
1988	Not Free	Autocracy
1989	Not Free	Autocracy
1990	Not Free	Autocracy
1991	Not Free	Autocracy
1992	Not Free	Autocracy
1993	Not Free	Autocracy
1994	Not Free	Autocracy
1995	Not Free	Anocracy
1996	Imperfectly Free	Anocracy
1997	Imperfectly Free	Anocracy
1998	Not Free	Anocracy
1999	Not Free	Anocracy
2000	Imperfectly Free	Anocracy
2001	Imperfectly Free	Anocracy
2002	Imperfectly Free	Democracy
2003	Imperfectly Free	Democracy
2004	Imperfectly Free	Democracy
2005	Imperfectly Free	Democracy
2006	Imperfectly Free	Democracy
2007	Imperfectly Free	Democracy
2008	Imperfectly Free	Democracy
2009	Imperfectly Free	Democracy
2010	Imperfectly Free	Democracy
2011	Imperfectly Free	Democracy
2012	Imperfectly Free	Democracy

exploitative occupations during the two world wars. The transition from a Soviet Bloc style authoritarian and strictly controlled press to a moderately stable and effective Western free media system took roughly a decade, but in some ways the actual transition began in 1985 with the death of Enver Hoxha, who had ruled for several decades. Calls for liberalization emerged shortly after his death, and the press was one of the institutions that benefitted from efforts to redress rising economic difficulties by seeking closer ties to the West. It is not clear how much geographic location aided or impeded the post-Socialist development of media, but the strategic location of Albania in relation to Greece, Italy, and the disintegrating Yugoslavia make Western intervention and external support of liberalization beyond official aid highly likely. Overall, the years since the fall of communism have been chaotic, marked by frequent short-term shifts in the political environment.

Chronology

1948–1995: Not Free

The early years of Socialist Albania were bloody, marked by imprisonment, purges, liquidations, and other acts aimed at completely eliminating any and all political opposition, and by 1948, control of the media was absolute. There is little evidence of any change until 1985 when some tentative debates over developing closer ties with the West begin to appear and there appears to be some, very slight, expansion in the topics of coverage. The fall of the Soviet bloc brought chaos to Albania, and 1990 to 1995 saw rapid, large, and repeated shifts in the media environment. Control, however, remained the default until roughly 1995.

The timing and duration of this transitional period is debatable, but by 1995, it was clear that direct government control was giving way to other coercive mechanisms. Media often reflected the interests of political groups, government determination to crack down on dissent, and economic difficulties.[1]

1996–1997: Imperfectly Free

Between swings from persecution of reporters to complete freedom and everything in between, the environment eventually settled into the situation where news media could provide a forum for debate more often than not. Throughout the rapid succession of government changes in 1996–1997, the media demonstrated a consistent ability to criticize both liberal and conservative political parties and politicians. Economic pressures during this period were immense, and many media outlets were compromised by ownership interests or other forms of economic coercion.

During these years, there were a number of attacks on independent journalists, some of which led to severe injuries, arrests, and in some cases death.[2] In 1997, thousands of citizens who lost money in pyramid schemes took to the streets in protest. Many journalists attempting to cover the story were either shot or beaten, and their equipment seized.[3]

1998–1999: Not Free

Ironically, the establishment of a constitutional guarantee of media freedom in 1998 occurred near the beginning of a conservative swing in the domestic political environment. A sustained effort to coerce media, both politically and economically, significantly compromised their ability to criticize conservative policies and leaders.

2000–2012: Imperfectly Free

In the run up to the externally monitored and accepted 2001 national elections, media demonstrated a clear ability to act as a forum for political competition and debate, and Albania officially moved into the ranks of Western-style democracies. With that, many of the issues and forces that threatened to derail media freedom were removed, and in 2002, media demonstrated the ability to carry their public sphere role forward into the daily conduct of democratic government.

Media Today

Economic issues probably represent the greatest threat to media freedom, with some difficulties in strongly partisan press outlets a second concern. It is not at all clear how the collapse of the Greek economy and Italian economic difficulties will affect Albania. It is also unclear how the elites from earlier authoritarian regimes might react to that situation, but a retreat from liberal political and social institutions is a constant possibility.

Notes

1. *World Press Freedom Review*, IPI Report (Vienna: International Press Institute, 1995).
2. *World Press Freedom Review*, IPI Report (Vienna: International Press Institute, 1996).
3. *World Press Freedom Review*, IPI Report (Vienna: International Press Institute, 1997).

Algeria: 1962–2012

Algeria Year by Year

Year	Media	Government
1962	Not Free	Autocracy
1963	Not Free	Autocracy
1964	Not Free	Autocracy
1965	Not Free	Autocracy
1966	Not Free	Autocracy
1967	Not Free	Autocracy
1968	Not Free	Autocracy
1969	Not Free	Autocracy
1970	Not Free	Autocracy
1971	Not Free	Autocracy
1972	Not Free	Autocracy
1973	Not Free	Autocracy
1974	Not Free	Autocracy
1975	Not Free	Autocracy
1976	Not Free	Autocracy
1977	Not Free	Autocracy
1978	Not Free	Autocracy
1979	Not Free	Autocracy
1980	Not Free	Autocracy
1981	Not Free	Autocracy
1982	Not Free	Autocracy
1983	Not Free	Autocracy
1984	Not Free	Autocracy
1985	Not Free	Autocracy
1986	Not Free	Autocracy
1987	Not Free	Autocracy
1988	Not Free	Autocracy

(Continued)

MEDIA FREEDOM HISTORY IN A NUTSHELL

- Algeria's military took over government shortly after independence and controlled the media
- In what is essentially an ongoing civil war, media remain restricted
- As of 2012, Algeria had eighty newspapers in the capital, many of which were privately owned, but whose owners had close ties to government; television and radio were state-owned (Freedom House Freedom of the Press 2013 Report)
- As of 2012 about 15 percent of Algerians had Internet access (International Telecommunication Union's 2012 ICT Indicators Database)

In Brief

In the half century since gaining independence from France, Algeria has been wracked by almost constant conflict and violence. In the context of that violence, media have been directly controlled or strictly regulated.

Chronology

1962–2012: Not Free

The presidency of Ben Bella lasted less than two years before he was overthrown by Colonel Houari Boumedienne. After Bouemedienne's death in 1976, the military appointed a new president and military rule, with a directly controlled media, continued through 1988.

Economic crisis in the mid 1980s, culminating with riots in 1988, presaged a shift in Algerian politics. During the 1988 riots more than 500 journalists resigned from the government party (the FLN), admitted that they had been pressured to alter the facts in the past, and vowed to report truthfully in the future.[1] The ban on political

(Continued)

Year	Media	Government
1989	Not Free	Anocracy
1990	Not Free	Anocracy
1991	Not Free	Anocracy
1992	Not Free	Autocracy
1993	Not Free	Autocracy
1994	Not Free	Autocracy
1995	Not Free	Anocracy
1996	Not Free	Anocracy
1997	Not Free	Anocracy
1998	Not Free	Anocracy
1999	Not Free	Anocracy
2000	Not Free	Anocracy
2001	Not Free	Anocracy
2002	Not Free	Anocracy
2003	Not Free	Anocracy
2004	Not Free	Anocracy
2005	Not Free	Anocracy
2006	Not Free	Anocracy
2007	Not Free	Anocracy
2008	Not Free	Anocracy
2009	Not Free	Anocracy
2010	Not Free	Anocracy
2011	Not Free	Anocracy
2012	Not Free	Anocracy

parties was lifted in 1989, and with that, partisan media began to emerge. The military retook power in 1992, banning street gatherings and placing extreme restrictions on the media, which remained in place throughout what was essentially a civil war. During the transition, a number of journalists were arrested, many foreign journalists were expelled or banned from entering the country, and Presidential Decree 92-320 was used to close down critical news outlets.[2] In 2011, the state of emergency was lifted but media remained restricted.

Media Today

Violence continues despite attempts at reconciliation and furthering democratic rule. The media remain heavily restricted. Insulting the president, the military, the judiciary, and the parliament remains a criminal offence. The 2012 media law appears to both limit and enhance media freedom. On the one hand, the law established requirements for media ownership, limitations on press coverage of security and criminal investigations, and imposed stiff fines for journalistic offences with prison sentences for failure to pay those fines. On the other hand, the law was supposed to put an end to prison sentences for journalistic offences. Thus, the impact of this law remains unclear.

Notes

1. *World Press Freedom Review*, IPI Report (Zurich: International Press Institute, 1988).
2. *World Press Freedom Review*, IPI Report (Vienna: International Press Institute, 1992).

Andorra: 1993–2012

Andorra Year by Year

Year	Media	Government
1993	Free	Democracy
1994	Free	Democracy
1995	Free	Democracy
1996	Free	Democracy
1997	Free	Democracy
1998	Free	Democracy
1999	Free	Democracy
2000	Free	Democracy
2001	Free	Democracy
2002	Free	Democracy
2003	Free	Democracy
2004	Free	Democracy
2005	Free	Democracy
2006	Free	Democracy
2007	Free	Democracy
2008	Free	Democracy
2009	Free	Democracy
2010	Free	Democracy
2011	Free	Democracy
2012	Free	Democracy

MEDIA FREEDOM HISTORY IN A NUTSHELL

- Andorra's media environment has to a great extent been shaped by its close relationship with neighboring France and Spain
- Since 1993, media have been free
- Andorra has a variety of publicly owned and privately owned print and broadcast news media; news media from France and Spain are also accessible
- As of 2012, more than 86 percent of Andorrans had Internet access (International Telecommunication Union's 2012 ICT Indicators Database)

Although Andorra had limited domestic news outlets in the early 1990s (two newspapers, three magazines, one public radio station, and one private radio station), publications from other countries were widely available, especially those from Andorra's neighbors—France and Spain.[2] By the mid-2000s, Andorra had several daily and weekly newspapers, one public radio and television station, and more than a dozen privately owned radio stations and half a dozen privately owned television stations.[3] Additionally, residents have access to news media from France and Spain. The Internet remains unrestricted, and most residents (more than 86 percent in 2012) enjoy Internet access.

Chronology

1993–2012: Free

Andorra's media environment has to a great extent been shaped by its close relationship with neighboring France and Spain. In 1993, the Principality of Andorra transitioned to a parliamentary democracy. The new constitution included provisions for freedom of expression and media freedom that were also respected in practice.[1]

Notes

1. *Andorra Human Rights Practices, 1993* (Washington, DC: U.S. Department of State, 1994). Available at http://dosfan.lib.uic.edu/ERC/democracy/1993_hrp_report/93hrp_report_eur/Andorra.html.
2. Ibid.
3. *Freedom of the Press* (Washington, DC: Freedom House, 2008). Available at http://www.freedomhouse.org/reports.

Angola: 1975–2012

Angola Year by Year

Year	Media	Government
1975	Not Free	Autocracy
1976	Not Free	Autocracy
1977	Not Free	Autocracy
1978	Not Free	Autocracy
1979	Not Free	Autocracy
1980	Not Free	Autocracy
1981	Not Free	Autocracy
1982	Not Free	Autocracy
1983	Not Free	Autocracy
1984	Not Free	Autocracy
1985	Not Free	Autocracy
1986	Not Free	Autocracy
1987	Not Free	Autocracy
1988	Not Free	Autocracy
1989	Not Free	Autocracy
1990	Not Free	Autocracy
1991	Not Free	Transition
1992	Not Free	Interregnum
1993	Not Free	Transition
1994	Not Free	Transition
1995	Not Free	Transition
1996	Not Free	Transition
1997	Not Free	Anocracy
1998	Not Free	Anocracy
1999	Not Free	Anocracy

MEDIA FREEDOM HISTORY IN A NUTSHELL

- For nearly three decades following its independence from Portugal, Angola was mired in civil war
- During the civil war, news media were tightly controlled by government, and since the ceasefire, news media have been restricted
- As of 2012, the government-controlled newspaper, television channel, and radio station were the only news media with national reach, and most owners of private media had close relationships to the government (Freedom House Freedom of the Press 2013 Report)
- As of 2012, less than 17 percent of Angolans had Internet access (International Telecommunication Union's 2012 ICT Indicators Database)

In Brief

Angola was effectively engaged in a civil war from the time it achieved independence in 1975 until the 2002 cease fire between government forces and rebels. During this period, news media were controlled by the government, and following the ceasefire they remain restricted.

Chronology

1975–2012: Not Free

Angola's transition to independence was tumultuous. The Portuguese withdrew, ceding independence to the people of Angola. Given the lack of a central government, different factions seized different territories, and the country plunged into civil war. By 1976, the People's Movement for the Liberation of Angola (MPLA) had control over most of the country, had nationalized all news outlets, and "the media were

Year	Media	Government
2000	Not Free	Anocracy
2001	Not Free	Anocracy
2002	Not Free	Anocracy
2003	Not Free	Anocracy
2004	Not Free	Anocracy
2005	Not Free	Anocracy
2006	Not Free	Anocracy
2007	Not Free	Anocracy
2008	Not Free	Anocracy
2009	Not Free	Anocracy
2010	Not Free	Anocracy
2011	Not Free	Anocracy
2012	Not Free	Anocracy

limited to disseminating official policy without critical comment or opposing viewpoints."[1] Angop, the country's official news agency, maintained a close relationship with TASS, the Soviet news agency.[2] Radio was a particularly popular medium, and Rádio Nacional de Angola broadcasts were available throughout the country. In the late 1980s, the opposition station Voice of Resistance of the Black Cockerel began broadcasting in central and southern Angola.

In 1991, the MPLA took steps toward creating a social democracy, and in 1992 held multiparty elections, but these were postponed as the civil war intensified. During this time journalists self-censored and stayed away from covering issues and events that might raise the ire of the government or the opposition. Even so many journalists were killed or kidnapped as the conflict continued.[3] President dos Santos, dubbed an "enemy of the press" by the Committee to Protect Journalists, who rose to power in 1979, remained in control of the country following the 2002 ceasefire between government forces and the National Union for the Total Independence of Angola (UNITA) rebels.[4] While the end of the twenty-seven-year civil war reduced some of the dangers for journalists, news media remained restricted.

Media Today

Although the constitution guarantees media freedom, in practice news media are restricted. Libel and defamation remain criminalized, with penalties that include prison terms and stiff fines. Although Angola does have privately owned media, the country's major media outlets—those with national reach—are government owned and operated. Journalists who criticize the government are vulnerable to lawsuits, prison sentences, and physical attacks.

Notes

1. Thomas Collelo, *Angola: A Country Study*. Federal Research Division (Washington, DC: Library of Congress, 1989). Available at http://lcweb2.loc.gov/frd/cs/.
2. Ibid.
3. *World Press Freedom Review*, IPI Report (Vienna: International Press Institute, 1993).
4. *World Press Freedom Review*, IPI Report (Vienna: International Press Institute, 2002), 8.

Antigua and Barbuda: 1982–2012

Antigua and Barbuda Year by Year

Year	Media	Government
1982	Imperfectly Free	Democracy
1983	Imperfectly Free	Democracy
1984	Imperfectly Free	Democracy
1985	Imperfectly Free	Democracy
1986	Imperfectly Free	Democracy
1987	Imperfectly Free	Democracy
1988	Imperfectly Free	Democracy
1989	Imperfectly Free	Democracy
1990	Imperfectly Free	Democracy
1991	Imperfectly Free	Democracy
1992	Imperfectly Free	Democracy
1993	Imperfectly Free	Democracy
1994	Imperfectly Free	Democracy
1995	Imperfectly Free	Democracy
1996	Imperfectly Free	Democracy
1997	Imperfectly Free	Democracy
1998	Imperfectly Free	Democracy
1999	Imperfectly Free	Democracy
2000	Imperfectly Free	Democracy
2001	Imperfectly Free	Democracy
2002	Imperfectly Free	Democracy
2003	Imperfectly Free	Democracy
2004	Imperfectly Free	Democracy
2005	Imperfectly Free	Democracy
2006	Imperfectly Free	Democracy

MEDIA FREEDOM HISTORY IN A NUTSHELL

- Since Antigua and Barbuda gained independence the media have been imperfectly free
- The country had one daily newspaper in 2012 (Freedom House *Freedom of the Press 2013 Report*)
- There are several regional and local television stations, as well as the availability of American television networks. ZDK radio is owned and operated by the Prime Minister and family
- As of 2012, 84 percent of Antiguans and Barbudans had Internet access (International Telecommunication Union's 2012 ICT Indicators Database)

In Brief

Antigua and Barbuda has long had limited but functionally free media.

Chronology

1982–2012: Imperfectly Free

Since Antigua and Barbuda gained independence in 1981, the media have been imperfectly free. There are constitutional provisions for media freedom, but defamation is a criminal offense and carries prison terms of up to three years. From 1982 to 2004, much of the broadcast media in Antigua were owned and operated by the family of then Prime Minister Lester Bird of the Antigua Labour Party; however newspapers were independently owned. In 1996, *The Daily Observer* newspaper started Observer Radio, but after just one day on-air, police seized the station's equipment.[1] After a five-year court battle, Observer Radio was allowed to resume broadcasting in 2001.[2] The elections of 2004 brought about a change of

2007	Imperfectly Free	Democracy
2008	Imperfectly Free	Democracy
2009	Imperfectly Free	Democracy
2010	Imperfectly Free	Democracy
2011	Imperfectly Free	Democracy
2012	Imperfectly Free	Democracy

administration under the United Progressive Party, but not a meaningful change in media freedom. The new administration struggled to gain control of the state-run television station from some employees who remained loyal to the Antigua Labor Party.[3] In 2007, the IAPA noted that much of the media, especially the radio stations, had been "hijacked by the political parties and their agents."[4]

Media Today

Media remain imperfectly free.

Notes

1. *General Assembly 1996* (Miami, FL: Inter American Press Association, 1996). Available at http://www.sipiapa.org/v4/archivo_de_asambleas.php?idioma=us.
2. *General Assembly 2001* (Miami, FL: Inter American Press Association, 2001). Available at http://www.sipiapa.org/v4/archivo_de_asambleas.php?idioma=us.
3. *Midyear Meeting 2005* (Miami, FL: Inter American Press Association, 2005). Available at http://www.sipiapa.org/v4/archivo_de_asambleas.php?idioma=us.
4. *Midyear Meeting 2007* (Miami, FL: Inter American Press Association, 2007). Available at http://www.sipiapa.org/v4/archivo_de_asambleas.php?idioma=us.

Argentina: 1948–2012

Argentina Year by Year

Year	Media	Government
1948	Not Free	Autocracy
1949	Not Free	Autocracy
1950	Not Free	Autocracy
1951	Not Free	Autocracy
1952	Not Free	Autocracy
1953	Not Free	Autocracy
1954	Not Free	Autocracy
1955	Not Free	Autocracy
1956	Free	Anocracy
1957	Free	Anocracy
1958	Free	Anocracy
1959	Free	Anocracy
1960	Imperfectly Free	Anocracy
1961	Imperfectly Free	Anocracy
1962	Imperfectly Free	Anocracy
1963	Imperfectly Free	Anocracy
1964	Imperfectly Free	Anocracy
1965	Imperfectly Free	Anocracy
1966	Imperfectly Free	Autocracy
1967	Imperfectly Free	Autocracy
1968	Imperfectly Free	Autocracy
1969	Not Free	Autocracy
1970	Imperfectly Free	Autocracy
1971	Imperfectly Free	Autocracy
1972	Imperfectly Free	Autocracy
1973	Imperfectly Free	Democracy
1974	Not Free	Democracy
1975	Not Free	Democracy

MEDIA FREEDOM HISTORY IN A NUTSHELL

- For much of Argentina's history news media have been imperfectly free
- Even during the periods of martial law prior to 1974, news media could and did criticize government
- In recent years the relationship between government and news media has become increasingly hostile
- As of 2011, there were 185 total daily newspapers, and 181 of them were paid-for dailies with a total average circulation of 1,354,000, hundreds of radio stations and dozens of television stations (World Association of Newspaper's 2012 World Newspaper Trends)
- As of 2012, about 56 percent of Argentinians had Internet access (International Telecommunication Union's 2012 ICT Indicators Database)

In Brief

Argentina has a long history of political upheaval, military dominance, and authoritarian leadership, but since its democratization in 1984, media have been imperfectly free. Prior to 1984, the state of media freedom varied under different regimes, but for the most part journalists were quite restricted.

Chronology

1948–1955: Not Free

Under the dictatorship of Juan Domingo Perón, Argentina experienced "the most drastic bullying and muzzling of the press" in Latin America.[1] A 1949 amendment to the Penal Code criminalized *desacato* (the disrespect of authorities). The IPI characterized this measure as "one of the worst" because any criticism was

Year	Media	Government
1976	Not Free	Autocracy
1977	Not Free	Autocracy
1978	Not Free	Autocracy
1979	Not Free	Autocracy
1980	Not Free	Autocracy
1981	Not Free	Autocracy
1982	Not Free	Autocracy
1983	Not Free	Democracy
1984	Imperfectly Free	Democracy
1985	Imperfectly Free	Democracy
1986	Imperfectly Free	Democracy
1987	Imperfectly Free	Democracy
1988	Imperfectly Free	Democracy
1989	Imperfectly Free	Democracy
1990	Imperfectly Free	Democracy
1991	Imperfectly Free	Democracy
1992	Imperfectly Free	Democracy
1993	Imperfectly Free	Democracy
1994	Imperfectly Free	Democracy
1995	Imperfectly Free	Democracy
1996	Imperfectly Free	Democracy
1997	Imperfectly Free	Democracy
1998	Imperfectly Free	Democracy
1999	Imperfectly Free	Democracy
2000	Imperfectly Free	Democracy
2001	Imperfectly Free	Democracy
2002	Imperfectly Free	Democracy
2003	Imperfectly Free	Democracy
2004	Imperfectly Free	Democracy
2005	Imperfectly Free	Democracy
2006	Imperfectly Free	Democracy
2007	Imperfectly Free	Democracy
2008	Imperfectly Free	Democracy
2009	Imperfectly Free	Democracy
2010	Imperfectly Free	Democracy
2011	Imperfectly Free	Democracy
2012	Imperfectly Free	Democracy

actionable, regardless of accuracy.[2] Perón commonly took over newspapers and then used them to publish propaganda for his party. In the early 1950s, the government expropriated the Buenos Aires daily newspaper *La Prensa* and demanded that the owners pay more than two million dollars in customs duties for imported newsprint.[3]

1956–1959: Free

In September of 1955, the military removed Perón from office, and in 1956 *La Prensa* and other newspapers were returned to their owners. During this time, most daily newspapers were supportive of the government, but "opposition views were loudly expressed particularly in the weekly papers such as *Palabra Argentina*, which was the principal mouthpiece of left-wing (some said neo-Perónist) views."[4]

1960–1968: Imperfectly Free

In 1959, Argentina entered a state of siege, but the government promised that the press would remain free. The Inter American Press Association (IAPA) noted that while communist publications were sanctioned, freedom of the press remained largely intact, "criticism of the government was freely exercised—intensely at times, and with severity—without any consequences."[5] Yet the IAPA acknowledged that doing journalism under a state of siege did make reporters more likely to self-censor.[6] During this time, journalists who wrote stories that were critical of government officials faced harassment, intimidation, and arrest on *desecato* (meaning disrespect) charges.[7] Additionally, the government imposed customs duties and taxes on imported newsprint and equipment newspapers needed in order to modernize.

1969: Not Free

In 1969, several publications were shut down and the restrictions on media freedom that had been building for a decade reached a point where the Association of Argentine News Organizations declared that freedom of the press no longer existed in Argentina.[8]

1970–1973: Imperfectly Free

There were some improvements in 1970 to the extent that the IAPA ascertained that press freedom was restored even though Argentina remained under martial law. Yet the government's discretionary powers put news media in a "precarious and dependent" situation.[9] Additionally, there were reports of local governments censoring news media. In 1972, a vaguely worded new law gave government the authority to punish news outlets for publishing news deemed to be from terrorist groups.[10] Yet, in spite (or perhaps because) of these challenges, the IAPA concluded the Argentine press remained free "and, perhaps more important, seemingly ready to fight for its sacred rights."[11]

In 1973, Perón was elected and returned to the Presidency.

1974–1983: Not Free

When Perón died in 1974, his wife and vice president, Maria Estela Martínez de Perón (Isabelita), became president. That same year, the number of attacks on journalists combined with government shutdowns and takeovers of newspapers created a threatening environment for journalists that discouraged critical reporting.

In 1976, a military coup ended the Presidency of Martínez and marked the beginning of Argentina's "dirty war" in which the new military government sought to transform society by getting rid of all subversive elements. The military restricted news coverage and closed down or seized control of many newspapers and magazines. During this time thousands of people were killed or disappeared (the National Commission on the Disappearance of Persons put the number of disappeared at 8,961, but other estimates are as high as 30,000). The situation continued to deteriorate in 1977 with "the detentions, kidnappings, disappearances, and killings—proved in one case—of journalists."[12]

1984–2012: Imperfectly Free

In 1983, Argentina transitioned to democracy with the election of President Raúl Alfonsin. One of the first actions of the new civilian government was to release sixteen journalists from prison.[13] Yet a number of newspapers remained in "intervention" (meaning government intervention and control) and journalists continued to face threats because laws that criminalized the reporting on acts of subversion remained in place.[14] By 1985, these laws were repealed, but some newspapers remained intervened. Additionally, many publishers had to slash the number of pages in their newspapers because newsprint remained in short supply due to limited production at the two Argentine plants (one of which was in part government owned) and the high customs duty on imported newsprint. In 1986, the government lowered the customs duty, but the costs of newsprint remained high.[15]

Media Today

The relationship between media and government remains contentious. In 2009, Argentina decriminalized media offenses (libel and slander by journalists). Yet the hostility between the news media and President Cristina Fernández de Kirchner is damaging the credibility of both the news media and government. According to the Committee to Protect Journalists, the citizens of Argentina are the victims in the battle between the President and the country's most powerful media conglomerate Grupo Clarin, because they are unable to trust Grupo Clarin's news outlets to provide objective information about government:

> On one side, Kirchner's critics accuse her of stifling press freedom by rewarding allied media and hammering—with regulation as well as advertising—unsympathetic outlets into silence. On the other side, many believe that Clarín has too much power and leverages its huge media holdings to further its private business interests.[16]

Thus, media remain imperfectly free in Argentina—able to criticize the government, but somewhat compromised in their ability to access and publish news and information.

Notes

1. *The Press in Authoritarian Countries*, IPI Survey (Zurich: International Press Institute, 1959), 164–65.
2. *Government Pressures on the Press*, IPI Survey (Zurich: International Press Institute, 1955), 43–4.
3. *Press of the Americas. Vol. 1 No. 1* (Zurich: International Press Institute, August 15, 1951), 3.
4. *The Press in Authoritarian Countries*, IPI Survey (Zurich: International Press Institute, 1959), 164–65.
5. "Report by Chairman of the Freedom of the Press Committee," *General Assembly Proceedings*, 1961 (Miami, FL: Inter American Press Association, 1962), 178.

6. "Report by Chairman of the Freedom of the Press Committee," *General Assembly Proceedings*, 1962 (Miami, FL: Inter American Press Association, 1963), 143.

7. Ibid.

8. "Report of the Committee on Freedom of the Press and Information," *General Assembly Proceedings*, 1969 (Miami, FL: Inter American Press Association, 1970).

9. "The Challenge to the Hemispheric Press," *IAPA News* (Miami, FL: Inter American Press Association, 1971), 5.

10. "Report of the Committee on Freedom of the Press and Information," *General Assembly Proceedings*, 1962 (Miami, FL: Inter American Press Association, 1973).

11. "Report of the Committee on Freedom of the Press and Information," *General Assembly Proceedings*, 1962 (Miami, FL: Inter American Press Association, 1974), B-5.

12. "Report of the Committee on Freedom of the Press and Information," *General Assembly Proceedings*, 1977 (Miami, FL: Inter American Press Association, 1978), Appendix, 2.

13. "World Press Freedom Review," *IPI Report*, December 1984 (Miami, FL: Inter American Press Association, 1984).

14. "Report of the Committee on Freedom of the Press and Information," *Midyear Meeting*, 1984 (Miami, FL: Inter American Press Association, 1985).

15. "Report of the Committee on Freedom of the Press and Information," *General Assembly Proceedings*, 1986 (Miami, FL: Inter American Press Association, 1987).

16. Sara Rafsky, *In Government-Media Fight, Argentine Journalism Suffers* (Committee to Protect Journalists Special Reports, 2012), para 3. Available at http://www.cpj.org/reports/2012/09/amid-government-media-fight-argentine-journalism-suffers.php.

Armenia 1991–2012

Armenia Year by Year

Year	Media	Government
1991	Not Free	Democracy
1992	Not Free	Democracy
1993	Not Free	Democracy
1994	Not Free	Democracy
1995	Not Free	Anocracy
1996	Not Free	Autocracy
1997	Not Free	Autocracy
1998	Imperfectly Free	Anocracy
1999	Imperfectly Free	Anocracy
2000	Imperfectly Free	Anocracy
2001	Imperfectly Free	Anocracy
2002	Not Free	Anocracy
2003	Not Free	Anocracy
2004	Not Free	Anocracy
2005	Not Free	Anocracy
2006	Not Free	Anocracy
2007	Not Free	Anocracy
2008	Not Free	Anocracy
2009	Not Free	Anocracy
2010	Not Free	Anocracy
2011	Not Free	Anocracy
2012	Not Free	Anocracy

In Brief

Development of a free media system in the late 1990s was more illusory than real. Libel laws are used to great effect to control news outlets, most of which are broadcast media.

MEDIA FREEDOM HISTORY IN A NUTSHELL

- War with Azerbaijan delayed and complicated any effort to liberalize the post-Soviet political and social environment
- European supported liberalization and media development initiatives did bring about a brief period of media freedom from 1998–2001
- Indirect but effective control of the media is well established and robust
- As of 2009, there were twelve daily newspapers, all of them were paid-for dailies, with a total average circulation of 42,000 (World Association of Newspaper's 2010 World Newspaper Trends)
- Armenia has a mix of state-owned and privately owned broadcast media
- As of 2011, about 32 percent of Armenians had Internet access (International Telecommunication Union's 2011 ICT Indicators Database)

Chronology

1991–1997: Not Free

Armenia established laws protecting media freedom when it gained independence from the Soviet Union in 1991, but these laws were not respected in practice. The conflict with Azerbaijan over the region of Nagorno-Karabakh dominated the early period of post-Soviet independence. Soviet-style media controls were maintained as part of the war effort, and it was not until the war ended in 1994 that reform became possible. Although most newspapers were affiliated with opposition groups, Armenian television remained under government control.[1]

In 1995, a privatization push included the media. Print media remained small and elitist, but broadcast media grew rapidly, eventually leading to twenty-five independent TV stations in what was a very small market of only 3.1 million people. European support for political and social development began during this period. Yet journalists continued to face threats. Several newspapers with ties to the opposition were closed down in 1995. Journalists fought back, and several hundred protested in front of the Presidential Palace, but the demonstration was short-lived and the papers remained closed.[2]

1998–2001: Imperfectly Free

Despite continued and growing domestic unrest, development of an independent media system continued and reached the point of being functionally free in 1998.

2002–2012: Not Free

Arguments that Armenian media freedom was nothing more than a façade built up for the purpose of establishing ties to Europe gained credence when, immediately after being made a full member of the Council of Europe in 2001, media restrictions returned. In particular in 2002, the government closed down the country's most popular privately owned television station.[3] Moreover, critical journalists were increasingly targeted with punitive lawsuits. There were notable convictions and imprisonment of journalists throughout these years. Claims of electoral irregularities and fraud followed in 2003.

Media Today

While media are nominally free, the lack of an independent judiciary allows the government to use libel laws to severely restrict reporting. Although libel was decriminalized in 2010, meaning that journalists would no longer face prison terms, there has been a subsequent rise in civil libel cases.[4] Conditions for journalists have improved in recent years, and Armenian media may soon become imperfectly free if this trend continues.

Notes

1. *World Press Freedom Review*, IPI Report (Vienna: International Press Institute, 1994).
2. *World Press Freedom Review*, IPI Report (Vienna: International Press Institute, 1995).
3. *Freedom of the Press* (Washington, DC: Freedom House, 2003). Available at http://freedomhouse.org/reports.
4. *Freedom of the Press* (Washington, DC: Freedom House, 2013). Available at http://freedomhouse.org/reports.

Australia 1948–2012

Australia Year by Year

Year	Media	Government
1948	Free	Democracy
1949	Free	Democracy
1950	Free	Democracy
1951	Free	Democracy
1952	Free	Democracy
1953	Free	Democracy
1954	Free	Democracy
1955	Free	Democracy
1956	Free	Democracy
1957	Free	Democracy
1958	Free	Democracy
1959	Free	Democracy
1960	Free	Democracy
1961	Free	Democracy
1962	Free	Democracy
1963	Free	Democracy
1964	Free	Democracy
1965	Free	Democracy
1966	Free	Democracy
1967	Free	Democracy
1968	Free	Democracy
1969	Free	Democracy
1970	Free	Democracy
1971	Free	Democracy
1972	Free	Democracy
1973	Free	Democracy
1974	Free	Democracy
1975	Free	Democracy

MEDIA FREEDOM HISTORY IN A NUTSHELL

- Australia has a long history of media freedom that dates back to its colonial years, yet the country lacks constitutional provisions for media freedom
- Media ownership is highly concentrated
- As of 2012, Australia had forty-eight total paid-for daily newspapers with an average circulation of 2,597,206 (World Association of Newspaper's 2012 World Newspaper Trends)
- Australia has a strong tradition of public broadcasting, but there are also many privately owned radio and television outlets
- As of 2011, about 79 percent of Australians had Internet access (International Telecommunication Union's 2011 ICT Indicators Database)

In Brief

Australia's first newspapers were censored by the colonial government, but in 1824, the first issue of the *Australian* was published without permission and with a call for press freedom:

> A free Press is the most legitimate, and at the same time, the most powerful weapon that can be employed to annihilate such influence, frustrate the designs of tyranny, and restrain the arm of oppression. Without its active and liberal cooperation the biased views of a party frequently preponderate, while the interests of the public languish and are overlooked.[1]

In spite of this early push for media freedom, Australia has no constitutional guarantee of press freedom, yet in practice media are free and the country has long been an exemplar of media freedom in the Asia-Pacific region.

Year	Media	Government
1976	Free	Democracy
1977	Free	Democracy
1978	Free	Democracy
1979	Free	Democracy
1980	Free	Democracy
1981	Free	Democracy
1982	Free	Democracy
1983	Free	Democracy
1984	Free	Democracy
1985	Free	Democracy
1986	Free	Democracy
1987	Free	Democracy
1988	Free	Democracy
1989	Free	Democracy
1990	Free	Democracy
1991	Free	Democracy
1992	Free	Democracy
1993	Free	Democracy
1994	Free	Democracy
1995	Free	Democracy
1996	Free	Democracy
1997	Free	Democracy
1998	Free	Democracy
1999	Free	Democracy
2000	Free	Democracy
2001	Free	Democracy
2002	Free	Democracy
2003	Free	Democracy
2004	Free	Democracy
2005	Free	Democracy
2006	Free	Democracy
2007	Free	Democracy
2008	Free	Democracy
2009	Free	Democracy
2010	Free	Democracy
2011	Free	Democracy
2012	Free	Democracy

Chronology

1948–2012: Free

Although news media in Australia began reporting independently during the colonial years, Australia did not formally adopt constitutional provisions or laws guaranteeing press freedom. Thus, Australia is one of very few countries where media freedom exists because of convention rather than through legislation.

After suffering newsprint rationing and restrictions on news coverage during World War II, members of the Australian Press Union were particularly outspoken for the need for increased press freedom and resistant to calls for greater press responsibility during debates at conferences held by the Empire Press Union (an organization of British-language newspapers from the Empire, renamed the Commonwealth Press Union in 1950).[2] At these conferences, the Australian Press Union delegates spoke out against government restrictions, not only in Australia, but also in other countries as well.

Although news media were functionally free, for decades the inconsistency of laws across the state governments challenged news media.[3] This was especially the case with Australia's defamation laws, which according to the IPI were among the harshest in the world, because in some states in order to defeat a defamation suit, journalists were required to prove that their reports were accurate and true and that their publication was in the public interest.[4] Thus, there were many cases in which politicians used defamation laws to threaten and punish journalists.[5] In 2006, the Uniform Defamation Laws established a common set of defamation policies and constrained such lawsuits to nonprofits, corporations with fewer than ten employees, and individuals.

The Australian Press Council, an independent and self-regulatory organization, was established in 1976 to promote press freedom and resolve complaints against print media. Broadcast media also have their advocates—1992 marked the founding of The Media Entertainment & Arts Alliance, a trade union and professional organization representing journalists and other workers in the broadcast, theater, film and entertainment industries, which among other issues, advocates for media freedom.

Since 2000, Australia has adopted several media-related laws, some of which expand and some of which constrain media freedom. In 2003, the Australian Security Intelligence Organization Act was amended to permit the government to imprison for up to five years journalists who failed to share information or sources regarding possible terrorist attacks. The Anti-terrorism Act of 2005 constrained news media from reporting on people who were detained under antiterrorism legislation. The years 2010 and 2011 saw the passage of laws that expanded journalists' ability to access information and protect sources.

Media Today

News media in Australia remain free, yet there is no countrywide legal provision for media freedom. In 2006, the State of Victoria adopted the Charter of Human Rights and Responsibilities, which included provisions for freedom of expression, but other states have not followed suit. Although the country now has consistent policies regarding defamation, civil defamation lawsuits remain a threat to journalists and news outlets. For example, in 2012 the News Corporation group was fined $339,000 (US $) for an article that characterized a former police officer as "corrupt."[6] Australia has a strong commitment to public broadcasting, although most media are privately owned. Concentration of ownership remains extremely high, with most print media owned by the News Corporation and the Fairfax Group. The Australian Communications and Media Authority has the authority to censor domestic Internet content.[7]

Notes

1. Quoted in "Freedom of the Press," Discover Collections, *The Australian*, October 14, 1824, 2, State Library of New South Wales, http://www.sl.nsw.gov.au/discover_collections/history_nation/justice/freedom_press/index.html.
2. Denis Cryle, "A British Legacy? The Empire Press Union and Freedom of the Press, 1940-1950," *History of Intellectual Culture* 4 (1).
3. *World Press Freedom Review*, IPI Report (Zurich: International Press Institute, December 1983).
4. *World Press Freedom Review*, IPI Report (Zurich: International Press Institute, December 1984).
5. *World Press Freedom Review*, IPI Report (Zurich: International Press Institute, December 1983).
6. *Freedom of the Press* (Washington, DC: Freedom House, 2013). Available at http://www.freedomhouse.org/reports.
7. Ibid.

Austria: 1948–2012

Austria Year by Year

Year	Media	Government
1948	Free	Democracy
1949	Free	Democracy
1950	Free	Democracy
1951	Free	Democracy
1952	Free	Democracy
1953	Free	Democracy
1954	Free	Democracy
1955	Free	Democracy
1956	Free	Democracy
1957	Free	Democracy
1958	Free	Democracy
1959	Free	Democracy
1960	Free	Democracy
1961	Free	Democracy
1962	Free	Democracy
1963	Free	Democracy
1964	Free	Democracy
1965	Free	Democracy
1966	Free	Democracy
1967	Free	Democracy
1968	Free	Democracy
1969	Free	Democracy
1970	Free	Democracy
1971	Free	Democracy
1972	Free	Democracy
1973	Free	Democracy
1974	Free	Democracy
1975	Free	Democracy
1976	Free	Democracy

(Continued)

> **MEDIA FREEDOM HISTORY IN A NUTSHELL**
>
> - Media free even as Austria was occupied by Allied Forces, including the Soviet Union, until 1955
> - One of the many well established Western-European free media regimes
> - Austria has a mix of publicly owned and privately owned broadcast and print media
> - As of 2011, there eighteen daily newspapers and fifteen paid-for dailies (World Association of Newspaper's 2012 World Newspaper Trends)
> - As of 2011, Internet media were unrestricted and about 73 percent of Austrians had Internet access (International Telecommunication Union's 2011 ICT Indicators Database)

In Brief

Austria is one of the many well-established free media regimes of Western Europe. It is consistently categorized as a free press regime by all the major indices. Press freedom was established as part of the Allied occupation of Austria. During the war, the allies identified it as part of the western sphere and committed to keeping it whole and democratic. Although the Soviets occupied the capital and governed 25 percent of the population, it is generally agreed that they never intended to try to bring Austria into the communist bloc. They clearly did hope to establish a Moscow-friendly government, and in all the regions they controlled, they installed sympathetic socialist politicians in all significant posts, but the Socialist party barely registered in the 1945 elections, and with a subsequent Soviet policy change, any real threat to the creation of a western liberal democratic regime all but vanished. The Soviets supported socialist and communist efforts until 1955, but their intent seemed

(Continued)

Year	Media	Government
1977	Free	Democracy
1978	Free	Democracy
1979	Free	Democracy
1980	Free	Democracy
1981	Free	Democracy
1982	Free	Democracy
1983	Free	Democracy
1984	Free	Democracy
1985	Free	Democracy
1986	Free	Democracy
1987	Free	Democracy
1988	Free	Democracy
1989	Free	Democracy
1990	Free	Democracy
1991	Free	Democracy
1992	Free	Democracy
1993	Free	Democracy
1994	Free	Democracy
1995	Free	Democracy
1996	Free	Democracy
1997	Free	Democracy
1998	Free	Democracy
1999	Free	Democracy
2000	Free	Democracy
2001	Free	Democracy
2002	Free	Democracy
2003	Free	Democracy
2004	Free	Democracy
2005	Free	Democracy

Year	Media	Government
2006	Free	Democracy
2007	Free	Democracy
2008	Free	Democracy
2009	Free	Democracy
2010	Free	Democracy
2011	Free	Democracy
2012	Free	Democracy

primarily focused on expropriating German industrial holdings in their zone of occupation.

Chronology

1948–2012: Free

Press freedom was established during the allied occupation, and by 1948, there was little question that the media were and would be free. There are some interesting aspects to the politics in the Soviet Occupied zones that are often overlooked in the discussion of early cold-war politics, but the Soviets signaled quite early that they were abandoning any effort to dominate Austria. This culminates with Austria joining the European Union in 1995, and there has been no real challenge to media freedom since.

Media Today

There are some issues over restrictions of expression of Nazi, anti-Semitic, and holocaust denial perspectives, but these are minor and do not threaten Austria's standing as a free press nation. Information in all forms flows freely into and out of Austria, particularly regarding German language media and German language audiences in neighboring countries.

Azerbaijan 1991–2012

Azerbaijan Year by Year

Year	Media	Government
1991	Not Free	Anocracy
1992	Not Free	Anocracy
1993	Not Free	Anocracy
1994	Not Free	Anocracy
1995	Not Free	Autocracy
1996	Not Free	Autocracy
1997	Not Free	Autocracy
1998	Not Free	Autocracy
1999	Not Free	Autocracy
2000	Not Free	Autocracy
2001	Not Free	Autocracy
2002	Not Free	Autocracy
2003	Not Free	Autocracy
2004	Not Free	Autocracy
2005	Not Free	Autocracy
2006	Not Free	Autocracy
2007	Not Free	Autocracy
2008	Not Free	Autocracy
2009	Not Free	Autocracy
2010	Not Free	Autocracy
2011	Not Free	Autocracy
2012	Not Free	Autocracy

In Brief

Oil rich, Azerbaijan has developed into what is essentially a hereditary dictatorship with Ilham Aliyev taking over the presidency from his father.

MEDIA FREEDOM HISTORY IN A NUTSHELL

- An oil rich authoritarian regime that strictly controls the media
- Some media outlets are nominally owned by opposition parties, but police state tactics prevent them from operating with any independence
- As of 2009, there were thirty-two daily newspapers, all were paid-for dailies, with a total average circulation of 120,000 (World Association of Newspaper's 2010 World Newspaper Trends)
- The government does not provide information regarding ownership of broadcast media, but most are government-owned and operated or effectively under government control
- As of 2011, about 50 percent of Azerbaijanis had Internet access (International Telecommunication Union's 2011 ICT Indicators Database)

War with Armenia defined the initial years of post-Soviet independence, and despite some gestures at liberalization, the government has never strayed far from an authoritarian, wartime footing. Media are dominated by TV and remain strictly controlled.

Chronology

1991–2012: Not Free

War, both internal and external defined the first decade of post-Soviet Azerbaijan. Although there was no formal system of censorship, the state initially owned and controlled almost all media.[1]

Post-war expansion of the media market extended media ownership beyond the government, but even though opposition parties owned media outlets, their ability to use them to criticize government was almost nonexistent.

What little freedom the media had to operate was further degraded when Ilham Aliyev took power.

By 2006, the continual and fierce harassment and arrests of media professionals effectively eliminated independent ownership of media in all but name. In protest over the continued maltreatment of journalists, members of the media and opposition groups joined in a hunger strike, but no changes were forthcoming.[2] Unable to even control their own newsrooms, opposition parties were unable to compete in the 2010 elections.

Media Today

Azerbaijan is on several media freedom and human rights watch lists and reports. Media are strictly controlled and there is no indication of any pressure for change.

Notes

1. *World Press Freedom Review*, IPI Report (Vienna: International Press Institute, 1994).
2. *Freedom of the Press* (Washington, DC: Freedom House, 2007). Available at http://freedomhouse.org/reports.

Bahamas: 1973–2012

Bahamas Year by Year

Year	Media	Government
1973	Free	Democracy
1974	Free	Democracy
1975	Free	Democracy
1976	Free	Democracy
1977	Free	Democracy
1978	Free	Democracy
1979	Free	Democracy
1980	Free	Democracy
1981	Free	Democracy
1982	Free	Democracy
1983	Free	Democracy
1984	Free	Democracy
1985	Free	Democracy
1986	Free	Democracy
1987	Free	Democracy
1988	Free	Democracy
1989	Free	Democracy
1990	Free	Democracy
1991	Free	Democracy
1992	Free	Democracy
1993	Free	Democracy
1994	Free	Democracy
1995	Free	Democracy
1996	Free	Democracy
1997	Free	Democracy
1998	Free	Democracy
1999	Free	Democracy
2000	Free	Democracy
2001	Free	Democracy
2002	Free	Democracy

Year	Media	Government
2003	Free	Democracy
2004	Free	Democracy
2005	Free	Democracy
2006	Free	Democracy
2007	Free	Democracy
2008	Free	Democracy
2009	Free	Democracy
2010	Free	Democracy
2011	Free	Democracy
2012	Free	Democracy

MEDIA FREEDOM HISTORY IN A NUTSHELL

- Since the Bahamas became an independent state in 1973, news media have been free

Chronology

1973–2012: Free

In 1973, the Bahamas became an independent state. Since then media have been free. While harsh libel laws remain in effect, they are almost never applied. The Bahamas have a mix of privately owned and state-owned media, but the state-owned Broadcasting Corporation of the Bahamas is for the most part editorially independent. There are some concerns about concentration of ownership. In 2007, three of the Bahamas four newspapers formed a partnership.[1]

Note

1. *Freedom of the Press* (Washington, DC: Freedom House, 2008). Available at http://www.freedomhouse.org/reports.

Bahrain: 1971–2012

Bahrain Year by Year

Year	Media	Government
1971	Not Free	Autocracy
1972	Not Free	Autocracy
1973	Not Free	Autocracy
1974	Not Free	Autocracy
1975	Not Free	Autocracy
1976	Not Free	Autocracy
1977	Not Free	Autocracy
1978	Not Free	Autocracy
1979	Not Free	Autocracy
1980	Not Free	Autocracy
1981	Not Free	Autocracy
1982	Not Free	Autocracy
1983	Not Free	Autocracy
1984	Not Free	Autocracy
1985	Not Free	Autocracy
1986	Not Free	Autocracy
1987	Not Free	Autocracy
1988	Not Free	Autocracy
1989	Not Free	Autocracy
1990	Not Free	Autocracy
1991	Not Free	Autocracy
1992	Not Free	Autocracy
1993	Not Free	Autocracy
1994	Not Free	Autocracy
1995	Not Free	Autocracy

In Brief

The monarchy directly controlled most news media until Bahrain became a constitutional monarchy in 2001. This political transition had little effect on the media environment, which remains not free.

Chronology

1972–2012: Not Free

A small but extremely wealthy hereditary monarchy, the Khalifa family exercised complete political control, including the ownership and operation of most news media. In 1965, six years prior to Bahrain's independence, a press law went into effect that required all newspapers to obtain a license from the Ministry of Information.[1] Bahrain's first daily newspaper began publishing in 1976.[2] In 2001, the Ministry of Information remained in control of most media, as evidenced by information

Year	Media	Government
1996	Not Free	Autocracy
1997	Not Free	Autocracy
1998	Not Free	Autocracy
1999	Not Free	Autocracy
2000	Not Free	Autocracy
2001	Not Free	Autocracy
2002	Not Free	Autocracy
2003	Not Free	Autocracy
2004	Not Free	Autocracy
2005	Not Free	Autocracy
2006	Not Free	Autocracy
2007	Not Free	Autocracy
2008	Not Free	Autocracy
2009	Not Free	Autocracy
2010	Not Free	Autocracy
2011	Not Free	Autocracy
2012	Not Free	Autocracy

minister's leadership of the Bahraini Journalists' Society.[3]

Technically, Bahrain was transformed into a constitutional monarchy in 2001, and some moderate evidence of liberalization and respect for human rights has been apparent, including the establishment of the first independent newspaper in 2002. However, the constitutional guarantee of freedom of expression was effectively gutted by the legal and religious qualifications attached to it, and it was all but meaningless in the face of a king who wielded unchecked political power. For example, the 2002 constitution allowed for freedom of speech and press "provided that the fundamental beliefs of Islamic doctrine are not infringed, the unity of the people is not prejudiced, and discord or sectarianism is not aroused."[4] Also in 2002, a new press law was adopted that seemed to limit the state's ability to close down publications, but vague language raised doubts about its effectiveness.[5] Moreover, the press law also made criticism of Islam or the king punishable by imprisonment of six months to five years.[6]

Media Today

Media are controlled and Bahrain shows no indication of moving toward a more liberal model. The government retains the authority to censor and close down critical news media and regulate Internet activity.

Notes

1. Helem Chapin Metz, *Bahrain: A Country Study*, Library of Congress Federal Research Division (Washington, DC: Library of Congress, 1993).
2. *World Press Trends* (Darmstadt, Germany: WAN-IFRA, 2010).
3. *Freedom of the Press* (Washington, DC: Freedom House, 2002). Available at http://www.freedomhouse.org/report/freedom-press/2002/bahrain.
4. *Constitution of the Kingdom of Bahrain*, 2002, Article 23.
5. *Freedom of the Press* (Washington, DC: Freedom House, 2003). Available at http://www.freedomhouse.org/report/freedom-press/2003/bahrain.
6. *World Press Trends* (Darmstadt, Germany: WAN-IFRA, 2010).

Bangladesh: 1972–2012

Bangladesh Year by Year

Year	Media	Government
1972	Not Free	Democracy
1973	Not Free	Democracy
1974	Not Free	Anocracy
1975	Not Free	Autocracy
1976	Not Free	Autocracy
1977	Not Free	Autocracy
1978	Not Free	Anocracy
1979	Not Free	Anocracy
1980	Not Free	Anocracy
1981	Not Free	Anocracy
1982	Not Free	Autocracy
1983	Not Free	Autocracy
1984	Not Free	Autocracy
1985	Not Free	Autocracy
1986	Not Free	Anocracy
1987	Not Free	Anocracy
1988	Not Free	Anocracy
1989	Not Free	Anocracy
1990	Not Free	Anocracy
1991	Not Free	Democracy
1992	Not Free	Democracy
1993	Not Free	Democracy
1994	Not Free	Democracy
1995	Not Free	Democracy
1996	Not Free	Democracy

MEDIA FREEDOM HISTORY IN A NUTSHELL

- When Bangladesh gained independence, media were tightly controlled
- Political reforms brought about improvements in the media environment in 2009
- Bangladesh remains one of the more dangerous countries in which to practice journalism
- As of 2012, there were 400 daily newspapers with a total average circulation of 1,550,000 (World Association of Newspaper's 2012 World Newspaper Trends)
- Television remains the most popular medium and most broadcast media are state owned
- As of 2011, about 5 percent of Bangladeshis had access to the Internet (International Telecommunication Union's 2011 ICT Indicators Database)

In Brief

Since Bangladesh gained independence, political instability has led to treacherous conditions for journalists. Although political reforms brought about a transition in the media environment from not free to imperfectly free in 2009, attacks on journalists remain a problem in Bangladesh.

Chronology

1971–2008: Not Free

From the beginning, those in power appreciated the potential of news media. During the war for independence, Bangladesh's independence was declared from a captured radio station.[1] According to the International Press Association, the new government promised in early 1972 that it would maintain press freedom, but journalists who criticized the government faced repercussions.[2] In

Year	Media	Government
1997	Not Free	Democracy
1998	Not Free	Democracy
1999	Not Free	Democracy
2000	Not Free	Democracy
2001	Not Free	Democracy
2002	Not Free	Democracy
2003	Not Free	Democracy
2004	Not Free	Democracy
2005	Not Free	Democracy
2006	Not Free	Democracy
2007	Not Free	Autocracy
2008	Not Free	Autocracy
2009	Imperfectly Free	Anocracy
2010	Imperfectly Free	Anocracy
2011	Imperfectly Free	Anocracy
2012	Imperfectly Free	Anocracy

1973, the Printing Press and Publication Law imposed prior restraint on newspapers.[3] During these years, the state controlled most broadcast media. Additionally, journalists were often victims of violent attacks at the hands of organized crime, security forces, and extremists groups.[4]

2009–2012: Imperfectly Free

The elections of 2008 brought a civilian government into power and subsequent political reforms led to improvements in the media environment. As the state of emergency restrictions were removed in 2009, media became imperfectly free.

Media Today

Though there are constitutional provisions for media freedom, the government does not always respect these in practice.[5] Recently, there have been increasing incidents in which journalists who are critical of government are harassed or detained under the 1974 Special Powers Act.[6] Most recently, bloggers have come under attack. In the spring of 2013, hundreds of thousands demonstrated in Dhaka, calling for the deaths of bloggers whose writing they deemed blasphemous.[7]

Notes

1. James Heitzman and Robert Worden, *Bangladesh: A Country Study* (Washington, DC: Library of Congress Federal Research Division, 1988). Available at http://lcweb2.loc.gov/frd/cs/.
2. *Annual Review of Press Freedom 1972*, IPI Report (Zurich: International Press Institute, January 1973).
3. *Annual Review of Press Freedom 1973*, IPI Report (Zurich: International Press Institute, January 1974).
4. *Freedom of the Press* (Washington, DC: Freedom House, 2005). Available at http://www.freedomhouse.org/report/freedom-press/2005/bangladesh.
5. *World Press Trends* (Darmstadt, Germany: WAN-IFRA, 2010).
6. *Freedom of the Press* (Washington, DC: Freedom House, 2013). Available at http://www.freedomhouse.org/report/freedom-press/2013/Bangladesh.
7. *In Bangladesh, Climate Worsens for Journalists* (Committee to Protect Journalists, 2013). Available at http://cpj.org/blog/2013/04/in-bangladesh-climate-worsens-for-journalists.php.

Barbados: 1967–2012

Barbados Year by Year

Year	Media	Government
1967	Free	Democracy
1968	Free	Democracy
1969	Free	Democracy
1970	Free	Democracy
1971	Free	Democracy
1972	Free	Democracy
1973	Free	Democracy
1974	Free	Democracy
1975	Free	Democracy
1976	Free	Democracy
1977	Free	Democracy
1978	Free	Democracy
1979	Free	Democracy
1980	Free	Democracy
1981	Free	Democracy
1982	Free	Democracy
1983	Free	Democracy
1984	Free	Democracy
1985	Free	Democracy
1986	Free	Democracy
1987	Free	Democracy
1988	Free	Democracy
1989	Free	Democracy
1990	Free	Democracy
1991	Free	Democracy

MEDIA FREEDOM HISTORY IN A NUTSHELL

- Since Barbados gained independence in 1966 media have been free
- As of 2010, there were two paid-for daily newspapers with a total average circulation of 48,000 (World Association of Newspaper's 2010 World Newspaper Trends)
- A government controlled television and radio broadcasting serviced operated in the country. There were six radio stations, two of them owned by CBS. CBS also owned the only television station (World Association of Newspaper's 2012 World Newspaper Trends)
- As of 2011, about 71.7 percent of Barbadians had Internet access (International Telecommunication Union's 2011 ICT Indicators Database)

Chronology

1967–2012: Free

Since Barbados gained independence in 1966, news media have been functionally free. In the late 1990s, the Barbados Parliament passed a new Defamation Act that provided increased protections for journalists. Barbados' only television station is owned and operated by the government, but there are privately owned newspapers and radio stations. Barbados does not have a Freedom of Information Act, and in 2013, members of the ruling Democratic Labour Party granted only limited access to the independent news media.[1] If this practice continues, media in Barbados may become imperfectly free.

Note

1. *Midyear Meeting 2013* (Miami, FL: Inter American Press Association, 2013). Available at http://www.sipiapa.org/v4/archivo_de_asambleas.php?idioma=us.

Year	Media	Government
1992	Free	Democracy
1993	Free	Democracy
1994	Free	Democracy
1995	Free	Democracy
1996	Free	Democracy
1997	Free	Democracy
1998	Free	Democracy
1999	Free	Democracy
2000	Free	Democracy
2001	Free	Democracy

Year	Media	Government
2002	Free	Democracy
2003	Free	Democracy
2004	Free	Democracy
2005	Free	Democracy
2006	Free	Democracy
2007	Free	Democracy
2008	Free	Democracy
2009	Free	Democracy
2010	Free	Democracy
2011	Free	Democracy
2012	Free	Democracy

Belarus: 1991–2012

Belarus Year by Year

Year	Media	Government
1991	Not Free	Democracy
1992	Not Free	Democracy
1993	Not Free	Democracy
1994	Not Free	Democracy
1995	Not Free	Anocracy
1996	Not Free	Autocracy
1997	Not Free	Autocracy
1998	Not Free	Autocracy
1999	Not Free	Autocracy
2000	Not Free	Autocracy
2001	Not Free	Autocracy
2002	Not Free	Autocracy
2003	Not Free	Autocracy
2004	Not Free	Autocracy
2005	Not Free	Autocracy
2006	Not Free	Autocracy
2007	Not Free	Autocracy
2008	Not Free	Autocracy
2009	Not Free	Autocracy
2010	Not Free	Autocracy
2011	Not Free	Autocracy
2012	Not Free	Autocracy

In Brief

Located in a strategically vital avenue for launching military campaigns into and out of Europe, the history of Belarus is a story of foreign occupation.

MEDIA FREEDOM HISTORY IN A NUTSHELL

- With the dissolution of the Soviet Union, media were unprepared and unable to adopt a liberal, professional position independent of government control
- Media remain strictly controlled
- As of 2009, the Belarus government said the country has 158 radio stations and seventy-one television stations; and while some of these are privately owned, few of them have national reach (World Association of Newspaper's 2010 World Newspaper Trends)
- As of 2011, there were 33 paid-for daily newspapers with a total average circulation of 1,814,000 (World Association of Newspaper's 2012 World Newspaper Trends)
- As of 2011 about 32 percent of Belarusians had Internet access (International Telecommunication Union's 2011 ICT Indicators Database)
- The government restricts and monitors Internet use (Freedom House)

In this light, the almost immediate re-imposition of authoritarian media controls following the dissolution of the Soviet Union is an unsurprising reflection of a country that has experienced centuries of authoritarian rule.

Chronology

1991–2012: Not Free

Except for a few months in 1918–1919, the dissolution of the Soviet Union created the first opportunity for self-rule in centuries. After generations of subjugation and authoritarian rule, the burst of liberalism that started in 1991 was short-lived, at least in part because the media had almost no experience as professionals independent of government and were unable to provide the arena needed to support competitive democratic elections. It could be argued that there was no force of liberalism that could have overcome the political and social habits established in centuries of authoritarian occupation, but other former Soviet republics in Europe managed the transition much more effectively; so political culture alone cannot explain the quick reestablishment of authoritarian rule. A dismal economic situation and lack of strong ethnic constituencies in the developed western democracies of the world were also probably significant factors.

In 1995, President Alexander Lukashenka claimed to support freedom of expression and announced that he would not tolerate censorship. Yet he later accused journalists of failing to support his plans for the country. The president persistently assaulted media freedom. These attacks included jamming the U.S. funded Radio Liberty for the first time since the Soviet Era and the closure of four leading independent newspapers.[1] Other independent newspapers had to be printed abroad because they did not have access to local printing presses.[2] In 1997, a reporter and cameraman for Russia's ORT television network were arrested for reporting that proceeds from smuggling were going directly into the presidential coffers.[3] Subsequently, authorities arrested fifteen journalists for peacefully protesting the imprisonment of the ORT journalists.[4] The government continued to use both new and old tools for harassing independent journalists, ranging from official warnings, interference in printing houses, arrests, bullying, and beatings, to advanced methods of demands that all newspapers be "re-registered."[5]

News media struggled financially as the economic situation weakened. Advertising is illegal in independent media, and state controlled media are funded directly by the state.[6]

Media Today

Media are so closely controlled that there is little chance of dissent or criticism. Criticism of the government or the president is considered a criminal offence, and libel convictions can result in long prison sentences.[7]

Notes

1. *World Press Freedom Review*, IPI Report (Vienna: International Press Institute, 1995).
2. Ibid.
3. *World Press Freedom Review*, IPI Report (Vienna: International Press Institute, 1997).
4. Ibid.
5. *World Press Freedom Review*, IPI Report (Vienna: International Press Institute, 1998).
6. *World Press Freedom Review*, IPI Report (Vienna: International Press Institute, 1999).
7. *Belarus* (Washington, DC: Freedom House, 2013). Available at http://www.freedomhouse.org/report/freedom-press/2013/belarus.

Belgium: 1948–2012

Belgium Year by Year

Year	Media	Government
1948	Free	Democracy
1949	Free	Democracy
1950	Free	Democracy
1951	Free	Democracy
1952	Free	Democracy
1953	Free	Democracy
1954	Free	Democracy
1955	Free	Democracy
1956	Free	Democracy
1957	Free	Democracy
1958	Free	Democracy
1959	Free	Democracy
1960	Free	Democracy
1961	Free	Democracy
1962	Free	Democracy
1963	Free	Democracy
1964	Free	Democracy
1965	Free	Democracy
1966	Free	Democracy
1967	Free	Democracy
1968	Free	Democracy
1969	Free	Democracy
1970	Free	Democracy
1971	Free	Democracy
1972	Free	Democracy
1973	Free	Democracy
1974	Free	Democracy
1975	Free	Democracy

MEDIA FREEDOM HISTORY IN A NUTSHELL

- Clearly free and independent media
- As of 2011, there were twenty-five daily newspapers, twenty-three were paid-for dailies with a total average circulation of 1,321,000 (World Association of Newspaper's 2012 World Newspaper Trends)
- Belgium has a variety of public and private radio and television stations
- As of 2011, about 78 percent of Belgiums had Internet access (International Telecommunication Union's 2011 ICT Indicators Database)

In Brief

Belgian media are unquestionably free and effective as political institutions enabling political competition and criticism of all parties in the political process. The only real notable aspect of Belgian media is the division between Dutch, German, and French speaking populations and the associated domestic media outlets. Some argue that the French language papers have more influence over policy and politics, but there is little evidence that this is significant.

Chronology

1948–2010: Free

There has been little if any challenge to media freedom in Belgium. There has been recent concern over increases in ownership concentration and the economic challenges facing small and medium circulation newspapers, but this is a common issue around the world.

Media Today

Free, developed, and effective.

Year	Media	Government
1976	Free	Democracy
1977	Free	Democracy
1978	Free	Democracy
1979	Free	Democracy
1980	Free	Democracy
1981	Free	Democracy
1982	Free	Democracy
1983	Free	Democracy
1984	Free	Democracy
1985	Free	Democracy
1986	Free	Democracy
1987	Free	Democracy
1988	Free	Democracy
1989	Free	Democracy
1990	Free	Democracy
1991	Free	Democracy
1992	Free	Democracy
1993	Free	Democracy
1994	Free	Democracy

Year	Media	Government
1995	Free	Democracy
1996	Free	Democracy
1997	Free	Democracy
1998	Free	Democracy
1999	Free	Democracy
2000	Free	Democracy
2001	Free	Democracy
2002	Free	Democracy
2003	Free	Democracy
2004	Free	Democracy
2005	Free	Democracy
2006	Free	Democracy
2007	Free	Democracy
2008	Free	Democracy
2009	Free	Democracy
2010	Free	Democracy
2011	Free	Democracy
2012	Free	Democracy

Belize: 1981–2012

Belize Year by Year

Year	Media	Government
1981	Imperfectly Free	Democracy
1982	Imperfectly Free	Democracy
1983	Imperfectly Free	Democracy
1984	Imperfectly Free	Democracy
1985	Imperfectly Free	Democracy
1986	Imperfectly Free	Democracy
1987	Imperfectly Free	Democracy
1988	Free	Democracy
1989	Free	Democracy
1990	Free	Democracy
1991	Free	Democracy
1992	Free	Democracy
1993	Free	Democracy
1994	Free	Democracy
1995	Free	Democracy
1996	Free	Democracy
1997	Free	Democracy
1998	Free	Democracy
1999	Free	Democracy
2000	Free	Democracy
2001	Free	Democracy
2002	Free	Democracy
2003	Free	Democracy
2004	Free	Democracy
2005	Free	Democracy
2006	Free	Democracy
2007	Free	Democracy
2008	Free	Democracy

MEDIA FREEDOM HISTORY IN A NUTSHELL

- Belizean media are closely tied to political parties, and this has led to a contentious relationship between government and opposition media
- As of 2012, there were no daily newspapers in Belize, but there were a number of weekly newspapers and a variety of television and radio stations (Freedom House, 2013 Freedom of the Press)
- As of 2012, about 25 percent of Belizeans had access to the Internet (Freedom House, 2013 Freedom of the Press)

In Brief

Belizean law provides for media freedom, and for the most part government respects these rights, but Belizean media are highly partisan, and this has created a tension between opposition media and government.

Chronology

1981–1987: Imperfectly Free

When Belize gained independence in 1981, there were few news outlets, and those that did exist were closely connected with political parties. During the 1980s, there were controversies regarding limited access to broadcast media for opposition parties and the dependence of newspapers on government advertising.[1]

1988–2012: Free

By 1988, media had diversified to the point that they were effectively free. Yet journalists continued to face pressure from criminal defamation laws.[2]

Year	Media	Government
2009	Free	Democracy
2010	Free	Democracy
2011	Free	Democracy
2012	Free	Democracy

Media Today

Media remain highly partisan, and there have been reports of intimidation of opposition media. Yet media remain vibrant and functionally free.[3]

Notes

1. Tim Merrill, *Belize: A Country Study* (Washington, DC: Library of Congress Federal Research Division, 1993). Available at http://lcweb2.loc.gov/frd/cs/.
2. *Freedom of the Press* (Washington, DC: Freedom House, 2003). Available at http://www.freedomhouse.org/report/freedom-press/2003/belize.
3. *Freedom of the Press* (Washington, DC: Freedom House, 2013). Available at http://www.freedomhouse.org/report/freedom-press/2013/belize.

Benin: 1960–2012

Benin Year by Year

Year	Media	Government
1960	Not Free	Anocracy
1961	Not Free	Anocracy
1962	Not Free	Anocracy
1963	Not Free	Anocracy
1964	Not Free	Anocracy
1965	Not Free	Autocracy
1966	Not Free	Autocracy
1967	Not Free	Autocracy
1968	Not Free	Autocracy
1969	Not Free	Autocracy
1970	Not Free	Anocracy
1971	Not Free	Anocracy
1972	Not Free	Autocracy
1973	Not Free	Autocracy
1974	Not Free	Autocracy
1975	Not Free	Autocracy
1976	Not Free	Autocracy
1977	Not Free	Autocracy
1978	Not Free	Autocracy
1979	Not Free	Autocracy
1980	Not Free	Autocracy
1981	Not Free	Autocracy
1982	Not Free	Autocracy
1983	Not Free	Autocracy
1984	Not Free	Autocracy

MEDIA FREEDOM HISTORY IN A NUTSHELL

- Although Benin gained its independence from France in 1960, the Beninese media were not functionally free until 1995—four years after the country transitioned to democracy
- As of 2010, there were thirty-eight paid-for daily newspapers with a total average circulation of 50,000, more than seventy-five radio stations (some private, some community, and some commercial) and one government-owned and five private television stations (World Association of Newspaper's 2010 World Newspaper Trends)
- As of 2011, about 3.5 percent of Beninese had Internet access (International Telecommunication Union's 2011 ICT Indicators Database)

In Brief

Beninese media were not free for the first three and a half decades following the country's independence. Since 1995, the Beninese media have been among the most free in Africa, yet they remain vulnerable to criminal libel charges and bribery.

Chronology

1960–1994: Not Free

Benin (formerly Dahomey) gained independence from France in 1960. During the early years, there were a number of regime changes and the country was for the most part under military control. There were few news outlets in the country, yet there is evidence that government did take steps to control media; in 1964, a press censorship commission was established.[1] In 1972, under the leadership of Mathieu Kerekou, the country adopted a government

Year	Media	Government
1985	Not Free	Autocracy
1986	Not Free	Autocracy
1987	Not Free	Autocracy
1988	Not Free	Autocracy
1989	Not Free	Autocracy
1990	Not Free	Anocracy
1991	Not Free	Democracy
1992	Not Free	Democracy
1993	Not Free	Democracy
1994	Not Free	Democracy
1995	Imperfectly Free	Democracy
1996	Imperfectly Free	Democracy
1997	Imperfectly Free	Democracy
1998	Imperfectly Free	Democracy
1999	Imperfectly Free	Democracy
2000	Imperfectly Free	Democracy
2001	Imperfectly Free	Democracy
2002	Free	Democracy
2003	Free	Democracy
2004	Free	Democracy
2005	Free	Democracy
2006	Free	Democracy
2007	Imperfectly Free	Democracy
2008	Imperfectly Free	Democracy
2009	Imperfectly Free	Democracy
2010	Imperfectly Free	Democracy
2011	Imperfectly Free	Democracy
2012	Imperfectly Free	Democracy

based on a "'scientific' Marxism-Leninism" and media came under complete government control and citizens' access to foreign news media was restricted.[2]

Benin transitioned to democracy with the elections of 1991, and though the new constitution included provisions for media freedom, the government retained control over "the most influential media" including the broadcast media and the country's only daily newspaper.[3] In 1991, Benin had about twenty privately owned newspapers and journalists for state-owned media as well as those at independent media did criticize government and persist in covering "sensitive matters."[4] Yet journalists who criticized government did face pressures. In 1992, several government journalists were transferred to different jobs and some independent journalists were charged with libel, imprisoned, and/or fined.[5]

1995–2001: Imperfectly Free

Although critical journalists typically faced harassment or imprisonment, in the run up to the 1996 elections restrictions were relaxed to the point where news media became imperfectly free.[6] Yet in 1998, several reporters and editors were sentenced to prison in retaliation for reports that criticized public officials.[7] During the 2001 elections that returned Mathieu Kerekou to power, the news media were able to report critically about both government and opposition.[8]

2002–2006: Free

By 2002, conditions for news media had improved to the point where news media could and did safely criticize the government.[9] Yet news media remained vulnerable to economic influence. Although the 1997 Press Law, which criminalized libel, remained in place, for the most part it went unused until 2006 when a journalist and editor of a privately owned newspaper were sentenced to six years behind bars for refusing to retract a story that accused a court employee of rape.[10]

2007–2012: Imperfectly Free

By 2007, the media environment declined to the point where media were imperfectly free. The number of criminal libel cases grew as news media became increasingly partisan and politically funded.[11] As media became more polarized, physical attacks on journalists increased.[12]

Media Today

Although the Beninese media are among the most free in Africa, media freedom continues to be somewhat restricted. In particular, libel remains a criminal offense punishable with prison terms and fines. Additionally, it is not unusual for political and economic elites to bribe journalists in exchange for favorable coverage.[13] Benin enjoys a mix of privately owned and state-owned media in both the broadcast and print sectors.

Notes

1. *The Toils of the Press*, IPI Report (Zurich: International Press Institute, January 1964).

2. *Country Reports on Human Rights Practices 1977* (Washington, DC: U.S. Department of State, 1978), 3.

3. *Country Reports on Human Rights Practices 1991* (Washington, DC: U.S. Department of State, 1992), 12.

4. Ibid.

5. *Country Reports on Human Rights Practices 1992* (Washington, DC: U.S. Department of State, 1993).

6. *World Press Freedom Review*, IPI Report (Vienna: International Press Institute, 1996).

7. *World Press Freedom Review*, IPI Report (Vienna: International Press Institute, 1998).

8. *Freedom of the Press* (Washington, DC: Freedom House, 2002). Available at http://www.freedom house.org/report/freedom-press/benin/2002.

9. *Freedom of the Press* (Washington, DC: Freedom House, 2003). Available at http://www.freedomhouse .org/report/freedom-press/benin/2003.

10. *Freedom of the Press* (Washington, DC: Freedom House, 2007). Available at http://www.freedomhouse .org/report/freedom-press/benin/2007.

11. *Freedom of the Press* (Washington, DC: Freedom House, 2008). Available at http://www.freedomhouse .org/report/freedom-press/benin/2008.

12. *Freedom of the Press* (Washington, DC: Freedom House, 2013). Available at http://www.freedomhouse .org/report/freedom-press/benin/2013.

13. Ibid.

Bhutan: 1971–2012

Bhutan Year by Year

Year	Media	Government
1971	Not Free	Autocracy
1972	Not Free	Autocracy
1973	Not Free	Autocracy
1974	Not Free	Autocracy
1975	Not Free	Autocracy
1976	Not Free	Autocracy
1977	Not Free	Autocracy
1978	Not Free	Autocracy
1979	Not Free	Autocracy
1980	Not Free	Autocracy
1981	Not Free	Autocracy
1982	Not Free	Autocracy
1983	Not Free	Autocracy
1984	Not Free	Autocracy
1985	Not Free	Autocracy
1986	Not Free	Autocracy
1987	Not Free	Autocracy
1988	Not Free	Autocracy
1989	Not Free	Autocracy
1990	Not Free	Autocracy
1991	Not Free	Autocracy
1992	Not Free	Autocracy
1993	Not Free	Autocracy
1994	Not Free	Autocracy

(Continued)

MEDIA FREEDOM HISTORY IN A NUTSHELL

- Isolated from the rest of the world for centuries, Bhutan's media were nonexistent or government-controlled until 2009, when Bhutan became a constitutional monarchy
- As of 2010, there was one paid-for daily newspaper with an average circulation of 18,000 and several weekly newspapers (World Association of Newspaper's 2010 World Newspaper Trends)
- The Bhutanese Broadcasting Service operates the country's only television stations, but there is a mix of state-owned and privately owned radio stations
- As of 2011, about 21 percent of Bhutanese had access to the Internet (International Telecommunication Union's 2011 ICT Indicators Database)

In Brief

This Himalayan kingdom was virtually isolated from the rest of the world for hundreds of years. Therefore, it has been slow to develop media, much less media freedom. For most of its history, Bhutan's media have been either nonexistent or government controlled. Bhutan's transition to a constitutional monarchy has led to improvements in the media environment, but news media continue to face significant restrictions.

Chronology

1971–2008: Not Free

Although Bhutan was first established as a theocracy in the 1600s and its hereditary monarchy was established in 1907, the kingdom allowed first Britain and then India to manage its foreign affairs until the country became a member of the

(Continued)

Year	Media	Government
1995	Not Free	Autocracy
1996	Not Free	Autocracy
1997	Not Free	Autocracy
1998	Not Free	Autocracy
1999	Not Free	Autocracy
2000	Not Free	Autocracy
2001	Not Free	Autocracy
2002	Not Free	Autocracy
2003	Not Free	Autocracy
2004	Not Free	Autocracy
2005	Not Free	Autocracy
2006	Not Free	Autocracy
2007	Not Free	Autocracy
2008	Not Free	Anocracy
2009	Imperfectly Free	Anocracy
2010	Imperfectly Free	Anocracy
2011	Imperfectly Free	Anocracy
2012	Imperfectly Free	Anocracy

United Nations in 1971. For most of its recent history, Bhutan had almost no news outlets. In 1967, the government began publishing *Kuensel* as a government newsletter, but in 1986, *Kuensel* was transformed and became the country's first newspaper, published weekly by the Bhutanese Ministry of Communications' Department of Information.[1] In 1973, the government established the Bhutan Broadcasting Service, which initially broadcast thirty hours per week of programing via shortwave radio and expanded in the 1990s with daily FM broadcasts.[2] Prior to 1999, Bhutan did not have any domestic television, and in 1989, the government took steps to keep citizens from viewing broadcasts from neighboring countries with a royal decree that antennas be taken down.[3]

Although Bhutan began to modernize, the media environment remained restricted, and in 1992, the National Security Act outlawed criticizing the king and the government. In 1999, the Bhutanese Broadcasting Service began operating the state-owned television station.[4] That same year Bhutan also gained Internet access.[5]

2009–2012: Imperfectly Free

When Jigme Khesar Namgyel Wangchuk became king in 2006, he quickly implemented reforms. In 2008, the country held parliamentary elections and ratified a new constitution, which included provisions for media freedom and the right to information.[6] Yet in practice media remained partially restricted.[7]

Media Today

Although Bhutan now has constitutional provisions for media freedom, in practice government sometimes pressures news media through the Bhutan InfoCom and Media Authority.[8] The Bhutanese media environment borders on being not free, largely because of economic pressures that make it difficult for private media to survive without government support. Both domestic television channels are state-owned, but Bhutan has a mix of state and privately owned radio stations and newspapers. As of 2011, more than 21 percent of Bhutanese had Internet access.

Notes

1. Andrea Matles Savada, *Bhutan: A Country Study* (Washington, DC: Library of Congress Federal Research Division, 1991). Available at http://lcweb2.loc.gov/frd/cs/cshome.html.
2. Ibid.
3. Ibid.
4. *Bhutan*, BBC Country Profiles (London, UK: British Broadcasting Company). Available at http://www.bbc.co.uk/news/world-south-asia-12484025.
5. *World Press Freedom Review*, IPI Report (Vienna: International Press Institute, 1999).
6. *Freedom of the Press* (Washington, DC: Freedom House, 2013). Available at http://www.freedomhouse.org/report/freedom-press/2013/bhutan.
7. Ibid.
8. Ibid.

Bolivia: 1948–2012

Bolivia Year by Year

Year	Media	Government
1948	Not Free	Autocracy
1949	Not Free	Autocracy
1950	Not Free	Autocracy
1951	Not Free	Autocracy
1952	Not Free	Autocracy
1953	Not Free	Autocracy
1954	Not Free	Autocracy
1955	Not Free	Autocracy
1956	Not Free	Autocracy
1957	Not Free	Autocracy
1958	Not Free	Autocracy
1959	Not Free	Autocracy
1960	Not Free	Autocracy
1961	Not Free	Autocracy
1962	Not Free	Autocracy
1963	Not Free	Autocracy
1964	Not Free	Autocracy
1965	Not Free	Autocracy
1966	Not Free	Autocracy
1967	Not Free	Autocracy
1968	Not Free	Autocracy
1969	Not Free	Autocracy
1970	Not Free	Autocracy
1971	Not Free	Autocracy
1972	Not Free	Autocracy
1973	Not Free	Autocracy
1974	Not Free	Autocracy
1975	Not Free	Autocracy
1976	Not Free	Autocracy

(Continued)

MEDIA FREEDOM HISTORY IN A NUTSHELL

- Until Bolivia democratized in 1982, media were highly controlled
- News organizations tend to be closely related to political parties
- Media are often caught in the middle of the struggle between the government and opposition
- Attacks against journalists often go unpunished
- As of 2009, there were twenty-seven paid-for daily newspapers with a total average circulation per issue of 155,000 (World Association of Newspaper's 2010 World Newspaper Trends)
- There are many radio and television, most of which are privately owned and functionally free
- As of 2012, about 34 percent of Bolivians had Internet access (International Telecommunication Union's 2012 ICT Indicators Database)

In Brief

Since it gained independence from Spain in 1825, Bolivia has had a tumultuous history with nearly 200 coups.[1] The media have often been caught in the middle of this political turmoil. Prior to 1982, the media were tightly controlled by government. Since Bolivia's democratization in 1982, media have been partly free. Bolivia's media enjoy more freedom than media in many other countries in the region, and Bolivians do have access to a wide range of print, broadcast and online media, both privately and publicly owned. Yet, in the wake of the ongoing struggle between the government and a separatist opposition, media tend to be partisan and the relationship between government and media remains contentious. Consequently, journalists for both public and private media are frequently harassed and threatened, and attacks against journalists often go unpunished.[2]

(Continued)

Year	Media	Government
1977	Not Free	Autocracy
1978	Not Free	Autocracy
1979	Not Free	Autocracy
1980	Not Free	Autocracy
1981	Not Free	Autocracy
1982	Imperfectly Free	Democracy
1983	Imperfectly Free	Democracy
1984	Imperfectly Free	Democracy
1985	Imperfectly Free	Democracy
1986	Imperfectly Free	Democracy
1987	Imperfectly Free	Democracy
1988	Imperfectly Free	Democracy
1989	Imperfectly Free	Democracy
1990	Imperfectly Free	Democracy
1991	Imperfectly Free	Democracy
1992	Imperfectly Free	Democracy
1993	Imperfectly Free	Democracy
1994	Imperfectly Free	Democracy
1995	Imperfectly Free	Democracy
1996	Imperfectly Free	Democracy
1997	Imperfectly Free	Democracy
1998	Imperfectly Free	Democracy
1999	Imperfectly Free	Democracy
2000	Imperfectly Free	Democracy
2001	Imperfectly Free	Democracy
2002	Free	Democracy
2003	Imperfectly Free	Democracy
2004	Imperfectly Free	Democracy
2005	Imperfectly Free	Democracy
2006	Imperfectly Free	Democracy
2007	Imperfectly Free	Democracy
2008	Imperfectly Free	Democracy
2009	Imperfectly Free	Democracy
2010	Imperfectly Free	Democracy
2011	Imperfectly Free	Democracy
2012	Imperfectly Free	Democracy

Chronology

1948–1981: Not Free

The Print Law of 1925 called for freedom of the press on the one hand, but on the other criminalized damaging reporting (even when it was truthful) and established a Jury of Print to judge accused journalists.[3] Newspapers for the most part were strictly controlled by the government; however, the daily *La Calle* was established by the Nationalist Revolutionary Movement (MNR) in the 1930s and is credited with facilitating mobilization for the MNR.[4] *La Calle* was influential to the point where it was eventually banned by the government in 1946.[5] The Revolution of 1952 ushered in an era of even more tightly controlled media as the MNR abolished all unfavorable media and created an official state newspaper.[6] Because of high poverty and illiteracy, radio, in particular community radio, was (and remains) a preferred source of news and information.[7]

1982–2001: Imperfectly Free

Following many coups and counter-coups, 1982 saw a remarkable transition in Bolivia, from a series of authoritarian governments to a fledgling democracy. This transition came about in the wake of growing unrest due to failure of three different military governments within fourteen months to address the country's economic problems.[8] The change came about as the military reconvened the Congress to elect a president. As a result of this democratization, government control of media relaxed and media became partly free. During this time, the number of newspapers, radio stations, and television stations increased dramatically, especially in preparation for the 1985 elections.[9] At the same time, both print and broadcast journalists faced significant restrictions. Since 1979, all journalists have been required to obtain a university degree and must register with the National Registry of Journalism.[10] Bolivian journalists faced (and continue to face) "some of the toughest defamation laws in the continent" as a result of the 1995 Telecommunications Act.[11] Additionally, journalists covering government corruption faced harassment and physical threats. Consequently, self-censorship was (and remains) common.

2002: Free

It appeared that media would enjoy greater freedom from government control in 2002 when President Jorge Quiroga Ramirez signed a declaration to establish media freedom. Initially, the media enjoyed increased freedom to the degree that they were briefly coded as "Free."[12]

2003–2012: Free

In 2003, mass protests prompted President Gonzalo Sánchez, who had just won the 2002 elections, to resign. His successor, President Carlos Mesa, was also forced to resign in 2005, as mass demonstrations continued. At issue was (and still is) a protracted struggle between the upper-middle class minority who controlled most of the country's natural gas reserves and reside in the eastern part of the country, in particular Santa Cruz, and the Indian majority who for the most part live in poverty in La Paz and the western highlands.[13] In 2003, after a brief period of increased openness, media freedom was again constrained to the point where media were only partly free, as the struggles between these groups intensified and both the minority-controlled government and the majority-controlled opposition sought to use the media to sway public opinion. As a result journalists faced harassment and attacks from both groups.[14]

Media Today

Though the political power shifted with the election of Bolivia's first indigenous president, opposition leader Evo Morales, in December of 2005, the media remain caught in the middle of this struggle between the new majority-controlled government and the now separatist opposition. According to Reporters Without Borders, the media often play a direct role in the conflict:

In Santa Cruz, attacks against the state press by the regionalist extreme right Unión Juvenil Cruceñista went on occasion as far as murder attempts, while some local privately-owned media like Radio Oriental called for racial hatred and murder of the president and some ministers, who like him, were of indigenous origin.[15]

Both state-controlled and private media faced threats and attacks from opposition and government supporters, respectively.[16] As a result, although Bolivia has greater media freedom than many other countries in the region, Bolivian journalists tend to avoid reporting on corruption, drug trafficking, and other controversial subjects.[17] In 2010, Bolivia passed an antiracism law that criminalized reporting that condones racism that critics claimed would have a chilling effect on media.[18]

Thus, though it is among the poorest countries in Latin America, Bolivia has a wide range of print, television, radio, and online media, both state-controlled and independently owned. The privately owned media will criticize the government, but attacks on journalists who engage in investigative reporting continue. Journalists accused of violations must go before the Press Tribunal, an independent agency. Journalists found guilty slander or defamation can be sentenced up to two years in prison, and those found guilty of insulting the president or vice president face sentences of up to three years.[19] Journalists are frequently targets of harassment, threats, and physical attacks.[20]

Although Bolivian laws provide for media freedom, and the government in general respects this, the relationship between government and media remains contentious. For example, President Evo Morales has been known to limit questioning to journalists from state-controlled and international media at his news conferences.[21] Internet media are not restricted by government, and as of 2012, about 34 percent of Bolivians had Internet access.[22] Media tend to be tied to government or opposition parties.

Notes

1. *Bolivia* (Washington, DC: CIA World Factbook, 2011).
2. *Country Report Bolivia* (Paris, France: Reporters Without Borders, 2011).
   Available at http://en.rsf.org/report-bolivia,168.html.
3. Gonzalo Soruco and Juliet Pinto, "The Mass Media in Bolivia," in *The Handbook of Spanish Language Media*, ed. Alan B. Albarran (New York: Routledge, 2009), 94.
4. Ibid.
5. Ibid.
6. Rex A. Hudson and Dennis M. Hanratty, *Bolivia: A Country Study* (Washington, DC: GPO for the Library of Congress, 1989). Available at http://lcweb2.loc.gov/frd/cs/botoc.html.

7. Soruco and Pinto, "The Mass Media in Bolivia," 95.
8. Hudson and Hanratty, *Bolivia: A Country Study*.
9. Ibid.
10. *Press Laws Database* (Miami, FL: Inter American Press Association, 1999). Available at http://www.sipiapa.org/projects/laws-bol.cfm.
11. Javier A. Galvan, *Culture and Customs of Bolivia* (Santa Barbara, CA: ABC-CLIO, LLC), 106–07.
12. Bolivian media were coded as "Partly Free" by both Freedom House and our coders.
13. Monty G. Marshall and Keith Jaggers, *Polity IV Country Report: Bolivia* (Societal-Systems Research Inc. and the Center of Systemic Peace). Available at http://www.systemicpeace.org/polity/Bolivia2010.pdf.
14. *Freedom of the Press* (Washington, DC: Freedom House, 2004). Available at http://www.freedomhouse.org/report-types/freedom-press.
15. *Country Report Bolivia* (Paris, France: Reporters Without Borders, 2011). Available at http://en.rsf.org/report-bolivia,168.html.
16. *Freedom of the Press* (Washington, DC: Freedom House, 2007). Available at http://www.freedomhouse.org/report-types/freedom-press.
17. *Bolivia 2007* (Paris, France: Reporters Without Borders, 2007). Available at http://en.rsf.org/bolivia-bolivia-01-02-2007,20528.html.
18. *Freedom of the Press* (Washington, DC: Freedom House, 2011). Available at http://www.freedomhouse.org/report-types/freedom-press.
19. *World Press Trends, WAN-IFRA/ZenithOptimedia* (Darmstadt, Germany: WAN-IFRA, 2010), 298.
20. Reporters Without Borders, 2011.
21. WAN-INFRA, 298.
22. *International Telecommunications Union* (Geneva, Switzerland: ICT Indicators Database, 2011) Available at http://www.itu.int/ITU-D/ict/statistics/.

Bosnia and Herzegovina: 1992–2012

Bosnia and Herzegovina Year by Year

Year	Media	Government
1992	Free	Anocracy
1993	Free	Anocracy
1994	Free	Anocracy
1995	Not Free	Foreign Interruption
1996	Not Free	Foreign Interruption
1997	Not Free	Foreign Interruption
1998	Imperfectly Free	Foreign Interruption
1999	Imperfectly Free	Foreign Interruption
2000	Imperfectly Free	Foreign Interruption
2001	Imperfectly Free	Foreign Interruption
2002	Imperfectly Free	Foreign Interruption
2003	Imperfectly Free	Foreign Interruption
2004	Imperfectly Free	Foreign Interruption
2005	Imperfectly Free	Foreign Interruption
2006	Imperfectly Free	Foreign Interruption
2007	Imperfectly Free	Foreign Interruption
2008	Imperfectly Free	Foreign Interruption
2009	Imperfectly Free	Foreign Interruption
2010	Imperfectly Free	Foreign Interruption
2011	Imperfectly Free	Foreign Interruption
2012	Imperfectly Free	Foreign Interruption

In Brief

Bosnia was left divided and traumatized by the bloody civil war that followed the dissolution of Yugoslavia. During the war only limited media

MEDIA FREEDOM HISTORY IN A NUTSHELL

- Civil war from 1992 to 1995 left the country divided and traumatized. During the war, limited press operated more or less freely in significant parts of the country
- Extensive post-war effort to build a Western-style professional media has had limited success
- Current media are heavily influenced by ownership or political backers and lacking qualities of professionalism but are functionally free
- As of 2009, there were twelve paid-for daily newspapers with a total average circulation of 190,000, forty-four television stations, and 144 radio stations (World Association of Newspaper's 2010 World Newspaper Trends)
- As of 2012, about 65 percent of Bosnians had Internet access (International Telecommunication Union's 2012 ICT Indicators Database)

were available, but some were able to function more or less freely. The post-war era saw a massive, externally supported effort to build a free and professional news media system, but success was limited.

Chronology

1992–1994: Free

Analysts may wish to code this war time period as missing data because it is debatable whether there was sufficient media activity to claim media were functional as a political force. However, when the media could and did operate during the war, they were free and critical. For much of the war, the media spectrum was limited to government-controlled television and radio, and few independent news agencies were able to publish throughout the worst of the conflict.[1]

Additionally many journalists attempting to cover the war were wounded or killed.[2]

1995–1997: Not Free

The Dayton peace accords that ended the war have defined Bosnia and Herzegovina in the years since. The country was effectively split into two self-governed regions, and every aspect of the governing body they share is legally bound to the preservation of the peace accords. The result is an almost indefinable political structure that functioned in many ways like an occupational government. The first years of the post-war period were dominated by an effort to enforce the peace, and even as Western powers began a massive effort to develop a professional and independent news media, media were limited and restricted to the point of control.

1998–2012: Imperfectly Free

The media development effort was successful to a degree. Like the odd political structures in place within the country, it is almost impossible to put a meaningful label on the nature of the media regime. It does for the most part function as a free press, but it is still constrained by the structures put in place with the Dayton peace accords and it shows signs of being politically and economically coerced.

These signs include the conviction of the editor-in-chief of one of the most prominent independent news magazines for criminal libel, as well as grenades exploding nearby the offices of the famous magazine, *Dani*.[3]

Media Today

The constitution of Bosnia and Herzegovina guarantees freedom of the press, but politicians exert continuous pressure on journalists and media outlets tend to be aligned with political parties.[4]

Most recent assessments of the media criticize their professionalism and indicate that media are significantly influenced by economic and political forces. Thus news media manage to remain functionally free, but this is a fragile freedom at best.

Notes

1. *World Press Freedom Review*, IPI Report (Vienna: International Press Institute, 1994).
2. *World Press Freedom Review*, IPI Report (Vienna: International Press Institute, 1993).
3. *World Press Freedom Review*, IPI Report (Vienna: International Press Institute, 1998).
4. *Freedom of the Press, Bosnia and Herzegovina* (Washington, DC: Freedom House, 2013). Available at http://www.freedomhouse.org/report/freedom-press/2013/bosnia-and-herzegovina.

Botswana: 1966–2012

Botswana Year by Year

Year	Media	Government
1966	Free	Democracy
1967	Free	Democracy
1968	Free	Democracy
1969	Free	Democracy
1970	Free	Democracy
1971	Free	Democracy
1972	Free	Democracy
1973	Free	Democracy
1974	Free	Democracy
1975	Free	Democracy
1976	Free	Democracy
1977	Free	Democracy
1978	Free	Democracy
1979	Free	Democracy
1980	Free	Democracy
1981	Free	Democracy
1982	Free	Democracy
1983	Free	Democracy
1984	Free	Democracy
1985	Free	Democracy
1986	Free	Democracy
1987	Free	Democracy
1988	Free	Democracy
1989	Free	Democracy

(Continued)

> **MEDIA FREEDOM HISTORY IN A NUTSHELL**
>
> - News media have been functionally free since Botswana gained independence in 1966, but state-owned media are far more accessible than privately owned media
> - As of 2010, there were two daily newspapers, one of them was a paid-for daily with a total average circulation of 76,000 (World Association of Newspaper's 2010 World Newspaper Trends)
> - State-owned radio and television are the primary sources of media
> - As of 2012, about 12 percent of Botswana had Internet access (International Telecommunication Union's 2012 ICT Indicators Database)

In Brief

Since gaining independence, Botswana has had a civilian government. Given this political context, it is not surprising that the news media have been functionally free. Botswana law provides for media freedom, and for the most part government respects this in practice; however, there are also a number of measures that allow government to limit media freedom—especially to preserve national security and promote public morality.[1]

Chronology

1966–1992: Free

After gaining independence from Britain in 1966, Botswana became a democracy, but it has been dominated by one party—the Botswana Democratic Party. The country's only daily newspaper was government owned, but editorially independent.[2] Yet there were reports of independent newspapers losing advertising following the

(Continued)

Year	Media	Government
1990	Free	Democracy
1991	Free	Democracy
1992	Free	Democracy
1993	Imperfectly Free	Democracy
1994	Imperfectly Free	Democracy
1995	Imperfectly Free	Democracy
1996	Imperfectly Free	Democracy
1997	Imperfectly Free	Democracy
1998	Imperfectly Free	Democracy
1999	Imperfectly Free	Democracy
2000	Imperfectly Free	Democracy
2001	Free	Democracy
2002	Free	Democracy
2003	Free	Democracy
2004	Free	Democracy
2005	Imperfectly Free	Democracy
2006	Imperfectly Free	Democracy
2007	Imperfectly Free	Democracy
2008	Imperfectly Free	Democracy
2009	Imperfectly Free	Democracy
2010	Imperfectly Free	Democracy
2011	Imperfectly Free	Democracy
2012	Imperfectly Free	Democracy

publication of articles that criticized government, and of journalists for independent publications having difficulty gaining access to government sources.[3] Moreover, foreign correspondents who engaged in critical reporting were sometimes detained by government.[4]

1993–2000: Imperfectly Free

By 1993, conditions had deteriorated to the point where media were imperfectly free. In particular, there were indications that the government-owned media were biased in a way that preserved the hegemony of the Botswana Democratic Party. Specifically, members of the opposition—the Botswana People's Party—claimed the Botswana Press Agency shunned coverage of its activities but provided ample coverage of the Botswana Democratic Party.[5] Additionally, journalists who criticized government faced libel suits, loss of advertising, and threats.[6]

Prior to 1999, all radio stations were government owned, but in 1999, the government granted a license to a private radio station.[7] In 2000, Botswana's state-owned television station began broadcasting.[8]

2001–2004: Free

The International Press Institute noted that in 2000, the government began to take a "softer approach" to the news media, and by 2001, this resulted in the media environment becoming effectively free.[9] The year 2001 also marked an important victory for independent media. Two newspapers filed a complaint in court after the government banned official advertising in the two newspapers. The judge ruled that the ban on advertising was unconstitutional.[10] Privately owned newspapers remained vibrant and critical of government, but state-owned media tended to be more supportive of government. Most broadcast media were state owned. In 2002, journalists established the Press Council of Botswana, as a form of self-regulation aimed at increasing professionalization.

2005–2012: Imperfectly Free

Government intolerance of critical reporting increased in 2005 to the extent that the media environment became imperfectly free. Also in 2005, two Zimbabwean journalists were expelled after criticizing the government in their reporting.[11] Although independent newspapers continued to report critically regarding government policies, they did not have the reach of the state-owned *Daily News*, which was distributed for free throughout the country. Similarly, privately owned broadcast media had far less range than their state-owned counterparts.

Media Today

Although independent media persist in critical reporting on government behavior and policies, the state-owned media have greater reach and influence. Critical journalists are subject to defamation suits and harassment. Although the internet is not restricted, most citizens cannot afford to access it.

Notes

1. *Freedom of the Press* (Washington, DC: Freedom House, 2013). Available at http://www.freedom house.org/report/freedom-press/2013/botswana.
2. *Country Reports on Human Rights Practices 1977* (Washington, DC: U.S. Department of State, 1978).
3. *Country Reports on Human Rights Practices 1989* (Washington, DC: U.S. Department of State, 1990).
4. *World Press Freedom Review*, IPI Report (Zurich: International Press Institute, 1990).
5. *World Press Freedom Review*, IPI Report (Vienna: International Press Institute, 1993).
6. *World Press Freedom Review*, IPI Report (Vienna: International Press Institute, 1999).
7. Ibid.
8. *World Press Freedom Review*, IPI Report (Vienna: International Press Institute, 2000).
9. *World Press Freedom Review*, IPI Report (Vienna: International Press Institute, 2001).
10. Ibid.
11. *Freedom of the Press* (Washington, DC: Freedom House, 2006). Available at http://www.freedom house.org/report/freedom-press/2006/botswana.

Brazil: 1948–2012

Brazil Year by Year

Year	Media	Government
1948	Free	Anocracy
1949	Free	Anocracy
1950	Free	Anocracy
1951	Free	Anocracy
1952	Free	Anocracy
1953	Free	Anocracy
1954	Free	Anocracy
1955	Free	Anocracy
1956	Free	Anocracy
1957	Free	Anocracy
1958	Free	Democracy
1959	Free	Democracy
1960	Free	Democracy
1961	Free	Anocracy
1962	Imperfectly Free	Anocracy
1963	Imperfectly Free	Anocracy
1964	Imperfectly Free	Anocracy
1965	Imperfectly Free	Autocracy
1966	Imperfectly Free	Autocracy
1967	Imperfectly Free	Autocracy
1968	Imperfectly Free	Autocracy
1969	Not Free	Autocracy
1970	Not Free	Autocracy
1971	Not Free	Autocracy
1972	Not Free	Autocracy
1973	Not Free	Autocracy
1974	Not Free	Anocracy
1975	Not Free	Anocracy

MEDIA FREEDOM HISTORY IN A NUTSHELL

- After World War II, Brazilian media were among the most free in the region
- From 1969 to 1977, the military government censored news media
- Although media are now functionally free, attacks on journalists remain a problem in Brazil
- Brazil is the largest media market in South America. As of 2011, Brazil had 4,835 total daily newspapers, 727 of them were paid-for dailies with a total average circulation per issue of 8,806,000 (World Association of Newspaper's 2012 World Newspaper Trends)
- The country is home to thousands of radio and television stations. Brazilian-made TV shows are aired worldwide (World Association of Newspaper's 2010 World Newspaper Trends)
- In 2012, 50 percent of Brazilians had Internet access (International Telecommunication Union's 2012 ICT Indicators Database)

In Brief

In the years following World War II, Brazilian media were among the most free in the region. Political turmoil brought about a decrease in media freedom in the early 1960s. Yet media remained imperfectly free even during mid-1960s when the military took control of the country. Although the government had the legal authority to censor the media, it did not do so until the late 1960s. For most of the 1970s, Brazilian media were severely restricted, but toward the end of the decade, the military censorship eased. Since then media have been imperfectly free, but attacks on journalists remain a problem.

Year	Media	Government
1976	Not Free	Anocracy
1977	Not Free	Anocracy
1978	Imperfectly Free	Anocracy
1979	Imperfectly Free	Anocracy
1980	Imperfectly Free	Anocracy
1981	Imperfectly Free	Anocracy
1982	Imperfectly Free	Anocracy
1983	Imperfectly Free	Anocracy
1984	Imperfectly Free	Anocracy
1985	Imperfectly Free	Democracy
1986	Imperfectly Free	Democracy
1987	Imperfectly Free	Democracy
1988	Imperfectly Free	Democracy
1989	Imperfectly Free	Democracy
1990	Imperfectly Free	Democracy
1991	Imperfectly Free	Democracy
1992	Imperfectly Free	Democracy
1993	Imperfectly Free	Democracy
1994	Imperfectly Free	Democracy
1995	Imperfectly Free	Democracy
1996	Imperfectly Free	Democracy
1997	Imperfectly Free	Democracy
1998	Imperfectly Free	Democracy
1999	Imperfectly Free	Democracy
2000	Imperfectly Free	Democracy
2001	Imperfectly Free	Democracy
2002	Imperfectly Free	Democracy
2003	Imperfectly Free	Democracy
2004	Imperfectly Free	Democracy
2005	Imperfectly Free	Democracy
2006	Imperfectly Free	Democracy
2007	Imperfectly Free	Democracy
2008	Imperfectly Free	Democracy
2009	Imperfectly Free	Democracy
2010	Imperfectly Free	Democracy
2011	Imperfectly Free	Democracy
2012	Imperfectly Free	Democracy

Chronology

1948–1961: Free

In a region where many countries had laws restricting press freedom, Brazil was a "happy exception," according to the International Press Association.[1] The newspaper industry in Brazil developed rapidly from the 1930s to the 1950s as literacy increased. In 1952, one newspaper director complained to the Inter American Press Association (IAPA) that the greatest threat to freedom of the press in Brazil was a worldwide shortage of newsprint at a time when the country's demand for it was increasing by about 30 percent each year.[2]

Brazil's first media empire emerged in the 1930s when Francisco de Assis Chateaubriand Bandeira de Melo established his Diários Associados newspaper chain. By the 1950s, Chateaubriand had expanded his holdings to include the Tupi Network.[3] In the 1920s, Irineu Marinho founded the O Globo newspaper in Rio, which with the acquisition of radio and television stations eventually became Globo Organization, Brazil's second media empire.

1962–1968: Imperfectly Free

The resignation of President Janio Quandros in August 1961 plunged Brazil into a political-military crisis. According to the Inter American Press Association, news media were censored for seventy-two hours following the resignation, but the censorship was lifted when newspaper publishers protested.[4]

In 1964, following antigovernment protests, President Goulart fled the country and the military took over. Under military control, political pressures on the press actually lessoned, according to IAPA.[5] Perhaps this happened because some newspapers supported the military's actions by calling for the ouster of Goulart.[6] Thus, news media remained functionally free, but there were concerns because the 1967 Press Law criminalized libel and slander and rendered such offenses punishable by up to three years in prison. The Inter American Press Association's Freedom of the Press Committee reported, "The government has the instruments to limit freedom of the press. It does not use them, has not yet used them, but they do exist."[7]

1969–1977: Not Free

In December 1968, Institutional Act 5 gave the president dictatorial powers including censorship of the media. In 1969, the government used the press law and national security law to punish journalists. Most were charged with political crimes rather than press crimes, but the end result had a chilling effect on news media.[8] By 1972, the government was practicing prior restraint. At first editors in Sao Paulo and Rio de Janeiro received phone calls from the federal police letting them know what information was prohibited. Then there were instances where federal police were dispatched to read newspapers as they came off the presses. For example, on August 24, 1972, a censor from the federal police arrived around midnight at the offices of *O Estado*. "The exits were blocked with police vehicles and men armed with machine guns so as to keep the issue from leaving the building. After reading and approving all the pages, the censor sent them to the General in charge of the Federal Police . . ."[9] The trucks carrying the newspapers were not allowed to leave until 3 AM.

1978–2012: Imperfectly Free

In 1978, conditions improved. While censorship remained constitutional, government no longer practiced it.[10] The year 1979 marked the creation of the Empresa Brasileira de Noticias, "whose aim is to monopolistically control all information concerning official activities in order to foster government objectives through manipulation of the media in general."[11] While there were attacks on journalists, for the most part news media were allowed to report freely.

In 1985, Brazil transitioned to a civilian government. The 1988 constitution included provisions for media freedom, but the 1967 Press Law was not overturned until 2009. Even so, the penal code still permitted sentences of two years imprisonment for criminal defamation.

Media Today

Brazil is the largest media market in South America. The country has a wide range of independently owned radio stations, television channels, newspapers, and magazines, but ownership remains highly concentrated. In particular, the Globo Organization dominates the television market. Although legal protections for journalists have improved in recent years (with the overturning of the 1967 Press Law), attacks on journalists remain a problem. According to Reporters Without Borders in 2012, eleven journalists were killed in Brazil.[12]

Notes

1. *Government Pressures on the Press*, IPI Survey (Zurich: International Press Institute. 1955), 35.
2. *Inter American Press Association Reports* (Miami, FL: Inter American Press Association, 1952), 1 (6).
3. Rex A. Hudson, *Brazil: A Country Study* (Washington DC: Library of Congress Federal Research Division, 1997). Available at http://lcweb2.loc.gov/frd/cs/cshome.html.
4. General Assembly Proceedings 1961. "Report by Chairman of the Freedom of the Press Committee." (Miami, FL: Inter American Press Association, 1962).
5. General Assembly Proceedings 1964. "Report by Chairman of the Freedom of the Press Committee." (Miami, FL: Inter American Press Association, 1965).
6. Rex A. Hudson, *Brazil: A Country Study* (Washington DC: Library of Congress Federal Research Division, 1997). Available at http://lcweb2.loc.gov/frd/cs/cshome.html.
7. General Assembly Proceedings 1966. "Report by Chairman of the Freedom of the Press Committee." (Miami, FL: Inter American Press Association, 1967), 186.
8. General Assembly Proceedings 1969. "Report by Chairman of the Freedom of the Press Committee." (Miami, FL: Inter American Press Association, 1970).
9. General Assembly Proceedings 1972. "Report by Chairman of the Freedom of the Press Committee." (Miami, FL: Inter American Press Association, 1973), 122–23.
10. General Assembly Proceedings 1978. "Report by Chairman of the Freedom of the Press Committee." (Miami, FL: Inter American Press Association, 1979).
11. General Assembly Proceedings 1979. "Report by Chairman of the Freedom of the Press Committee." (Miami, FL: Inter American Press Association, 1980), 2-a.
12. *Brazil* (Paris, France: Reporters Without Borders, July 2013). Available at http://en.rsf.org/report-brazil,169.html.

Brunei: 1984–2012

Brunei Year by Year

Year	Media	Government
1984	Not Free	Autocracy
1985	Not Free	Autocracy
1986	Not Free	Autocracy
1987	Not Free	Autocracy
1988	Not Free	Autocracy
1989	Not Free	Autocracy
1990	Not Free	Autocracy
1991	Not Free	Autocracy
1992	Not Free	Autocracy
1993	Not Free	Autocracy
1994	Not Free	Autocracy
1995	Not Free	Autocracy
1996	Not Free	Autocracy
1997	Not Free	Autocracy
1998	Not Free	Autocracy
1999	Not Free	Autocracy
2000	Not Free	Autocracy
2001	Not Free	Autocracy
2002	Not Free	Autocracy
2003	Not Free	Autocracy
2004	Not Free	Autocracy
2005	Not Free	Autocracy
2006	Not Free	Autocracy
2007	Not Free	Autocracy
2008	Not Free	Autocracy
2009	Not Free	Autocracy
2010	Not Free	Autocracy
2011	Not Free	Autocracy
2012	Not Free	Autocracy

MEDIA FREEDOM HISTORY IN A NUTSHELL

- Brunei has been ruled by the same family for more than six centuries, and that family either owns or controls most media
- As of 2009, there were three paid-for daily newspapers with a total average circulation of 41,000 (World Association of Newspaper's 2010 World Newspaper Trends)
- The government owns all domestic broadcast media, but Bruneians can also access Malaysian media
- As of 2012, about 60 percent Bruneians of had access to the Internet (International Telecommunication Union's 2012 ICT Indicators Database)

In Brief

Brunei gained independence from Britain in 1984, but this constitutional sultanate has been ruled by the same family for more than 600 years, and that family strictly controls all news media.

Chronology

1984–2012: Not Free

Since 1962, Brunei has been ruled under emergency powers that restrict media freedom.[1] The sultan's family owns or controls most domestic media. Radio Television Brunei is state controlled and operates all the country's broadcast media, but broadcasts from Malaysia are available. Journalists who criticize the sultan, his family, or his Malay Muslim Monarchy ideology face fines, and those whose reporting is deemed false or malicious face imprisonment of up to three years.[2] Internet service providers and content producers are also liable for material that is found offensive or against public interest.[3]

Media Today

The few news outlets that Brunei has are owned or controlled by the sultan and his family.[4] There is nothing to suggest that this will change in the near future.

Notes

1. *World Press Trends* (Darmstadt, Germany: WAN-IFRA, 2010).
2. *Freedom of the Press* (Washington, DC: Freedom House, 2013). Available at http://www.freedomhouse.org/report/freedom-press/2013/brunei.
3. Ibid.
4. *Brunei*, BBC Country Profiles (London, UK: British Broadcasting Company). Available at http://www.bbc.co.uk/news/world-asia-pacific-12990064.

Bulgaria: 1948–2012

Bulgaria Year by Year

Year	Media	Government
1948	Not Free	Autocracy
1949	Not Free	Autocracy
1950	Not Free	Autocracy
1951	Not Free	Autocracy
1952	Not Free	Autocracy
1953	Not Free	Autocracy
1954	Not Free	Autocracy
1955	Not Free	Autocracy
1956	Not Free	Autocracy
1957	Not Free	Autocracy
1958	Not Free	Autocracy
1959	Not Free	Autocracy
1960	Not Free	Autocracy
1961	Not Free	Autocracy
1962	Not Free	Autocracy
1963	Not Free	Autocracy
1964	Not Free	Autocracy
1965	Not Free	Autocracy
1966	Not Free	Autocracy
1967	Not Free	Autocracy
1968	Not Free	Autocracy
1969	Not Free	Autocracy
1970	Not Free	Autocracy
1971	Not Free	Autocracy

(Continued)

MEDIA FREEDOM HISTORY IN A NUTSHELL

- A Soviet-bloc country with directly controlled press until 1989
- Authoritarian control continued until 1994
- Social and economic crises lead to a sudden transition to an imperfect, but functionally free press regime.
- Analysts disagree on the continued significance of minor issues related to media freedom
- As of 2011, there were sixty-two daily newspapers, sixty-one of them were paid-for dailies with a total average circulation per issue of 827,000 (World Association of Newspaper's 2012 World Newspaper Trends)
- Bulgaria has many radio and television stations, including both publicly owned and privately owned
- As of 2012, about 55 percent of Bulgarians have Internet access (International Telecommunication Union's 2012 ICT Indicators Database)

In Brief

The communists managed to hold significant power and control in this Soviet bloc state, including control of the media, until 1994. The subsequent transition to a free press regime was sudden and has been robust. Though media are imperfectly free, there is little indication that there could be a reversion to authoritarian control.

Chronology

1948–1994: Not Free

A Soviet single party system with complete control of the media was in place until 1989. In 1988, as many as twenty newspapers were closed down because they "lacked sufficient readers."[1] Elections in 1989 kept the communists in power,

(Continued)

Year	Media	Government
1972	Not Free	Autocracy
1973	Not Free	Autocracy
1974	Not Free	Autocracy
1975	Not Free	Autocracy
1976	Not Free	Autocracy
1977	Not Free	Autocracy
1978	Not Free	Autocracy
1979	Not Free	Autocracy
1980	Not Free	Autocracy
1981	Not Free	Autocracy
1982	Not Free	Autocracy
1983	Not Free	Autocracy
1984	Not Free	Autocracy
1985	Not Free	Autocracy
1986	Not Free	Autocracy
1987	Not Free	Autocracy
1988	Not Free	Autocracy
1989	Not Free	Autocracy
1990	Not Free	Democracy
1991	Not Free	Democracy
1992	Not Free	Democracy
1993	Not Free	Democracy
1994	Not Free	Democracy
1995	Imperfectly Free	Democracy
1996	Imperfectly Free	Democracy
1997	Imperfectly Free	Democracy
1998	Imperfectly Free	Democracy
1999	Imperfectly Free	Democracy
2000	Imperfectly Free	Democracy
2001	Imperfectly Free	Democracy
2002	Free	Democracy
2003	Imperfectly Free	Democracy

but a sustained period of social and economic turmoil eroded their power and ability to control the media. In the same year, and for the first time ever, a Bulgarian leader met and heard a group of radical intellectuals who demanded genuine human rights, freedom of speech and the press, freedom to publish, and the release of political prisoners.[2] No action was taken but the fact that the meeting was held at all was encouraging to proponents of media freedom.

1995–2001: Imperfectly Free

The abruptness of the transition to a functionally free media regime was almost as remarkable as the effectiveness of the change. Yet although journalists were functionally free, they still faced threats and intimidation when they criticized government officials.[3] The foundation for critical media began growing almost immediately after the fall of the Berlin Wall, but it was not until the slowly growing economic and social turmoil reached crisis proportions that the media broke free and became a key factor in forcing the reforms enacted in 1997.

2002: Free

The push for liberalization peaked in 2002, when Bulgaria was briefly listed as a clearly free media country.

2003–2012: Imperfectly Free

A conservative push, particularly regarding the use of libel laws and other legal challenges to try to limit critical content, pulled the Bulgarian media back into the imperfectly free category.

Media Today

Analysts agree that the news media operate freely and are effective as an arena for political debate, but they disagree on just how free media are. Freedom House lists media as partly free while professional organizations such as the European Journalism Centre indicate that media are clearly free. All, however, are concerned about extent to which recent authoritarian pressures may have compromised its status as a free press. Still, there appears to be little reason to expect that media freedom is vulnerable or under threat.

Year	Media	Government
2004	Imperfectly Free	Democracy
2005	Imperfectly Free	Democracy
2006	Imperfectly Free	Democracy
2007	Imperfectly Free	Democracy
2008	Imperfectly Free	Democracy
2009	Imperfectly Free	Democracy
2010	Imperfectly Free	Democracy
2011	Imperfectly Free	Democracy
2012	Imperfectly Free	Democracy

Notes

1. *World Press Freedom Review,* IPI Report (Zurich: International Press Institute, 1987).
2. *World Press Freedom Review,* IPI Report (Zurich: International Press Institute, 1989).
3. *World Press Freedom Review,* IPI Report (Vienna: International Press Institute, 1995).

Burkina Faso: 1960–2012

Burkina Faso Year by Year

Year	Media	Government
1960	Not Free	Autocracy
1961	Not Free	Autocracy
1962	Not Free	Autocracy
1963	Not Free	Autocracy
1964	Not Free	Autocracy
1965	Not Free	Autocracy
1966	Not Free	Autocracy
1967	Not Free	Autocracy
1968	Not Free	Autocracy
1969	Not Free	Autocracy
1970	Not Free	Anocracy
1971	Not Free	Anocracy
1972	Not Free	Anocracy
1973	Not Free	Anocracy
1974	Not Free	Anocracy
1975	Not Free	Anocracy
1976	Not Free	Anocracy
1977	Not Free	Anocracy
1978	Imperfectly Free	Anocracy
1979	Imperfectly Free	Anocracy
1980	Imperfectly Free	Autocracy
1981	Imperfectly Free	Autocracy
1982	Not Free	Autocracy
1983	Not Free	Autocracy
1984	Not Free	Autocracy

MEDIA FREEDOM HISTORY IN A NUTSHELL

- After nearly three decades of military coups and restricted news media, Burkinabé media became functionally free in 1991
- As of 2009, there were five paid-for daily newspapers with a total average circulation per issue of 36,000 (World Association of Newspaper's 2010 World Newspaper Trends)
- Burkinabé media include both government-controlled and privately owned broadcast and print news outlets
- As of 2012, about 4 percent of Burkinabé had access to the Internet (International Telecommunication Union's 2012 ICT Indicators Database)

In Brief

Coups and political instability led to a hostile media environment for most of the three decades following Burkina Faso's independence from France in 1960. In the early 1990s, under international and domestic pressures, President Blaise Compaoré implemented limited political reforms and lifted some of the restrictions on media, prompting the emergence of independent news media. Thus, media have been imperfectly free since 1991.

Chronology

1960–1977: Not Free

After gaining independence from France in 1960, Burkina Faso, then known as Upper Volta, spent nearly a decade under the dictatorship of Maurice Yameogo, followed by two decades under military regimes that seized power through a series of coups. During these turbulent years,

Year	Media	Government
1985	Not Free	Autocracy
1986	Not Free	Autocracy
1987	Not Free	Autocracy
1988	Not Free	Autocracy
1989	Not Free	Autocracy
1990	Not Free	Autocracy
1991	Imperfectly Free	Anocracy
1992	Imperfectly Free	Anocracy
1993	Imperfectly Free	Anocracy
1994	Imperfectly Free	Anocracy
1995	Imperfectly Free	Anocracy
1996	Imperfectly Free	Anocracy
1997	Imperfectly Free	Anocracy
1998	Imperfectly Free	Anocracy
1999	Imperfectly Free	Anocracy
2000	Imperfectly Free	Anocracy
2001	Imperfectly Free	Anocracy
2002	Imperfectly Free	Anocracy
2003	Imperfectly Free	Anocracy
2004	Imperfectly Free	Anocracy
2005	Imperfectly Free	Anocracy
2006	Imperfectly Free	Anocracy
2007	Imperfectly Free	Anocracy
2008	Imperfectly Free	Anocracy
2009	Imperfectly Free	Anocracy
2010	Imperfectly Free	Anocracy
2011	Imperfectly Free	Anocracy
2012	Imperfectly Free	Anocracy

news media were either government-controlled or strictly restricted.

1978–1981: Imperfectly Free

The country's transition from military rule and the 1977 constitution brought about improvements in civil liberties to the extent that by 1978, news media were at least functionally free.[1] Both the state-owned daily newspaper and the privately owned daily newspaper reported critically on government policies; however, the government did censor negative articles that named the president or government ministers.[2] The political liberalization that followed the 1978 elections began to grind to a halt when Colonel Zerbo seized power in 1980 in a bloodless coup. Yet the news media remained functionally free under Zerbo.

1982–1990: Not Free

Following the coup of 1982, news media were again restricted, and in 1984, the military government issued a decree granting the national news agency control over all news media.[3]

1991–2012: Imperfectly Free

Captain Blaise Compaoré, who seized power in a 1987 coup, came under increasing international and domestic pressure to reform. In response, in 1991, he introduced a multiparty constitution and held elections, which he won. One of his first concessions was to make some provisions for independent news media. Thus, Burkina Faso's first independent radio station, Horizon FM, began broadcasting on December 31, 1990.[4] Yet these reforms were limited. Although the 1990 Information Code had provided for media freedom, journalists and newspapers were not allowed to defend themselves against defamation charges.[5] In spite of these restrictions, competition from independent media brought about improvements in state-owned media. [6]

In 1993, journalists gained the right to defend themselves in libel cases, which lead to increased media independence.[7] Yet in 1998, the media's relationship with Compaoré became contentious when newspaper editor Norbert Zongo and three others were murdered and the killings were connected to Zongo's investigative reporting regarding the death of the president's brother's driver.[8] The public was outraged and responded with protests and strikes.

Media Today

Burkina Faso has constitutional provisions for media freedom, and these are generally respected, but journalists who criticize government are vulnerable to harassment. The relationship between

President Blaise Compaoré and the news media remains contentious. On the 10th anniversary of Zongo's murder (December 2008), thousands demonstrated calling for the killers to be punished.[9] Although the Zongo murder underscored the dangers of reporting critically about the Compaoré regime, media remain imperfectly free.

Notes

1. *Country Reports on Human Rights Practices for 1979* (Washington, DC: U.S. Department of State, 1980).
2. Ibid.
3. *World Press Freedom Review*, IPI Report (Zurich: International Press Institute, 1984).
4. R. Geekie, "Interview: Moustapha Thiombiano, African radio pioneer," *Africa Report* 37 (1): 10.
5. *World Press Freedom Review*, IPI Report (Vienna: International Press Institute, 1996).
6. Jenifer Whitten-Woodring, *The Fabled Fourth Estate: Media Freedom, Democracy and Human Rights* (University of Southern California, 2010), Dissertation.
7. *Country Reports on Human Rights Practices for 1994* (Washington, DC: U.S. Department of State, 1995).
8. *World Report 2009* (Paris, France: Reporters Without Borders, 2009).
9. Ibid.

Burundi: 1962–2012

Burundi Year by Year

Year	Media	Government
1962	Not Free	Anocracy
1963	Not Free	Anocracy
1964	Not Free	Anocracy
1965	Not Free	Anocracy
1966	Not Free	Autocracy
1967	Not Free	Autocracy
1968	Not Free	Autocracy
1969	Not Free	Autocracy
1970	Not Free	Autocracy
1971	Not Free	Autocracy
1972	Not Free	Autocracy
1973	Not Free	Autocracy
1974	Not Free	Autocracy
1975	Not Free	Autocracy
1976	Not Free	Autocracy
1977	Not Free	Autocracy
1978	Not Free	Autocracy
1979	Not Free	Autocracy
1980	Not Free	Autocracy
1981	Not Free	Autocracy
1982	Not Free	Autocracy
1983	Not Free	Autocracy
1984	Not Free	Autocracy
1985	Not Free	Autocracy

(Continued)

MEDIA FREEDOM HISTORY IN A NUTSHELL

- Burundian media have been consistently restricted since the country gained independence in 1962—first under a series of military regimes and most recently under a fledgling democracy
- As of 2009, there was one paid-for daily newspaper with a total average circulation of 20,000 (World Association of Newspaper's 2010 World Newspaper Trends)
- Only the government-controlled broadcast media have national reach, but there are privately owned television and radio stations
- As of 2012, about 1 percent of Burundians had access to the Internet (International Telecommunication Union's 2012 ICT Indicators Database)

In Brief

Since Burundi gained independence from Belgium in 1962, it has been torn by ethnic conflict between the Hutu and the Tutsi that has left hundreds of thousands dead. Given this political turmoil and social intolerance, it is not surprising that Burundian news media have been and remain restricted, even though the country did democratize in 2005.

Chronology:

1962–2012: Not Free

For a few years immediately following independence, Burundi was a constitutional monarchy, but as tensions increased between ethnic groups in 1966, a coup transformed Burundi into a military state. During these years, news media have remained strictly controlled.[1] Even during a brief period of political liberalization in the early

(Continued)

Year	Media	Government
1986	Not Free	Autocracy
1987	Not Free	Autocracy
1988	Not Free	Autocracy
1989	Not Free	Autocracy
1990	Not Free	Autocracy
1991	Not Free	Autocracy
1992	Not Free	Anocracy
1993	Not Free	Anocracy
1994	Not Free	Anocracy
1995	Not Free	Anocracy
1996	Not Free	Anocracy
1997	Not Free	Anocracy
1998	Not Free	Anocracy
1999	Not Free	Anocracy
2000	Not Free	Anocracy
2001	Not Free	Anocracy
2002	Not Free	Anocracy
2003	Not Free	Anocracy
2004	Not Free	Anocracy
2005	Not Free	Democracy
2006	Not Free	Democracy
2007	Not Free	Democracy
2008	Not Free	Democracy
2009	Not Free	Democracy
2010	Not Free	Democracy
2011	Not Free	Democracy
2012	Not Free	Democracy

1990s under President Pierre Buyoya, the news media were not free. Restrictions of media were especially strict during Burundi's many violent transitions. For example, during the 1993 coup when President Ndadaye was taken from his home and assassinated, the military also seized control of the radio station and took it off air.[2] Although control of Burundi changed hands through many coups, suppression of the news media remained constant. While President Buyoya (who returned to power in 1996) took steps to mitigate the ethnic conflict and implement democratic reforms, he did not ease restrictions on the news media. In fact, Burundi has passed a number of laws aimed at muzzling the media. Two cases in point are the 1997 Press Law, which prohibits the distribution of information that promotes civil disobedience, and the 2003 Media Law, which provides for prison terms and fines for those who disseminate information that insults the president.[3]

Media Today

Although Burundi transitioned to democracy in 2005 with the election of a President Nkurunziza and the ratification of a new constitution, which provides for media freedom, news media in Burundi remain restricted. Journalists who criticize government face defamation charges, harassment, and in some cases, physical attacks. Although Burundi has a mix of privately owned and government-owned media, only the government-owned radio and television stations reach the entire country, and the government-owned newspaper is the only one that publishes on a regular basis. Internet penetration is miniscule (about 1 percent), but mobile phone penetration is increasing and could eventually increase access to online media.

Notes

1. *World Press Freedom Review*, IPI Report (Zurich: International Press Institute, 1990).
2. *World Press Freedom Review*, IPI Report (Vienna: International Press Institute,1993).
3. *Freedom of the Press* (Washington, DC: Freedom House, 2013). Available at http://www.freedomhouse.org/report/freedom-press/2013/burundi.

Cambodia: 1953–2012

Cambodia Year by Year

Year	Media	Government
1953	Not Free	Anocracy
1954	Not Free	Autocracy
1955	Not Free	Autocracy
1956	Not Free	Autocracy
1957	Not Free	Autocracy
1958	Not Free	Autocracy
1959	Not Free	Autocracy
1960	Not Free	Autocracy
1961	Not Free	Autocracy
1962	Not Free	Autocracy
1963	Not Free	Autocracy
1964	Not Free	Autocracy
1965	Not Free	Autocracy
1966	Not Free	Autocracy
1967	Not Free	Autocracy
1968	Not Free	Autocracy
1969	Not Free	Autocracy
1970	Not Free	Autocracy
1971	Not Free	Autocracy
1972	Not Free	Anocracy
1973	Not Free	Anocracy
1974	Not Free	Anocracy
1975	Not Free	Anocracy
1976	Not Free	Autocracy
1977	Not Free	Autocracy

(Continued)

MEDIA FREEDOM HISTORY IN A NUTSHELL

- Cambodian news media have had little freedom since the country gained independence in 1953
- When media have not been government-controlled, they have been dependent on and closely tied to political parties
- As of 2009, there were 100 daily newspapers, twenty-two of them were paid-for dailies with a total average circulation per issue of 58,000 (World Association of Newspaper's 2010 World Newspaper Trends)
- There were nine television stations and fifty radio stations most of which were controlled by the Cambodian People's Party (World Association of Newspaper's 2010 World Newspaper Trends)
- As of 2012, about 5 percent of Cambodians had Internet access (International Telecommunication Union's 2012 ICT Indicators Database)

In Brief

Cambodia's 1993 constitution guarantees media freedom, but there are also laws that constrain journalists, including vaguely worded provisions that criminalize defamation and incitement. For most of the country's recent history, Cambodian media have been effectively controlled by government.

Chronology

1953–1991: Not Free

When Cambodia gained independence from France in 1953, a number of newspapers emerged, but most of them were closely linked to political parties.[1] By the mid-1960s, Prince Sihanouk controlled the media "by alternating cash rewards with punitive action."[2] In 1970, Sihanouk announced that foreign journalists would not be allowed in Cambodia.[3] From 1970

(Continued)

Year	Media	Government
1978	Not Free	Autocracy
1979	Not Free	Foreign Interruption
1980	Not Free	Foreign Interruption
1981	Not Free	Foreign Interruption
1982	Not Free	Foreign Interruption
1983	Not Free	Foreign Interruption
1984	Not Free	Foreign Interruption
1985	Not Free	Foreign Interruption
1986	Not Free	Foreign Interruption
1987	Not Free	Foreign Interruption
1988	Not Free	Anocracy
1989	Not Free	Anocracy
1990	Not Free	Anocracy
1991	Not Free	Anocracy
1992	Imperfectly Free	Anocracy
1993	Imperfectly Free	Anocracy
1994	Not Free	Anocracy
1995	Not Free	Anocracy
1996	Not Free	Anocracy
1997	Not Free	Autocracy
1998	Not Free	Anocracy
1999	Not Free	Anocracy
2000	Not Free	Anocracy
2001	Not Free	Anocracy
2002	Not Free	Anocracy
2003	Not Free	Anocracy
2004	Not Free	Anocracy
2005	Not Free	Anocracy
2006	Imperfectly Free	Anocracy
2007	Imperfectly Free	Anocracy
2008	Not Free	Anocracy
2009	Not Free	Anocracy
2010	Not Free	Anocracy
2011	Not Free	Anocracy
2012	Not Free	Anocracy

to 1975, following the 1970 coup led by Prime Minister Lon Nol, there was a brief period of press expansion during which Cambodia had between twenty to thirty daily newspapers.[4] In 1975, any semblance of media freedom vanished as the Khmer Rouge gained control of the country. Under the Khmer Rouge leader Pol Pot, all independent media were silenced and print media and radio were used to disseminate propaganda, as the Khmer Rouge oversaw the killing of hundreds of thousands and many others perished from starvation and disease.[5] In 1979, the Vietnamese overthrew Pol Pot, and the pro-Vietnamese People's Republic of Kampuchea (PRK) gained control of the country. Under this new regime, news media remained under government control.

1992–1993: Imperfectly Free

Following the withdrawal of the Vietnamese troops in 1989 and the peace agreement that brought the United Nations transitional authority to Cambodia in 1991, independent news outlets began to emerge, and by 1992, the media environment improved to the point where media were imperfectly free.[6] In 1993, the monarchy was restored and Sihanouk was once again king.

1994–2005: Not Free

By 1994, attacks on journalists, including the murders of several newspaper editors, increased to the point where news media were not free.[7] Although the number of newspapers increased from about ten in 1992 to more than forty by the end of 1994, most media were highly partisan, and most broadcast media were either owned by government officials or their associates.[8] The 1995 press law outlawed the publication of news that might threaten political stability and gave government the power to suspend newspapers for up to thirty days.[9]

2006–2007: Imperfectly Free

By 2006, attacks on journalists were less frequent and defamation was decriminalized.[10] Consequently, the environment for Cambodian media became imperfectly free, but just barely so.

2008–2012: Not Free

In 2008, attacks on journalists increased to the point where news media were not free.[11] In

2010, Cambodia adopted a new penal code, which criminalized defamation and the publication or distribution of information that could "create serious turmoil in society."[12] In 2012, Mam Sonando, owner of Beehive Radio, was sentenced to twenty years in prison on charges that he was inciting rebellion. The charges were connected to Sonando's coverage of human rights violations.[13] Sonando was released in March of 2013 after an appeals court reduced his conviction to a lesser charge.

Media Today

Cambodian media remain closely tied to and dependent on political parties. Journalists who criticize public officials face harassment, punitive lawsuits, and imprisonment.

Notes

1. Ham Samnang, "Cambodian Media in a Post-Socialist Situation," in *Media Fortunes Changing Times*, ed. Russell H. K. Heng (Singapore: Institute of Southeast Asian Studies, 2002).
2. Ibid., 28.
3. *World Press Freedom Review*, IPI Report (Zurich: International Press Institute, 1970).
4. Samnang, "Cambodian Media in a Post-Socialist Situation."
5. Ibid.
6. *World Press Freedom Review*, IPI Report (Vienna: International Press Institute, 1992).
7. *World Press Freedom Review*, IPI Report (Vienna: International Press Institute, 1994).
8. Samnang, "Cambodian Media in a Post-Socialist Situation."
9. *Freedom of the Press* (Washington, DC: Freedom House, 2013). Available at http://www.freedomhouse.org/report/freedom-press/2013/cambodia.
10. *Freedom of the Press* (Washington, DC: Freedom House, 2007). Available at http://www.freedomhouse.org/report/freedom-press/2007/cambodia.
11. *Freedom of the Press* (Washington, DC: Freedom House, 2009). Available at http://www.freedomhouse.org/report/freedom-press/2009/cambodia.
12. *Freedom of the Press* (Washington, DC: Freedom House, 2011). Available at http://www.freedomhouse.org/report/freedom-press/2011/cambodia.
13. *Cambodia Reduces Jail Term of Journalist Sonando* (Committee to Protect Journalists, 2013). Available at http://www.cpj.org/2013/03/cambodia-reduces-jail-term-of-journalist-sonando.php#more.

Cameroon: 1960–2012

Cameroon Year by Year

Year	Media	Government
1960	Not Free	Autocracy
1961	Not Free	Autocracy
1962	Not Free	Autocracy
1963	Not Free	Autocracy
1964	Not Free	Autocracy
1965	Not Free	Autocracy
1966	Not Free	Autocracy
1967	Not Free	Autocracy
1968	Not Free	Autocracy
1969	Not Free	Autocracy
1970	Not Free	Autocracy
1971	Not Free	Autocracy
1972	Not Free	Autocracy
1973	Not Free	Autocracy
1974	Not Free	Autocracy
1975	Not Free	Autocracy
1976	Not Free	Autocracy
1977	Not Free	Autocracy
1978	Not Free	Autocracy
1979	Not Free	Autocracy
1980	Not Free	Autocracy
1981	Not Free	Autocracy
1982	Not Free	Autocracy
1983	Not Free	Autocracy
1984	Not Free	Autocracy

MEDIA FREEDOM HISTORY IN A NUTSHELL

- Cameroonian news media have been subject to government control since the country gained independence in 1960
- As of 2009, there were five paid-for daily newspapers with a total average circulation per issue of 75,000 (World Association of Newspaper's 2010 World Newspaper Trends)
- Government retains control over most broadcast media; although Cameroon has a number of independent nonlicensed rural radio stations, they are not permitted to broadcast political commentary
- As of 2012, about 6 percent of Cameroonians had Internet access (International Telecommunication Union's 2012 ICT Indicators Database)

In Brief

Since Cameroon gained independence in 1960, news media have been effectively under government control.

Chronology

1960–2012: Not Free

In the mid-1960s, shortly after Cameroon won independence from France, it merged with parts of the country that had been under British and German control. Though this unification produced some political stability, it did not promote media freedom. For the first three decades, Cameroon was a one-party state under the Cameroon People's Democratic Movement, and during these years the press was subject to government control.[1] Journalists who criticized government officials were subject to harassment and arrest.[2] In 1990, political parties were legalized and print media no longer had to obtain licenses. Yet news media

Year	Media	Government
1985	Not Free	Autocracy
1986	Not Free	Autocracy
1987	Not Free	Autocracy
1988	Not Free	Autocracy
1989	Not Free	Autocracy
1990	Not Free	Autocracy
1991	Not Free	Autocracy
1992	Not Free	Anocracy
1993	Not Free	Anocracy
1994	Not Free	Anocracy
1995	Not Free	Anocracy
1996	Not Free	Anocracy
1997	Not Free	Anocracy
1998	Not Free	Anocracy
1999	Not Free	Anocracy
2000	Not Free	Anocracy
2001	Not Free	Anocracy
2002	Not Free	Anocracy
2003	Not Free	Anocracy
2004	Not Free	Anocracy
2005	Not Free	Anocracy
2006	Not Free	Anocracy
2007	Not Free	Anocracy
2008	Not Free	Anocracy
2009	Not Free	Anocracy
2010	Not Free	Anocracy
2011	Not Free	Anocracy
2012	Not Free	Anocracy

remained under control during this transition as English language programs were banned and a new law required that all independent newspapers be approved by government officials prior to publication.[3] Opposition parties boycotted the first several elections, and Paul Biya has been president since 1982. Senior members of the Cameroon People's Democratic Movement have used their influence to have journalists arrested and detained.[4] Prior to 2007, the state-owned Cameroon Radio Television was the only licensed broadcaster.

Media Today

The 1996 constitution has provisions for media freedom, but in practice the Cameroonian news media are restricted. Both defamation and libel are criminal offenses punishable by harsh fines and prison terms. Broadcast media remain for the most part under government control, though since 2007, the government has granted licenses to two television stations and one radio station.[5] There are a number of rural radio stations that are permitted to operate without licenses, but political discussions are prohibited on these outlets.[6] Cameroon's one national newspaper is state-owned, but there are a number of privately owned regional newspapers. Print media remain subject to prior restraint under a law that has been in place since 1990, and in 2012, a presidential decree gave the National Communication Council the power to ban media outlets.[7]

Notes

1. *Country Reports on Human Rights Practices 1977* (Washington, DC: U.S. Department of State, 1978).
2. *World Press Freedom Review*, IPI Report (Zurich: International Press Institute, 1988).
3. *World Press Freedom Review*, IPI Report (Zurich: International Press Institute, 1990).
4. *World Press Trends* (Darmstadt, Germany: WAN-IFRA, 2010).
5. *Cameroon*, World Fact Book (Washington, DC: CIA, 2013). Available at https://www.cia.gov/library/publications/the-world-factbook/geos/cm.html.
6. *Freedom of the Press* (Washington, DC: Freedom House, 2013). Available at http://www.freedomhouse.org/report/freedom-press/2013/cameroon.
7. Ibid.

Canada: 1948–2012

Canada Year by Year

Year	Media	Government
1948	Free	Democracy
1949	Free	Democracy
1950	Free	Democracy
1951	Free	Democracy
1952	Free	Democracy
1953	Free	Democracy
1954	Free	Democracy
1955	Free	Democracy
1956	Free	Democracy
1957	Free	Democracy
1958	Free	Democracy
1959	Free	Democracy
1960	Free	Democracy
1961	Free	Democracy
1962	Free	Democracy
1963	Free	Democracy
1964	Free	Democracy
1965	Free	Democracy
1966	Free	Democracy
1967	Free	Democracy
1968	Free	Democracy
1969	Free	Democracy
1970	Free	Democracy
1971	Free	Democracy
1972	Free	Democracy
1973	Free	Democracy
1974	Free	Democracy
1975	Free	Democracy

MEDIA FREEDOM HISTORY IN A NUTSHELL

- Canada is an exemplar of media freedom
- As of 2012, there were 109 daily newspapers, 95 of them were paid-for dailies with a total average circulation per issue of 6,011,066 (World Association of Newspaper's 2012 World Newspaper Trends)
- There are almost 2,000 licensed radio stations in Canada, many of them commercial. There are many television stations (BBC News Country Profiles, 2013)
- As of 2012, about 87 percent of Canadians had access to the Internet (International Telecommunication Union's 2012 ICT Indicators Database)

In Brief

The 1982 constitution provides for media freedom and the Canadian government respects this in practice.

Chronology

1948–2012: Free

Although Canada's first newspaper, the *Halifax Gazette*, began publishing in 1752, press freedom did not emerge in Canada until the early 1800s.[1] By the end of the 1850s, then British North America had close to 300 newspapers. In addition to print media, broadcast media have flourished in Canada. Moreover, public broadcasting has been an important source for news since the Canadian Broadcasting Corporation began broadcasting in the 1930s.[2]

Journalists in Canada rarely face physical attacks. According to the Committee to Protect Journalists (CPJ), two journalists have been

Year	Media	Government
1976	Free	Democracy
1977	Free	Democracy
1978	Free	Democracy
1979	Free	Democracy
1980	Free	Democracy
1981	Free	Democracy
1982	Free	Democracy
1983	Free	Democracy
1984	Free	Democracy
1985	Free	Democracy
1986	Free	Democracy
1987	Free	Democracy
1988	Free	Democracy
1989	Free	Democracy
1990	Free	Democracy
1991	Free	Democracy
1992	Free	Democracy
1993	Free	Democracy
1994	Free	Democracy
1995	Free	Democracy
1996	Free	Democracy
1997	Free	Democracy
1998	Free	Democracy
1999	Free	Democracy
2000	Free	Democracy
2001	Free	Democracy
2002	Free	Democracy
2003	Free	Democracy
2004	Free	Democracy
2005	Free	Democracy
2006	Free	Democracy
2007	Free	Democracy
2008	Free	Democracy
2009	Free	Democracy
2010	Free	Democracy
2011	Free	Democracy
2012	Free	Democracy

killed in connection to their work since CPJ began tracking these attacks in 1992.[3] In 1995, sportscaster Brian Smith was fatally shot by Jeffrey Arenburg, who subsequently turned himself in. Perhaps the greatest blemish on Canada's media freedom record is the 1998 death of Tara Singh Hayer. Hayer, the publisher of the *Indo-Canadian Times*, was gunned down following his persistent coverage of the 1985 Air India bombing. To date, there have been no arrests in connection with his killing.

Like many countries, in recent years Canada has come under criticism for concentration of media ownership. In addition, access to government information is somewhat limited. Although Canada's 1983 Access to Information Act requires that requests for government information be answered within thirty days, the Canadian Journalists for Free Expression reported that in 2012 nearly 45 percent of requests were not answered within this time limit.[4]

Media Today

Canadian news media are by and large free. Hate speech is prohibited, and access to government information remains an issue, but journalists can and do report critically on government policies and actions.[5]

Notes

1. Paul Nesbitt-Larking, *Politics, Society and the Media* (University of Toronto Press, 2007).
2. *Canada*, BBC Country Profiles (London, UK: British Broadcasting Company, 2013). Available at http://www.bbc.co.uk/news/world-us-canada-16841120.
3. *2 Journalists Killed in Canada since 1992/Motive Confirmed* (Committee to Protect Journalists, 2013). Available at http://cpj.org/killed/americas/canada/.
4. *Assessing Access 2012–13*, Review of Free Expression in Canada (Canadian Journalist for Free Expression, 2013). Available at http://www.cjfe.org/sites/default/files/2013_CJFE_Review-of-free-expression-in-Canada.pdf.
5. *Freedom of the Press* (Washington, DC: Freedom House, 2013). Available at http://www.freedomhouse.org/report/freedom-press/.

Cape Verde: 1975–2012

Cape Verde Year by Year

Year	Media	Government
1975	Not Free	Anocracy
1976	Not Free	Anocracy
1977	Not Free	Anocracy
1978	Not Free	Anocracy
1979	Not Free	Anocracy
1980	Not Free	Anocracy
1981	Not Free	Anocracy
1982	Not Free	Anocracy
1983	Not Free	Anocracy
1984	Not Free	Anocracy
1985	Not Free	Anocracy
1986	Not Free	Anocracy
1987	Not Free	Anocracy
1988	Not Free	Anocracy
1989	Not Free	Anocracy
1990	Not Free	Anocracy
1991	Imperfectly Free	Democracy
1992	Imperfectly Free	Democracy
1993	Imperfectly Free	Democracy
1994	Imperfectly Free	Democracy
1995	Imperfectly Free	Democracy
1996	Imperfectly Free	Democracy
1997	Imperfectly Free	Democracy
1998	Imperfectly Free	Democracy

MEDIA FREEDOM HISTORY IN A NUTSHELL

- For a decade and a half after gaining independence, Cape Verde was a one-party state with controlled media
- When Cape Verde democratized in 1991, news media became imperfectly free; the media environment continued to improve, and today Cape Verdean media are among the most free in Africa and the world
- As of 2009, there were twelve total paid-for, nondaily newspapers (World Association of Newspaper's 2010 World Newspaper Trends)
- Cape Verde has a mix of state-run and privately owned television and radio stations
- As of 2012, about 35 percent of Cape Verdeans had Internet access (International Telecommunication Union's 2012 ICT Indicators Database)

In Brief

For the first decade and a half following independence, the ruling party controlled Cape Verdean media. When the country democratized in the early 1990s, media became first imperfectly free, and then free.

Chronology

1975–1990: Not Free

After gaining independence from Portugal in 1975, Cape Verde was a single party republic and most media were owned or controlled by the African Party for the Independence of Guinea-Bissau and Cape Verde, and privately owned media exercised "prudent restraint."[1] In 1980, following a coup in Guinea-Bissau, Cape Verde relinquished plans to unify with that country and

Year	Media	Government
1999	Imperfectly Free	Democracy
2000	Imperfectly Free	Democracy
2001	Imperfectly Free	Democracy
2002	Imperfectly Free	Democracy
2003	Imperfectly Free	Democracy
2004	Imperfectly Free	Democracy
2005	Imperfectly Free	Democracy
2006	Free	Democracy
2007	Free	Democracy
2008	Free	Democracy
2009	Free	Democracy
2010	Free	Democracy
2011	Free	Democracy
2012	Free	Democracy

the ruling party was renamed the African Party for the Independence of Cape Verde. Restrictions on news media remained intact: "The news media (radio and newspaper) are government monopolies. New is edited to reinforce support for the government's economic development programs and foreign policy."[2]

1991–2005: Imperfectly Free

In 1990, the government lifted the ban on opposition parties, and the country held its first multiparty elections in 1991. Although the government owned the media with the widest reach—radio, television, and the most popular newspaper—these media covered both government and opposition perspectives.[3] Yet in 1991, the government began to withhold advertising from opposition news media.[4] Journalists who criticized government were vulnerable to lawsuits.[5]

In the 2000s, the availability of independent newspapers increased, but the African Party for the Independence of Cape Verde continued to control most of the privately owned media, and many journalists engaged in self-censorship.[6]

2006–2012: Free

By 2006, the environment had improved to the point where Cape Verdean news media were free. Attacks and lawsuits against journalists were rare.[7]

Media Today

Cape Verde is an exemplar of media freedom in Africa. In fact, Reporters Without Borders ranks the Cape Verdean media as more free than media in Australia, the United Kingdom, the United States, and France.[8]

Notes

1. *Country Reports on Human Rights Practices for 1977* (Washington, DC: U.S. Department of State, 1978), 19.
2. *Country Reports on Human Rights Practices for 1981* (Washington, DC: U.S. Department of State, 1981), 45.
3. *Country Reports on Human Rights Practices for 1991* (Washington, DC: U.S. Department of State, 1992).
4. Ibid.
5. *World Press Freedom Review*, IPI Report (Vienna: International Press Institute, 1994).
6. *Freedom of the Press* (Washington, DC: Freedom House, 2004). Available at http://www.freedomhouse.org/report/freedom-press/2004/cape-verde.
7. *Freedom of the Press* (Washington, DC: Freedom House, 2007). Available at http://www.freedomhouse.org/report/freedom-press/2007/cape-verde.
8. *2013 World Press Freedom Index: Dashed Hopes After Spring* (Paris, France: Reporters Without Borders, 2013). Available at http://en.rsf.org/press-freedom-index-2013,1054.html.

Central African Republic: 1960–2012

Central African Republic Year by Year

Year	Media	Government
1960	Not Free	Autocracy
1961	Not Free	Autocracy
1962	Not Free	Autocracy
1963	Not Free	Autocracy
1964	Not Free	Autocracy
1965	Not Free	Autocracy
1966	Not Free	Autocracy
1967	Not Free	Autocracy
1968	Not Free	Autocracy
1969	Not Free	Autocracy
1970	Not Free	Autocracy
1971	Not Free	Autocracy
1972	Not Free	Autocracy
1973	Not Free	Autocracy
1974	Not Free	Autocracy
1975	Not Free	Autocracy
1976	Not Free	Autocracy
1977	Not Free	Autocracy
1978	Not Free	Autocracy
1979	Not Free	Autocracy
1980	Not Free	Autocracy
1981	Not Free	Autocracy
1982	Not Free	Autocracy
1983	Not Free	Autocracy
1984	Not Free	Autocracy

MEDIA FREEDOM HISTORY IN A NUTSHELL

- Since the Central African Republic gained independence in 1960, news media have for the most part been government controlled or restricted
- As of 2009, there were thirty daily newspapers, six of them were paid-for dailies with a total average circulation per issue of 5,000 (World Association of Newspaper's 2010 World Newspaper Trends)
- Radio is the most important news medium, and there are both state-run and privately owned stations; there is also a mix of state-run and privately owned television
- As of 2012, about 3 percent of Central Africans had Internet access (International Telecommunication Union's 2012 ICT Indicators Database)

In Brief

Political instability and extreme poverty have contributed to a poor media environment in the Central African Republic. Since gaining independence in 1960, news media have with few exceptions been restricted or directly under government control.

Chronology

1960–1992: Not Free

For the first three decades after gaining independence from France, the Central African Republic had a series of mostly military governments—including fourteen years under Jean-Bedel Bokassa, who proclaimed himself Emperor and was notorious for his brutality, including the massacre of school children. During these tumultuous years, news media were government controlled.

Year	Media	Government
1985	Not Free	Autocracy
1986	Not Free	Autocracy
1987	Not Free	Autocracy
1988	Not Free	Autocracy
1989	Not Free	Autocracy
1990	Not Free	Autocracy
1991	Not Free	Autocracy
1992	Not Free	Autocracy
1993	Imperfectly Free	Anocracy
1994	Imperfectly Free	Anocracy
1995	Imperfectly Free	Anocracy
1996	Not Free	Anocracy
1997	Not Free	Anocracy
1998	Not Free	Anocracy
1999	Not Free	Anocracy
2000	Not Free	Anocracy
2001	Not Free	Anocracy
2002	Not Free	Anocracy
2003	Not Free	Anocracy
2004	Not Free	Anocracy
2005	Not Free	Anocracy
2006	Imperfectly Free	Anocracy
2007	Not Free	Anocracy
2008	Not Free	Anocracy
2009	Not Free	Anocracy
2010	Not Free	Anocracy
2011	Not Free	Anocracy
2012	Not Free	Anocracy

1993–1995: Imperfectly Free

In 1993, the Central African Republic held its first democratic elections. As part of this process, the Prime Minister ordered that the media should be opened to the opposition during the campaign and then fired the Minister of Communication for censoring the media.[1]

During the campaign, members of the opposition were allowed to criticize the government on government-controlled broadcast media, but government media remained most supportive of President Kolingba. After Kolingba was defeated by Ange-Felix Patasse, the media environment became more open.[2]

1996–2005: Not Free

In 1996, civilian protests and mutinies by unpaid soldiers erupted. As the country edged close to civil war, the government clamped down on media freedom, and journalists who criticized the government risked harassment, imprisonment, and exile.[3] Unrest continued in the early 2000s with general strikes, riots, and attempted coups. Broadcast media were for the most part state controlled, and privately owned newspapers were restricted by harsh libel laws.[4] In 2003, Francois Bozize seized control in a coup that was widely supported by the news media.[5]

2006: Imperfectly Free

A press law decriminalizing libel and slander went into effect in 2005, and the 2005 constitution included provisions for media freedom. By 2006, the government respected these legal changes in practice to the extent that the media environment became imperfectly free. Yet journalists who criticized government remained vulnerable to some defamation suits.[6]

2007–2012: Not Free

The improvements in the media environment were short-lived. In 2007, in the wake of increased threats from armed conflict in the north, the government sought to stifle criticism, in particular allegations of human rights abuses, and regulate media with the establishment of the High Communications Council (HCC). Just one month after the HCC was created, the leader of an editors' group was fined and imprisoned for two months for criticizing the HCC.[7]

Media Today

In theory, the High Council for Communications is supposed to be an independent agency that promotes media freedom, but in practice the government seems to control the HCC.[8] Some journalists persist in criticizing the government, and sometimes they are threatened or harassed for doing so, but sometimes there are no repercussions; consequently, self-censorship is widespread.[9] Journalists also face threats from the rebel group, the Lord's Resistance Army.[10] There are a number of independent dailies and one state-owned biweekly newspaper, as well as one state-run television station and one privately owned television. Because of poverty and low literacy rates, radio remains the most accessible medium, and the country has a mix of state-run, private, church-run and UN-backed radio stations.

Notes

1. *World Press Freedom Review*, IPI Report (Vienna: International Press Institute, 1993).
2. *Country Reports on Human Rights Practices for 1993* (Washington, DC: U.S. Department of State, 1994). Available at http://dosfan.lib.uic.edu/ERC/democracy/1993_hrp_report/93hrp_report_africa/CentralAfricanRepublic.html.
3. *World Press Freedom Review*, IPI Report (Vienna: International Press Institute, 1997).
4. *Freedom of the Press* (Washington, DC: Freedom House, 2002). Available at http://www.freedomhouse.org/report/freedom-press/2002/central-african-republic.
5. *Freedom of the Press* (Washington, DC: Freedom House, 2004). Available at http://www.freedomhouse.org/report/freedom-press/2004/central-african-republic.
6. *Freedom of the Press* (Washington, DC: Freedom House, 2007). Available at http://www.freedomhouse.org/report/freedom-press/2007/central-african-republic.
7. *World Press Freedom Review*, IPI Report (Vienna: International Press Institute, 2007).
8. *Freedom of the Press* (Washington, DC: Freedom House, 2013). Available at http://www.freedomhouse.org/report/freedom-press/2013/central-african-republic.
9. Ibid.
10. Ibid.

Chad: 1960–2012

Chad Year by Year

Year	Media	Government
1960	Not Free	Autocracy
1961	Not Free	Autocracy
1962	Not Free	Autocracy
1963	Not Free	Autocracy
1964	Not Free	Autocracy
1965	Not Free	Autocracy
1966	Not Free	Autocracy
1967	Not Free	Autocracy
1968	Not Free	Autocracy
1969	Not Free	Autocracy
1970	Not Free	Autocracy
1971	Not Free	Autocracy
1972	Not Free	Autocracy
1973	Not Free	Autocracy
1974	Not Free	Autocracy
1975	Not Free	Autocracy
1976	Not Free	Autocracy
1977	Not Free	Autocracy
1978	Not Free	Anocracy
1979	Not Free	Anocracy
1980	Not Free	Anocracy
1981	Not Free	Anocracy
1982	Not Free	Anocracy
1983	Not Free	Anocracy
1984	Not Free	Anocracy
1985	Not Free	Autocracy
1986	Not Free	Autocracy
1987	Not Free	Autocracy

(Continued)

MEDIA FREEDOM HISTORY IN A NUTSHELL

- Wracked by almost constant civil war, Chad has been essentially ruled by dictators and warlords since independence
- A U.S.- and French-backed effort to build democratic government led to a fragile period of media freedom from 1990 to 1997
- Return to civil war brought back government control of the media in 1998, and since then media have remained strictly controlled through what has effectively become a permanent state of emergency
- As of 2009, there were five paid-for, nondaily newspapers with a total average circulation per issue of 4,000 (World Association of Newspaper's 2010 World Newspaper Trends)
- There is a mix of privately owned and state-owned radio, but the only domestic television station is government owned
- As of 2012, about 2 percent of Chadians had Internet access (International Telecommunication Union's 2012 ICT Indicators Database)

In Brief

Chad's history is defined by the constant struggle between a Christian/animist south and a Muslim north. A brief period of media freedom accompanied a U.S.- and French-backed leader and democratization effort. This again ended in civil war and there is little indication that any return to media freedom might be eminent.

Chronology

1960–1989: Not Free

Following its independence from France in 1960, Chad's presidency was essentially a French-backed dictatorship and Chad was either caught

(Continued)

Year	Media	Government
1988	Not Free	Autocracy
1989	Not Free	Autocracy
1990	Imperfectly Free	Autocracy
1991	Imperfectly Free	Anocracy
1992	Imperfectly Free	Anocracy
1993	Imperfectly Free	Anocracy
1994	Imperfectly Free	Anocracy
1995	Imperfectly Free	Anocracy
1996	Imperfectly Free	Anocracy
1997	Imperfectly Free	Anocracy
1998	Not Free	Anocracy
1999	Not Free	Anocracy
2000	Not Free	Anocracy
2001	Not Free	Anocracy
2002	Not Free	Anocracy
2003	Not Free	Anocracy
2004	Not Free	Anocracy
2005	Not Free	Anocracy
2006	Not Free	Anocracy
2007	Not Free	Autocracy
2008	Not Free	Anocracy
2009	Not Free	Anocracy
2010	Not Free	Anocracy
2011	Not Free	Anocracy
2012	Not Free	Anocracy

up in a civil war or about to enter one. The government remained on a war footing at almost all times and strictly censored the media. In 1989, the newspaper *Contact* became the first privately owned publication in Chad.[1]

1990–1997: Imperfectly Free

Idriss Déby, leader of the Patriotic Salvation Movement (MPS), seized control of the government from rival ethnic-based warlords in 1990. Backed by the United States and France, he implemented a democratization program. Media freedom was established early in this process, but what little media existed was based in areas around the capital, which was also Déby's political stronghold. The government vigorously used libel and other legal mechanisms to intimidate the press, but most media in the south were supportive of Déby and governmental power was limited in the rest of the country. The result was effectively free media. Yet there were confrontations between the government and journalists. In 1992, the government accused journalists of provoking a coup, and that same year journalists called for President Déby to investigate the deaths of two journalists.[2]

1998–2012: Not Free

The return of civil war also brought an increase in governmental efforts to control the media, with little subtlety. Journalists and other media professionals who were critical of the government were prosecuted using libel laws, slander statutes, and other mechanisms. The declaration of a state of emergency effectively ended all but the most tenuous façade of media freedom as the government implemented strict censorship and significantly increased the legal penalties for libel, slander, and other loopholes used to control media.

Media Today

Media are strictly controlled. There were some indications in 2010 that some change may have been possible when a new law put an end to prison sentences for defamation.[3] Yet recent political arrests indicate that there is little hope of significant liberalization in the near future.

Notes

1. *World Press Freedom Review*, IPI Report (Zurich: International Press Institute, 1989).
2. *World Press Freedom Review*, IPI Report (Vienna: International Press Institute, 1992).
3. *Freedom of the Press* (Washington, DC: Freedom House, 2013). Available at http://www.freedomhouse .org/report/freedom-press/2013/chad.

Chile: 1948–2012

Chile Year by Year

Year	Media	Government
1948	Free	Democracy
1949	Free	Democracy
1950	Free	Democracy
1951	Free	Democracy
1952	Free	Democracy
1953	Free	Democracy
1954	Free	Democracy
1955	Free	Anocracy
1956	Free	Anocracy
1957	Free	Anocracy
1958	Free	Anocracy
1959	Free	Anocracy
1960	Free	Anocracy
1961	Free	Anocracy
1962	Free	Anocracy
1963	Free	Anocracy
1964	Free	Democracy
1965	Free	Democracy
1966	Free	Democracy
1967	Free	Democracy
1968	Free	Democracy
1969	Free	Democracy
1970	Free	Democracy
1971	Free	Democracy
1972	Free	Democracy
1973	Not Free	Autocracy
1974	Not Free	Autocracy

(Continued)

MEDIA FREEDOM HISTORY IN A NUTSHELL

- With the exception of the years under the General Pinochet dictatorship (1973–1989), Chilean news media have been among the most free in South America
- News organizations tend to be closely related to political parties
- As of 2011, there were sixty-five daily newspapers, sixty of which were paid-for dailies with a total average circulation per issue of 581,000 (World Association of Newspaper's 2012 World Newspaper Trends)
- There are many radio and television stations, most of which are privately owned and functionally free
- Chile was the first country in the world to pass a net-neutrality law, and Internet media are unrestricted
- As of 2012, about 61 percent of Chileans had Internet access (International Telecommunication Union's 2012 ICT Indicators Database)

In Brief

With the exception of the years under the dictatorship of General Augusto Pinochet Ugarte, the Chilean media have been free or imperfectly free. Since the adoption of the 1833 constitution, Chile has for the most part had a constitutional government with more democratic tendencies and political stability than many of its neighbors. In keeping with this political history, the Chilean news media reflect a wide range of ideologies, though they are often closely tied to political parties.

Chronology

1948–Early 1972: Free

Well before 1948, Chilean newspapers served as a vibrant source of political information

(Continued)

Year	Media	Government
1975	Not Free	Autocracy
1976	Not Free	Autocracy
1977	Not Free	Autocracy
1978	Not Free	Autocracy
1979	Not Free	Autocracy
1980	Not Free	Autocracy
1981	Not Free	Autocracy
1982	Not Free	Autocracy
1983	Not Free	Autocracy
1984	Not Free	Autocracy
1985	Not Free	Autocracy
1986	Not Free	Autocracy
1987	Not Free	Autocracy
1988	Not Free	Anocracy
1989	Not Free	Democracy
1990	Imperfectly Free	Democracy
1991	Imperfectly Free	Democracy
1992	Imperfectly Free	Democracy
1993	Imperfectly Free	Democracy
1994	Imperfectly Free	Democracy
1995	Imperfectly Free	Democracy
1996	Imperfectly Free	Democracy
1997	Imperfectly Free	Democracy
1998	Imperfectly Free	Democracy
1999	Imperfectly Free	Democracy
2000	Imperfectly Free	Democracy
2001	Imperfectly Free	Democracy
2002	Free	Democracy
2003	Free	Democracy
2004	Free	Democracy
2005	Free	Democracy
2006	Free	Democracy
2007	Free	Democracy
2008	Free	Democracy
2009	Free	Democracy
2010	Free	Democracy
2011	Free	Democracy
2012	Free	Democracy

reflecting a wide range of political ideologies. From the right-leaning *El Mercurio* (established in 1827) to the Communist *El Siglo*, Chile's news media tended to be closely (or directly in the case of *El Siglo*) related to political parties.[1] Compared to news media in other countries during this time, the Chilean media were remarkably free, but they did face some challenges. The *desacato* (disrespect) clause of the Law of March 20, 1925, effectively criminalized criticism of government. During the 1950s, several journalists were arrested and some were convicted under this clause, but in almost every case the charges were dismissed and the convictions overturned.[2] Although the government controlled access to newsprint, the Chilean press successfully challenged the constitutionality of the government commission that rationed newsprint.[3] In short, when their freedom was threatened, Chilean journalists often prevailed in the courts.

Late 1972–1989: Not Free

By late 1972, Chilean news media faced increasing constraints as President Allende sought to silence a growing opposition movement and a vibrant opposition news media. In October of 1972, the government seized control of all 125 radio stations in the country.[4] The relationship between the Allende Government and the opposition media became increasingly hostile. The government responded to critical news stories with suppression of advertising and other economic pressures.[5] With the military coup d'état, the suppression of the media became absolute.

General Pinochet's regime constantly attacked any sections of the media showing signs of opposition, never hesitating to resort to violence when already repressive press laws failed to achieve their aims. After September 1986, the government could rely on no less than three legal instruments to curb freedom of speech: the State of Emergency, in force since 1973, which "restricted" freedom of information and opinion; the State of Risk of Internal Peace Perturbation (March 1981), which could prohibit the launching, publishing and distribution of new[s]papers and magazines; and the State of Siege (1986), which allowed "suspension" of information and "restriction" of opinions, and the censoring of mail and other communications.[6]

1990–2001: Imperfectly Free

In 1989, as Chile transitioned to democracy with multiparty elections, newspapers that had closed with the coup began to reemerge.[7] Yet the reappearance of independent news media was accompanied by attacks on journalists as well as lawsuits against journalists. [8]

2002–2012: Free

The Press Law, passed in 2001, did away with most, but not all, of the insult laws that were so often used against journalists (the *desacato* laws remained in effect until 2005).[9]

Media Today

Chilean news media remain free, plentiful, and for the most part privately owned. As of 2009, Chile had fifty-three paid-for daily newspapers.[10] One point of concern is the extremely high concentration of ownership of media—especially newspapers and radio, which is the most accessible medium for the poor and illiterate. According to Freedom House, 95 percent of Chilean newspapers are owned by two companies and 55 percent of commercial radio stations are owned by three companies.[11] Government does not restrict the Internet, and in 2010, Chile became the first country to pass a net-neutrality law, which makes it illegal for Internet service providers to censor or limit access to online content.[12] According to the International Telecommunication Union, 61 percent of Chileans have access to the Internet.[13]

Notes

1. Rex A. Hudson, *Chile: A Country Study* (Washington, DC: GPO for the Library of Congress, 1994). Available at http://lcweb2.loc.gov/frd/cs/cltoc.html.
2. *Government Pressures on the Press* (Zurich: International Press Institute, 1955), 36.
3. Ibid., 72.
4. *IPI 1973 Press Freedom Report* (Zurich: International Press Institute, January 1973), 6.
5. *Press Freedom Report 1974* (Zurich: International Press Institute, January 1974), 12.
6. Kit Coppard, *The Defense of Press Freedom: A History of the International Press Institute Part II: 1976–1988* (Zurich: International Press Institute, 1988), 57–8.
7. *World Press Freedom Review*, IPI Report (Zurich: International Press Institute, December 1989), 5.
8. *World Press Freedom Review*, IPI Report (Zurich: International Press Institute, December 1990), 7; and *World Press Freedom Review*, IPI Report (Zurich: International Press Institute, December 1991), 7.
9. *Freedom of the Press* (Washington, DC: Freedom House, 2003). Available at http://www.freedomhouse.org/report/freedom-press/2003/chile; and *Freedom of the Press* (Washington, DC: Freedom House, 2006). Available at http://www.freedomhouse.org/report/freedom-press/2006/chile.
10. *World Press Trends* (Darmstadt, Germany: WAN-IFRA, 2010), 366.
11. *Freedom of the Press* (Washington, DC: Freedom House, 2011). Available at http://www.freedomhouse.org/report/freedom-press/2011/chile.
12. Ibid.
13. *ICT Indicators Database* (Geneva, Switzerland: International Telecommunications Union, 2012). Available at http://www.itu.int/ITU-D/ict/statistics/.

China: 1948–2012

China Year by Year

Year	Media	Government
1948	Imperfectly Free	Anocracy
1949	Not Free	Autocracy
1950	Not Free	Autocracy
1951	Not Free	Autocracy
1952	Not Free	Autocracy
1953	Not Free	Autocracy
1954	Not Free	Autocracy
1955	Not Free	Autocracy
1956	Not Free	Autocracy
1957	Not Free	Autocracy
1958	Not Free	Autocracy
1959	Not Free	Autocracy
1960	Not Free	Autocracy
1961	Not Free	Autocracy
1962	Not Free	Autocracy
1963	Not Free	Autocracy
1964	Not Free	Autocracy
1965	Not Free	Autocracy
1966	Not Free	Autocracy
1967	Not Free	Autocracy
1968	Not Free	Autocracy
1969	Not Free	Autocracy
1970	Not Free	Autocracy
1971	Not Free	Autocracy
1972	Not Free	Autocracy
1973	Not Free	Autocracy
1974	Not Free	Autocracy
1975	Not Free	Autocracy
1976	Not Free	Autocracy
1977	Not Free	Autocracy
1978	Not Free	Autocracy
1979	Not Free	Autocracy

MEDIA FREEDOM HISTORY IN A NUTSHELL

- During the civil war, there were enough free media in the urban centers for the country to be considered imperfectly free
- Victory by the communists in 1949 included an imposition of direct controls on the media
- As China began to reopen to the West in the 1970s and 1980s, information from Western media began to filter in
- The nature of government control shifted to a more indirect system, but media content remains strictly regulated; news outlets have commercialized, but government maintains a majority stake in all media outlets
- As of 2012, China had 970 total paid-for daily newspapers with an average circulation per issue of 116,321,000, and many radio and television stations (World Association of Newspaper's 2012 World Newspaper Trends)
- As of 2012, about 42 percent of Chinese had Internet access (International Telecommunication Union's 2012 ICT Indicators Database)

In Brief

While the coding of China rates it as consistently Not Free, the nature of government control has evolved significantly over this period because the ruling communist party has had to cope with changes in its engagement with the west, its industrial growth, and advances in information technology.

Chronology

1948: Imperfectly Free

Capturing the last year of the revolutionary period, 1948 largely reflects the nationalist government's lack of ability to implement government control in the major urban centers it still controlled.

Year	Media	Government
1980	Not Free	Autocracy
1981	Not Free	Autocracy
1982	Not Free	Autocracy
1983	Not Free	Autocracy
1984	Not Free	Autocracy
1985	Not Free	Autocracy
1986	Not Free	Autocracy
1987	Not Free	Autocracy
1988	Not Free	Autocracy
1989	Not Free	Autocracy
1990	Not Free	Autocracy
1991	Not Free	Autocracy
1992	Not Free	Autocracy
1993	Not Free	Autocracy
1994	Not Free	Autocracy
1995	Not Free	Autocracy
1996	Not Free	Autocracy
1997	Not Free	Autocracy
1998	Not Free	Autocracy
1999	Not Free	Autocracy
2000	Not Free	Autocracy
2001	Not Free	Autocracy
2002	Not Free	Autocracy
2003	Not Free	Autocracy
2004	Not Free	Autocracy
2005	Not Free	Autocracy
2006	Not Free	Autocracy
2007	Not Free	Autocracy
2008	Not Free	Autocracy
2009	Not Free	Autocracy
2010	Not Free	Autocracy
2011	Not Free	Autocracy
2012	Not Free	Autocracy

1949–2012: Not Free

Communist victory brought direct governmental editorial control over the media. Control was all but absolute until the combination of economic reforms, limited opening to the west, and advancing media technologies allowed some information from western media to begin penetrating urban centers. Hotels catering to Westerners carried some western news for guests, and during the Tiananmen Square uprising, fax machines were used by students in the West to transmit Western media reports to protesting students.

Responding to the infiltration of external media reports, the Chinese government began altering the way in which it controlled media content, shifting from direct editorial control to indirect, punishment-based methods.

By 1995, a significant portion of the media had become nominally independent of the ruling party, but indirect controls were established.

The effort to control the influx of information through the Internet essentially marked a return of direct governmental control over the media. Sometimes dubbed the Great Firewall of China, there has been some debate over the extent that the government was actually able to control the influx of new media content. Crackdowns and harsh punishments for editors who defied party edicts have been reported, and there have been several notable prosecutions of dissidents.

Media Today

The Chinese government puts considerable effort into controlling media within China and limiting the influx of information from the west. Although media have been allowed to commercialize, by law, the government maintains a majority stake in all news outlets.[1] Thus far, the government has managed to balance the need for the information flows necessary to support its technological industries and developing economy against the authoritarian need to control information. Replacing Western Internet resources, such as social networking and Internet search engines, with Chinese alternatives has thus far proven effective enough, but the long-term viability of such efforts to control information remains an open question. Editorial control of media, particularly print news media, is increasingly falling into the hands of Western-trained, Chinese professionals. Further, Western academics are becoming an increasingly salient part of the teaching of journalism and other media fields in Macau and Hong Kong universities.

Note

1. *Freedom of the Press* (Washington, DC: Freedom House, 2013). Available at http://freedomhouse.org/report/freedom-press/2013/china.

Colombia: 1948–2012

Colombia Year by Year

Year	Media	Government
1948	Not Free	Anocracy
1949	Not Free	Anocracy
1950	Not Free	Anocracy
1951	Not Free	Anocracy
1952	Not Free	Anocracy
1953	Not Free	Anocracy
1954	Not Free	Anocracy
1955	Not Free	Anocracy
1956	Not Free	Anocracy
1957	Not Free	Democracy
1958	Imperfectly Free	Democracy
1959	Imperfectly Free	Democracy
1960	Imperfectly Free	Democracy
1961	Imperfectly Free	Democracy
1962	Imperfectly Free	Democracy
1963	Imperfectly Free	Democracy
1964	Imperfectly Free	Democracy
1965	Imperfectly Free	Democracy
1966	Imperfectly Free	Democracy
1967	Imperfectly Free	Democracy
1968	Imperfectly Free	Democracy
1969	Imperfectly Free	Democracy
1970	Imperfectly Free	Democracy
1971	Imperfectly Free	Democracy
1972	Imperfectly Free	Democracy
1973	Imperfectly Free	Democracy
1974	Imperfectly Free	Democracy
1975	Imperfectly Free	Democracy

MEDIA FREEDOM HISTORY IN A NUTSHELL

- During Colombia's undeclared civil war, La Violencia (1948–1958), media were censored, but after that media were functionally free for decades
- Colombia remains one of the most dangerous countries for journalists, and from 2000 to 2005 these dangers reached a point where journalists could not function freely
- As of 2011, Colombia had sixty-one daily newspapers, fifty-seven of them were paid-for dailies with an average circulation per issue of 1,530,000. In addition, Colombia has many privately owned radio and television stations (World Association of Newspaper's 2012 World Newspaper Trends)
- As of 2012, 49 percent of Colombians had Internet access (International Telecommunication Union's 2012 ICT Indicators Database)

In Brief

Internal conflict in Colombia has long made it one of the most dangerous countries in the world for journalists. In spite of these challenges, media in Colombia have functioned freely for most of its recent history.

Chronology

1948–1957: Not Free

In 1948, media freedom and other civil liberties were suspended as Colombia plunged into an undeclared civil war known as *La Violencia* in which more than 200,000 people were killed.[1] During this period, the government had the power to invoke prior censorship.

1958–1999: Imperfectly Free

In May 1957, Rojas Pinilla (who had assumed the presidency in the 1953 coup) resigned amid

Year	Media	Government
1976	Imperfectly Free	Democracy
1977	Imperfectly Free	Democracy
1978	Imperfectly Free	Democracy
1979	Imperfectly Free	Democracy
1980	Imperfectly Free	Democracy
1981	Imperfectly Free	Democracy
1982	Imperfectly Free	Democracy
1983	Imperfectly Free	Democracy
1984	Imperfectly Free	Democracy
1985	Imperfectly Free	Democracy
1986	Imperfectly Free	Democracy
1987	Imperfectly Free	Democracy
1988	Imperfectly Free	Democracy
1989	Imperfectly Free	Democracy
1990	Imperfectly Free	Democracy
1991	Imperfectly Free	Democracy
1992	Imperfectly Free	Democracy
1993	Imperfectly Free	Democracy
1994	Imperfectly Free	Democracy
1995	Imperfectly Free	Democracy
1996	Imperfectly Free	Democracy
1997	Imperfectly Free	Democracy
1998	Imperfectly Free	Democracy
1999	Imperfectly Free	Democracy
2000	Not Free	Democracy
2001	Not Free	Democracy
2002	Not Free	Democracy
2003	Not Free	Democracy
2004	Not Free	Democracy
2005	Not Free	Democracy
2006	Imperfectly Free	Democracy
2007	Imperfectly Free	Democracy
2008	Imperfectly Free	Democracy
2009	Imperfectly Free	Democracy
2010	Imperfectly Free	Democracy
2011	Imperfectly Free	Democracy
2012	Imperfectly Free	Democracy

mass protests and strikes. In 1958, as Colombia transitioned to a civilian government, freedom of the press was restored to all but a few regions of the country.[2] From time to time government restricted broadcast media during periods of unrest and in response to attacks by insurgent groups. Yet print media remained functionally free.[3]

2000–2005: Not Free

By 2000, the armed conflict in Colombia reached levels that made it impossible for journalists to function freely because they were often the targets of insurgent groups. In 2000 alone, seven journalists were killed.[4] According to a poll conducted in 2000, 25 percent of Colombian editors had received threats.[5]

2006–2012: Imperfectly Free

Though journalists were still subject to violent attacks and threats, many of them persisted in reporting on the "parapolitica" scandal that revealed links between prominent politicians and the United Self-Defense Forces of Colombia (AUC), a paramilitary group. Thus, even though Colombia remained one of the most dangerous countries for journalists (according to the Committee to Protect Journalists), journalists were able to report critically about the actions of powerful elites.

Media Today

Colombia has many privately owned print and broadcast media outlets, though ownership is highly concentrated. A new trend in Colombia is the emergence of news organizations that are exclusively digital.[6] The government does operate three commercial television stations and one radio network. Colombia remains a dangerous country for journalists, especially in the regions that are controlled by insurgent groups and drug traffickers. In spite of these dangers, journalists continue to report on government corruption. In addition to physical threats, journalists are often the targets of lawsuits aimed at intimidating and silencing them.[7]

Notes

1. Rex A. Hudson, *Colombia: A Country Study* (Washington, DC: Library of Congress Federal

Research Division, 2010). Available at http://lcweb2.loc.gov/frd/cs/.

2. *General Assembly Proceedings 1958* (Miami, FL: Inter American Press Association, 1959). Report of the Committee on Freedom of the Press.

3. *General Assembly Proceedings 1980* (Miami, FL: Inter American Press Association, 1982). Report of the Committee on Freedom of the Press and Information.

4. *Killed since 1992* (Committee to Protect Journalists). Available at http://cpj.org/killed/.

5. *56 General Assembly Reports* (Miami, FL: Inter American Press Association, 2000). Available at http://www.sipiapa.org/v4/archivo_de_asambleas.php?idioma=us.

6. *Freedom of the Press* (Washington, DC: Freedom House, 2012). Available at http://www.freedomhouse.org/report/freedom-press/freedom-press-2012.

7. *Midyear Meeting* (Miami, FL: Inter American Press Association, 2013). Available at http://www.sipiapa.org/v4/archivo_de_asambleas.php?idioma=us.

Comoros: 1975–2012

Comoros Year by Year

Year	Media	Government
1975	Not Free	Anocracy
1976	Not Free	Anocracy
1977	Not Free	Anocracy
1978	Not Free	Anocracy
1979	Not Free	Anocracy
1980	Not Free	Anocracy
1981	Not Free	Anocracy
1982	Not Free	Autocracy
1983	Not Free	Autocracy
1984	Not Free	Autocracy
1985	Not Free	Autocracy
1986	Not Free	Autocracy
1987	Not Free	Autocracy
1988	Not Free	Autocracy
1989	Not Free	Autocracy
1990	Not Free	Anocracy
1991	Not Free	Anocracy
1992	Not Free	Anocracy
1993	Imperfectly Free	Anocracy
1994	Imperfectly Free	Anocracy
1995	Imperfectly Free	Anocracy
1996	Imperfectly Free	Anocracy
1997	Imperfectly Free	Anocracy
1998	Imperfectly Free	Anocracy

(Continued)

MEDIA FREEDOM HISTORY IN A NUTSHELL

- During the first decade after independence, there were almost no news outlets in Comoros
- In the mid-1980s, Comoros gained its first national radio station and newspaper, but these were government controlled
- In the early 1990s, the emergence of privately owned broadcast and print media improved the media environment to imperfectly free
- As of 2009, there were seven paid-for nondaily newspapers (World Association of Newspaper's 2010 World Newspaper Trends)
- Comoros has a mix of independent and government-controlled broadcast media
- As of 2012, about 6 percent of Comorans had Internet access (International Telecommunication Union's 2012 ICT Indicators Database)

In Brief

Since Comoros gained independence from France in 1975, it has experienced more than twenty coups or attempted coups. Because of this political instability, prior to the mid-1980s, there were almost no news outlets and those that did exist were either directly controlled by government or strictly restricted. In the mid-1980s, following a United Nations Educational Scientific and Cultural Organization study that identified Comoros as the only member state without print and electronic media, France provided funding to start a newspaper.[1] By the early 1990s, Comorans had access to a mix of government-owned and privately owned print and broadcast media and the media environment had improved to the point that media were imperfectly free.

(Continued)

Year	Media	Government
1999	Imperfectly Free	Anocracy
2000	Imperfectly Free	Anocracy
2001	Imperfectly Free	Anocracy
2002	Imperfectly Free	Anocracy
2003	Imperfectly Free	Anocracy
2004	Imperfectly Free	Democracy
2005	Imperfectly Free	Democracy
2006	Imperfectly Free	Democracy
2007	Imperfectly Free	Democracy
2008	Imperfectly Free	Democracy
2009	Imperfectly Free	Democracy
2010	Imperfectly Free	Democracy
2011	Imperfectly Free	Democracy
2012	Imperfectly Free	Democracy

Chronology

1975–1992: Not Free

Political instability and years of military rule created an inhospitable climate for news media. Prior to 1984, this impoverished, three-island country had no national media. The state-run Radio Comoros could only be heard on Njazidja, but with funding from France, the station acquired a new transmitter and began broadcasting to all three islands.[2] In 1985, again with backing from France, a state-owned newspaper, *Al Watwany*, began publishing, and the privately owned *L'Archipel* began publishing in 1988.[3] In 1990, a law went into effect that not only made it easier to start up newspapers and magazines but also gave the government the authority to exercise prepublication censorship.[4] Because nearly 85 percent of the population was illiterate, radio was the most accessible and popular medium, and the state maintained strict control over Radio Comoros until the early 1990s.[5]

1993–2012: Imperfectly Free

In the early 1990s, several privately owned radio stations began broadcasting in Comoros.[6] Additionally, Comorans could access radio and television broadcasts from neighboring Mayotte (an overseas department and region of France), and independently owned newspapers were able to publish without government censorship.[7] Even so, political instability continued, and as a result, journalists continued to face pressures. For example in 1996, the editor of the government-owned newspaper was arrested in connection to reporting on judicial corruption.[8] When he was released on bail and persisted in covering the alleged corruption, the newspaper was banned indefinitely.[9]

Media Today

The Comoran 2001 constitution includes provisions for media freedom, and these are usually, but not always, respected in practice. Journalists remain vulnerable to libel and defamation charges and often self-censor.[10]

Notes

1. Helen Chapin Metz, "Indian Ocean—Comoros." *Country Studies* (Washington, DC: Library of Congress Federal Research Division, 1994). Available at http://lcweb2.loc.gov/frd/cs/kmtoc.html.
2. Ibid.
3. Ibid.
4. *Country Reports on Human Rights Practices for 1992* (Washington, DC: U.S. Department of State, 1993). Available at https://archive.org/details/countryreportson1992unit.
5. *World Press Freedom Review*, IPI Report (Vienna: International Press Institute, 1993).
6. Ibid.
7. *Comoros Human Rights Practices, 1993* (Washington, DC: U.S. Department of State, 1994). Available at http://dosfan.lib.uic.edu/ERC/democracy/1993_hrp_report/93hrp_report_africa/Comoros.html.
8. *World Press Freedom Review*, IPI Report (Vienna: International Press Institute, 1996).
9. Ibid.
10. *Freedom of the Press* (Washington, DC: Freedom House, 2013). Available at http://www.freedomhouse.org/report/freedom-press/2013/comoros/.

Congo, Democratic Republic of the: 1960–2012

DRC Year by Year

Year	Media	Government
1960	Not Free	Anocracy
1961	Not Free	Anocracy
1962	Not Free	Anocracy
1963	Not Free	Anocracy
1964	Not Free	Autocracy
1965	Not Free	Autocracy
1966	Not Free	Autocracy
1967	Not Free	Autocracy
1968	Not Free	Autocracy
1969	Not Free	Autocracy
1970	Not Free	Autocracy
1971	Not Free	Autocracy
1972	Not Free	Autocracy
1973	Not Free	Autocracy
1974	Not Free	Autocracy
1975	Not Free	Autocracy
1976	Not Free	Autocracy
1977	Not Free	Autocracy
1978	Not Free	Autocracy
1979	Not Free	Autocracy
1980	Not Free	Autocracy
1981	Not Free	Autocracy
1982	Not Free	Autocracy

(Continued)

MEDIA FREEDOM HISTORY IN A NUTSHELL

- Media have not been free in the Democratic Republic of the Congo (formerly Zaire) since the country gained independence in 1960
- As of 2009, there were twelve paid-for daily newspapers with a total average circulation per issue of 50,000 (World Association of Newspaper's 2010 World Newspaper Trends)
- The country has a mix of government-owned and privately owned broadcast media
- As of 2012, about 2 percent of the Congolese had Internet access (International Telecommunication Union's 2012 ICT Indicators Database)

In Brief

Since the Democratic Republic of the Congo (DRC) gained independence in 1960, media have been directly controlled or restricted by the government. Political instability and violence continue to make the DRC a dangerous place for journalists.

Chronology

1960–2012: Not Free

Shortly after gaining independence from Belgium, the DRC plunged into civil war. During these tumultuous years, what few media existed were restricted by the government.

In 1965, Joseph Mobutu seized control of the country in a coup. Interestingly prior to entering politics, Mobutu had worked as a journalist and his connections helped garner him favorable coverage from the Belgium media.[1] Controlling mass media was a key aspect of Mobutu's efforts

(Continued)

Year	Media	Government
1983	Not Free	Autocracy
1984	Not Free	Autocracy
1985	Not Free	Autocracy
1986	Not Free	Autocracy
1987	Not Free	Autocracy
1988	Not Free	Autocracy
1989	Not Free	Autocracy
1990	Not Free	Autocracy
1991	Not Free	Autocracy
1992	Not Free	Anocracy
1993	Not Free	Anocracy
1994	Not Free	Anocracy
1995	Not Free	Anocracy
1996	Not Free	Anocracy
1997	Not Free	Anocracy
1998	Not Free	Anocracy
1999	Not Free	Anocracy
2000	Not Free	Anocracy
2001	Not Free	Anocracy
2002	Not Free	Anocracy
2003	Not Free	Anocracy
2004	Not Free	Anocracy
2005	Not Free	Anocracy
2006	Not Free	Anocracy
2007	Not Free	Anocracy
2008	Not Free	Anocracy
2009	Not Free	Anocracy
2010	Not Free	Anocracy
2011	Not Free	Anocracy
2012	Not Free	Anocracy

to establish and maintain control of the country, which he renamed Zaire:

Television news follows the official order of protocol, meaning that all news of President Mobutu, however routine, comes before any news of the prime minister, which in turn precedes any news of other ministers. At the height of the cult of personality in the late 1970s and early 1980s, each television news broadcast began with the president's face appearing, godlike, in a bank of clouds.[2]

Yet by the end of the 1980s, it was not possible for Mobutu to prevent citizens from gaining access to broadcasts from Brazzaville (Republic of the Congo).[3] In 1990, the government ended its official censorship, but journalists remained fearful of repercussions if they offended the government.[4] Although Mobutu's power over the country (which was renamed the Democratic Republic of the Congo in 1997) waned as civil war erupted in the mid-1990s, journalists who criticized government continued to faced threats, harassment, arrest, and torture.[5,6]

Since 1996, many African states have participated in the conflict that persists in the DRC, making the DRC a very dangerous place for journalists. For example, in 1999, the International Press Institute reported that more than seventy media workers were threatened, detained, tortured, or attacked.[7] In 2002, the government banned more than one hundred news organizations and twenty-five journalists were imprisoned.[8] More recently, in 2012, the DRC-based group Journalists in Danger reported that eight journalists had been killed and hundreds more imprisoned since 2007.[9]

Media Today

Although the 2005 constitution has provisions for media freedom, the government has failed to respect these in practice. Civil unrest continues to contribute to an inhospitable media environment. The High Authority on Media (a government agency) has the authority to suspend local media for hate speech and other violations.[10] The DRC has a mix of government-owned and privately owned print and broadcast media, and very few Congolese (less than 2 percent in 2011) have Internet access.

Notes

1. Sandra W. Meditz and Tim Merrill, *Zaire: A Country Study* (Washington, DC: Library of Congress

Federal Research Division, 1993). Available at http://lcweb2.loc.gov/frd/cs/.

2. Ibid. "The Media," para. 7.

3. Ibid.

4. *World Press Freedom Review*, IPI Report (Zurich: International Press Institute, 1991).

5. *World Press Freedom Review*, IPI Report (Vienna: International Press Institute, 1993).

6. *World Press Freedom Review*, IPI Report (Vienna: International Press Institute, 1996).

7. *World Press Freedom Review*, IPI Report (Vienna: International Press Institute, 1999).

8. *Freedom of the Press* (Washington, DC: Freedom House, 2002). Available at http://www.freedom house.org/report/freedom-press/2002/congo-democratic-republic-kinshasa.

9. *Media Sustainability Index 2012: Democratic Republic of the Congo* (Washington, DC: IREX, 2012). Available at http://www.irex.org/sites/default/files/u115/DRC.pdf.

10. *Freedom of the Press* (Washington, DC: Freedom House, 2013). Available at http://www.freedom house.org/report/freedom-press/2013/congo-democratic-republic-kinshasa.

Congo, Republic of the: 1960–2012

Congo Year by Year

Year	Media	Government
1960	No Media	Anocracy
1961	No Media	Anocracy
1962	No Media	Anocracy
1963	No Media	Autocracy
1964	No Media	Autocracy
1965	No Media	Autocracy
1966	No Media	Autocracy
1967	No Media	Autocracy
1968	No Media	Autocracy
1969	Not Free	Autocracy
1970	Not Free	Autocracy
1971	Not Free	Autocracy
1972	Not Free	Autocracy
1973	Not Free	Autocracy
1974	Not Free	Autocracy
1975	Not Free	Autocracy
1976	Not Free	Autocracy
1977	Not Free	Autocracy
1978	Not Free	Autocracy
1979	Not Free	Autocracy
1980	Not Free	Autocracy
1981	Not Free	Autocracy
1982	Not Free	Autocracy
1983	Not Free	Autocracy
1984	Not Free	Autocracy

MEDIA FREEDOM HISTORY IN A NUTSHELL

- Under a one-party government, the few Congolese media that existed were directly controlled until 1991
- For most of the 1990s, civil unrest plagued the country and government continued to restrict news media
- The 2001 constitution provides for media freedom and the government somewhat respects this in practice, but journalists continue to face pressures and often self-censor
- As of 2009, there were five paid-for daily newspapers with a total average circulation per issue of 8,000 (World Association of Newspaper's 2010 World Newspaper Trends)
- There is a mix of privately owned and government-owned broadcast media
- As of 2012, about 6 percent of Congolese had Internet access (International Telecommunication Union's 2012 ICT Indicators Database)

In Brief

For more than three decades postindependence, the Congolese media were either directly controlled or restricted by the government. Since the mid-1990s, civil unrest has created an inhospitable climate for journalists. Yet, since 2001, media have been imperfectly free, but self-censorship is common practice among Congolese journalists.

Chronology

1960–1993: Not Free

Just a few years after gaining independence from France, the Republic of the Congo (also called Congo-Brazzaville) experienced a series of coups and became a one-party state, first under the socialist National Revolutionary

Year	Media	Government
1985	Not Free	Autocracy
1986	Not Free	Autocracy
1987	Not Free	Autocracy
1988	Not Free	Autocracy
1989	Not Free	Autocracy
1990	Not Free	Autocracy
1991	Not Free	Anocracy
1992	Not Free	Anocracy
1993	Not Free	Anocracy
1994	Imperfectly Free	Anocracy
1995	Imperfectly Free	Anocracy
1996	Imperfectly Free	Anocracy
1997	Not Free	Autocracy
1998	Not Free	Autocracy
1999	Not Free	Autocracy
2000	Not Free	Autocracy
2001	Imperfectly Free	Anocracy
2002	Imperfectly Free	Anocracy
2003	Imperfectly Free	Anocracy
2004	Imperfectly Free	Anocracy
2005	Imperfectly Free	Anocracy
2006	Imperfectly Free	Anocracy
2007	Imperfectly Free	Anocracy
2008	Imperfectly Free	Anocracy
2009	Imperfectly Free	Anocracy
2010	Imperfectly Free	Anocracy
2011	Imperfectly Free	Anocracy
2012	Imperfectly Free	Anocracy

Movement in 1964, and then under the Marxist-leaning Congolese Labor Party (PCT) from 1968 to 1991. Prior to 1969, news media were virtually nonexistent. From 1969 to 1991, the news media that did exist were censored and almost all were government owned and operated.[1] In 1980, there was some improvement in the media environment when the government lifted the ban on thirty foreign publications.[2] Although foreign journalists were allowed in the country, like all journalists, they were forced to follow government guidelines in their reporting, and the State Censorship Board examined the content of all print media.[3]

In the 1990s, the government began to move away from Marxism, and in 1992, the Congo held its first multiparty election and Denis Sassou-Nguesso who had been president since 1979 was defeated. In part the power struggle that followed was played out in the struggle to control the media. Although print media provided critical coverage before and after the 1992 election, it was the government-owned radio and television stations that reached most of the public and at least one reporter who used these media to criticize government was fired.[4] Additionally, the military initially resisted the power transition and took over the country's primary radio and television stations in January and May of 1992.[5] In 1993, as civil unrest erupted in the Republic of the Congo, government censorship of news media became "pervasive" and there was almost no news coverage of the opposition during the elections.[6]

1994–1996: Imperfectly Free

Although government maintained control over broadcast media, censorship decreased and opposition newspapers provided critical coverage of the government.[7] Additionally, there was increased coverage of the opposition by the government-owned radio and television and political debates were broadcast.[8] Yet journalists continued to face pressures. For example, in 1996, the manager of an independent newspaper was imprisoned for four months on libel charges connected to the paper's coverage of alleged embezzlement by the management of the national social security fund.[9]

1997–2000: Not Free

In 1997, civil war broke out and conditions deteriorated to the point where the media were not free. Journalists who criticized the government faced libel charges, imprisonment, threats, and attacks. Under the 1996 Press Law, journalists convicted of defamation faced heavy fines and up to five years in prison. Violence against journalists went unpunished. For example, in 1997, a Radio France International reporter in Brazzaville had to evacuate to Gabon with his family after their home was attacked repeatedly.[10] In 1998, Radio Liberté reporter Fabien Fortuné Bitoumbo was fatally shot by a militia group.[11]

2001–2012: Imperfectly Free

In 2001, the Congolese adopted a new constitution that included guarantees of media freedom and an amendment that ended the requirement of prison terms for defamation convictions.[12] Government respect for media freedom increased to the point where media were imperfectly free, but government continued to operate most broadcast media.

Media Today

Independent newspapers do include critical coverage of government policies and actions, but the government-operated broadcast media are far more accessible to most Congolese. Although the constitution provides for media freedom, journalists are vulnerable to criminal charges for incitement and hate speech. Thus, "Congolese journalists survive through self-censorship—not only for their own safety, but to preserve their friendships with government officials, who own 80 percent of the lucrative media outlets. This is the price that journalists pay to keep their jobs, especially in the public media."[13]

Notes

1. *Country Reports on Human Rights Practices for 1980* (Washington, DC: U.S. Department of State, 1981). Available at http://babel.hathitrust.org/cgi/pt?id=mdp.39015014143476;view=1up;seq=79.
2. Ibid.
3. *World Press Freedom Review*, IPI Report (Zurich: International Press Institute, 1990).
4. *World Press Freedom Review*, IPI Report (Vienna: International Press Institute, 1992).
5. *Country Reports on Human Rights Practices for 1992* (Washington, DC: U.S. Department of State, 1993). Available at https://ia600305.us.archive.org/27/items/countryreportson1992unit/country reportson1992unit_bw.pdf.
6. *Country Reports on Human Rights Practices for 1993* (Washington, DC: U.S. Department of State, 1994). Available at http://dosfan.lib.uic.edu/ERC/democracy/1993_hrp_report/93hrp_report_africa/Congo.html.
7. *Country Reports on Human Rights Practices for 1994* (Washington, DC: U.S. Department of State, 1995). Available at http://dosfan.lib.uic.edu/ERC/democracy/1994_hrp_report/94hrp_report_africa/Congo.html.
8. Ibid.
9. *World Press Freedom Review*, IPI Report (Vienna: International Press Institute, 1996).
10. *World Press Freedom Review*, IPI Report (Vienna: International Press Institute, 1997).
11. *Journalists Killed Since 1992* (Committee to Protect Journalists, 2013). Available at http://cpj.org/killed/.
12. *Freedom of the Press* (Washington, DC: Freedom House, 2002). Available at http://www.freedomhouse.org/report/freedom-press/2002/congo-republic-brazzaville.
13. *Media Sustainability Index 2012: Republic of the Congo* (IREX, 2012), 85. Available at http://www.irex.org/sites/default/files/u128/RepCongo.pdf.

Costa Rica: 1948–2012

Costa Rica Year by Year

Year	Media	Government
1948	Free	Democracy
1949	Free	Democracy
1950	Free	Democracy
1951	Free	Democracy
1952	Free	Democracy
1953	Free	Democracy
1954	Free	Democracy
1955	Free	Democracy
1956	Free	Democracy
1957	Free	Democracy
1958	Free	Democracy
1959	Free	Democracy
1960	Free	Democracy
1961	Free	Democracy
1962	Free	Democracy
1963	Free	Democracy
1964	Free	Democracy
1965	Free	Democracy
1966	Free	Democracy
1967	Free	Democracy
1968	Free	Democracy
1969	Free	Democracy
1970	Free	Democracy
1971	Free	Democracy
1972	Free	Democracy
1973	Free	Democracy
1974	Free	Democracy

(Continued)

MEDIA FREEDOM HISTORY IN A NUTSHELL

- Media in Costa Rica have long been among the freest in Central America
- As of 2012, there were six paid-for daily newspapers with a total average circulation per issue of 153,000 (World Association of Newspaper's 2012 World Newspaper Trends)
- Costa Rica has a mix of public and privately owned broadcast media
- As of 2012, about 48 percent of Costa Ricans had Internet access (International Telecommunication Union's 2012 ICT Indicators Database)

In Brief

With the country's first law guaranteeing press freedom dating back to 1835, Costa Rican media have long been among the freest in Latin America.

Chronology

1948–2012: Free

In the build-up to the elections of 1948, newspapers were caught up in the ideological fight between communists and anticommunists.[1] When anticommunist newspaper publisher Otilio Ulate Blanco won, supporters of President Rafael Angel Calderon Guradia refused hand over power and a six-week civil war ensued. In 1949, Ulate was able to assume the presidency, and in the aftermath of the civil war, the army was disbanded. Following the civil war, the media that had previously had strong connections to political parties became more independent.[2]

Although Costa Rican media have consistently been among the freest, if not the freest, in Central America, the country's 1902 press law

(Continued)

Year	Media	Government
1975	Free	Democracy
1976	Free	Democracy
1977	Free	Democracy
1978	Free	Democracy
1979	Free	Democracy
1980	Free	Democracy
1981	Free	Democracy
1982	Free	Democracy
1983	Free	Democracy
1984	Free	Democracy
1985	Free	Democracy
1986	Free	Democracy
1987	Free	Democracy
1988	Free	Democracy
1989	Free	Democracy
1990	Free	Democracy
1991	Free	Democracy
1992	Free	Democracy
1993	Free	Democracy
1994	Free	Democracy
1995	Free	Democracy
1996	Free	Democracy
1997	Free	Democracy
1998	Free	Democracy
1999	Free	Democracy
2000	Free	Democracy
2001	Free	Democracy
2002	Free	Democracy
2003	Free	Democracy
2004	Free	Democracy

Year	Media	Government
2005	Free	Democracy
2006	Free	Democracy
2007	Free	Democracy
2008	Free	Democracy
2009	Free	Democracy
2010	Free	Democracy
2011	Free	Democracy
2012	Free	Democracy

included harsh *desacato* provisions under which journalists found guilty of defamation faced prison terms. In 2010, the Supreme Court struck down portions of this law. Yet defamation remained criminalized, and those convicted faced steep fines.

Media Today

Costa Rican media remain free. There were some concerns regarding the 2012 Law on Information-Technology Crimes, which included prison terms for the publication of "confidential political information." This law was amended in 2013, and prison terms were eliminated for the publication or broadcasting of information in the public interest or information contained in public documents, records, and databases.[3]

Notes

1. Rick Rockwell and Noreene Janus, *Media Power in Central America* (Urbana: University of Illinois Press, 2003).
2. Ibid.
3. *2013 General Assembly of the IAPA* (Miami, FL: Inter American Press Association, 2013), para. 1. Available at http://www.sipiapa.org/en/asamblea/costa-rica-126/?i=1.

Côte d'Ivoire: 1960–2012

Côte d'Ivoire Year by Year

Year	Media	Government
1960	Not Free	Autocracy
1961	Not Free	Autocracy
1962	Not Free	Autocracy
1963	Not Free	Autocracy
1964	Not Free	Autocracy
1965	Not Free	Autocracy
1966	Not Free	Autocracy
1967	Not Free	Autocracy
1968	Not Free	Autocracy
1969	Not Free	Autocracy
1970	Not Free	Autocracy
1971	Not Free	Autocracy
1972	Not Free	Autocracy
1973	Not Free	Autocracy
1974	Not Free	Autocracy
1975	Not Free	Autocracy
1976	Not Free	Autocracy
1977	Not Free	Autocracy
1978	Not Free	Autocracy
1979	Not Free	Autocracy
1980	Not Free	Autocracy
1981	Not Free	Autocracy
1982	Not Free	Autocracy
1983	Not Free	Autocracy

(Continued)

MEDIA FREEDOM HISTORY IN A NUTSHELL

- Ivorian media have been directly controlled or restricted by government since the country gained independence in 1960
- As of 2009, there were twenty-nine paid-for daily newspapers with a total average circulation per issue of 200,000 (World Association of Newspaper's 2010 World Newspaper Trends)
- In 2004, privately owned radio stations were prohibited from providing news coverage and privately owned television was prohibited altogether; these provisions were overturned in 2012, but government has yet to grant licenses for privately-owned television
- As of 2012, about 2 percent of Ivoirians had Internet access (International Telecommunication Union's 2012 ICT Indicators Database)

In Brief

Throughout nearly four decades of one-party rule followed by a more than a decade of civil unrest, Ivorian media have been either directly controlled or restricted by government.

Chronology

1963–2012: Not Free

For more than thirty years after gaining independence from France in 1960, the Côte d'Ivoire was a one-party state under President Felix Houphouet-Boigny and the Democratic Party of Côte d'Ivoire (PDCI). During these years, all media were government-owned and controlled.[1] In 1986, there was a move to increase media independence, but the Minister of Information threatened to fire journalists who failed to act as public servants.[2] Nevertheless, privately owned newspapers

(Continued)

Year	Media	Government
1984	Not Free	Autocracy
1985	Not Free	Autocracy
1986	Not Free	Autocracy
1987	Not Free	Autocracy
1988	Not Free	Autocracy
1989	Not Free	Autocracy
1990	Not Free	Autocracy
1991	Not Free	Autocracy
1992	Not Free	Autocracy
1993	Not Free	Autocracy
1994	Not Free	Autocracy
1995	Not Free	Autocracy
1996	Not Free	Autocracy
1997	Not Free	Autocracy
1998	Not Free	Autocracy
1999	Not Free	Anocracy
2000	Not Free	Anocracy
2001	Not Free	Anocracy
2002	Not Free	Interregnum
2003	Not Free	Interregnum
2004	Not Free	Interregnum
2005	Not Free	Interregnum
2006	Not Free	Interregnum
2007	Not Free	Transition
2008	Not Free	Transition
2009	Not Free	Transition
2010	Not Free	Interregnum
2011	Not Free	Anocracy
2012	Not Free	Anocracy

became available in the late 1980s, and foreign newspapers were also available.[3] Yet, like their Ivorian counterparts, foreign journalists were vulnerable to arrest—especially if they covered protests.[4] As President Houphouet-Boigny's health deteriorated, journalists who questioned his succession were arrested.[5] Upon Houphouet-Boigny's death in 1993, Henri Konan Bedie, also with the PDCI, became president, and under his leadership news media remained restricted.[6] In 1999, Bedie was overthrown in a coup led by Robert Guei and the media environment deteriorated.[7] Although Guei initially claimed the presidency, a popular uprising forced him out and Laurent Gbagbo was proclaimed president in 2000. Yet civil unrest continued, and in 2002, the country descended into civil war and the media environment deteriorated as journalists working for domestic and foreign media alike faced threats and attacks from both government and opposition forces.[8] The government used the rebellion to justify further reductions of media freedom to promote national unity.[9] In 2004, a law was passed prohibiting privately owned television stations and restricting privately owned radio stations to entertainment and cultural programming.[10] Also in 2004, defamation penalties were revised so that journalists convicted of defamation no longer faced imprisonment, but they were still subject to harsh fines.[11]

Media Today

Civil unrest remains a problem and Ivorian news media remain restricted. In 2012, conditions for journalists did improve and reports of attacks on journalists decreased.[12] In particular, the government agreed to permit privately owned television stations and news coverage on privately owned radio stations.[13] Yet it remains to be seen if the government will actually grant licenses for privately owned television stations.

Notes

1. Robert E. Handloff, *Cote D'Ivoire/Ivory Coast: A Country Study* (Washington, DC: Library of Congress Federal Research Division, 1988). Available at http://lcweb2.loc.gov/frd/cs/.
2. Ibid.
3. *World Press Freedom Review*, IPI Report (Zurich: International Press Institute, 1989).
4. *World Press Freedom Review*, IPI Report (Zurich: International Press Institute, 1990).
5. Ibid.

6. *World Press Freedom Review,* IPI Report (Vienna: International Press Institute, 1994).

7. *World Press Freedom Review,* IPI Report (Vienna: International Press Institute, 1999).

8. *Freedom of the Press* (Washington, DC: Freedom House, 2004). Available at http://www.freedom house.org/report/freedom-press/2004/c%C3% B4te-divoire.

9. *World Press Trends* (Darmstadt, Germany: WAN-IFRA, 2010).

10. *Freedom of the Press* (Washington, DC: Freedom House, 2005). Available at http://www.freedom house.org/report/freedom-press/2005/c%C3% B4te-divoire

11. Ibid.

12. *Freedom of the Press* (Washington, DC: Freedom House, 2013). Available at http://www.freedom house.org/report/freedom-press/2013/c%C3% B4te-divoire.

13. Ibid.

Croatia: 1993–2012

Croatia Year by Year

Year	Media	Government
1993	Free	Anocracy
1994	Free	Anocracy
1995	Not Free	Anocracy
1996	Not Free	Anocracy
1997	Not Free	Anocracy
1998	Not Free	Anocracy
1999	Not Free	Anocracy
2000	Imperfectly Free	Democracy
2001	Imperfectly Free	Democracy
2002	Imperfectly Free	Democracy
2003	Imperfectly Free	Democracy
2004	Imperfectly Free	Democracy
2005	Imperfectly Free	Democracy
2006	Imperfectly Free	Democracy
2007	Imperfectly Free	Democracy
2008	Imperfectly Free	Democracy
2009	Imperfectly Free	Democracy
2010	Imperfectly Free	Democracy
2011	Imperfectly Free	Democracy
2012	Imperfectly Free	Democracy

MEDIA FREEDOM HISTORY IN A NUTSHELL

- During the nearly decade-long war that followed the dissolution of Yugoslavia, media within Croat-controlled territories were reasonably free, but limited by wartime constraints, and therefore unable to effectively function as a free press
- Media freedom was established throughout the country at the end of the war, but it remains economically threatened
- As of 2011, there were sixteen paid-for daily newspapers with a total average circulation per issue of 457,341 (World Association of Newspaper's 2010 World Newspaper Trends)
- Croatia has around 150 radio stations and more than twenty television channels, but only a fraction of these are licensed for national coverage
- As of 2012, about 63 percent of Croatian citizens had Internet access (International Telecommunication Union's 2012 ICT Indicators Database)

country under authoritarian rule. Media freedom was part of that liberal culture and was well supported by the western European powers that intervened in the war. Yet during the war the media were often compromised by the pragmatics of war, to the point that they did not effectively function as a free press. By most accounts, the media regime that was established after the war is of a high standard, but is threatened by economic and political forces.

In Brief

Croatia is a country born in the war that followed the dissolution of Yugoslavia, and in many ways the Croats represented the liberal Western opposite of the Serbian effort to forcefully reunite the

Chronology

1992: Missing Data

The dissolution of Yugoslavia was particularly difficult for Croatia because Serbia tried to keep it as part of a Serbian-controlled country, often using a large Serbian ethnic minority within Croatia to try to force the issue. The first outbreak of civil war started in 1991, and 1992 is the year in which a UN ceasefire briefly interrupted the war and allowed the space to establish an independent and internationally recognized government. It is all but impossible to apply a meaningful label to the media context at this time because news media were in the middle of the struggle over defining the politics of the country.[1]

1993–1994: Free

Civil war returned, but after the ceasefire, the Croat majority effectively controlled over three-quarters of the country. The national government was built on a western democratic political model, including a strong commitment to media freedom. The degree to which media freedom existed in the Serbian dominated sections of the country is debatable, but in the capital and in the national political arena, media freedom was dominant. With increasing pressure from the West, Croatia's tightly controlled state television halted its vilification of Bosnia's Muslims and transitioned to focusing on the merits and benefits of cooperation between Croats and Muslims against the common Serbian enemy.[2]

1995–1999: Not Free

Media freedom became a victim of the civil war, and the remainder of the war was fought with a tightly, but indirectly controlled press. During the campaign for the 1995 elections, television stations covered only the ruling party, the Croatian Democratic Union, and there was no mention of other parties except for a special program that presented "brief news."[3] In 1996, the regime introduced harsh new sedition laws,

and immediately used them to punish journalists and threaten independent newspapers with bankruptcy.[4]

2000–2012: Imperfectly Free

Military victory in the civil war enabled the Croats to establish political institutions, including media freedom, without significant compromise to the Serbian minorities. Some aspects of media freedom that were problematic during the brief period of media freedom earlier, such as inciting unrest, were placed under legal restrictions and scrutiny, but the real imperfection in the press freedom of the post war media is their vulnerability to economic influence.

Media Today

Economic issues are the primary concern for Croatian media freedom. Media outlets have grown increasingly commercial and entertainment-oriented. Consequently, professionalism in journalism has suffered as media chase audience in search of revenue. While this is a common concern around the world, it appears to be disproportionately affecting a country that is both small and still struggling with the economic consequences of a war that destroyed as much as a third of its infrastructure.

Notes

1. *World Press Freedom Review* (Vienna: International Press Institute, 1992).
2. *World Press Freedom Review* (Vienna: International Press Institute, 1993).
3. *World Press Freedom Review* (Vienna: International Press Institute, 1995).
4. *World Press Freedom Review* (Vienna: International Press Institute, 1996).

Cuba: 1948–2012

Cuba Year by Year

Year	Media	Government
1948	Imperfectly Free	Anocracy
1949	Imperfectly Free	Anocracy
1950	Imperfectly Free	Anocracy
1951	Imperfectly Free	Anocracy
1952	Not Free	Anocracy
1953	Not Free	Anocracy
1954	Imperfectly Free	Autocracy
1955	Imperfectly Free	Autocracy
1956	Imperfectly Free	Autocracy
1957	Not Free	Autocracy
1958	Not Free	Autocracy
1959	Not Free	Anocracy
1960	Not Free	Anocracy
1961	Not Free	Autocracy
1962	Not Free	Autocracy
1963	Not Free	Autocracy
1964	Not Free	Autocracy
1965	Not Free	Autocracy
1966	Not Free	Autocracy
1967	Not Free	Autocracy
1968	Not Free	Autocracy
1969	Not Free	Autocracy
1970	Not Free	Autocracy
1971	Not Free	Autocracy
1972	Not Free	Autocracy
1973	Not Free	Autocracy
1974	Not Free	Autocracy
1975	Not Free	Autocracy

MEDIA FREEDOM HISTORY IN A NUTSHELL

- Other than two brief periods in the late 1940s and the mid-1950s, news media in Cuba have been directly controlled by government
- Today the Cuban media remain among the world's most restricted
- As of 2011, there were nineteen paid for daily newspapers with a total average circulation per issue of 1,800,000 (World Association of Newspaper's 2012 World Newspaper Trends)
- The government considers print and electronic media state property
- As of 2012, about 26 percent of Cubans had Internet access, which for the most part is restricted to the country's intranet (International Telecommunication Union's 2012 ICT Indicators Database)

In Brief

After a series of military governments, in the mid- to late-1940s Cuba had a democratic government. Though these administrations were marred by allegations of corruption, political instability, and violence, they did for the most part respect media freedom. The 1952 coup d'état brought an end to media freedom. Initially there were expectations that the Revolution led by Fidel Castro would bring a return of media freedom, but these hopes were quickly dashed. Cuba remains today one of the world's most restricted media environments.

Chronology

1948–1951: Imperfectly Free

In 1948, Carlos Prío Socarrás was elected president of Cuba, and during his tenure, news

Year	Media	Government
1976	Not Free	Autocracy
1977	Not Free	Autocracy
1978	Not Free	Autocracy
1979	Not Free	Autocracy
1980	Not Free	Autocracy
1981	Not Free	Autocracy
1982	Not Free	Autocracy
1983	Not Free	Autocracy
1984	Not Free	Autocracy
1985	Not Free	Autocracy
1986	Not Free	Autocracy
1987	Not Free	Autocracy
1988	Not Free	Autocracy
1989	Not Free	Autocracy
1990	Not Free	Autocracy
1991	Not Free	Autocracy
1992	Not Free	Autocracy
1993	Not Free	Autocracy
1994	Not Free	Autocracy
1995	Not Free	Autocracy
1996	Not Free	Autocracy
1997	Not Free	Autocracy
1998	Not Free	Autocracy
1999	Not Free	Autocracy
2000	Not Free	Autocracy
2001	Not Free	Autocracy
2002	Not Free	Autocracy
2003	Not Free	Autocracy
2004	Not Free	Autocracy
2005	Not Free	Autocracy
2006	Not Free	Autocracy
2007	Not Free	Autocracy
2008	Not Free	Autocracy
2009	Not Free	Autocracy
2010	Not Free	Autocracy
2011	Not Free	Autocracy
2012	Not Free	Autocracy

media were for the most part free. Yet Prío's presidency was marred by allegations of corruption.

1952–1953: Not Free

In 1952, Fulgencio Batista y Zaldívar seized control of the country in a coup and imposed censorship on the news media.[1]

1954–1956: Imperfectly Free

In 1954, the government revoked Public Order Decree 997 that had restricted broadcast media and which Batista had signed just one year earlier; thus, exiled Cubans were invited to return home for the November 1954 elections.[2]

1957–2012: Not Free

In 1957, political unrest prompted government to suspend constitutional guarantees and implement censorship of both domestic and foreign news media.[3] In 1959, Fidel Castro and his rebel army seized control of the country and the headline of the Inter American Press Association's Press of the Americas Report proclaimed "Batista Ousted; Censorship Ends."[4] Yet, by 1960, the IAPA concluded that Castro's government had no respect for press freedom.[5] Furthermore, by 1961, there was no pretense of media freedom in Cuba:

In a shameful acknowledgement that the government aims at full control of the press, Castro requested "more coordination between the government agencies and the information media, with the understanding that the press, at the service of the revolution, must brush aside every pretension of exclusiveness."[6]

This regime of media censorship continued as Castro handed over power to his brother Raul Castro in 2008.

Media Today

Cuban media remain among the most restricted in the world. Private ownership of media is prohibited, critical journalists risk harassment and arrest, and those convicted of subversion or acting against the state face long prison terms or even death.[7] The Committee to Protect Journalists placed Cuba in ninth place on its 2012 list of most censored countries.[8] Although some Cubans have Internet access (about 26 percent in 2012), most can only access the very limited Cuban intranet, and those who access the Internet illegally risk a five-year prison sentence.[9]

Notes

1. *World Press Freedom Review*, IPI Report (Zurich: International Press Institute, 1952).
2. *Press of the Americas* (Miami, FL: Inter American Press Association, 1954).
3. *Press of the Americas* (Miami, FL: Inter American Press Association, 1957).
4. *Press of the Americas* (Miami, FL: Inter American Press Association, 1959).
5. *Press of the Americas* (Miami, FL: Inter American Press Association, 1960).
6. *Report by Chairman of the Freedom of the Press Committee*, 1961 General Assembly Proceedings (Miami, FL: Inter American Press Association, 1962), 185.
7. *Freedom of the Press* (Washington, DC: Freedom House, 2013). Available at http://www.freedomhouse.org/report/freedom-press/2013/cuba.
8. *Attacks on the Press: Journalism on the Front Lines in* 2012 (Committee to Protect Journalists, 2013). Available at http://www.cpj.org/2013/02/attacks-on-the-press-in-2012-cuba.php.
9. *Freedom of the Press* (Washington, DC: Freedom House, 2013). Available at http://www.freedomhouse.org/report/freedom-press/2013/cuba.

Cyprus: 1960–2012

Cyprus Year by Year

Year	Media	Government
1960	Not Free	Democracy
1961	Not Free	Democracy
1962	Not Free	Democracy
1963	Not Free	Anocracy
1964	Not Free	Anocracy
1965	Not Free	Anocracy
1966	Not Free	Anocracy
1967	Not Free	Anocracy
1968	Not Free	Democracy
1969	Not Free	Democracy
1970	Not Free	Democracy
1971	Not Free	Democracy
1972	Not Free	Democracy
1973	Not Free	Democracy
1974	Not Free	Democracy
1975	Not Free	Democracy
1976	Imperfectly Free	Democracy
1977	Free	Democracy
1978	Free	Democracy
1979	Free	Democracy
1980	Free	Democracy
1981	Free	Democracy
1982	Free	Democracy
1983	Free	Democracy

(Continued)

MEDIA FREEDOM HISTORY IN A NUTSHELL

- The Greek/Turkish cleavage is the defining aspect of Cypriot politics
- Prior to the physical partition of the island, Greek leaders used media control as part of an effort to retain political control of the island
- After partition, the Greek half of the island quickly transitioned to a democracy with a free media
- As of 2009, there were twenty-two paid-for daily newspapers with a total average circulation per issue of 100,000 (World Association of Newspaper's 2010 World Newspaper Trends)
- Private television and radio stations compete with state-owned broadcasters.
- As of 2012, about 61 percent of Cypriots had Internet access (International Telecommunication Union's 2012 ICT Indicators Database)

In Brief

Cypriot politics are dominated by the conflict between Greek and Turkish communities. Prior to the division of the island in 1974, the Greeks used authoritarian methods, including media controls, to retain control of government. As soon as the island was partitioned, effectively removing the Turkish residents from Cypriot politics, the Greek half of the island quickly shifted to a liberal democratic model including media freedom.

The Turkish Cyprus enclave declared independence but is only recognized by Turkey and is not coded here.

Chronology

1960–1975: Not Free

A power sharing agreement between Greek and Turkish communities was central to the

(Continued)

Year	Media	Government
1984	Free	Democracy
1985	Free	Democracy
1986	Free	Democracy
1987	Free	Democracy
1988	Free	Democracy
1989	Free	Democracy
1990	Free	Democracy
1991	Free	Democracy
1992	Free	Democracy
1993	Free	Democracy
1994	Free	Democracy
1995	Free	Democracy
1996	Free	Democracy
1997	Free	Democracy
1998	Free	Democracy
1999	Free	Democracy
2000	Free	Democracy
2001	Free	Democracy
2002	Free	Democracy
2003	Free	Democracy
2004	Free	Democracy
2005	Free	Democracy
2006	Free	Democracy
2007	Free	Democracy
2008	Free	Democracy
2009	Free	Democracy
2010	Free	Democracy
2011	Free	Democracy
2012	Free	Democracy

agreement on the constitution that led to the establishment of an independent Cyprus. Media were limited and owned by the government. Nominally they were to be run using a BBC-style public service model. But before any signs of media independence materialized, constitutional changes proposed by the Greek-led government of Makarios in 1963 threatened the power sharing guarantees and violence erupted. UN peacekeepers arrived and ended the violence. The Turkish community withdrew from the power sharing agreement and media control was exercised by the Greek-dominated government.

A 1974 coup attempt, backed by the military Junta in Greece, failed but triggered a Turkish military intervention that resulted in the partition of the island. The Greek-dominated government in the south remained the recognized government, but an independent Turkish administration was established in the north.

The division of island effectively removed the Turkish population from the Cypriot political calculus. Without this fundamental cleavage threatening the wealthier Greek population's hold on political power, Greek Cyprus began a swift transition to a truly democratic system and media controls were relaxed.

1976: Imperfectly Free

Media effectively shifted to a BBC-style public service model (in which publicly owned media were editorially independent) and a small but free collection of independent print outlets.

1977–2012: Free

By 1977, media on the Greek half of the island were clearly free and independent of government control and provided an arena for debate and political competition. The 1989 Press Law allowed the establishment of privately owned radio stations and protected journalists' rights to keep sources confidential.[1]

Media Today

Cyprus remains divided and the Greek half of the island remains clearly democratic with an independent media.

Note

1. *Cyprus, Country Studies* (Washington, DC: Library of Congress, 1991). Available at http://lcweb2.loc.gov/cgi-bin/query/D?cstdy:2:./temp/~frd_crY6.

Czech Republic: 1993–2012

Czech Republic Year by Year

Year	Media	Government
1993	Missing Data	Democracy
1994	Free	Democracy
1995	Imperfectly Free	Democracy
1996	Imperfectly Free	Democracy
1997	Imperfectly Free	Democracy
1998	Imperfectly Free	Democracy
1999	Imperfectly Free	Democracy
2000	Imperfectly Free	Democracy
2001	Imperfectly Free	Democracy
2002	Free	Democracy
2003	Free	Democracy
2004	Free	Democracy
2005	Free	Democracy
2006	Free	Democracy
2007	Free	Democracy
2008	Free	Democracy
2009	Free	Democracy
2010	Free	Democracy
2009	Free	Democracy
2010	Free	Democracy
2011	Free	Democracy
2012	Free	Democracy

In Brief

The transition from single-party communist controlled media to free media occurred primarily in the three years that Czechoslovakia continued as a unified country after the fall of the Berlin wall. Following some modest challenges

---

MEDIA FREEDOM HISTORY IN A NUTSHELL

- Free media were a major force in the peaceful dissolution of Czechoslovakia and have been sustained
- Challenges to media freedom have largely been eliminated and the Czech Republic has developed a free media environment of the highest standard
- There are more than eighty radio stations, twelve of which have national reach, as well as several television channels, some public and some private
- As of 2011, there were eighty-two daily newspapers, eighty of which were paid-for dailies with a total average circulation per issue of 1,052,000 (World Association of Newspaper's 2012 World Newspaper Trends)
- As of 2012, about 75 percent of citizens had Internet access (International Telecommunication Union's 2012 ICT Indicators Database)

---

during the late 1990s, the media have developed into a stable political institution that is free and of a high professional standard.

Chronology:

1993: Missing Data

The year 1993 was a transition year in which political institutions for an independent Czech Republic were being formulated. The imperfect but free media of Czechoslovakia appeared to be the default during this period but there is enough uncertainty to leave this as an uncoded transitional year.

1994: Free

The Czech Republic initially established a higher standard of media freedom than existed in Czechoslovakia. A crucial development was the establishment of the first nationwide private TV channel in post-communist central Europe.[1] Yet in some ways these standards may have been overly ambitious, or overly idealistic, for a country that had such a limited history of professional independent media. Political leaders struggled with how to work effectively in a free media environment, and challenges to media slowly grew in significance. For example, in 1994 in an interview with *Forbes* magazine, Prime Minister Vaclav Klaus stated that "the greatest enemies of humanity are journalists."[1]

1995–2001: Imperfectly Free

Political and economic pressures challenged the media enough to categorize this period as imperfectly free, but the professional development of the free and independent media continued. The increasing success of political and economic leaders who adapted to the free media environment and the continuing growth of connections to Western Europe limited the effect of these imperfections.

In 1995, a new law was supposed to be a major development toward safeguarding a free press, but the final version of the bill omitted two provisions considered important to press freedom including the provision that would have protected journalists from having to reveal their sources.[2] In 1999, a poll showed that just over half of Czechs were convinced that the media were free, while almost 40 percent believed the opposite.[3]

2002–2012: Free

The transition from imperfectly free to free categories is gradual and indistinct. Development toward a more robust free media regime is clear both before and after this date, and by 2006, it is the clearly equal to the professional and political standard across the developed democracies of Western Europe.

Media Today

Media are clearly free and function to a standard comparable to longstanding European democracies.

Notes

1. *World Press Freedom Review*, IPI Report (Vienna: International Press Institute, 1994).
2. *World Press Freedom Review*, IPI Report (Vienna: International Press Institute, 1995).
3. *World Press Freedom Review*, IPI Report (Vienna: International Press Institute, 1999).

Czechoslovakia: 1948–1992

Czechoslovakia Year by Year

Year	Media	Government
1948	Not Free	Autocracy
1949	Not Free	Autocracy
1950	Not Free	Autocracy
1951	Not Free	Autocracy
1952	Not Free	Autocracy
1953	Not Free	Autocracy
1954	Not Free	Autocracy
1955	Not Free	Autocracy
1956	Not Free	Autocracy
1957	Not Free	Autocracy
1958	Not Free	Autocracy
1959	Not Free	Autocracy
1960	Not Free	Autocracy
1961	Not Free	Autocracy
1962	Not Free	Autocracy
1963	Not Free	Autocracy
1964	Not Free	Autocracy
1965	Not Free	Autocracy
1966	Not Free	Autocracy
1967	Not Free	Autocracy
1968	Not Free	Autocracy
1969	Not Free	Autocracy
1970	Not Free	Autocracy
1971	Not Free	Autocracy
1972	Not Free	Autocracy
1973	Not Free	Autocracy
1974	Not Free	Autocracy

(Continued)

MEDIA FREEDOM HISTORY IN A NUTSHELL

- From 1948 to 1989, under the Communist Party of Czechoslovakia, all media were government controlled.
- Following a nationwide protest in late 1989—dubbed the Velvet Revolution—democracy and media freedom emerged
- Czechoslovakia's peaceful split to the Czech Republic and Slovakia in 1992 was dubbed the Velvet Divorce

In Brief

Under communist rule from 1948 to 1989, all media were government controlled. In the brief period between the fall of the communist regime and the dissolution of Czechoslovakia, media were imperfectly free.

Chronology

1948–1989: Not Free

Czechoslovakia reemerged as a sovereign state after World War II and in 1948 became a communist regime. During these years, all media were controlled by the party and private ownership was for the most part forbidden.[1] For three months, restrictions on the media were lifted during the 1968 Prague Spring.[2]

1990–1992: Imperfectly Free

With the fall of the Communist regime, the Federal Press and Information Office was abolished and independent news media began to emerge. Although the government maintained ownership of all domestic television and most domestic radio, it relinquished editorial control

(Continued)

Year	Media	Government
1975	Not Free	Autocracy
1976	Not Free	Autocracy
1977	Not Free	Autocracy
1978	Not Free	Autocracy
1979	Not Free	Autocracy
1980	Not Free	Autocracy
1981	Not Free	Autocracy
1982	Not Free	Autocracy
1983	Not Free	Autocracy
1984	Not Free	Autocracy
1985	Not Free	Autocracy
1986	Not Free	Autocracy
1987	Not Free	Autocracy
1988	Not Free	Autocracy
1989	Not Free	Autocracy
1990	Imperfectly Free	Democracy
1991	Imperfectly Free	Democracy
1992	Imperfectly Free	Democracy

to the management of each station.[3] Also in 1990, for the first time Czechoslovakians could legally listen to broadcasts from Radio Free Europe, CNN, and the BBC.[4] In 1991, privately owned broadcast media became legal, but newspapers reported increasing financial difficulties from newsprint shortages and high taxes.[5]

Media Today

On January 1, 1993, Czechoslovakia peacefully separated into two independent countries—the Czech Republic and Slovakia.

Notes

1. Ihor Gawdiak, *Czechoslovakia: A Country Study* (Washington, DC: Library of Congress Federal Research Division, 1987). Available at http://lcweb2 .loc.gov/frd/cs/.
2. Ibid.
3. *Country Reports on Human Rights Practices for 1990* (Washington, DC: U.S. Department of State, 1991). Available at https://archive.org/details/ countryreportson1990unit.
4. *World Press Freedom Review*, IPI Report (Zurich: International Press Institute, 1990).
5. *World Press Freedom Review*, IPI Report (Zurich: International Press Institute, 1991).

Denmark: 1948–2012

Denmark Year by Year

Year	Media	Government
1948	Free	Democracy
1949	Free	Democracy
1950	Free	Democracy
1951	Free	Democracy
1952	Free	Democracy
1953	Free	Democracy
1954	Free	Democracy
1955	Free	Democracy
1956	Free	Democracy
1957	Free	Democracy
1958	Free	Democracy
1959	Free	Democracy
1960	Free	Democracy
1961	Free	Democracy
1962	Free	Democracy
1963	Free	Democracy
1964	Free	Democracy
1965	Free	Democracy
1966	Free	Democracy
1967	Free	Democracy
1968	Free	Democracy
1969	Free	Democracy
1970	Free	Democracy
1971	Free	Democracy
1972	Free	Democracy
1973	Free	Democracy

(Continued)

MEDIA FREEDOM HISTORY IN A NUTSHELL

- An exemplar of a free media society.
- In 2005, a Danish magazine published controversial cartoons of the Prophet Muhammad sparking outrage and anti-Danish sentiment across much of the Middle East
- As of 2011, there were thirty-two daily newspapers, thirty of which are paid-for dailies (World Association of Newspaper's 2012 World Newspaper Trends)
- Denmark has a mix of public and commercial radio stations and television channels (Freedom House's 2013 Freedom of the Press Report)
- As of 2012, Internet media were unrestricted and 93 percent of Danish citizens had Internet access (International Telecommunication Union's 2012 ICT Indicators Database)

In Brief

An exemplar of media freedom in almost every respect.

Chronology

1948–2012: Free

There has been little threat to the robustness of the free media as an essential aspect of Danish politics and society. There was some debate over the 2005 publication of controversial cartoons that depicted the Prophet Muhammad and caused a severe global crisis for Denmark. The repercussions included attacks on Danish embassies in the Middle East and condemnations from the UN Secretary General and former U.S. President Bill Clinton.[1]

(Continued)

Year	Media	Government
1974	Free	Democracy
1975	Free	Democracy
1976	Free	Democracy
1977	Free	Democracy
1978	Free	Democracy
1979	Free	Democracy
1980	Free	Democracy
1981	Free	Democracy
1982	Free	Democracy
1983	Free	Democracy
1984	Free	Democracy
1985	Free	Democracy
1986	Free	Democracy
1987	Free	Democracy
1988	Free	Democracy
1989	Free	Democracy
1990	Free	Democracy
1991	Free	Democracy
1992	Free	Democracy
1993	Free	Democracy
1994	Free	Democracy
1995	Free	Democracy
1996	Free	Democracy
1997	Free	Democracy

Year	Media	Government
1998	Free	Democracy
1999	Free	Democracy
2000	Free	Democracy
2001	Free	Democracy
2002	Free	Democracy
2003	Free	Democracy
2004	Free	Democracy
2005	Free	Democracy
2006	Free	Democracy
2007	Free	Democracy
2008	Free	Democracy
2009	Free	Democracy
2010	Free	Democracy
2011	Free	Democracy
2012	Free	Democracy

Media Today

Danish media are free, robust, diverse, and continue to provide an exemplar.

Note

1. *Denmark*, Media Landscape Reports (Maastricht, The Netherlands: European Journalism Centre, 2013). Available at http://ejc.net/media_landscapes/denmark.

Djibouti: 1977–2012

Djibouti Year by Year

Year	Media	Government
1977	Not Free	Autocracy
1978	Not Free	Autocracy
1979	Not Free	Autocracy
1980	Not Free	Autocracy
1981	Not Free	Autocracy
1982	Not Free	Autocracy
1983	Not Free	Autocracy
1984	Not Free	Autocracy
1985	Not Free	Autocracy
1986	Not Free	Autocracy
1987	Not Free	Autocracy
1988	Not Free	Autocracy
1989	Not Free	Autocracy
1990	Not Free	Autocracy
1991	Not Free	Autocracy
1992	Not Free	Autocracy
1993	Not Free	Autocracy
1994	Not Free	Autocracy
1995	Imperfectly Free	Autocracy
1996	Imperfectly Free	Autocracy
1997	Imperfectly Free	Autocracy
1998	Imperfectly Free	Autocracy
1999	Not Free	Anocracy
2000	Not Free	Anocracy

(Continued)

MEDIA FREEDOM HISTORY IN A NUTSHELL

- With the exception of four years during the 1990s, Djiboutian media have been controlled or restricted by government
- As of 2009, there was one paid-for daily newspaper with a total average circulation per issue of 5,000 (World Association of Newspaper's 2010 World Newspaper Trends)
- As of 2012, Djibouti had no privately owned Internet service providers, newspapers, radio stations, or television stations (Freedom House's 2013 Freedom of the Press Report)
- As of 2012, about 8 percent of Djiboutians had Internet access (Freedom House's 2013 Freedom of the Press Report)

In Brief

Djiboutian media are among the most restricted in Africa. Except for a brief period in the 1990s, news media have been controlled by government. Journalists who criticize government risk imprisonment, and consequently, self-censorship is common. The government owns and operates virtually all domestic media.

Chronology

1977–1994: Not Free

Formerly the French Territory of the Afars and the Issas, Djibouti gained independence in 1977. Under President Hassan Gouled Aptidon's Issa-dominated People's Rally for Progress (RPP) party, Djibouti was an authoritarian one-party state. Although there were no reports of overt government censorship in the late 1970s, media were government-owned and supportive of government policies, yet somewhat critical of local

(Continued)

Year	Media	Government
2001	Not Free	Anocracy
2002	Not Free	Anocracy
2003	Not Free	Anocracy
2004	Not Free	Anocracy
2005	Not Free	Anocracy
2006	Not Free	Anocracy
2007	Not Free	Anocracy
2008	Not Free	Anocracy
2009	Not Free	Anocracy
2010	Not Free	Anocracy
2011	Not Free	Anocracy
2012	Not Free	Anocracy

institutions.[1] In 1992, Djibouti adopted a new constitution that included provisions for media freedom, but the RPP maintained control over broadcast media and the country's most popular newspaper.[2] Still, opposition media began to emerge when the Party for Democratic Renewal (PRD) began publishing its own newspaper, *Le Renouveau*.[3] The constitution also called for multiparty elections, but the Afar-led Front for the Restoration of Unity and Democracy (FRUD) was banned from participating and the RPP continued to hold all important government positions. Consequently, unrest soon gave way to civil war.

1995–1998: Imperfectly Free

A 1994 power-sharing agreement between the government and FRUD was supposed to end the civil war, but a radical faction of FRUD continued to rebel. Yet by 1995, the media environment had improved to the point where media were imperfectly free. Opposition newspapers, which were critical of the government, circulated freely, but government retained control of broadcast media and the most popular newspaper, *La Nation*.[4] Djiboutians also had access to foreign broadcasts and print media.

1999–2012: Not Free

In 1999, after President Aptidon announced he would not run again, Ismael Omar Gelleh of the RPP was elected president. That same year, the government shutdown two opposition newspapers for six months and arrested the editors after the papers published a letter in which a FRUD leader claimed responsibility for the downing of an army helicopter.[5] Although President Gelleh signed a peace agreement with the FRUD in 2000, thereby ending the civil war, some unrest continued and the government prohibited the importation of two Somaliland newspapers.[6] Throughout the first decade of the 2000s, the government continued to crackdown on critical news outlets, closing down newspapers and imprisoning journalists on charges of distributing false information or defamation.[7]

Media Today

Djiboutian media remain restricted. The government owns and controls the only Internet service provider, all domestic broadcast media and the most popular newspaper. Since the early 2000s, the media environment has deteriorated and Djibouti is now "one of the few countries on the continent without any independent or privately owned newspapers."[8]

Notes

1. *Country Reports on Human Rights Practices for 1980* (Washington, DC: U.S. Department of State, 1981). Available at http://babel.hathitrust.org/cgi/pt?id=mdp.39015014143476;view=1up;seq=1.
2. *World Press Freedom Review* (Vienna: International Press Institute, 1993).
3. Ibid.
4. *Country Reports on Human Rights Practices for 1995* (Washington, DC: U.S. Department of State, 1996). Available at http://dosfan.lib.uic.edu/ERC/democracy/1995_hrp_report/95hrp_report_toc.html.
5. *Country Reports on Human Rights Practices for 2000* (Washington, DC: U.S. Department of State, 2001). Available at http://www.state.gov/j/drl/rls/hrrpt/2000/index.htm.
6. Ibid.
7. *Freedom of the Press* (Washington, DC: Freedom House, 2002).
8. *Freedom of the Press* (Washington, DC: Freedom House, 2013).

Dominica: 1978–2012

Dominica Year by Year

Year	Media	Government
1978	In Transition	In Transition
1979	Free	In Transition
1980	Free	Democracy
1981	Free	Democracy
1982	Free	Democracy
1983	Free	Democracy
1984	Free	Democracy
1985	Free	Democracy
1986	Free	Democracy
1987	Free	Democracy
1988	Free	Democracy
1989	Free	Democracy
1990	Free	Democracy
1991	Free	Democracy
1992	Free	Democracy
1993	Free	Democracy
1994	Free	Democracy
1995	Free	Democracy
1996	Free	Democracy
1997	Free	Democracy
1998	Free	Democracy
1999	Free	Democracy
2000	Free	Democracy
2001	Free	Democracy

(Continued)

MEDIA FREEDOM HISTORY IN A NUTSHELL

- Dominican news media have been free since independence
- Dominica has several independently owned weekly newspapers, but no daily newspaper
- Dominicans have access to both privately owned and state-owned radio stations and cable television
- As of 2012, more than 55 percent of Dominicans had Internet access (International Telecommunication Union's 2012 ICT Indicators Database)

In Brief

In spite of political turmoil in the first years following independence, news media in Dominica have remained free.

Chronology

1979–2012: Free

Shortly after Dominica gained independence from the United Kingdom, Prime Minister Patrick John tried to enact a press law that would have restricted the island's independently owned newspapers and another measure that would have prohibited strikes by government employees.[1] When thousands of people protested the proposed laws in front of the Assembly building, security forces opened fire, killing two people and wounding nine.[2] In response, the opposition called for a general strike that paralyzed the country for three weeks, and eventually, after all of his cabinet members resigned, John was forced out. Throughout the political turmoil, Dominica's three weekly newspapers were independent and critical of John and his

(Continued)

Year	Media	Government
2002	Free	Democracy
2003	Free	Democracy
2004	Free	Democracy
2005	Free	Democracy
2006	Free	Democracy
2007	Free	Democracy
2008	Free	Democracy
2009	Free	Democracy
2010	Free	Democracy
2011	Free	Democracy
2012	Free	Democracy

government.[3] The island's only radio station was government owned and operated, but did provide coverage of the opposition as well as the government.[4] Before Dominica could recover from this political turmoil, in August 1979, Hurricane David devastated the island and destroyed its banana crop. In August 1980, just before Eugenia Charles became prime minister, Hurricane Allen struck and destroyed the banana crop. In spite of the difficulties, government continued to respect media freedom. In 1981, a state of emergency was declared after an attempted coup, and for several months news coverage of the coup plot had to be reviewed by cabinet secretary, but none of the news stories were blocked.[5] Over the years, some journalists have been sued for libel or defamation, but by and large, the Dominican news media have remained free since independence.

Media Today

The Dominican constitution has provisions for media freedom, and the government respects these in practice. The island has four weekly papers, cable television, and a mix of privately owned and government-owned radio stations. More than half of the Dominicans have Internet access, and the Internet is unrestricted.

Notes

1. Parry Bellot, *International News: Roseau, Dominica* (The Associated Press, June 19, 1979).
2. Ibid.
3. *Country Reports on Human Rights for 1979* (Washington, DC: U.S. Department of State, 1980). Available at http://babel.hathitrust.org/cgi/pt?id=mdp.39015014188273;view=1up;seq=312.
4. Ibid.
5. *Country Reports on Human Rights for 1981* (Washington, DC: U.S. Department of State, 1982). Available at http://babel.hathitrust.org/cgi/pt?id=mdp.39015039359891;view=1up;seq=424.

Dominican Republic: 1948–2012

Dominican Republic Year by Year

Year	Media	Government
1948	Not Free	Autocracy
1949	Not Free	Autocracy
1950	Not Free	Autocracy
1951	Not Free	Autocracy
1952	Not Free	Autocracy
1953	Not Free	Autocracy
1954	Not Free	Autocracy
1955	Not Free	Autocracy
1956	Not Free	Autocracy
1957	Not Free	Autocracy
1958	Not Free	Autocracy
1959	Not Free	Autocracy
1960	Not Free	Autocracy
1961	Imperfectly Free	Anocracy
1962	Imperfectly Free	Democracy
1963	Imperfectly Free	Anocracy
1964	Imperfectly Free	Anocracy
1965	Imperfectly Free	Anocracy
1966	Imperfectly Free	Anocracy
1967	Imperfectly Free	Anocracy
1968	Imperfectly Free	Anocracy
1969	Imperfectly Free	Anocracy
1970	Imperfectly Free	Anocracy
1971	Imperfectly Free	Anocracy
1972	Imperfectly Free	Anocracy
1973	Imperfectly Free	Anocracy
1974	Imperfectly Free	Anocracy

(Continued)

MEDIA FREEDOM HISTORY IN A NUTSHELL

- Under the Trujillo dictatorship news media were restricted
- Following Trujillo's assassination and the subsequent regime change, news media became functionally free
- Journalists who criticize government sometimes face threats, harassment, or imprisonment
- As of 2012, the Dominican Republic had five daily newspapers, more than 300 radio and forty television stations, most of which were privately owned (Freedom House's 2013 Freedom of the Press Report)
- Roughly 45 percent of the country had Internet access in 2012 (International Telecommunication Union's 2012 ICT Indicators Database)

In Brief

During the Trujillo regime, the Dominican media were heavily restricted. In the early 1960s, independent media emerged and became a vibrant arena for political competition. Since then the media environment has straddled the border between imperfectly free and free. For the most part journalists are able to criticize government, but sometimes they face repercussions. Consequently, self-censorship is common.

Chronology

1948–1960: Not Free

Under the dictatorship of Rafael Leonidas Trujillo, all news media were restricted, and no opposition media were tolerated.[1] Additionally, foreign journalists (including the President of the Inter American Press Association) who were deemed "undesirable" were barred from the Dominican Republic.[2]

(Continued)

Year	Media	Government
1975	Imperfectly Free	Anocracy
1976	Imperfectly Free	Anocracy
1977	Imperfectly Free	Anocracy
1978	Free	Democracy
1979	Free	Democracy
1980	Free	Democracy
1981	Free	Democracy
1982	Free	Democracy
1983	Free	Democracy
1984	Free	Democracy
1985	Free	Democracy
1986	Free	Democracy
1987	Free	Democracy
1988	Free	Democracy
1989	Free	Democracy
1990	Free	Democracy
1991	Free	Democracy
1992	Free	Democracy
1993	Free	Democracy
1994	Imperfectly Free	Anocracy
1995	Imperfectly Free	Anocracy
1996	Imperfectly Free	Democracy
1997	Free	Democracy
1998	Free	Democracy
1999	Free	Democracy
2000	Free	Democracy
2001	Free	Democracy
2002	Imperfectly Free	Democracy
2003	Imperfectly Free	Democracy
2004	Imperfectly Free	Democracy
2005	Imperfectly Free	Democracy
2006	Imperfectly Free	Democracy
2007	Imperfectly Free	Democracy
2008	Imperfectly Free	Democracy
2009	Imperfectly Free	Democracy
2010	Imperfectly Free	Democracy
2011	Imperfectly Free	Democracy
2012	Imperfectly Free	Democracy

1961–1977: Imperfectly Free

Following the assassination of Trujillo, the Dominican Republic went through a "communications revolution" in which radio became accessible even in the remote regions of the country, and newspapers and television also extended their reach.[3]

Although the coverage of news stories was not always entirely professional, and although there had been attempts by government and the military over the years to intimidate, or even to close down, some papers and stations, by and large the Dominican media had been remarkably free, independent, and diverse since 1961. They performed an important educational function in the country, and they exerted an important influence in mobilizing the country politically. In fact, the mass media had become one of the most important bulwarks of Dominican democracy.[4]

Although media were functionally free, there were some threats. The Inter American Press Association noted that after three decades of dictatorship and controlled media, political leaders continued to seek to control news media.[5]

In 1963, a military coup overthrew President Juan Bosch, but the three-man civilian junta that replaced him for the most part kept its promise to maintain media freedom.[6] In 1965, civil war broke out when Bosch's supporters tried to reclaim the presidency for him. Eventually the United States intervened (motivated in part by concerns about communist support for Bosch). During this conflict, there were some restrictions on media freedom and several papers had to suspend publication.[7] When the conflict ended and Joaquin Balaguer was elected president, media remained independent and somewhat critical of government. "Such criticism was just candid enough to be discernible to readers and listeners but tactfully discreet enough to avoid a repressive backlash."[8]

1978–1993: Free

In the 1978 elections, Antonio Guzman defeated Balaguer, and under his leadership, the media environment improved to the point that the media were fully free.[9] In 1986, Balaguer returned to power.

1994–1996: Imperfectly Free

Balaguer was reelected to his seventh term in 1994, but there were allegations of fraud, and after mass protests, Balaguer agreed to limit his term to two years. In the aftermath of the election, there were several incidents in which police detained and/or beat journalists.[10] Shortly after the elections, Narcisco Gonzalez, a journalist and professor who had been critical of President Balaguer, disappeared. Years later, in 2012, the Inter-American Court of Human Rights ruled that the government was responsible.[11] In 1995, reporter Juan Carlos Vasquez was gunned down by an off-duty policeman who was charged with murder. These incidents, though isolated, likely had a chilling effect on the news media.

1997–2001: Free

In 1996, Leonel Fernandez was elected president, and though there were some complaints of police attacks on journalists, by and large the media were vibrant and free.[12]

2002–2012: Imperfectly Free

In 2002, the media environment deteriorated to the point that media were only imperfectly free. Although news media were for the most part able to criticize the government, those that did risked losing advertising revenue.[13] Newspapers also faced increased taxes on newsprint.[14] Thus, journalists tended to self-censor.

Media Today

The 2010 constitution provides for media freedom, but the government sometimes disregards these provisions in practice. At the end of 2013, the Constitutional Court was considering a petition to annul articles of a law that allows prison terms for libel and defamation convictions.[15] Journalists remain vulnerable to attacks and harassment.[16] Although ownership is concentrated, the Dominican Republic has hundreds of radio stations, a several dozen television stations, five daily newspapers, and an increasing range of online media.[17]

Notes

1. *State of the Press*, 1956 Annual Meeting (Miami, FL: Inter American Press Association, 1957).
2. *World Press Freedom Review* (Zurich: International Press Institute, 1958), month/page number not visible, slide 81 on 1958 reports pdf.
3. Richard A. Haggerty, *Dominican Republic: A Country Study* (Washington, DC: Library of Congress Federal Research Division, 1989). Available at http://lcweb2.loc.gov/frd/cs/.
4. Ibid. "The Media," para. 8.
5. *Report by Committee on Freedom of the Press*, 1962 General Meeting (Miami, FL: Inter American Press Association, 1963).
6. *Report by Committee on Freedom of the Press*, 1963 General Meeting (Miami, FL: Inter American Press Association, 1964).
7. *Press Freedom in 1965: The Gains Outweighed the Losses*, IPI Report (Zurich: International Press Institute, 1966).
8. Marvin Alisky, "Mass Media in the Dominican Republic," in *Mass Media and the Caribbean*, ed. Stuart H. Surlin and Walter C. Soderlund (New York: Gordon and Breach Science Publishers, 1990), 179.
9. Ibid.
10. *Country Reports on Human Rights Practices for 1994* (Washington, DC: U.S. Department of State, 1995). Available at http://dosfan.lib.uic.edu/ERC/democracy/1994_hrp_report/94hrp_report_toc.html.
11. Emily Willard, *Forced Disappearance in the Dominican Republic* (The National Security Archive, 2013). Available at http://www2.gwu.edu/~nsarchiv/NSAEBB/NSAEBB429/.
12. *World Press Freedom Review*, IPI Report (Vienna: International Press Institute, 1998), 76.
13. *Freedom of the Press* (Washington, DC: Freedom House, 2003).
14. Ibid.
15. *General Assembly* (Miami, FL: Inter American Press Association, 2013). Available at http://www.sipiapa.org/en/asambleas.
16. *Freedom of the Press* (Washington, DC: Freedom House, 2013).
17. Ibid.

Ecuador: 1948–2012

Ecuador Year by Year

Year	Media	Government
1948	Not Free	Anocracy
1949	Not Free	Anocracy
1950	Not Free	Anocracy
1951	Not Free	Anocracy
1952	Not Free	Anocracy
1953	Not Free	Anocracy
1954	Not Free	Anocracy
1955	Not Free	Anocracy
1956	Not Free	Anocracy
1957	Free	Anocracy
1958	Free	Anocracy
1959	Free	Anocracy
1960	Free	Anocracy
1961	Free	Anocracy
1962	Free	Anocracy
1963	Free	Anocracy
1964	Free	Anocracy
1965	Free	Anocracy
1966	Free	Anocracy
1967	Free	Anocracy
1968	Free	Anocracy
1969	Free	Anocracy
1970	Free	Anocracy
1971	Free	Anocracy
1972	Imperfectly Free	Anocracy
1973	Imperfectly Free	Anocracy
1974	Imperfectly Free	Anocracy
1975	Imperfectly Free	Anocracy

MEDIA FREEDOM HISTORY IN A NUTSHELL

- Ecuador's history of political instability has often led to a contentious relationship between government and news media
- Although most news media outlets are independently owned, journalists who criticize the government have faced threats, fines, and imprisonment
- The Communication Organic Law passed in 2013 gave the government new authority to regulate news media and punish journalists
- As of 2011, Ecuador had 47 daily newspapers with an average circulation per issue of 697,000 (World Association of Newspaper's 2012 World Newspaper Trends)
- Radio is the most prevalent medium and is dominated by the private sector (World Association of Newspaper's 2010 World Newspaper Trends)
- As of 2012, 35 percent of Ecuadorians had Internet access (International Telecommunication Union's 2012 ICT Indicators Database)

In Brief

Political turmoil has made it difficult for media to function freely:

Perhaps the most consistent element of Ecuador's republican history has been its political instability. In just over a century and a half, there have been no fewer than eighty-six changes of government, making for an average of 1.75 years in power for each regime.[1]

News media are often caught up in these political struggles.

Year	Media	Government
1976	Imperfectly Free	Anocracy
1977	Imperfectly Free	Anocracy
1978	Imperfectly Free	Anocracy
1979	Imperfectly Free	Democracy
1980	Imperfectly Free	Democracy
1981	Imperfectly Free	Democracy
1982	Imperfectly Free	Democracy
1983	Imperfectly Free	Democracy
1984	Imperfectly Free	Democracy
1985	Imperfectly Free	Democracy
1986	Imperfectly Free	Democracy
1987	Imperfectly Free	Democracy
1988	Free	Democracy
1989	Free	Democracy
1990	Free	Democracy
1991	Free	Democracy
1992	Free	Democracy
1993	Free	Democracy
1994	Free	Democracy
1995	Free	Democracy
1996	Free	Democracy
1997	Free	Democracy
1998	Free	Democracy
1999	Free	Democracy
2000	Free	Democracy
2001	Free	Democracy
2002	Imperfectly Free	Democracy
2003	Imperfectly Free	Democracy
2004	Imperfectly Free	Democracy
2005	Imperfectly Free	Democracy
2006	Imperfectly Free	Democracy
2007	Imperfectly Free	Anocracy
2008	Imperfectly Free	Anocracy
2009	Imperfectly Free	Anocracy
2010	Imperfectly Free	Anocracy
2011	Imperfectly Free	Anocracy
2012	Not Free	Anocracy

Chronology

1948–1956: Not Free

Although many news media were independently owned, and therefore not under direct control of government, during this period government successfully controlled media, often through indirect means such as harassment and intimidation and economic pressures. There were frequent reports of attacks on journalists, including the bombing of a reporter's home in Guayaquil in 1952.[2] In 1953, progovernment protesters raided the offices of two major opposition newspapers in Guayaquil, and rather than punish the protesters, the government arrested a publisher and several journalists.[3] In addition to these attacks, the government boosted the price of newsprint for opposition newspapers and sometimes banned them or forced them to close.[4]

1957–1971: Free

In 1956, President-elect Camilo Ponce Enríquez pledged that he would restore freedom of the press to his country because "a free press constitutes the most powerful means of maintaining world peace and developing a civilization that can live in harmony."[5] When he took office in 1957, Ponce made good on this pledge.

1972–1987: Imperfectly Free

In 1972, the military overthrew President José Maria Velasco Ibarra and replaced him with a military junta lead by General Guillermo Rodriguez Lara. While news media remained functionally free, journalists were subject to government pressure. For example in 1973, Rodriguez Lara encouraged reporters to engage in "a noble and well understood self-censorship."[6] In 1978, the military government prepared to return the country to constitutional rule and made it clear that a free press would be an important part of the transition, yet the government warned that it would not tolerate any criticism of armed forces.[7] The 1979 Constitution included provisions for freedom of expression, but media ownership was highly concentrated.

1988–2001: Free

In 1987, the government tried to silence opposition radio and television stations, but as President Febres Cordero's popularity deteriorated, the government lost its power to pressure and stifle independent media. In 1988, President Borja took office and took steps to improve media freedom and make the government more accessible to journalists.[8]

2002–2011: Imperfectly Free

In February of 2002, the war in Colombia prompted unrest and antigovernment protests in the Ecuadoran border provinces of Sucumbios and Orellana. In response, President Gustavo Noboa declared a state of emergency, suspended media freedom and shut down four radio stations.[9]

In 2003, President Lucio Gutiérrez, a former coup leader, took office. His administration was considerably more aggressive toward, and far less accessible to, news media. For example Gutiérrez pressured *El Comercio*, a daily newspaper, to reveal its sources for a story that connected a donation to Gutiérrez's campaign to drug trafficking money.[10] (The newspaper refused.)

2012: Not Free

In 2011, President Rafael Correa referred to reporters as "assassins with ink."[11] The relationship between the government and news media became increasingly contentious in 2012. Journalists who criticized the government were charged with libel and defamation, and several faced steep fines and prison sentences. Correa also used his line-item veto power to modify an electoral reform law and restrain the media's coverage of election campaigns. In June of 2013, the Ecuadoran National Assembly passed the Communication Organic Law that established the Council for the Regulation and Development of Information and the Department of Information and Communication, both of which have the authority to regulate and punish news media. Additionally the Communication Organic Law established new crimes including "'media lynching,' defined as the repeated dissemination of information with the aim of discrediting or reducing the credibility of individuals or legal entities."[12] This legislation was widely condemned by media freedom monitoring groups. Ironically, in 2012—the same year media freedom decreased within Ecuador—the government granted asylum to WikiLeaks founder Julian Assange in the Ecuadoran embassy in London.

Media Today

Although most media outlets are privately owned, the government effectively constrains media freedom through laws and practices. The relationship between media and government remains combative. Libel and defamation are criminal offenses. Journalists who criticize the government face threats, fines, and imprisonment.

Notes

1. Dennis M. Hanratty, *Ecuador: A Country Study* (Washington, DC: GPO for the Library of Congress, 1989). Available at http://lcweb2.loc.gov/frd/cs/ectoc.html.
2. *News of the World Press*, IPI Report (Zurich: International Press Institute, November 1952), 8.
3. *Government Pressures on the Press* (Zurich: International Press Institute, 1955), 102.
4. Ibid.
5. *Freedom in Ecuador Pledged* (Miami, FL: Inter American Press Association, September 1956), 4.
6. *Press Freedom Report*, IPI Report (Zurich: International Press Institute, 1973), 8.
7. *World Press Freedom Review*, IPI Report (Zurich: International Press Institute, 1978), 7.
8. Hanratty, *Ecuador: A Country Study*.
9. *Country Report: Ecuador*, 58th General Assembly, Lima Peru Reports and Resolutions (Miami, FL: Inter American Press Association, 2002). Available at http://www.sipiapa.org/v4/archivo_de_asambleas.php?idioma=us.
10. *Freedom of the Press* (Washington, DC: Freedom House, 2004). Available at http://www.freedomhouse.org/report/freedom-press/2004/ecuador
11. *Freedom of the Press* (Washington, DC: Freedom House, 2012). Available at http://www.freedomhouse.org/report/freedom-press/2012/ecuador.
12. *IAPA Protests New 'Press Crimes' Enacted by Ecuador's President Correa* (Miami, FL: Inter American Press Association, June 24, 2013). Available at http://www.sipiapa.org/v4/comunicados_de_prensa.php?seccion=detalles&id=4899&idioma=us.

Egypt: 1948–2012

Egypt Year by Year

Year	Media	Government
1948	Not Free	Anocracy
1949	Not Free	Anocracy
1950	Not Free	Anocracy
1951	Not Free	Anocracy
1952	Not Free	Autocracy
1953	Not Free	Autocracy
1954	Not Free	Autocracy
1955	Not Free	Autocracy
1956	Not Free	Autocracy
1957	Not Free	Autocracy
1958	Not Free	Autocracy
1959	Not Free	Autocracy
1960	Not Free	Autocracy
1961	Not Free	Autocracy
1962	Not Free	Autocracy
1963	Not Free	Autocracy
1964	Not Free	Autocracy
1965	Not Free	Autocracy
1966	Not Free	Autocracy
1967	Not Free	Autocracy
1968	Not Free	Autocracy
1969	Not Free	Autocracy
1970	Not Free	Autocracy
1971	Not Free	Autocracy
1972	Not Free	Autocracy
1973	Not Free	Autocracy
1974	Not Free	Autocracy

(Continued)

MEDIA FREEDOM HISTORY IN A NUTSHELL

- As a hereditary monarchy and then an authoritarian regime, government maintained indirect control of the large media establishment
- The state of emergency imposed during the Six Day War included full control of the media. This was not revoked until 2011
- As of 2012, Egypt had upwards of 500 periodicals, almost all of which had remained under strict government control during the Mubarak regime (Freedom House's 2013 Freedom of the Press report)
- Since February of 2011, at least sixteen television stations began to operate. However, it remains difficult to effectively analyze ownership and financial patterns (Freedom House's 2013 Freedom of the Press report)
- As of 2012, 44 percent of Egyptians had regular access to the Internet, and almost 70 percent had access to mobile phones (Freedom House's 2013 Freedom of the Press report)

In Brief

Prior to the late 2000s, Egyptian media were controlled—either directly or indirectly—by government. In 2007, President Hosni Mubarak relaxed some of the restrictions on news media, but by 2010, the restrictions returned. Following the mass protests of 2011 and the resignation of Mubarak, there was a burst of media freedom and new independent outlets emerged. Yet in the power struggle that ensued in 2012, media were once again restricted.

Chronology

1948–2006: Not Free

Even though Egypt gained independence from Britain in 1922, the legacy of British rule

(Continued)

Year	Media	Government
1975	Not Free	Autocracy
1976	Not Free	Autocracy
1977	Not Free	Autocracy
1978	Not Free	Autocracy
1979	Not Free	Autocracy
1980	Not Free	Autocracy
1981	Not Free	Autocracy
1982	Not Free	Autocracy
1983	Not Free	Autocracy
1984	Not Free	Autocracy
1985	Not Free	Autocracy
1986	Not Free	Autocracy
1987	Not Free	Autocracy
1988	Not Free	Autocracy
1989	Not Free	Autocracy
1990	Not Free	Autocracy
1991	Not Free	Autocracy
1992	Not Free	Autocracy
1993	Not Free	Autocracy
1994	Not Free	Autocracy
1995	Not Free	Autocracy
1996	Not Free	Autocracy
1997	Not Free	Autocracy
1998	Not Free	Autocracy
1999	Not Free	Autocracy
2000	Not Free	Autocracy
2001	Not Free	Autocracy
2002	Not Free	Autocracy
2003	Not Free	Autocracy
2004	Not Free	Autocracy
2005	Not Free	Anocracy
2006	Not Free	Anocracy
2007	Imperfectly Free	Anocracy
2008	Imperfectly Free	Anocracy
2009	Imperfectly Free	Anocracy
2010	Not Free	Anocracy
2011	Imperfectly Free	In Transition
2012	Not Free	In Transition

and the continued presence of the British military were evident in the variety of newspapers being published, including several in English. The hereditary monarchy exerted significant, but indirect control. A 1953 military coup led to Gamal Abdel Nasser seizing power, but he retained the status quo of the government relationship with the press until the Six Day War in June of 1967.[1]

During the Six Day War, Nasser imposed a state of emergency and shifted from exerting indirect control to direct control over media.[2]

Hosni Mubarak became president in October 1981, after the assassination of President Anwar Sadat. Mubarak—unlike his two predecessors—moved toward more press freedom and lifted many of the restrictions and censorship. In particular, restrictions on some opposition press were relaxed.[3]

The result was a return to the indirect controls practiced before the Six Day War.

In 1996, significant changes in laws marked the end of Mubarak's toleration of a somewhat independent media. New definitions of libel and increased penalties were coupled with increased prosecution of journalists and resulted in a return of full and direct control of the media by the government.[4] Concessions were made in response to protests, but prosecutions did not abate.

In 2004, pro-reform demonstrations led to a referendum that allowed multiple candidates to stand for elections. This was the beginning of a democratic shift in Egyptian politics, and it included an easing of the strict government restrictions on the news media.[5]

2007–2009: Imperfectly Free

It is clear that there was continued easing of media restrictions after 2004. Although several opposition parties were openly publishing newspapers, Egypt only barely attained a functionally free media system during this period. Critical reporting in party newspapers was tolerated, but journalists were still frequently the subject of arrest and harassment.[6]

2010: Not Free

A relatively modest deterioration in conditions for the media, apparently driven by the military, brought Egypt clearly back into the restricted category. Arrest and detention was relatively common, and the violent intimidation of journalists was frequently noted.[7]

2011: Imperfectly Free

Following the mass protests at the beginning of 2011, Hosni Mubarak was forced out of the presidency in February. Bolstered by the apparent success of the protests, independent news outlets sprung up in Egypt.

2012: Not Free

The media quickly became caught in the political power struggles between opponents and supporters of the Muslim Brotherhood. As both sides sought to influence and intimidate the media, the environment deteriorated to the point that the media were not free.

Media Today

The wave of revolts and unrest commonly called the *Arab Spring* established the political power of new forms of communication, and with the elections that followed, it briefly it appeared that Egypt might respond by shifting to a free media environment. The military's reassertion of control and the violence that followed dashed that hope, and the state of emergency that has technically been in place since 1967 has been reasserted.

Notes

1. *The Freedom of the Press*, IPI Report (Zurich: International Press Institute, October 1953).
2. *News of the World's Press: Arab-Israel War Tests the Press*, IPI Report (Zurich: International Press Institute, July/August 1967).
3. *World Press Freedom Review*, IPI Report (Zurich: International Press Institute, December1983).
4. *World Press Freedom Review*, IPI Report (Vienna: International Press Institute, December 1996/ January 1997).
5. *Freedom of the Press* (Washington, DC: Freedom House, 2005).
6. *Freedom of the Press* (Washington, DC: Freedom House, 2008).
7. *Freedom of the Press* (Washington, DC: Freedom House, 2011).

El Salvador: 1948–2012

El Salvador Year by Year

Year	Media	Government
1948	Not Free	In Transition
1949	Not Free	In Transition
1950	Imperfectly Free	Autocracy
1951	Imperfectly Free	Autocracy
1952	Imperfectly Free	Autocracy
1953	Imperfectly Free	Autocracy
1954	Imperfectly Free	Autocracy
1955	Imperfectly Free	Autocracy
1956	Imperfectly Free	Anocracy
1957	Imperfectly Free	Anocracy
1958	Imperfectly Free	Anocracy
1959	Imperfectly Free	Anocracy
1960	Imperfectly Free	Anocracy
1961	Imperfectly Free	Anocracy
1962	Imperfectly Free	Anocracy
1963	Imperfectly Free	Anocracy
1964	Imperfectly Free	Anocracy
1965	Imperfectly Free	Anocracy
1966	Imperfectly Free	Anocracy
1967	Imperfectly Free	Anocracy
1968	Imperfectly Free	Anocracy
1969	Imperfectly Free	Anocracy
1970	Imperfectly Free	Anocracy
1971	Imperfectly Free	Anocracy
1972	Imperfectly Free	Anocracy
1973	Imperfectly Free	Anocracy
1974	Imperfectly Free	Anocracy
1975	Imperfectly Free	Anocracy

MEDIA FREEDOM HISTORY IN A NUTSHELL

- In spite of a nondemocratic government, Salvadoran media were functionally free during the 1950s, 1960s, and much of the 1970s

- In the late 1970s, the media environment deteriorated as conflict intensified

- With the reestablishment of peace in the early 1990s, media freedom returned to El Salvador

- As of 2012, El Salvador had four daily newspapers (Freedom House's 2013 Freedom of the Press report)

- With the exception of one state-run radio station, all broadcast media are privately owned

- In 2012, almost 26 percent of the country had Internet access (International Telecommunication Union's 2012 ICT Indicators Database)

In Brief

For much of El Salvador's recent history, news media have been imperfectly free—even when other civil liberties have been restricted. This is likely due to the power of the Salvadoran media oligarchy. Yet, when conflict escalated in the late 1970s, journalists were vulnerable to attacks by both sides and media were not free.

Chronology

1948–1949: Not Free

When General Salvador Castaneda Castro tried to extend his term as president in 1948, he was overthrown by a group of younger officers who called themselves the Juventud Militar.[1] During these years under military rule, news media were restricted.

Year	Media	Government
1976	Imperfectly Free	Anocracy
1977	Imperfectly Free	Autocracy
1978	Not Free	Autocracy
1979	Not Free	Anocracy
1980	Not Free	Anocracy
1981	Not Free	Anocracy
1982	Not Free	Anocracy
1983	Not Free	Anocracy
1984	Not Free	Democracy
1985	Not Free	Democracy
1986	Not Free	Democracy
1987	Not Free	Democracy
1988	Not Free	Democracy
1989	Not Free	Democracy
1990	Not Free	Democracy
1991	Not Free	Democracy
1992	Not Free	Democracy
1993	Imperfectly Free	Democracy
1994	Imperfectly Free	Democracy
1995	Imperfectly Free	Democracy
1996	Imperfectly Free	Democracy
1997	Imperfectly Free	Democracy
1998	Imperfectly Free	Democracy
1999	Imperfectly Free	Democracy
2000	Imperfectly Free	Democracy
2001	Imperfectly Free	Democracy
2002	Imperfectly Free	Democracy
2003	Imperfectly Free	Democracy
2004	Imperfectly Free	Democracy
2005	Imperfectly Free	Democracy
2006	Imperfectly Free	Democracy
2007	Imperfectly Free	Democracy
2008	Imperfectly Free	Democracy
2009	Imperfectly Free	Democracy
2010	Imperfectly Free	Democracy
2011	Imperfectly Free	Democracy
2012	Imperfectly Free	Democracy

1950–1977: Imperfectly Free

In 1950, as the military junta moved to hold open elections, restrictions on news media were relaxed to the point where media were imperfectly free.[2] In 1961, a military coup brought the right-wing National Conciliation Party into power, and although many civil liberties were limited at this time, the Inter American Press Association noted that the press remained free.[3] In part, this was probably due to the power of El Salvador's media oligarchy.[4]

1978–1992: Not Free

In the late 1970s, media freedom deteriorated as conflict erupted between the government and left-wing Farabundo Marti National Liberation Front (FMLN).[5] Throughout the 1980s, as the country descended into civil war, journalists faced threats from many quarters as the FMLN attacks intensified and the U.S.-backed government's army supported death squads that killed thousands of people.[6]

1993–2012: Imperfectly Free

The media environment improved in the early 1990s, as the FMLN was recognized as a political party and a peace agreement was reached. Yet, in October 1993, there were a number of violent attacks on journalists and news outlets as the country prepared for the 1994 elections.[7] In the late 1990s, the attacks on journalists declined, but journalists continued to face pressures and new laws limited journalists' access to the courts.[8] In 2011, El Salvador decriminalized libel, defamation, and slander.

Media Today

El Salvador has constitutional provisions for media freedom, and the government for the most part respects these in practice. Attacks on journalists are less frequent than they were in the 1990s, but they are not unheard of. El Salvador has four daily newspapers, five television stations (all of which are privately owned), and numerous radio stations. More than a fourth of Salvadorans have Internet access, and online news media continue to emerge and garner public attention.

Notes

1. Richard A. Haggarty, *El Salvador: A Country Study* (Washington, DC: Library of Congress Federal Research Division, 2013). Available at http://lcweb2 .loc.gov/frd/cs/.
2. *IAPA Reports* (Miami, FL: Inter American Press Association, February 1952).
3. *Freedom of the Press Committee Report*, 1963 General Assembly (Miami, FL: Inter American Press Association. 1964).
4. Catherine Salzman and Ryan Salzman, "The Media in Central America: Costa Richa, El Salvadore, Guatemala, Honduras, Nicaragua and Panama," in *The Handbook of Spanish Language Media*, ed. Alan B. Albarran (New York: Routledge, 2009).
5. *Report of the Committee on Freedom of the Press and Information*, 1978 General Assembly (Miami, FL: Inter American Press Association, 1979).
6. Salzman and Salzman, "The Media in Central America: Costa Richa, El Salvadore, Guatemala, Hondoras, Nicaragua and Panama."
7. *1993 General Assembly* (Miami, FL: Inter American Press Association, 1993). Available at http://www .sipiapa.org/en/asamblea/el-salvador-76/.
8. *World Press Freedom Review*, IPI Report (Vienna: International Press Institute, December 1998).

Equatorial Guinea: 1969–2012

Equatorial Guinea Year by Year

Year	Media	Government
1969	Not Free	Autocracy
1970	Not Free	Autocracy
1971	Not Free	Autocracy
1972	Not Free	Autocracy
1973	Not Free	Autocracy
1974	Not Free	Autocracy
1975	Not Free	Autocracy
1976	Not Free	Autocracy
1977	Not Free	Autocracy
1978	Not Free	Autocracy
1979	Not Free	Autocracy
1980	Not Free	Autocracy
1981	Not Free	Autocracy
1982	Not Free	Autocracy
1983	Not Free	Autocracy
1984	Not Free	Autocracy
1985	Not Free	Autocracy
1986	Not Free	Autocracy
1987	Not Free	Autocracy
1988	Not Free	Autocracy
1989	Not Free	Autocracy
1990	Not Free	Autocracy
1991	Not Free	Autocracy
1992	Not Free	Autocracy

(Continued)

MEDIA FREEDOM HISTORY IN A NUTSHELL

- Since independence, Equatorial Guinea has been ruled by repressive dictators who have maintained tight control over the Equatoguinean media
- As of 2013, Equatorial Guinea had one state-owned newspaper and several privately owned newspapers, one state-run television station, one state-run radio station, and one radio station owned by the President's son (BBC News Country Profiles)
- As of 2012, about 14 percent of Equatoguineans had Internet access (Freedom House's Report on Freedom of the Press 2013)

In Brief

Since gaining independence from Spain in 1968, Equatorial Guinea has been ruled by two repressive dictators, and both regimes have exerted tight control over media.

Chronology

1969–2012: Not Free

Franciso Macias Nguema became the first president of the Equatorial Guinea when the country gained independence in 1968. During Macias's tenure, newspapers "ceased to exist" and the government owned and operated all broadcast media.[1] Little changed for the news media when Macias was overthrown in 1979 in a coup lead by his nephew Teodoro Obiang Nguema Mbasogo.[2] Under Nguema, media have remained controlled.

Media Today

Nguema is now Africa's longest serving leader, and Reporters Without Borders characterizes him

(Continued)

Year	Media	Government
1993	Not Free	Autocracy
1994	Not Free	Autocracy
1995	Not Free	Autocracy
1996	Not Free	Autocracy
1997	Not Free	Autocracy
1998	Not Free	Autocracy
1999	Not Free	Autocracy
2000	Not Free	Autocracy
2001	Not Free	Autocracy
2002	Not Free	Autocracy
2003	Not Free	Autocracy
2004	Not Free	Autocracy
2005	Not Free	Autocracy
2006	Not Free	Autocracy
2007	Not Free	Autocracy
2008	Not Free	Autocracy
2009	Not Free	Autocracy
2010	Not Free	Autocracy
2011	Not Free	Autocracy
2012	Not Free	Autocracy

as a "predator of press freedom."[3] All broadcast media are either government owned and operated or owned by the president's family.[4] Although there are several privately owned newspapers, they lack the financial and technical capacity to publish with any regularity.[5] According to Freedom House, the Internet is now the primary source of news from the opposition, but only about 14 percent of Equatoguineans have Internet access.[6]

Notes

1. *Country Reports on Human Rights Practices for 1979* (Washington, DC: U.S. Department of State, 1980), 64. Available at http://babel.hathitrust.org/cgi/pt?id=mdp.39015014188273;view=1up;seq=76.
2. Ibid.
3. *World Report: Equatorial Guinea* (Paris, France: Reporters Without Borders, 2012). Available at http://en.rsf.org/report-equatorial-guinea,21.html.
4. Ibid.
5. Ibid.
6. *Freedom of the Press* (Washington, DC: Freedom House, 2013). Available at http://www.freedomhouse.org/report/freedom-press/2013/equatorial-guinea.

Eritrea: 1993–2012

Eritrea Year by Year

Year	Media	Government
1993	Not Free	Autocracy
1994	Not Free	Autocracy
1995	Not Free	Autocracy
1996	Not Free	Autocracy
1997	Not Free	Autocracy
1998	Not Free	Autocracy
1999	Not Free	Autocracy
2000	Not Free	Autocracy
2001	Not Free	Autocracy
2002	Not Free	Autocracy
2003	Not Free	Autocracy
2004	Not Free	Autocracy
2005	Not Free	Autocracy
2006	Not Free	Autocracy
2007	Not Free	Autocracy
2008	Not Free	Autocracy
2009	Not Free	Autocracy
2010	Not Free	Autocracy
2011	Not Free	Autocracy
2012	Not Free	Autocracy

In Brief

Since Eritrea gained independence, its media have been among the most censored in the world. In 2001, the government prohibited private and foreign ownership of media.

> **MEDIA FREEDOM HISTORY IN A NUTSHELL**
>
> - Eritrean media are among the world's most censored
> - In 2001, the government prohibited private ownership of media
> - As of 2013, an estimated twenty-eight journalists remained imprisoned without charges, many of them had been held since 2001 (Committee to Protect Journalists)
> - As of 2013, Eritrea had four newspapers, one television station and two radio stations—all of which are run by the government or the ruling party (BBC News Country Profiles)
> - As of 2012, about 8 percent of Eritreans had access to the Internet (International Telecommunication Union's 2012 ICT Indicators Database)

Chronology

1993–2012: Not Free

Following a bloody three-decade fight for independence from Ethiopia, Eritrea officially became independent in 1993, but Eritrean media remained restricted. President Isaias Afworki maintained tight control over the news media via the Ministry of Information and Culture.[1] Although Eritrea became involved in conflict in the mid-1990s, first with Yemen and then with Ethiopia, independent newspapers and magazines emerged. Yet the 1997 press law required that all media reflect "the objective reality of Eritrea."[2] The government retained control of all broadcast media. Also in 1997, *Agence France Press* reporter Ruth Simon was arrested and held without trial for twenty months on allegations that she disseminated false information.

In 2001, President Afworki closed down all independent news media and imprisoned a number of journalists—according to media monitors at least fourteen.[3,4] In 2006, as many as nine journalists for the state-run media were arrested.[5] In all, the Committee to Protect Journalists estimates that twenty-eight journalists, most of whom were never charged, remain imprisoned in secret locations in Eritrea, and it is feared that some of them have died.[6]

Media Today

Reporters Without Borders has placed Eritrea at the bottom of its 2013 Press Freedom Index—just below North Korea.[7] In 2012, the Committee to Protect Journalists identified Eritrea as the world's "most censored country."[8] Calls for reform from nongovernment organizations and the United Nations have gone unheeded.

Notes

1. *World Press Freedom Review*, IPI Report (Vienna: International Press Institute, November/December 1995).
2. *World Press Freedom Review*, IPI Report (Vienna: International Press Institute, 1999), 24.
3. *World Press Freedom Review*, IPI Report (Vienna: International Press Institute, 2001).
4. *World Press Freedom Review*, IPI Report (Vienna: International Press Institute, 2002).
5. *World Press Freedom Review*, IPI Report (Vienna: International Press Institute, 2006).
6. *Attacks on the Press 2012: Eritrea* (Committee to Protect Journalists, 2012). Available at https://cpj.org/africa/eritrea/.
7. *2013 World Press Freedom Index: Dashed Hopes After Spring* (Paris, France: Reporters Without Borders, 2013). Available at http://en.rsf.org/press-freedom-index-2013,1054.html.
8. *Attacks on the Press 2012: Eritrea*.

Estonia: 1991–2012

Estonia Year by Year

Year	Media	Government
1991	In Transition	Democracy
1992	Not Free	Democracy
1993	Not Free	Democracy
1994	Not Free	Democracy
1995	Free	Democracy
1996	Free	Democracy
1997	Free	Democracy
1998	Free	Democracy
1999	Free	Democracy
2000	Free	Democracy
2001	Free	Democracy
2002	Free	Democracy
2003	Free	Democracy
2004	Free	Democracy
2005	Free	Democracy
2006	Free	Democracy
2007	Free	Democracy
2008	Free	Democracy
2009	Free	Democracy
2010	Free	Democracy
2011	Free	Democracy
2012	Free	Democracy

In Brief

True independence was delayed by the occupation by Russian troops, but once full independence

MEDIA FREEDOM HISTORY IN A NUTSHELL

- It took three years of peaceful political struggle after independence to establish free media, but then a steady transition was made to a commercial media system
- Support from Scandinavia appears to have prevented the rebound toward control in response to authoritarian counter challenges
- The notable language division between ethnic Russians and Estonians led to different media consumption patterns
- Estonia has a mix of private and public radio stations and television channels
- As of 2011, there were twelve paid-for daily newspapers with a total average circulation per issue of 204,400 (World Association of Newspaper's 2012 World Newspaper Trends)
- As of 2012, about 79 percent of Estonians had Internet access (International Telecommunication Union's 2012 ICT Indicators Database)

was secured, media freedom was established and has been sustained and developed since. Media consumption patterns are notably different in ethnic Estonian and ethnic Russian populations, with a free flow of information into the country providing variety.

Chronology

1991: In Transition

As with other former Soviet Republics, 1991 was a disrupted and unsettled transitional year that was impossible to define. Estonia was far less disrupted by the dissolution of the USSR than other former Soviet Republics, but a long tradition of Western ties and minor but constant efforts to resist Soviet control meant that the government had somewhat limited interest in enforcing authoritarian control.

The press began to transition to an independent sector. One at a time, newspapers became privately owned under an agreement with the government.[1]

1992–1994: Not Free

Occupied by Russian military forces, this period was marked by peaceful but persistent negotiations that led to the withdrawal of foreign forces. During this time, challenges to media control were limited. Media remained heavily restricted to the point of almost complete governmental control. Even though the country enjoyed the most developed press of all the Baltic States, publishers protested in 1993 against a proposed sales tax on newspapers.[2]

1995–2012: Free

A free media regime was established almost immediately upon withdrawal of Russian troops. Heavily supported by Scandinavian countries, there was little if any counter push by conservative forces and the continued development of a commercial media has been a clear feature in the years since independence. By 1995, Estonia had more television channels and newspapers per citizen than most countries;

however, it faced financial difficulties as the price of publishing rose.[3]

Media Today

Media Freedom is robust and information is readily available, but Estonia faces all the difficulties associated with a very small market, economic pressures, limited ability to commercially support competitive outlets, and ownership concentration. Support from the Scandinavian countries has been vital, but it remains to be seen how the development in Estonia can be sustained as that external support is wound down. It is also unclear how the Russian-speaking minority will factor into that future. They currently consume primarily foreign media but may become more assertive in their demand for locally generated Russian-language media if the decline in Scandinavian economic support threatens Estonian language outlets.

Notes

1. *Estonia*, Media Landscape Reports (Maastricht, The Netherlands: European Journalism Centre, 2013). Available at http://ejc.net/media_landscapes/Estonia.
2. *World Press Freedom Review*, IPI Report (Vienna: International Press Institute, 1993).
3. *World Press Freedom Review*, IPI Report (Vienna: International Press Institute, 1995).

Ethiopia: 1948–2012

Ethiopia Year by Year

Year	Media	Government
1948	Not Free	Autocracy
1949	Not Free	Autocracy
1950	Not Free	Autocracy
1951	Not Free	Autocracy
1952	Not Free	Autocracy
1953	Not Free	Autocracy
1954	Not Free	Autocracy
1955	Not Free	Autocracy
1956	Not Free	Autocracy
1957	Not Free	Autocracy
1958	Not Free	Autocracy
1959	Not Free	Autocracy
1960	Not Free	Autocracy
1961	Not Free	Autocracy
1962	Not Free	Autocracy
1963	Not Free	Autocracy
1964	Not Free	Autocracy
1965	Not Free	Autocracy
1966	Not Free	Autocracy
1967	Not Free	Autocracy
1968	Not Free	Autocracy
1969	Not Free	Autocracy
1970	Not Free	Autocracy
1971	Not Free	Autocracy

(Continued)

MEDIA FREEDOM HISTORY IN A NUTSHELL

- Ethiopian news media have always been controlled or restricted by government
- As of 2013, Ethiopia had a mix of state-owned and privately owned newspapers, one state-owned television network, and a mix of state-owned and privately owned radio stations (BBC News Country Profiles)
- As of 2012, less than 2 percent of Ethiopians had access to the Internet (International Telecommunication Union's 2012 ICT Indicators Database)

In Brief

Although Ethiopia has experienced several regime changes since World War II, the lack of government respect for media freedom has remained consistent.

Chronology

1948–2012: Not Free

With the exception of the Italian occupation from 1936 to 1941, Ethiopia was never colonized. Although there were newspapers dating back to the 1800s and Emperor Haile Selassie imported printing presses in the early 1930s, these were "nationally oriented" publications.[1] Radio and television broadcasts became available in the 1940s and the 1960s respectively, but the imperial government maintained tight control over all media.

Following a two-year famine that left an estimated 200,000 dead, a military group known as the Derg staged a coup and overthrew Haile Selassie in 1974. Although one of the first actions of this new government was to abolish censorship, conflict

(Continued)

Year	Media	Government
1972	Not Free	Autocracy
1973	Not Free	Autocracy
1974	Not Free	Anocracy
1975	Not Free	Autocracy
1976	Not Free	Autocracy
1977	Not Free	Autocracy
1978	Not Free	Autocracy
1979	Not Free	Autocracy
1980	Not Free	Autocracy
1981	Not Free	Autocracy
1982	Not Free	Autocracy
1983	Not Free	Autocracy
1984	Not Free	Autocracy
1985	Not Free	Autocracy
1986	Not Free	Autocracy
1987	Not Free	Autocracy
1988	Not Free	Autocracy
1989	Not Free	Autocracy
1990	Not Free	Autocracy
1991	Not Free	Interregnum
1992	Not Free	In Transition
1993	Not Free	In Transition
1994	Not Free	In Transition
1995	Not Free	Anocracy
1996	Not Free	Anocracy
1997	Not Free	Anocracy
1998	Not Free	Anocracy
1999	Not Free	Anocracy
2000	Not Free	Anocracy
2001	Not Free	Anocracy
2002	Not Free	Anocracy
2003	Not Free	Anocracy

with what was then the Eritrean province prompted the government to crack down on news media and expel several foreign correspondents.[2,3] In 1977, a military coup established a Marxist one-party state under the leadership of Colonel Mengistu Haile Miriam who orchestrated the rounding up and killing of thousands of suspected opponents in what was called the "Red Terror." By the end of the 1970s, all news media were once again government owned and controlled, and the only views expressed were those of the government.[4]

In 1991, the Ethiopian People's Revolutionary Democratic Front seized control of the country, and the 1992 Press Law abolished censorship. Hopes that the new government would respect media freedom led to an eruption of privately owned media, and by 1994, there were nearly one hundred independent newspapers.[5] Yet in late 1993, the government began cracking down on these news outlets and arresting journalists.[6]

In 2005, unrest erupted following disputed elections, and the news media were caught in the middle of the crisis. The government issued a list of people who were accused of treason that included both publishers and journalists, and several dozen were arrested.[7] In 2007, the government released fifteen journalists who had been imprisoned in connection with the 2005 unrest, but others remained behind bars.[8]

Media Today

The government owns and controls the only Internet service provider, the only television station, and most radio stations.[9] Ethiopia has a mix of government-owned and privately owned newspapers, but journalists who criticize the government risk imprisonment.[10]

Notes

1. Thomas P. Ofcansky and LaVerle Berry, "Haile Selassie: The Prewar Period, 1930-36," *Ethiopia: A Country Study* (Washington, DC: Library of Congress Federal Research Division, 1991), Para. 5. Available at http://lcweb2.loc.gov/frd/cs/.
2. *World Press Freedom Review*, IPI Report (Zurich: International Press Institute, January 1975).
3. *World Press Freedom Review*, IPI Report (Zurich: International Press Institute, December 1975).
4. *Country Reports on Human Rights Practices for 1979* (Washington, DC: U.S. Department of State,

Year	Media	Government
2004	Not Free	Anocracy
2005	Not Free	Anocracy
2006	Not Free	Anocracy
2007	Not Free	Anocracy
2008	Not Free	Anocracy
2009	Not Free	Anocracy
2010	Not Free	Anocracy
2011	Not Free	Anocracy
2012	Not Free	Anocracy

1980). Available at http://babel.hathitrust.org/cgi/pt?id=mdp.39015014188273;view=1up;seq=81.

5. *World Press Freedom Review*, IPI Report (Vienna: International Press Institute, December 1994).

6. *World Press Freedom Review*, IPI Report (Vienna: International Press Institute, November/December 1995).

7. *World Press Freedom Review*, IPI Report (Vienna: International Press Institute, 2005).

8. *World Press Freedom Review*, IPI Report (Vienna: International Press Institute, 2007).

9. *Ethiopia*, BBC News Country Profiles (London, UK: British Broadcasting Company, 2013). Available at http://www.bbc.co.uk/news/world-africa-13349401.

10. *Attacks on the Press 2012: Ethiopia* (Committee to Protect Journalists, 2013). Available at http://www.cpj.org/2013/02/attacks-on-the-press-in-2012-ethiopia.php.

Fiji: 1970–2012

Fiji Year by Year

Year	Media	Government
1970	Imperfectly Free	Democracy
1971	Imperfectly Free	Democracy
1972	Imperfectly Free	Democracy
1973	Imperfectly Free	Democracy
1974	Imperfectly Free	Democracy
1975	Imperfectly Free	Democracy
1976	Imperfectly Free	Democracy
1977	Imperfectly Free	Democracy
1978	Imperfectly Free	Democracy
1979	Imperfectly Free	Democracy
1980	Imperfectly Free	Democracy
1981	Imperfectly Free	Democracy
1982	Imperfectly Free	Democracy
1983	Imperfectly Free	Democracy
1984	Imperfectly Free	Democracy
1985	Imperfectly Free	Democracy
1986	Imperfectly Free	Democracy
1987	Not Free	Anocracy
1988	Not Free	Anocracy
1989	Imperfectly Free	Anocracy
1990	Imperfectly Free	Anocracy
1991	Imperfectly Free	Anocracy
1992	Imperfectly Free	Anocracy
1993	Imperfectly Free	Anocracy

MEDIA FREEDOM HISTORY IN A NUTSHELL

- For the first decade and a half after independence, Fijian media were functionally free
- In 1987, a coup put an end to democratic rule and media freedom and marked the beginning of a power struggle between indigenous Fijians and those of Indian descent
- In 1989, the political situation stabilized and media became functionally free
- Since the 2006 military coup, Commodore Frank Bainimarama has controlled the country, and the media environment has deteriorated to the point that the Fijian news media are no longer free
- As of 2013, Fiji had two privately owned dailies and several weekly newspapers; there are two privately owned television channels and a mix of public and private radio stations (BBC News Country Profiles)
- As of 2012, about 38 percent of Fijians had Internet access (International Telecommunication Union's 2012 ICT Indicators Database)

In Brief

Although at times the Fijian news media have been among the freest in the Pacific Islands, all too often they have been caught in the middle of tensions and power struggles between indigenous Fijians and those descended of Indian immigrants. Since independence the country has experienced several coups, and the most recent, in 2006 by Commodore Frank Bainimarama, has led to a deterioration of media freedom. Human rights organizations have criticized the 2013 Constitution as failing to protect a number of rights, including freedom of expression.

Year	Media	Government
1994	Imperfectly Free	Anocracy
1995	Imperfectly Free	Anocracy
1996	Imperfectly Free	Anocracy
1997	Imperfectly Free	Anocracy
1998	Imperfectly Free	Anocracy
1999	Imperfectly Free	Democracy
2000	Not Free	Anocracy
2001	Imperfectly Free	Anocracy
2002	Free	Anocracy
2003	Free	Anocracy
2004	Free	Democracy
2005	Free	Democracy
2006	Imperfectly Free	Anocracy
2007	Imperfectly Free	Anocracy
2008	Imperfectly Free	Anocracy
2009	Not Free	Anocracy
2010	Not Free	Anocracy
2011	Not Free	Anocracy
2012	Not Free	Anocracy

Chronology

1970–1986: Imperfectly Free

Upon gaining independence from Britain in 1970, Fiji news media were somewhat limited, but functionally free.[1] By 1979, Fiji had one radio station, which following the British model was operated by an independent broadcasting commission. Additionally, the country had a couple of independent newspapers.[2]

1987–1988: Not Free

Just one moth after the April 1987 election in which ethnic Indians prevailed, Colonel Sitweni Rabuka seized control of the country in a coup with the goal of restoring control of the country to indigenous Fijians. During this transition, the country's two daily newspapers were closed down but were allowed to reopen within a week.[3] But in October 1987, after a second coup staged by Rabuka, the deputy publisher of the *Fiji Sun*, Jim Carney, was arrested and eventually expelled from Fiji.[4] Colonel Rabuka subsequently announced that newspapers would be allowed to publish with "military oversight" and the military took over all radio programming.[5] By the end of 1987, Fiji had an interim civilian government, but the military remained heavily involved.

1989–1999: Imperfectly Free

By 1989, the media environment had improved to the degree that news media were imperfectly free. Although self-censorship remained common, independent newspapers and broadcast media were not censored by government.[6] Throughout the 1990s news media remained imperfectly free, but comparatively among the freest in the Pacific Islands.[7] Yet, following the 1999 election of Prime Minister Mahendra Chaudhry, the relationship between news media and government soured as Chaudhry sought to reign in critical news media using a variety of tactics from denying the work permits of foreign journalists to limiting government advertising to the *Daily Post* (of which the government was the primary shareholder).[8,9]

2000: Not Free

The year 2000 was marked by political upheaval as rebel leader George Speight attempted a coup and held hostage Chaudhry and members of his administration. Journalists were caught in the middle of the power struggle that ensued; some were harassed, others attacked, and several were kidnapped.[10]

2001: Imperfectly Free

In 2001, democracy returned to Fiji as elections were held, and the media were again functionally free, although journalists continued to face pressures in the ongoing power struggle between indigenous Fijians and those of Indian descent.[11]

2002–2005: Free

As Fiji's political situation continued to stabilize, the media environment improved to the point that the news media were free.[12] Yet there were lingering concerns about the independence of the news media and the ability of the government to exert its influence.[13]

2006–2008: Imperfectly Free

Following his 2006 military coup, Commodore Frank Bainimarama made it clear that he had "zero tolerance for media criticism."[14] Although the military government restored some semblance of media freedom once the transition was complete, media continued to face limitations.

2009–2012: Not Free

In 2009, President Josefa Iloilo suspended the constitution and imposed Public Emergency Regulations that prohibited criticism of the government and gave the government the authority to censor print and broadcast media on a daily basis.[15] In 2010, the Media Industry Development Decree established a new regulatory authority and a media tribunal to hear cases of journalists accused of acting against "public interest or public order" and impose prison sentences or fines.[16] That same year the government also issued a decree criminalizing sedition and defining it as "any criticism of government."[17] Although the government lifted the emergency regulations in early 2012, thereby removing government censors from the newsrooms, the decrees of 2010 remained in place.[18] Thus, by the end of the first decade of the 2000s, the Fijian media were not free.

Media Today

The Fijian news media remain restricted. The 2013 Constitution has been criticized by human rights organization as restricting a number of civil rights including freedom of speech.[19] The new Constitution leaves in place the decrees that previously limited media freedom. Fiji continues to have a mix of public and private radio stations as well as two privately owned television channels. As of 2013, Fiji had two privately owned daily newspapers and several weeklies. Nearly 38 percent of Fijians have Internet access, but there are reports that the government monitors Internet traffic to crack down on those who criticize the government in blogs.[20]

There are plans to hold elections in 2014, which the military government claims will be free, but whether the Fijian media will be able serve as an arena for political competition during this process remains to be seen.

Notes

1. *World Press Freedom Review*, IPI Report (Zurich: International Press Institute, December 1987).
2. *Country Reports on Human Rights Practices for 1979* (Washington, DC: U.S. Department of State, 1980). Available at http://babel.hathitrust.org/cgi/pt?id=mdp.39015014188273;view=1up;seq=460.
3. *World Press Freedom Review*, IPI Report (Zurich: International Press Institute, December 1987).
4. Ibid.
5. Ibid., 9.
6. *Country Reports on Human Rights Practices for 1990* (Washington, DC: U.S. Department of State, 1990). Available at https://archive.org/stream/countryreportson1989unit#page/842/mode/2up/search/fiji.
7. *Attacks on the Press 1999* (Committee to Protect Journalists, 1999). Available at http://cpj.org/2000/03/attacks-on-the-press-1999-fiji.php.
8. Ibid.
9. *World Press Freedom Review*, IPI Report (Vienna: International Press Institute, 1999).
10. Ann K. Cooper, *Radio Journalists Harassed for Reporting on Military* (Committee to Protect Joualists, 2000). Available at http://cpj.org/2000/10/radio-journalists-harassed-for-reporting-on-milita.php.
11. *Attacks on the Press 2001* (Committee to Protect Journalists, 2001). Available at httpcpj.org/2002/03/attacks-on-the-press-2001-fiji.php.
12. *Freedom of the Press* (Washington, DC: Freedom House, 2003). Available at httpwww.freedomhouse.org/report/freedom-press/2003/Fiji.
13. Ibid.
14. *Freedom of the Press* (Washington, DC: Freedom House, 2007). Available at httpwww.freedomhouse.org/report/freedom-press/2007/fiji.
15. *Freedom of the Press* (Washington, DC: Freedom House, 2010). Available at httpfreedomhouse.org/report/freedom-press/2011/fiji.
16. Ibid.
17. Ibid.
18. Madeline Earp, *Fiji's Emergency Ends, but Media Oppression Continues* (Committee to Protect Journalists, 2012). Available at http://www.cpj.org/blog/2012/01/fijis-emergency-ends-but-media-oppression-continue.
19. *Fiji: New Constitution Fails to Protect Fundamental Human Rights* (London, UK: Amnesty International, September 4, 2013). Available at http://www.amnesty.org/en/news/fiji-new-constitution-fails-protect-fundamental-human-rights-2013-09-04.
20. *Freedom of the Press* (Washington, DC: Freedom House, 2013). Available at http://www.freedomhouse.org/report/freedom-press/2013/fiji.

Finland: 1948–2012

Finland Year by Year

Year	Media	Government
1948	Imperfectly Free	Democracy
1949	Imperfectly Free	Democracy
1950	Imperfectly Free	Democracy
1951	Imperfectly Free	Democracy
1952	Imperfectly Free	Democracy
1953	Imperfectly Free	Democracy
1954	Imperfectly Free	Democracy
1955	Imperfectly Free	Democracy
1956	Imperfectly Free	Democracy
1957	Imperfectly Free	Democracy
1958	Imperfectly Free	Democracy
1959	Imperfectly Free	Democracy
1960	Imperfectly Free	Democracy
1961	Imperfectly Free	Democracy
1962	Imperfectly Free	Democracy
1963	Imperfectly Free	Democracy
1964	Imperfectly Free	Democracy
1965	Imperfectly Free	Democracy
1966	Imperfectly Free	Democracy
1967	Imperfectly Free	Democracy
1968	Imperfectly Free	Democracy
1969	Imperfectly Free	Democracy
1970	Imperfectly Free	Democracy
1971	Imperfectly Free	Democracy
1972	Imperfectly Free	Democracy
1973	Imperfectly Free	Democracy
1974	Imperfectly Free	Democracy

(Continued)

MEDIA FREEDOM HISTORY IN A NUTSHELL

- Clearly a free media throughout, but issues related to ownership concentration and Cold War diplomacy move it into the imperfect category
- Gradual economic changes and the end of the Cold War eliminate these issues and it becomes a robust exemplar of a free media system
- Finland has a mix of public and private radio stations and television channels
- As of 2011, there were forty-nine daily newspapers, forty-eight of which were paid-for dailies with a total average circulation per issue of 1,780,000 (World Association of Newspaper's 2012 World Newspaper Trends)
- As of 2012, about 91 percent of citizens had Internet access (International Telecommunication Union's 2012 ICT Indicators Database)

In Brief

Today Finland is often considered one of the best examples of a free media system and it has been a free media regime for the duration of this data. Yet it is unclear how much concentration of media ownership and Cold War politics compromised media effectiveness as a forum for critical political competition.

Chronology

1948–1994: Imperfectly Free

Finland has always occupied what might be called an uncomfortable position between East and West. Ethnically and linguistically connected to the East but culturally tied to Scandinavia in the West, it was part of the Kingdom of Sweden for 700 years, conquered and made part of the Russian Empire for a century, fought against first

(Continued)

Year	Media	Government
1975	Imperfectly Free	Democracy
1976	Imperfectly Free	Democracy
1977	Imperfectly Free	Democracy
1978	Imperfectly Free	Democracy
1979	Imperfectly Free	Democracy
1980	Imperfectly Free	Democracy
1981	Imperfectly Free	Democracy
1982	Imperfectly Free	Democracy
1983	Imperfectly Free	Democracy
1984	Imperfectly Free	Democracy
1985	Imperfectly Free	Democracy
1986	Imperfectly Free	Democracy
1987	Imperfectly Free	Democracy
1988	Imperfectly Free	Democracy
1989	Imperfectly Free	Democracy
1990	Imperfectly Free	Democracy
1991	Imperfectly Free	Democracy
1992	Imperfectly Free	Democracy
1993	Imperfectly Free	Democracy
1994	Imperfectly Free	Democracy
1995	Free	Democracy
1996	Free	Democracy
1997	Free	Democracy
1998	Free	Democracy
1999	Free	Democracy
2000	Free	Democracy
2001	Free	Democracy
2002	Free	Democracy
2003	Free	Democracy
2004	Free	Democracy
2005	Free	Democracy
2006	Free	Democracy
2007	Free	Democracy
2008	Free	Democracy

Year	Media	Government
2009	Free	Democracy
2010	Free	Democracy
2011	Free	Democracy
2012	Free	Democracy

the Soviets and then the Germans during World War II, and in 1948, signed a treaty of cooperation and friendship with the Soviet Union that in many ways was similar to those signed by Warsaw Pact countries. A liberal democracy with a free press, Finland had to distance itself from the West to ease Soviet concerns. Fear of provoking the Soviets was a significant aspect of all of Finnish politics, including the functioning of its press. Further complicating this situation was a concentration of media ownership, combined with the country's economic dependence on the USSR during most of the Cold War. The degree to which these imperfections mattered in any practical sense is debatable, but the media's ability to criticize on certain subjects was certainly limited by this overwhelming political concern with the USSR and the economic reality that the handful of major owners all had some level of engagement in the country's economic dependence on the Soviet Union. In the 1980s, Finland began actively pursuing expanded economic ties to the West and, with the rise of Gorbachev, both the political and economic concerns gradually faded. The key word here, however, is gradual.

1995–2012: Free

Change was gradual and there is no event or point of demarcation for this shift to clearly free. Regarding policy, or media ownership and the politics of being the only western democratic nation to directly border Russia, there was no overt reaction to the fall of the Berlin Wall or the dissolution of the Soviet Union, but by 1995, it was clear that neither mattered to media organizations in Finland.

Media Today

An exemplar of media freedom and often at the top of scale measures.

France: 1948–2012

France Year by Year

Year	Media	Government
1948	Free	Democracy
1949	Free	Democracy
1950	Free	Democracy
1951	Free	Democracy
1952	Free	Democracy
1953	Free	Democracy
1954	Free	Democracy
1955	Free	Democracy
1956	Free	Democracy
1957	Free	Democracy
1958	Free	Anocracy
1959	Free	Anocracy
1960	Free	Anocracy
1961	Free	Anocracy
1962	Free	Anocracy
1963	Free	Anocracy
1964	Free	Anocracy
1965	Free	Anocracy
1966	Free	Anocracy
1967	Free	Anocracy
1968	Free	Anocracy
1969	Free	Democracy
1970	Free	Democracy
1971	Free	Democracy

(Continued)

MEDIA FREEDOM HISTORY IN A NUTSHELL

- A Free and independent press
- As of 2011, there were 120 daily newspapers, 83 of which were paid-for dailies with a total average circulation per issue of 9,485,000 (World Association of Newspaper's 2012 World Newspaper Trends)
- France has more than 1,000 radio stations and a variety of public and private television channels
- As of 2012, about 83 percent of citizens had Internet access (International Telecommunication Union's 2012 ICT Indicators Database)

In Brief

France is a well-established free media regime that boasts one of the most prominent newspapers in the world *(Le Monde)* and one of the big international wire services *(Agence France-Presse)*.

Chronology

1948–2012: Free

There is little to say about media freedom in France other than it has proven to be one of the most robust aspects of a sometimes-volatile political context. Throughout the periods of frequent shifting of governments and other changes that have characterized French politics, the media have been consistently free and critical.

Media Today

There have been no substantive challenges to the French media's ability or willingness to publish stories critical of government or elites and nothing to suggest a threat to their robustness as a political institution.

(Continued)

Year	Media	Government	Year	Media	Government
1972	Free	Democracy	1993	Free	Democracy
1973	Free	Democracy	1994	Free	Democracy
1974	Free	Democracy	1995	Free	Democracy
1975	Free	Democracy	1996	Free	Democracy
1976	Free	Democracy	1997	Free	Democracy
1977	Free	Democracy	1998	Free	Democracy
1978	Free	Democracy	1999	Free	Democracy
1979	Free	Democracy	2000	Free	Democracy
1980	Free	Democracy	2001	Free	Democracy
1981	Free	Democracy	2002	Free	Democracy
1982	Free	Democracy	2003	Free	Democracy
1983	Free	Democracy	2004	Free	Democracy
1984	Free	Democracy	2005	Free	Democracy
1985	Free	Democracy	2006	Free	Democracy
1986	Free	Democracy	2007	Free	Democracy
1987	Free	Democracy	2008	Free	Democracy
1988	Free	Democracy	2009	Free	Democracy
1989	Free	Democracy	2010	Free	Democracy
1990	Free	Democracy	2011	Free	Democracy
1991	Free	Democracy	2012	Free	Democracy
1992	Free	Democracy			

Gabon: 1961–2012

Gabon Year by Year

Year	Media	Government
1961	Not Free	Autocracy
1962	Not Free	Autocracy
1963	Not Free	Autocracy
1964	Not Free	Autocracy
1965	Not Free	Autocracy
1966	Not Free	Autocracy
1967	Not Free	Autocracy
1968	Not Free	Autocracy
1969	Not Free	Autocracy
1970	Not Free	Autocracy
1971	Not Free	Autocracy
1972	Not Free	Autocracy
1973	Not Free	Autocracy
1974	Not Free	Autocracy
1975	Not Free	Autocracy
1976	Not Free	Autocracy
1977	Not Free	Autocracy
1978	Not Free	Autocracy
1979	Not Free	Autocracy
1980	Not Free	Autocracy
1981	Not Free	Autocracy
1982	Not Free	Autocracy
1983	Not Free	Autocracy
1984	Not Free	Autocracy

(Continued)

MEDIA FREEDOM HISTORY IN A NUTSHELL

- From 1961 to 1990, Gabon was a one-party state and the government controlled all news media
- In the early 1990s, as Gabon transitioned to a multiparty system, the government allowed some media freedom, and independent news media emerged
- As of 2009, there was one paid-for daily newspaper and nine paid-for nondaily newspapers with a daily total average circulation per issue of 20,000 (World Association of Newspaper's 2010 World Newspaper Trends)
- The government owned and operated two radio and two television stations. Seven radio and four television stations were privately owned and operated (World Association of Newspaper's 2010 World Newspaper Trends)
- As of 2012, about 9 percent of Gabonese had Internet access (International Telecommunication Union's 2012 ICT Indicators Database)

In Brief

With the exception of the 1990s, Gabonese media have been either directly controlled or effectively restricted by government. After more than four decades as president, Omar Bongo died in 2009, only to be replaced by his son, and little changed for the news media.

Chronology

1961–1990: Not Free

Shortly after Gabon gained independence from France in 1960, it became a one-party state under the leadership of El Hadj Omar Bongo Ondimba, and the media were government controlled.[1]

(Continued)

Year	Media	Government
1985	Not Free	Autocracy
1986	Not Free	Autocracy
1987	Not Free	Autocracy
1988	Not Free	Autocracy
1989	Not Free	Autocracy
1990	Not Free	Autocracy
1991	Imperfectly Free	Anocracy
1992	Imperfectly Free	Anocracy
1993	Imperfectly Free	Anocracy
1994	Imperfectly Free	Anocracy
1995	Imperfectly Free	Anocracy
1996	Imperfectly Free	Anocracy
1997	Imperfectly Free	Anocracy
1998	Not Free	Anocracy
1999	Not Free	Anocracy
2000	Not Free	Anocracy
2001	Not Free	Anocracy
2002	Not Free	Anocracy
2003	Not Free	Anocracy
2004	Not Free	Anocracy
2005	Not Free	Anocracy
2006	Not Free	Anocracy
2007	Not Free	Anocracy
2008	Not Free	Anocracy
2009	Not Free	Anocracy
2010	Not Free	Anocracy
2011	Not Free	Anocracy
2012	Not Free	Anocracy

1991–1997: Imperfectly Free

In the early 1990s, following mass protests, Gabon transitioned to a multiparty system. As part of this process, restrictions on news media were removed and opposition newspapers began publishing.[2] Although President Bongo encouraged journalists to criticize government officials and expose corruption, newspapers that did so were vulnerable to defamation lawsuits.[3]

1998–2012: Not Free

In 1998, President Bongo was reelected, but there were allegations of election fraud. When a privately owned radio station with ties to the opposition broadcast a call-in show featuring some of these allegations, the station's transmissions were scrambled and its phone lines were cut off.[4] The government subsequently banned the broadcasting of political programs. In 2003, the government suspended several privately owned newspapers.[5] In 2009, President Bongo died and his son Ali Ben Bongo was elected, but the media environment remained unchanged.

Media Today

Although Gabon has constitutional provisions for media freedom, the government does not respect these in practice. Journalists who criticize government are vulnerable to threats and lawsuits.[6] Both of Gabon's daily newspapers are government controlled, but the Gabonese do have access to privately owned weekly newspapers, most of which have ties to the opposition parties and publish only sporadically. Gabon has a mix of privately owned and government-owned broadcast media. In 2012, less than 10 percent of Gabonese had Internet access.

Notes

1. *Country Reports on Human Rights Practices for 1979* (Washington, DC: U.S. Department of State, 1980). Available at http://babel.hathitrust.org/cgi/pt?id=mdp.39015014188273;view=1up;seq=85.
2. *Country Reports on Human Rights Practices for 1990* (Washington, DC: U.S. Department of State, 1991). Available at http://babel.hathitrust.org/cgi/pt?id=ien.35556020518650;view=1up;seq=149.
3. *World Press Freedom Review*, IPI Report (Zurich: International Press Institute, 1991).
4. *World Press Freedom Review*, IPI Report (Vienna: International Press Institute, 1998).
5. *CPJ Protests Deteriorating State of Press Freedom* (Committee to Protect Journalists, 2003). Available at http://cpj.org/2003/09/cpj-protests-deteriorating-state-of-press-freedom.php
6. *Freedom of the Press* (Washington, DC: Freedom House, 2013). Available at http://www.freedomhouse.org/report/freedom-press/2013/gabon.

Gambia, The: 1965–2012

The Gambia Year by Year

Year	Media	Government
1965	Free	Democracy
1966	Free	Democracy
1967	Free	Democracy
1968	Free	Democracy
1969	Free	Democracy
1970	Free	Democracy
1971	Free	Democracy
1972	Free	Democracy
1973	Free	Democracy
1974	Free	Democracy
1975	Free	Democracy
1976	Free	Democracy
1977	Free	Democracy
1978	Free	Democracy
1979	Free	Democracy
1980	Free	Democracy
1981	Free	Democracy
1982	Free	Democracy
1983	Free	Democracy
1984	Free	Democracy
1985	Free	Democracy
1986	Free	Democracy
1987	Free	Democracy
1988	Free	Democracy

(Continued)

MEDIA FREEDOM HISTORY IN A NUTSHELL

- After nearly three decades of media freedom, The Gambia experienced a military coup
- Since the 1994 military coup, journalists have been restricted and those who criticize the government risk arrest, imprisonment, and violent attacks
- As of 2009, there were three paid-for daily newspapers with a total average circulation per issue of 4,000 (World Association of Newspaper's 2010 World Newspaper Trends)
- The Gambia has one state-owned television station and a mix of state-owned and privately owned broadcast media
- As of 2012, about 12 percent of Gambians had Internet access (International Telecommunication Union's 2012 ICT Indicators Database)

In Brief

After nearly three decades of democracy and media freedom, a military coup in 1994 ushered in a repressive regime that does not tolerate critical news media.

Chronology

1965–1994: Free

Upon gaining independence from the United Kingdom in 1965, The Gambia transitioned to a multiparty democracy and the media were free.

1995–2012: Not Free

In 1994, Lt. Yaya Jammeh seized power in a bloodless coup. Although Jammeh claimed to welcome media scrutiny, critical journalists faced arrest, imprisonment, and deportation.[1,2]

(Continued)

Year	Media	Government
1989	Free	Democracy
1990	Free	Democracy
1991	Free	Democracy
1992	Free	Democracy
1993	Free	Democracy
1994	Free	Autocracy
1995	Not Free	Autocracy
1996	Not Free	Autocracy
1997	Not Free	Anocracy
1998	Not Free	Anocracy
1999	Not Free	Anocracy
2000	Not Free	Anocracy
2001	Not Free	Anocracy
2002	Not Free	Anocracy
2003	Not Free	Anocracy
2004	Not Free	Anocracy
2005	Not Free	Anocracy
2006	Not Free	Anocracy
2007	Not Free	Anocracy
2008	Not Free	Anocracy

Year	Media	Government
2009	Not Free	Anocracy
2010	Not Free	Anocracy
2011	Not Free	Anocracy
2012	Not Free	Anocracy

In 2004, Deyda Hydara, an editor known for his criticism of Jammeh's government, was fatally shot. That same year, the government passed legislation criminalizing "inaccurate news" and sedition.[3]

Media Today

Journalists who criticize the government risk arrest, imprisonment, and violence. The government routinely shuts down critical news media.[4] The Gambia has several privately owned newspapers, one state-owned television station, and a mix of state-owned and privately owned radio stations.

Notes

1. *World Press Freedom Review*, IPI Report (Vienna: International Press Institute, 1994).
2. *World Press Freedom Review*, IPI Report (Vienna: International Press Institute, 1995).
3. *World Press Freedom Review*, IPI Report (Vienna: International Press Institute, 2005).
4. *Freedom of the Press* (Washington, DC: Freedom House, 2013). Available at http://www.freedomhouse.org/report/freedom-press/2013/gambia.

Georgia: 1991–2012

Georgia Year by Year

Year	Media	Government
1991	Not Free	Anocracy
1992	Not Free	Anocracy
1993	Not Free	Anocracy
1994	Not Free	Anocracy
1995	Imperfectly Free	Anocracy
1996	Imperfectly Free	Anocracy
1997	Imperfectly Free	Anocracy
1998	Imperfectly Free	Anocracy
1999	Imperfectly Free	Anocracy
2000	Imperfectly Free	Anocracy
2001	Imperfectly Free	Anocracy
2002	Imperfectly Free	Anocracy
2003	Imperfectly Free	Anocracy
2004	Imperfectly Free	Democracy
2005	Imperfectly Free	Democracy
2006	Imperfectly Free	Democracy
2007	Imperfectly Free	Democracy
2008	Imperfectly Free	Democracy
2009	Imperfectly Free	Democracy
2010	Imperfectly Free	Democracy
2011	Imperfectly Free	Democracy
2012	Imperfectly Free	Democracy

In Brief

Internal conflict has plagued Georgia since it gained independence from the Soviet Union.

MEDIA FREEDOM HISTORY IN A NUTSHELL

- Despite internal conflicts, Georgia moved quickly to a democratic political system including media freedom
- The 1994 constitution established media freedom
- Media are highly politicized and have difficulty with unofficial influences on content, but are also critical of leadership and government and are clearly, if imperfectly free
- As of 2009, there were ten paid-for daily newspapers with a total average circulation per issue of 43,000 (World Association of Newspaper's 2010 World Newspaper Trends)
- As of 2012, about 46 percent of Georgians had Internet access (International Telecommunication Union's 2012 ICT Indicators Database)

Still, it progressed relatively quickly to a new constitution that established media freedom in 1994 and has sustained a functional, though imperfect media system since.

Chronology

1991–1994: Not Free

The first years of post-Soviet independence were marked by conflict between government and separatist forces in Abkhazia and a secessionist movement in South Ossetia. The first president was deposed as a result of fighting in Tbilidi, and Eduard Shevardnadze became the leader of the Georgian Parliament. During these years, there were a number of attacks on journalists, and at the end of 1993, all newspapers ceased publishing for two weeks because of a paper shortage.[1] Still, despite these difficulties, progress toward a democratic system was steady and a new Constitution was adopted in 1994, establishing media freedom and leading to competitive elections in 1995 and the election of Shevardnadze to the restored presidency.

1995: Imperfectly Free

By 1995, the media environment improved to the point where media were imperfectly free. Attacks on journalists decreased, but independent newspapers continued to struggle financially.[2] There was some indication of authoritarian efforts by Shevardnadze, including suggestions of voter intimidation and other voting irregularities, but the media remained functionally free and were a key part of the 2003 "Rose Revolution" that ended Shevardnadze's rule and led to the election of a new president.

Media Today

Television is the dominant medium. News is highly politicized, and its content is often critical of government and governing officials, but it is also compromised by excessive ownership interference in content and editorial policy. Unofficial influence on media is an ongoing concern, but the news media's function as an arena for democratic political competition appears to be robust.

Notes

1. *World Press Freedom Review*, IPI Report (Vienna: International Press Institute, 1994).
2. *World Press Freedom Review*, IPI Report (Vienna: International Press Institute, 1995).

Germany: 1948–2012

East Germany Year by Year

Year	Media	Government
1948	Not Free	Autocracy
1949	Not Free	Autocracy
1950	Not Free	Autocracy
1951	Not Free	Autocracy
1952	Not Free	Autocracy
1953	Not Free	Autocracy
1954	Not Free	Autocracy
1955	Not Free	Autocracy
1956	Not Free	Autocracy
1957	Not Free	Autocracy
1958	Not Free	Autocracy
1959	Not Free	Autocracy
1960	Not Free	Autocracy
1961	Not Free	Autocracy
1962	Not Free	Autocracy
1963	Not Free	Autocracy
1964	Not Free	Autocracy
1965	Not Free	Autocracy
1966	Not Free	Autocracy
1967	Not Free	Autocracy
1968	Not Free	Autocracy
1969	Not Free	Autocracy
1970	Not Free	Autocracy
1971	Not Free	Autocracy

(Continued)

MEDIA FREEDOM HISTORY IN A NUTSHELL

- After years of Nazi-controlled and manipulated media, followed by the destruction of World War II, Germany was divided and occupied
- East Germany became an authoritarian Soviet-style state with government-controlled media
- As West Germany's media system was rebuilt, it was initially controlled by Allied Forces
- Free and independent media began to emerge in the West in the 1950s
- With the decline of the Soviet Union, East and West Germany were reunified in 1990
- As of 2011, there were 350 paid-for daily newspapers with a total average circulation per issue of 18,021,000 (World Association of Newspaper's 2012 World Newspaper Trends).
- Germany has a wide range of public and private broadcast media, including nine regional public service broadcasters and two national public radio stations that are financed and managed by independent organizations (Freedom House, Freedom of the Press 2013)
- As of 2012, about 84 percent of Germans had Internet access (International Telecommunication Union's 2012 ICT Indicators Database)

In Brief

At the end of World War II, Germany's media systems were destroyed and the country was divided and occupied. East Germany became integrated into the Soviet system and all news media were controlled by the Sozialistiche Einheitspartei Deutschlands. Initially, as West Germany's media were rebuilt, they were controlled by the Allied Command. In the late 1940s and early 1950s, independent newspapers began to emerge, followed by radio and then television. By 1955, German media were free. In 1990, Germany was reunified and media freedom spread to the East.

(Continued)

Year	Media	Government
1972	Not Free	Autocracy
1973	Not Free	Autocracy
1974	Not Free	Autocracy
1975	Not Free	Autocracy
1976	Not Free	Autocracy
1977	Not Free	Autocracy
1978	Not Free	Autocracy
1979	Not Free	Autocracy
1980	Not Free	Autocracy
1981	Not Free	Autocracy
1982	Not Free	Autocracy
1983	Not Free	Autocracy
1984	Not Free	Autocracy
1985	Not Free	Autocracy
1986	Not Free	Autocracy
1987	Not Free	Autocracy
1988	Not Free	Autocracy
1989	Not Free	Autocracy
1990	Not Free	Autocracy

Germany (West and Unified) Year by Year

Year	Media	Government
1948	In Transition	Occupied
1949	Imperfectly Free	Democracy
1950	Imperfectly Free	Democracy
1951	Imperfectly Free	Democracy
1952	Imperfectly Free	Democracy
1953	Imperfectly Free	Democracy
1954	Imperfectly Free	Democracy
1955	Free	Democracy
1956	Free	Democracy
1957	Free	Democracy

Chronology: East Germany

1948–1990: Not Free

As East Germany transitioned to a Soviet-style authoritarian regime, the Sozialistiche Einheitspartei Deutschlands took control over all news media. Although domestic news media were censored, the government was unable to keep citizens from tuning in to broadcast media from West Germany.[1]

In the fall of 1989, as the Soviet Union began to fall apart, the East German government stopped restricting citizens from crossing into West Germany and the Berlin Wall was dismantled. As Germany moved toward unification, media freedom was restored.

Chronology: Germany (West)

1949–1954: Imperfectly Free

At the end of World War II, Germany was divided and occupied. The western part of Germany was under Allied control and eventually became the Bundesrepublik Deutschland, also known as West Germany. During this occupation, media were subject to Allied control. By 1950s, newspapers were no longer required to obtain licenses except in West Berlin, and in 1955, the Allied Commanders handed over the licensing responsibilities of print media to the West Berlin Senate.[2] Even in the early to mid-1950s, radio broadcasting was closely monitored and stations were forced to carry programming from *Voice of America* six days a week.[3] Additionally, movie theaters were required to show the British-American newsreel *Welt im Film* until 1949.[4] To avoid Nazi-style media manipulation, public radio (and later public television) was decentralized and regionalized, and according to U.S. advisement, members of the boards of directors were offered courses that encouraged "democratic radio management."[5]

1955–2012: Free

By the mid-1950s, free and independent news media had emerged.[6]

In 1980s, new legislation permitted privately owned radio and television to apply for licenses.

In 1990, Germany was unified and media freedom was restored to the eastern part of the country.

Year	Media	Government
1958	Free	Democracy
1959	Free	Democracy
1960	Free	Democracy
1961	Free	Democracy
1962	Free	Democracy
1963	Free	Democracy
1964	Free	Democracy
1965	Free	Democracy
1966	Free	Democracy
1967	Free	Democracy
1968	Free	Democracy
1969	Free	Democracy
1970	Free	Democracy
1971	Free	Democracy
1972	Free	Democracy
1973	Free	Democracy
1974	Free	Democracy
1975	Free	Democracy
1976	Free	Democracy
1977	Free	Democracy
1978	Free	Democracy
1979	Free	Democracy
1980	Free	Democracy
1981	Free	Democracy
1982	Free	Democracy
1983	Free	Democracy
1984	Free	Democracy
1985	Free	Democracy

Year	Media	Government
1986	Free	Democracy
1987	Free	Democracy
1988	Free	Democracy
1989	Free	Democracy
1990	Free	Democracy
1991	Free	Democracy
1992	Free	Democracy
1993	Free	Democracy
1994	Free	Democracy
1995	Free	Democracy
1996	Free	Democracy
1997	Free	Democracy
1998	Free	Democracy
1999	Free	Democracy
2000	Free	Democracy
2001	Free	Democracy
2002	Free	Democracy
2003	Free	Democracy
2004	Free	Democracy
2005	Free	Democracy
2006	Free	Democracy
2007	Free	Democracy
2008	Free	Democracy
2009	Free	Democracy
2010	Free	Democracy
2011	Free	Democracy
2012	Free	Democracy

Media Today

The German constitution provides for media freedom and the government respects this in practice. Yet hate speech and Holocaust denial are prohibited. Although journalists are rarely attacked, in recent years there have been some reports of political and economic elites pressuring journalists and news organizations.[7] As Europe's largest economy, Germany enjoys one of the most advanced telecommunications systems in the world. Although newspaper circulations have declined in the last two decades, Germany has about 350 newspapers, as well as hundreds of television and radio stations.

Notes

1. *East Germany* (Washington, DC: Library of Congress Country Studies, 1987). Available at http://lcweb2.loc.gov/frd/cs/
2. *World Press Freedom Review*, IPI Report (Zurich: International Press Institute, January 1955).
3. David Braden Posner, "Blurred Sovereignty: The German-American Media Relationship in the Postwar Era," in *The United States and Germany in the Era of the Cold War, 1945–1968: A Handbook*, Vol. 1, ed. Detlef Junker (Cambridge, UK: Cambridge University Press, 2004), 594–600.
4. Ibid.
5. Jessica C.E. Gienow-Hecht, "American Cultural Policy in the Federal Republic of Germany, 1949–1968," in *The United States and Germany in the Era of the Cold War, 1945-1968: A Handbook*, Vol. 1, ed. Detlef Junker (Cambridge, UK: Cambridge University Press, 2004), 401–08.
6. *Germany* (Washington, DC: Library of Congress Country Studies, 1995). Available at http://lcweb2.loc.gov/frd/cs/.
7. *Freedom of the Press* (Washington, DC: Freedom House, 2012). Available at http://www.freedomhouse.org/report/freedom-press/2012/germany.

Ghana: 1957–2012

Ghana Year by Year

Year	Media	Government
1957	Imperfectly Free	Autocracy
1958	Imperfectly Free	Autocracy
1959	Imperfectly Free	Autocracy
1960	Not Free	Autocracy
1961	Not Free	Autocracy
1962	Not Free	Autocracy
1963	Not Free	Autocracy
1964	Not Free	Autocracy
1965	Not Free	Autocracy
1966	Imperfectly Free	Autocracy
1967	Imperfectly Free	Autocracy
1968	Imperfectly Free	Autocracy
1969	Imperfectly Free	Anocracy
1970	Imperfectly Free	Anocracy
1971	Imperfectly Free	Anocracy
1972	Not Free	Autocracy
1973	Not Free	Autocracy
1974	Not Free	Autocracy
1975	Not Free	Autocracy
1976	Not Free	Autocracy
1977	Not Free	Autocracy
1978	Not Free	Anocracy
1979	Free	Democracy
1980	Free	Democracy

(Continued)

MEDIA FREEDOM HISTORY IN A NUTSHELL

- After gaining independence, Ghana experienced quite a bit of political instability, which led to a number of transitions in media freedom in Ghana
- Since the country transitioned to a multiparty system in the early 1990s, the media have been functionally free and highly partisan
- As of 2012, Ghana had four daily newspapers, two of which were privately owned, more than two dozen television stations (some subscription-based, but most free-to-air) and hundreds of radio stations (both state-owned and privately owned) (Freedom House Freedom of the Press Report 2013)
- As of 2012, about 17 percent of Ghanaians had Internet access (International Telecommunication Union's 2012 ICT Indicators Database)

In Brief

Political instability has led to many transitions in the Ghanaian media environment, but since the early 1990s, when the country adopted a new constitution and a multiparty system, the media have been at least functionally free. The media remain highly partisan but provide an arena for political competition.

Chronology

1957–1959: Imperfectly Free

Upon gaining independence from Britain in 1957, Ghana initially had media that were at least functionally free and newspapers that were outspoken about government actions. Yet problems quickly emerged, and by the end of the year, the new government had expelled two journalists.[1] In 1959, the government circulated a bill that

(Continued)

Year	Media	Government
1981	Free	Autocracy
1982	Not Free	Autocracy
1983	Not Free	Autocracy
1984	Not Free	Autocracy
1985	Not Free	Autocracy
1986	Not Free	Autocracy
1987	Not Free	Autocracy
1988	Not Free	Autocracy
1989	Not Free	Autocracy
1990	Not Free	Autocracy
1991	Not Free	Anocracy
1992	Not Free	Anocracy
1993	Imperfectly Free	Anocracy
1994	Imperfectly Free	Anocracy
1995	Imperfectly Free	Anocracy
1996	Imperfectly Free	Anocracy
1997	Imperfectly Free	Anocracy
1998	Imperfectly Free	Anocracy
1999	Imperfectly Free	Anocracy
2000	Imperfectly Free	Anocracy
2001	Free	Democracy
2002	Free	Democracy
2003	Free	Democracy
2004	Free	Democracy
2005	Free	Democracy
2006	Free	Democracy
2007	Free	Democracy
2008	Free	Democracy
2009	Free	Democracy
2010	Free	Democracy
2011	Free	Democracy
2012	Free	Democracy

would render making a false statement about the country or its government punishable by as many as fifteen years in prison.[2]

1960–1965: Not Free

In 1960, a new censorship law gave the president the power to order precensorship of newspapers and President Kwame Nkrumah quickly used the measure on the country's only opposition newspaper.[3] In 1964, Ghana became a one-party state and media censorship continued.

1966–1971: Imperfectly Free

In 1966, the military staged a coup and overthrew Nkrumah. The new government freed a number of imprisoned journalists, and an opposition newspaper that had been banned resumed publishing.[4]

1972–1978: Not Free

In 1972, Colonel Ignatius Acheampong seized power in a military coup and banned political parties. Although the government officially allowed press freedom and there were opposition newspapers, the government retained ownership of all broadcast media and the country's two most popular dailies.[5] Additionally, the government did restrict media coverage of issues where its interests were "significantly involved" and the "Prohibition of Rumors Decree," which criminalized the insulting of government officials, remained in effect.[6]

1979–1981: Free

In 1979, the media environment improved as Ghana prepared to elect a new president. According to the International Press Institute, "Newspapers took an active part in publicizing the elections for a U.S.-style president and administration to take over from the junior army and air force officers who seized power from the outgoing military regime in order to supervise a 'clean-up' of corruption in the senior ranks."[7]

1982–1992: Not Free

In December of 1981, Jerry Rawlings seized control of Ghana in a coup and the media environment quickly deteriorated. The government maintained control over the broadcast media and restricted independent newspapers through intimidation and by limiting their supply of newsprint.[8] In 1983, two independent newspapers closed after their offices were attacked, and there were also reports of journalists being beaten and detained.[9,10]

In 1992, journalists pressured the Ghanaian government to allow media freedom in practice as the country adopted a new constitution that included provisions for media freedom and transitioned to a multiparty system.[11]

1993–2000: Imperfectly Free

In 1993, the establishment of the independent National Media Commission—with the aim of ensuring media freedom for both private and state media—marked the return of media freedom to Ghana.[12] Yet both radio and television remained state owned and tended to avoid criticizing the president and government policies.[13]

2001–2012: Free

In 2000, a Supreme Court ruled that the president could no longer designate the heads of the state-owned media, and shortly thereafter, the state media became noticeably more critical of government.[14] Additionally, in the early 2000s, the number of libel suits decreased and there were few if any reports of attacks on journalists such that by 2001, the media environment had improved to the point that the media were free.

Media Today

Ghana has constitutional provisions for media freedom and the government respects these in practice. Although the media are highly partisan, they represent a range of views and therefore provide a platform for political competition.

Ghana has a mix of state-owned and privately owned print and broadcast media, and even the state-owned media remain for the most part editorially independent. As of 2012, about 17 percent of Ghanaians had Internet access.

Notes

1. *News of the World Press*, IPI Report (Zurich: International Press Institute, September/October 1957).
2. *Bill on False Statements on Ghana or Government*, IPI Report (Zurich: International Press Institute, July 1959).
3. *Toils of the Press*, IPI Report (Zurich: International Press Institute, 1960).
4. Per Monsen, *1.966 Ended Badly for the Free Press: Brazil, Argentina Cause Concern*, IPI Report (Zurich: International Press Institute, January 1967).
5. *A Year of Fragile Press Freedom*, IPI Report (Zurich: International Press Institute, January 1972).
6. *Country Reports on Human Rights Practices for 1977* (Washington, DC: U.S. Department of State, 1978), 43.
7. *World Press Freedom Review*, IPI Report (Zurich: International Press Institute, 1979), 6.
8. *Country Reports on Human Rights Practices for 1983* (Washington, DC: U.S. Department of State, 1984). Available at http://babel.hathitrust.org/cgi/pt?id=mdp.39015014227832;view=1up;seq=161.
9. Ibid.
10. *World Press Freedom Review*, IPI Report (Zurich: International Press Institute, 1984).
11. *World Press Freedom Review*, IPI Report (Zurich: International Press Institute, 1991).
12. *Ghana*, Country Studies (Washington, DC: Library of Congress, 1994). Available at http://lcweb2.loc.gov/frd/cs/.
13. *Ghana*, Country Reports on Human Rights (Washington, DC: U.S. Department of State, 1993).
14. *Ghana*, Country Reports on Human Rights (Washington, DC: U.S. Department of State, 2002).

Greece: 1948–2012

Greece Year by Year

Year	Media	Government
1948	Not Free	Democracy
1949	Not Free	Anocracy
1950	Not Free	Anocracy
1951	Not Free	Anocracy
1952	Not Free	Anocracy
1953	Not Free	Anocracy
1954	Not Free	Anocracy
1955	Not Free	Anocracy
1956	Not Free	Anocracy
1957	Not Free	Anocracy
1958	Not Free	Anocracy
1959	Not Free	Anocracy
1960	Not Free	Anocracy
1961	Not Free	Anocracy
1962	Not Free	Anocracy
1963	Not Free	Anocracy
1964	Not Free	Anocracy
1965	Not Free	Anocracy
1966	Not Free	Anocracy
1967	Not Free	Autocracy
1968	Not Free	Autocracy
1969	Not Free	Autocracy
1970	Not Free	Autocracy
1971	Not Free	Autocracy
1972	Not Free	Autocracy
1973	Not Free	Autocracy
1974	Not Free	Anocracy

MEDIA FREEDOM HISTORY IN A NUTSHELL

- Although Greece democratized in the mid-1970s, media were not functionally free until the mid-1990s
- Greece's history of restricting the press in the name of domestic political stability raises questions about the future of media freedom in Greece as economic struggles continue to fuel protests
- Greece has more than 1,000 radio stations and a mix of public and private television stations
- As of 2011, there were forty-four daily newspapers, forty-two of which were paid-for dailies with a total average circulation per issue of 1,119,550 (World Association of Newspaper's 2012 World Newspaper Trends)
- As of 2012, about 56 percent of citizens had Internet access (International Telecommunication Union's 2012 ICT Indicators Database)

In Brief

During the Cold War, authoritarian rule was the norm as the United States financed and armed right-wing governments and parties in the name of anticommunism. Political stability was often the issue that seemed to lead to the suppression of media criticism and the justification of the use of economic and legal means to coerce news outlets away from divisive issues and commentary. Anti-U.S. sentiment began to shape politics in the late 1970s and early 1980s, but the socialist government elected in 1981 was nearly as authoritarian as the right wing government it replaced, and media remained too restricted to function freely until 1996.

Year	Media	Government
1975	Not Free	Democracy
1976	Not Free	Democracy
1977	Not Free	Democracy
1978	Not Free	Democracy
1979	Not Free	Democracy
1980	Not Free	Democracy
1981	Not Free	Democracy
1982	Not Free	Democracy
1983	Not Free	Democracy
1984	Not Free	Democracy
1985	Not Free	Democracy
1986	Not Free	Democracy
1987	Not Free	Democracy
1988	Not Free	Democracy
1989	Not Free	Democracy
1990	Not Free	Democracy
1991	Not Free	Democracy
1992	Not Free	Democracy
1993	Not Free	Democracy
1994	Not Free	Democracy
1995	Not Free	Democracy
1996	Imperfectly Free	Democracy
1997	Imperfectly Free	Democracy
1998	Imperfectly Free	Democracy
1999	Imperfectly Free	Democracy
2000	Imperfectly Free	Democracy
2001	Imperfectly Free	Democracy
2002	Free	Democracy
2003	Free	Democracy
2004	Free	Democracy
2005	Free	Democracy
2006	Free	Democracy
2007	Free	Democracy
2008	Free	Democracy
2009	Free	Democracy
2010	Free	Democracy
2011	Free	Democracy
2012	Imperfectly Free	Democracy

Chronology

1948–1995: Not Free

It was almost inevitable that the Cold War would dominate the post-World War II politics of Greece. Communist-controlled resistance fighters emerged from the war as the most powerful faction in the country, and three neighboring communist states joined the communist bloc. A civil war ensued between the communists and the U.K.-backed nationalist government. Moreover, anticommunist politics led the United States to give extensive aid to the Greek government, which allowed it to overwhelm the communist forces in 1949. Elections were held shortly after the end of the civil war, but media were heavily restricted and there was little opportunity to contest the U.S.-backed conservatives. This began to break down in the 1960s, as the government became both more centrist and unstable, but media remained controlled. Media were also seen as a tool of conservative forces that were backed economically by the United States. Both legislation and financial support from the government were used as means of control. All broadcast media were state run.

In 1967, a coup on the eve of elections brought a right wing military junta to power. Civil liberties were suppressed, and what freedom the already heavily restricted media had was eliminated. It is unclear if there was direct U.S. backing of the coup, but the junta claimed U.S. support as a way of deterring opposition. The belief that the United States was involved would have effects in the slow adoption of effective media freedom even after legal and economic liberalization of the media began in the 1980s. All television and radio were state run.

In 1975, following a disastrous attempt to intervene in Cyprus, the military junta fell and a more moderate, elected government eased direct controls on the media but kept the press highly restricted both through legislation that limited threats to stability and through economic coercion with government economic supports of the industry. A socialist government was elected in 1980, and, ironically, in the mid-1980s, Greece began a process of developing a market-based media system by deregulating aspects of ownership. Direct state control of broadcast media was eased in the mid-1980s, and privately owned channels began to appear. The press, however, was heavily partisan, and both legislative and economic mechanisms were used to limit the ability of wealth, largely conservative owners of these news outlets from undermining or destabilizing the government. It is unclear if United States President Reagan's neoanticommunist policies included support of any kind for socialist political opponents in Greece, but the history of U.S. involvement made it easy to understand the socialist government's belief that it needed to restrict the actions of the new cadre of wealthy media owners. A robust economy under the socialist government further limited populist pressures to liberalize content restrictions.

There was extreme political instability in 1989, with two parliamentary elections held in a matter of months. This led to an increase in restrictions on the press, largely in the name of stability. The fear of instability was exacerbated by the brutal war in the former Yugoslavia, just to Greece's north.

With the Cold War over and the Prime minister responsible for the latest round of media restrictions in poor health, a process of liberalization began in 1995. It was notable that the overt use of news media outlets for partisan political purposes had diminished significantly in the decade since market reforms were introduced.

During the transition in 1995, there were a number of attacks on news media. Journalists were subject to death threats, imprisonment, fines, and in a few cases, bombings.[1] One of the biggest stories of 1995 was when George Kouris published a nude picture of the Prime Minister's wife in his daily newspaper. The journalist quickly went into hiding after hearing the prosecutor's order for his arrest.[1]

1996–2001: Imperfectly Free

Elections in 1996 were notable for the robustness and diversity of the campaign coverage and marked the end of efforts to restrict the media. Media were still subject to influence and partisan leanings were evident, but they were functionally free. Journalists did still face some pressures. For example in 1996, Parliament accused some privately owned television channels of dispersing Turkish propaganda, but the television companies fought back and accused

the government of attempting to silence the media.[2]

2002–2011: Free

Pressures on news media continued to lessen, and by 2002, Greek media were mostly free.[3] Although the Constitution had provisions guaranteeing media freedom and these were for the most part respected in practice, from time to time the government put pressure on news media, and insults against the president remained a criminal offence, punishable by fines and/or imprisonment. Nearly all the newspapers were privately owned.[4]

2012: Imperfectly Free

Economic declines and government efforts to quell political dissent created an increasingly hostile environment for news media, to the extent that Greek media became imperfectly free. There were increasing reports of attacks on journalists. In addition, economic difficulties led to closures and cutbacks at both print and broadcast news organizations, which subsequently limited citizens' access to accurate information about Greece's economic and political struggles.[5]

Media Today

Greek media are imperfectly free and remain vulnerable to economic and political coercion. Ownership is highly concentrated. The history of restricting the press in the name of domestic political stability raises fears that legislative restrictions could be imposed as part of any crisis response.

Notes

1. *World Press Freedom Review*, IPI Report (Vienna: International Press Institute, 1995).
2. *World Press Freedom Review*, IPI Report (Vienna: International Press Institute, 1996).
3. *Greece* (Washington, DC: Freedom House, 2003). Available at http://www.freedomhouse.org/report/freedom-press/2003/Greece.
4. *Greece*, Media Landscape Reports (Maastricht, The Netherlands: European Journalism Centre, 2013). Available at http://ejc.net/media_landscapes/greece.
5. *Greece* (Washington, DC: Freedom House, 2013). Available at http://www.freedomhouse.org/report/freedom-press/2013/greece.

Grenada: 1974–2012

Grenada Year by Year

Year	Media	Government
1974	Not Free	Democracy
1975	Not Free	Democracy
1976	Not Free	Democracy
1977	Not Free	Democracy
1978	Not Free	Democracy
1979	Not Free	Anocracy
1980	Not Free	Anocracy
1981	Not Free	Anocracy
1982	Not Free	Anocracy
1983	Not Free	Anocracy
1984	Not Free	Democracy
1985	Imperfectly Free	Democracy
1986	Imperfectly Free	Democracy
1987	Imperfectly Free	Democracy
1988	Imperfectly Free	Democracy
1989	Imperfectly Free	Democracy
1990	Imperfectly Free	Democracy
1991	Imperfectly Free	Democracy
1992	Imperfectly Free	Democracy
1993	Free	Democracy
1994	Free	Democracy
1995	Free	Democracy
1996	Free	Democracy
1997	Free	Democracy

(Continued)

MEDIA FREEDOM HISTORY IN A NUTSHELL

- Following independence, news media in Grenada were not free—largely due to political instability
- After a coup and then a U.S. invasion in 1983, elections were held in 1984
- As Grenada democratized, media became functionally free in 1985
- Grenada has a several independent newspapers
- The Grenadian Broadcasting Network (GBN) is partially owned by the government and runs the country's major television and radio stations, and additional stations are privately owned (BBC News Country Profiles)
- As of 2012, about 42 percent of Grenadians had Internet access (International Telecommunication Union's 2012 ICT Indicators Database)

In Brief

Upon independence, Grenadian news media were not free, largely because of corruption and political instability. Since the 1984 elections Grenada has experienced political stability and news media have been functionally free.

Chronology

1974–1984: Not Free

Upon gaining independence from Britain, Grenada adopted a constitution that called for media freedom, but the government of Prime Minister Eric Gairy did not respect this in practice. Although Gairy was ousted in a coup led by Maurice Bishop in 1979, the news media continued to be restricted. In 1979, the government closed down Grenada's only privately owned newspaper on the grounds that it was a threat to national security.[1] In 1980, the government suppressed a newspaper sponsored by the Catholic

(Continued)

Year	Media	Government
1998	Free	Democracy
1999	Free	Democracy
2000	Free	Democracy
2001	Free	Democracy
2002	Free	Democracy
2003	Free	Democracy
2004	Free	Democracy
2005	Free	Democracy
2006	Free	Democracy
2007	Free	Democracy
2008	Free	Democracy
2009	Free	Democracy
2010	Free	Democracy
2011	Free	Democracy
2012	Free	Democracy

Church and accused the Church of serving as "an instrument of destabilization."[2]

In 1983, Maurice Bishop was executed following a coup led by Deputy Prime Minister Bernard Coard and General Hudson Austin. A U.S. military intervention removed Austin and Coard, and in 1984, elections were held and Herbert Blaize was elected Prime Minister.

1985–1992: Imperfectly Free

By 1985, the media environment had improved to the point where the media were imperfectly free. The Inter American Press Association noted the country now had a "pluralistic press" with five newspapers, one of which was put out by the opposition Maurice Bishop Patriotic Movement.[3]

1993–2012: Free

The media environment continued to improve, and by 1993, the media were free.[4]

Media Today

The Grenadian media remain vibrant and pluralistic. The constitution has provisions for media freedom, which the government usually respects in practice. In July 2012, the Parliament decriminalized libel and defamation.[5] Grenada has a variety of privately owned newspapers. The Grenada Broadcasting Network is partially owned by the government and runs the country's primary television and radio stations, but there are several privately owned radio stations and one privately owned television station.[6]

Notes

1. *Country Reports on Human Rights Practices for 1979* (Washington, DC: U.S. State Department, 1980). Available at http://babel.hathitrust.org/cgi/pt?id=mdp.39015014188273;view=1up;seq=337.
2. *Country Reports on Human Rights Practices for 1980* (Washington, DC: U.S. State Department, 1981), 438. Available at http://babel.hathitrust.org/cgi/pt?id=mdp.39015014143476;view=1up;seq=450.
3. *Report of the Committee on Freedom of the Press and Information*, Midyear Meeting (Zurich: Inter American Press Association, 1986), 3.
4. *Country Reports on Human Rights for 1993* (Washington, DC: U.S. State Department, 1994). Available at http://dosfan.lib.uic.edu/ERC/democracy/1993_hrp_report/93hrp_report_ara/Grenada.html.
5. *Grenada*, Country Reports on Human Rights (Washington, DC: U.S. State Department, 2012). Available at http://www.state.gov/j/drl/rls/hrrpt/humanrightsreport/index.htm?year=2012&dlid=204452.
6. Ibid

Guatemala: 1948–2012

Guatemala Year by Year

Year	Media	Government
1948	Imperfectly Free	Anocracy
1949	Imperfectly Free	Anocracy
1950	Imperfectly Free	Anocracy
1951	Imperfectly Free	Anocracy
1952	Imperfectly Free	Anocracy
1953	Imperfectly Free	Anocracy
1954	Imperfectly Free	Autocracy
1955	Not Free	Autocracy
1956	Not Free	Autocracy
1957	Not Free	Autocracy
1958	Not Free	Anocracy
1959	Not Free	Anocracy
1960	Not Free	Anocracy
1961	Not Free	Anocracy
1962	Not Free	Anocracy
1963	Not Free	Anocracy
1964	Not Free	Anocracy
1965	Not Free	Anocracy
1966	Not Free	Anocracy
1967	Not Free	Anocracy
1968	Not Free	Anocracy
1969	Not Free	Anocracy
1970	Not Free	Anocracy
1971	Not Free	Anocracy

(Continued)

MEDIA FREEDOM HISTORY IN A NUTSHELL

- The 1954 U.S.-backed coup marked the end of a period of democratic reforms and media freedom
- As Guatemala descended into a civil war that lasted more than three and a half decades and left as many as 200,000 dead, the country became one of the most dangerous in the region for journalists
- Although the 1996 peace agreement brought an end to the war, it took several years for media freedom to return to Guatemala, and the country's media environment remains precarious as the country teeters on the border of imperfectly free and not free
- As of 2013, Guatemala had four independently owned daily newspapers, four television stations owned by the same company, and several private and one state-owned radio station (BBC News Country Profiles)
- As of 2012, about 16 percent of Guatemalans had Internet access (International Telecommunication Union's 2012 ICT Indicators Database)

In Brief

From the mid-1940s to the mid-1950s, Guatemala went through a series of democratic reforms and the media were imperfectly free. Following the 1954 U.S.-backed coup, Guatemala descended into a long civil war during which Guatemala became one of the most dangerous countries in Latin America for journalists. Although the 1996 peace agreement brought an end to the civil war, media freedom did not return to the country until 1999, and since then state of media freedom has been precarious at best.

Chronology

1948–1954: Imperfectly Free

Guatemala's first major newspaper *La Hora* has a history of criticizing government that dates

(Continued)

Year	Media	Government
1972	Not Free	Anocracy
1973	Not Free	Anocracy
1974	Not Free	Anocracy
1975	Not Free	Anocracy
1976	Not Free	Anocracy
1977	Not Free	Anocracy
1978	Not Free	Anocracy
1979	Not Free	Anocracy
1980	Not Free	Anocracy
1981	Not Free	Anocracy
1982	Not Free	Autocracy
1983	Not Free	Autocracy
1984	Not Free	Autocracy
1985	Not Free	Anocracy
1986	Not Free	Anocracy
1987	Not Free	Anocracy
1988	Not Free	Anocracy
1989	Not Free	Anocracy
1990	Not Free	Anocracy
1991	Not Free	Anocracy
1992	Not Free	Anocracy
1993	Not Free	Anocracy
1994	Not Free	Anocracy
1995	Not Free	Anocracy
1996	Not Free	Democracy
1997	Not Free	Democracy
1998	Not Free	Democracy
1999	Imperfectly Free	Democracy
2000	Imperfectly Free	Democracy
2001	Imperfectly Free	Democracy
2002	Imperfectly Free	Democracy
2003	Not Free	Democracy

back to its start in 1920 near the end of the dictatorship of Manuel Estrada Cabrera.[1] Then the paper, which marked the beginning of a publishing dynasty for owner Clemente Marroquín Rojas, "challenged the central government by publishing stories about army massacres of peasants and covered union battles against government forces and the nation's business elite."[2] Even so, in the 1930s and early 1940s, media were not free during the dictatorship of General Jorge Ubico Castañeda, and *La Hora* was closed down and Marroquin was exiled until Ubico was overthrown in 1944. Following Ubico's ouster, President Juan José Arevalo brought a number of social-democratic reforms to Guatemala, such that by 1948 and until 1954, news media were functionally free.[3]

1955–1998: Not Free

Following the 1954 U.S.-backed coup, conditions for news media deteriorated and news media were no longer free to criticize the government about issues of importance. Though the Inter American Press Association continued to declare that Guatemala had freedom of the press in its annual meetings until 1963, the organization acknowledged in 1956 that the government had shut down a procommunist student newspaper and an opposition paper.[4] (It is important to note here that during these years the IAPA saw its mission of promoting press freedom as being closely connected to the fight against communism.) In 1960, civil war erupted between the U.S.-backed army and leftist insurgents and continued through 1996. During these decades as an estimated 200,000 or more people were killed or disappeared, Guatemala was one of the most dangerous countries in the region for journalists. The International Press Institute reported that at least eighty journalists died during the conflict.[5]

Although the 1996 peace agreement marked the end of the civil war, Guatemala remained a perilous place for journalists. In 1997 alone four journalists were murdered and journalists continued to face threats and harassment.[6] Moreover critical news outlets risked losing advertising revenue.[7]

1999–2002: Imperfectly Free

By 1999, the media environment had improved to the degree that media were functionally free,

Year	Media	Government
2004	Imperfectly Free	Democracy
2005	Imperfectly Free	Democracy
2006	Imperfectly Free	Democracy
2007	Imperfectly Free	Democracy
2008	Imperfectly Free	Democracy
2009	Imperfectly Free	Democracy
2010	Imperfectly Free	Democracy
2011	Imperfectly Free	Democracy
2012	Imperfectly Free	Democracy

but journalists continued to face threats and attacks from "drug traffickers, corrupt officials and other criminal elements intent on silencing the media."[8]

2003: Not Free

In 2003, there were a number of violent attacks on journalists that prompted Freedom House to downgrade its rating of the media environment.[9] These attacks included the kidnapping of four journalists by former paramilitary fighters to extract payment from the government (they were later released unharmed).[10]

2004–2012: Imperfectly Free

Although attacks on news media remained a problem, by 2004, the frequency and viciousness of these acts declined to the point where media were again imperfectly free. In spite of the ongoing threats, the news media persisted in acting independently and providing critical coverage of the government, the military, and drug traffickers.[11]

Media Today

The Guatemalan constitution has provisions for media freedom; though the government respects these for the most part, journalists continue to face threats, punitive lawsuits, and attacks. These threats come not only from corrupt government officials, but also from organized crime.[12] In addition to these negative pressures, there are allegations that the government influences media by advertising only with supportive news outlets.[13] Thus, Guatemala remains on the border of being imperfectly free and not free.

Notes

1. Rick Rockwell and Noreene Janus, *Media Power in Central America* (Chicago: University of Illinois Press, 2003).
2. Ibid., 101.
3. *Press of the Americas* (Miami, FL: Inter American Press Association, April 1, 1954).
4. *1956 General Assembly* (Miami, FL: Inter American Press Association, 1957).
5. *World Press Freedom Review*, IPI Report (Vienna: International Press Institute, 1998).
6. Ibid.
7. *World Press Freedom Review*, IPI Report (Vienna: International Press Institute, 1999).
8. Ibid.
9. *Freedom of the Press* (Washington, DC: Freedom House, 2004). Available at http://freedomhouse .org/report/freedom-press/2004/guatemala.
10. *Four Journalists Abducted by Former Paramilitaries* (Committee to Protect Journalists, 2013). Available at http://cpj.org/2003/10/four-journalists-abducted-by-former-paramilitaries-1.php.
11. *Guatemala*, Country Reports on Human Rights (Washington, DC: U.S. State Department, 2005). Available at http://www.state.gov/j/drl/rls/hrrpt/2004/41762.htm.
12. *Guatemala*, Country Reports on Human Rights (Washington, DC: U.S. State Department, 2013). Available at http://www.state.gov/j/drl/rls/hrrpt/humanrightsreport/index.htm#wrapper.
13. Ibid.

Guinea: 1958–2012

Guinea Year by Year

Year	Media	Government
1958	Not Free	Autocracy
1959	Not Free	Autocracy
1960	Not Free	Autocracy
1961	Not Free	Autocracy
1962	Not Free	Autocracy
1963	Not Free	Autocracy
1964	Not Free	Autocracy
1965	Not Free	Autocracy
1966	Not Free	Autocracy
1967	Not Free	Autocracy
1968	Not Free	Autocracy
1969	Not Free	Autocracy
1970	Not Free	Autocracy
1971	Not Free	Autocracy
1972	Not Free	Autocracy
1973	Not Free	Autocracy
1974	Not Free	Autocracy
1975	Not Free	Autocracy
1976	Not Free	Autocracy
1977	Not Free	Autocracy
1978	Not Free	Autocracy
1979	Not Free	Autocracy
1980	Not Free	Autocracy
1981	Not Free	Autocracy
1982	Not Free	Autocracy
1983	Not Free	Autocracy

MEDIA FREEDOM HISTORY IN A NUTSHELL

- Since independence, Guinea has been under authoritarian rule
- With the exception of a brief period of political openness in 2010, media have not been free
- The only daily newspaper is state owned, but there are private newspapers, which publish less frequently (BBC News Country Profiles)
- The only television outlet is state owned
- Radio remains the most accessible medium and there is a mix of state-owned and privately owned stations
- State-owned media reported almost exclusively on the Council for Democracy and Development (CNDD). Private and state radio remain the most important media outlets (World Association of Newspaper's 2010 World Newspaper Trends)
- As of 2012, less than 2 percent of Guineans had Internet access (International Telecommunication Union's 2012 ICT Indicators Database)

In Brief

Since gaining independence from France, Guinea has been ruled by authoritarian governments. With the exception of a brief period of political openness in 2010, media have not been free.

Chronology

1958–2009: Not Free

After gaining independence from France in 1958, Guinea became a one-party socialist state led by President Ahmed Sekou Toure, and news media were government controlled. When Toure died in 1984, the military seized control of the country, Lansana Conte was named President, and news media remained restricted.[1] In the early

Year	Media	Government
1984	Not Free	Autocracy
1985	Not Free	Autocracy
1986	Not Free	Autocracy
1987	Not Free	Autocracy
1988	Not Free	Autocracy
1989	Not Free	Autocracy
1990	Not Free	Autocracy
1991	Not Free	Anocracy
1992	Not Free	Anocracy
1993	Not Free	Anocracy
1994	Not Free	Anocracy
1995	Not Free	Anocracy
1996	Not Free	Anocracy
1997	Not Free	Anocracy
1998	Not Free	Anocracy
1999	Not Free	Anocracy
2000	Not Free	Anocracy
2001	Not Free	Anocracy
2002	Not Free	Anocracy
2003	Not Free	Anocracy
2004	Not Free	Anocracy
2005	Not Free	Anocracy
2006	Not Free	Anocracy
2007	Not Free	Anocracy
2008	Not Free	Anocracy
2009	Not Free	Anocracy
2010	Imperfectly Free	Anocracy
2011	Not Free	Anocracy
2012	Not Free	Anocracy

arrest, and physical attacks.[4,5] In 2008, President Conte died and the military seized control of the country. In 2009, the military opened fire on a rally at a stadium, killing more than 150 people and injuring as many as 1,200. This political violence prompted the African Union, the European Union, and the United States to impose sanctions on Guinea.

2010: Imperfectly Free

In 2010, as Guinea prepared for presidential election and adopted a new constitution with provisions for media freedom, the media environment improved to the degree that the media were imperfectly free.[6]

2011–2012: Not Free

Ethnic tensions and increasing unrest slowed down Guinea's efforts to democratize, and the government failed in practice to respect the constitutional provisions for media freedom.

Media Today

While Guinea has constitutional provisions for media freedom, the government does not respect these measures in practice. Although Guinea has independent newspapers, these publications are not accessible to the majority of Guineans because approximately 59 percent of them cannot read. Although radio is an accessible medium and there are private radio stations, journalists who criticize government are vulnerable to harassment and radio broadcasts have been suspended.[7]

Notes

1. *World Press Freedom Review*, IPI Report (Zurich: International Press Institute, December 1990).
2. *World Press Freedom Review*, IPI Report (Zurich: International Press Institute, December 1991).
3. *World Press Freedom Review*, IPI Report (Vienna: International Press Institute, December 1994).
4. *World Press Freedom Review*, IPI Report (Vienna: International Press Institute, November/December 1995).
5. *World Press Freedom Review*, IPI Report (Vienna: International Press Institute, 1996).
6. *Freedom of the Press* (Washington, DC: Freedom House, 2013). Available at http://www.freedomhouse.org/report/freedom-press/2011/guinea.
7. *Guinea*, Country Reports on Human Rights (Washington, DC: U.S. State Department, 2012).

1990s, privately owned newspapers began to emerge in Guinea.[2] In December of 1993, Guinea held its first free elections amid a great deal of unrest, and the news media were attacked because they were caught in the middle of the conflict.[3] Government retained control over broadcast media, and journalists working for independent newspapers were vulnerable to lawsuits, threats,

Guinea-Bissau: 1974–2012

Guinea-Bissau Year by Year

Year	Media	Government
1974	Not Free	Autocracy
1975	Not Free	Autocracy
1976	Not Free	Autocracy
1977	Not Free	Autocracy
1978	Not Free	Autocracy
1979	Not Free	Autocracy
1980	Not Free	Autocracy
1981	Not Free	Autocracy
1982	Not Free	Autocracy
1983	Not Free	Autocracy
1984	Not Free	Autocracy
1985	Not Free	Autocracy
1986	Not Free	Autocracy
1987	Not Free	Autocracy
1988	Not Free	Autocracy
1989	Not Free	Autocracy
1990	Not Free	Autocracy
1991	Imperfectly Free	Autocracy
1992	Imperfectly Free	Autocracy
1993	Imperfectly Free	Autocracy
1994	Imperfectly Free	Anocracy
1995	Not Free	Anocracy
1996	Not Free	Anocracy
1997	Not Free	Anocracy
1998	Not Free	Anocracy

MEDIA FREEDOM HISTORY IN A NUTSHELL

- Since independence, political instability has led to a precarious media environment
- Although the country experienced periods in early 1990s and the late-2000s when media were imperfectly free, the political uncertainty made the freedom during these periods tenuous at best
- As of 2013, there were two weekly newspapers (one state and one independent), two television stations (one state and one run by RTP, the Portuguese public broadcaster), and a mix of private and state-run radio stations (BBC News Country Profiles)
- As of 2012, about 3 percent of Guinea-Bissauans had Internet access (International Telecommunication Union's 2012 ICT Indicators Database)

In Brief

Since independence, Guinea-Bissau has experienced many coups and much corruption. This political turmoil has made it difficult for news media to fulfill any sort of watchdog role. Although the media environment has shifted between not free and imperfectly free, the situation for news media has always been precarious at best—largely due to the political instability. Financial difficulties also limit the ability of both state and independent print and broadcast media to provide reliable news coverage.

Chronology

1974–1990: Not Free

Upon gaining independence from Portugal in 1974, Guinea-Bissau became a one-party state under the control of Luis Cabral and the African

Year	Media	Government
1999	Not Free	Anocracy
2000	Not Free	Anocracy
2001	Not Free	Anocracy
2002	Not Free	Anocracy
2003	Not Free	Anocracy
2004	Imperfectly Free	Anocracy
2005	Imperfectly Free	Democracy
2006	Imperfectly Free	Democracy
2007	Imperfectly Free	Democracy
2008	Imperfectly Free	Democracy
2009	Imperfectly Free	Democracy
2010	Imperfectly Free	Democracy
2011	Imperfectly Free	Democracy
2012	Not Free	Democracy

Party for the Independence of Guinea and Cape Verde (PAIGC). Although the constitution called for media freedom, the government did not respect this in practice, and all media were controlled by government.[1] Joao Bernardo Vieira seized power in a military coup in 1980, and the news media remained government controlled.[2]

In 1990, the government began to move toward a multiparty system and there were signs of the beginnings of a tolerance for some media freedom.[3]

1991–1994: Imperfectly Free

In 1991, the Assembly adopted legislation on media freedom and the state-owned media were allowed to operate with greater independence.[4] The country held its first multiparty elections in 1994, but there was no change in leadership as João Bernardo Vieira won the presidency.

1995–2003: Not Free

The media environment deteriorated in 1995, as one independent newspaper was shut down and its editor was detained and severely beaten as he tried to leave the country.[5] Opposition leaders were given little coverage by the state-owned media, and there were other reports of journalists being questioned by government officials regarding their news coverage to the extent that journalists seeking to avoid problems engaged in self-censorship.[6]

In 1998, as conflict erupted between President Vieira and the military, news media remained restricted.[7] Although Vieira was defeated in 1999 and elections were held in 2000, newly elected President Kumba Yala had a contentious relationship with the independent news media.[8] Continued political turmoil led to continued restrictions on Bissau-Ginean media throughout the early 2000s, as those in power sought to silence the opposition. These included arrests of journalists and the closure of an opposition radio station in 2003.[9]

2004–2011: Imperfectly Free

In September of 2003, President Yala was ousted in a military coup and, as the interim government relaxed controls on news media, independent radio stations resumed broadcasting.[10] The media environment remained imperfectly free as the political turmoil continued—including the 2009 assassination of President Vieira who had returned to power in 2005, several mutinies, and the U.S. government's implication of top military officials in drug trafficking.

2012: Not Free

In 2012, the media environment deteriorated following a coup and the new government's restrictions on coverage of the coup and the protests that followed.[11]

Media Today

Media remain restricted in Guinea-Bissau. Given the country's history of political upheaval, the media environment could certainly change, but whether it will change for the better is difficult to predict. Financial challenges also make it difficult for both state and independent media to function. One promising sign was the interim government's reversal of its decision to expel Radio-Télévision Portugaise journalist Fernando Gomes in late 2012.[12] At the end of 2013, the interim government remained in power as elections were postponed until 2014. Guinea-Bissau has a mix of private and state-run print and broadcast media. As of 2012, less than 3 percent of Bissau-Guineans had Internet access.

Notes

1. *Country Reports on Human Rights Practices for 1977* (Washington, DC: U.S. State Department, 1978). Available at http://babel.hathitrust.org/cgi/pt?id=mdp.39015078705632;view=1up;seq=62.

2. *Country Reports on Human Rights Practices for 1980* (Washington, DC: U.S. State Department, 1981). Available at http://babel.hathitrust.org/cgi/pt?id=mdp.39015014143476;view=1up;seq=130.

3. *Guinea-Bissau*, Country Reports on Human Rights (Washington, DC: U.S. State Department, 1991).

4. *World Press Freedom Review*, IPI Report (Zurich: International Press Institute, 1991).

5. *Guinea-Bissau*, Country Reports on Human Rights (Washington, DC: U.S. State Department, 1995).

6. *World Press Freedom Review*, IPI Report (Vienna: International Press Institute, November/December 1995).

7. *World Press Freedom Review*, IPI Report (Vienna: International Press Institute, 1998).

8. *Guinea-Bissau*, Country Reports on Human Rights (Washington, DC: U.S. State Department, 2002).

9. *Freedom of the Press* (Washington, DC: Freedom House, 2004). Available at http://www.freedomhouse.org/report/freedom-press/2004/guinea-bissau.

10. *World Press Freedom Review*, IPI Report (Vienna: International Press Institute, 2005).

11. *Freedom of the Press* (Washington, DC: Freedom House, 2013). Available at http://www.freedomhouse.org/report/freedom-press/2013/guinea-bissau.

12. *Government Reverses Decision to Expel RTP Bureau Chief* (Paris, France: Reporters Without Borders, 2012). Available at http://en.rsf.org/guinee-bissau-rtp-bureau-chief-deported-amid-02-11-2012,43630.html.

Guyana: 1967–2012

Guyana Year by Year

Year	Media	Government
1967	Not Free	Anocracy
1968	Not Free	Anocracy
1969	Not Free	Anocracy
1970	Not Free	Anocracy
1971	Not Free	Anocracy
1972	Not Free	Anocracy
1973	Not Free	Anocracy
1974	Not Free	Anocracy
1975	Not Free	Anocracy
1976	Not Free	Anocracy
1977	Not Free	Anocracy
1978	Not Free	Anocracy
1979	Not Free	Anocracy
1980	Not Free	Autocracy
1981	Not Free	Autocracy
1982	Not Free	Autocracy
1983	Not Free	Autocracy
1984	Not Free	Autocracy
1985	Not Free	Autocracy
1986	Not Free	Autocracy
1987	Not Free	Autocracy
1988	Not Free	Autocracy
1989	Not Free	Autocracy
1990	Not Free	Autocracy

(Continued)

MEDIA FREEDOM HISTORY IN A NUTSHELL

- After independence Guyanese media were controlled by government
- As the country democratized in the early 1990s, these restrictions slowly gave way and media became imperfectly free
- As of 2009, there were three paid-for daily newspapers with an average circulation per issue of 30,000 (World Association of Newspaper's 2010 World Newspaper Trends)
- There are more than twenty television stations, most of which are privately owned and functionally free
- The government owns and operates the country's only radio stations (but there were indications that independent stations might be permitted to begin broadcasting in 2012)
- As of 2012, about 34 percent of Guyanese had Internet access (International Telecommunication Union's 2012 ICT Indicators Database)

In Brief

After Guyana gained independence from Britain in 1966, the government tightly controlled all media using a variety of legal, political, and economic restrictions. As the country began to democratize in the early 1990s, these restrictions slowly gave way. The government does own and operate a major newspaper, television station, and (as of this writing) all the country's radio stations, but there are also independently owned newspapers and television stations that span the spectrum of political views. While Guyanese news media are for the most part free, those who criticize the government have faced libel suits and advertisement bans.

(Continued)

Year	Media	Government
1991	Not Free	Autocracy
1992	Not Free	Democracy
1993	Not Free	Democracy
1994	Not Free	Democracy
1995	Imperfectly Free	Democracy
1996	Imperfectly Free	Democracy
1997	Imperfectly Free	Democracy
1998	Imperfectly Free	Democracy
1999	Imperfectly Free	Democracy
2000	Imperfectly Free	Democracy
2001	Imperfectly Free	Democracy
2002	Imperfectly Free	Democracy
2003	Imperfectly Free	Democracy
2004	Imperfectly Free	Democracy
2005	Imperfectly Free	Democracy
2006	Imperfectly Free	Democracy
2007	Imperfectly Free	Democracy
2008	Imperfectly Free	Democracy
2009	Imperfectly Free	Democracy
2010	Imperfectly Free	Democracy
2011	Imperfectly Free	Democracy
2012	Imperfectly Free	Democracy

Chronology

1966–1994: Not Free

Shortly after Guyana gained independence from Britain in 1966, the parliament passed the National Security Act, which gave the government leeway to censor and suppress all communications and methods of communication.[1] For the next three and a half decades, government efforts to control all media were persistent and successful:

In the 1970s, the government of Forbes Burnham virtually took over Guyanese

mass media, purchasing newspapers, nationalizing broadcasting, and harassing the opposition with legislative, economic, and physical sanctions. By the end of the decade, the government, by then socialist owned both dailies—the *Guyana Chronicle* and the *Citizen*—both radio stations, and the new television service.[2]

In addition to outright ownership, the government controlled news media through more covert means including fining critical news organizations for libel, limiting access to newsprint and printing presses by requiring that publishers obtain licenses to import these items, and creating conditions that discouraged foreign advertising on radio.[3] Journalists working for the few remaining independent newspapers were often harassed, threatened, and attacked. One of the most egregious attacks was in 1979, when pro-government thugs beat photographer Bernard Darke to death as he covered a protest at a police station.[4] Darke, a Jesuit missionary, had long provided pictures to the *Catholic Standard* (a weekly newspaper and one of the few not owned by the government) as well as Catholic newspapers in other countries.[5]

1995–2012: Imperfectly Free

The elections of 1992 were deemed the first to be free and fair since Guyana gained independence, yet the Guyanese media remained mostly under government control.[6] During the following three years, though, the government began to loosen its grip and independent newspapers began to report more critically of government. At the same time, Guyana gained more privately owned television stations (for a total of twelve in 1995), at least two of which did not shy away from negative news coverage of government.[7] Still the government maintained ownership and control over the country's only radio station.

Following the 1997 election, which was deemed free and fair, the media landscape continued to improve. In particular there were increasing numbers of independent newspapers and television stations that provided coverage from a variety of political perspectives.[8] However, the state maintained ownership of all of Guyanese radio stations and did not grant any requests for radio frequency allocations.[9] Until January 1999, the Ministry of Information censored Internet content and restricted access, but since then the Internet has been unrestricted.[10]

Media Today

Guyana has vibrant and robust news media, but news organizations that are critical of government continue to face advertising boycotts and libel suits.[11] In early 2012, the state monopoly of radio continued, although the government recently approved some license applications.[12] Guyana has three paid-for daily newspapers (as of 2009), twenty-three television stations, and two radio stations (as of 2010).[13,14] The Internet is not restricted, and nearly 30 percent of Guyanese have Internet access (as of 2010).[15]

Notes

1. *World Press Freedom Review*, IPI Report (Zurich: International Press Institute, February 1967), 16.
2. John A Lent, "Mass Media and Socialist Governments in the Commonwealth Caribbean," *Human Rights Quarterly* 4, no. 3 (1982): 371.
3. Ibid., 373.
4. *World Press Freedom Review*, IPI Report (Zurich: International Press Institute, December 1979), 10.
5. Ibid.
6. *Background Notes on Countries of the World: Guyana* (Washington, DC: U.S. Department of State, 2011). Available at http://www.state.gov/r/pa/ei/bgn/1984.htm.
7. *Guyana Country Report on Human Rights Practices, 1995* (Washington, DC: U.S. Department of State, 1996).
8. *Guyana Country Report on Human Rights Practices, 1998* (Washington, DC: U.S. Department of State, 1999). Available at http://www.state.gov/www/global/human_rights/1998_hrp_report/guyana.html.
9. Ibid.
10. *Guyana Country Report on Human Rights Practices, 1999* (Washington, DC: U.S. Department of State, 2000). Available at http://www.state.gov/j/drl/rls/hrrpt/1999/390.htm.
11. *Freedom of the Press* (Washington, DC: Freedom House, 2011). Available at http://www.freedomhouse.org/report/freedom-press/2011/guyana.
12. "Guyana's Press freedom ranking Remains Unchanged," KNEWS (Georgetown, Guyana: Kaieteur News, January 26, 2012). Available at http://www.kaieteurnewsonline.com/2012/01/26/guyana%E2%80%99s-press-freedom-ranking-remains-unchanged/.
13. *World Press Trends* (Darmstadt, Germany: WAN-IFRA, 2010), 542.
14. *Freedom of the Press* (Washington, DC: Freedom House, 2011).
15. *ICT Indicators Database* (Geneva, Switzerland: International Telecommunications Union, 2011). Available at http://www.itu.int/ITU-D/ict/statistics/.

Haiti: 1948–2012

Haiti Year by Year

Year	Media	Government
1948	Not Free	Anocracy
1949	Not Free	Anocracy
1950	Not Free	Anocracy
1951	Not Free	Anocracy
1952	Not Free	Anocracy
1953	Not Free	Anocracy
1954	Not Free	Anocracy
1955	Not Free	Anocracy
1956	Not Free	Anocracy
1957	Not Free	Anocracy
1958	Not Free	Autocracy
1959	Not Free	Autocracy
1960	Not Free	Autocracy
1961	Not Free	Autocracy
1962	Not Free	Autocracy
1963	Not Free	Autocracy
1964	Not Free	Autocracy
1965	Not Free	Autocracy
1966	Not Free	Autocracy
1967	Not Free	Autocracy
1968	Not Free	Autocracy
1969	Not Free	Autocracy
1970	Not Free	Autocracy
1971	Not Free	Autocracy
1972	Not Free	Autocracy
1973	Not Free	Autocracy
1974	Not Free	Autocracy
1975	Not Free	Autocracy

MEDIA FREEDOM HISTORY IN A NUTSHELL

- Decades of dictatorship and political instability left Haiti without media freedom until the mid-1990s
- Following U.S. and then U.N. intervention, media became imperfectly free in 1995
- In the early 2000s, as the number of attacks on journalists mounted, the media environment deteriorated
- With the elections of 2006, media became functionally free and have remained so in spite of the devastation of the 2010 earthquake
- Radio remains Haiti's most important medium, and the country has several hundred privately owned stations, most of which are local
- Haiti has two independently owned daily newspapers and three privately owned television channels in addition to one government-owned station (BBC News Country Profiles)
- As of 2012, about 11 percent of Haitians had Internet access (International Telecommunication Union's 2012 ICT Indicators Database)

In Brief

Decades of dictatorship and political instability combined more recently with devastating storms and the catastrophic 2010 earthquake have created a hostile environment for the Haitian news media. After decades of government restriction, media became somewhat free in the mid-1990s as the United States and then the UN intervened. In the early 2000s, media freedom was compromised as political tensions increased. With the restoration of democracy in 2006, news media were once again functionally free.

Year	Media	Government
1976	Not Free	Autocracy
1977	Not Free	Autocracy
1978	Not Free	Autocracy
1979	Not Free	Autocracy
1980	Not Free	Autocracy
1981	Not Free	Autocracy
1982	Not Free	Autocracy
1983	Not Free	Autocracy
1984	Not Free	Autocracy
1985	Not Free	Autocracy
1986	Not Free	In Transition
1987	Not Free	In Transition
1988	Not Free	Autocracy
1989	Not Free	Autocracy
1990	Not Free	Democracy
1991	Not Free	Autocracy
1992	Not Free	Autocracy
1993	Not Free	Autocracy
1994	Not Free	Democracy
1995	Imperfectly Free	Democracy
1996	Imperfectly Free	Democracy
1997	Imperfectly Free	Democracy
1998	Imperfectly Free	Democracy
1999	Imperfectly Free	In Transition
2000	Not Free	Anocracy
2001	Not Free	Anocracy
2002	Not Free	Anocracy
2003	Not Free	Anocracy
2004	Not Free	In Transition
2005	Not Free	In Transition
2006	Imperfectly Free	Anocracy
2007	Imperfectly Free	Anocracy
2008	Imperfectly Free	Anocracy
2009	Imperfectly Free	Anocracy
2010	Imperfectly Free	Interregnum
2011	Imperfectly Free	Interregnum
2012	Imperfectly Free	Interregnum

Chronology

1948–1994: Not Free

Following the Revolution of 1946—which was sparked in part by the jailing of editors of a Marxist journal—Haiti experienced a series of failed presidents and military coups. During these power struggles, media were for the most part not free.[1] In 1957, when François "Papa Doc" Duvalier became president, he promised that he would respect press freedom,[2] but by 1958, the Inter American Press Association concluded that there was no freedom of the press in Haiti after police destroyed the offices of two newspapers, a journalists was beaten, a foreign correspondent was expelled, and three Haitian journalists were each sentenced to five years in prison.[3] In addition to controlling the media, Duvalier exerted his power over rural areas of the country through a militia commonly known as the Tonton Macoutes, which terrorized and killed those who were thought to be against Duvalier. Upon Duvalier's death in 1971, his son, Jean-Claude "Baby Doc" Duvalier assumed control of the country and media remained restricted. Following mass demonstrations in 1986, Baby Doc fled the country. As the political turmoil continued, journalists were caught in the crossfire. In 1987 and 1988, there were reports of violent attacks on radio stations, and a number of journalists were wounded, at least one fatally, as they tried to document the unrest in the country.[4,5] With the 1990 election of Jean-Bertrand Aristide, there were hopes that the media environment would improve, but the situation for media actually deteriorated following a military coup in 1991. The Inter American Press Association noted that the country's most important medium, radio, was particularly hard hit as several stations were attacked and equipment was destroyed.[6]

1995–1999: Imperfectly Free

The media environment improved in the last quarter of 1994, when, under the threat of a U.S. invasion, the military relinquished control of the country and U.S. forces (later replaced by UN Peacekeepers) stepped in to facilitate the transition to a civilian government.[7] By 1995, with the help of foreign media assistance programs, several independent radio stations resumed broadcasting and privately owned newspapers resumed publishing. Yet journalists for state-run print and broadcast media continued to face pressure from the government.[8] Although conditions had improved, by the late 1990s, there were signs of trouble including allegations of police brutality against journalists, especially those covering drug trafficking and corruption.[9]

2000–2005: Not Free

By 2000, conditions had deteriorated to the point that media were not free. The Committee to Protect Journalists reported a number of attacks on journalists including the murder of *Radio Haiti* owner Jean Léopold Dominique, arguably the country's most prominent journalist.[10] Threats drove some reporters out of the country and others into hiding.[11] Conditions remained grim for journalists through 2005, as conflict erupted between government security forces and armed gangs with ties to former President Aristide.[12]

2006–2012: Imperfectly Free

With the 2006 elections, democracy and some media freedom returned to Haiti.[13] In 2010, a catastrophic earthquake left as many as 300,000 dead and destroyed much of Haiti's infrastructure.

Media Today

Poverty, corruption, political instability, and the devastation following the 2010 earthquake make Haiti a difficult place in which to practice journalism. Haiti has constitutional provisions for media freedom, which the government for the most part respects, but journalists continue to face threats. In 2013, there were a number of attacks on journalists and two were murdered, though it is unknown if they were killed because of their work.[14] Because of these threats, self-censorship remains common practice among Haitian journalists.[15]

Radio remains Haiti's primary news medium, and there are several hundred stations operating in the country—most of them local and privately owned. Poverty and poor infrastructure continue to limit Haitians' access to television, but the country does have three privately owned channels in addition to the government-owned station. Although circulation is limited, Haiti has two privately owned daily newspapers. About 11 percent of Haitians have Internet access.

Notes

1. Richard A. Haggerty, *Haiti: A Country Study* (Washington, DC: Library of Congress Federal Research Division, 1989). Available at http://lcweb2.loc.gov/frd/cs/.

2. *Report of the Committee on Freedom of the Press*, 1957 Annual Meeting (Miami, FL: Inter American Press Association, 1958).

3. Ibid.

4. *World Press Freedom Review*, IPI Report (Zurich: International Press Institute, December 1987).

5. *World Press Freedom Review*, IPI Report (Zurich: International Press Institute, December 1988).

6. *Haiti*, 1991 General Assembly (Miami, FL: Inter American Press Association, 1991). Available at http://www.sipiapa.org/en/asamblea/haiti-83/.

7. *World Press Freedom Review*, IPI Report (Vienna: International Press Institute, December 1994).

8. *World Press Freedom Review*, IPI Report (Vienna: International Press Institute, November/December 1995).

9. *World Press Freedom Review*, IPI Report (Vienna: International Press Institute, 1999).

10. *Attacks on the Press* (Committee to Protect Journalists, 2000). Available at http://cpj.org/2001/03/attacks-on-the-press-2000-haiti.php.

11. Ibid.

12. *Freedom of the Press* (Washington, DC: Freedom House, 2006). Available at http://www.freedomhouse.org/report/freedom-press/2006/haiti.

13. *Freedom of the Press* (Washington, DC: Freedom House, 2007). Available at http://www.freedomhouse.org/report/freedom-press/2007/haiti.

14. *Haiti*, 2013 General Assembly (Miami, FL: Inter American Press Association, 2013). Available at http://www.sipiapa.org/en/asamblea/haiti-130/?i=1.

15. *Freedom of the Press* (Washington, DC: Freedom House, 2013). Available at http://www.freedomhouse.org/report/freedom-press/2013/haiti.

Honduras: 1948–2012

Honduras Year by Year

Year	Media	Government
1948	Not Free	Anocracy
1949	Not Free	Anocracy
1950	Imperfectly Free	Anocracy
1951	Imperfectly Free	Anocracy
1952	Imperfectly Free	Anocracy
1953	Imperfectly Free	Anocracy
1954	Imperfectly Free	Anocracy
1955	Imperfectly Free	Anocracy
1956	Imperfectly Free	Anocracy
1957	Imperfectly Free	Anocracy
1958	Imperfectly Free	Anocracy
1959	Imperfectly Free	Anocracy
1960	Imperfectly Free	Anocracy
1961	Imperfectly Free	Anocracy
1962	Imperfectly Free	Anocracy
1963	Not Free	Anocracy
1964	Not Free	Anocracy
1965	Not Free	Anocracy
1966	Not Free	Anocracy
1967	Imperfectly Free	Anocracy
1968	Imperfectly Free	Anocracy
1969	Imperfectly Free	Anocracy
1970	Imperfectly Free	Anocracy
1971	Imperfectly Free	Anocracy
1972	Imperfectly Free	Anocracy
1973	Not Free	Anocracy
1974	Not Free	Anocracy
1975	Not Free	Anocracy

(Continued)

MEDIA FREEDOM HISTORY IN A NUTSHELL

- Five families control most of the Honduran media, and as economic elites, these families have close ties to the government and military
- The Honduran media environment has shifted between not free and imperfectly free for decades, but since the 2009 coup, media are not free
- As of 2013, there were nine paid-for daily newspapers as well as a number of privately owned broadcast media (Freedom House's Report on Freedom of the Press 2013)
- As of 2012, about 18 percent of Hondurans had Internet access (International Telecommunication Union's 2012 ICT Indicators Database)

In Brief

Most Honduran media are controlled by five families, for the most part Arab Hondurans whose families immigrated to Honduras in the early 1900s.[1] These families, known as the *turcos*, gained immense wealth largely because of their investment in industry and then invested in the country's media.[2] As economic elites, they have tended to use their media to protect their own interests. "This means they will usually support an institutionalized hierarchy or oligarchy rather than open the media system to nation building, democratic forces, or the true marketplace of ideas."[3] The military controlled the government until the mid-1980s, and during these years, although there were some periods where the media were imperfectly free, for the most part media were not free. From the mid-1980s to 2008, media were on the border of imperfectly free and not free. Since the 2009 coup, journalists have faced threats from government, opposition, and organized crime, and as a result Honduras has become one of the most dangerous countries for journalists.

(Continued)

Year	Media	Government
1976	Not Free	Anocracy
1977	Not Free	Anocracy
1978	Not Free	Anocracy
1979	Not Free	Anocracy
1980	Not Free	In Transition
1981	Not Free	In Transition
1982	Not Free	Democracy
1983	Not Free	Democracy
1984	Not Free	Democracy
1985	Not Free	Anocracy
1986	Not Free	Anocracy
1987	Not Free	Anocracy
1988	Not Free	Anocracy
1989	Not Free	Democracy
1990	Not Free	Democracy
1991	Not Free	Democracy
1992	Not Free	Democracy
1993	Not Free	Democracy
1994	Imperfectly Free	Democracy
1995	Imperfectly Free	Democracy
1996	Imperfectly Free	Democracy
1997	Imperfectly Free	Democracy
1998	Imperfectly Free	Democracy
1999	Imperfectly Free	Democracy
2000	Imperfectly Free	Democracy
2001	Imperfectly Free	Democracy
2002	Imperfectly Free	Democracy
2003	Imperfectly Free	Democracy
2004	Imperfectly Free	Democracy
2005	Imperfectly Free	Democracy
2006	Imperfectly Free	Democracy
2007	Imperfectly Free	Democracy
2008	Imperfectly Free	Democracy
2009	Not Free	Democracy
2010	Not Free	Democracy
2011	Not Free	Democracy
2012	Not Free	Democracy

Chronology

1948–1949: Not Free

As part of his effort to consolidate his power, President-turned-dictator Tiburcio Carías Andino began to crack down on opposition media in the mid-1930s.[4]

1950–1962: Imperfectly Free

Carías's hand-picked successor, Juan Manuel Gálvez, implemented a number of reforms including the restoration of press freedom.[5] Following an uprising in 1956, when media were censored for about twenty days, there was a military coup, but the new military government allowed the news media to remain functionally free.[6]

1963–1966: Not Free

Instead of holding elections as scheduled in 1963, the military staged a coup led by Colonel López Arellano who then claimed the presidency. During these years of military rule, media were restricted and there were reports of journalists being imprisoned and newspaper premises being destroyed.[7]

1967–1972: Imperfectly Free

By 1967, the military government tolerated some press freedom. The Inter American Press Association noted that the National Congress had repealed an earlier law restricting press freedom.[8] As conflict escalated between Honduras and El Salvador, Salvadoran newspapers were not allowed into the country.[9]

1973–1993: Not Free

In the early 1970s, the media environment began to deteriorate, and by the mid-1970s, media were no longer free.[10] The military pressured the country's two main political parties to close their newspapers, and in 1972, established the Collegium of Journalists with mandatory membership for all Honduran journalists.[11] In 1973, the government issued a decree that those who published false reports deemed harmful to the national economy could be imprisoned for up to three years and fined, but when the Inter American Press Association complained, the government vowed not to use the decree against journalists.[12] In 1975, a Ministry of Information was established that initially attempted to force newspapers to carry government-dictated news, but Honduran news media protested and the government backed down.[13] Even so, most news media remained in the hands of five families who were closely tied to the military and unlikely to criticize the government.

In 1981, Honduras transitioned to a civilian government with the election of Roberto Suazo Cordova, but in reality, the military remained in power with strong support from the United States as the United States used Honduras as a base to train counter-revolutionaries from Nicaragua and El Salvador.

In the early 1990s, concerns grew that media freedom was being compromised by military pressures.[14] In 1991, the government threatened to press criminal charges against journalists who were not licensed by the Collegium.[15] In 1993, there were allegations that a number of government agencies had paid reporters for favorable coverage, and some media observers estimated that half of all journalists had accepted payoffs.[16]

1994–2008: Imperfectly Free

At the end of 1993, there were hopes that newly elected President Carlos Roberto Reina, a lawyer and human rights advocate, would have greater respect for press freedom.[17] While these hopes were dashed in early 1994 when Reina ordered the news media to stop providing news coverage of the Presidential Office, the media environment did improve to the point that the media were functionally free, but only barely so.[18] In 1999, more allegations surfaced about journalists accepting payoffs to provide favorable coverage and suppress other stories.[19] Additionally, there were several reports of journalists being pressured and threatened by government officials following critical news coverage.[20] Moreover, the penal code criminalized libel and insulting of public officials and made these crimes punishable by up to four years in prison; offending the president carried a prison term of up to twelve years.[21]

2009–2012: Not Free

In the late 2000s, the Honduran media environment declined as the relationship between the news media and President Manuel Zelaya became increasingly contentious. Journalists faced threats not only from government but also from organized crime.[22] In 2009, Zelaya was ousted in a military coup and attacks on journalists increased as the conflict between the military and Zelaya's supporters intensified.[23]

Media Today

Attacks on journalists remain a problem and often go unpunished.[24] Although Honduras has a wide range of privately owned media, the attacks on journalists tend to intimidate journalists and encourage self-censorship. Honduras has as many as nine daily newspapers, as well as a number of privately owned television and radio stations.[25] Access to online media remains limited as only about 18 percent of Hondurans have Internet access.[26]

Notes

1. Rick Rockwell and Noreene Janus, *Media Power in Central America* (Chicago: University of Illinois Press, 2003).
2. Ibid.
3. Ibid., 48.
4. Tim Merrill, *Honduras: A Country Study* (Washington, DC: Library of Congress Federal Research Division, 1993). Available at http://lcweb2.loc.gov/frd/cs/.
5. Ibid.
6. *State of the Press*, 1956 Annual Meeting (Miami, FL: Inter American Press Association, 1957).
7. *Report by the Committee on Freedom of the Press*, 1965 Annual Meeting (Miami, FL: Inter American Press Association, 1966).
8. *Report of the Committee on Freedom of the Press*, 1967 Annual Meeting (Miami, FL: Inter American Press Association, 1968).
9. *Report of the Committee on Freedom of the Press*, 1969 Annual Meeting (Miami, FL: Inter American Press Association, 1970).
10. Kim Quaile Hill and Patricia A. Hurley, "Freedom of the Press in Latin America: A Thirty-Year Survey," *Latin American Research Review* 15, no. 2 (1980): 212–18.
11. Rockwell and Janus, *Media Power in Central America*.
12. *Report of the Committee on Freedom of the Press*, 1974 Annual Meeting (Miami, FL: Inter American Press Association, 1975).
13. *Report of the Committee on Freedom of the Press*, 1976 Annual Meeting (Miami, FL: Inter American Press Association, 1977).
14. *Freedom of the Press Report* (Miami, FL: Inter American Press Association, 1991).
15. *Honduras*, 1991 General Assembly (Miami, FL: Inter America Press Association, 1991). Available at http://www.sipiapa.org/en/asamblea/honduras-81/.

16. Merrill, *Honduras: A Country Study,* 7.
17. *World Press Freedom Review,* IPI Report (Vienna: International Press Institute, 1993).
18. *World Press Freedom Review,* IPI Report (Vienna: International Press Institute, 1994).
19. *World Press Freedom Review,* IPI Report (Vienna: International Press Institute, 1999).
20. Ibid.
21. *World Press Freedom Review,* IPI Report (Vienna: International Press Institute, 2001).
22. *Honduras,* 2008 General Assembly (Miami, FL: Inter American Press Association, 2008). Available at http://www.sipiapa.org/en/asamblea/honduras-38/.
23. *Honduras,* 2009 General Assembly (Miami, FL: Inter American Press Association, 2009). Available at http://www.sipiapa.org/en/asamblea/honduras-44/.
24. *Honduras,* 2013 General Assembly (Miami, FL: Inter American Press Association, 2013). Available at http://www.sipiapa.org/en/asamblea/honduras-124/?i=1.
25. *Freedom of the Press* (Washington, DC: Freedom House, 2013). Available at http://freedomhouse.org/report/freedom-press/2013/honduras.
26. *ICT Indicators Database* (Geneva, Switzerland: International Telecommunication Union, 2012).

Hungary: 1948–2012

Hungary Year by Year

Year	Media	Government
1948	Not Free	Autocracy
1949	Not Free	Autocracy
1950	Not Free	Autocracy
1951	Not Free	Autocracy
1952	Not Free	Autocracy
1953	Not Free	Autocracy
1954	Not Free	Autocracy
1955	Not Free	Autocracy
1956	Not Free	Revolution
1957	Not Free	Autocracy
1958	Not Free	Autocracy
1959	Not Free	Autocracy
1960	Not Free	Autocracy
1961	Not Free	Autocracy
1962	Not Free	Autocracy
1963	Not Free	Autocracy
1964	Not Free	Autocracy
1965	Not Free	Autocracy
1966	Not Free	Autocracy
1967	Not Free	Autocracy
1968	Not Free	Autocracy
1969	Not Free	Autocracy
1970	Not Free	Autocracy
1971	Not Free	Autocracy

(Continued)

MEDIA FREEDOM HISTORY IN A NUTSHELL

- A single party Soviet Bloc state with complete government control of the media until the fall of the Berlin Wall
- Transition to a functionally free press took six years
- Media freedom advocates continue to pressure the Hungarian government to rescind the restrictive 2010 media law
- As of 2011, there were thirty-one daily newspapers, thirty of which were paid-for dailies with a total average circulation per issue of 1,379,000 (World Association of Newspaper's 2012 World Newspaper Trends)
- Hungary has a mix of publicly and privately owned radio stations and television channels
- As of 2012, about 72 percent of Hungarians had access to the Internet (International Telecommunication Union's 2012 ICT Indicators Database)

In Brief

Hungary's rather tumultuous time as part of the communist bloc had little practical effect on government control of the media. Hungary was the first of the Eastern European nations to begin liberalizing, but the transition to a free media regime was slow, taking almost eight years.

Chronology

1948–1994: Not Free

As part of the communist bloc, government directly controlled media. Even during the revolution in 1956 control simply shifted to the revolutionaries, it did not end.

Hungary began the process of breaking away from the Soviet Bloc earlier than most of

(Continued)

Year	Media	Government
1972	Not Free	Autocracy
1973	Not Free	Autocracy
1974	Not Free	Autocracy
1975	Not Free	Autocracy
1976	Not Free	Autocracy
1977	Not Free	Autocracy
1978	Not Free	Autocracy
1979	Not Free	Autocracy
1980	Not Free	Autocracy
1981	Not Free	Autocracy
1982	Not Free	Autocracy
1983	Not Free	Autocracy
1984	Not Free	Autocracy
1985	Not Free	Autocracy
1986	Not Free	Autocracy
1987	Not Free	Autocracy
1988	Not Free	Anocracy
1989	Not Free	Anocracy
1990	Not Free	Democracy
1991	Not Free	Democracy
1992	Not Free	Democracy
1993	Not Free	Democracy
1994	Not Free	Democracy
1995	Imperfectly Free	Democracy
1996	Imperfectly Free	Democracy
1997	Imperfectly Free	Democracy
1998	Imperfectly Free	Democracy
1999	Imperfectly Free	Democracy
2000	Imperfectly Free	Democracy
2001	Imperfectly Free	Democracy
2002	Free	Democracy
2003	Free	Democracy

the rest of Eastern Europe, but the transition to functionally free media was slow. This was partly due to concessions made to the communist party as part of negotiating a peaceful transition to democratic rule. The poor showing of the communists in the 1990s provided an impetus to eliminate most of these concessions to the former communists, but economic issues, particularly regarding public versus private property, took precedence. Media development began and was quietly supported by Western powers. Thus, a cadre of media professionals and institutions began to emerge during this period.

1995–2001: Imperfectly Free

Indications that media were beginning to function as a free and critical voice first appeared in the 1994 elections, but it was not until the neocommunist winners of the election confirmed a commitment to economic reform and a free press as part of a continuing process of liberalization that media became functionally free.

2002–2010: Free

Media continued to gain freedom and, by 2002, were at the point where they were coded "Free," but the media remained at the edge of "Free" and "Imperfectly Free" as evidenced by the Freedom House codes. In 2010, concerns about media freedom grew as lawmakers passed a new media law.

2011-2012: Imperfectly Free

With the beginning of 2011, Hungary's new media law went into effect, which established the National Media and Infocommunications Authority (NMHH), made up of political appointees, to oversee the news media. Under this new law, fines could be imposed on journalists and news organizations for "imbalanced news coverage" and for publishing or broadcasting content deemed immoral.[1] By the end of 2011, the courts struck down a measure of the law that would have forced journalists to reveal their sources, and in 2012, print and online media were exempted from NMHH sanctioning powers. Yet media observers contend these provisions have had a chilling effect on news media and have encouraged journalists to self-censor.[2]

Year	Media	Government
2004	Free	Democracy
2005	Free	Democracy
2006	Free	Democracy
2007	Free	Democracy
2008	Free	Democracy
2009	Free	Democracy
2010	Free	Democracy
2011	Imperfectly Free	Democracy
2012	Imperfectly Free	Democracy

Media Today

Hungary media are functionally free media, but they are under economic stress, and it appears that development toward a high standard of professional and nonpartisan reporting has been stalled. However, there is no indication that the media are in danger of losing their ability to act as a critical voice in domestic politics.

Notes

1. *Attacks on the Press in 2011* (Committee to Protect Journalists, 2012). Available at http://cpj .org/2012/02/attacks-on-the-press-in-2011-hungary .php.
2. *Freedom of the Press* (Washington, DC: Freedom House, 2012). Available at http://www.freedom house.org/reports.

Iceland: 1948–2012

Iceland Year by Year

Year	Media	Government
1948	Free	Democracy
1949	Free	Democracy
1950	Free	Democracy
1951	Free	Democracy
1952	Free	Democracy
1953	Free	Democracy
1954	Free	Democracy
1955	Free	Democracy
1956	Free	Democracy
1957	Free	Democracy
1958	Free	Democracy
1959	Free	Democracy
1960	Free	Democracy
1961	Free	Democracy
1962	Free	Democracy
1963	Free	Democracy
1964	Free	Democracy
1965	Free	Democracy
1966	Free	Democracy
1967	Free	Democracy
1968	Free	Democracy
1969	Free	Democracy
1970	Free	Democracy
1971	Free	Democracy
1972	Free	Democracy
1973	Free	Democracy
1974	Free	Democracy
1975	Free	Democracy

MEDIA FREEDOM HISTORY IN A NUTSHELL

- Since Iceland became independent in 1944, it has been an exemplar of media freedom
- As of 2011, there was one paid-for daily newspaper with an average circulation per issue of 480,000 (World Association of Newspaper's 2012 World Newspaper Trends), but the country also has a very popular free daily newspaper
- The Icelandic National Broadcasting Service (RUV) provides national radio and television service, but the privately owned media 365 has gained popularity in recent years
- As of 2012, about 96 percent of Icelanders had Internet access (International Telecommunication Union's 2012 ICT Indicators Database)

In Brief

Iceland is considered a bastion of media freedom. Yet there are some concerns that recent legislation aimed at curbing hate speech may impose some constraints on news media.

Chronology

1948–2012: Free

Since Iceland became independent from Denmark in 1944, media have been free. Starting in the 1910s, newspapers had close ties to political parties.[1] It was not until the 1960s that news media began to transfer away from a partisan-driven model to a market-driven model.[2] In 2001, *Frettabladid*, a free daily newspaper, began publishing. Prior to 1986, the only radio and television broadcaster was the state-run RÚV, which has traditionally been nonpartisan.[3] Since 1986, private broadcast media have been permitted, and in recent years, the privately held 365 media

Year	Media	Government
1976	Free	Democracy
1977	Free	Democracy
1978	Free	Democracy
1979	Free	Democracy
1980	Free	Democracy
1981	Free	Democracy
1982	Free	Democracy
1983	Free	Democracy
1984	Free	Democracy
1985	Free	Democracy
1986	Free	Democracy
1987	Free	Democracy
1988	Free	Democracy
1989	Free	Democracy
1990	Free	Democracy
1991	Free	Democracy
1992	Free	Democracy
1993	Free	Democracy
1994	Free	Democracy
1995	Free	Democracy
1996	Free	Democracy
1997	Free	Democracy
1998	Free	Democracy
1999	Free	Democracy
2000	Free	Democracy
2001	Free	Democracy
2002	Free	Democracy
2003	Free	Democracy
2004	Free	Democracy
2005	Free	Democracy
2006	Free	Democracy

Year	Media	Government
2007	Free	Democracy
2008	Free	Democracy
2009	Free	Democracy
2010	Free	Democracy
2011	Free	Democracy
2012	Free	Democracy

conglomerate has gained popularity.[4] Over the years, media observers have found the Icelandic news media to be among the freest in the world. The constitution includes provision for media freedom, which the government respects in practice, but there are some concerns that the 2011 media control law will limit media freedom because it prohibits news coverage that might promote hate speech and requires that news outlets document their editorial strategies.[5]

Media Today

Although concentration of ownership—in particular the dominance of 365 media—is an issue for the Icelandic media, the country does have a range of independent, partisan and public media. In addition, the majority of Icelanders have Internet access.

Notes

1. Birgir Gudmundsson, *Media Landscapes: Iceland* (Maastricht, The Netherlands: European Journalism Centre, 2013). Available at http://ejc.net/media_landscapes/iceland.
2. Ibid.
3. Ibid.
4. Ibid.
5. *Country Reports on Human Rights Practices 2012* (Washington, DC: U.S. Department of State, 2013). Available at http://www.state.gov/j/drl/rls/hrrpt/.

India: 1948–2012

India Year by Year

Year	Media	Government
1948	Imperfectly Free	In Transition
1949	Imperfectly Free	In Transition
1950	Imperfectly Free	Democracy
1951	Imperfectly Free	Democracy
1952	Imperfectly Free	Democracy
1953	Imperfectly Free	Democracy
1954	Imperfectly Free	Democracy
1955	Imperfectly Free	Democracy
1956	Imperfectly Free	Democracy
1957	Imperfectly Free	Democracy
1958	Imperfectly Free	Democracy
1959	Imperfectly Free	Democracy
1960	Imperfectly Free	Democracy
1961	Imperfectly Free	Democracy
1962	Imperfectly Free	Democracy
1963	Imperfectly Free	Democracy
1964	Imperfectly Free	Democracy
1965	Imperfectly Free	Democracy
1966	Imperfectly Free	Democracy
1967	Imperfectly Free	Democracy
1968	Imperfectly Free	Democracy
1969	Imperfectly Free	Democracy
1970	Imperfectly Free	Democracy
1971	Imperfectly Free	Democracy
1972	Imperfectly Free	Democracy
1973	Imperfectly Free	Democracy
1974	Imperfectly Free	Democracy

MEDIA FREEDOM HISTORY IN A NUTSHELL

- India has a long history of media freedom, but people who are poor, illiterate, or in rural or conflict-prone areas may not have access to independent media
- As of 2012, India had 4,397 total paid-for daily newspapers with an average circulation per issue of 112,891,676 (World Association of Newspaper's 2012 World Newspaper Trends)
- India has hundreds of television channels, many of which carry news
- The only radio outlet allowed to broadcast news is the state-owned AM network
- As of 2012, about 13 percent of Indians had Internet access (International Telecommunication Union's 2012 ICT Indicators Database)

In Brief

India has a long history of media freedom, yet it also has a long history of media restriction. With the exception of a couple of years in the mid-1970s, India has had independent and functionally free news media, but not all Indians have access to these media. Those who cannot read, those who are poor, those who live in rural areas, and those who live in conflict-prone regions tend to have limited access to independent news. Newspapers and television are widely available to those who can afford them and those who can read, but radio, which is generally more accessible, is limited. Only the government-owned AM radio is allowed to broadcast news. The government has also been known to block access to texting, online content, and social media in conflict prone regions.

Year	Media	Government
1975	Not Free	Democracy
1976	Not Free	Democracy
1977	Not Free	Democracy
1978	Imperfectly Free	Democracy
1979	Imperfectly Free	Democracy
1980	Imperfectly Free	Democracy
1981	Imperfectly Free	Democracy
1982	Imperfectly Free	Democracy
1983	Imperfectly Free	Democracy
1984	Imperfectly Free	Democracy
1985	Imperfectly Free	Democracy
1986	Imperfectly Free	Democracy
1987	Imperfectly Free	Democracy
1988	Imperfectly Free	Democracy
1989	Imperfectly Free	Democracy
1990	Imperfectly Free	Democracy
1991	Imperfectly Free	Democracy
1992	Imperfectly Free	Democracy
1993	Imperfectly Free	Democracy
1994	Imperfectly Free	Democracy
1995	Imperfectly Free	Democracy
1996	Imperfectly Free	Democracy
1997	Imperfectly Free	Democracy
1998	Imperfectly Free	Democracy
1999	Imperfectly Free	Democracy
2000	Imperfectly Free	Democracy
2001	Imperfectly Free	Democracy
2002	Imperfectly Free	Democracy
2003	Imperfectly Free	Democracy
2004	Imperfectly Free	Democracy
2005	Imperfectly Free	Democracy
2006	Imperfectly Free	Democracy
2007	Imperfectly Free	Democracy
2008	Imperfectly Free	Democracy
2009	Imperfectly Free	Democracy
2010	Imperfectly Free	Democracy
2011	Imperfectly Free	Democracy
2012	Imperfectly Free	Democracy

Chronology

1948–1974: Imperfectly Free

India's press flourished after independence. Under British rule, the norm of freedom of the press had been established and a number of newspapers had been launched.[1] Yet the British partitioning of the subcontinent into India (mostly Hindu) and Pakistan (mostly Muslim) set the stage for future conflicts that would lead to restrictions of media freedom. As it was, the partition process led to communal violence and hundreds of thousands of people were killed.

Since independence, the story of media freedom in India has been a tale of two media systems: one for the mostly rural poor and one for the mostly urban rich. In a study conducted in the late 1970s, Graham Jones of the International Press Institute wrote that the gap was substantial. "The poor press, largely in the smaller towns, makes do with poor resources—low investment, inadequate management, rickety machines, ageing type, untrained correspondents. Its poverty makes it vulnerable to advertisers, politicians, crooks and temptation."[2]

Yet even national newspapers serving mostly urban readers were subject to government pressures. In 1953, the government withheld advertising from the *Times of India* following critical news coverage.[3]

While print media were for the most part independently owned, the government maintained a monopoly on radio, which was established in 1936.[4] Likewise, India's Ministry of Information and Broadcasting controlled the country's television network Doordarshan, which began broadcasting in 1959.[5]

In 1974, there were several indications that the media environment was deteriorating, as opposition to the government increased and tensions between the government and the press increased. A shortage of newsprint led to the closure of a number of smaller newspapers and magazines, there were allegations that government and police were complicit in a mob attack that destroyed a newspaper office in the state of Bihar, and the government was believed to have pressured the owners of the *Hindustan Times* into firing the paper's editor.[6]

1975–1977: Not Free

In 1975, Prime Minister Indira Gandhi convinced the president to declare a state of emergency—complete with press censorship—after she was found guilty of electoral malpractice. Gandhi claimed the limitations on press freedom were temporary until the opposition became more "responsible."[7] Yet the restrictions continued in 1976, as government employed a number of tactics aimed at silencing critical media, including detaining journalists, shutting off power to newspaper offices, and putting government nominees on newspaper executive boards.[8]

1978–2012: Imperfectly Free

After the state of emergency was lifted in 1977, the media environment improved and media were once again imperfectly free. Yet there were concerns that restrictions could return as Gandhi returned to power.[9]

The 1980s were a period of tremendous growth for news media, fueled in part by the increases in literacy and consumerism. The number of daily newspapers increased from 214 in 1950 to 2,856 in 1990.[10] Newspapers were vibrant and uncensored, but they were much less accessible to the rural poor and illiterate. While radio was more accessible, the government maintained its monopoly over broadcast media, and the opposition claimed that these media favored the government.[11]

In the mid- to late-1990s as tensions increased in Kashmir, journalists in that region faced threats and attacks from both separatist and government forces, and the government banned reporting from the shrine of Chrar-e-Sharif, which was destroyed in May of 1995.[12]

Media Today

Most media freedom monitors describe India's media as the freest in South Asia, and while this is probably true, it is also true that media freedom in India varies, depending on the medium, the level of conflict in the region, and along the rural-urban divide. Independent news is widely available to those who live in urban areas, those who can read, and those who can afford it, but news media are far less accessible to those who live in rural areas or conflict-prone regions, and those who are poor or illiterate. In other words,

little has changed since the 1970s, when the International Press Institute identified the gap between the "poor press" and the "rich press." Although there are privately owned FM radio stations, they are prohibited from broadcasting news—only the state-owned AM radio is allowed to do that.[13] Though community radio stations have been allowed since 2006, there were only 140 at the end of 2012.[14] India's television options have increased dramatically in the last couple of decades, and hundreds of channels are now available. Journalists and citizens in conflict-prone regions, in particular Jammu and Kashmir, experience far less freedom than those in other regions. In the name of preventing violence, the government has been known to block texting capabilities, online access, and social media accounts.[15]

Notes

1. James Heitzman and Robert L. Worden, *India: A Country Study* (Washington, DC: Library of Congress Federal Research Division, 1995). Available at http://lcweb2.loc.gov/frd/cs/cshome.html.
2. Graham Jones, *The Toiling World: Nurturing a Healthy Press for India's Rural Millions* (Zurich: International Press Institute in association with Friedrich-Naumann-Stiftung, 1979).
3. *World Press Freedom Review*, IPI Report (Zurich: International Press Institute, January 1953).
4. Heitzman and Worden, *India: A Country Study*.
5. Ibid.
6. *World Press Freedom Review*, IPI Report (Zurich: International Press Institute, December 1974).
7. *World Press Freedom Review*, IPI Report (Zurich: International Press Institute, December 1975).
8. *World Press Freedom Review*, IPI Report (Zurich: International Press Institute, December 1976).
9. *World Press Freedom Review*, IPI Report (Zurich: International Press Institute, December 1978).
10. Heitzman and Worden, *India: A Country Study*.
11. *Country Reports on Human Rights Practices 1980* (Washington, DC: U.S. Department of State, 1981).
12. *World Press Freedom Review*, IPI Report (Zurich: International Press Institute, December 1995).
13. *Freedom of the Press* (Washington, DC: Freedom House, 2013). Available at http://www.freedomhouse.org/report/freedom-press/2013/india.
14. Ibid.
15. Ibid.

Indonesia: 1950–2012

Indonesia Year by Year

Year	Media	Government
1950	Not Free	Anocracy
1951	Not Free	Anocracy
1952	Not Free	Anocracy
1953	Not Free	Anocracy
1954	Not Free	Anocracy
1955	Not Free	Anocracy
1956	Not Free	Anocracy
1957	Not Free	Anocracy
1958	Not Free	Anocracy
1959	Not Free	Anocracy
1960	Not Free	Anocracy
1961	Not Free	Anocracy
1962	Not Free	Anocracy
1963	Not Free	Anocracy
1964	Not Free	Anocracy
1965	Not Free	Anocracy
1966	Not Free	Autocracy
1967	Not Free	Autocracy
1968	Not Free	Autocracy
1969	Not Free	Autocracy
1970	Not Free	Autocracy
1971	Not Free	Autocracy
1972	Not Free	Autocracy
1973	Not Free	Autocracy
1974	Not Free	Autocracy
1975	Not Free	Autocracy

(Continued)

MEDIA FREEDOM HISTORY IN A NUTSHELL

- For nearly fifty years following independence, Indonesian news media were restricted, usually in the name of nationalism and national security
- Media restrictions eased in 1998 as Indonesia democratized
- Media today are functionally free, but journalists are subject to attacks and punitive lawsuits
- As of 2012, Indonesia had 400 total paid-for daily newspapers with an average circulation per issue of 2,217,434 (World Association of Newspaper's 2012 World Newspaper Trends)
- Indonesia has a wide range of privately-owned broadcast media that compete with the public networks; television is Indonesia's most prominent medium (BBC News Country Profiles)
- As of 2012, about 15 percent of Indonesians had Internet access (International Telecommunication Union's 2012 ICT Indicators Database)

In Brief

After Indonesia gained independence from the Dutch, nationalism was used as justification for imposing restrictions on the Dutch press, and these restrictions also affected the domestic press. Media restrictions increased as the government became increasingly authoritarian and repressive. When President Suharto rose to power, there were initial hopes that media would be free, but media suppression continued as Suharto sought to minimize domestic conflict. Following Suharto's ouster in 1998, media restrictions eased as Indonesia democratized. Although journalists remain vulnerable to physical attacks and punitive lawsuits, media remain functionally free.

(Continued)

Year	Media	Government
1976	Not Free	Autocracy
1977	Not Free	Autocracy
1978	Not Free	Autocracy
1979	Not Free	Autocracy
1980	Not Free	Autocracy
1981	Not Free	Autocracy
1982	Not Free	Autocracy
1983	Not Free	Autocracy
1984	Not Free	Autocracy
1985	Not Free	Autocracy
1986	Not Free	Autocracy
1987	Not Free	Autocracy
1988	Not Free	Autocracy
1989	Not Free	Autocracy
1990	Not Free	Autocracy
1991	Not Free	Autocracy
1992	Not Free	Autocracy
1993	Not Free	Autocracy
1994	Not Free	Autocracy
1995	Not Free	Autocracy
1996	Not Free	Autocracy
1997	Not Free	Autocracy
1998	Imperfectly Free	Anocracy
1999	Imperfectly Free	Democracy
2000	Imperfectly Free	Democracy
2001	Imperfectly Free	Democracy
2002	Imperfectly Free	Democracy
2003	Imperfectly Free	Democracy
2004	Imperfectly Free	Democracy
2005	Imperfectly Free	Democracy
2006	Imperfectly Free	Democracy
2007	Imperfectly Free	Democracy
2008	Imperfectly Free	Democracy
2009	Imperfectly Free	Democracy
2010	Imperfectly Free	Democracy
2011	Imperfectly Free	Democracy
2012	Imperfectly Free	Democracy

Chronology

1950–1997: Not Free

Following occupation by Japan during World War II, Indonesia declared independence in 1945 but was not granted independence by the Dutch until 1949, after four years of fighting. Under the leadership of Indonesia's first president, Sukarno, censorship of the media was initially motivated by nationalism and aimed at Dutch newspapers, but the measures taken restricted all news outlets. For example in 1952, a press law was proposed that would have prohibited foreign ownership of newspapers and "limit the rights of all Indonesian papers reflecting 'foreign influence.'"[1] Though Sukarno's government was established as a constitutional democracy, it became increasingly authoritarian and there was a corresponding increase in the restriction of news media.[2]

Following a failed coup in 1965 and the retaliatory killing of an estimated 600,000 to 1 million people (according to Indonesia's National Commission on Human Rights), Sukarno relinquished his powers to General Suharto. Under Suharto's leadership, the media environment initially improved, but when rioting erupted in 1974, the government closed down a number of publications and criticism of government and senior officials was generally not tolerated.[3] These and other media restrictions were justified as necessary to preserve political stability and national security. "The acronym SARA—*suku* (ethnicity), *agama* (religion), *ras* (race), and *antargolongan* (social relations)—listed the prohibited subjects, to which could be added less than adulatory references to the president and his family."[4] Thus, the media that were not directly run by the government were effectively controlled by it.

1998–2012: Imperfectly Free

In 1998, following the Asian economic crisis, dissatisfaction with Suharto intensified and at the same time, government restrictions on news media eased, so that the news media were able to cover the protests and calls for reform.[5] Eventually Suharto was forced to resign and hand over power to Bacharuddin Jusuf Habibie. Habibie promised political forms and the government did take steps to improve media freedom, including the revoking of the 1984 decree that gave the Minister of Information the authority cancel newspaper publication licenses. Yet the government did retain the right to suspend licenses.[6] Habibie also opened the media market, thereby facilitating the emergence of many new publications and allowed private radio stations to provide their own news coverage and reduced the required broadcasting of government-produced news to three times a day instead of fourteen times a day.[7]

Media Today

Although the Indonesian news media offer diverse views and lively coverage, journalists and news organizations are vulnerable to defamation suits. Journalists are also subject to attacks from both government and nongovernment actors, especially in the province of West Papua.[8] Television is Indonesia's most popular medium and the public network has competition from a number of private networks. Indonesia has a wide range of private and public radio stations, and several hundred privately owned newspapers. About 15 percent of Indonesians have internet access.

Notes

1. *News of the World Press: Indonesian Squeeze* (Zurich: International Press Institute, October 1952), 8.
2. *Country Reports on Human Rights Practices for 1979* (Washington, DC: U.S. Department of State, 1980). Available at http://babel.hathitrust.org/cgi/pt?id=mdp.39015078705632;view=1up;seq=249
3. Ibid.
4. William H. Frederick and Robert L. Worden, "*The Media.*" *Indonesia: A Country Study* (Washington, DC: Library of Congress Federal Research Division, 1992), Para. 1. Available at http://lcweb2.loc.gov/frd/cs/.
5. *Country Reports on Human Rights Practices 1998* (Washington, DC: U.S. Department of State, 1999). Available at http://www.state.gov/www/global/human_rights/1998_hrp_report/indonesi.html.
6. Ibid.
7. *World Press Freedom Review*, IPI Report (Vienna: International Press Institute, December 1998).
8. *Freedom of the Press* (Washington, DC: Freedom House, 2013). Available at http://www.freedomhouse.org/report/freedom-press/2013/indonesia.

Iran: 1948–2012

Iran Year by Year

Year	Media	Government
1948	Imperfectly Free	Anocracy
1949	Imperfectly Free	Anocracy
1950	Imperfectly Free	Anocracy
1951	Imperfectly Free	Anocracy
1952	Not Free	Anocracy
1953	Not Free	Anocracy
1954	Not Free	Autocracy
1955	Not Free	Autocracy
1956	Not Free	Autocracy
1957	Not Free	Autocracy
1958	Not Free	Autocracy
1959	Not Free	Autocracy
1960	Not Free	Autocracy
1961	Not Free	Autocracy
1962	Not Free	Autocracy
1963	Not Free	Autocracy
1964	Not Free	Autocracy
1965	Not Free	Autocracy
1966	Not Free	Autocracy
1967	Not Free	Autocracy
1968	Not Free	Autocracy
1969	Not Free	Autocracy
1970	Not Free	Autocracy
1971	Not Free	Autocracy
1972	Not Free	Autocracy
1973	Not Free	Autocracy
1974	Not Free	Autocracy
1975	Not Free	Autocracy

MEDIA FREEDOM HISTORY IN A NUTSHELL

- Post-war Iran had a democratic government including media freedom
- A U.S.- and British-backed coup installed the Shah as a dictator, eliminating media freedom
- The Iranian revolution replaced the Shah's dictatorship with an Islamic fundamentalist government that strictly controls the media
- As of 2012, there were 180 paid-for daily newspapers, with an average circulation per issue of 1,575,000 (World Association of Newspaper's 2012 World Newspaper Trends)
- Radio and television provide news for many citizens, but the government holds a monopoly on all official news (Freedom House's Freedom of the Press Report 2013)
- As of 2012, about 26 percent of Iranians had Internet access (International Telecommunication Union's 2012 ICT Indicators Database)

In Brief

A U.S.- and British-backed coup replaced a democratic regime with free media with the dictatorship of the Shah, who eliminated media freedom. He was later replaced by an Islamic fundamentalist government that strictly controls the media.

Chronology

1948–1951: Imperfectly Free

Occupied by Allied forces during World War II, Iran had a well-established democratic system, including functionally free media after the end of the war. In 1950, newly elected Prime Minister Ali Razmara was assassinated and Mohammad Mosaddegh became prime minister. In 1951, Mosaddegh led a campaign that nationalized the

Year	Media	Government
1976	Not Free	Autocracy
1977	Not Free	Autocracy
1978	Not Free	Autocracy
1979	Not Free	Anocracy
1980	Not Free	Anocracy
1981	Not Free	Anocracy
1982	Not Free	Autocracy
1983	Not Free	Autocracy
1984	Not Free	Autocracy
1985	Not Free	Autocracy
1986	Not Free	Autocracy
1987	Not Free	Autocracy
1988	Not Free	Autocracy
1989	Not Free	Autocracy
1990	Not Free	Autocracy
1991	Not Free	Autocracy
1992	Not Free	Autocracy
1993	Not Free	Autocracy
1994	Not Free	Autocracy
1995	Not Free	Autocracy
1996	Not Free	Autocracy
1997	Not Free	Anocracy
1998	Not Free	Anocracy
1999	Not Free	Anocracy
2000	Not Free	Anocracy
2001	Not Free	Anocracy
2002	Not Free	Anocracy
2003	Not Free	Anocracy
2004	Not Free	Autocracy
2005	Not Free	Autocracy
2006	Not Free	Autocracy
2007	Not Free	Autocracy
2008	Not Free	Autocracy
2009	Not Free	Autocracy
2010	Not Free	Autocracy
2011	Not Free	Autocracy
2012	Not Free	Autocracy

oil industry and the resulting embargo and domestic power struggle forced Shah Mohammad Reza, the constitutional monarch, to flee.

1952–2012: Not Free

A U.S.- and British-backed coup ousted Mosaddegh and installed a military government that was effectively controlled by the Shah. Media controls were put in place. The government did not directly control the media, but strict censorship rules were enforced by the Savak, the Shah's notorious secret police. In the late 1960s, the Shah led an unpopular secularization and development campaign that alienated the Islamic clergy and ultimately led to his ouster.

The Iranian revolution sent the Shah and his family into exile, brought Islamic fundamentalist Ayatollah Ruhollah Khomeini to power, and the media became directly controlled. After the release of the U.S. embassy staff who had been held hostage since the revolution, the method of media control shifted from direct to indirect, but the degree of censorship remained extreme. The U.S. imposition of trade sanctions sparked some domestic criticism in Iran and several nominally independent newspapers were shut down or effectively put under direct control of the religious elite.

Media Today

All broadcast media are controlled by the Islamic Republic of Iran Broadcasting (IRIB). Some print media outlets remain nominally independent, but any deviation from very narrow parameters of coverage quickly leads to arrest. There are reports that between 2009 and 2012 as many as forty publications were shut down.[1]

Note

1. *Country Reports on Human Rights Practices 2012* (Washington, DC: U.S. Department of State, 2013). Available at http://www.state.gov/j/drl/rls/hrrpt/humanrightsreport/index.htm#wrapper.

Iraq: 1948–2012

Iraq Year by Year

Year	Not Free	Government
1948	Not Free	Anocracy
1949	Not Free	Anocracy
1950	Not Free	Anocracy
1951	Not Free	Anocracy
1952	Not Free	Anocracy
1953	Not Free	Anocracy
1954	Not Free	Anocracy
1955	Not Free	Anocracy
1956	Not Free	Anocracy
1957	Not Free	Anocracy
1958	Not Free	Anocracy
1959	Not Free	Anocracy
1960	Not Free	Anocracy
1961	Not Free	Anocracy
1962	Not Free	Anocracy
1963	Not Free	Anocracy
1964	Not Free	Anocracy
1965	Not Free	Anocracy
1966	Not Free	Anocracy
1967	Not Free	Anocracy
1968	Not Free	Autocracy
1969	Not Free	Autocracy
1970	Not Free	Autocracy
1971	Not Free	Autocracy
1972	Not Free	Autocracy
1973	Not Free	Autocracy
1974	Not Free	Autocracy
1975	Not Free	Autocracy

MEDIA FREEDOM HISTORY IN A NUTSHELL

- Media were directly controlled by authoritarian dictators of one form or another until Saddam Hussein was ousted by the United States
- Media development efforts during the U.S. military occupation increased the diversity of media sources but did not establish a free media environment
- External media are widely available, which establishes some pragmatic limits on the extent of government control that is possible
- As of 2013, Iraq had a wide range of privately owned print and broadcast media in addition to state-run print and broadcast news outlets
- As of 2012, about 7 percent of Iraqis had Internet access (International Telecommunication Union's 2012 ICT Indicators Database)

In Brief

Autocratic rule, including strict control of the media, has been the norm for modern Iraq. During the U.S. occupation, an effort was made to construct a viable and effective domestic media system as part of a democratic government, but media freedom remains elusive.

Chronology

1948–2012: Not Free

Authoritarian rule with strict media control has been the norm in modern Iraq. The hereditary monarchy was overthrown in 1958 in a military coup, and a series of coups and dictators marked the struggle between the military and the Arab Socialist Baath party for control of the government. Baathist Saddam Hussein took power in 1979 and remained in control until he was ousted in a U.S. invasion in 2003.

Year	Not Free	Government
1976	Not Free	Autocracy
1977	Not Free	Autocracy
1978	Not Free	Autocracy
1979	Not Free	Autocracy
1980	Not Free	Autocracy
1981	Not Free	Autocracy
1982	Not Free	Autocracy
1983	Not Free	Autocracy
1984	Not Free	Autocracy
1985	Not Free	Autocracy
1986	Not Free	Autocracy
1987	Not Free	Autocracy
1988	Not Free	Autocracy
1989	Not Free	Autocracy
1990	Not Free	Autocracy
1991	Not Free	Autocracy
1992	Not Free	Autocracy
1993	Not Free	Autocracy
1994	Not Free	Autocracy
1995	Not Free	Autocracy
1996	Not Free	Autocracy
1997	Not Free	Autocracy
1998	Not Free	Autocracy
1999	Not Free	Autocracy
2000	Not Free	Autocracy
2001	Not Free	Autocracy
2002	Not Free	Autocracy
2003	Not Free	Foreign Interruption
2004	Not Free	Foreign Interruption
2005	Not Free	Foreign Interruption
2006	Not Free	Foreign Interruption

Year	Not Free	Government
2007	Not Free	Foreign Interruption
2008	Not Free	Foreign Interruption
2009	Not Free	Foreign Interruption
2010	Not Free	Anocracy
2011	Not Free	Anocracy
2012	Not Free	Anocracy

During its military occupation of Iraq, the United States spent a great deal trying to develop a media system as part of a democratic Iraq. The availability of media, particularly print media, soared, but there was little evidence that a free media system would ever develop except perhaps in the autonomous Kurdish enclaves in the very northern edge of the country. Ongoing ethnic strife and violence bordering on civil war provided ample justifications for government restrictions on media. In the early 2000s, Iraq was a very dangerous place for journalists. The International Press Institute reported that more than twenty journalists were killed in 2005 alone.[1]

Media Today

While the domestic media remain restricted, external news media are easily accessible, particularly satellite television. Although this does not enable domestic criticism and debates in the media, it does place some practical limits on how extensive restrictions on the media can be. While harassment and threats against journalists were common, no journalists were killed in 2012.[2]

Notes

1. *World Press Freedom Review*, IPI Report (Vienna: International Press Institute, 2005).
2. *Freedom of the Press* (Washington, DC: Freedom House, 2013). Available at http://freedomhouse.org/report/freedom-press/2013/iraq.

Ireland: 1948–2012

Ireland Year by Year

Year	Media	Government
1948	Free	Democracy
1949	Free	Democracy
1950	Free	Democracy
1951	Free	Democracy
1952	Free	Democracy
1953	Free	Democracy
1954	Free	Democracy
1955	Free	Democracy
1956	Free	Democracy
1957	Free	Democracy
1958	Free	Democracy
1959	Free	Democracy
1960	Free	Democracy
1961	Free	Democracy
1962	Free	Democracy
1963	Free	Democracy
1964	Free	Democracy
1965	Free	Democracy
1966	Free	Democracy
1967	Free	Democracy
1968	Free	Democracy
1969	Free	Democracy
1970	Free	Democracy
1971	Free	Democracy
1972	Free	Democracy
1973	Free	Democracy
1974	Free	Democracy
1975	Free	Democracy

MEDIA FREEDOM HISTORY IN A NUTSHELL

- A robust and effective free media system
- As of 2011, there were ten daily newspapers, nine of which were paid-for dailies with a total average circulation of 643,077 (World Association of Newspaper's 2012 World Newspaper Trends)
- There are a variety of radio stations and television channels, some of which are publically owned and some of which are privately owned
- As of 2012, about 79 percent of citizens had Internet access (International Telecommunication Union's 2012 ICT Indicators Database)

In Brief

Ireland has long enjoyed a robust and effective free media system, although there have been some issues with defamation laws being used to pressure journalists.

Chronology

1948–2012: Free

There are few if any substantive challenges to media freedom, which was established in Ireland's 1937 constitution. Ireland's defamation laws, which "place the burden of proof on defendants," have been used to pressure journalists, but in 2009, the time limit for bringing defamation suits decreased from six years to one year.[1] However, the 2009 Defamation Act also rendered blasphemy a criminal offense punishable with fines.[2]

Media Today

Ireland is an exemplar of how a free media can function effectively in a highly religious nation.

Year	Media	Government
1976	Free	Democracy
1977	Free	Democracy
1978	Free	Democracy
1979	Free	Democracy
1980	Free	Democracy
1981	Free	Democracy
1982	Free	Democracy
1983	Free	Democracy
1984	Free	Democracy
1985	Free	Democracy
1986	Free	Democracy
1987	Free	Democracy
1988	Free	Democracy
1989	Free	Democracy
1990	Free	Democracy
1991	Free	Democracy
1992	Free	Democracy
1993	Free	Democracy
1994	Free	Democracy
1995	Free	Democracy
1996	Free	Democracy
1997	Free	Democracy

Year	Media	Government
1998	Free	Democracy
1999	Free	Democracy
2000	Free	Democracy
2001	Free	Democracy
2002	Free	Democracy
2003	Free	Democracy
2004	Free	Democracy
2005	Free	Democracy
2006	Free	Democracy
2007	Free	Democracy
2008	Free	Democracy
2009	Free	Democracy
2010	Free	Democracy
2011	Free	Democracy
2012	Free	Democracy

Ireland has a wide range of print, broadcast and online news media.

Notes

1. *Freedom of the Press* (Washington, DC: Freedom House, 2013). Available at http://www.freedom house.org/reports.
2. Ibid.

Israel: 1948–2012

Israel Year by Year

Year	Media	Government
1948	Free	Democracy
1949	Free	Democracy
1950	Free	Democracy
1951	Free	Democracy
1952	Free	Democracy
1953	Free	Democracy
1954	Free	Democracy
1955	Free	Democracy
1956	Free	Democracy
1957	Free	Democracy
1958	Free	Democracy
1959	Free	Democracy
1960	Free	Democracy
1961	Free	Democracy
1962	Free	Democracy
1963	Free	Democracy
1964	Free	Democracy
1965	Free	Democracy
1966	Free	Democracy
1967	Free	Democracy
1968	Free	Democracy
1969	Free	Democracy
1970	Free	Democracy
1971	Free	Democracy
1972	Free	Democracy
1973	Free	Democracy
1974	Free	Democracy
1975	Free	Democracy

In Brief

A parliamentary democracy with a robust free media system, Israel has been in a constant state of war with its Arab neighbors for the entirety of its existence. While the fighting has not been constant, it has been frequent.

Chronology

1948–1997: Free

From the day of its initial independence, Israel has had a robust democracy with a well-established and diverse free media system.

1998–2001: Imperfectly Free

An escalation of the Palestinian conflict, including a significant surge in suicide bombings, followed the election of Binyamin Netanyahu as prime minister. The resulting emphasis on domestic security included some potential threats to media freedom. There was never any indication that media freedom was truly in jeopardy,

Year	Media	Government
1976	Free	Democracy
1977	Free	Democracy
1978	Free	Democracy
1979	Free	Democracy
1980	Free	Democracy
1981	Free	Democracy
1982	Free	Democracy
1983	Free	Democracy
1984	Free	Democracy
1985	Free	Democracy
1986	Free	Democracy
1987	Free	Democracy
1988	Free	Democracy
1989	Free	Democracy
1990	Free	Democracy
1991	Free	Democracy
1992	Free	Democracy
1993	Free	Democracy
1994	Free	Democracy
1995	Free	Democracy
1996	Free	Democracy
1997	Free	Democracy
1998	Imperfectly Free	Democracy
1999	Imperfectly Free	Democracy
2000	Imperfectly Free	Democracy
2001	Imperfectly Free	Democracy
2002	Free	Democracy
2003	Free	Democracy
2004	Free	Democracy
2005	Free	Democracy
2006	Free	Democracy
2007	Free	Democracy
2008	Imperfectly Free	Democracy
2009	Free	Democracy
2010	Free	Democracy
2011	Free	Democracy
2012	Imperfectly Free	Democracy

and this coding should be considered as barely falling into the imperfectly free category.

2002–2007: Free

The lifting of some of the security related ·restrictions on reporting signaled the clear return to free media.

2008: Imperfectly Free

Escalating conflict with the Palestinians led to some media restrictions, in particular foreign journalists were prohibited from entering the Gaza Strip (domestic journalists had already been restricted from the area since 2006).[1] Again, the concerns over these changes in the media environment may be overstated as these restrictions only marginally compromised media freedom.

2009–2011: Free

Concerns over threats to Israel's media freedom eased as the travel restrictions were lifted.[2]

2012: Imperfectly Free

Concerns about government interference with news media increased slightly in 2012 when a reporter was indicted for possessing state secrets and the state-run Israel Broadcasting Authority required that every program hosted by government critic Keren Neubach include a "balancing" journalist.[3] In addition, the increasing popularity of a free newspaper, *Israel Hayom*, threatened the sustainability of commercial newspapers.[4]

Media Today

Israeli media are by and large free and diverse, yet there are concerns about concentration of ownership and government infringement on media freedom due to the ongoing conflict between Israel and its neighbors.

Notes

1. *Freedom of the Press* (Washington, DC: Freedom House, 2009). Available at http://freedomhouse.org/report/freedom-press/2009/israel.
2. *Freedom of the Press* (Washington, DC: Freedom House, 2010). Available at http://freedomhouse.org/report/freedom-press/2010/israel.
3. *Freedom of the Press* (Washington, DC: Freedom House, 2013). Available at http://freedomhouse.org/report/freedom-press/2013/israel.
4. Ibid.

Italy: 1948–2012

Italy Year by Year

Year	Media	Government
1948	Free	Democracy
1949	Free	Democracy
1950	Free	Democracy
1951	Free	Democracy
1952	Free	Democracy
1953	Free	Democracy
1954	Free	Democracy
1955	Free	Democracy
1956	Free	Democracy
1957	Free	Democracy
1958	Free	Democracy
1959	Free	Democracy
1960	Free	Democracy
1961	Free	Democracy
1962	Free	Democracy
1963	Free	Democracy
1964	Free	Democracy
1965	Free	Democracy
1966	Free	Democracy
1967	Free	Democracy
1968	Free	Democracy
1969	Free	Democracy
1970	Free	Democracy
1971	Free	Democracy
1972	Free	Democracy
1973	Free	Democracy
1974	Free	Democracy
1975	Free	Democracy

MEDIA FREEDOM HISTORY IN A NUTSHELL

- Despite almost continuous political instability and corruption, Italy has sustained a functionally free press since the end of World War II
- Media moguls who are also political leaders have complicated media issues lately, both by overtly using the media to influence government and attempting to protect media interests with legislation
- As of 2011, there were 103 paid-for daily newspapers with a total average circulation per issue of 5,691,000 (World Association of Newspaper's 2012 World Newspaper Trends)
- Italy has a variety of state-owned and private-owned radio and television stations, but ownership is highly concentrated, such that when media mogul Silvio Berlusconi served as prime minister he effectively controlled 90 percent of the country's broadcast media
- As of 2012, about 58 percent of Italians had Internet access (International Telecommunication Union's 2012 ICT Indicators Database)

In Brief

Media in Italy are functionally free, but inappropriate linkages between media ownership and political office plague an effort to bring Italian news media up to the high standards of most of the rest of Europe.

Chronology

1948–2002: Free

Despite corruption, criminal influence, and political instability, Italian media remain free and able to criticize government and leaders.

Year	Media	Government
1976	Free	Democracy
1977	Free	Democracy
1978	Free	Democracy
1979	Free	Democracy
1980	Free	Democracy
1981	Free	Democracy
1982	Free	Democracy
1983	Free	Democracy
1984	Free	Democracy
1985	Free	Democracy
1986	Free	Democracy
1987	Free	Democracy
1988	Free	Democracy
1989	Free	Democracy
1990	Free	Democracy
1991	Free	Democracy
1992	Free	Democracy
1993	Free	Democracy
1994	Free	Democracy
1995	Free	Democracy
1996	Free	Democracy
1997	Free	Democracy
1998	Free	Democracy
1999	Free	Democracy
2000	Free	Democracy
2001	Free	Democracy
2002	Free	Democracy
2003	Imperfectly Free	Democracy
2004	Imperfectly Free	Democracy
2005	Imperfectly Free	Democracy
2006	Free	Democracy
2007	Free	Democracy
2008	Imperfectly Free	Democracy
2009	Imperfectly Free	Democracy
2010	Imperfectly Free	Democracy
2011	Imperfectly Free	Democracy
2012	Imperfectly Free	Democracy

2003–2005: Imperfectly Free

High concentration of ownership and political pressures somewhat compromise media independence, but media remain functionally free. Prime Minister Silvio Berlusconi, who was also a media tycoon with ownership of the three largest TV networks, made several blatant and rather clumsy attempts to use legislation and other acts of government to manipulate the parameters governing the switch to digital TV transmission to sustain dominance of the media landscape within Italy. Subsequent attempts to limit media ownership and promote diversity of media failed, and Berlusconi continued to overtly use media dominance to assert influence.

2006–2007: Free

The 2006 elections changed the political landscape, as Silvio Berlusconi's center right party was narrowly defeated. Since he was no longer prime minister, Berlusconi could no longer control state television, though he did continue to have significant holdings in private broadcast media.[1]

2008–2012: Imperfectly Free

Silvio Berlusconi was reelected and once again became prime minister. Journalists who criticized the government were targeted with libel charges. Berlusconi's ownership of private media combined with his political power over state-owned media gave him control over most of Italy's broadcast media. Although Berlusconi resigned in 2011, Italian news media remained vulnerable to political control for a variety of reasons, including licensing procedures.

Media Today

There is sufficient diversity of news sources other than television to assert that media remain effectively free. However, the predominance of Berlusconi's Mediaset Group—a highly partisan news outlet with a blatantly manipulative owner who is intimately involved in government—has cast serious doubts on the robustness of free media in Italy.

Note

1. *Freedom of the Press* (Washington, DC: Freedom House, 2007). Available at http://www.freedomhouse.org/reports.

Jamaica: 1962–2012

Jamaica Year by Year

Year	Media	Government
1962	Free	Democracy
1963	Free	Democracy
1964	Free	Democracy
1965	Free	Democracy
1966	Free	Democracy
1967	Free	Democracy
1968	Free	Democracy
1969	Free	Democracy
1970	Free	Democracy
1971	Free	Democracy
1972	Free	Democracy
1973	Free	Democracy
1974	Free	Democracy
1975	Free	Democracy
1976	Free	Democracy
1977	Free	Democracy
1978	Free	Democracy
1979	Free	Democracy
1980	Free	Democracy
1981	Free	Democracy
1982	Free	Democracy
1983	Free	Democracy
1984	Free	Democracy
1985	Free	Democracy
1986	Free	Democracy
1987	Free	Democracy
1988	Free	Democracy
1989	Free	Democracy

MEDIA FREEDOM HISTORY IN A NUTSHELL

- Jamaica has a long history of media freedom, but journalists have at times been threatened and attacked
- Criminal libel and defamation laws have compromised media freedom, but in 2013 these measures were repealed
- As of 2012, there were there were 3 paid-for daily newspapers with a total average circulation per issue of 115,000 (World Association of Newspaper's 2010 World Newspaper Trends)
- Jamaica had more than twenty radio stations, three television stations, and multiple cable stations operating in the country (Freedom House's Report on Freedom of the Press 2013)
- As of 2012 about 47% of Jamaicans had internet access (International Telecommunication Union's 2012 ICT Indicator's Database)

In Brief

Although Jamaica has enjoyed democracy and political stability since gaining independence, poverty and crime are widespread. While political power has shifted between the People's National Party (PNP) and the Jamaica Labour Party (JLP), the Jamaican media have remained free, though at times journalists and news organizations have faced attacks, threats, and punitive lawsuits. Recently, the Jamaican Parliament decriminalized defamation.

Chronology

1962–1995: Free

In 1958, Jamaica and other British Caribbean colonies formed the Federation of the West Indies, and the members of Inter American Press

Year	Media	Government
1990	Free	Democracy
1991	Free	Democracy
1992	Free	Democracy
1993	Free	Democracy
1994	Free	Democracy
1995	Free	Democracy
1996	Imperfectly Free	Democracy
1997	Free	Democracy
1998	Free	Democracy
1999	Free	Democracy
2000	Imperfectly Free	Democracy
2001	Imperfectly Free	Democracy
2002	Free	Democracy
2003	Free	Democracy
2004	Free	Democracy
2005	Free	Democracy
2006	Free	Democracy
2007	Free	Democracy
2008	Free	Democracy
2009	Free	Democracy
2010	Free	Democracy
2011	Free	Democracy
2012	Free	Democracy

1996: Imperfectly Free

In the mid-1990s, the media environment began to deteriorate as threats and harassment of journalists increased.[6] Critical news organizations were vulnerable to libel suits, and in 1996, Jamaica's oldest newspaper, the *Gleaner*, was ordered to pay $2.5 million to the former Minister of Tourism.[7]

1997–1999: Free

The media environment improved in 1997, and there were no incidents during the 1997 general elections.[8]

2000–2001: Imperfectly Free

In the early 2000s, media freedom was somewhat compromised by journalists' lack of access to government documents and information.[9]

2002–2012: Free

In 2002, the Parliament passed the Access to Information Act, which improved journalists' ability to report on government actions.[10] Moreover, there were no restrictions on news media during the 2002 elections. Yet libel laws and violent crime remained a problem, and there were some concerns that journalists self-censored to avoid being targeted.[11]

Media Today

The Jamaican government respects the constitutional provisions for media freedom. In November of 2013, the Jamaican Parliament decriminalized defamation following a campaign by the International Press Institute to repeal criminal defamation in the Caribbean. Jamaica has three privately owned daily newspapers and a wide range of independent broadcast media.

Notes

Association applauded when the committee on Freedom of the Press announced the Federation media were free.[1] When Jamaica withdrew from the Federation and became independent in 1962, its new constitution provided for media freedom, and the government respected these provisions in practice.[2]

In 1988, the government decided to sell off the state-owned broadcast media, but in 1989, there was a change in government and the new government canceled the sale of the national AM station and began accepting applications for a new radio station and a new television station.[3]

In the 1990s, there were increased reports of police harassment of journalists.[4] Allegations of fraud and political violence followed the 1993 elections.[5]

1. *Report of the Committee on Freedom of the Press*, 1958 Annual Meeting (Miami, FL: Inter American Press Association, 1959).
2. *Report of the Committee on Freedom of the Press*, 1962 Annual Meeting (Miami, FL: Inter American Press Association, 1963).
3. *World Press Freedom Review*, IPI Report (Zurich: International Press Institute, December 1990).
4. Ibid.

5. *Jamaica Country Report on Human Rights Practices, 1995* (Washington, DC: U.S. Department of State, 1996). Available at http://dosfan.lib.uic.edu/ERC/democracy/1995_hrp_report/95hrp_report_ara/Jamaica.html.

6. *Jamaica Country Report on Human Rights Practices, 1996* (Washington, DC: U.S. Department of State, 1997). Available at http://www.state.gov/www/global/human_rights/1996_hrp_report/jamaica.html.

7. *World Press Freedom Review*, IPI Report (Vienna: Inter American Press Association, 1996).

Available at http://www.sipiapa.org/en/asamblea/caribbean-22/.

8. *Attacks on the Press in 1997, Jamaica* (Committee to Protect Journalists, 1997). Available at http://www.cpj.org/attacks97/americas/americas97setter.html.

9. *Attacks on the Press in 2001* (Committee to Protect Journalists, 2001). Available at http://cpj.org/2002/03/attacks-on-the-press-2001-jamaica.php.

10. *World Press Freedom Review*, IPI Report (Vienna: International Press Institute, 2002).

11. Ibid.

Japan: 1952–2012

Japan Year by Year

Year	Media	Government
1952	Free	Democracy
1953	Free	Democracy
1954	Free	Democracy
1955	Free	Democracy
1956	Free	Democracy
1957	Free	Democracy
1958	Free	Democracy
1959	Free	Democracy
1960	Free	Democracy
1961	Free	Democracy
1962	Free	Democracy
1963	Free	Democracy
1964	Free	Democracy
1965	Free	Democracy
1966	Free	Democracy
1967	Free	Democracy
1968	Free	Democracy
1969	Free	Democracy
1970	Free	Democracy
1971	Free	Democracy
1972	Free	Democracy
1973	Free	Democracy
1974	Free	Democracy
1975	Free	Democracy
1976	Free	Democracy
1977	Free	Democracy
1978	Free	Democracy

(Continued)

MEDIA FREEDOM HISTORY IN A NUTSHELL

- A robust and economically vibrant free media system
- Minor issues regarding a cultural deference to authority and collusion between economic and political elites are often a point of discussion
- As of 2011, there were a total of 106 daily newspapers, 105 of them were paid-for daily newspapers, with an average circulation of 47,777,910 (World Association of Newspaper's 2012 World Newspaper Trends)
- Japan has four national commercial television networks as well as public television and a mix of commercial and public radio
- As of 2012, about 79 percent of Japanese had Internet access (International Telecommunication Union's 2012 ICT Indicators Database)

In Brief

American Occupational forces established a parliamentary democratic system, including free media. A robust and economically vibrant free media system has continued to this day.

Chronology

1952–2012: Free

With a clearly free and economically robust media system, discussions and debates regarding Japan have centered on nuances regarding the effects of a cultural deference to authority. Some self-censorship and muting of criticism has been apparent, but any claim that this threatens the basic functions of free media would be difficult to justify. Even this minor issue faded with the first electoral loss of the predominant Liberal Democratic Party in 1993. The shift in public opinion regarding the party was largely attributed to the news media.[1]

(Continued)

Year	Media	Government
1979	Free	Democracy
1980	Free	Democracy
1981	Free	Democracy
1982	Free	Democracy
1983	Free	Democracy
1984	Free	Democracy
1985	Free	Democracy
1986	Free	Democracy
1987	Free	Democracy
1988	Free	Democracy
1989	Free	Democracy
1990	Free	Democracy
1991	Free	Democracy
1992	Free	Democracy
1993	Free	Democracy
1994	Free	Democracy
1995	Free	Democracy
1996	Free	Democracy
1997	Free	Democracy
1998	Free	Democracy
1999	Free	Democracy
2000	Free	Democracy
2001	Free	Democracy
2002	Free	Democracy

Year	Media	Government
2003	Free	Democracy
2004	Free	Democracy
2005	Free	Democracy
2006	Free	Democracy
2007	Free	Democracy
2008	Free	Democracy
2009	Free	Democracy
2010	Free	Democracy
2011	Free	Democracy
2012	Free	Democracy

Media Today

Japan has constitutional provisions for media freedom and the government respects these in practice. Japanese media face the same challenges as the media in other developed countries, although the effects of technological change are perhaps slightly more acute in what is arguably the most technologically sophisticated populace on the globe. Economic difficulties have also been more extensive and more challenging in Japan than in other developed countries.

Note

1. *World Press Freedom Review*, IPI Report (Vienna: International Press Institute, December 1993).

Jordan: 1948–2012

Jordan Year by Year

Year	Media	Government
1948	Not Free	Autocracy
1949	Not Free	Autocracy
1950	Not Free	Autocracy
1951	Not Free	Autocracy
1952	Not Free	Autocracy
1953	Not Free	Autocracy
1954	Not Free	Autocracy
1955	Not Free	Autocracy
1956	Not Free	Autocracy
1957	Not Free	Autocracy
1958	Not Free	Autocracy
1959	Not Free	Autocracy
1960	Not Free	Autocracy
1961	Not Free	Autocracy
1962	Not Free	Autocracy
1963	Not Free	Autocracy
1964	Not Free	Autocracy
1965	Not Free	Autocracy
1966	Not Free	Autocracy
1967	Not Free	Autocracy
1968	Not Free	Autocracy
1969	Not Free	Autocracy
1970	Not Free	Autocracy
1971	Not Free	Autocracy
1972	Not Free	Autocracy
1973	Not Free	Autocracy
1974	Not Free	Autocracy

(Continued)

MEDIA FREEDOM HISTORY IN A NUTSHELL

- A consistently diverse but restricted media system
- A 2003 Audio Visual Law put an end to the government monopoly on terrestrial broadcasting, which has led to an increase in the number of private radio stations; however, terrestrial television stations are still under state control (Freedom House, 2013)
- As of 2013, Jordan had five daily newspapers, all of which were privately owned (BBC News Country Profiles)
- All Jordanian television channels are state-run, but there is a mix of state-run and privately owned radio
- As of 2012, about 53 percent of Jordanians had Internet access (International Telecommunication Union's 2012 ICT Indicators Database)

In Brief

Jordan represents an island of relative stability in an otherwise volatile region. A reasonably progressive and benevolent hereditary monarchy allows a diverse but restricted media system.

Chronology

1948–2012: Not Free

While the media have always been diverse, and the BBC has long been allowed to broadcast in Jordan, criticism of the monarchy, religion and state institutions is strictly forbidden. Since 1999, journalists must belong to the Jordan Press Association to practice in the country.[1]

Media Today

Self-censorship is apparent, and the government has been quite active in blocking access to news

(Continued)

Year	Media	Government
1975	Not Free	Autocracy
1976	Not Free	Autocracy
1977	Not Free	Autocracy
1978	Not Free	Autocracy
1979	Not Free	Autocracy
1980	Not Free	Autocracy
1981	Not Free	Autocracy
1982	Not Free	Autocracy
1983	Not Free	Autocracy
1984	Not Free	Autocracy
1985	Not Free	Autocracy
1986	Not Free	Autocracy
1987	Not Free	Autocracy
1988	Not Free	Autocracy
1989	Not Free	Anocracy
1990	Not Free	Anocracy
1991	Not Free	Anocracy
1992	Not Free	Anocracy
1993	Not Free	Anocracy
1994	Not Free	Anocracy
1995	Not Free	Anocracy
1996	Not Free	Anocracy
1997	Not Free	Anocracy
1998	Not Free	Anocracy
1999	Not Free	Anocracy

Year	Media	Government
2000	Not Free	Anocracy
2001	Not Free	Anocracy
2002	Not Free	Anocracy
2003	Not Free	Anocracy
2004	Not Free	Anocracy
2005	Not Free	Anocracy
2006	Not Free	Anocracy
2007	Not Free	Anocracy
2008	Not Free	Anocracy
2009	Not Free	Anocracy
2010	Not Free	Anocracy
2011	Not Free	Anocracy
2012	Not Free	Anocracy

websites. This accelerated with the Arab Spring uprisings, but the Queen herself is known to use social media as a diplomatic tool. The 2012 Press and Publications Law requires licenses for Internet news outlets and gives government the authority to block websites.[2]

Notes

1. *World Press Freedom Review*, IPI Report (Vienna: International Press Institute, December 1999).
2. *Attacks on the Press in 2012, Jordan* (Committee to Protect Journalists, 2013). Available at http://www.cpj.org/2013/02/attacks-on-the-press-in-2012-jordan.php.

Kazakhstan: 1991–2012

Kazakhstan Year by Year

Year	Media	Government
1991	Not Free	Anocracy
1992	Not Free	Anocracy
1993	Not Free	Anocracy
1994	Not Free	Anocracy
1995	Not Free	Anocracy
1996	Not Free	Anocracy
1997	Not Free	Anocracy
1998	Not Free	Anocracy
1999	Not Free	Anocracy
2000	Not Free	Anocracy
2001	Not Free	Anocracy
2002	Not Free	Autocracy
2003	Not Free	Autocracy
2004	Not Free	Autocracy
2005	Not Free	Autocracy
2006	Not Free	Autocracy
2007	Not Free	Autocracy
2008	Not Free	Autocracy
2009	Not Free	Autocracy
2010	Not Free	Autocracy
2011	Not Free	Autocracy
2012	Not Free	Autocracy

In Brief

Some effort is occasionally made to feign or mimic the superficial trappings of democratic governance, but Kazakhstan is a dictatorship that strictly controls the media.

> ### MEDIA FREEDOM HISTORY IN A NUTSHELL
>
> - Under the dictatorship of Nursultan Nazarbayev, media have been restricted
> - Attempts to present the façade of democratic government have led to occasional shifts to method of indirect control
> - Although Kazakhstan has a range of state-run and private print and broadcast media, most news outlets are controlled or influenced by the president and members of his family (BBC News Country Profiles)
> - As of 2012, about 53 percent of Kazakhs had Internet access (International Telecommunication Union's 2012 ICT Indicators Database)

Chronology

1991–2012: Not Free

Since Kazakhstan declared independence from the Soviet Union in 1991, Nursultan Nazarbayev has been president. Although the government has frequently shifted between direct control and the use of indirect methods of coercion to control the media, there has been little if any substantive change to the nature of the media in the country. The dictatorship of Nursultan Nazarbayev has led an extensive shift from a command-based Soviet economy to a market economy, but there has been no evidence of liberalization of the political environment. In 2012, following unrest and strikes, the government launched a crackdown on critical news media and closed down as many as forty opposition news outlets.[1]

Media Today

With a history of authoritarian rule and occupation that goes back to the first imposition of a semblance of government by the Mongols, there is little if any experience with or domestic demand for more liberal social or political institutions and the media is likely to remain controlled for the foreseeable future. Although there are privately owned print and broadcast media, most news outlets depend on government subsidies and many media companies are owned by people with close ties to government.[2]

Notes

1. *Freedom of the Press* (Washington, DC: Freedom House, 2013). Available at http://freedomhouse.org/report/freedom-press/2013/kazakhstan.
2. *Country Reports on Human Rights Practices 2012* (Washington, DC: U.S. Department of State, 2013). Available at http://www.state.gov/j/drl/rls/hrrpt/humanrightsreport/index.htm#wrapper.

Kenya: 1963–2012

Kenya Year by Year

Year	Media	Government
1963	Not Free	Anocracy
1964	Not Free	Anocracy
1965	Not Free	Anocracy
1966	Not Free	Anocracy
1967	Not Free	Anocracy
1968	Not Free	Anocracy
1969	Not Free	Autocracy
1970	Not Free	Autocracy
1971	Not Free	Autocracy
1972	Not Free	Autocracy
1973	Not Free	Autocracy
1974	Not Free	Autocracy
1975	Not Free	Autocracy
1976	Not Free	Autocracy
1977	Not Free	Autocracy
1978	Not Free	Autocracy
1979	Not Free	Autocracy
1980	Not Free	Autocracy
1981	Not Free	Autocracy
1982	Not Free	Autocracy
1983	Not Free	Autocracy
1984	Not Free	Autocracy
1985	Not Free	Autocracy
1986	Not Free	Autocracy
1987	Not Free	Autocracy
1988	Not Free	Autocracy

(Continued)

MEDIA FREEDOM HISTORY IN A NUTSHELL

- For most of the three decades following independence, Kenya was a one-party state and the news media were restricted
- As Kenya transitioned to a multiparty system, news media began to provide more critical coverage of political events, but attacks and harassment of journalists increased
- As Kenya democratized in the early 2000s, conditions for news media slowly improved
- As of 2012, there were eight paid-for daily newspapers with an average circulation of 310,000 (World Association of Newspaper's 2012 World Newspaper Trends)
- There were six private television broadcasters and numerous private radio stations; International news media are also widely available in the country (Freedom House's Report on Freedom of the Press 2013)
- As of 2012, about 32 percent of Kenyans had Internet access (International Telecommunication Union's 2012 ICT Indicators Database)

In Brief

Following independence, Kenya soon became a one party state and media were restricted. As Kenya transitioned to a multiparty system, news media became more aggressive in providing political news coverage, and journalists faced attacks and harassment. Following Kenya's democratization in the early 2000s, the media environment gradually improved to the point where media became imperfectly free.

Chronology

1963–1993: Not Free

Shortly after Kenya gained independence, Minister of Information Ramogi Oneko promised

(Continued)

Year	Media	Government
1989	Not Free	Autocracy
1990	Not Free	Autocracy
1991	Not Free	Anocracy
1992	Not Free	Anocracy
1993	Not Free	Anocracy
1994	Imperfectly Free	Anocracy
1995	Imperfectly Free	Anocracy
1996	Imperfectly Free	Anocracy
1997	Not Free	Anocracy
1998	Not Free	Anocracy
1999	Not Free	Anocracy
2000	Not Free	Anocracy
2001	Not Free	Anocracy
2002	Not Free	Democracy
2003	Not Free	Democracy
2004	Not Free	Democracy
2005	Imperfectly Free	Democracy
2006	Imperfectly Free	Democracy
2007	Imperfectly Free	Democracy
2008	Imperfectly Free	Democracy
2009	Imperfectly Free	Democracy
2010	Imperfectly Free	Democracy
2011	Imperfectly Free	Democracy
2012	Imperfectly Free	Democracy

that media would be free provided they "co-operated with the Government for the good of Kenya."[1] Although news media were not subject to formal censorship, self-censorship was common and the government provided guidelines for news coverage of certain political issues.[2] Moreover, the Public Security Act gave government the authority to detain people for political reasons.[3] Prior to 1991, Kenya was in effect a one-party state. In 1991, President Daniel Moi agreed to allow a transition to a multiparty system, and as the media began to provide more critical political news coverage, some journalists were threatened and others were arrested.[4] In 1993, the threats and attacks continued and the government confiscated the printing press of

a company that printed several independent publications.[5]

1994–1996: Imperfectly Free

Following Kenya's transition to a multiparty system, news media became more aggressive about covering politics and attacks on journalists and news organizations increased.[6] Although there was some self-censorship, news media persisted in criticizing government, and in mid-1994, government pressures on the press began to decrease.[7] Thus, more by force of journalistic will than by improved government practices, news media became imperfectly free, but only barely so.

1997–2004: Not Free

In 1997, as the country prepared for elections at the end of the year, journalists faced increased attacks and harassment.[8] President Moi won the elections. In the early 2000s, Moi and other officials filed a number of libel and defamation suits against critical newspapers.[9] When the elections of 2002 brought an end to the Kanu Party's four decades in power, there were hopes that the media environment would improve, but critical journalists still faced threats, lawsuits, and arrest, and the government did not repeal the 2002 Media Bill, which among other things mandated that publishers purchase an insurance bond prior to publishing.[10] In 2004, the government cracked down on tabloid newspapers, confiscating thousands of publications and arresting news vendors.[11]

2005–2012: Imperfectly Free

In the mid-2000s, the media environment improved as the independent radio stations became available and journalists faced fewer threats and attacks.[12] Even so, the relationship between President Mwai Kibaki and the news media became contentious, and journalists were arrested on libel charges.[13] In 2007, the Parliament passed the Kenya Media Law, which established a council to regulate media. That same year, broadcast media were not allowed to provide live news coverage following the disputed 2007 elections and the violence that ensued.

Media Today

Although Kenyan newspapers often provide critical news coverage, journalists remain vulnerable to attacks and punitive lawsuits. While there are some independent radio and television stations, the state-run Kenya Broadcasting Corporation stations have greater reach, especially in rural areas.[14] Although poor infrastructure has limited Internet access, mobile phone penetration is increasing and will likely improve access to online news.[15]

Notes

1. *The Toils of the Press*, IPI Report (Zurich: International Press Institute, November 1963), 11.
2. *Country Reports on Human Rights Practices for 1977* (Washington, DC: U.S. Department of State, 1978). Available at http://babel.hathitrust.org/cgi/pt?id=mdp.39015078705632;view=1up;seq=68.
3. Ibid.
4. *Country Reports on Human Rights Practices for 1992* (Washington, DC: U.S. Department of State, 1993). Available at https://archive.org/details/countryreportson1992unit.
5. *Country Reports on Human Rights Practices for 1993* (Washington, DC: U.S. Department of State, 1994). Available at http://dosfan.lib.uic.edu/ERC/democracy/1993_hrp_report/93hrp_report_africa/Kenya.htm.
6. *World Press Freedom Review*, IPI Report (Vienna: International Press Institute, 1993).
7. *Country Reports on Human Rights Practices for 1994* (Washington, DC: U.S. Department of State, 1995). Available at http://dosfan.lib.uic.edu/ERC/democracy/1994_hrp_report/94hrp_report_africa/Kenya.htm.
8. *World Press Freedom Review*, IPI Report (Vienna: International Press Institute, December 1997).
9. *Attacks on the Press in 2001 Kenya* (Committee to Protect Journalists, 2001). Available at http://cpj.org/2002/03/attacks-on-the-press-2001-kenya.php.
10. *Freedom of the Press* (Washington, DC: Freedom House, 2004). Available at http://www.freedomhouse.org/report/freedom-press/2004/kenya.
11. *Freedom of the Press* (Washington, DC: Freedom House, 2005). Available at http://www.freedomhouse.org/report/freedom-press/2005/kenya.
12. *Freedom of the Press* (Washington, DC: Freedom House, 2006). Available at http://www.freedomhouse.org/report/freedom-press/2006/kenya.
13. *World Press Freedom Review*, IPI Report (Vienna: International Press Institute, 2005).
14. *Country Reports on Human Rights Practices 2012* (Washington, DC: U.S. Department of State, 2013). Available at http://www.state.gov/j/drl/rls/hrrpt/humanrightsreport/index.htm#wrapper.
15. *Freedom of the Press* (Washington, DC: Freedom House, 2013). Available at http://www.freedomhouse.org/report/freedom-press/2013/kenya.

Kiribati: 1979–2012

Kiribati Year by Year

Year	Media	Government
1979	Imperfectly Free	In Transition
1980	Imperfectly Free	In Transition
1981	Imperfectly Free	In Transition
1982	Imperfectly Free	Democracy
1983	Imperfectly Free	Democracy
1984	Imperfectly Free	Democracy
1985	Imperfectly Free	Democracy
1986	Imperfectly Free	Democracy
1987	Imperfectly Free	Democracy
1988	Imperfectly Free	Democracy
1989	Imperfectly Free	Democracy
1990	Imperfectly Free	Democracy
1991	Imperfectly Free	Democracy
1992	Imperfectly Free	Democracy
1993	Imperfectly Free	Democracy
1994	Not Free	Democracy
1995	Not Free	Democracy
1996	Not Free	Democracy
1997	Not Free	Democracy
1998	Not Free	Democracy
1999	Not Free	Democracy
2000	Imperfectly Free	Democracy
2001	Imperfectly Free	Democracy
2002	Imperfectly Free	Democracy
2003	Imperfectly Free	Democracy

MEDIA FREEDOM HISTORY IN A NUTSHELL

- Since gaining independence, Kiribati has had imperfectly free media, with the exception of the mid-1990s when the government resisted efforts to establish privately owned media
- Most Kiribati media are state-owned and run by the Broadcasting and Publications Authority, which is supposed to be editorially independent, but has been subject to government manipulation
- As of 2009, there were three paid-for non-daily newspapers with an average circulation of 4,000 (World Association of Newspaper's 2010 World Newspaper Trends)
- Kiribati has one state-run radio station and one privately owned radio station
- As of 2012, about 11 percent of Kiribati had Internet access (International Telecommunication Union's 2012 ICT Indicators Database)

In Brief

Formerly the Gilbert Islands, Kiribati was renamed in 1979 when it gained independence from the United Kingdom. Kiribati's thirty-three atolls span more than 2,400 miles from east to west and more than 1,200 miles north to south, yet, with a population of around 103,000, it is a small media market and has no domestic television. Most Kiribati media are state-owned or owned by government officials. With the exception of five years when the government resisted efforts to establish privately owned media, Kiribati has had imperfectly free media. Kiribati is at risk from rising sea levels.

Chronology

1979–1993: Imperfectly Free

Upon gaining independence from the United Kingdom in 1979, Kiribati adopted a constitution

Year	Media	Government
2004	Imperfectly Free	Democracy
2005	Imperfectly Free	Democracy
2006	Imperfectly Free	Democracy
2007	Imperfectly Free	Democracy
2008	Imperfectly Free	Democracy
2009	Imperfectly Free	Democracy
2010	Imperfectly Free	Democracy
2011	Imperfectly Free	Democracy
2012	Imperfectly Free	Democracy

that provided for media freedom and the government appeared to respect this in practice; however, Kiribati's only radio station and newspaper were government owned and operated by the Broadcasting and Publications Authority (BPA).[1] There is some evidence that government manipulated the BPA to gain favorable coverage.[2]

1994–1999: Not Free

During his campaign for president, Teburoro Tito promised to allow the BPA to operate independently and freely, yet when he was elected in 1994, he ordered the BPA to stop airing a critical program on *Radio Kiribati* and to limit access of the opposition to both the radio station and the newspaper.[3]

In 1999, former President Ieremia Tabai tried to start a new radio station, but was fined for bringing communication equipment into the country without a license.[4] That same year, the government banned New Zealand journalist Michael Field from Kiribati in response to his critical reporting.[5] Tabai had to wait nearly four years before the government granted his license to start the radio station.

2000–2012: Imperfectly Free

When he was unable to start up his radio station, Tabai began publishing a weekly newspaper, the *Kiribati Newstar*, in 2000.[6] In 2002, an amendment to the Newspaper Registration Act, which gave the government the authority to shut down

newspapers it determined were offensive, defamatory, or inflammatory, was viewed as a move against *Newstar*.[7] Yet the government never used this authority, and the amendment was repealed several years later. In 2003, Tabai was granted a license and *Newair* FM began broadcasting.[8] In 2006, a state radio reporter was fired when he refused to name his sources for a story on government corruption.[9] Thus in the 2000s, Kiribati gained independent news media, but the government continually made some efforts to control media.

Media Today

While there are no formal restrictions on media freedom, Kiribati is a very small media market and much of the media are state-run or owned by government officials. Although the Broadcasting and Publications Authority is supposed to be editorially independent, over the years the government has manipulated it. Moreover, most of the independent media are owned by Ieremia Tabai who is a former president and current Member of Parliament.[10]

Notes

1. *Country Reports on Human Rights Practices for 1985* (Washington, DC: U.S. Department of State, 1986). Available at http://babel.hathitrust.org/cgi/pt?id=mdp.39015011233270;view=1up;seq=7.
2. Taberannang Korauaba, "Small Pacific States and Media Freedom: A Kiribati Case Study," *Pacific Journalism Review* 13, no. 1 (2007): 29–38.
3. Ibid.
4. *World Press Freedom Review*, IPI Report (Vienna: International Press Institute, 1999).
5. Ibid.
6. *World Press Freedom Review*, IPI Report (Vienna: International Press Institute, 2000).
7. *World Press Freedom Review*, IPI Report (Vienna: International Press Institute, 2003).
8. *Freedom of the Press* (Washington, DC: Freedom House, 2004). Available at http://www.freedomhouse.org/report/freedom-press/2004/kiribati.
9. *World Press Freedom Review*, IPI Report (Vienna: International Press Institute, 2006).
10. *Country Report on Human Rights Practices, 2012* (Washington, DC: U.S. Department of State, 2013). Available at http://www.state.gov/j/drl/rls/hrrpt/humanrightsreport/index.htm#wrapper.

Kosovo: 2008–2012

Kosovo Year by Year

Year	Media	Government
2008	Imperfectly Free	Democracy
2009	Imperfectly Free	Democracy
2010	Imperfectly Free	Democracy
2011	Imperfectly Free	Democracy
2012	Imperfectly Free	Democracy

In Brief

Media are in a highly volatile state and face a tremendous number of challenges in making the transition to a free media system.

Chronology

2008–2012: Imperfectly Free

Kosovo is one of the few countries to have a media system remain for any length of time at the border between functionally free and restricted. External, primarily European, efforts to foster the development of free media appear to be balanced against a domestic backdrop of indifference and suspicion.

Media Today

The massive expansion from a single, government-controlled source of news to hundreds of

> **MEDIA FREEDOM HISTORY IN A NUTSHELL**
>
> - Media are at the border of being imperfectly free and restricted
> - As of 2011, there were nine paid-for daily newspapers with a total average circulation per issue of 32,000 (World Association of Newspaper's 2012 World Newspaper Trends)
> - Kosovo had more than one hundred licensed radio stations and twenty-two television stations (World Association of Newspaper's 2012 World Newspaper Trends)
> - As of 2011, about 20 percent of citizens had Internet access (Freedom House's 2012 Freedom of the Press Report)

tiny, economically untenable media sources in this very small country has created a situation that is ripe for coercion and manipulation. The inevitable contraction will be a challenge for supporters of further liberalization. Further complicating matters is the tremendous social and political divide between Albanian and Serbian language communities and a centuries-long history of authoritarian rule of one sort or another that is probably the explanation for the tepid domestic demands for free and professional media.

Kuwait: 1961–2012

Kuwait Year by Year

Year	Media	Government
1961	Not Free	Autocracy
1962	Not Free	Autocracy
1963	Not Free	Autocracy
1964	Not Free	Autocracy
1965	Not Free	Autocracy
1966	Not Free	Autocracy
1967	Not Free	Autocracy
1968	Not Free	Autocracy
1969	Not Free	Autocracy
1970	Not Free	Autocracy
1971	Not Free	Autocracy
1972	Not Free	Autocracy
1973	Not Free	Autocracy
1974	Not Free	Autocracy
1975	Not Free	Autocracy
1976	Not Free	Autocracy
1977	Not Free	Autocracy
1978	Not Free	Autocracy
1979	Not Free	Autocracy
1980	Not Free	Autocracy
1981	Not Free	Autocracy
1982	Not Free	Autocracy
1983	Not Free	Autocracy
1984	Not Free	Autocracy
1985	Not Free	Autocracy
1986	Not Free	Autocracy
1987	Not Free	Autocracy
1988	Not Free	Autocracy

(Continued)

MEDIA FREEDOM HISTORY IN A NUTSHELL

- A former British Protectorate, independent Kuwait is a hereditary monarchy that has always had a diverse, but restricted media
- Criticism of government has always been outlawed
- The Emir restricted the media to the point of full control in 1976 and 1986
- As of 2012, there were seventeen paid-for daily newspapers with an average circulation of 961,000 (Freedom House's Freedom of the Press 2013)
- Kuwait has a mix of state-owned and private broadcast media
- As of 2012, about 79 percent of Kuwaitis had Internet access (International Telecommunication Union's 2012 ICT Indicators Database)

In Brief

Although it is a hereditary monarchy, Kuwait's media are reasonably diverse for such a small market. Moreover since it was liberated from Iraq in the first Gulf War, Kuwait has been reasonably open to external news sources, but arrests remain a common punishment for criticism of the government or Islam and a variety of other taboo subjects.

Chronology

1961–2012: Not Free

A British protectorate since 1899, Kuwait gained independence in 1961. Yet the British influence was clearly evident in the variety of media available in such a small market and the quasi-democratic political structures such as the National Assembly that were established with the constitution. BBC media are allowed to broadcast in the

• 257

(Continued)

Year	Media	Government
1989	Not Free	Autocracy
1990	Not Free	Foreign Interruption
1991	Not Free	Autocracy
1992	Not Free	Autocracy
1993	Not Free	Autocracy
1994	Not Free	Autocracy
1995	Not Free	Autocracy
1996	Not Free	Autocracy
1997	Not Free	Autocracy
1998	Not Free	Autocracy
1999	Not Free	Autocracy
2000	Not Free	Autocracy
2001	Not Free	Autocracy
2002	Not Free	Autocracy
2003	Not Free	Autocracy
2004	Not Free	Autocracy
2005	Not Free	Autocracy
2006	Not Free	Autocracy
2007	Not Free	Autocracy
2008	Not Free	Autocracy
2009	Not Free	Autocracy
2010	Not Free	Autocracy
2011	Not Free	Autocracy
2012	Not Free	Autocracy

country, but domestic news is restricted. Criticism of the Royal Family, government, Islam, and other disruptive coverage are all criminal offenses and remain so to this day.

In 1976, the Emir suspended the National Assembly and imposed strict censorship of news media. What specific combination of factors that led to this action is unclear. However, the subsequent actions taken to marginalize the significant non-Kuwaiti population in the country, particularly the Palestinians, is likely associated with the rather harsh antidemocratic action by the Royal Family.

In 1981, The National Assembly was reconstituted, and with that, some of the more severe media controls were eased.

In 1986, The National Assembly was again suspended and media controls returned. During the Iraqi invasion and occupation, Iraq imposed absolute control over the media and churned out extensive propaganda. Much of this was aimed at gaining the support of the significant Palestinian population, which had suffered greatly since 1976.

The liberation of Kuwait from Iraqi occupation by the United States led to a reestablishment of the National Assembly and related semiautonomous media. However, the war was used to justify the expulsion or extreme marginalization of most of the non-Kuwaiti population. The rhetoric used by the Kuwaiti Royal family in this process, and the coverage in the domestic media, suggested that government had assumed direct control during the years after the war. The U.S. Department of State assessments of the political situation in Kuwait during this period border on propaganda, and almost all assessments since the war appear to be politically tinted in one way or another. It is clear, however, that despite some descriptions that may suggest otherwise, Kuwait never had free media.

In 1996, the International Press Institute reported that all Kuwaiti newspapers were censored and that eighteen journalists had been jailed in Kuwait since 1991, allegedly for their role in abetting the Iraqi occupation.[1] Even the U.S. Department of State reported in 2000 that "the Press Law prohibits the publication of any direct criticism of the Amir, official government communications with other states, and material that serves to 'attack religions' or 'incite people to commit crimes, creates hatred, or spreads dissension among the populace.'"[2]

Media Today

Media are reasonably diverse for such a small market, but arrests are still a common punishment for criticism of the government, Islam, and a variety of other taboo subjects.

Notes

1. *World Press Freedom Review*, IPI Report (Vienna: International Press Institute, December 1996)
2. *Country Reports on Human Rights Practices 1999* (Washington, DC: U.S. Department of State, 2000). Available at http://www.state.gov/www/global/human_rights/1999_hrp_report/kuwait.html.

Kyrgyzstan: 1991–2012

Kyrgyzstan Year by Year

Year	Media	Government
1991	Imperfectly Free	Anocracy
1992	Imperfectly Free	Anocracy
1993	Imperfectly Free	Anocracy
1994	Imperfectly Free	Anocracy
1995	Not Free	Anocracy
1996	Not Free	Anocracy
1997	Not Free	Anocracy
1998	Not Free	Anocracy
1999	Not Free	Anocracy
2000	Not Free	Anocracy
2001	Not Free	Anocracy
2002	Not Free	Anocracy
2003	Not Free	Anocracy
2004	Not Free	Anocracy
2005	Not Free	Anocracy
2006	Not Free	Anocracy
2007	Not Free	Anocracy
2008	Not Free	Anocracy
2009	Not Free	Anocracy
2010	Not Free	Democracy
2011	Not Free	Democracy
2012	Not Free	Democracy

In Brief

An agrarian society that claims 1995 as the millennial anniversary of its founding, Kyrgyzstan's modern history is dominated by its incorporation in and departure from the Soviet Union.

MEDIA FREEDOM HISTORY IN A NUTSHELL

- A brief period of liberal government and society, including media freedom, followed independence from the Soviet Union
- Authoritarian impulses gained momentum, effectively ending media freedom in 1995
- As of 2013, Kyrgyzstan had three daily newspapers, all of which were privately owned, as well as a number of privately owned weeklies and one government-owned triweekly (BBC News Country Profiles)
- Kyrgyzstan has a mix of privately owned and state-run broadcast media
- As of 2012, about 22 percent of Kyrgyz had Internet access (International Telecommunication Union's 2012 ICT Indicators Database)

Chronology

1991–1994: Imperfectly Free

Unlike the other former Soviet republics in Central Asia, a liberal period followed secession from the Soviet Union. This included multiparty elections, and the media freedom needed to allow an active public sphere and engaged civil society. This moment of freedom quickly faded as economic difficulties and the struggle to sustain a stable government led to increasing authoritarianism. Constant and sometimes violent conflict with Uzbekistan and Tajikistan over the disputed Ferghana valley further strained the effort to establish a liberal government.

1995–2012: Not Free

A crack down on journalists investigating or reporting corruption was the triggering event for the change to a not free press, but President

Askar Akayev's government had already taken a decidedly authoritarian turn in late 1994. His 1995 reelection by an overwhelming and, for all intents and purposes, impossible margin effectively exposed the liberal trappings of government and society as a pretense. After the government sued and then shut down a newspaper, journalists were encouraged to self-censor.[1] Corruption and government protection of friendly business interests further hindered the economy, which floundered on the verge of collapse. The 2005 "Tulip Revolution" ousted Askar Akayev but little changed.

Media Today

Plagued by corruption and organized crime, government in Kyrgyzstan is largely a game of playing foreign powers against one another in pursuit of the cash needed to support the graft and bribery needed to sustain power. Journalists and dissidents are harassed, arrested, and have disappeared, and elections have fallen far short of international democratic standards. Changes in leadership have to this date shown little real indication of change, and as the U.S. involvement in Afghanistan winds down, the decreasing need for a compliant Kyrgyzstan government will inevitably lead to decline in that source of support, and the ability to sustain the current patronage system is questionable.

Note

1. *World Press Freedom Review*, IPI Report (Vienna: International Press Institute, November/December 1995).

Laos: 1954–2012

Laos Year by Year

Year	Media	Government
1954	Not Free	Anocracy
1955	Not Free	Anocracy
1956	Not Free	Anocracy
1957	Not Free	Democracy
1958	Not Free	Democracy
1959	Not Free	Democracy
1960	Not Free	Anocracy
1961	Not Free	Anocracy
1962	Not Free	Anocracy
1963	Not Free	Anocracy
1964	Not Free	Anocracy
1965	Not Free	Anocracy
1966	Not Free	Anocracy
1967	Not Free	Anocracy
1968	Not Free	Anocracy
1969	Not Free	Anocracy
1970	Not Free	Anocracy
1971	Not Free	Anocracy
1972	Not Free	Anocracy
1973	Not Free	Anocracy
1974	Not Free	Anocracy
1975	Not Free	Autocracy
1976	Not Free	Autocracy
1977	Not Free	Autocracy
1978	Not Free	Autocracy
1979	Not Free	Autocracy
1980	Not Free	Autocracy

(Continued)

MEDIA FREEDOM HISTORY IN A NUTSHELL

- Long a colonial battleground, independent Laos has experienced chaos, civil war, autocratic rule, and controlled media
- As of 2009, Laos had a total of four paid for daily newspapers with an average circulation of 10,000 (World Association of Newspaper's 2010 World Newspaper Trends)
- Domestic television and radio broadcasts are closely controlled by the government; however, Laotians do have access to foreign broadcasts coming into the country (World Association of Newspaper's 2010 World Newspaper Trends)
- As of 2012, 11 percent of Laotians had Internet access (International Telecommunication Union's 2012 ICT Indicators Database)

In Brief

The modern history of Laos could be called a tragedy of colonialism. From French colonial occupation, to Japanese military conquest and occupation, to the return of the French, Laos was a battleground for colonial powers. Even after independence was attained in 1954, it was the target of the most massive aerial bombing campaign in history as the United States attempted to sustain a western aligned proxy regime in South Vietnam as part of the neocolonial super power struggle.

Chronology

1954–2012: Not Free

Laos has long history of controlled news media, dating back to the years of French colonialization. Authoritarian rule, or chaos, has been the norm over the last half century. Early attempts

(Continued)

Year	Media	Government
1981	Not Free	Autocracy
1982	Not Free	Autocracy
1983	Not Free	Autocracy
1984	Not Free	Autocracy
1985	Not Free	Autocracy
1986	Not Free	Autocracy
1987	Not Free	Autocracy
1988	Not Free	Autocracy
1989	Not Free	Autocracy
1990	Not Free	Autocracy
1991	Not Free	Autocracy
1992	Not Free	Autocracy
1993	Not Free	Autocracy
1994	Not Free	Autocracy
1995	Not Free	Autocracy
1996	Not Free	Autocracy
1997	Not Free	Autocracy
1998	Not Free	Autocracy
1999	Not Free	Autocracy
2000	Not Free	Autocracy
2001	Not Free	Autocracy
2002	Not Free	Autocracy
2003	Not Free	Autocracy
2004	Not Free	Autocracy
2005	Not Free	Autocracy

Year	Media	Government
2006	Not Free	Autocracy
2007	Not Free	Autocracy
2008	Not Free	Autocracy
2009	Not Free	Autocracy
2010	Not Free	Autocracy
2011	Not Free	Autocracy
2012	Not Free	Autocracy

at elections created fragile governments that succumbed to external pressures easily and collapsed quickly. A coup in 1960 all but ended any pretense at democratic governance. Laos became a key battlefield in the Vietnam War, and the country was divided and governed by military leaders. The end of the war brought an authoritarian communist regime to power. Centralized control of the economy was abandoned after the fall of the Soviet Union, but the communist party still controls all elements of government.[1]

Media Today

What limited media exist in Laos have been strictly controlled by government. Media from outside of Laos appear to be allowed in the country.

Note

1. Andrea Matles Savada, *Laos: A Country Study* (Washington, DC: Library of Congress Federal Research Division, 1994). Available at http://lcweb2.loc.gov/frd/cs/.

Latvia: 1992–2012

Latvia Year by Year

Year	Media	Government
1992	Free	Democracy
1993	Free	Democracy
1994	Free	Democracy
1995	Imperfectly Free	Democracy
1996	Imperfectly Free	Democracy
1997	Imperfectly Free	Democracy
1998	Imperfectly Free	Democracy
1999	Free	Democracy
2000	Free	Democracy
2001	Free	Democracy
2002	Free	Democracy
2003	Free	Democracy
2004	Free	Democracy
2005	Free	Democracy
2006	Free	Democracy
2007	Free	Democracy
2008	Free	Democracy
2009	Free	Democracy
2010	Free	Democracy
2011	Free	Democracy
2012	Free	Democracy

In Brief

Latvia has long been the most strategically and economically important of the three Baltic States, having the deepest ports, the largest city, and the

MEDIA FREEDOM HISTORY IN A NUTSHELL

- Media freedom was quickly and fully adopted after independence from the Soviet Union
- Challenges and threats to media freedom emerged during the severe economic crisis that followed independence, but media freedom was sustained
- As of 2011, there were thirteen paid-for daily newspapers with a total average circulation per issue of 340,000 (World Association of Newspaper's 2012 World Newspaper Trends)
- Latvia had one state-owned television station and one radio station. Privately owned television and radio stations also operate in the country
- As of 2012, about 74 percent of Latvians had Internet access (International Telecommunication Union's 2012 ICT Indicators Database)

most significant industrial base of the three. It hosted the most significant of Soviet military installations. As a result, there was a large Russian population in Latvia. Thus, the Soviets exerted far greater efforts to control the country during its incorporation in the Soviet Union, and they were less inclined to accede to its push for independence. In response to independence, Latvia made a massive and in many ways radical push to install western style political and economic institutions, including press freedom.

Chronology

1992–1994: Free

Press freedom was a critical part of Latvia's radical westernization after it gained independence from the Soviet Union. Press freedom was seen as one of the key tools to fight against corruption in the quickly privatizing economy.

Although Latvia gained independence, it still had fragments of the Soviet era, in particular the Media Law, which listed several categories of information that may not be published. However, Latvian media were among the most free in the former Soviet Union.[1]

1995–1998: Imperfectly Free

A severe economic crisis was both part of Latvia's radical post-Soviet reformation and a result of several of the economic measures employed. The media did not escape this crisis, but the effect on the media was limited by strong support from reformers who saw media freedom and transparence as a powerful tool against the use of political power to seize wealth and other forms of corruption that plagued many of the other former Soviet countries. Mafia groups also presented a major threat to journalists in Latvia. Their use of violent methods to protect their interests and silence others contributed to an imperfectly free media system.[2]

1999–2012: Free

The gradual success and consolidation of the radical reform agenda effectively ended the most significant challenges to free media. In addition in the mid-2000s, several companies began to offer free newspapers to people on the streets and on public transportation.[3]

Media Today

Limited market size, which is further split between Russian and Latvian languages, is a long-term concern for the health of the Latvian media. A lesser but still significant concern lies in the slowly decreasing concerns over corruption and how that might erode the steadfast commitment to press freedom. Distinct differences exist between the journalistic cultures of Russian and Latvian media outlets, with Latvian outlets far more clear regarding the distinction between reporting and opinion.

Paragraph 100 of the 1991 reinstated constitution states that "each person shall have the right to freedom of speech, which includes the right to freely acquire, possess and distribute information and to express his or her opinions. Censorship is prohibited."[4]

Notes

1. *World Press Freedom Review*, IPI Report (Vienna: International Press Institute, 1993).
2. *World Press Freedom Review*, IPI Report (Vienna: International Press Institute, 1995).
3. *Latvia*, Media Landscape Reports (Maastricht, The Netherlands: European Journalism Centre, 2013). Available at http://ejc.net/media_landscapes/latvia#link_509.
4. Ibid.

Lebanon: 1948–2012

Lebanon Year by Year

Year	Media	Government
1948	Imperfectly Free	Anocracy
1949	Imperfectly Free	Anocracy
1950	Imperfectly Free	Anocracy
1951	Imperfectly Free	Anocracy
1952	Imperfectly Free	Anocracy
1953	Imperfectly Free	Anocracy
1954	Imperfectly Free	Anocracy
1955	Imperfectly Free	Anocracy
1956	Imperfectly Free	Anocracy
1957	Imperfectly Free	Anocracy
1958	Imperfectly Free	Anocracy
1959	Imperfectly Free	Anocracy
1960	Imperfectly Free	Anocracy
1961	Imperfectly Free	Anocracy
1962	Imperfectly Free	Anocracy
1963	Imperfectly Free	Anocracy
1964	Imperfectly Free	Anocracy
1965	Imperfectly Free	Anocracy
1966	Imperfectly Free	Anocracy
1967	Imperfectly Free	Anocracy
1968	Imperfectly Free	Anocracy
1969	Imperfectly Free	Anocracy
1970	Imperfectly Free	Anocracy
1971	Imperfectly Free	Anocracy

(Continued)

MEDIA FREEDOM HISTORY IN A NUTSHELL

- From 1948 to 1975, a dynamic and diverse free media environment was compromised by corruption and unofficial influence, but media were still functionally free
- Civil war from 1975 to 1990 devastated the country and the media system
- Civil war ended in 1990, but it took a decade before the political and media system recovered enough to restore media freedom
- After a failed first effort, media freedom returned in 2004
- Media quickly developed after the withdrawal of Syrian troops in 2005 and are now robust, diverse, and functionally free
- Most news outlets are closely tied to political parties (World Association of Newspapers' World Press Trends 2012 Report)
- As of 2012, Lebanon had seventeen daily newspapers, and newspapers reached about 38 percent of the population (World Association of Newspapers' World Press Trends 2012 Report)
- Lebanon has a mix of state-run and independent broadcast media
- Unlike many countries in the region, Lebanon does not appear to filter Internet content; as of 2012, more than 61 percent of Lebanese had Internet access (International Telecommunication Union's 2012 ICT Indicators Database)

In Brief

For more than three decades following its independence from France in 1943, Lebanon had media that were functionally free. From 1975 to 1998, as the country went through civil war, Syrian occupation, and then Israeli occupation, media were limited and for the most part restricted. As Lebanon democratized in 2005, media became functionally free.

(Continued)

Year	Media	Government
1972	Imperfectly Free	Anocracy
1973	Imperfectly Free	Anocracy
1974	Imperfectly Free	Anocracy
1975	Imperfectly Free	Anocracy
1976	Not Free	Interregnum
1977	Not Free	Interregnum
1978	Not Free	Interregnum
1979	Not Free	Interregnum
1980	Not Free	Interregnum
1981	Not Free	Interregnum
1982	Not Free	Interregnum
1983	Not Free	Interregnum
1984	Not Free	Interregnum
1985	Not Free	Interregnum
1986	Not Free	Interregnum
1987	Not Free	Interregnum
1988	Not Free	Interregnum
1989	Not Free	Interregnum
1990	Not Free	Foreign Interruption
1991	Not Free	Foreign Interruption
1992	Not Free	Foreign Interruption
1993	Not Free	Foreign Interruption
1994	Not Free	Foreign Interruption
1995	Not Free	Foreign Interruption
1996	Not Free	Foreign Interruption
1997	Not Free	Foreign Interruption
1998	Not Free	Foreign Interruption
1999	Imperfectly Free	Foreign Interruption
2000	Imperfectly Free	Foreign Interruption
2001	Not Free	Foreign Interruption
2002	Not Free	Foreign Interruption
2003	Not Free	Foreign Interruption

Chronology

1948–1975: Imperfectly Free

A power sharing agreement, which advantaged the Christian community by guaranteeing it control of the presidency, was the basis for a democratic regime that included media freedom. Media were diverse and reasonably robust but often compromised by unofficial influence and pressure to avoid coverage that would disturb the relatively fragile government. Media freedom survived the 1958 clashes, but fell in the conflagration of the 1975 civil war.

1976–1998 Not Free

Media all but disappeared as the civil war raged. Syrian troops invaded and at least some Syrian military presence remained in the country until 2005.

The 1982 Israeli invasion of southern Lebanon coincided with a reduction in the intensity of the civil war in the rest of the country and some semblance of functional media began to reappear, but outlets were heavily censored by the faction that controlled their location. Fighting continued until the formal end of the civil war in 1990. It took two years for the Lebanese Armed Forces to reassert control over just two-thirds of the country, and the degree to which the government had any influence over the southern portion of the country, which was dominated by the South Lebanon Army, is debatable. Elections were held in 1992, but even the process of disbanding and disarming the many militias took several years and was never fully completed.

1999–2000: Imperfectly Free

The collapse of the South Lebanon Army and the beginning of Israel's withdrawal from southern Lebanon marked the return to a reasonable degree of central government control over most of the country. Media restrictions were relaxed, and more important, the very real threats of violence toward journalists who might criticize or offend the more radical factions eased considerably to the point where the media were functionally but imperfectly free. In fact, by 1999, Lebanon's media were among the freest in the Middle East.[1]

Year	Media	Government
2004	Imperfectly Free	Foreign Interruption
2005	Imperfectly Free	Democracy
2006	Imperfectly Free	Democracy
2007	Imperfectly Free	Democracy
2008	Imperfectly Free	Democracy
2009	Imperfectly Free	Democracy
2010	Imperfectly Free	Democracy
2011	Imperfectly Free	Democracy
2012	Imperfectly Free	Democracy

2001–2003: Not Free

By 2001, the government appeared to be unable to exert sufficient control over Hezbollah forces in the south to keep them from attacking Israel. It is unclear if this exposure of weakness was associated with the rise in violence against journalists, but in 2001, there were increased reports of the government censoring television news and threatening journalists, thereby encouraging self-censorship.[2]

2004–2012: Imperfectly Free

The 2004 protests against continued Syrian occupation marked the return of media freedom. After Syrian troops left, private media developed rapidly and offered increasingly diverse viewpoints.[3]

Media Today

Media are now best described as diverse and dynamic. Critical coverage is tolerated. Restrictions against coverage that will incite sectarian strife have created a grey area where some legitimate criticisms and debates are suppressed.

Notes

1. *World Press Freedom Review*, IPI Report (Vienna: International Press Institute, 1999).
2. *Country Reports on Human Rights Practices 2001* (Washington, DC: U.S. Department of State, 2002). Available at http://www.state.gov/j/drl/rls/hrrpt/2001/nea/8270.htm.
3. *Freedom of the Press* (Washington, DC: Freedom House, 2005). Available at http://www.freedomhouse.org/report/freedom-press/2005/lebanon.

Lesotho: 1966–2012

Lesotho Year by Year

Year	Media	Government
1966	Not Free	Democracy
1967	Not Free	Democracy
1968	Not Free	Democracy
1969	Not Free	Democracy
1970	Not Free	Autocracy
1971	Not Free	Autocracy
1972	Not Free	Autocracy
1973	Not Free	Autocracy
1974	Not Free	Autocracy
1975	Not Free	Autocracy
1976	Not Free	Autocracy
1977	Not Free	Autocracy
1978	Not Free	Autocracy
1979	Not Free	Autocracy
1980	Not Free	Autocracy
1981	Not Free	Autocracy
1982	Not Free	Autocracy
1983	Not Free	Autocracy
1984	Not Free	Autocracy
1985	Not Free	Autocracy
1986	Not Free	Autocracy
1987	Not Free	Autocracy
1988	Not Free	Autocracy
1989	Not Free	Autocracy
1990	Not Free	Autocracy

MEDIA FREEDOM HISTORY IN A NUTSHELL

- Postindependence, the government controlled most media for two and half decades
- As Lesotho democratized in the mid-1990s, media became imperfectly free, but political instability remains a threat
- State-owned print and broadcast media tend to reflect the government's point of view, but independent media are critical of government
- As of 2012, there were no daily newspapers, but there were several independent weekly newspapers; in addition to state-run radio and television, there were eight private radio stations (Freedom House's Report on Freedom of the Press 2013)
- As of 2012, about 5 percent of Basotho had Internet access (International Telecommunication Union's 2012 ICT Indicators Database)

In Brief

After independence the government maintained control over most news outlets, and a 1938 proclamation prohibiting criticism of the government remained in effect. In 1986, a military coup marked the beginning of a period of political instability. The 1993 elections brought about the return of a civilian government and the emergence of functionally free media. Political unrest following the disputed 1998 elections led to a suspension of media freedom, but since 1999, Basotho media have been functionally free.

Chronology

1966–1992: Not Free

After gaining independence from Britain in 1966, the Kingdom of Lesotho (formerly Basutoland) was led by King Moshoeshoe II and

Year	Media	Government
1991	Not Free	Autocracy
1992	Not Free	Autocracy
1993	Imperfectly Free	Democracy
1994	Imperfectly Free	Democracy
1995	Imperfectly Free	Democracy
1996	Imperfectly Free	Democracy
1997	Imperfectly Free	Democracy
1998	Not Free	Interregnum
1999	Imperfectly Free	In Transition
2000	Imperfectly Free	In Transition
2001	Imperfectly Free	In Transition
2002	Imperfectly Free	Democracy
2003	Imperfectly Free	Democracy
2004	Imperfectly Free	Democracy
2005	Imperfectly Free	Democracy
2006	Imperfectly Free	Democracy
2007	Imperfectly Free	Democracy
2008	Imperfectly Free	Democracy
2009	Imperfectly Free	Democracy
2010	Imperfectly Free	Democracy
2011	Imperfectly Free	Democracy
2012	Imperfectly Free	Democracy

Chief Leabua Jonathan as prime minister. The government controlled the radio station and most newspapers. Though there were some independent newspapers that were sometimes critical of government, these were small publications without much reach.[1] Additionally, Lesotho had a proclamation dating back to 1938 that prohibited criticism of the government.[2] Although Lesotho adopted a Human Rights Act in 1983, which called for freedom of expression, this same act made it clear that national security trumped freedom of expression.[3]

Chief Jonathan was ousted in a 1986 coup, and the new leader Major-General Justin Lekhanya banned politics and political discussion, but the effects of this ban were apparently minimal.[4] According to the International Press Institute, the independent press—mostly small church publications—did sometimes criticize government, but journalists working for the state-owned media faced detention if they engaged in critical reporting.[5] In 1991, Lekhanya was ousted and the ban on political activity was lifted.

1993–1997: Imperfectly Free

In the build-up to the 1993 elections, restrictions on news media eased and all political parties were granted free time on the government-controlled broadcast media.[6] After the elections, the new government appeared to encourage independent reporting by the government-owned media.[7] Thus, the media environment improved to the point that the media were imperfectly free. Yet political instability continued with infighting in the military, and eventually the elected government was replaced with a new government appointed by King Letsie that put the King as head of state. In spite of these transitions, the media remained for the most part functionally free, but only just so. Journalists reporting on the political turmoil were sometimes attacked.[8]

1998: Not Free

Riots that erupted following the disputed 1998 elections were eventually subdued by troops from the Southern African Development Community, but journalists caught in the middle were attacked and harassed.[9] Additionally, journalists for the public radio station were threatened with dismissal if they covered opposition protests.[10] A number of newspaper offices were looted and some were burned.[11] Thus, the media environment deteriorated to the point where it was not possible for journalists to safely criticize the government.

1999–2012: Imperfectly Free

As the political turmoil subsided and the South African Development Community troops withdrew from Lesotho, attacks and threats against journalists subsided and media were once again functionally free.

Yet defamation remained criminalized and journalists for independent media had difficulty gaining access to government information.[12] In 2002, Prime Minister Pakalitha Mosisili won a second term, but unlike 1998, there were no riots.

Media Today

Although the constitution guarantees freedom of expression, there are several laws that limit media freedom including the Sedition Proclamation of 1938, which prohibits criticism of government. There are also laws that prohibit government workers from providing information and laws that limit journalists' abilities to protect their sources.[13] Consequently, journalists and news outlets are vulnerable to punitive lawsuits and steep fines. Therefore, self-censorship is common. Attacks on journalists have become less frequent. Lesotho has a mix of government-owned and independent media. About 5 percent of Basotho have Internet access.

Notes

1. *Country Reports on Human Rights Practices for 1977* (Washington, DC: U.S. Department of State, 1978). Available at http://babel.hathitrust.org/cgi/pt?id=mdp.39015078705632;view=1up;seq=72.

2. *Freedom of the Press* (Washington, DC: Freedom House, 2003). Available at http://www.freedomhouse.org/report/freedom-press/2003/lesotho.

3. *Country Reports on Human Rights Practices 1990* (Washington, DC: U.S. Department of State, 1991). Available at https://archive.org/stream/countryreportson1990unit/countryreportson1990unit_djvu.txt.

4. Ibid.

5. *World Press Freedom Review*, IPI Report (Zurich: International Press Institute, 1987).

6. *Country Reports on Human Rights Practices 1993* (Washington, DC: U.S. Department of State, 1994). Available at http://dosfan.lib.uic.edu/ERC/democracy/1993_hrp_report/93hrp_report_africa/Lesotho.html.

7. Ibid.

8. *World Press Freedom Review*, IPI Report (Vienna: International Press Institute, December 1994).

9. *World Press Freedom Review*, IPI Report (Vienna: International Press Institute, December 1998).

10. Ibid.

11. *Country Reports on Human Rights Practices 1998* (Washington, DC: U.S. Department of State, 1999). Available at http://www.state.gov/www/global/human_rights/1998_hrp_report/lesotho.html.

12. *Attacks on the Press 2000 Lesotho* (Committee to Protect Journalists, 2000). Available at http://www.cpj.org/2001/03/attacks-on-the-press-2000-lesotho.php.

13. *Freedom of the Press* (Washington, DC: Freedom House, 2013). Available at http://www.freedomhouse.org/report/freedom-press/2013/lesotho.

Liberia: 1948–2012

Liberia Year by Year

Year	Media	Government
1948	Not Free	Autocracy
1949	Not Free	Autocracy
1950	Not Free	Autocracy
1951	Not Free	Autocracy
1952	Not Free	Autocracy
1953	Not Free	Autocracy
1954	Not Free	Autocracy
1955	Not Free	Autocracy
1956	Not Free	Autocracy
1957	Not Free	Autocracy
1958	Not Free	Autocracy
1959	Not Free	Autocracy
1960	Not Free	Autocracy
1961	Not Free	Autocracy
1962	Not Free	Autocracy
1963	Not Free	Autocracy
1964	Not Free	Autocracy
1965	Not Free	Autocracy
1966	Not Free	Autocracy
1967	Not Free	Autocracy
1968	Not Free	Autocracy
1969	Not Free	Autocracy
1970	Not Free	Autocracy
1971	Not Free	Autocracy

(Continued)

MEDIA FREEDOM HISTORY IN A NUTSHELL

- Although credited with modernizing Liberia, President Tubman used his increasing powers to control and restrict news media from 1944 until his death in 1971
- For much of the 1970s, media were functionally free under President Tolbert
- Media freedom ended in the 1980s shortly after Samuel Doe seized control of the country
- Political upheaval and civil war kept media restrictions in place for the 1990s and early 2000s
- Even as Liberia democratized in 2006, media did not become functionally free until 2010
- Liberia has a mix of independent and government print and broadcast media
- Because of poverty and illiteracy, radio remains the most popular medium
- As of 2012, Liberia had fifteen privately owned radio stations, fifty community radio stations and six television stations (Freedom House's Report on Freedom of the Press 2013)
- As of 2012, about 4 percent of Liberians had Internet access (International Telecommunication Union's 2012 ICT Indicators Database)

In Brief

Although Liberia experienced dramatic modernization during the 1944 to 1971 tenure of President Tubman, Tubman had little tolerance for criticism from independent media and used his power to control most news outlets. Conditions for media improved somewhat in the 1970s under President Tolbert. The 1980 coup ushered in a period of political instability and media control. Civil war during much of the 1990s and early 2000s created a hostile media environment that was slow to improve even after Liberia democratized in 2006. Since 2010,

(Continued)

Year	Media	Government
1972	Imperfectly Free	Autocracy
1973	Imperfectly Free	Autocracy
1974	Imperfectly Free	Autocracy
1975	Imperfectly Free	Autocracy
1976	Imperfectly Free	Autocracy
1977	Imperfectly Free	Autocracy
1978	Imperfectly Free	Autocracy
1979	Imperfectly Free	Autocracy
1980	Imperfectly Free	Autocracy
1981	Imperfectly Free	Autocracy
1982	Not Free	Autocracy
1983	Not Free	Autocracy
1984	Not Free	Autocracy
1985	Not Free	Autocracy
1986	Not Free	Autocracy
1987	Not Free	Autocracy
1988	Not Free	Autocracy
1989	Not Free	Autocracy
1990	Not Free	Interregnum
1991	Not Free	Interregnum
1992	Not Free	Interregnum
1993	Not Free	Interregnum
1994	Not Free	Interregnum
1995	Not Free	Interregnum
1996	Not Free	In Transition
1997	Not Free	Anocracy
1998	Not Free	Anocracy
1999	Not Free	Anocracy
2000	Not Free	Anocracy
2001	Not Free	Anocracy
2002	Not Free	Anocracy
2003	Not Free	In Transition

media have been functionally free, but only barely so.

Chronology

1948–1971: Not Free

Established as a settlement for freed slaves in 1821, with little consideration for the indigenous population, Liberia was initially a one-party state controlled by Americo-Liberians who represented about 5 percent of the population. The founding of Liberia's press was facilitated in 1825 by a donation from the Massachusetts Colonization Society to purchase a hand-operated press.[1] Although Liberia historically had an opposition press and a number of independent newspapers were launched in the 1940s and early 1950s, many of them failed in part because of the hostile environment created by the ruling National True Whig Party.[2] Libeling the president or other government officials carried harsh penalties.[3] President from 1944 to 1971, William Tubman is credited with modernizing Liberia and introducing universal suffrage, yet his regime was also quite autocratic and he had a contentious relationship with the news media:

> As he faced imminent defeat in the presidential election of 1955, Tubman resorted to sheer gangsterism to cow the opposition and to muzzle the press. Independent newspapers were physically attacked by agents of the government, especially after a phantom plot was contrived to incriminate and jail the leading opposition figures.[4]

Though there was significant modernization during Tubman's tenure, there was also a corresponding increase in government power resulting to a large extent from increased foreign investment in Liberia.[5] The government used some of this power to extend its tentacles into the media environment in the form of subsidies and in many cases direct ownership.[6]

1972–1981: Imperfectly Free

When Tubman died in 1971, William Tolbert became president, and though he too had a contentious relationship with independent media, under his leadership, controls on news media were relaxed to the point that media became functionally free.[7]

Year	Media	Government
2004	Not Free	In Transition
2005	Not Free	In Transition
2006	Not Free	Democracy
2007	Not Free	Democracy
2008	Not Free	Democracy
2009	Not Free	Democracy
2010	Imperfectly Free	Democracy
2011	Imperfectly Free	Democracy
2012	Imperfectly Free	Democracy

During the rest of the 1970s, media remained imperfectly free. "The Tolbert regime encouraged discussion of national issues and the news media openly criticized government policies and corruption up to but not including the presidency."[8] This was apparently true even as tensions increased with the rice riots in the late 1970s.[9]

In 1980, Tolbert was assassinated in a military coup led by Samuel K. Doe, and ten days later, journalists were invited to document the execution of thirteen members of Tolbert's administration.[10] As Liberia's first indigenous ruler, there were some hopes that Doe and his People's Redemption Council would bring about positive change. Initially, the Doe regime promised that media would be free with the caveat that journalists would be held responsible for their reporting.[11] During the first year after the coup, news media were for the most part free to criticize the government, but in late 1981, the government began to tighten controls.[12]

1982–2009: Not Free

In the early 1980s, a government decree called for death by firing squad for anyone seeking to oppose or criticize government policies.[13] Yet Doe also publically encouraged journalists to engage in watchdog reporting, provided they got their facts right.[14] There were also reports of critical journalists being detained and publications being closed down.[15] Thus by 1982, conditions had deteriorated and news media were not free.

In 1989, Charles Taylor led an uprising and the country descended into civil war. In 1990,

after Doe was executed, the International Press Institute predicted that "Whoever takes over the hot seat at the Executive Mansion will continue to silence Liberia's beleaguered press. There is no hope for freedom of the press or any other freedom, in a country where the rule of law comes from the barrel of a gun."[16]

In spite of a 1995 peace agreement, fighting continued on and off through 1996. In 1997, Taylor was elected president. Yet the peace was short-lived as fighting broke out again in 1999 and continued through much of 2003, until troops from both Nigeria and the United States intervened and Taylor fled the country. Through all this political upheaval, Taylor's regime did not tolerate criticism from media.

In 2006, Ellen Johnson Sirleaf was inaugurated, becoming Africa's first elected female head of state and the world's first elected black female head of state. Although Sirleaf's election marked the beginning of democracy in Liberia, it did not bring about media freedom. There were a number of reports of violence against journalists, and the International Press Institute suggested some of these attacks were motivated by the ongoing war of words between Sirleaf and the media.[17]

2010–2012: Imperfectly Free

Conditions for news media slowly improved, and by 2010, media were functionally free. This was due in part to Liberia's adoption of a freedom of information law.[18] Yet libel remained a criminal offense and a number of journalists were targeted with punitive lawsuits.

Media Today

Media remain functionally free, and there are signs that the environment is improving. These include a decrease in attacks on journalists and fewer libel cases in 2012.[19] Liberia has a mix of privately owned and government owned print and broadcast media. Because of poverty and illiteracy, radio remains the most popular medium. Internet access remained extremely limited in 2012.

Notes

1. Ayodeji Olukoju, *Culture and Customs of Liberia* (Westport, CT: Greenwood Press, 2006).
2. Ibid.

3. Ibid.

4. Ibid., 53.

5. Carl Patrick Burrowes, *Power and Press Freedom in Liberia, 1830-1970: The Impact of Globalization and Civil Society on Media-Government Relations* (Trenton, NJ, and Asmara, Eritria: African World Press).

6. Ibid.

7. Olukoju, *Culture and Customs of Liberia.*

8. *Country Reports on Human Rights Practices 1980* (Washington, DC: U.S. Department of State, 1981). Available at http://babel.hathitrust.org/cgi/pt?id=mdp.39015014143476;view=1up;seq=159.

9. *Country Reports on Human Rights Practices for 1979* (Washington, DC: U.S. Department of State, 1980). Available at http://babel.hathitrust.org/cgi/pt?id=mdp.39015014188273;view=1up;seq=9.

10. "1980: Deposed Ministers Executed in Liberia," On This Day—1950–2005: April 22, *BBC News* (London, UK: British Broadcasting Company). Available at http://news.bbc.co.uk/onthisday/hi/dates/stories/april/22/newsid_2525000/2525477.stm.

11. Olukoju, *Culture and Customs of Liberia.*

12. *Country Reports on Human Rights Practices for 1981* (Washington, DC: U.S. Department of State, 1982). Available at http://babel.hathitrust.org/cgi/pt?id=mdp.39015039359891;view=1up;seq=157.

13. *Country Reports on Human Rights Practices for 1983* (Washington, DC: U.S. Department of State, 1984). Available at http://babel.hathitrust.org/cgi/pt?id=mdp.39015014227832;view=1up;seq=7.

14. Ibid.

15. Ibid.

16. *World Press Freedom Review*, IPI Report (Zurich: International Press Institute, December 1990), 20.

17. *World Press Freedom Review*, IPI Report (Vienna: International Press Institute, 2006).

18. *Freedom of the Press* (Washington, DC: Freedom House, 2011). Available at http://www.freedom house.org/report/freedom-press/2011/liberia.

19. *Freedom of the Press* (Washington, DC: Freedom House, 2013). Available at http://www.freedom house.org/report/freedom-press/2013/liberia.

Libya: 1951–2012

Libya Year by Year

Year	Media	Government
1951	Imperfectly Free	Autocracy
1952	Imperfectly Free	Autocracy
1953	Imperfectly Free	Autocracy
1954	Imperfectly Free	Autocracy
1955	Imperfectly Free	Autocracy
1956	Imperfectly Free	Autocracy
1957	Imperfectly Free	Autocracy
1958	Imperfectly Free	Autocracy
1959	Imperfectly Free	Autocracy
1960	Imperfectly Free	Autocracy
1961	Imperfectly Free	Autocracy
1962	Imperfectly Free	Autocracy
1963	Imperfectly Free	Autocracy
1964	Imperfectly Free	Autocracy
1965	Imperfectly Free	Autocracy
1966	Imperfectly Free	Autocracy
1967	Imperfectly Free	Autocracy
1968	Imperfectly Free	Autocracy
1969	Not Free	Autocracy
1970	Not Free	Autocracy
1971	Not Free	Autocracy
1972	Not Free	Autocracy
1973	Not Free	Autocracy
1974	Not Free	Autocracy
1975	Not Free	Autocracy
1976	Not Free	Autocracy
1977	Not Free	Autocracy
1978	Not Free	Autocracy

(Continued)

MEDIA FREEDOM HISTORY IN A NUTSHELL

- Following independence under the leadership of King Idris, Libyan media were functionally free
- When Muammar Gaddafi seized power in 1969, he also seized control of all news media
- Following Gaddafi's ouster in 2011, media freedom returned to Libya, but the country remains a dangerous place for journalists because they are often attacked by militia groups
- As of 2012, there were two public daily newspapers and a number of weekly and monthly newspapers (Freedom House's Report on Freedom of the Press 2013)
- As of 2012, there were three main public radio stations and more than a dozen private stations, as well as four public television stations and five private stations (Freedom House's Report on Freedom of the Press 2013)
- As of 2012, about 20 percent of Libyans had Internet access (International Telecommunication Union's 2012 ICT Indicators Database)

In Brief

Following independence, Libyan media were functionally free until Colonel Muammar Gaddafi seized power in 1969. Under Gaddafi, Libyan media were among the most controlled in the world. With the fall of Gaddafi in 2011, the media environment has improved dramatically and media are now functionally free. Yet, as Libya's new government struggles to establish rule of law, the country is a dangerous place for journals.

Chronology

1951–1968: Imperfectly Free

Following the end of Italian occupation in 1943, Libya was under UN administration until it

(Continued)

Year	Media	Government
1979	Not Free	Autocracy
1980	Not Free	Autocracy
1981	Not Free	Autocracy
1982	Not Free	Autocracy
1983	Not Free	Autocracy
1984	Not Free	Autocracy
1985	Not Free	Autocracy
1986	Not Free	Autocracy
1987	Not Free	Autocracy
1988	Not Free	Autocracy
1989	Not Free	Autocracy
1990	Not Free	Autocracy
1991	Not Free	Autocracy
1992	Not Free	Autocracy
1993	Not Free	Autocracy
1994	Not Free	Autocracy
1995	Not Free	Autocracy
1996	Not Free	Autocracy
1997	Not Free	Autocracy
1998	Not Free	Autocracy
1999	Not Free	Autocracy
2000	Not Free	Autocracy
2001	Not Free	Autocracy
2002	Not Free	Autocracy
2003	Not Free	Autocracy
2004	Not Free	Autocracy
2005	Not Free	Autocracy
2006	Not Free	Autocracy
2007	Not Free	Autocracy
2008	Not Free	Autocracy
2009	Not Free	Autocracy
2010	Not Free	Autocracy
2011	Imperfectly Free	Autocracy
2012	Imperfectly Free	Autocracy

was granted independence in 1951 under King Idris al-Sanusi. Known as a spiritual man committed to the ideals of peaceful coexistence and tolerance, King Idris has been compared to Mahatma Gandhi and Nelson Mandela. Media were free under his rule, but his close ties to Britain troubled many. Some attributed his ouster to his failure to produce a male heir, but more pragmatic issues that created or exacerbated deep divisions in the country are more likely culprits. The development of an oil exporting industry not only increased the wealth of the country, but also led to significant corruption and increased the already extreme disparities in the distribution of wealth between elites and lower classes, and between coastal communities and the Bedouin tribes of the Sahara. It is notable that despite the oil wealth, Libya had the lowest standard of living in Africa. All these issues were factors behind the revolt that deposed of the King.

1969–2010: Not Free

In 1969, Colonel Muammar Gaddafi staged a swift and bloodless coup when King Idris traveled overseas for medical treatment. Ruling as a dictator, he seized control of the media and all news outlets were strictly controlled throughout his rule.

2011–2012: Imperfectly Free

In 2011, Gaddafi was overthrown in a popular uprising-turned-civil-war that lasted six months and ended with the killing of Gaddafi. As Libya transitioned to a new government, the media environment became much more open and a number of new print and broadcast media outlets were launched.[1] Although media freedom improved dramatically, there were a number of attacks on journalists, often by local militias.[2]

Media Today

As Libya's new government struggles to establish rule of law, the country remains a dangerous place for journalists.[3] That said, media remain functionally free. Yet there are indications that this freedom is tenuous, and the situation could change as Libya establishes its policies regarding media licensing and regulation.

Notes

1. *Freedom of the Press* (Washington, DC: Freedom House, 2013). Available at http://freedomhouse.org/report/freedom-press/2013/libya
2. *Attacks on the Press: Libya* (Committee to Project Journalists, 2013). Available at http://cpj.org/2013/02/attacks-on-the-press-in-2012-libya.php.
3. Ibid.

Liechtenstein: 1990–2012

Liechtenstein Year by Year

Year	Media	Government
1990	Free	Democracy
1991	Free	Democracy
1992	Free	Democracy
1993	Free	Democracy
1994	Free	Democracy
1995	Free	Democracy
1996	Free	Democracy
1997	Free	Democracy
1998	Free	Democracy
1999	Free	Democracy
2000	Free	Democracy
2001	Free	Democracy
2002	Free	Democracy
2003	Free	Democracy
2004	Free	Democracy
2005	Free	Democracy
2006	Free	Democracy
2007	Free	Democracy
2008	Free	Democracy
2009	Free	Democracy
2010	Free	Democracy
2011	Free	Democracy
2012	Free	Democracy

MEDIA FREEDOM HISTORY IN A NUTSHELL

- Although there is little information about Liechtenstein media, since the country joined the UN in 1990, it is clear that media have been free
- As of 2009, there were two paid-for daily newspapers with a total average circulation of 20,000 (World Association of Newspaper's 2010 World Newspaper Trends)
- Despite a local television station and state-run radio station, the country relies heavily on media from neighboring countries
- As of 2012, about 90 percent of Liechtensteiners had Internet access (International Telecommunication Union's 2012 ICT Indicators Database)

In Brief

The tiny Principality of Liechtenstein is home to about 37,000 and is touted as having one of the "freest media environments in the world."[1] Yet given its small size, Liechtenstein has been overlooked by most organizations that track media freedom, consequently we only have data for Liechtenstein since 1990, the year it joined the UN. Indeed since 1990, Liechtenstein media have been free.

Chronology

1990–2012: Free

Liechtenstein's constitution has provisions for media freedom, which the government respects in practice. In 2004, the government took over the country's primary radio station when the private owner ran into financial difficulties.

Media Today

While Liechtensteiners have access to domestic media, including two daily newspapers connected to the country's two political parties and one primary radio station and a television station, they also have access to print and broadcast media from other countries, especially neighboring Switzerland and Austria. Liechtenstein has strong anti–hate speech laws—racial or ethnic insults are punishable by up to two years imprisonment.[2]

Notes

1. *Freedom of the Press* (Washington, DC: Freedom House, 2004). Available at http://www.freedom house.org/report/freedom-press/2004/liechtenstein.
2. *Country Reports on Human Rights Practices 2012* (Washington, DC: U.S. Department of State, 2013).

Lithuania: 1991–2012

Lithuania Year by Year

Year	Media	Government
1991	Not Free	Democracy
1992	Not Free	Democracy
1993	Not Free	Democracy
1994	Not Free	Democracy
1995	Imperfectly Free	Democracy
1996	Imperfectly Free	Democracy
1997	Free	Democracy
1998	Free	Democracy
1999	Free	Democracy
2000	Free	Democracy
2001	Free	Democracy
2002	Free	Democracy
2003	Free	Democracy
2004	Free	Democracy
2005	Free	Democracy
2006	Free	Democracy
2007	Free	Democracy
2008	Free	Democracy
2009	Free	Democracy
2010	Free	Democracy
2011	Free	Democracy
2012	Free	Democracy

In Brief

Despite spending the majority of its history as a part of Poland or occupied by either German or Russian empires or states, Lithuania is the most

---

MEDIA FREEDOM HISTORY IN A NUTSHELL

- The transition to a free media environment took several years after independence from the Soviet Union
- Despite political instability and significant economic crises, press freedom has been maintained
- As of 2011, there were seventeen paid-for daily newspapers with a total average circulation of 261,000 (World Association of Newspaper's 2012 World Newspaper Trends)
- Lithuania's television and radio stations are all privately owned
- As of 2012, about 68 percent of Lithuanians had Internet access (International Telecommunication Union's 2012 ICT Indicators Database)

---

ethnically and linguistically homogeneous of the three Baltic countries. As with many of the other former Soviet states, the media played a key role in the political liberalization that preceded and followed the collapse of the Soviet Union. Lithuania declared independence in 1990, and was the first of the Baltic States to be free of Russian troops. Yet the country appears to have endured far more political instability in the post-Soviet period and corruption has been a salient part of that instability.

Chronology

1991–1994: Not Free

There was a modest amount of media privatization and liberalization that preceded independence and this continued, albeit slowly, after independence from the Soviet Union. During this period, organized crime became an increasing threat to journalists. For example, in 1993,

Vytautas Lingys, one of the country's leading crime reporters, was assassinated following his investigation into mafia activity in Lithuania.[1] Lingys' killing did seem to have a chilling effect on news media coverage of organized crime.[2]

1995–1996: Imperfectly Free

The gradual approach to liberalization eventually instilled enough confidence to support significant foreign investment in Lithuanian media and media gradually became functionally free. There is no obvious or clear-cut moment to identify this change within the overall trend, but media content became increasing critical of all elites during this period, with significant coverage of issues related to corruption and improper use of political power for economic gains. Yet organized crime remained a threat to media freedom. In 1995, the largest daily, *Lietuvos Rytas*, was bombed, and the attack was likely related to reporting on the Kaunas mafia.[3]

1997–2012: Free

Again there is no clear-cut event or date to mark the culmination of the gradual reform process for the media, but by 1997, it was clear that Lithuania's media had effectively reached a reasonable standard of professional conduct and independence that matched its western European peers. Moreover, with the passage of the Mass Media Law, the funding for state-run radio and TV networks was safeguarded.[4]

Media Today

Small market issues are significant concerns, but less so than the other Baltic States. The Lithuanian-speaking population is large enough to justify the translation and publication of Lithuanian editions of several foreign periodicals, and it appears to be large enough to sustain commercial free media. Continued political instability and challenges regarding corruption are more significant concerns. Thus far, media freedom has not been compromised.

Notes

1. *World Press Freedom Review*, IPI Report (Vienna: International Press Institute, 1993), 38.
2. Ibid.
3. *World Press Freedom Review*, IPI Report (Vienna: International Press Institute, 1995), 68.
4. *World Press Freedom Review*, IPI Report (Vienna: International Press Institute, 1996/1997), 59.

Luxembourg: 1948–2012

Luxembourg Year by Year

Year	Not Free	Government
1948	Free	Democracy
1949	Free	Democracy
1950	Free	Democracy
1951	Free	Democracy
1952	Free	Democracy
1953	Free	Democracy
1954	Free	Democracy
1955	Free	Democracy
1956	Free	Democracy
1957	Free	Democracy
1958	Free	Democracy
1959	Free	Democracy
1960	Free	Democracy
1961	Free	Democracy
1962	Free	Democracy
1963	Free	Democracy
1964	Free	Democracy
1965	Free	Democracy
1966	Free	Democracy
1967	Free	Democracy
1968	Free	Democracy
1969	Free	Democracy
1970	Free	Democracy
1971	Free	Democracy
1972	Free	Democracy
1973	Free	Democracy
1974	Free	Democracy

(Continued)

MEDIA FREEDOM HISTORY IN A NUTSHELL

- Luxembourg has a long history of media freedom
- As of 2012, there were eight paid-for daily newspapers with a total average circulation of 111,590 and three free daily newspapers (World Association of Newspaper's 2012 World Newspaper Trends)
- Luxembourg's radio and television stations are often enjoyed beyond its borders
- As of 2012, about 92 percent of Luxembourgers had Internet access (International Telecommunication Union's 2012 ICT Indicators Database)

In Brief

One of the founding countries of the European Economic Community (which later became the EU), Luxembourg has a long tradition of media freedom.

Chronology

1948–2012: Free

Luxembourg's media environment has been open, vibrant, and diverse for decades. In fact, unlike most small countries, which tend to be influenced by foreign media, Luxembourg's broadcast media are often consumed by audiences in neighboring countries.[1] A media law passed in 1991 did away with RTL media group's monopoly in radio and television, but to date, RTL's television station has not received significant competition, probably because of the small size of the media market.[2]

Media Today

In spite of Luxembourg's small population—estimated at fewer than 515,000 in 2013[3]—the

(Continued)

Year	Not Free	Government
1975	Free	Democracy
1976	Free	Democracy
1977	Free	Democracy
1978	Free	Democracy
1979	Free	Democracy
1980	Free	Democracy
1981	Free	Democracy
1982	Free	Democracy
1983	Free	Democracy
1984	Free	Democracy
1985	Free	Democracy
1986	Free	Democracy
1987	Free	Democracy
1988	Free	Democracy
1989	Free	Democracy
1990	Free	Democracy
1991	Free	Democracy
1992	Free	Democracy
1993	Free	Democracy
1994	Free	Democracy
1995	Free	Democracy
1996	Free	Democracy
1997	Free	Democracy
1998	Free	Democracy
1999	Free	Democracy
2000	Free	Democracy
2001	Free	Democracy
2002	Free	Democracy

Year	Not Free	Government
2003	Free	Democracy
2004	Free	Democracy
2005	Free	Democracy
2006	Free	Democracy
2007	Free	Democracy
2008	Free	Democracy
2009	Free	Democracy
2010	Free	Democracy
2011	Free	Democracy
2012	Free	Democracy

country has a number of daily newspapers (8 paid-for and 3 free).[4] In part this is because most newspapers have close ties to political parties, but also because the government has subsidized print media.[5] Luxembourg also has privately owned broadcast media. More than 90 percent of Luxembourgers have Internet access.

Notes

1. *Freedom of the Press* (Washington, DC: Freedom House, 2013). Available at http://freedomhouse .org/report/freedom-press/2008/Luxembourg.
2. Mario Hirsch, *Media Landscapes: Luxembourg* (Maastricht, The Netherlands: European Journalism Centre, 2013). Available at http://ejc.net/media_ landscapes/luxembourg#link_144.
3. *Luxembourg* (Washington, DC: CIA World Factbook, 2013). Available at http://www.cia.gov/ library/publications/the-world-factbook/geos/lu .html.
4. *World Press Trends* (Darmstadt, Germany: WAN-IFRA, 2012).
5. Hirsch, *Media Landscapes: Luxembourg.*

Macedonia: 1994–2012

Macedonia Year by Year

Year	Media	Government
1994	Not Free	Democracy
1995	Not Free	Democracy
1996	Not Free	Democracy
1997	Imperfectly Free	Democracy
1998	Imperfectly Free	Democracy
1999	Imperfectly Free	Democracy
2000	Imperfectly Free	Democracy
2001	Imperfectly Free	Democracy
2002	Imperfectly Free	Democracy
2003	Imperfectly Free	Democracy
2004	Imperfectly Free	Democracy
2005	Imperfectly Free	Democracy
2006	Imperfectly Free	Democracy
2007	Imperfectly Free	Democracy
2008	Imperfectly Free	Democracy
2009	Imperfectly Free	Democracy
2010	Imperfectly Free	Democracy
2011	Imperfectly Free	Democracy
2012	Imperfectly Free	Democracy

MEDIA FREEDOM HISTORY IN A NUTSHELL

- Media freedom was pursued as part of a larger effort at political liberalization and development
- The move to media freedom stalled well short of a European standard for a free and independent press
- Authoritarian political efforts are methodically eliminating media freedom
- As of 2011, there were thirteen daily newspapers, twelve of them were paid-for daily newspapers, with a total average circulation of 280,000 (World Association of Newspaper's 2010 World Newspaper Trends).
- Macedonian Radio and Television is the sole public broadcaster, and as of 2009, the country had seventy-eight private television stations and seventy independent radio stations (World Association of Newspaper's 2010 World Newspaper Trends)
- As of 2011, about 56.70 percent of Macedonians had Internet access (International Telecommunication Union's 2011 ICT Indicators Database)

assertion of Macedonian distinctness from Greece continues to be a salient aspect of politics as Greece opposed the creation of an independent Macedonia out of the former Yugoslavian province because of fears that it would create/empower a secessionist movement in the Greek province of Macedonia. This tension continues.

Chronology

1994–1996: Not Free

Greece opposed the creation of an independent Macedonia and subsequent Macedonian efforts to join the EU and other European political and economic organizations. While this has not been a deterministic factor, it did increase the

In Brief

Macedonians claim a 2,500-year history as a distinct nation of people, and in almost any discussion of a Macedonian perspective on history, someone will be quick to point out that Alexander the Great was Macedonian, not Greek. That

challenges facing those pursuing a more democratic and liberal Macedonia. It impeded the early political and economic development support offered by some European organizations and generally raised additional barriers to using inclusion in European organizations and structures as a way of supporting liberalization. This generally slowed efforts to transition from authoritarian media structures to an independent and free media system.

The media restrictions that were in place prior to Macedonia's 1991 declaration of independence remained strong. A case in point, in 1996, the director of state television was fired for "political reasons."[1]

1997–2012: Imperfectly Free

Macedonia is a small media market, thus it has been difficult to develop and sustain a commercial free media system. Yet, even with an expectation that there would have to be some level of ongoing government support, the development of the media system stalled well short of a general European standard for a free and independent news media. Media are highly partisan and funding is hidden and almost certainly politically driven. Media professionals and outlets struggle constantly against the regulatory and economic coercion of political elites. In 2011, several opposition media outlets owned by Velija Ramkovski were closed down when Ramkovski was arrested and his assets were frozen.[2] He was subsequently convicted of tax evasion and money laundering.

Media Today

For all intents and purposes, media freedom is in the process of disappearing in Macedonia with the most notable act being the forced closure of opposition-friendly media outlets. Thus, while the constitution guarantees freedom of speech and access to information, in practice journalists face many pressures.[3]

Notes

1. *World Press Freedom Review*, IPI Report (Vienna: International Press Institute, 1996).
2. *Freedom of the Press* (Washington, DC: Freedom House, 2013). Available at http://www.freedom house.org/reports.
3. *Macedonia*, BBC Country Profiles (London, UK: British Broadcasting Company, August 2013). Available at http://www.bbc.co.uk/news/world-europe-17551488.

Madagascar: 1960–2012

Madagascar Year by Year

Year	Media	Government
1960	Imperfectly Free	Anocracy
1961	Imperfectly Free	Anocracy
1962	Imperfectly Free	Anocracy
1963	Imperfectly Free	Anocracy
1964	Imperfectly Free	Anocracy
1965	Imperfectly Free	Anocracy
1966	Imperfectly Free	Anocracy
1967	Imperfectly Free	Anocracy
1968	Imperfectly Free	Anocracy
1969	Imperfectly Free	Anocracy
1970	Imperfectly Free	Anocracy
1971	Imperfectly Free	Anocracy
1972	Imperfectly Free	Anocracy
1973	Not Free	Anocracy
1974	Not Free	Anocracy
1975	Not Free	Autocracy
1976	Not Free	Autocracy
1977	Not Free	Autocracy
1978	Not Free	Autocracy
1979	Not Free	Autocracy
1980	Not Free	Autocracy
1981	Not Free	Autocracy
1982	Not Free	Autocracy

(Continued)

MEDIA FREEDOM HISTORY IN A NUTSHELL

- Following independence, media were functionally free, though subject to some pressures from government
- Following mass protests in the early 1970s, Madagascar became a one-party state, and the government controlled all broadcast media and censored the newspapers
- As the country democratized in the early 1990s, censorship was abolished and media became functionally free
- In 2009, a power struggle between rival media moguls-turned-politicians mushroomed into a coup and media have not been free since
- The future of media freedom remained unclear following the elections held at the end of 2013
- As of 2012, there were thirteen daily private newspapers and more than 300 radio and television stations (Freedom House's Freedom of the Press 2013)
- As of 2012, about 2 percent of Malagasy had Internet access (International Telecommunication Union's 2012 ICT Indicators Database)

In Brief

The fourth largest island in the world, Madagascar, gained independence from France in 1960. Though Malagasy media were functionally free for more than a decade after independence, they were controlled during the 1970s and 1980s when Madagascar became a one-party state. As the country democratized in the 1990s, media were once again functionally free and the independent media market expanded. In 2009, a power struggle between rival media moguls-turned-politicians mushroomed into a coup and media have not been free since.

(Continued)

Year	Media	Government
1983	Not Free	Autocracy
1984	Not Free	Autocracy
1985	Not Free	Autocracy
1986	Not Free	Autocracy
1987	Not Free	Autocracy
1988	Not Free	Autocracy
1989	Not Free	Autocracy
1990	Imperfectly Free	Autocracy
1991	Imperfectly Free	Anocracy
1992	Imperfectly Free	Democracy
1993	Imperfectly Free	Democracy
1994	Imperfectly Free	Democracy
1995	Imperfectly Free	Democracy
1996	Imperfectly Free	Democracy
1997	Imperfectly Free	Democracy
1998	Imperfectly Free	Democracy
1999	Imperfectly Free	Democracy
2000	Imperfectly Free	Democracy
2001	Imperfectly Free	Democracy
2002	Imperfectly Free	Democracy
2003	Imperfectly Free	Democracy
2004	Imperfectly Free	Democracy
2005	Imperfectly Free	Democracy
2006	Imperfectly Free	Democracy
2007	Imperfectly Free	Democracy
2008	Imperfectly Free	Democracy
2009	Not Free	Anocracy
2010	Not Free	Anocracy
2011	Not Free	Anocracy
2012	Not Free	Anocracy

Chronology

1960–1972: Imperfectly Free

Just prior to officially gaining independence from France, Madagascar's assembly approved a press law that gave the government the authority to confiscate newspapers.[1] In the early 1960s, Madagascar's first president, Philibert Tsiranana, sought to consolidate his power and minimize the power of his opposition. To that end his administration temporarily banned several newspapers in retaliation for criticizing the government, and the editor of an opposition paper was arrested on charges of violating the press laws.[2,3] In spite of these actions, the International Press Institute reported that newspapers were thriving.[4]

In 1972, as unrest swept through the country, anticolonial sentiments ran high and protesters burned the offices of a French-language newspaper.[5] When he was unable to quell the unrest, Tsiranana handed over power to the military.

1973–1989: Not Free

As the political turmoil continued, the media environment deteriorated. Following a 1975 coup, Lieutenant-Commander Didier Ratsiraka took control of the country and under martial law all political expression was prohibited.[6] Ratsiraka's regime did not tolerate criticism of the president or the "Socialist Revolution" government.[7] The government owned all broadcast media, and newspapers were subject to prepublication censorship.[8]

In the late 1980s, as Ratsiraka moved away from socialism and toward a market economy, he reduced the restrictions on news media, and in 1989 ceased prepublication censorship.[9] Yet the government maintained control over broadcast media.

1990–2008: Imperfectly Free

In the early 1990s, following prodemocracy demonstrations, Ratsiraka implemented democratic reforms including officially abolishing censorship and allowing members of the opposition to appear on the state-run broadcast media.[10] Ratsiraka lost in the 1992 presidential elections, but he was reelected in 1996. By the mid-1990s, privately owned radio and television stations were competing with the state-run broadcast media. Throughout the 1990s and early 2000s, Madagascar was known for having media that were freer than most in Africa. During this period, both Marc Ravalomanana and Andry Rajoelina established media empires, which they leveraged to gain political power. Ravalomanana became president in 2002, and Rajoelina became mayor of the capital, Antananarivo. In 2008, the government closed down Rajoelina's television station after it aired an interview with Ratsiraka. The closure prompted a social media campaign calling for the reopening of the station.[11]

2009–2012: Not Free

In 2009, what started as a protest over the closure of Rajoelina's television station mobilized into an opposition movement against Ravalomanana, and Rajoelina declared himself to be in charge of the country.[12] Throughout the power struggle, both men used their media as weapons and, as the Committee to Protect Journalists reported, Malagasy journalists were caught in the middle:

> Viva Radio, for example, aired the names and addresses of people identified as "stealing" taxpayer money during the Ravalomanana regime, leading mobs to burn one home and attack a number of others. Transcripts of programs on the Ravalomanana-owned Radio Mada, reviewed by CPJ, included incendiary commentary that threatened retaliation against perceived opponents of the president. The few media outlets that sought to cover protests and other events in a neutral way were attacked by extremists from both sides.[13]

Eventually, Rajoelina prevailed after gaining support for the military. Following the coup, many broadcast news outlets were closed down.[14] Although (or perhaps because) Rajoelina came to power through the media, his regime did not respect press freedom and used censorship, intimidation, and defamation charges to silence critical media.[15]

Media Today

While the broadcast media shut down in the wake of the coup remain closed, there are still several

hundred radio and television stations. Yet only the government-owned broadcast media have national reach.[16] Only 2 percent of Malagasy had Internet access in 2012. The future of media freedom was unclear in early 2014. With oversight from the international community, presidential elections were held at the end of 2013 after both Rajoelina and Ravalomanana agreed not to run.

Notes

1. *The Toils of the Press*, IPI Report (Zurich: International Press Institute, April 1959).
2. *The Toils of the Press*, IPI Report (Zurich: International Press Institute, December 1962).
3. *The Toils of the Press*, IPI Report (Zurich: International Press Institute, December 1963).
4. *Sixteen Newspapers Thrive*, IPI Report (Zurich: International Press Institute, November 1964).
5. Peter J. Schraeder, "Madagascar: A Country Study," in *Indian Ocean*, ed. Helen Chapin Metz (Washington, DC: Library of Congress Federal Research Division). Available at http://lcweb2.loc.gov/frd/cs/cshome.html.
6. Ibid.
7. *Country Reports on Human Rights Practices for 1987* (Washington, DC: U.S. Department of State, 1988). Available at http://babel.hathitrust.org/cgi/pt?id=mdp.39015013385052;view=1up;seq=1.
8. Ibid.
9. *Country Reports on Human Rights Practices for 1989* (Washington, DC: U.S. Department of State, 1990). Available at https://archive.org/stream/countryreportson1989unit/countryreportson1989unit_djvu.txt.
10. Ibid.
11. *Attacks on the Press 2009: Madagascar* (Committee to Protect Journalists, 2010). Available at http://www.cpj.org/2010/02/attacks-on-the-press-2009-madagascar.php.
12. Ibid.
13. Ibid., para. 9.
14. *Freedom of the Press* (Washington, DC: Freedom House, 2013). Available at http://www.freedomhouse.org/report/freedom-press/2013/madagascar.
15. Ibid.
16. Ibid.

Malawi: 1964–2012

Malawi Year by Year

Year	Media	Government
1964	Not Free	Autocracy
1965	Not Free	Autocracy
1966	Not Free	Autocracy
1967	Not Free	Autocracy
1968	Not Free	Autocracy
1969	Not Free	Autocracy
1970	Not Free	Autocracy
1971	Not Free	Autocracy
1972	Not Free	Autocracy
1973	Not Free	Autocracy
1974	Not Free	Autocracy
1975	Not Free	Autocracy
1976	Not Free	Autocracy
1977	Not Free	Autocracy
1978	Not Free	Autocracy
1979	Not Free	Autocracy
1980	Not Free	Autocracy
1981	Not Free	Autocracy
1982	Not Free	Autocracy
1983	Not Free	Autocracy
1984	Not Free	Autocracy
1985	Not Free	Autocracy
1986	Not Free	Autocracy
1987	Not Free	Autocracy

MEDIA FREEDOM HISTORY IN A NUTSHELL

- For the three decades following independence, Malawi was a one-party state with media that were controlled and censored
- For most of the 1990s and early 2000s media were right on the border between being imperfectly free and not free
- Media today are functionally free, but still somewhat restricted
- As of 2012, there were eight independent newspapers, including two dailies; however, few Malawians read them (Freedom House's Report on Freedom of the Press 2013)
- Radio is most popular source for news, and though the state-controlled radio and TV stations are the only broadcast media with national reach, the availability of privately-owned broadcast media continues to increase (Freedom House's Freedom of the Press 2013)
- As of 2012, about 4 percent of Malawians had Internet access (International Telecommunication Union's 2012 ICT Indicators Database)

In Brief

For the first three decades following independence, Malawi was a one-party state with a leader who did not tolerate any dissent. Journalists who dared to criticize him put their lives at risk. As Malawi transitioned to democracy in the mid-1990s, media conditions improved, but journalists still faced substantial restrictions during most of the 1990s. Though conditions improved to the point that media were functionally free in 2003, in reality throughout much of the 1990s and early 2000s, the media environment has hovered on the border of imperfectly free and not free.

Year	Media	Government
1988	Not Free	Autocracy
1989	Not Free	Autocracy
1990	Not Free	Autocracy
1991	Not Free	Autocracy
1992	Not Free	Autocracy
1993	Not Free	Autocracy
1994	Not Free	Democracy
1995	Imperfectly Free	Democracy
1996	Not Free	Democracy
1997	Not Free	Democracy
1998	Not Free	Democracy
1999	Not Free	Democracy
2000	Not Free	Democracy
2001	Not Free	Anocracy
2002	Not Free	Anocracy
2003	Imperfectly Free	Anocracy
2004	Imperfectly Free	Democracy
2005	Imperfectly Free	Democracy
2006	Imperfectly Free	Democracy
2007	Imperfectly Free	Democracy
2008	Imperfectly Free	Democracy
2009	Imperfectly Free	Democracy
2010	Imperfectly Free	Democracy
2011	Imperfectly Free	Democracy
2012	Imperfectly Free	Democracy

Chronology

1964–1994: Not Free

After gaining independence from Britain, Malawi became a one-party state under Dr. Hastings Kamuzu Banda. As President Banda sought to consolidate his power, freedom of expression and freedom of the press were greatly restricted. The government controlled and censored all media.[1] In 1971, Banda became the Life President of Malawi and those who criticized him were subject to detention.[2] Critical journalists were persecuted and in some cases murdered.[3] In 1993, after nearly three decades in power, Banda became ill and his one-party system was rejected by voters. Yet as the country prepared for multi-party elections, hundreds of publications were banned.[4] In 1994, Bakili Muluzi was elected. One of his first moves was to repeal a law that mandated imprisonment for reporting false news.[5]

1995: Imperfectly Free

Under President Muluzi, conditions initially improved for journalists, to the point where media were functionally free. Yet there were still reports of journalists being threatened and harassed.[6]

1996–2002: Not Free

Although Muluzi pledged to respect media freedom when he took office, by 1996, it was clear that he had no intention of following through on this promise. Instead, Muluzi chose to punish critical journalists and news outlets with threats and defamation charges rather than the physical violence employed by his predecessor.[7] During these years, there were a number of reports of journalists being attacked, harassed, and threatened by members of the government and their supporters. Yet some journalists persisted in critical reporting of the government. Thus, Malawian media really hovered between being not free and imperfectly free during these years

2003–2012: Imperfectly Free

In 2003, conditions for news media improved somewhat as the Director of Public Prosecution ordered police to stop arbitrarily arresting reporters and cleared a journalist who had been charged with publishing potentially disruptive information.[8] Even so, journalists continued to face a number of restrictions, to the point that media were only just barely functionally free. While newspapers, especially those with ties to the opposition, were critical of government, most broadcast media were state-owned and tended to provide preferential coverage of the government.[9] While privately owned radio stations were available, their news coverage was restricted, and in 2003, the government mandated that community radio stations cease broadcasting news.[10]

Media Today

Malawian media remain functionally free, but still face many restrictions. In 2012, the lawmakers repealed a law that had allowed the government to ban the publication or dissemination of material considered "contrary to the public interest."[11] Radio is the dominant medium in Malawi, and though the state controls the only radio and television stations that have national reach, privately owned broadcast media continue to emerge. In 2012 alone, fifteen new broadcasting licenses were awarded.[12] Although independent newspapers continue to represent a range of views, few people read them because they are expensive and many of them are published in English, which most Malawians cannot read.[13]

Notes

1. *Country Reports on Human Rights Practices for 1977* (Washington, DC: U.S. Department of State, 1978).

2. Ibid.
3. *World Press Freedom Review*, IPI Report (Vienna: International Press Institute, December 1996/ January 1997).
4. *World Press Freedom Review*, IPI Report (Vienna: International Press Institute, 1994).
5. Ibid.
6. *World Press Freedom Review*, IPI Report (Vienna: International Press Institute, 1995).
7. *World Press Freedom Review*, IPI Report (Vienna: International Press Institute, 1996).
8. *Freedom of the Press* (Washington, DC: Freedom House, 2004). Available at http://www.freedom house.org/report/freedom-press/2004/malawi.
9. Ibid.
10. Ibid.
11. *Country Reports on Human Rights Practices for 2012* (Washington, DC: U.S. Department of State, 2013). Available at http://www.state.gov/j/drl/rls/ hrrpt/humanrightsreport/index.htm#wrapper.
12. Ibid.
13. *Freedom of the Press* (Washington, DC: Freedom House, 2013). Available at http://www.freedom house.org/report/freedom-press/2013/malawi.

Malaysia: 1957–2012

Malaysia Year by Year

Year	Media	Government
1957	Imperfectly Free	Democracy
1958	Imperfectly Free	Democracy
1959	Imperfectly Free	Democracy
1960	Imperfectly Free	Democracy
1961	Imperfectly Free	Democracy
1962	Imperfectly Free	Democracy
1963	Imperfectly Free	Democracy
1964	Imperfectly Free	Democracy
1965	Imperfectly Free	Democracy
1966	Imperfectly Free	Democracy
1967	Imperfectly Free	Democracy
1968	Imperfectly Free	Democracy
1969	Not Free	Anocracy
1970	Not Free	Anocracy
1971	Not Free	Anocracy
1972	Not Free	Anocracy
1973	Not Free	Anocracy
1974	Not Free	Anocracy
1975	Not Free	Anocracy
1976	Not Free	Anocracy
1977	Not Free	Anocracy
1978	Not Free	Anocracy
1979	Not Free	Anocracy
1980	Not Free	Anocracy
1981	Not Free	Anocracy
1982	Not Free	Anocracy
1983	Not Free	Anocracy

(Continued)

MEDIA FREEDOM HISTORY IN A NUTSHELL

- The British colonizers installed a parliamentary democracy, including an independent press
- Racial politics, with the majority Malay pitted against the economically and politically powerful ethnic Chinese, brought an end to effective democratic governance in 1969
- While some of the democratic structures remain, the government is authoritarian and the press is severely restricted
- As of 2012, Malaysia had thirty-two total paid-for daily newspapers with an average circulation per issue of 2,547,346 (World Association of Newspaper's 2012 World Newspaper Trends)
- Although there is a mix of state-owned and privately owned broadcast media, paid-for television was particularly popular (World Association of Newspaper's 2010 World Newspaper Trends)
- As of 2012, about 66 percent of Malaysians had Internet access (International Telecommunication Union's 2012 ICT Indicators Database)

In Brief

The Federation of Malaya that was granted independence from Britain in 1957 bears little resemblance to its modern incarnation. It wasn't until 1963 that the British colonies of Sabah, Sarawak, and Singapore joined to bring it up to fourteen provinces. Singapore then departed in 1965, leaving the current thirteen provinces that form Malaysia. For the first decade after independence, media were imperfectly free, but in 1969, domestic conflict led to a deterioration of media freedom. Racial politics have been significant, with the majority Malay people rallying against the wealth and power held by ethnic Chinese and to a lesser degree ethnic Indian populations in

(Continued)

Year	Media	Government
1984	Not Free	Anocracy
1985	Not Free	Anocracy
1986	Not Free	Anocracy
1987	Not Free	Anocracy
1988	Not Free	Anocracy
1989	Not Free	Anocracy
1990	Not Free	Anocracy
1991	Not Free	Anocracy
1992	Not Free	Anocracy
1993	Not Free	Anocracy
1994	Not Free	Anocracy
1995	Not Free	Anocracy
1996	Not Free	Anocracy
1997	Not Free	Anocracy
1998	Not Free	Anocracy
1999	Not Free	Anocracy
2000	Not Free	Anocracy
2001	Not Free	Anocracy
2002	Not Free	Anocracy
2003	Not Free	Anocracy
2004	Not Free	Anocracy
2005	Not Free	Anocracy
2006	Not Free	Anocracy
2007	Not Free	Anocracy
2008	Not Free	Democracy
2009	Not Free	Democracy
2010	Not Free	Democracy
2011	Not Free	Democracy
2012	Not Free	Democracy

the country. While democratic structures are still nominally in place, authoritarian rule with controlled media remains the norm.

Chronology

1957–1968: Imperfectly Free

During the first, rather tumultuous decade of independence, the parliamentary democracy installed by the departing British managed to continue to function with reasonable effect. Media, though limited and provincial, were reasonably independent, as evidenced by the coverage of the conflicts between provinces in the federation, including the peaceful departure of Singapore. The exception was in areas placed in a state of emergency in the fight against localized communist insurgencies.

1969–2012: Not Free

Anti-Chinese riots marked the effective end of the limited and imperfect media freedom that had held for a decade in Malaysia. Media restrictions were part of the government effort to maintain control.[1] The 1969 amendment to the 1948 Sedition Act, which prohibited any action promoting ill will and hostility between the races of Malaysia, made it all but impossible to cover the racial conflicts within the country. In 1972, an official secrets act allowed the government to designate almost anything as an official secret, making investigative journalism, or even routine coverage, all but impossible. This included all business dealings with government and government officials. An extended economic boom brought increasing wealth and rapid urbanization to Malaysia and with that, a growing consumer demand for media products. Some government control was eased, but the use of the official secrets act still prevents media from functioning freely.

Media Today

Malaysia appears to have settled into a relatively stable, somewhat authoritarian system with just enough democratic elements that it is now considered a democracy. External media products and information appear to be reasonably accessible, but the use of secrecy, the internal security act, and the threat of extended detainment without charge has a powerful chilling effect that prevents any kind of real examination of government and government officials.

Note

1. *Country Reports on Human Rights Practices for 1977* (Washington, DC: U.S. Department of State, 1978). Available at http://babel.hathitrust.org/cgi/pt?id=mdp.39015078705632;view=1up;seq=1.

Maldives: 1965–2012

Maldives Year by Year

Year	Media	Government
1965	Not Free	Anocracy
1966	Not Free	Anocracy
1967	Not Free	Anocracy
1968	Not Free	Democracy
1969	Not Free	Democracy
1970	Not Free	Democracy
1971	Not Free	Democracy
1972	Not Free	Democracy
1973	Not Free	Anocracy
1974	Not Free	Anocracy
1975	Not Free	Anocracy
1976	Not Free	Anocracy
1977	Not Free	Anocracy
1978	Not Free	Anocracy
1979	Not Free	Anocracy
1980	Not Free	Anocracy
1981	Not Free	Anocracy
1982	Not Free	Anocracy
1983	Not Free	Anocracy
1984	Not Free	Anocracy
1985	Not Free	Anocracy
1986	Not Free	Anocracy
1987	Not Free	Anocracy
1988	Not Free	Autocracy
1989	Not Free	Autocracy
1990	Not Free	Autocracy
1991	Not Free	Autocracy

(Continued)

MEDIA FREEDOM HISTORY IN A NUTSHELL

- Shortly after independence, the Maldives became an Islamic republic
- After more than four decades of government restrictions, the Maldivian media became imperfectly free in 2008
- The government maintained a monopoly on broadcast media until 2007 when the country's first private television and radio stations were permitted to begin broadcasting (Freedom House's Freedom of the Press 2013)
- As of 2009, there were six paid-for daily newspapers with a total average circulation per issue of 21,000 (World Association of Newspaper's 2010 World Newspaper Trends)
- As of 2012, about 39 percent of Maldivians had Internet access (International Telecommunication Union's 2012 ICT Indicators Database)

In Brief

A collection of islands and atolls in the Indian Ocean that total about 115 square miles, the Maldives is an isolated country, about 400 miles from its closest neighbor. Shortly after independence, the Maldives became an Islamic republic. For more than four decades, the government had little tolerance for criticism and media were strictly restricted. In 2008, media became functionally free as the Maldives held democratic elections and adopted a constitution that provides for media freedom. Yet that freedom is now in question because of political unrest.

Chronology

1965–2007: Not Free

Given its isolation, there is very little information about the Maldivian news media in the

(Continued)

Year	Media	Government
1992	Not Free	Autocracy
1993	Not Free	Autocracy
1994	Not Free	Autocracy
1995	Not Free	Autocracy
1996	Not Free	Autocracy
1997	Not Free	Autocracy
1998	Not Free	Autocracy
1999	Not Free	Autocracy
2000	Not Free	Autocracy
2001	Not Free	Autocracy
2002	Not Free	Autocracy
2003	Not Free	Autocracy
2004	Not Free	Autocracy
2005	Not Free	Autocracy
2006	Not Free	Autocracy
2007	Not Free	Autocracy
2008	Imperfectly Free	Anocracy
2009	Imperfectly Free	Anocracy
2010	Imperfectly Free	Anocracy
2011	Imperfectly Free	Anocracy
2012	Imperfectly Free	Autocracy

years immediately following independence. In 1965, the Maldives had an elected sultanate, but in 1968, it became a republic. In spite of changes in the form of government, in practice the country was ruled in an authoritarian manner.[1] Additionally, the Maldives had a "long history of banishment of influential persons for political reasons" to remote and sparsely inhabited islands or atolls.[2] This practice likely encouraged self-censorship of media. The constitution called for press freedom provided Islamic and civil law were not violated, and there were a number of laws limiting media freedom including one that prohibited "the arousal of ill feelings against a lawfully formed government."[3] All publications were required to register with the government.[4] The government's radio station Voice of Maldives was established in 1962, and in 1978, the government established *Television Maldives*.

In 1990, there was some government discussion about media freedom, but that same year the government pressured two newspapers to close.[5,6]

2008–2012: Imperfectly Free

The government relinquished its monopoly on broadcast media in 2007, and several privately owned radio stations and one television station began broadcasting.[7] Then in 2008, Maldives held its first multiparty elections and adopted a new constitution that protected media freedom, though only to the extent that "is not contrary to any tenet of Islam."[8] Thus, conditions improved to the point that media were functionally free.

Media Today

Media remain imperfectly free, but their continued freedom is questionable due to political unrest. In early 2012, the democratically elected president was forced to resign in what appeared to be a coup. There were a number of attacks against journalists, and several news outlets were closed.[9] As Internet penetration has increased, the Communication Authority of the Maldives has blocked content that is deemed to be pornographic or anti-Islamic.[10]

Notes

1. *Country Reports on Human Rights Practices for 1979* (Washington, DC: U.S. Department of State, 1980). Available at http://babel.hathitrust.org/cgi/pt?id=mdp.39015014188273.
2. Ibid.
3. Ibid., 793.
4. Ibid.
5. Karl Ryavec, "Maldives," in *Indian Ocean*, ed. Helen Chapin Metz (Washington, DC: Library of Congress Federal Research Division, 1994). Available at http://lcweb2.loc.gov/frd/cs/mvtoc.html.
6. *Country Reports on Human Rights Practices for 1990* (Washington, DC: U.S. Department of State, 1991). Available at https://archive.org/stream/countryreportson1990unit/countryreportson1990unit_djvu.txt.
7. *Freedom of the Press* (Washington, DC: Freedom House, 2008. Available at http://www.freedomhouse.org/report/freedom-press/2008/maldives.
8. Constitution of the Republic of Maldives, 2008), 3. Available at http://www.maldivesinfo.gov.mv/home/upload/downloads/Compilation.pdf.
9. *Freedom of the Press* (Washington, DC: Freedom House, 2013). Available at http://freedomhouse.org/report/freedom-press/2013/maldives.
10. Ibid.

Mali: 1960–2012

Mali Year by Year

Year	Media	Government
1960	Not Free	Autocracy
1961	Not Free	Autocracy
1962	Not Free	Autocracy
1963	Not Free	Autocracy
1964	Not Free	Autocracy
1965	Not Free	Autocracy
1966	Not Free	Autocracy
1967	Not Free	Autocracy
1968	Not Free	Autocracy
1969	Not Free	Autocracy
1970	Not Free	Autocracy
1971	Not Free	Autocracy
1972	Not Free	Autocracy
1973	Not Free	Autocracy
1974	Not Free	Autocracy
1975	Not Free	Autocracy
1976	Not Free	Autocracy
1977	Not Free	Autocracy
1978	Not Free	Autocracy
1979	Not Free	Autocracy
1980	Not Free	Autocracy
1981	Not Free	Autocracy
1982	Not Free	Autocracy
1983	Not Free	Autocracy

(Continued)

MEDIA FREEDOM HISTORY IN A NUTSHELL

- Authoritarian rulers directly controlled the media until a 1991 coup initiated the transition to democracy
- Democracy and a free media were quickly established, with free elections in 1992
- Media face challenges of professionalism and unofficial forms of influence but are clearly free
- Recent political instability is threatening media freedom
- Radio remains the most popular medium, and Mali has a mix of private and public; the only television with national reach is state run
- Following the conflict in the north and the coup in 2012, a number of news outlets ceased publishing and broadcasting; 30 newspapers and about 300 radio stations remained (Freedom House's Report on Freedom of the Press 2013
- As of 2012, about 2 percent of Malians had Internet access (International Telecommunication Union's 2012 ICT Indicators Database)

In Brief

Mali successfully made the transition from dictatorship to democracy in 1991, and despite issues with market size and economic struggles, it has sustained free media. Yet media freedom is currently in jeopardy due to recent political instability.

Chronology

1961–1991: Not Free

A socialist, single-party state was declared shortly after independence from France, and media were directly controlled by the party. Despite a military coup in 1968, the establishment of a constitution and elections in 1979, media remained directly controlled.

(Continued)

Year	Media	Government
1984	Not Free	Autocracy
1985	Not Free	Autocracy
1986	Not Free	Autocracy
1987	Not Free	Autocracy
1988	Not Free	Autocracy
1989	Not Free	Autocracy
1990	Not Free	Autocracy
1991	Not Free	Anocracy
1992	Imperfectly Free	Democracy
1993	Imperfectly Free	Democracy
1994	Imperfectly Free	Democracy
1995	Free	Democracy
1996	Free	Democracy
1997	Free	Democracy
1998	Free	Democracy
1999	Free	Democracy
2000	Free	Democracy
2001	Free	Democracy
2002	Free	Democracy
2003	Free	Democracy
2004	Free	Democracy
2005	Free	Democracy
2006	Free	Democracy
2007	Free	Democracy
2008	Free	Democracy
2009	Free	Democracy
2010	Free	Democracy
2011	Free	Democracy
2012	Imperfectly Free	Democracy

1992–1994 Imperfectly Free

Student-led rioting in 1991 eventually led to a coup that implemented competitive democratic elections. Media were freed from direct government control, but the fledgling free media struggled with unofficial efforts to influence content, and many of the new papers were sponsored by political parties. A civil war against the Tuareg tribes was limited to the north, and most of the country had an imperfect press that was free to criticize government and officials.

1995–2011: Free

The 1995 peace agreement with the Tuareg rebels in the north was taken as the signal that the steady development of the political environment had reached the point where media were clearly and fully functional as an arena of political competition and critics of government that provided an effective check on leadership. Lack of professionalism was a serious issue, and the media environment remained close to the border of free and imperfectly free.

2012: Imperfectly Free

In 2012, most news outlets in northern Mali were closed down as militant groups seized control of the region. Subsequently, media in southern Mali were suppressed as the government was overthrown in a military coup:

> This included a temporary suspension of the constitution, arbitrary arrests of journalists, the takeover of the state broadcaster, and restrictions on reporting on the coup in the south; the closure or takeover of nearly all outlets and the imposition of Islamic law in the north; and harassment and attacks on journalists in both regions.[1]

Media Today

In 2013, following intervention by French troops, northern Mali was largely retaken from the rebels. After elections in the summer of 2013, democracy and media freedom appeared to be restored, though flare-ups of conflict continued in the north. At the end of 2013, the fate of media freedom in Mali remained unclear.

Note

1. *Freedom of the Press* (Washington, DC: Freedom House 2013). Available at http://freedomhouse.org/report/freedom-press/2013/mali.

Malta: 1965–2012

Malta Year by Year

Year	Media	Government
1965	Free	Democracy
1966	Free	Democracy
1967	Free	Democracy
1968	Free	Democracy
1969	Free	Democracy
1970	Free	Democracy
1971	Free	Democracy
1972	Free	Democracy
1973	Free	Democracy
1974	Free	Democracy
1975	Free	Democracy
1976	Free	Democracy
1977	Free	Democracy
1978	Free	Democracy
1979	Free	Democracy
1980	Free	Democracy
1981	Free	Democracy
1982	Free	Democracy
1983	Free	Democracy
1984	Free	Democracy
1985	Free	Democracy
1986	Free	Democracy
1987	Free	Democracy

(Continued)

MEDIA FREEDOM HISTORY IN A NUTSHELL

- Malta has a long history of media freedom
- Media outlets tend to be partisan, and many have direct connections to political parties or the Catholic Church
- As of 2012, there were five paid-for daily newspapers and mix of state-run and independent broadcast media (Freedom House's Freedom of the Press 2013)
- As of 2012, about 70 percent of Maltese had Internet access (International Telecommunication Union's 2012 ICT Indicators Database)

In Brief

Malta has a long history of media freedom, but this freedom is somewhat constrained by laws that prohibit offending the Roman Catholic Church, Malta's official religion, and those that criminalize defamation, hate speech, and obscene speech. News outlets tend to be partisan, reflecting their close ties to political parties and, in some cases, the Catholic Church.

Chronology

1965–2012: Free

Long before Malta gained independence, press censorship was banned in 1839. Newspapers have traditionally had strong ties to political parties, and they reflect the bilingual culture with some published in English and others published in Maltese.[1] Rediffusion Ltd., a British company, enjoyed a monopoly in the Maltese radio market with cable radio from 1935 until the early 1970s.[2] Rediffusion also launched Malta Television in 1962. In part,

(Continued)

Year	Media	Government
1988	Free	Democracy
1989	Free	Democracy
1990	Free	Democracy
1991	Free	Democracy
1992	Free	Democracy
1993	Free	Democracy
1994	Free	Democracy
1995	Free	Democracy
1996	Free	Democracy
1997	Free	Democracy
1998	Free	Democracy
1999	Free	Democracy
2000	Free	Democracy
2001	Free	Democracy
2002	Free	Democracy
2003	Free	Democracy
2004	Free	Democracy
2005	Free	Democracy
2006	Free	Democracy
2007	Free	Democracy
2008	Free	Democracy
2009	Free	Democracy
2010	Free	Democracy
2011	Free	Democracy
2012	Free	Democracy

these early broadcasting ventures were launched in response to the availability of Italian broadcasts, which in the case of radio in the 1930s included Fascist propaganda.[3] By the mid-1970s, Malta had terrestrial radio stations and broadcasting was nationalized.[4] In the early 1990s, both radio and television were pluralized, and since then Malta has developed a range of broadcast media, with some owned by the state and others owned by political parties and the Catholic Church.[5]

Media Today

Although the government for the most part respects the provisions for media freedom in the constitution, Malta has some laws that limit this freedom. In particular, it is against the law to insult the country's official religion, the Roman Catholic Church.[6] Moreover, defamation, hate speech, and obscene speech are criminalized.[7] That said, Malta has a range of independent media that are free to criticize the government. News outlets tend to be partisan because most have ties to political parties or the Catholic Church.[8]

Notes

1. Joseph Borg, *Media Landscapes: Malta* (Maastricht, The Netherlands: European Journalism Centre, December 2013). Available at http://ejc.net/media_landscapes/malta.
2. Ibid.
3. *Malta*, BBC Country Profiles (London, UK: British Broadcasting Company, 2012). Available at http://www.bbc.co.uk/news/world-europe-17598077.
4. Borg *Media Landscapes: Malta*.
5. Ibid.
6. *Freedom of the Press* (Washington, DC: Freedom House, 2013). Available at http://freedomhouse.org/report/freedom-press/2013/malta.
7. Ibid.
8. Ibid.

Marshall Islands: 1986–2012

Marshall Islands Year by Year

Year	Media	Government
1986	Free	Democracy
1987	Free	Democracy
1988	Free	Democracy
1989	Free	Democracy
1990	Free	Democracy
1991	Free	Democracy
1992	Free	Democracy
1993	Free	Democracy
1994	Free	Democracy
1995	Free	Democracy
1996	Free	Democracy
1997	Free	Democracy
1998	Free	Democracy
1999	Free	Democracy
2000	Free	Democracy
2001	Free	Democracy
2002	Free	Democracy
2003	Free	Democracy
2004	Free	Democracy
2005	Free	Democracy
2006	Free	Democracy
2007	Free	Democracy
2008	Free	Democracy
2009	Free	Democracy
2010	Free	Democracy
2011	Free	Democracy
2012	Free	Democracy

MEDIA FREEDOM HISTORY IN A NUTSHELL

- The Marshall Islands have limited, but relatively free media
- As of 2013, Marshallese media included one private newspaper and one government newspaper, a mix of government and religious radio, and one government television station; U.S. military broadcast media are also accessible in parts of the country (BBC News Country Profiles)
- As of 2012, about 10 percent of Marshallese had Internet access (International Telecommunication Union's 2012 ICT Indicators Database)

In Brief

The Marshall Islands consist of 29 atolls and five islands that together add up to only 70 square miles, but are spread out over 750,000 square miles in the Central Pacific. Given its population (estimated at under 70,000 in 2013[1]), the media market is small. Media are for the most part free.

Rising sea levels are a threat to this island state.

Chronology

1986–2012: Free

After several decades of U.S. occupation following World War II, the Marshall Islands gained independence in 1986. In the 1940s and 1950s, the United States tested nuclear weapons on the Islands of Bikini and Enewetak, and the United States still maintains a base and missile test range on the Kwajalean atoll. For the most part, Marshallese media have been sparse but functionally free. In addition to private and government domestic media, U.S. forces radio and television reach some parts of the country.

Media Today

Marshallese media remain free. There is one weekly private newspaper and one monthly government newspaper. There are government and church-owned radio stations, and state-run television. In some parts of the country, U.S. military broadcast media are available.[2] Internet access is limited.

Notes

1. *Marshall Islands* (Washington, DC: CIA World Factbook, 2013). Available at https://www.cia.gov/library/publications/the-world-factbook/geos/rm.html.
2. *Freedom of the Press* (Washington, DC: Freedom House, 2013). Available at http://www.freedomhouse.org/report/freedom-world/2013/marshall-islands.

Mauritania: 1960–2012

Mauritania Year by Year

Year	Media	Government
1960	Not Free	Anocracy
1961	Not Free	Anocracy
1962	Not Free	Autocracy
1963	Not Free	Autocracy
1964	Not Free	Autocracy
1965	Not Free	Autocracy
1966	Not Free	Autocracy
1967	Not Free	Autocracy
1968	Not Free	Autocracy
1969	Not Free	Autocracy
1970	Not Free	Autocracy
1971	Not Free	Autocracy
1972	Not Free	Autocracy
1973	Not Free	Autocracy
1974	Not Free	Autocracy
1975	Not Free	Autocracy
1976	Not Free	Autocracy
1977	Not Free	Autocracy
1978	Not Free	Autocracy
1979	Not Free	Autocracy
1980	Not Free	Autocracy
1981	Not Free	Autocracy
1982	Not Free	Autocracy
1983	Not Free	Autocracy

(Continued)

MEDIA FREEDOM HISTORY IN A NUTSHELL

- Coups and coup attempts fill any discussion of the history of Mauritania
- Authoritarian rulers controlled or restricted the media until recently
- Instability continued after the 2005 coup freed the media, but the media have continued to function in an imperfect but free manner
- Mauritania has a mix of state-run and independent newspapers as well as a mix of public and private broadcast media; the number of private radio and television outlets is increasing since the government began granting licenses in 2011
- As of 2012, about 5 percent of Mauritanians had Internet access (International Telecommunication Union's 2012 ICT Indicators Database)

In Brief

After long history of authoritarian rule following independence from France, Mauritania has showed signs of democratization and the emergence of an imperfect but functionally free media. The situation appears fragile and the media face many challenges.

Chronology

1961–2005: Not Free

War, civil war, rebellions, and coups fill most descriptions of Mauritanian government during this period, but through it all, what little media existed in this impoverished nation were controlled by government or its proxies. The coup that led to the 1992 election of Colonel Taya as president seemed to signal a shift in the political environment. This included some loosening of

(Continued)

Year	Media	Government
1984	Not Free	Autocracy
1985	Not Free	Autocracy
1986	Not Free	Autocracy
1987	Not Free	Autocracy
1988	Not Free	Autocracy
1989	Not Free	Autocracy
1990	Not Free	Autocracy
1991	Not Free	Autocracy
1992	Not Free	Autocracy
1993	Not Free	Autocracy
1994	Not Free	Autocracy
1995	Not Free	Autocracy
1996	Not Free	Autocracy
1997	Not Free	Autocracy
1998	Not Free	Autocracy
1999	Not Free	Autocracy
2000	Not Free	Autocracy
2001	Not Free	Autocracy
2002	Not Free	Autocracy
2003	Not Free	Autocracy
2004	Not Free	Autocracy
2005	Not Free	Anocracy
2006	Imperfectly Free	Anocracy
2007	Imperfectly Free	Anocracy
2008	Imperfectly Free	Anocracy
2009	Imperfectly Free	Anocracy
2010	Imperfectly Free	Anocracy
2011	Imperfectly Free	Anocracy
2012	Imperfectly Free	Anocracy

media controls and a shift to a restricted model rather than direct government control of news media.

The 1995 deterioration of the political environment, which would eventually lead to a series of coups just after the turn of the century, prompted a return to direct control of the media.

In 2002, media restrictions were eased, as much a result of an inability to enforce restrictions as an intentional act. Coup attempts and foiled coup attempts were frequent.

2006–2012: Imperfectly Free

A 2005 military coup ousted President Taya, and in something of a surprise, the military council that stepped in to rule the country eased media restrictions in 2006 and began the process of democratization.[1] In 2011, the government of President Mohamed Ould Abdelaziz announced a plan to liberalize media and approved a number of new privately owned radio and television stations, ending the government's monopoly on broadcast media.[2]

Media were limited, unprofessional, and plagued by corruption, but there was sufficient competition among those trying to influence content to create an effectively free media.

Media Today

The media system is fragile, unprofessional, and impoverished, but it has proven to be more robust than Mauritania's other attempted democratic reforms.

Notes

1. *World Press Freedom Review*, IPI Report (Zurich: International Press Institute, 2006).
2. *Freedom of the Press* (Washington, DC: Freedom House, 2012). Available at http://www.freedom house.org/report/freedom-press/2012/mauritania.

Mauritius: 1968–2012

Mauritius Year by Year

Year	Media	Government
1968	Imperfectly Free	Democracy
1969	Imperfectly Free	Democracy
1970	Not Free	Democracy
1971	Not Free	Democracy
1972	Not Free	Democracy
1973	Not Free	Democracy
1974	Not Free	Democracy
1975	Not Free	Democracy
1976	Imperfectly Free	Democracy
1977	Imperfectly Free	Democracy
1978	Imperfectly Free	Democracy
1979	Imperfectly Free	Democracy
1980	Imperfectly Free	Democracy
1981	Imperfectly Free	Democracy
1982	Imperfectly Free	Democracy
1983	Imperfectly Free	Democracy
1984	Imperfectly Free	Democracy
1985	Imperfectly Free	Democracy
1986	Imperfectly Free	Democracy
1987	Imperfectly Free	Democracy
1988	Imperfectly Free	Democracy
1989	Imperfectly Free	Democracy
1990	Imperfectly Free	Democracy
1991	Imperfectly Free	Democracy

(Continued)

MEDIA FREEDOM HISTORY IN A NUTSHELL

- With the exception of the early 1970s, Mauritian media have been functionally free
- As of 2009, there were 4 paid-for daily newspapers with a total average circulation per issue of 105,000 (World Association of Newspaper's 2010 World Newspaper Trends)
- The state-owned Mauritius Broadcasting Corporation (MBC) radio and TV often reflect government views, but there are some privately owned radio stations (British Broadcasting Company)
- As of 2012, about 42 percent of Mauritians had Internet access (International Telecommunication Union's 2012 ICT Indicators Database)

In Brief

Since gaining independence from Britain in 1968, Mauritius has been a multiparty democracy. With the exception of the early 1970s, Mauritian media have been functionally free. News media are published and broadcast in several languages because of the ethnically diverse population. In addition to the Indo-Mauritian majority, there are Creoles, Sino-Mauritians, and Franco-Mauritians.

Chronology

1968–1969: Imperfectly Free

Upon gaining independence from Britain, Mauritius was a multiparty democracy with media that were functionally free, but with some limitations due to libel and slander laws.

1970–1975: Not Free

In the early 1970s, as the opposition group, the Mauritian Militant Movement (MMM)

(Continued)

Year	Media	Government
1992	Imperfectly Free	Democracy
1993	Imperfectly Free	Democracy
1994	Imperfectly Free	Democracy
1995	Imperfectly Free	Democracy
1996	Imperfectly Free	Democracy
1997	Imperfectly Free	Democracy
1998	Imperfectly Free	Democracy
1999	Imperfectly Free	Democracy
2000	Free	Democracy
2001	Free	Democracy
2002	Free	Democracy
2003	Free	Democracy
2004	Free	Democracy
2005	Free	Democracy
2006	Free	Democracy
2007	Free	Democracy
2008	Free	Democracy
2009	Free	Democracy
2010	Free	Democracy
2011	Free	Democracy
2012	Free	Democracy

gained momentum and held a series of strikes, the government (led by the Mauritius Labor Party) declared a state of emergency and introduced the Public Order Act, which banned some types of political activity.[1] Under the state of emergency, news media were censored. "All chief editors had to submit a proof of their newspaper before printing to allow the police censors to cut out things like the mere mention of MMM and the General Workers Federation (GWF) leaders and even the slightest criticism of government."[2] Yet by the mid-1970, these controls were removed, and in 1975, an opposition paper was allowed to resume publication.[3]

1976–1999: Imperfectly Free

The state of emergency was lifted in 1976, and as multiparty elections were held at the end of the year, the Mauritian media were once again functionally free and highly partisan.[4] There were a number of privately owned newspapers, most of which had ties to political parties or religious organizations, and while most were published in French, some were published in Chinese and English.[5] The government maintained a monopoly over the country's radio and television stations, which offered broadcasts in twelve languages.[6]

2000–2012: Free

In the 2000 elections campaign, Mauritian media presented a diverse range of views and were able to criticize the government.[7] The government maintained its monopoly on broadcast media until 2002, when private radio stations were allowed to begin broadcasting.[8]

Although the media functioned freely, there were some problems. In 2005, the International Press Institute noted that the government would refuse to talk to certain reporters and often engaged in the practice of "blackout," which entailed denying the media all information about a particular subject.[9] Also in 2005, the government began to decrease its advertising in newspapers published by La Sentinelle Group, and in 2010, the government agencies boycotted their subscriptions to one the group's newspapers.[10] Thus, by 2011, media were close to being imperfectly free.

Media Today

Media freedom improved in 2012, as the government ended its boycott of La Sentinelle Group's publications.[11] Mauritian media remain vibrant, highly partisan but representative of diverse views, and free to engage in watchdog reporting. Though there are privately owned newspapers as well as a mix of government and privately owned radio stations, the government still controls the country's only television network. Yet Mauritians can access foreign television networks if they have a cable subscription. The Internet is generally unrestricted, and about 42 percent of Mauritians had Internet access in 2012.

Notes

1. Anthony Toth, "Mauritius: Country Profile," in *Indian Ocean*, ed. Helen Chapin Metz (Washington, DC: Library of Congress Federal Research Division, 1994). Available at http://lcweb2.loc.gov/frd/cs/cshome.html.

2. Sydney Selvon, *A New Comprehensive History of Mauritius*, vol. 1 (Printed in Mauritius: MDSelvon), 215.

3. Ibid.

4. *Country Reports for Human Rights Practices for 1979* (Washington, DC: U.S. Department of State, 1980). Available at http://babel.hathitrust.org/cgi/pt?id=mdp.39015014188273;view=1up;seq=1.

5. Toth, "Mauritius: Country Profile."

6. Ibid.

7. *World Press Freedom Review*, IPI Report (Vienna: International Press Institute, 2000).

8. *World Press Freedom Review*, IPI Report (Vienna: International Press Institute, 2005).

9. Ibid.

10. *Country Reports on Human Rights Practices for 2010: Mauritius* (Washington, DC: U.S. Department of State, 2011). Available at http://www.state.gov/j/drl/rls/hrrpt/2010/af/154359.htm.

11. *Country Reports on Human Rights Practices for 2012: Mauritius* (Washington, DC: U.S. Department of State, 2013). Available at http://www.state.gov/j/drl/rls/hrrpt/humanrightsreport/index.htm#wrapper.

Mexico: 1948–2012

Mexico Year by Year

Year	Media	Government
1948	Imperfectly Free	Autocracy
1949	Imperfectly Free	Autocracy
1950	Imperfectly Free	Autocracy
1951	Imperfectly Free	Autocracy
1952	Imperfectly Free	Autocracy
1953	Imperfectly Free	Autocracy
1954	Imperfectly Free	Autocracy
1955	Imperfectly Free	Autocracy
1956	Imperfectly Free	Autocracy
1957	Imperfectly Free	Autocracy
1958	Imperfectly Free	Autocracy
1959	Imperfectly Free	Autocracy
1960	Imperfectly Free	Autocracy
1961	Imperfectly Free	Autocracy
1962	Imperfectly Free	Autocracy
1963	Imperfectly Free	Autocracy
1964	Imperfectly Free	Autocracy
1965	Imperfectly Free	Autocracy
1966	Imperfectly Free	Autocracy
1967	Imperfectly Free	Autocracy
1968	Imperfectly Free	Autocracy
1969	Imperfectly Free	Autocracy
1970	Imperfectly Free	Autocracy
1971	Imperfectly Free	Autocracy
1972	Imperfectly Free	Autocracy
1973	Imperfectly Free	Autocracy
1974	Imperfectly Free	Autocracy
1975	Imperfectly Free	Autocracy

MEDIA FREEDOM HISTORY IN A NUTSHELL

- Although ruled by a single party for decades, Mexico had media that were functionally free
- As Mexico democratized and launched a war against the drug cartels, violence against journalists increased to the point that media were no longer free in 2010
- As of 2012, there were 505 paid-for daily newspapers with a total average circulation per issue of 4,800,000 (World Association of Newspaper's 2012 World Newspaper Trends)
- In 2012, two media companies controlled 85 percent of the television stations and about a dozen family owned companies controlled most radio stations (Freedom House's Report on Freedom of the Press 2013)
- As of 2012, about 38 percent of Mexicans had Internet access (International Telecommunication Union's 2012 ICT Indicators Database)

In Brief

The case of Mexico and its media illustrates that democracy and media freedom do not always go hand-in-hand. For decades under the rule of a single party, Mexico was an autocratic state with media that were at least somewhat free. Then as Mexico democratized media freedom deteriorated because of violence against journalists and the government's inability or unwillingness to punish those responsible. Since 2010, media have been restricted as journalists continue to be harassed and attacked by both police (usually local) and drug traffickers.

Chronology

1948–2009: Imperfectly Free

Starting in 1929 and continuing for more than seven decades, the Institutional

Year	Media	Government
1976	Imperfectly Free	Autocracy
1977	Imperfectly Free	Anocracy
1978	Imperfectly Free	Anocracy
1979	Imperfectly Free	Anocracy
1980	Imperfectly Free	Anocracy
1981	Imperfectly Free	Anocracy
1982	Imperfectly Free	Anocracy
1983	Imperfectly Free	Anocracy
1984	Imperfectly Free	Anocracy
1985	Imperfectly Free	Anocracy
1986	Imperfectly Free	Anocracy
1987	Imperfectly Free	Anocracy
1988	Imperfectly Free	Anocracy
1989	Imperfectly Free	Anocracy
1990	Imperfectly Free	Anocracy
1991	Imperfectly Free	Anocracy
1992	Imperfectly Free	Anocracy
1993	Imperfectly Free	Anocracy
1994	Imperfectly Free	Anocracy
1995	Imperfectly Free	Anocracy
1996	Imperfectly Free	Anocracy
1997	Imperfectly Free	Democracy
1998	Imperfectly Free	Democracy
1999	Imperfectly Free	Democracy
2000	Imperfectly Free	Democracy
2001	Imperfectly Free	Democracy
2002	Imperfectly Free	Democracy
2003	Imperfectly Free	Democracy
2004	Imperfectly Free	Democracy
2005	Imperfectly Free	Democracy
2006	Imperfectly Free	Democracy
2007	Imperfectly Free	Democracy
2008	Imperfectly Free	Democracy
2009	Imperfectly Free	Democracy
2010	Not Free	Democracy
2011	Not Free	Democracy
2012	Not Free	Democracy

Revolutionary Party (PRI) ruled Mexico. Under the PRI, media were for the most part independently owned and free from direct government censorship. But a different, more subtle form of control was practiced dating back to the years following World War II, "when presidents Manuel Avila-Camacho (1940–1946) and Miguel Aleman (1946–1952) encouraged the corruption of the news media and the consolidation of media ownership in the hands of sympathetic owners."[1] Thus, some opposition media were tolerated and some criticism of government was permitted, but criticism or ridicule of an incumbent president was unacceptable. "Among the many unwritten rules is one that journalists are expected to respect the image of the president and other high-level government officials."[2] Newspapers and broadcast media were also dependent on government advertising and subsidies.

In the late 1970s and early 1980s independent print media emerged in Mexico, in part prompted by increased professionalization among journalists and in part a long-term effect of the 1968 and 1971 deadly government crackdowns on student protesters.[3] Thus, in the 1980s, there was a notable increase in media criticism of government that some credit with paving the way to Mexico's democratization.[4] As the government withdrew its advertising and subsidies from critical news media, some outlets folded, but others survived and became more reliant on sales. In order to maintain and increase their audience, Mexican news media discovered that scandals attracted readers, viewers and listeners.[5] Consequently, Mexican news media became increasingly engaged in watchdog reporting in the 1990s. This was particularly apparent in the media coverage of the 1994 government suppression of the rebellion in Chiapas.

In the 1997 elections, the PRI lost its majority in the lower house of parliament, and in 2000, it lost the presidency. Yet as Mexico democratized and the government moved against the drug cartels, it became an increasingly dangerous country for journalists, especially those covering organized crime and government corruption. Between 1997 and 2013, sixty-five journalists were killed, and in twenty-seven cases, the Committee to Protect Journalists confirmed that the killings were directly linked to their work.[6] Others simply disappeared, and still more fled the country. As violence against journalists increased, these crimes usually went unpunished, with the government either unable or unwilling to intervene. The attacks had a chilling effect on the Mexican media, and journalists admitted to practicing self-censorship.[7]

2010–2012: Not Free

By 2010, cartel violence against journalists escalated to the point where media were no longer free. In September of that year, the Juárez newspaper *El Diario* effectively surrendered to the Cartels, with a front page editorial after a photographer was gunned down at a mall:

> Under the headline, "What do you want from us?," the editorial pleads for the cartels to stop killing journalists, and asks them to clarify what journalists are allowed to publish in order to avoid adding to the long list of reporters killed in Mexico in the last decade. In a bold move, the paper addresses the cartels directly, and even recognizes their power in Ciudad Juárez. "You are the de facto authorities in this city, since our legitimate representatives have been unable to prevent our colleagues from being killed," the editorial reads in Spanish.[8]

The drug cartels employed a variety of controls over news media, including bribery, threats, and attacks, and sometimes forced news outlets to carry their news releases and propaganda.[9] Thus, though Mexico remained a democracy in the early 2010s, news media were not able to function as a fourth estate. In the 2012 elections, the PRI regained the presidency with the victory of Enrique Pena Nieto.

Media Today

Mexican media continue to be restricted and Mexico remains one of the most dangerous countries in the world for journalists. In addition to systematic violence and impunity, journalists are still constrained by defamation laws in some states even though defamation has been decriminalized at the federal level.[10] On a positive note, a 2012 constitutional amendment rendered crimes against journalists a federal offense.

Mexico has a wide range of privately owned print media. Ownership of broadcast media remains highly concentrated. As of 2012, 85 percent of Mexico's television stations were owned by either Televisa or TV Azteca.[11]

Notes

1. Chappell Lawson, *Building the Fourth Estate: Democratization and the Rise of a Free Press in Mexico* (Ewing, NJ: University of California Press, 2002), 26.
2. Tim L. Merril and Ramón Miró, "The Church," *Mexico: A Country Study* (Washington, DC: Library of Congress Federal Research Division, 1996), para. 9. Available at http://lcweb2.loc.gov/frd/cs/cshome.html.
3. Lawson, *Building the Fourth Estate: Democratization and the Rise of a Free Press in Mexico.*
4. Ibid.
5. Ibid.
6. *29 Journalists Killed in Mexico Since 1992/Motive Confirmed* (Committee to Protect Journalists, 2014). Available at http://cpj.org/killed/americas/mexico/.
7. *Country Reports on Human Rights Practices 2009* (Washington, DC: U.S. Department of State, 2010) Available at http://www.state.gov/j/drl/rls/hrrpt/2009/wha/136119.htm.
8. José Barbeito, "Paper Will Curb Coverage to Protect Reporters' Lives in Juárez," CPJ Blog: Press Freedom News and Views (Committee to Protect Journalists, 2010), para. 2. Available at http://cpj.org/blog/2010/09/paper-will-curb-coverage-to-protect-reporters-live.php.
9. *Freedom of the Press* (Washington, DC: Freedom House, 2011). Available at http://freedomhouse.org/report/freedom-press/2011/mexico.
10. *Freedom of the Press* (Washington, DC: Freedom House, 2013). Available at http://freedomhouse.org/report/freedom-press/2013/mexico.
11. Ibid.

Micronesia, Federated States of: 1986–2012

Micronesia Year by Year

Year	Media	Government
1986	Free	Democracy
1987	Free	Democracy
1988	Free	Democracy
1989	Free	Democracy
1990	Free	Democracy
1991	Free	Democracy
1992	Free	Democracy
1993	Free	Democracy
1994	Free	Democracy
1995	Free	Democracy
1996	Free	Democracy
1997	Free	Democracy
1998	Free	Democracy
1999	Free	Democracy
2000	Free	Democracy
2001	Free	Democracy
2002	Free	Democracy
2003	Free	Democracy
2004	Free	Democracy
2005	Free	Democracy
2006	Free	Democracy
2007	Free	Democracy
2008	Free	Democracy
2009	Free	Democracy
2010	Free	Democracy
2011	Free	Democracy
2012	Free	Democracy

MEDIA FREEDOM HISTORY IN A NUTSHELL

- Since gaining independence in 1986, Micronesian media have been limited but free
- Micronesia does not have any daily newspapers, but it does have regularly published government newsletters and at least one independent nondaily newspaper
- Each state has its own government-run radio station, and there is one radio station operated by the Baptist Church; cable and satellite television are available in some areas (BBC News Country Profiles)
- As of 2012, 26 percent of Micronesians had Internet access (International Telecommunication Union's 2012 ICT Indicators Database)

In Brief

The Federated States of Micronesia is made up of hundreds of islands and atolls scattered over one million square miles in the Central Pacific. Given its small population (about 106,000 in 2013[1]) Micronesia is a small media market, and while media are limited, they are for the most part free.

Chronology

1986–2012: Free

Following Japanese occupation during World War II, the United Nations placed Micronesia under U.S. administration in 1947. In 1986, Micronesia was granted independence through an agreement with the United States, which gave the United States the right to establish military bases in Micronesia in exchange for economic assistance. In the late 1980s, Micronesia had one privately owned newspaper and one privately owned religious-based radio station.[2] By the mid-1990s some of Micronesia's four states had local television programming and subscription-based cable television, and each state had its own radio station.[3] Newsletters published by the national government and the state governments were also available.[4] By 2005, privately owned newspapers were available in some states, and satellite television was increasingly available.[5]

Media Today

Micronesian media remain free but limited. It is difficult for this small remote market to sustain much domestic media. Each of the four states and the national government publish newsletters. In 2012, there was at least one privately owned newspaper. Each state has its own radio station, and an additional radio station is run by the Baptist Church.[6] About one-fourth of the population has Internet access.

Notes

1. *Federated States of Micronesia* (Washington, DC: CIA World Factbook, 2013). Available at https://www.cia.gov/library/publications/the-world-factbook/geos/fm.html.

2. *Country Reports on Human Rights Practices for 1988* (Washington, DC: U.S. Department of State, 1989). Available at https://archive.org/stream/countryreportson1988unit#page/880/mode/2up/search/Micronesia.

3. *Country Reports on Human Rights Practices for 1995* (Washington, DC: U.S. Department of State, 1996). Available at http://dosfan.lib.uic.edu/ERC/democracy/1995_hrp_report/95hrp_report_eap/Micronesia.html.

4. Ibid.

5. *Country Reports on Human Rights Practices for 2005* (Washington, DC: U.S. Department of State, 2006). Available at http://www.state.gov/j/drl/rls/hrrpt/2005/61618.htm.

6. *Micronesia*, BBC Country Profiles (London, UK: British Broadcasting Company, 2013). Available at http://www.bbc.co.uk/news/world-asia-pacific-15519476.

Moldova: 1992–2012

Moldova Year by Year

Year	Media	Government
1992	Not Free	Anocracy
1993	Not Free	Democracy
1994	Not Free	Democracy
1995	Imperfectly Free	Democracy
1996	Imperfectly Free	Democracy
1997	Imperfectly Free	Democracy
1998	Not Free	Democracy
1999	Not Free	Democracy
2000	Not Free	Democracy
2001	Imperfectly Free	Democracy
2002	Imperfectly Free	Democracy
2003	Not Free	Democracy
2004	Not Free	Democracy
2005	Not Free	Democracy
2006	Not Free	Democracy
2007	Not Free	Democracy
2008	Not Free	Democracy
2009	Not Free	Democracy
2010	Imperfectly Free	Democracy
2011	Imperfectly Free	Democracy
2012	Imperfectly Free	Democracy

MEDIA FREEDOM HISTORY IN A NUTSHELL

- Independence from the Soviet Union brought civil unrest and a restricted press
- A democratic electoral system was established, but it wasn't until after the first election that an imperfect but free media system was established
- Media have swung back and forth between restricted and imperfectly free, but authoritarian political influences have never been far removed
- As of 2011, there were 248 daily newspapers, 7 of them were paid-for daily newspapers with a total average circulation per issue of 400,000 (World Association of Newspaper's 2010 World Newspaper Trends)
- Moldova had forty-six radio stations, thirty-eight television stations, and 166 cable providers (World Association of Newspaper's 2010 World Newspaper Trends)
- As of 2012, about 43 percent of Moldavians had Internet access (International Telecommunication Union's 2012 ICT Indicators Database)

In Brief

Despite targeted aid from European programs intent on aiding Eastern European transitions to democratic rule and developing liberal social institutions such as free media, Moldova is still dominated by the authoritarian legacy of Soviet rule. Independence was accompanied by war over the attempted succession of eastern, Russian-dominated parts of the country, and significant territory is still effectively under Russian occupation and outside the rule of the central government. A largely Turkish region within the country gained significant autonomy, including a right to secede if Moldavia should attempt to become part of Romania. This is a significant concern because the cultural ties with Romania are so close that Moldavian language is all but indistinguishable from Romanian.

Chronology

1992–1994: Not Free

During what was essentially a civil war, efforts were made to establish an independent media capable of supporting free and fair electoral competition. These efforts met with limited success, and it is notable that the first post-Soviet election was held without effective free media. In addition, Parliament passed a Press Law in 1994 that legal experts argued was more representative of a fascist regime.[1] During this time, there were reports of increased government harassment of the opposition press.[2]

1995–1997: Imperfectly Free

The first post-Soviet election brought a centrist party to power, and the media became sufficiently independent to consider them to be imperfectly free. However, as that centrist party began to splinter, a rapid growth in partisan media alignments threatened media effectiveness and ultimately resulted in a press that was unable to support critical debate. New restrictive press laws came into effect in 1995, as well as controversial provisions that enabled the state to control broadcasting licenses and frequencies. Despite these barriers, independent newspapers began gaining ground.[3]

1998–2000: Not Free

With the electoral landscape shifting away from parties and candidates that might support a continued push for liberalization, media freedom quickly declined. Media were still nominally independent, but by 1998, self-censorship, economic hardship, and political pressure had eliminated any realistic ability to air criticisms of government or rulers. Most major newspapers relied on financing by the state or political parties because of the poor economic situation, limiting their independence.[4]

2001–2002: Imperfectly Free

In the 2001 elections, the Communist party won an outright majority. Despite campaigning on developing closer ties to Russia, the Communist government pursued closer ties to the West. The ties it sought with the West were primarily economic, but part of that effort included a brief relaxation of efforts to dominate the media.

2003–2009: Not Free

The return of unrest in the country ended the use of liberalization as part of the effort to build economic ties with the West, and a period of intense restriction and intense pressure from government led to a period that some labeled the nadir of freedom in Moldova. Media remained as a political instrument used by the Communist government. The lack of financial stability, scarce management, and increased self-censorship caused the media to be dependent on the government and political influence.

2010–2012: Imperfectly Free

Despite the on again off again authoritarian pressures on the media, the basic structure of Moldovan media retained elements, such as a commercial business model, that enabled them to function as an imperfect but effectively free system when the opportunity arose. In 2010, technology appears to have created just such an opportunity, and despite an absence of liberalization from the government, the media are increasingly acting as a forum for debate and criticism. New online media channels and investment by foreign media outlets have played a role in the rise of independent media.[6]

Media Today

It is unclear if technology will enable the transition to a sustained free media environment or if this most recent trend represents another brief swing toward liberalism. If Moldova is to truly develop a free media environment, it will need to overcome the Soviet tradition of government control of news media and develop an editorially independent public broadcast system.[7,8]

Notes

1. *World Press Freedom Review*, IPI Report (Vienna: International Press Institute, 1994).
2. Ibid.
3. *World Press Freedom Review*, IPI Report (Vienna: International Press Institute, 1995).
4. *World Press Freedom Review*, IPI Report (Vienna: International Press Institute, 1999).
5. *Moldova*, Media Landscape Reports (Maastricht, The Netherlands: European Journalism Centre, 2013). Available at http://ejc.net/media_landscapes/moldova.
6. *World Press Freedom Review*, IPI Report (Vienna: International Press Institute, 1999).
7. Ibid.
8. *Moldova*, Media Landscape Reports.

Monaco: 1993–2012

Monaco Year by Year

Year	Media	Government
1993	Imperfectly Free	Democracy
1994	Imperfectly Free	Democracy
1995	Imperfectly Free	Democracy
1996	Imperfectly Free	Democracy
1997	Imperfectly Free	Democracy
1998	Imperfectly Free	Democracy
1999	Imperfectly Free	Democracy
2000	Imperfectly Free	Democracy
2001	Imperfectly Free	Democracy
2002	Imperfectly Free	Democracy
2003	Imperfectly Free	Democracy
2004	Imperfectly Free	Democracy
2005	Imperfectly Free	Democracy
2006	Imperfectly Free	Democracy
2007	Imperfectly Free	Democracy
2008	Imperfectly Free	Democracy
2009	Imperfectly Free	Democracy
2010	Imperfectly Free	Democracy
2011	Imperfectly Free	Democracy
2012	Imperfectly Free	Democracy

MEDIA FREEDOM HISTORY IN A NUTSHELL

- Monaco's constitution guarantees media freedom, but it is against the law to insult the ruling family
- Monegasque media are limited, but functionally free
- As of 2013, Monaco had one government-owned weekly newspaper, one privately owned television station, and several privately owned radio stations
- Foreign media are widely available
- As of 2012, 87 percent of Monegasques had Internet access (International Telecommunication Union's 2012 ICT Indicators Database)

In Brief

The Principality of Monaco is a constitutional monarchy that has been ruled by the Grimaldi family for more than seven centuries. In 1993, it joined the United Nations. Although the constitution has provisions for media freedom, it is against the law to insult the royal family. Given its small market size (estimated population for 2013 was 30,500[1]), domestic media are limited. In spite of the restrictions on domestic media, foreign print and broadcast media are widely available.

Chronology

1993–2012: Imperfectly Free

Very little information is available about the Monegasque media prior to the 1990s, but it was probably imperfectly free. Although Monaco's 1962 constitution guaranteed of freedom of expression, there were also laws prohibiting insulting the ruling family.[2] Given the small market, domestic media were limited to several small publications, but foreign print and broadcast media were not subject to these restrictions and were widely available.[3] Monaco is home to broadcast media that are heard way beyond its borders. In the 1960s, Radio Monte-Carlo began broadcasting from Monaco into France, and in the 1970s, it began broadcasting in Italy.

Media Today

Monegasque media remain functionally free. Monaco has one government-owned weekly newspaper, several privately owned radio stations, and one private television station.[4] A large portion of the Monegasques (87 percent) have Internet access.

Notes

1. *Monaco* (Washington, DC: CIA World Factbook, 2013). Available at https://www.cia.gov/library/publications/the-world-factbook/geos/mn.html.
2. *Country Reports on Human Rights Practices for 1993* (Washington, DC: U.S. Department of State, 1994). Available at http://dosfan.lib.uic.edu/ERC/democracy/1993_hrp_report/93hrp_report_eur/Monaco.html.
3. Ibid.
4. *Monaco*, Country Profiles (London, UK: British Broadcasting Company, 2013). Available at http://www.bbc.co.uk/news/world-europe-17616158.

Mongolia: 1948–2012

Mongolia Year by Year

Year	Media	Government
1948	Not Free	Autocracy
1949	Not Free	Autocracy
1950	Not Free	Autocracy
1951	Not Free	Autocracy
1952	Not Free	Autocracy
1953	Not Free	Autocracy
1954	Not Free	Autocracy
1955	Not Free	Autocracy
1956	Not Free	Autocracy
1957	Not Free	Autocracy
1958	Not Free	Autocracy
1959	Not Free	Autocracy
1960	Not Free	Autocracy
1961	Not Free	Autocracy
1962	Not Free	Autocracy
1963	Not Free	Autocracy
1964	Not Free	Autocracy
1965	Not Free	Autocracy
1966	Not Free	Autocracy
1967	Not Free	Autocracy
1968	Not Free	Autocracy
1969	Not Free	Autocracy
1970	Not Free	Autocracy
1971	Not Free	Autocracy

(Continued)

MEDIA FREEDOM HISTORY IN A NUTSHELL

- Media were directly controlled by a single party, communist regime until the fall of the Soviet Union
- Media in the capital were a key part of a quick and peaceful transition to a multiparty democracy with free media
- Politics and media are concentrated in the capital, with limited impact on the rural way of life that dominates the country
- As of 2009, Mongolia had a total of fifteen paid-for daily newspapers with an average circulation per issue of 49,000 (according to the World Association of Newspaper's 2010 World Newspaper Trends)
- Mongolia's public-service television and radio broadcasters compete with private television and radio services (World Association of Newspaper's 2010 World Newspaper Trends)
- As of 2012, about 16 percent of Mongolians had Internet access (International Telecommunication Union's 2012 ICT Indicators Database)

In Brief

Landlocked and isolated from most of the world, Mongolia occupied the uncomfortable position as a Soviet buffer against China. During this time, Mongolia was dominated politically and militarily by the Soviets, but it had more significant economic and cultural ties to China. Since the fall of the Soviet Union, Mongolia has established and managed to maintain a multiparty democracy, including imperfect but functionally free media. The degree to which any of this matters outside of Ulan Bator, the capital city, is an open question, because most of the country is still the domain of rural, semi-nomadic herders.

(Continued)

Year	Media	Government
1972	Not Free	Autocracy
1973	Not Free	Autocracy
1974	Not Free	Autocracy
1975	Not Free	Autocracy
1976	Not Free	Autocracy
1977	Not Free	Autocracy
1978	Not Free	Autocracy
1979	Not Free	Autocracy
1980	Not Free	Autocracy
1981	Not Free	Autocracy
1982	Not Free	Autocracy
1983	Not Free	Autocracy
1984	Not Free	Autocracy
1985	Not Free	Autocracy
1986	Not Free	Autocracy
1987	Not Free	Autocracy
1988	Not Free	Autocracy
1989	Imperfectly Free	Autocracy
1990	Imperfectly Free	Anocracy
1991	Imperfectly Free	Anocracy
1992	Imperfectly Free	Democracy
1993	Imperfectly Free	Democracy
1994	Imperfectly Free	Democracy
1995	Imperfectly Free	Democracy
1996	Imperfectly Free	Democracy
1997	Imperfectly Free	Democracy
1998	Imperfectly Free	Democracy
1999	Imperfectly Free	Democracy
2000	Imperfectly Free	Democracy
2001	Imperfectly Free	Democracy
2002	Imperfectly Free	Democracy
2003	Imperfectly Free	Democracy

Chronology

1948–1988: Not Free

Directly controlled by the Soviets until 1960, Mongolia was essentially a Soviet satellite state, hosting Soviet troops for most of the time until the collapse of the Soviet Union. Single party communist politics included the direct control of the media.[1]

1989–2012: Imperfectly Free

The collapse of the Soviet Union prompted an almost immediate shift in Mongolian politics toward democracy, led by independent and active media. Starting in 1988, the government began to tolerate some criticism in the media.[2] By 1990, the Soviet style politburo was forced to resign, political parties were legalized, and media freedom was for the most part respected.[3] A number of independent newspapers were launched, but the government maintained control over the distribution of newsprint, and some opposition media claimed low allocations of newsprint made it difficult them to publish as often as the newspaper owned by the government's party.[4]

Media Today

Media function relatively freely in a democratic environment that appears to be persistently unstable. Riots followed the 2008 election, and corruption appears to be rife. However, the influx of wealth from the development of Gobi Desert mineral resources has created something of a boom around the capital and minimized the extent of unrest. The vast rural areas have little access to media, and only minimal impact on the politics in the capital. Defamation is a criminal offense, and critical journalists are often targeted with punitive lawsuits, and threats; consequently, self-censorship is common.[5] In rural areas, the state-run radio is the dominant medium, and since 2005, there has been a shift toward a public broadcasting model for state-owned broadcast media.[6]

Notes

1. Morris Rossabi, *Modern Mongolia: From Khans to Commissars to Capitalists* (Berkeley and Los Angeles: University of California Press).

Year	Media	Government
2004	Imperfectly Free	Democracy
2005	Imperfectly Free	Democracy
2006	Imperfectly Free	Democracy
2007	Imperfectly Free	Democracy
2008	Imperfectly Free	Democracy
2009	Imperfectly Free	Democracy
2010	Imperfectly Free	Democracy
2011	Imperfectly Free	Democracy
2012	Imperfectly Free	Democracy

2. *Country Reports on Human Rights Practices for 1989* (Washington, DC: U.S. Department of State, 1990). Available at https://archive.org/details/country reportson1989unit.

3. *Country Reports on Human Rights Practices for 1990* (Washington, DC: U.S. Department of State, 1991). Available at https://archive.org/details/country reportson1990unit.

4. Ibid.

5. *Freedom of the Press* (Washington, DC: Freedom House, 2013). Available at http://www.freedom house.org/report/freedom-press/2013/mongolia.

6. Ibid.

Montenegro: 2006–2012

Montenegro Year by Year

Year	Media	Government
2006	Imperfectly Free	Democracy
2007	Imperfectly Free	Democracy
2008	Imperfectly Free	Democracy
2009	Imperfectly Free	Democracy
2010	Imperfectly Free	Democracy
2011	Imperfectly Free	Democracy
2012	Imperfectly Free	Democracy

MEDIA FREEDOM HISTORY IN A NUTSHELL

- Media are free, but face the challenges of a very small market, as well as some authoritarian legacies of communist Yugoslavia
- As of 2011, there were 4 paid-for daily newspapers with a total average circulation per issue of 62,000, as well as 38 radio stations, and 37 television stations; the only news agency, Mina News Agency, was privately owned (World Association of Newspaper's 2012 World Newspaper Trends)
- As of 2012, about 57 percent of Montenegrins had Internet access (International Telecommunication Union's 2012 ICT Indicators Database)

In Brief

Montenegro was the last of the former Yugoslav republics to split from Serbia. As a result of a referendum, it declared its independence and peacefully separated from Serbia in 2006.

Chronology

2006–2012: Imperfectly Free

Even before separation from Serbia, Montenegrin media were far freer than those of Serbia. They effectively enabled a political debate over the referendum of secession and have been consistently, if imperfectly, free since.

Media Today

Media face all the challenges of a very small national market. Those challenges make the media vulnerable to influence by political and economic elites but a commitment to media freedom appears to enjoy broad support across this small mountainous country.

Morocco: 1956–2012

Morocco Year by Year

Year	Media	Government
1956	Not Free	Anocracy
1957	Not Free	Anocracy
1958	Not Free	Anocracy
1959	Not Free	Anocracy
1960	Not Free	Anocracy
1961	Not Free	Anocracy
1962	Not Free	Anocracy
1963	Not Free	Anocracy
1964	Not Free	Anocracy
1965	Not Free	Autocracy
1966	Not Free	Autocracy
1967	Not Free	Autocracy
1968	Not Free	Autocracy
1969	Not Free	Autocracy
1970	Not Free	Autocracy
1971	Not Free	Autocracy
1972	Not Free	Autocracy
1973	Not Free	Autocracy
1974	Not Free	Autocracy
1975	Not Free	Autocracy
1976	Not Free	Autocracy
1977	Not Free	Autocracy
1978	Not Free	Autocracy
1979	Not Free	Autocracy

(Continued)

MEDIA FREEDOM HISTORY IN A NUTSHELL

- Media have always been diverse but restricted
- Media restrictions were eased enough to allow a brief period of media freedom in 2002, but were almost immediately re-imposed
- As of 2011, Morocco had 36 paid-for daily newspapers with an average circulation per issue of 340,000 (World Association of Newspapers' World Press Trends 2012)
- The government controls most broadcast media; however, satellite television is widely available
- As of 2012, about 55 percent of Moroccans had Internet access (International Telecommunication Union's 2012 ICT Indicators Database)

In Brief

While the domestic political history of Morocco has been eventful, media have remained diverse but heavily restricted.

Chronology

1957–2001: Not Free

With independence, Sultan Mohammed became king and carried forward many of the media restrictions and methods of control that the French had used. The intensity of the restrictions ranged from the use of libel statutes and other legal mechanisms to suppress criticism, to periods of martial law and severe criminal penalties imposed on journalists and publishers. However, the general method of indirect control remained the same.

2002: Imperfectly Free

The 1991 ceasefire that ended of the long running conflict over Western Sahara started a

(Continued)

Year	Media	Government
1980	Not Free	Autocracy
1981	Not Free	Autocracy
1982	Not Free	Autocracy
1983	Not Free	Autocracy
1984	Not Free	Autocracy
19;85	Not Free	Autocracy
1986	Not Free	Autocracy
1987	Not Free	Autocracy
1988	Not Free	Autocracy
1989	Not Free	Autocracy
1990	Not Free	Autocracy
1991	Not Free	Autocracy
1992	Not Free	Autocracy
1993	Not Free	Autocracy
1994	Not Free	Autocracy
1995	Not Free	Autocracy
1996	Not Free	Autocracy
1997	Not Free	Autocracy
1998	Not Free	Autocracy
1999	Not Free	Autocracy
2000	Not Free	Autocracy
2001	Not Free	Autocracy
2002	Imperfectly Free	Autocracy
2003	Not Free	Autocracy

Year	Media	Government
2004	Not Free	Autocracy
2005	Not Free	Autocracy
2006	Not Free	Autocracy
2007	Not Free	Autocracy
2008	Not Free	Autocracy
2009	Not Free	Autocracy
2010	Not Free	Autocracy
2011	Not Free	Autocracy
2012	Not Free	Autocracy

gradual process of democratization that led to the first election of an opposition-led government in 1998 and culminated in the relaxation of media restrictions in 2002. Specifically new legislation made it easier to start up newspapers and magazines and reduced the length of sentences for press crimes.[1]

2003–2012: Not Free

Media controls were restored when suicide bombers attacked several sites in Casablanca.

Media Today

Media remain diverse but restricted.

Note

1. *Freedom of the Press* (Washington, DC: Freedom House, 2003). Available at http://www.freedom house.org/report/freedom-press/2003/morocco.

Mozambique: 1975–2012

Mozambique Year by Year

Year	Media	Government
1975	Not Free	Autocracy
1976	Not Free	Autocracy
1977	Not Free	Autocracy
1978	Not Free	Autocracy
1979	Not Free	Autocracy
1980	Not Free	Autocracy
1981	Not Free	Autocracy
1982	Not Free	Autocracy
1983	Not Free	Autocracy
1984	Not Free	Autocracy
1985	Not Free	Autocracy
1986	Not Free	Autocracy
1987	Not Free	Autocracy
1988	Not Free	Autocracy
1989	Not Free	Autocracy
1990	Not Free	Autocracy
1991	Not Free	Autocracy
1992	Imperfectly Free	Autocracy
1993	Imperfectly Free	Autocracy
1994	Imperfectly Free	Anocracy
1995	Imperfectly Free	Anocracy
1996	Not Free	Anocracy
1997	Not Free	Anocracy
1998	Not Free	Anocracy

(Continued)

MEDIA FREEDOM HISTORY IN A NUTSHELL

- Upon independence, Mozambique became a one-party state and the government owned and controlled all media
- In the late 1970s, conflict with the RENAMO group escalated into civil war. which continued into the 1990s
- To end the conflict, the government transitioned to a multiparty system in the early 1990s, and media controls were relaxed
- As independent media emerged, the government stepped up restrictions, but by the end of the 1990s, media were functionally free
- As of 2012, there were three paid-for daily newspapers with a combined estimated print run of 30,000 copies (World Association of Newspaper's 2012 World Newspaper Trends)
- Although Mozambique has a mix of state-owned and private broadcast media, the state-run media still dominate (Freedom House's Report on Freedom of the Press 2013)
- As of 2012, about 5 percent of Mozambicans had Internet access (International Telecommunication Union's 2012 ICT Indicators Database)

In Brief

One of the poorest countries in the world, upon independence, Mozambique became a one-party state with controlled media. Shortly thereafter, the RENAMO rebel group mobilized with backing from the apartheid governments of Rhodesia and South Africa, and the conflict escalated into a prolonged civil war. In the early 1990s, in a move to end the conflict, the country transitioned to a multiparty system, and the government relaxed its hold on media. As independent media emerged, the government grew intolerant of media criticism, and by the mid-1990s, the

(Continued)

Year	Media	Government
1999	Imperfectly Free	Anocracy
2000	Imperfectly Free	Anocracy
2001	Imperfectly Free	Anocracy
2002	Imperfectly Free	Anocracy
2003	Imperfectly Free	Anocracy
2004	Imperfectly Free	Anocracy
2005	Imperfectly Free	Anocracy
2006	Imperfectly Free	Anocracy
2007	Imperfectly Free	Anocracy
2008	Imperfectly Free	Anocracy
2009	Imperfectly Free	Anocracy
2010	Imperfectly Free	Anocracy
2011	Imperfectly Free	Anocracy
2012	Imperfectly Free	Anocracy

government was using indirect means to restrict news media. Yet by the end of the 1990s, media ownership had diversified and news media were functionally free as they covered the 1999 elections campaign. Since then, media have remained imperfectly free.

Chronology

1976–1991: Not Free

Upon gaining independence from Portugal, Mozambique became a one-party state under Samora Machel. The Front for the Liberation of Mozambique (FRELIMO) party did not tolerate public criticism, and those who did so risked being sent to "reeducation" centers.[1] All media were government controlled.[2]

The governments of Rhodesia and South Africa backed the Mozambican National Resistance Movement (RENAMO) in retaliation for Mozambican support of militant groups fighting their apartheid governments, and civil war erupted in 1977. During this conflict, which lasted into the early 1990s, the South African government broadcast propaganda into Mozambique.[3] In 1986, Machel was killed in a plane crash, and

the FRELIMO Central Committee named Joaquim Chissano president. Chissano instituted a number of reforms, but in the late 1980s, all media remained government owned.

Chissano's government introduced a new constitution that went into effect at the end of 1990 and set the stage for the transition to a multiparty system as a means to end the conflict with RENAMO. Although the constitution had provisions for media freedom, it also gave government the right to restrict news media for national security and other reasons. And there was no immediate move to establish media freedom.[4] In 1991, a new press law specified that truth was not an adequate defense in cases of defamation of the President. Although there were some improvements in media freedom in 1991, almost all media remained government-owned and all advertising had to be approved by the Ministry of Information, which kept the media economically dependent on the government.[5]

1992–1995: Imperfectly Free

In 1992, FRELIMO and RENAMO signed a peace agreement, and conditions improved to the point that news media were functionally free, but only barely so. Most media remained government-owned with government-appointed directors, and there were reports that the government used its influence to bring at least one newspaper back in line following a series of critical reports.[6] In 1994, Mozambique held its first multiparty elections and Chissano won.

1996–1998: Not Free

In spite of difficult economic conditions, independent news media had emerged by the mid-1990s, including an independent news cooperative, Medicoop, and privately owned broadcast media, but most of these news outlets, and those that were government-owned, were not available beyond the capital.[7] Additionally, perhaps in response to the potential threat of independent news media, the government became less tolerant of media criticism and there were reports of journalists being harassed and attacked.[8,9] Thus by 1996, news media were restricted to the point that they were not free.

In the late 1990s, the media environment began to improve and journalists—even those working for state-owned media—began to report more independently and critically about the government.[10] Yet those who did so risked being threatened and harassed.[11]

1999–2012: Imperfectly Free

By 1999, media ownership had diversified to the point where there were more privately owned commercial outlets (about 36 percent) than state-owned media (about 34 percent), and most remaining media were owned by religious-oriented nonprofits (about 28 percent).[12] Still, only the government-owned broadcast media had national reach. During 1999, the media environment improved dramatically as news outlets covered the elections campaign. Media observers reported the state-owned media's coverage was far more balanced than it had been during 1994 campaign.[13] Yet there were still allegations that these media favored incumbent President Chissano, who did in fact win.[14]

Media Today

Mozambican media remain imperfectly free. Yet there are concerns that the tensions between FRELIMO and RENAMO (which flared up at the end of 2013) might lead to another civil war. Though the constitution provides for media freedom, government has the authority to constrain the media to protect national security, and libel and defamation remain criminal offenses, punishable with imprisonment and fines. Although Mozambique has independent print and broadcast media, the print media have limited readership and the state-owned broadcast media reach larger audiences than the private broadcast media.[15] Internet access remains extremely limited.

Notes

1. *Country Reports on Human Rights Practices for 1977* (Washington, DC: U.S. Department of State, 1978), 83. Available at http://babel.hathitrust.org/cgi/pt?id=mdp.39015078705632;view=1up;seq=4.
2. Ibid.
3. *World Press Freedom Review*, IPI Report (Zurich: International Press Institute, 1987).
4. *Country Reports on Human Rights Practices for 1990* (Washington, DC: U.S. Department of State, 1991). Available at http://www.archive.org/details/countryreportson1990unit.
5. *World Press Freedom Review*, IPI Report (Zurich: International Press Institute, 1991).
6. *Country Reports on Human Rights Practices for 1992* (Washington, DC: U.S. Department of State, 1993). Available at https://archive.org/details/countryreportson1992unit.
7. *World Press Freedom Review*, IPI Report (Vienna: International Press Institute, 1995).
8. *Country Reports on Human Rights Practices for 1996* (Washington, DC: U.S. Department of State, 1997). Available at http://babel.hathitrust.org/cgi/pt?id=mdp.39015078291708;view=1up;seq=1.
9. *World Press Freedom Review*, IPI Report (Vienna: International Press Institute, 1996).
10. *World Press Freedom Review*, IPI Report (Vienna: International Press Institute, 1998).
11. Ibid.
12. *Country Reports on Human Rights Practices for 1999* (Washington, DC: U.S. Department of State, 2000). Available at http://www.state.gov/www/global/human_rights/1999_hrp_report/mozambiq.html.
13. *World Press Freedom Review*, IPI Report (Vienna: International Press Institute, 1999).
14. Ibid.
15. *Freedom of the Press* (Washington, DC: Freedom House, 2013). Available at http://www.state.gov/www/global/human_rights/1999_hrp_report/mozambiq.html.

Myanmar (Burma): 1948–2012

Myanmar (Burma) Year by Year

Year	Media	Government
1948	Imperfectly Free	Democracy
1949	Imperfectly Free	Democracy
1950	Imperfectly Free	Democracy
1951	Imperfectly Free	Democracy
1952	Imperfectly Free	Democracy
1953	Imperfectly Free	Democracy
1954	Imperfectly Free	Democracy
1955	Imperfectly Free	Democracy
1956	Imperfectly Free	Democracy
1957	Imperfectly Free	Democracy
1958	Imperfectly Free	Democracy
1959	Imperfectly Free	Democracy
1960	Imperfectly Free	Democracy
1961	Imperfectly Free	Democracy
1962	Not Free	Autocracy
1963	Not Free	Autocracy
1964	Not Free	Autocracy
1965	Not Free	Autocracy
1966	Not Free	Autocracy
1967	Not Free	Autocracy
1968	Not Free	Autocracy
1969	Not Free	Autocracy
1970	Not Free	Autocracy
1971	Not Free	Autocracy
1972	Not Free	Autocracy

MEDIA FREEDOM HISTORY IN A NUTSHELL

- Despite a variety of insurgencies, the British legacy of democracy and media freedom held for over a decade
- A coup brought a military government to power in 1962, and media became strictly controlled
- In 2012, the government stopped prepublication censorship, but it remains to be seen whether recent dramatic changes in the political landscape will bring about lasting change in the media environment
- As of 2009, Myanmar had a total of six paid-for dailies with a total average circulation per issue of 420,000 (according to the World Association of Newspaper's 2010 World Newspaper Trends)
- All domestic broadcast media remain under government control, but foreign radio stations are accessible and are an important source of information
- As of 2012, about 1 percent of Burmese had Internet access (according to the International Telecommunication Union's 2012 ICT Indicators Database)

In Brief

Myanmar, also referred to as Burma, has essentially been locked in a state of civil war since the end of World War II. Even the early period, when the democratic institutions and media freedom bequeathed by the British remained in place and were moderately functional, the degree to which it could be said that the country was democratic or the media were free is debatable. The 1962 military coup brought an end to any pretense of democracy and media freedom. Since the 2010 elections Myanmar has undergone some dramatic changes and become more open politically. Whether these changes will be long term or lead to media freedom remains to be seen.

Year	Media	Government
1973	Not Free	Autocracy
1974	Not Free	Autocracy
1975	Not Free	Autocracy
1976	Not Free	Autocracy
1977	Not Free	Autocracy
1978	Not Free	Autocracy
1979	Not Free	Autocracy
1980	Not Free	Autocracy
1981	Not Free	Autocracy
1982	Not Free	Autocracy
1983	Not Free	Autocracy
1984	Not Free	Autocracy
1985	Not Free	Autocracy
1986	Not Free	Autocracy
1987	Not Free	Autocracy
1988	Not Free	Autocracy
1989	Not Free	Autocracy
1990	Not Free	Autocracy
1991	Not Free	Autocracy
1992	Not Free	Autocracy
1993	Not Free	Autocracy
1994	Not Free	Autocracy
1995	Not Free	Autocracy
1996	Not Free	Autocracy
1997	Not Free	Autocracy
1998	Not Free	Autocracy
1999	Not Free	Autocracy
2000	Not Free	Autocracy
2001	Not Free	Autocracy
2002	Not Free	Autocracy
2003	Not Free	Autocracy
2004	Not Free	Autocracy
2005	Not Free	Autocracy
2006	Not Free	Autocracy

Chronology

1949–1961: Imperfectly Free

The British colonial legacy included democratic institutions and free media, but a constant state of civil war against multiple insurgencies limited the extent to which that applied to significant portions of the country. Even in the capital, the pragmatics of fighting against insurgents limited freedoms to the point that the country could only barely be called free or democratic.

1962–2012: Not Free

A full-fledged military regime seized power through a coup in 1962, and all pretense of democracy or media freedom was eliminated. For five decades the military junta ruled Myanmar with an iron fist and media were either government owned or completely controlled.

In 2010, for the first time in two decades, the Myanmar held elections, and though there were allegations of fraud as the military-backed Union Solidarity and Development Party was victorious, these elections marked the beginning of a period of remarkable change and increasing political openness. Just days after the election, prodemocracy leader Aung San Suu Kyi was released from house arrest, and in 2012, she was elected to parliament. The government suddenly appeared willing to tolerate some media freedom.

Media Today

In the wake of the dramatic political changes in Myanmar, the prospects for media freedom remain unclear. Yet it appears that Myanmar is edging toward becoming imperfectly free. In 2012, the government halted prepublication censorship. Although most domestic broadcast media remained government run at the end of 2013, foreign broadcasts were accessible. Privately owned newspapers are permitted. In spite of these promising developments, there were some troubling signs in 2013. A journalist was sentenced to three months in prison after being convicted of defamation in connection with reporting on judicial corruption.[1] Also in 2013, the July issue of *Time Magazine*, which featured a Burmese Buddhist monk on the cover with the headline "The Face of Buddhist Terror," was banned.[2] Thus, Burmese journalists work in an

Year	Media	Government
2007	Not Free	Autocracy
2008	Not Free	Autocracy
2009	Not Free	Autocracy
2010	Not Free	Autocracy
2011	Not Free	Autocracy
2012	Not Free	Autocracy

environment that is precarious at best. The government has eased its controls on the Internet so that people can now access international news, but only about 1 percent of the population has Internet access.

Notes

1. *Journalist Gets Three-Month Jail Sentence for Her Reporting* (Paris, France: Reporters Without Borders, December 23, 2013). Available at http://en.rsf.org/burma-journalist-gets-three-month-jail-23-12-2013,45663.html.
2. *Time Magazine Censored Twice Over for Coverage Of Radical Buddhists* (Paris, France: Reporters Without Borders, June 26, 2013). Available at http://en.rsf.org/burma-time-magazine-censored-twice-over-26-06-2013,44860.html

Namibia: 1990–2012

Namibia Year by Year

Year	Media	Government
1990	Imperfectly Free	Democracy
1991	Imperfectly Free	Democracy
1992	Imperfectly Free	Democracy
1993	Imperfectly Free	Democracy
1994	Imperfectly Free	Democracy
1995	Imperfectly Free	Democracy
1996	Imperfectly Free	Democracy
1997	Imperfectly Free	Democracy
1998	Imperfectly Free	Democracy
1999	Imperfectly Free	Democracy
2000	Imperfectly Free	Democracy
2001	Imperfectly Free	Democracy
2002	Imperfectly Free	Democracy
2003	Imperfectly Free	Democracy
2004	Free	Democracy
2005	Free	Democracy
2006	Free	Democracy
2007	Free	Democracy
2008	Free	Democracy
2009	Imperfectly Free	Democracy
2010	Imperfectly Free	Democracy
2011	Imperfectly Free	Democracy
2012	Imperfectly Free	Democracy

MEDIA FREEDOM HISTORY IN A NUTSHELL

- Since independence, Namibian media have been functionally free, but at times government has been less tolerant of media criticism
- As of 2012, there were five daily national newspapers, as well as five independent weeklies, one biweekly and about a dozen monthly magazines (Freedom House's Report on Freedom of the Press 2013)
- Although the state-run broadcast media remain dominant, in 2012, there were more than twenty private and community radio stations (Freedom House's Report on Freedom of the Press 2013)
- As of 2012, about 13 percent of Namibians had Internet access (International Telecommunication Union's 2012 ICT Indicators Database)

In Brief

After three-quarters of a century under white South African rule, Namibia gained independence in 1990. Though it is a multiparty democracy, Namibia has been ruled by the South West Africa People's Organization (SWAPO) since independence. Namibian news media have always been functionally free, though at times, especially during elections, SWAPO has been less tolerant of media criticism.

Chronology

1990–2003: Imperfectly Free

Upon independence, Namibia became a multiparty democracy with a constitution that called for media freedom. Print media functioned freely and provided a wide range of views, though many had ties to political parties, including those in support of apartheid and those against it.[1] In late 1990, a grenade attack devastated the offices of *The Namibian*, a newspaper known for its anti-apartheid stance. The government-owned National Broadcasting Corporation controlled all broadcast media, but these stations did give the opposition some coverage.[2] By the mid-1990s, it was finances rather than government that limited media freedom. In particular, the company Die Republikein, which owned most of the country's newspapers and the countries only private printing presses, tended to favor the perspective of the white minority.[3] Also in the mid-1990s, privately owned radio stations began broadcasting.[4]

2004–2008: Free

By 2004, Namibia was known as "one of the media-friendliest countries" in Africa.[5] With a mix of private and state-run media, Namibia's media environment offered a wide range of perspectives, yet there were still allegations that the government influenced and interfered with the state-run broadcast media.[6]

2009–2012: Imperfectly Free

In 2009, conditions for news media deteriorated as the government established the Communication Regulatory Authority of Namibia to oversee the country's communications and media:

> The CRAN's other duties include setting up a licensing framework for both telecommunications and broadcasting, determining interconnection tariffs, allocating radio and telecommunication frequencies, promoting competition in the telecommunications industry, and establishing telecommunications data (such as Internet and telephone) interception centers.[7]

Additionally, during the 2009 elections campaign, the relationship between the SWAPO and the news media became increasingly contentious, to the point that a government official warned the editor of *The Namibian* that she would "be held responsible for the wrongdoings of her white ancestors if she was not more careful of the paper's reporting on SWAPO leaders."[8] Moreover, the National Broadcasting Corporation ceased airing call-in radio programs.[9]

Media Today

Namibian media remain imperfectly free. While the constitution provides for media freedom, it also allows government to limit these freedoms to preserve public morality, public order, and national security.[10] Namibia has a mix of privately owned and state-owned print and broadcast media. Though Internet content is unrestricted, the majority of Namibians do not have access. Moreover, the 2009 Communications Act remains in effect and gives government the authority to intercept text messages, emails, and phone calls.[11]

Notes

1. *World Press Freedom Review*, IPI Report (Zurich: International Press Institute, December 1990).
2. *Country Reports on Human Rights Practices for 1990* (Washington, DC: U.S. Department of State, 1991).
3. *World Press Freedom Review*, IPI Report (Vienna: International Press Institute, December 1993).
4. *Country Reports on Human Rights Practices for 1994* (Washington, DC: U.S. Department of State, 1995). Available at http://dosfan.lib.uic.edu/ERC/democracy/1994_hrp_report/94hrp_report_africa/Nambia.html.
5. *World Press Freedom Review*, IPI Report (Vienna: International Press Institute, 2005).
6. Ibid.
7. *Country Reports on Human Rights Practices for 2009* (Washington, DC: U.S. Department of State, 2010), sec. 2, para. 2. Available at http://www.state.gov/j/drl/rls/hrrpt/2009/af/135968.htm.
8. *Freedom of the Press* (Washington, DC: Freedom House, 2010), para. 7. Available at http://www.freedomhouse.org/report/freedom-press/2010/namibia.
9. Ibid.
10. *Freedom of the Press* (Washington, DC: Freedom House, 2013). Available at http://freedomhouse.org/report/freedom-press/2013/namibia.
11. Ibid.

Nauru: 1968–2012

Nauru Year by Year

Year	Media	Government
1968	Free	Democracy
1969	Free	Democracy
1970	Free	Democracy
1971	Free	Democracy
1972	Free	Democracy
1973	Free	Democracy
1974	Free	Democracy
1975	Free	Democracy
1976	Free	Democracy
1977	Free	Democracy
1978	Free	Democracy
1979	Free	Democracy
1980	Free	Democracy
1981	Free	Democracy
1982	Free	Democracy
1983	Free	Democracy
1984	Free	Democracy
1985	Free	Democracy
1986	Free	Democracy
1987	Free	Democracy
1988	Free	Democracy
1989	Free	Democracy
1990	Free	Democracy

(Continued)

MEDIA FREEDOM HISTORY IN A NUTSHELL

- Since gaining independence from Australia in 1968, Nauru has had limited but free media

- Nauru has government-owned radio and television as well as several independent weekly publications and foreign media are widely available (Freedom House's Report on Freedom of the World 2013)

- As of 2011, 54 percent of Nauruans had Internet access (according to the International Telecommunication Union's 2012 ICT Indicators Database)

In Brief

This South Pacific island is the smallest republic in the world. With only eight square miles and a population of 9,488, Nauru's media market is tiny but free.[1]

Chronology

1968–2012: Free

Since gaining independence from Australia in 1968, Nauru has had limited but free media.

Media Today

Nauruan media remain free. The government owns the radio and television stations, but there are several nondaily domestic newspapers and foreign media are available.[2]

(Continued)

Year	Media	Government
1991	Free	Democracy
1992	Free	Democracy
1993	Free	Democracy
1994	Free	Democracy
1995	Free	Democracy
1996	Free	Democracy
1997	Free	Democracy
1998	Free	Democracy
1999	Free	Democracy
2000	Free	Democracy
2001	Free	Democracy
2002	Free	Democracy
2003	Free	Democracy
2004	Free	Democracy

Year	Media	Government
2005	Free	Democracy
2006	Free	Democracy
2007	Free	Democracy
2008	Free	Democracy
2009	Free	Democracy
2010	Free	Democracy
2011	Free	Democracy
2012	Free	Democracy

Notes

1. *Nauru* (Washington, DC: CIA World Factbook, 2014). Available at https://www.cia.gov/library/publications/the-world-factbook/geos/nr.html.
2. *Freedom of the Press* (Washington, DC: Freedom House, 2013). Available at http://www.freedomhouse.org/report/freedom-world/2013/nauru-0.

Nepal: 1948–2012

Nepal Year by Year

Year	Media	Government
1948	No Media	Anocracy
1949	No Media	Anocracy
1950	No Media	Anocracy
1951	No Media	Autocracy
1952	No Media	Autocracy
1953	No Media	Autocracy
1954	No Media	Autocracy
1955	No Media	Autocracy
1956	No Media	Autocracy
1957	No Media	Anocracy
1958	No Media	Anocracy
1959	No Media	Anocracy
1960	Not Free	Autocracy
1961	Not Free	Autocracy
1962	Not Free	Autocracy
1963	Not Free	Autocracy
1964	Not Free	Autocracy
1965	Not Free	Autocracy
1966	Not Free	Autocracy
1967	Not Free	Autocracy
1968	Not Free	Autocracy
1969	Not Free	Autocracy
1970	Not Free	Autocracy
1971	Not Free	Autocracy
1972	Not Free	Autocracy
1973	Not Free	Autocracy
1974	Not Free	Autocracy

(Continued)

In Brief

An extreme of isolationism that is driven by both geography and philosophical tenets saw Nepal completely shut off from the world for significant periods of its history. By 1960, it was clear that the media that existed in Nepal were not free, although the government tactics for controlling media shifted from absolute control to less conspicuous, but equally effective restrictions. From 1980 to 1992, Nepal experienced a rare decade of functionally free media as reforms were implemented, but by 1993, unrest prompted the government to limit media freedom and these restrictions remained in place until 2006 when

(Continued)

Year	Media	Government
1975	Not Free	Autocracy
1976	Not Free	Autocracy
1977	Not Free	Autocracy
1978	Not Free	Autocracy
1979	Not Free	Autocracy
1980	Imperfectly Free	Autocracy
1981	Imperfectly Free	Anocracy
1982	Imperfectly Free	Anocracy
1983	Imperfectly Free	Anocracy
1984	Imperfectly Free	Anocracy
1985	Imperfectly Free	Anocracy
1986	Imperfectly Free	Anocracy
1987	Imperfectly Free	Anocracy
1988	Imperfectly Free	Anocracy
1989	Imperfectly Free	Anocracy
1990	Imperfectly Free	Anocracy
1991	Imperfectly Free	Anocracy
1992	Imperfectly Free	Anocracy
1993	Not Free	Anocracy
1994	Not Free	Anocracy
1995	Not Free	Anocracy
1996	Not Free	Anocracy
1997	Not Free	Anocracy
1998	Not Free	Anocracy
1999	Not Free	Democracy
2000	Not Free	Democracy
2001	Not Free	Democracy
2002	Not Free	Autocracy
2003	Not Free	Autocracy
2004	Not Free	Autocracy
2005	Not Free	Autocracy
2006	Imperfectly Free	Democracy
2007	Imperfectly Free	Democracy
2008	Imperfectly Free	Democracy
2009	Imperfectly Free	Democracy
2010	Imperfectly Free	Democracy
2011	Imperfectly Free	Democracy
2012	Imperfectly Free	Democracy

King Gyanendra was forced to reinstate Parliament and the new government reversed a number of laws that had restricted the media.

Chronology

1948–1959: No Media

Though the Rana dynasty lasted over a century, from 1846 to 1953, and Nepal joined the United Nations in 1955, it is difficult to code its media prior to 1960. In fact, it is difficult to say that Nepal had any media of significance prior to the emergence of democratic reform movements in the 1950s. These reform movements resulted in a new constitution and democratic elections in 1959. The relationship between government and the limited media that existed in and around the capital during this time is unclear.

1960–1979: Not Free

The elections of 1959 offered only the briefest and most limited flirtations with democracy and the reassertion of monarchical power, sometimes referred to as a royal coup, eliminated the fledgling democracy and made it clear that media would not be allowed to function outside strict parameters set by the government.

In 1968, as part of the effort to unify a country of isolated mountain villages, direct control of the media became part of a campaign to establish a single language for Nepal as a way of creating a more robust national identity. The one nation one language campaign faded after a few years, and the media returned to the previous status quo of indirect but still strict control.

Gradually increasing unrest led the monarchy to assert more control over the media in 1975, but this had little effect. By 1979, student unrest had grown to the point that King Birendra was forced to call for a referendum on the future of the government.

1980–1992: Imperfectly Free

While the option of a parliamentary democracy did not win majority support in the referendum, and the monarchy continued, reforms were implemented in response to the referendum. This included the appointment of a prime minister as well as a relaxing of restrictions on media and other liberalizing measures. Ironically, this marked the most liberal period the country would see for some time. In 1990, the establishment of a multiparty democracy and contested elections began the swift return to authoritarian rule.

1993–2005: Not Free

Unrest and strong support for the communist party, which advocated single party governance, led to repressive policies and a return of the dominance of the monarchy. By 1995, civil war had erupted as Maoists tried to bring down the monarchy. Then the monarchy faced threats from within when Crown Prince Dipendra gunned down a large part of the royal family and then killed himself in 2001, bringing Prince Gyanendra to the throne. In 2005, Gyanendra took total control, sacked the government, and declared a state of emergency. As Gyanendra engaged in a propaganda war with the Maoists, journalists and news outlets were attacked by both sides. Gyanendra prohibited radio stations from carrying news, and Maoists bombed the state-owned television station.[1] Journalists who tried to cover the growing unrest were often beaten, arrested, and detained, and journalists also faced threats and attacks from the Maoists.[2] In early 2006, the army seized control of a number of radio stations and police shut off the power of an independent radio station that had covered the Maoists.[3] Elections in early 2006 were little more than a charade, and by April, the monarchy was collapsing.

2006–2012: Imperfectly Free

Eventually, in April 2006, massive protests forced the king to reinstate Parliament and with it returned some semblance of media freedom.[4] The media, however, were limited and largely absent outside the capital. Maoists won a simple majority in the 2008 elections and have ruled over the republic of Nepal since. They appear to have abandoned the one-state party stance that was problematic in the early 1990s, but democracy and related freedoms appear to be quite fragile.

Media Today

Nepal suffers an extreme version of the small market issues plaguing many of the small countries around the world. With only 150 radio stations servicing a population of 30 million, it is safe to say that there is little media penetration of Nepali society. The fragility of democratic structures and norms creates a precarious situation for the media.

Notes

1. *World Press Freedom Review*, IPI Report (Vienna: International Press Institute, 2006).
2. Ibid.
3. Ibid.
4. Ibid.

Netherlands: 1948–2012

Netherlands Year by Year

Year	Media	Government
1948	Free	Democracy
1949	Free	Democracy
1950	Free	Democracy
1951	Free	Democracy
1952	Free	Democracy
1953	Free	Democracy
1954	Free	Democracy
1955	Free	Democracy
1956	Free	Democracy
1957	Free	Democracy
1958	Free	Democracy
1959	Free	Democracy
1960	Free	Democracy
1961	Free	Democracy
1962	Free	Democracy
1963	Free	Democracy
1964	Free	Democracy
1965	Free	Democracy
1966	Free	Democracy
1967	Free	Democracy
1968	Free	Democracy
1969	Free	Democracy
1970	Free	Democracy
1971	Free	Democracy
1972	Free	Democracy
1973	Free	Democracy
1974	Free	Democracy
1975	Free	Democracy

MEDIA FREEDOM HISTORY IN A NUTSHELL

- The Netherlands has provided a longstanding and robust example of a free media system
- As of 2011, there were thirty-two daily newspapers, twenty-nine were paid-for daily newspapers with a total average circulation per issue of 4,106,000 (World Association of Newspaper's 2012 World Newspaper Trends)
- Each province has its own public television and radio station, and there are also a number of privately owned broadcast media
- As of 2012, about 93 percent of the Dutch had Internet access (International Telecommunication Union's 2012 ICT Indicators Database)

In Brief

The Netherlands has a longstanding tradition of media freedom. It can claim one of the first newspapers and the first free media environment, because it was one of the primary sources of banned publications that smugglers transported into England and across Europe in the early years of the printing press.

Chronology

1948–2012: Free

From almost the moment it was liberated from Nazi occupation, The Netherlands reestablished its free media and has provided a model of information freedom. Freedom of the press and freedom of speech are guaranteed by the constitution, and these rights are respected in practice.[1]

Media Today

Media face the same challenges as the other established free media regimes around the world.

Year	Media	Government
1976	Free	Democracy
1977	Free	Democracy
1978	Free	Democracy
1979	Free	Democracy
1980	Free	Democracy
1981	Free	Democracy
1982	Free	Democracy
1983	Free	Democracy
1984	Free	Democracy
1985	Free	Democracy
1986	Free	Democracy
1987	Free	Democracy
1988	Free	Democracy
1989	Free	Democracy
1990	Free	Democracy
1991	Free	Democracy
1992	Free	Democracy
1993	Free	Democracy
1994	Free	Democracy

Year	Media	Government
1995	Free	Democracy
1996	Free	Democracy
1997	Free	Democracy
1998	Free	Democracy
1999	Free	Democracy
2000	Free	Democracy
2001	Free	Democracy
2002	Free	Democracy
2003	Free	Democracy
2004	Free	Democracy
2005	Free	Democracy
2006	Free	Democracy
2007	Free	Democracy
2008	Free	Democracy
2009	Free	Democracy
2010	Free	Democracy
2011	Free	Democracy
2012	Free	Democracy

Internet editions of the national newspapers struggle to maintain sufficient advertising and subscription revenue to remain viable. The significant Dutch-speaking population of Belgium creates a Dutch language market that should be large enough to sustain a diverse and commercial Dutch media. Newspapers remain popular, particularly with older citizens. Yet the Internet is gaining ground, especially with younger generations.[2] Nearly all Dutch enjoy Internet access.

Notes

1. *The Netherlands*, BBC Country Profiles (London, UK: British Broadcasting Company, 2013). Available at http://www.bbc.co.uk/news/world-europe-17741366.
2. *The Netherlands*, Media Landscape Reports (Maastricht, The Netherlands: European Journalism Centre, 2013. Available at http://ejc.net/media_landscapes/the-netherlands.

New Zealand: 1948–2012

New Zealand Year by Year

Year	Media	Government
1948	Free	Democracy
1949	Free	Democracy
1950	Free	Democracy
1951	Free	Democracy
1952	Free	Democracy
1953	Free	Democracy
1954	Free	Democracy
1955	Free	Democracy
1956	Free	Democracy
1957	Free	Democracy
1958	Free	Democracy
1959	Free	Democracy
1960	Free	Democracy
1961	Free	Democracy
1962	Free	Democracy
1963	Free	Democracy
1964	Free	Democracy
1965	Free	Democracy
1966	Free	Democracy
1967	Free	Democracy
1968	Free	Democracy
1969	Free	Democracy
1970	Free	Democracy
1971	Free	Democracy
1972	Free	Democracy
1973	Free	Democracy
1974	Free	Democracy
1975	Free	Democracy

MEDIA FREEDOM HISTORY IN A NUTSHELL

- A robust free media system that struggles with small market difficulties
- Consolidation of newspaper ownership into two groups and continuing financial struggles have raised concerns
- Once a paragon of public service broadcasting, deregulation and commercialization have marginalized this form of news
- Financial difficulties plague commercial news broadcasters, and the future of the market is unclear, but the commitment to liberal political values remains robust
- As of 2012, New Zealand had twenty-one total paid-for daily newspapers with an average circulation per issue of 596,370 (World Association's 2012 World Newspaper Trends)
- New Zealand has liberal state owned and private television broadcasters operating in the country
- As of 2012, nearly 90 percent of New Zealanders had Internet access (International Telecommunication Union's 2012 ICT Indicators Database)

In Brief

The most isolated of western democracies, New Zealand was one of the first countries in the world to give the vote to women and has a longstanding and robust commitment to liberal politics. A rugged, mountainous country, with only four million inhabitants spread across the equivalent of the entire west coast of the United States, it is only with the advent of satellite television that a diverse broadcast television market could be established. Even so, the small market is an extreme challenge to any commercial model.

Year	Media	Government
1976	Free	Democracy
1977	Free	Democracy
1978	Free	Democracy
1979	Free	Democracy
1980	Free	Democracy
1981	Free	Democracy
1982	Free	Democracy
1983	Free	Democracy
1984	Free	Democracy
1985	Free	Democracy
1986	Free	Democracy
1987	Free	Democracy
1988	Free	Democracy
1989	Free	Democracy
1990	Free	Democracy
1991	Free	Democracy
1992	Free	Democracy
1993	Free	Democracy
1994	Free	Democracy
1995	Free	Democracy
1996	Free	Democracy
1997	Free	Democracy
1998	Free	Democracy
1999	Free	Democracy
2000	Free	Democracy
2001	Free	Democracy
2002	Free	Democracy
2003	Free	Democracy
2004	Free	Democracy
2005	Free	Democracy

Year	Media	Government
2006	Free	Democracy
2007	Free	Democracy
2008	Free	Democracy
2009	Free	Democracy
2010	Free	Democracy
2011	Free	Democracy
2012	Free	Democracy

Chronology

1948–2012: Free

Print media have been free and independent since the very first days of western colonization, and broadcast media functioned on an independent public service model until the 1980s. A severe financial crisis in the 1980s, nearly resulting in national bankruptcy, coincided with technological advances to disrupt these longstanding traditions. Broadcast media were deregulated, and the state-owned television and radio stations were pushed toward a commercial model even as satellite television opened up new and affordable channels for broadcast.

Media Today

Small market challenges dominate the New Zealand media landscape. Even with massive consolidation in the ownership of the regional newspapers, print media struggle to be commercially viable and the primary independent commercial television news provider recently went into receivership. The country's commitment to liberal political values is fierce, and there is no real expectation that media freedom will be curtailed, but finding a viable model in the modern media environment will remain a challenge.

Nicaragua: 1948–2012

Nicaragua Year by Year

Year	Media	Government
1948	Not Free	Autocracy
1949	Not Free	Autocracy
1950	Not Free	Autocracy
1951	Not Free	Autocracy
1952	Not Free	Autocracy
1953	Not Free	Autocracy
1954	Not Free	Autocracy
1955	Not Free	Autocracy
1956	Not Free	Autocracy
1957	Not Free	Autocracy
1958	Not Free	Autocracy
1959	Not Free	Autocracy
1960	Not Free	Autocracy
1961	Not Free	Autocracy
1962	Not Free	Autocracy
1963	Not Free	Autocracy
1964	Not Free	Autocracy
1965	Not Free	Autocracy
1966	Not Free	Autocracy
1967	Not Free	Autocracy
1968	Not Free	Autocracy
1969	Not Free	Autocracy
1970	Not Free	Autocracy
1971	Not Free	Autocracy
1972	Not Free	Autocracy
1973	Not Free	Autocracy
1974	Not Free	Autocracy
1975	Not Free	Autocracy

MEDIA FREEDOM HISTORY IN A NUTSHELL

- Following decades of dictatorship and restricted media, Nicaragua experienced a brief period of media freedom after the Sandinista victory
- In 1982, as the new government faced increased threats from the U.S.-backed Contra rebels, it restricted media freedom
- As the conflict decreased and Nicaragua democratized in 1990, media became imperfectly free
- As of 2009, there were six paid-for daily newspapers with a total average circulation per issue of 170,000 (World Association of Newspaper's 2010 World Newspaper Trends)
- Nicaragua has more than one hundred radio stations; ownership of television is highly concentrated (Freedom House's Freedom of the Press 2013)
- As of 2012, about 14 percent of Nicaraguans had Internet access (International Telecommunication Union's 2012 ICT Indicators Database)

In Brief

One of the poorest countries in the Western Hemisphere (second only to Haiti), Nicaragua's media have long been controlled by the country's political elites, in particular the Chamorro and Sacasa families. Throughout the Somoza dictatorship news media were restricted, though the government was not always able to silence the critical voice of the Chamorro family's newspaper *La Prensa*. In the early 1980s, hopes that the Sandinista victory would bring about media freedom faded as the new government introduced a series of restrictions followed by a declaration of a state of emergency when it came under attack by the U.S.-backed Contras. In 1990, as the conflict decreased and Nicaragua democratized,

Year	Media	Government
1976	Not Free	Autocracy
1977	Not Free	Autocracy
1978	Not Free	Autocracy
1979	Not Free	Anocracy
1980	Imperfectly Free	Anocracy
1981	Imperfectly Free	Anocracy
1982	Not Free	Anocracy
1983	Not Free	Anocracy
1984	Not Free	Anocracy
1985	Not Free	Anocracy
1986	Not Free	Anocracy
1987	Not Free	Anocracy
1988	Not Free	Anocracy
1989	Not Free	Anocracy
1990	Imperfectly Free	Democracy
1991	Imperfectly Free	Democracy
1992	Imperfectly Free	Democracy
1993	Imperfectly Free	Democracy
1994	Imperfectly Free	Democracy
1995	Imperfectly Free	Democracy
1996	Imperfectly Free	Democracy
1997	Imperfectly Free	Democracy
1998	Imperfectly Free	Democracy
1999	Imperfectly Free	Democracy
2000	Imperfectly Free	Democracy
2001	Imperfectly Free	Democracy
2002	Imperfectly Free	Democracy
2003	Imperfectly Free	Democracy
2004	Imperfectly Free	Democracy
2005	Imperfectly Free	Democracy
2006	Imperfectly Free	Democracy
2007	Imperfectly Free	Democracy
2008	Imperfectly Free	Democracy
2009	Imperfectly Free	Democracy
2010	Imperfectly Free	Democracy
2011	Imperfectly Free	Democracy
2012	Imperfectly Free	Democracy

media became functionally free. The status of the media remains precarious because of the contentious relationship between the opposition press and President Ortega.

Chronology

1948–1979: Not Free

Dictator Anastasio "Tacho" Somoza Garcia had very little tolerance for critical news media. During his tenure (1937–1956), opposition papers were firebombed or closed down.[1] None of this changed when Somoza was killed because he was succeeded by his sons. The Somoza government controlled the country's only television station from 1955 until 1962, when it allowed Octavio Sacasa Sarria to start Nicaragua's first commercial station.[2] Neither Somoza nor his sons were able to completely silence *La Prensa*, the newspaper owned by the politically powerful Chamorro family:

> In the 1960s Pedro Chamorro Cardenal took control of the family newspaper, working to become the journalistic nuisance of the Somoza regimes. He particularly enraged Tachito Somoza, who responded by ordering that *La Prensa* submit to government censors. Whenever international human rights groups and media organizations, such as the Inter-American Press Association (IAPA), managed to pressure Somoza into relenting and sending the censors home, Chamorro would respond with a fresh series of broadsides. Somoza would then impose a new round of censorship. This cycle continued for years, and Chamorro received wide international recognition for his role as the opposition critic of the thin-skinned dictator.[3]

Chamorro was a longtime member of the IAPA and used his connections with the organization to draw international attention to the transgressions of the Somoza regime. In 1978, when Pedro Chamorro Cardenal was assassinated, his killing fueled anti-Somoza sentiment and helped mobilize support for the Sandinista National Liberation Front (FSLN). In 1979, Anastasio "Tachito" Somoza fled the country and the National Guard surrendered.

1980–1981: Imperfectly Free

Initially after the victory of the FSLN, media were functionally free, but the new Government of National Reconstruction soon took steps to restrain media with a series of decrees requiring prior censorship of stories deemed likely to threaten internal security.[4] "The scope of these decrees was broadened to include news on scarcities, labor and popular unrest, counter-revolutionary activities, armed attacks on the government and reporting on electioneering."[5] These decrees were used on several occasions to close down *La Prensa*. Although the FSLN had seized control over Nicaragua's television stations, there were a number of privately owned radio stations that provided independent news coverage.[6]

1982–1989: Not Free

In March 1982, as the U.S.-backed Contra rebels began attacking Nicaragua, the government declared a state of emergency and, initially, all broadcast news was prohibited and stations were required to carry announcements from the government.[7] Although these restrictions were soon lifted, they were replaced with prior censorship. In particular, *La Prensa* was persistently censored, and in 1986, the paper was closed down.[8]

In the late 1980s, the government reached a peace agreement with the Contras.

1990–2012: Imperfectly Free

In preparation for the 1990 elections, President Daniel Ortega allowed *La Prensa* to resume publishing. Before leaving office, Ortega repealed a number of laws restricting media freedom, which paved the way for the FSLN to maintain a media presence after Violeta Barrios de Chamorro, the widow of Pedro Chamorro, won the elections, becoming the first elected female head of state in the Americas.[9] Under President Chamorro, media were functionally free.[10] Yet in the mid and late 1990s, there were a number of reports of journalists and news outlets being attacked by former Contras, Sandinistas, and police. There were also several libel convictions.

In 2001, a law went into effect requiring all journalists to have credentials from the Nicaraguan Journalists Colegio.[11] In 2006, former President Daniel Ortega won the elections, and with his return to power, the media environment deteriorated, as news outlets and the rest of the country became polarized between those who supporting and those against Ortega and the FSLN. The Committee to Protect Journalists characterized the situation as a "media war."[12]

Media Today

Nicaraguan media remain free, though they are constrained by the contentious relationship between independent media and the Ortega administration. Journalists remain vulnerable to punitive lawsuits, because both libel and defamation remain criminal offenses. Because of poverty and illiteracy, radio remains the primary source of news for most of the population. Nicaragua has a mix of government-owned and private broadcast media, though most television stations are owned by two media groups, one controlled by President Ortega's family and one owned by Angel Gonzalez of Mexico.[13] Though the Chamorro family has long dominated the Nicaraguan newspaper market, its holdings decreased in 2011 when the country's second largest paper, *El Nuevo Diario*, came under new ownership.[14]

Notes

1. Rick J. Rockwell and Noreene Janus, *Media Power in Central America* (Urbana and Chicago: University of Illinois Press).
2. Ibid.
3. Ibid., 73.
4. *Country Reports on Human Rights Practices 1981* (Washington, DC: U.S. Department of State, 1982). Available at http://babel.hathitrust.org/cgi/pt?id=mdp.39015039359891;view=1up;seq=504.
5. Ibid., 488.
6. Ibid.
7. *Report of the Committee on Freedom of the Press and Information*, 1982 General Assembly (Miami, FL: Inter American Press Association, 1983).
8. Rockwell and Janus, *Media Power in Central America*.
9. Ibid.
10. *World Press Freedom Review*, IPI Report (Vienna: International Press Institute, December 1993).
11. *Mid-year Meeting: Nicaragua* (Miami, FL: Inter American Press Association, 2001). Available at http://www.sipiapa.org/en/asamblea/nicaragua-53/.
12. Carlos Lauria and Joel Simon, *Nicaragua Special Report: Daniel Ortega's Media War*. Available at http://cpj.org/reports/2009/07/daniel-ortegas-media-war.php#more.
13. *Freedom of the Press* (Washington, DC: Freedom House, 2013). Available at http://freedomhouse.org/report/freedom-press/2013/nicaragua.
14. Ibid.

Niger: 1961–2012

Niger Year by Year

Year	Media	Government
1961	Not Free	Autocracy
1962	Not Free	Autocracy
1963	Not Free	Autocracy
1964	Not Free	Autocracy
1965	Not Free	Autocracy
1966	Not Free	Autocracy
1967	Not Free	Autocracy
1968	Not Free	Autocracy
1969	Not Free	Autocracy
1970	Not Free	Autocracy
1971	Not Free	Autocracy
1972	Not Free	Autocracy
1973	Not Free	Autocracy
1974	Not Free	Autocracy
1975	Not Free	Autocracy
1976	Not Free	Autocracy
1977	Not Free	Autocracy
1978	Not Free	Autocracy
1979	Not Free	Autocracy
1980	Not Free	Autocracy
1981	Not Free	Autocracy
1982	Not Free	Autocracy
1983	Not Free	Autocracy
1984	Not Free	Autocracy

(Continued)

MEDIA FREEDOM HISTORY IN A NUTSHELL

- Ruled by dictators until 1989, Nigerien media were directly controlled
- Unrest and an inability to enforce restrictions on the media brought about a functionally free media system, which was part of the process that forced constitutional change in 1992
- Economic strife and coups have lead to significant swings between restricted and imperfectly free media
- Media are fragile, economically stressed, and vulnerable to government pressures
- Radio remains the most accessible medium
- Niger has a mix of state-run and independent print and broadcast media, including several dozen newspapers, three private and two government television stations, and a number of private radio stations in addition to the government station (Freedom House's Report on Freedom of the Press 2013)
- As of 2012, only 1 percent of Nigeriens had Internet access (International Telecommunication Union's 2012 ICT Indicators Database)

In Brief

Impoverished and frequently drought stricken, Niger has been fraught with political instability since gaining independence. Following nearly three decades of autocratic rule and controlled media, Nigerien media became imperfectly free as the country began to democratize, and the first independent newspaper began publishing in 1990. Since then, political instability, coups, and rebellion have led to continual shifts between imperfectly free and not free media. Since the 2010 coup and subsequent transition to democracy, media have been functionally free.

(Continued)

Year	Media	Government
1985	Not Free	Autocracy
1986	Not Free	Autocracy
1987	Not Free	Autocracy
1988	Not Free	Autocracy
1989	Not Free	Autocracy
1990	Imperfectly Free	Autocracy
1991	Imperfectly Free	In Transition
1992	Imperfectly Free	Democracy
1993	Imperfectly Free	Democracy
1994	Imperfectly Free	Democracy
1995	Imperfectly Free	Democracy
1996	Imperfectly Free	Autocracy
1997	Not Free	Autocracy
1998	Not Free	Autocracy
1999	Not Free	Anocracy
2000	Not Free	Anocracy
2001	Imperfectly Free	Anocracy
2002	Imperfectly Free	Anocracy
2003	Imperfectly Free	Anocracy
2004	Imperfectly Free	Democracy
2005	Imperfectly Free	Democracy
2006	Imperfectly Free	Democracy
2007	Not Free	Democracy
2008	Not Free	Democracy
2009	Not Free	Anocracy
2010	Imperfectly Free	Anocracy
2011	Imperfectly Free	Democracy
2012	Imperfectly Free	Democracy

Chronology

1961–1989: Not Free

After gaining independence from France in 1960, Niger was under the dictatorial rule of President Hamani Diori. Diori's presidency ended with a military coup, and military rule followed. Throughout these years, media were directly controlled.

1990–1996: Imperfectly Free

The new constitution adopted in 1989 included democratic political structures and press freedom, but it was a one-party system, and in practice, the government pressured the news media.[1] In 1990, Niger's first independent newspaper began publishing.[2] Also in the early 1990s, strikes and demonstrations exposed the government's inability to prevent the publication of opposition news and led to an effectively free but highly partisan and unprofessional media system. Continued unrest led to the legalization of opposition parties and a new constitution in 1992.

1997–2000: Not Free

A 1996 coup brought back military rule and a ban on all political parties. There were a number of reports of journalists being threatened, harassed, or attacked and news outlets being shut down.[3] Severe media restrictions were put in place, but direct control of the media was impossible.

2001–2006: Imperfectly Free

The 1999 constitution establishing a set of checks and balances between the legislature and executive was approved in a referendum. Elections followed, and a gradual easing of media restrictions shifted the balance back to an imperfectly free, highly partisan competitive system.

2007–2009: Not Free

Economic strife brought a return of strikes, and a Tuareg rebellion erupted in the north. The president suspended the constitution, and media restrictions were put in place. In particular, media were banned from covering the rebellion, and journalists who did so risked arrest and the closure of their news organizations.[4]

2010–2012: Imperfectly Free

A 2010 military coup restored media freedom, and its leaders promised a return to democratic government. As restrictions eased and the transitional government decriminalized media offenses, attacks and harassment of journalists became less frequent.[5]

Media Today

Democratic rule was restored in 2011, and media have remained functionally free. Yet financial strife and domestic unrest are a constant threat. In addition to a state-run daily newspaper, Niger has several dozen independent newspapers. Although Niger has a mix of private and state-run broadcast media, the state radio and television remain dominant.[6] Only about 1 percent of Nigeriens have Internet access.[7]

Notes

1. *Country Reports on Human Rights Practices for 1990* (Washington, DC: U.S. Department of State, 1991). Available at https://archive.org/details/countryreportson1990unit.

2. *World Press Freedom Review*, IPI Report (Vienna: International Press Institute, December 1996/January 1997).

3. Ibid.

4. *World Press Freedom Review*, IPI Report (Vienna: International Press Institute, 2007).

5. *Freedom of the Press* (Washington, DC: Freedom House, 2011). Available at http://www.freedomhouse.org/report/freedom-press/2011/niger.

6. *Freedom of the Press* (Washington, DC: Freedom House, 2013). Available at http://www.freedomhouse.org/report/freedom-press/2013/niger.

Nigeria: 1960–2012

Nigeria Year by Year

Year	Media	Government
1960	Imperfectly Free	Democracy
1961	Imperfectly Free	Democracy
1962	Imperfectly Free	Democracy
1963	Imperfectly Free	Democracy
1964	Imperfectly Free	Democracy
1965	Imperfectly Free	Democracy
1966	Imperfectly Free	Autocracy
1967	Imperfectly Free	Autocracy
1968	Imperfectly Free	Autocracy
1969	Imperfectly Free	Autocracy
1970	Imperfectly Free	Autocracy
1971	Imperfectly Free	Autocracy
1972	Imperfectly Free	Autocracy
1973	Imperfectly Free	Autocracy
1974	Imperfectly Free	Autocracy
1975	Imperfectly Free	Autocracy
1976	Imperfectly Free	Autocracy
1977	Imperfectly Free	Autocracy
1978	Imperfectly Free	Anocracy
1979	Not Free	Democracy
1980	Not Free	Democracy
1981	Not Free	Democracy
1982	Not Free	Democracy
1983	Not Free	Democracy
1984	Not Free	Autocracy

MEDIA FREEDOM HISTORY IN A NUTSHELL

- Since independence, Nigeria has experienced a number of coups and internal conflict, yet for nearly two decades following independence, media were functionally free

- The media environment deteriorated in the late 1970s and early 1980s, and media were not free again until 2002, when the availability of independent media increased to the point that media were once again able to function freely

- Radio is the most popular medium; though the government owns the only national radio and television networks, there are privately owned radio and television stations

- As of 2010, Nigeria had twenty-eight paid-for daily newspapers (World Association of Newspapers' World Press Trends 2011)

- As of 2012, about 33 percent of Nigerians had Internet access (International Telecommunication Union's 2012 ICT Indicators Database)

In Brief

Political instability and coups have contributed to a contentious media environment in Nigeria, yet independent news media have persisted in providing critical news coverage of government. For nearly two decades after independence, news media were imperfectly free. Although the 1979 elections brought a brief return of civilian rule to Nigeria, restrictions on news media increased to the point that media were not free. By 2002, the availability of independent print and broadcast media increased to the extent that media were again functionally free. Yet journalists remain vulnerable to threats, attacks, and punitive lawsuits.

Year	Media	Government
1985	Not Free	Autocracy
1986	Not Free	Autocracy
1987	Not Free	Autocracy
1988	Not Free	Autocracy
1989	Not Free	Anocracy
1990	Not Free	Anocracy
1991	Not Free	Anocracy
1992	Not Free	Anocracy
1993	Not Free	Autocracy
1994	Not Free	Autocracy
1995	Not Free	Autocracy
1996	Not Free	Autocracy
1997	Not Free	Autocracy
1998	Not Free	Anocracy
1999	Not Free	Anocracy
2000	Not Free	Anocracy
2001	Not Free	Anocracy
2002	Imperfectly Free	Anocracy
2003	Imperfectly Free	Anocracy
2004	Imperfectly Free	Anocracy
2005	Imperfectly Free	Anocracy
2006	Imperfectly Free	Anocracy
2007	Imperfectly Free	Anocracy
2008	Imperfectly Free	Anocracy
2009	Imperfectly Free	Anocracy
2010	Imperfectly Free	Anocracy
2011	Imperfectly Free	Anocracy
2012	Imperfectly Free	Anocracy

Chronology

1960–1978: Imperfectly Free

Shortly after Nigeria gained independence from Britain, media freedom came under question when the new Federal Minister of Information announced that he was prepared to discipline journalists who engaged in "destructive criticism" of the country.[1] He subsequently stated that he regretted his statement had been viewed as an attempt to stifle the news media.[2] Thus, the media were functionally free.

A coup in 1966 brought Nigeria under military control and political parties were banned, but media for the most part remained imperfectly free. Though the military government owned all broadcast media, there were two independent newspapers, and all media engaged in criticism of government policies.[3]

1979–2001: Not Free

The 1979 elections saw a return to civilian rule for Nigeria but increased restrictions on news media. The 1978 Nigerian Press Council Decree No. 31 required registration of all journalists, established a code of conduct, and imposed penalties on journalists who were not in compliance.[4] The government retained control over all broadcast media, but there were privately owned newspapers. Although there was no overt censorship, in 1981 the government temporarily shut down three opposition newspapers, and the editors were arrested on charges of sedition.[5] Though the charges were later dismissed, this was seen as an effort to muzzle the news media.[6]

Political instability and coups continued, and news media remained restricted, though some outlets continued to criticize government in spite of the potential repercussions. In 1993 when the military annulled the election results, news outlets that persisted in publishing those results faced vicious reprisals, offices were ransacked, and journalists were detained.[7] At the end of the year, General Sani Abacha seized control of the country, and in his first address to the country, emphasized that he would not tolerate criticism from the news media.[8] Following Abacha's death in 1998, Olusegun Obasanjo was elected president. Political turmoil, ethnic violence, and tribal conflict continued in the late 1990s and early 2000s, all contributing to a contentious relationship between media and government.

2002–2012: Imperfectly Free

By 2002, government interference had diminished and independent print and broadcast media were providing coverage that reflected diverse perspectives and included criticism of government. Although journalists remained vulnerable to criminal defamation charges and, in the northern states under Islamic law, harsh penalties for a range of media offenses, news outlets were for the most part functionally free.[9]

Media Today

The 1999 constitution guarantees media freedom, and the government for the most part respects this in practice. Yet Nigerian journalists are vulnerable to punitive lawsuits in connection with a range of press offenses, including defamation, sedition, and publication of false news.[10] Threats and attacks against journalists remain a problem. In 2012, two journalists were murdered, though it is not known if their killings were linked to their work.[11]

Notes

1. *The Toils of the Press*, IPI Report (Zurich: International Press Institute, February 1960), 8.

2. *The Toils of the Press*, IPI Report (Zurich: International Press Institute, March 1960).

3. *Country Reports on Human Rights Practices for 1977* (Washington, DC: U.S. Department of State, 1978). Available at http://babel.hathitrust.org/cgi/pt?id=mdp.39015078705632;view=1up;seq=3.

4. *Country Reports on Human Rights Practices for 1979* (Washington, DC: U.S. Department of State, 1980). Available at http://babel.hathitrust.org/cgi/pt?id=mdp.39015014188273;view=1up;seq=9.

5. *Country Reports on Human Rights Practices for 1981* (Washington, DC: U.S. Department of State, 1982). Available at http://babel.hathitrust.org/cgi/pt?id=mdp.39015039359891;view=1up;seq=5.

6. Ibid.

7. *World Press Freedom Review*, IPI Report (Vienna: International Press Institute, December 1993).

8. Ibid.

9. *Freedom of the Press* (Washington, DC: Freedom House, 2033). Available at http://www.freedomhouse.org/report/freedom-press/2003/nigeria.

10. Ibid.

11. Ibid.

North Korea: 1948–2012

North Korea Year by Year

Year	Media	Government
1948	Not Free	Autocracy
1949	Not Free	Autocracy
1950	Not Free	Autocracy
1951	Not Free	Autocracy
1952	Not Free	Autocracy
1953	Not Free	Autocracy
1954	Not Free	Autocracy
1955	Not Free	Autocracy
1956	Not Free	Autocracy
1957	Not Free	Autocracy
1958	Not Free	Autocracy
1959	Not Free	Autocracy
1960	Not Free	Autocracy
1961	Not Free	Autocracy
1962	Not Free	Autocracy
1963	Not Free	Autocracy
1964	Not Free	Autocracy
1965	Not Free	Autocracy
1966	Not Free	Autocracy
1967	Not Free	Autocracy
1968	Not Free	Autocracy
1969	Not Free	Autocracy
1970	Not Free	Autocracy
1971	Not Free	Autocracy

(Continued)

MEDIA FREEDOM HISTORY IN A NUTSHELL

- The last bastion of a Communist system of complete control of the media
- Media are treated as a propaganda machine for the hereditary dictatorship
- Access to foreign media is against the law, but there are some indications that such access has increased in the last two decades
- As of 2009, North Korea had a total of fifteen paid-for daily newspapers, with a total average circulation per issue of 4,500,000 (The World Association of Newspaper's 2010 World Newspaper Trends)
- There were four television stations in 2003; however, radio is the most widely used medium in the country with forty-one stations. Only news that favors the regime is permitted and all international news is jammed (The World Association of Newspaper's 2010 World Newspaper Trends)
- Internet access is limited to high ranking elites

In Brief

A hereditary dictatorship that exercises complete and absolute control over the media.

Chronology

1948–2012: Not Free

The government controls all aspects of the media. Yet there is some evidence that North Korean access to foreign media has increased since the late 1990s.[1] In particular, North Koreans are able to access radio news from outside the country using modified radios.[2] Of course, it is illegal to own these modified radios, and the punishments for doing do can be severe, but there are some indications that enforcement

(Continued)

Year	Media	Government
1972	Not Free	Autocracy
1973	Not Free	Autocracy
1974	Not Free	Autocracy
1975	Not Free	Autocracy
1976	Not Free	Autocracy
1977	Not Free	Autocracy
1978	Not Free	Autocracy
1979	Not Free	Autocracy
1980	Not Free	Autocracy
1981	Not Free	Autocracy
1982	Not Free	Autocracy
1983	Not Free	Autocracy
1984	Not Free	Autocracy
1985	Not Free	Autocracy
1986	Not Free	Autocracy
1987	Not Free	Autocracy
1988	Not Free	Autocracy
1989	Not Free	Autocracy
1990	Not Free	Autocracy
1991	Not Free	Autocracy
1992	Not Free	Autocracy
1993	Not Free	Autocracy
1994	Not Free	Autocracy
1995	Not Free	Autocracy
1996	Not Free	Autocracy
1997	Not Free	Autocracy
1998	Not Free	Autocracy
1999	Not Free	Autocracy

Year	Media	Government
2000	Not Free	Autocracy
2001	Not Free	Autocracy
2002	Not Free	Autocracy
2003	Not Free	Autocracy
2004	Not Free	Autocracy
2005	Not Free	Autocracy
2006	Not Free	Autocracy
2007	Not Free	Autocracy
2008	Not Free	Autocracy
2009	Not Free	Autocracy
2010	Not Free	Autocracy
2011	Not Free	Autocracy
2012	Not Free	Autocracy

of these policies has decreased somewhat in recent years.[3]

Media Today

Media remain a well-used propaganda arm of the government, and there is no expectation of change absent a fall of the dictatorship. It is against the law for citizens to access foreign media. Radios and televisions must be registered, and they are supposed to be limited to receiving domestic channels, which are state-controlled.[4] Most citizens do not have Internet access.

Notes

1. Nat Kretchun and Jane Kim, *A Quiet Opening: North Koreans in a Changing Media Environment* (Washington, DC: InterMedia, 2012).
2. Ibid.
3. Ibid.
4. Ibid.

Norway: 1948–2012

Norway Year by Year

Year	Media	Government
1948	Free	Democracy
1949	Free	Democracy
1950	Free	Democracy
1951	Free	Democracy
1952	Free	Democracy
1953	Free	Democracy
1954	Free	Democracy
1955	Free	Democracy
1956	Free	Democracy
1957	Free	Democracy
1958	Free	Democracy
1959	Free	Democracy
1960	Free	Democracy
1961	Free	Democracy
1962	Free	Democracy
1963	Free	Democracy
1964	Free	Democracy
1965	Free	Democracy
1966	Free	Democracy
1967	Free	Democracy
1968	Free	Democracy
1969	Free	Democracy
1970	Free	Democracy
1971	Free	Democracy
1972	Free	Democracy
1973	Free	Democracy
1974	Free	Democracy

(Continued)

**MEDIA FREEDOM HISTORY
IN A NUTSHELL**

- Norway is an exemplar of media freedom with a significant public service media component
- As of 2011, there were seventy-three paid-for daily newspapers, with a total average circulation per issue of 1,725,032 (World Association of Newspaper's 2012 World Newspaper Trends)
- Press freedom is guaranteed by the constitution and public radio and TV broadcast without official interference; Norway's public broadcaster (NRK) competes with private broadcasters for listeners and viewers (BBC Country Reports)
- As of 2012, about 95 percent of Norwegians had Internet access (International Telecommunication Union's 2012 ICT Indicators Database)

In Brief

Norway is an exemplar of a free media environment with a significant public service component. Freedom of expression is constitutionally guaranteed, and in 2004, the Norwegian Parliament amended the constitution to instruct the government to promote diversity in the media and public debate for the purpose of more protection of freedom of expression.[1]

Chronology

1948–2012: Free

For the most part, there have been no significant challenges to media freedom. In 1999, the European Court of Human Rights heard complaints concerning the country's defamation law. In two rulings, Norway was deemed to be in breach of the Convention for the Protection of Human Rights.[2] The European Court of Human

(Continued)

Year	Media	Government
1975	Free	Democracy
1976	Free	Democracy
1977	Free	Democracy
1978	Free	Democracy
1979	Free	Democracy
1980	Free	Democracy
1981	Free	Democracy
1982	Free	Democracy
1983	Free	Democracy
1984	Free	Democracy
1985	Free	Democracy
1986	Free	Democracy
1987	Free	Democracy
1988	Free	Democracy
1989	Free	Democracy
1990	Free	Democracy
1991	Free	Democracy
1992	Free	Democracy
1993	Free	Democracy
1994	Free	Democracy
1995	Free	Democracy
1996	Free	Democracy
1997	Free	Democracy
1998	Free	Democracy
1999	Free	Democracy
2000	Free	Democracy
2001	Free	Democracy
2002	Free	Democracy
2003	Free	Democracy
2004	Free	Democracy
2005	Free	Democracy
2006	Free	Democracy

Year	Media	Government
2007	Free	Democracy
2008	Free	Democracy
2009	Free	Democracy
2010	Free	Democracy
2011	Free	Democracy
2012	Free	Democracy

Rights also ruled in 2008 that Norway's ban on campaign advertisements was a violation of freedom of expression, but the government defended the policy on the grounds that it allows candidates equal access to news media regardless of their resources.[3]

Media Today

With only 4.8 million people, Norway faces the same economic and technological difficulties that challenge other small media markets. In particular, the worldwide financial decline in 2008 led to diminished advertising revenues.[4] A relatively high level of wealth and public support for government sponsorship of the media should see Norwegian media through in the near term, but the prevalence of English literacy across the population exposes Norwegian language commercial efforts to competition from foreign outlets.

Notes

1. *Norway*, Media Landscape Reports (Maastricht, The Netherlands: European Journalism Centre, 2013). Available at http://ejc.net/media_landscapes/norway.
2. *World Press Freedom Review*, IPI Report (Vienna: International Press Institute, 1999).
3. *Freedom of the Press* (Washington, DC: Freedom House, 2012). Available at http://www.freedomhouse.org/reports.z.
4. *Norway*, Media Landscape Reports.

Oman: 1948–2012

Oman Year by Year

Year	Media	Government
1948	Not Free	Autocracy
1949	Not Free	Autocracy
1950	Not Free	Autocracy
1951	Not Free	Autocracy
1952	Not Free	Autocracy
1953	Not Free	Autocracy
1954	Not Free	Autocracy
1955	Not Free	Autocracy
1956	Not Free	Autocracy
1957	Not Free	Autocracy
1958	Not Free	Autocracy
1959	Not Free	Autocracy
1960	Not Free	Autocracy
1961	Not Free	Autocracy
1962	Not Free	Autocracy
1963	Not Free	Autocracy
1964	Not Free	Autocracy
1965	Not Free	Autocracy
1966	Not Free	Autocracy
1967	Not Free	Autocracy
1968	Not Free	Autocracy
1969	Not Free	Autocracy
1970	Not Free	Autocracy

(Continued)

MEDIA FREEDOM HISTORY IN A NUTSHELL

- Oman has a long tradition of controlled media
- Omanis have limited access to external media sources
- As of 2012, Oman had ten daily newspapers, two state-run and eight private (World Association of Newspapers' World Press Trends 2012)
- The only domestic television station is state-run, but satellite television is available and provides access to foreign broadcasts including Al-Jazeera
- There is a mix of state-run and private radio stations
- The government limits access to Internet content; as of 2012, about 60 percent of Omanis had Internet access (International Telecommunication Union's 2012 ICT Indicators Database)

In Brief

The Sultanate of Oman has been ruled by the Al Bu Said family since 1749. This hereditary monarchy continues to control all media. The Internet and some external media sources are allowed in the country, but strict censorship is in place.

Chronology

1948–2012: Not Free

From 1932 until 1970, Sultan Said bin Taimur kept Oman isolated from the rest of the world. His regime directly controlled all media and access to external media was essentially forbidden. In 1970, the Sultan was ousted by his son Sultan Qaboos bin Said who began to liberalize and modernize the country, but these efforts had little effect on media. Oman's 1984 Press and Publication Law gave the government

(Continued)

Year	Media	Government
1971	Not Free	Autocracy
1972	Not Free	Autocracy
1973	Not Free	Autocracy
1974	Not Free	Autocracy
1975	Not Free	Autocracy
1976	Not Free	Autocracy
1977	Not Free	Autocracy
1978	Not Free	Autocracy
1979	Not Free	Autocracy
1980	Not Free	Autocracy
1981	Not Free	Autocracy
1982	Not Free	Autocracy
1983	Not Free	Autocracy
1984	Not Free	Autocracy
1985	Not Free	Autocracy
1986	Not Free	Autocracy
1987	Not Free	Autocracy
1988	Not Free	Autocracy
1989	Not Free	Autocracy
1990	Not Free	Autocracy
1991	Not Free	Autocracy
1992	Not Free	Autocracy
1993	Not Free	Autocracy
1994	Not Free	Autocracy
1995	Not Free	Autocracy
1996	Not Free	Autocracy
1997	Not Free	Autocracy
1998	Not Free	Autocracy
1999	Not Free	Autocracy
2000	Not Free	Autocracy
2001	Not Free	Autocracy
2002	Not Free	Autocracy

Year	Media	Government
2003	Not Free	Autocracy
2004	Not Free	Autocracy
2005	Not Free	Autocracy
2006	Not Free	Autocracy
2007	Not Free	Autocracy
2008	Not Free	Autocracy
2009	Not Free	Autocracy
2010	Not Free	Autocracy
2011	Not Free	Autocracy
2012	Not Free	Autocracy

the power to censor all domestic and foreign media.[1] The 1996 Basic Law guaranteed press freedom, but the government did not respect this in practice.[2]

In the early 2000s, though the government continued to restrict all privately owned newspapers and directly control all broadcast media, the growth of satellite TV and the Internet forced a modest shift in policies toward indirect control of media. However, media were still heavily censored and there was extensive filtering of Internet content. Yet citizens with satellite TV did gain access to Al-Jazeera and other foreign broadcasts.

Media Today

Slight concessions have been made in regard to the reality of external media penetration into the country, but strict censorship laws control media content. A number of media offenses remain criminalized and punishable with steep fines or imprisonment.[3]

Notes

1. *World Press Freedom Review*, IPI Report (Vienna: International Press Institute, December 1998).
2. Ibid.
3. *Freedom of the Press* (Washington, DC: Freedom House, 2013). Available at http://www.freedomhouse.org/report/freedom-press/2013/oman.

Pakistan: 1948–2012

Pakistan Year by Year

Year	Media	Government
1948	Not Free	Anocracy
1949	Not Free	Anocracy
1950	Not Free	Anocracy
1951	Not Free	Anocracy
1952	Not Free	Anocracy
1953	Not Free	Anocracy
1954	Not Free	Anocracy
1955	Not Free	Anocracy
1956	Not Free	Democracy
1957	Not Free	Democracy
1958	Not Free	Autocracy
1959	Not Free	Autocracy
1960	Not Free	Autocracy
1961	Not Free	Autocracy
1962	Not Free	Anocracy
1963	Not Free	Anocracy
1964	Not Free	Anocracy
1965	Not Free	Anocracy
1966	Not Free	Anocracy
1967	Not Free	Anocracy
1968	Not Free	Anocracy
1969	Not Free	Anocracy
1970	Not Free	Anocracy
1971	Not Free	Anocracy
1972	Not Free	Anocracy
1973	Not Free	Democracy
1974	Not Free	Democracy

(Continued)

MEDIA FREEDOM HISTORY IN A NUTSHELL

- Despite a façade of civil liberties and democratic institutions, civil war and military rule have kept media heavily restricted or controlled for most of Pakistan's history
- The late 1980s brought a period of substance to democratic institutions, including media freedom
- Media have weathered ongoing political upheavals better than other democratic elements of society, to the point of functioning freely under military rule in the early 2000s
- Media are currently restricted, but institutionally well situated to act freely if restrictions are lifted
- As of 2011, Pakistan had 330 total paid-for daily newspapers with an average circulation per issue of 6,100,000 (World Association of Newspaper's 2011 World Newspaper Trends)
- The government controls the dominant radio and television stations, but there are private radio stations and cable and satellite television
- As of 2012, about 10 percent of Pakistanis had Internet access (International Telecommunication Union's 2012 ICT Indicators Database)

In Brief

For the first four decades of Pakistan's existence, media were restricted. Since 1989, media have gone through periods of being imperfectly free and not free as the political landscape has shifted. Currently, media are restricted and Pakistan is one of the more dangerous countries in the world for journalists.

Chronology

1948–1988: Not Free

Terms like *Communal Violence* or *Sectarian Unrest* are often used to describe the events and situations that followed independence from

(Continued)

Year	Media	Government
1975	Not Free	Democracy
1976	Not Free	Democracy
1977	Not Free	Autocracy
1978	Not Free	Autocracy
1979	Not Free	Autocracy
1980	Not Free	Autocracy
1981	Not Free	Autocracy
1982	Not Free	Autocracy
1983	Not Free	Autocracy
1984	Not Free	Autocracy
1985	Not Free	Anocracy
1986	Not Free	Anocracy
1987	Not Free	Anocracy
1988	Not Free	Democracy
1989	Imperfectly Free	Democracy
1990	Imperfectly Free	Democracy
1991	Imperfectly Free	Democracy
1992	Imperfectly Free	Democracy
1993	Imperfectly Free	Democracy
1994	Imperfectly Free	Democracy
1995	Imperfectly Free	Democracy
1996	Not Free	Democracy
1997	Not Free	Democracy
1998	Not Free	Democracy
1999	Not Free	Autocracy
2000	Imperfectly Free	Autocracy
2001	Imperfectly Free	Autocracy
2002	Imperfectly Free	Anocracy
2003	Imperfectly Free	Anocracy
2004	Not Free	Anocracy
2005	Not Free	Anocracy
2006	Not Free	Anocracy
2007	Not Free	Anocracy
2008	Not Free	Anocracy
2009	Not Free	Anocracy
2010	Not Free	Democracy
2011	Not Free	Democracy
2012	Not Free	Democracy

British colonial rule and the separation of the Muslim-dominated East and West Pakistan from India. However, these are clearly euphemisms that cannot come close to representing the hundreds of thousands of people killed and the millions made homeless. Following independence, Pakistan was on a war footing, with media strictly controlled.

In 1957, the creation of a constitution that included freedom of speech as a fundamental right instigated a shift in the nature of the government's relationship with the media. While no real freedom of the press or the media was allowed, the nature of government control shifted to support the pretense of media freedom. That pretense was a necessary part of maintaining and strengthening diplomatic relationships with the west. Eventually, the growth of commercial media, particularly printed media, provided a mechanism for creating some freedoms.

In 1977, the façade of democratic institutions collapsed when a disputed election led to riots, followed by a military coup led by General Zia ul-Haq. Military rule under Zia, who became president in 1978, included media restrictions. In 1979, Zia formally imposed censorship of all newspapers and opposition newspapers were shut down.[1]

The run-up to the elections of 1986 included an easing of media controls and a reassertion of some independence by commercial print media. While they were not free from extreme governmental influence, they did function without direct government control, creating a foundation for free media. In 1988, General Zia was killed in a plane crash.

1989–1995: Imperfectly Free

The election of Benazir Bhutto as Prime Minister in November of 1988 was quickly followed by significant easing of government restrictions on the media. Bhutto's tenure was short lived. She was dismissed in 1990 following charges of corruption and incompetence but returned to office after winning reelection in 1993. During this tumultuous period, print media continued to function independently of national government control. However, regional variations became notable, particularly in relation to religious versus secular issues.

1996–1999: Not Free

In 1996, Bhutto was again forced from office by charges of corruption and incompetence and restrictions were placed on the media. There were also numerous reports of journalists being attacked and newspapers being raided and shut down.[2] Bhutto and her husband were convicted in April 1999, and by the end of the year, another coup returned Pakistan to military rule.

2000–2003: Imperfectly Free

Military rule brought an easing of restrictions on the media, and the period from 2000 to 2004 provides one of the better examples of how authoritarian leaders can use free media as a means of monitoring public demands and adjusting their rule to placate significant portions of the population. While General Pervez Musharraf's administration reduced the import duty imposed on newsprint and did away with quota on newsprint, it did little protect journalists and news outlets from attacks and harassment.[3]

2004–2012: Not Free

Renewed restrictions on the media were most easily explained as spillover from the Afghan war between the United States and the Taliban. However, tensions between Muslim fundamentalism in the outlying regions and the more secular and cosmopolitan urban areas were already evident. While media were not free, no effort was made to dismantle the institutions that would enable a free press to function if the political will emerged.

Media Today

Journalism remains a perilous profession in Pakistan. The Committee to Protect Journalists listed Pakistan as the deadliest country for journalists in 2010 and 2011, the third deadliest in 2012, and one of the deadliest in 2013.[4] Many journalists have been threatened or attacked, sometimes by militant groups and sometimes by security forces, intelligence, or military.[5] In addition to threats, the government has a number of legal mechanisms for punishing or restraining media including blasphemy laws, the Defamation Act, and the Official Secrets Act.[6]

In spite of these restrictions, Pakistan has about 350 daily newspapers. The government controls the only free broadcast media with national reach, and while there are private radio stations, they are prohibited from providing news coverage.[7] Foreign news services are available on cable and satellite television. About 10 percent of Pakistanis have Internet access.

Unlike the other states that border Afghanistan, which have benefitted from the wealth brought to them through cooperation with the U.S. military efforts, the Afghan war has been difficult for Pakistan. Pakistan's government has been put in a precarious position of trying to balance the strong domestic sympathies for the Taliban against the international politics that drive it to support the U.S. war effort. The winding down of the Afghan war may ease the internal tensions in the country and enhance the possibilities for media freedom.

Notes

1. *Country Reports on Human Rights Practices for 1979* (Washington, DC: US Department of State, 1980). Available at http://babel.hathitrust.org/cgi/pt?id=mdp.39015014188273.
2. *World Press Freedom Review*, IPI Report (Vienna: International Press Institute, December 1996/January 1997).
3. *World Press Freedom Review*, IPI Report (Vienna: International Press Institute, 2000).
4. *53 Journalists Killed in Pakistan since 1992/Motive Confirmed* (Committee to Protect Journalists, 2013). Available at http://cpj.org/killed/asia/pakistan.
5. Sumit Galhotra, *In Pakistan, Another Journalist Breaks His Silence* (Committee to Protect Journalists, December 9, 2013). Available at http://www.cpj.org/blog/2013/12/in-pakistan-another-journalist-breaks-his-silence.php.
6. *Freedom of the Press* (Washington, DC: Freedom House, 2013). Available at http://www.freedomhouse.org/report/freedom-press/2013/pakistan.
7. Ibid.

Palau: 1994–2012

Palau Year by Year

Year	Media	Government
1994	Imperfectly Free	Democracy
1995	Imperfectly Free	Democracy
1996	Imperfectly Free	Democracy
1997	Imperfectly Free	Democracy
1998	Imperfectly Free	Democracy
1999	Imperfectly Free	Democracy
2000	Imperfectly Free	Democracy
2001	Imperfectly Free	Democracy
2002	Imperfectly Free	Democracy
2003	Imperfectly Free	Democracy
2004	Imperfectly Free	Democracy
2005	Imperfectly Free	Democracy
2006	Imperfectly Free	Democracy
2007	Imperfectly Free	Democracy
2008	Imperfectly Free	Democracy
2009	Imperfectly Free	Democracy
2010	Imperfectly Free	Democracy
2011	Imperfectly Free	Democracy
2012	Imperfectly Free	Democracy

MEDIA FREEDOM HISTORY IN A NUTSHELL

- Although Palauan media are limited due to the small population, they are functionally free
- Palau has three independent weekly newspapers, one government-owned radio station, and several private radio stations; although there are no domestic television stations, cable TV is widely available
- No estimates were available regarding Internet penetration, but in 2012, Palau did have four Internet hosts

of about 21,108,[1] it is a small media market. Thus media are limited but functionally free.

Chronology

1994–2012: Imperfectly Free

While the government respects media freedom, media are limited but functionally free.

Media Today

Palauan media remain limited but functionally free. There are three independent weekly newspapers, one government-owned radio station, and several private radio stations.[2] Although there is no terrestrial television, many residents have access to cable television.

In Brief

Palau consists of more than 300 islands totaling 188 square miles in the Western Pacific Ocean. After World War II, the United States administered Palau as a UN Trust Territory. In 1994, Palau gained full independence after reaching an agreement with the United States, which gives Palau financial assistance and the United States the responsibility of defending Palau and the right to maintain military bases there. With a population

Notes

1. *Palau* (Washington, DC: CIA World Factbook, 2013). Available at https://www.cia.gov/library/publications/the-world-factbook/geos/ps.html.
2. *Palau*, BBC Country Profiles (London, UK: British Broadcasting Company, 2012). Available at http://www.bbc.co.uk/news/world-middle-east-15446662.

Panama: 1948–2012

Panama Year by Year

Year	Media	Government
1948	Imperfectly Free	Anocracy
1949	Imperfectly Free	Anocracy
1950	Imperfectly Free	Anocracy
1951	Imperfectly Free	Anocracy
1952	Imperfectly Free	Anocracy
1953	Imperfectly Free	Anocracy
1954	Imperfectly Free	Anocracy
1955	Imperfectly Free	Anocracy
1956	Imperfectly Free	Anocracy
1957	Imperfectly Free	Anocracy
1958	Imperfectly Free	Anocracy
1959	Imperfectly Free	Anocracy
1960	Imperfectly Free	Anocracy
1961	Imperfectly Free	Anocracy
1962	Imperfectly Free	Anocracy
1963	Imperfectly Free	Anocracy
1964	Imperfectly Free	Anocracy
1965	Imperfectly Free	Anocracy
1966	Imperfectly Free	Anocracy
1967	Imperfectly Free	Anocracy
1968	Imperfectly Free	Autocracy
1969	Not Free	Autocracy
1970	Not Free	Autocracy
1971	Not Free	Autocracy

(Continued)

MEDIA FREEDOM HISTORY IN A NUTSHELL

- In the 1940s, 1950s, and 1960s, Panamanian media were functionally free and dominated by the oligarchy known as the Twenty Families
- In 1968, General Omar Torrijos seized control of the country and restricted all news media
- Following the U.S. invasion of Panama and the ouster of General Noriega, media freedom was restored in the early 1990s
- As of 2012, there were at least five paid-for daily newspapers (Freedom House's Report on Freedom of the Press 2013)
- With the exception of one state-owned television network and one radio station, all media outlets in the country are privately owned, including more than one hundred radio stations and many national television networks (Freedom House's Report on Freedom of the Press 2013)
- As of 2012, about 45 percent of Panamanians had Internet access (International Telecommunication Union's 2012 ICT Indicators Database)

In Brief

Panama's history has to a large degree been shaped by the strategic importance of its location, between the continents of North and South America and the Pacific and Atlantic Oceans. Consequently, the United States has maintained a special interest in Panama's politics, which in turn has influenced the relationship between the Panamanian media and politics. Traditionally, media in Panama have been partisan and controlled by the oligarchy known as the *Twenty Families*. For most of the 1940s, 1950s, and 1960s media were functionally free. Following the 1968 coup, dictator Omar Torrijos seized control of news media, and media freedom did not return until the U.S. troops ousted General Manuel

(Continued)

Year	Media	Government
1972	Not Free	Autocracy
1973	Not Free	Autocracy
1974	Not Free	Autocracy
1975	Not Free	Autocracy
1976	Not Free	Autocracy
1977	Not Free	Autocracy
1978	Not Free	Autocracy
1979	Not Free	Autocracy
1980	Not Free	Autocracy
1981	Not Free	Autocracy
1982	Not Free	Anocracy
1983	Not Free	Anocracy
1984	Not Free	Autocracy
1985	Not Free	Autocracy
1986	Not Free	Autocracy
1987	Not Free	Autocracy
1988	Not Free	Autocracy
1989	Not Free	Democracy
1990	Imperfectly Free	Democracy
1991	Imperfectly Free	Democracy
1992	Imperfectly Free	Democracy
1993	Imperfectly Free	Democracy
1994	Imperfectly Free	Democracy
1995	Imperfectly Free	Democracy
1996	Imperfectly Free	Democracy
1997	Imperfectly Free	Democracy
1998	Imperfectly Free	Democracy
1999	Imperfectly Free	Democracy
2000	Imperfectly Free	Democracy
2001	Imperfectly Free	Democracy
2002	Imperfectly Free	Democracy
2003	Imperfectly Free	Democracy

Year	Media	Government
2004	Imperfectly Free	Democracy
2005	Imperfectly Free	Democracy
2006	Imperfectly Free	Democracy
2007	Imperfectly Free	Democracy
2008	Imperfectly Free	Democracy
2009	Imperfectly Free	Democracy
2010	Imperfectly Free	Democracy
2011	Imperfectly Free	Democracy
2012	Imperfectly Free	Democracy

Noriega. Since 1990, Panamanian media have been functionally free.

Chronology

1948–1968: Imperfectly Free

Most media were owned by competing and powerful political elites and were therefore functionally free, but also targeted by their owners' political opponents. In the early 1940s, former President Harmodia Arias used his newspapers to back his brother Arnulfo Arias, who was elected President in 1940 and reelected in 1948 and then deposed.[1] Thus, members of the Arias family were major players in both media and politics. Throughout the 1940s, 1950s, and 1960s, there are reports of journalists and news outlets being attacked, but generally news media were able to function freely according to reports from the Inter American Press Association and Latin American area experts.[2]

In 1968, Arnulfo Arias was again elected president only to be ousted within days of taking office in a military coup led by General Omar Torrijos Herrera.

1969–1989: Not Free

After taking control of the country in October 1968, General Torrijos and the military took steps to control the media, first taking over the Arias family's newspapers and closing down two radio stations owned by associates of Arnulfo Arias, and then establishing media censors to control all media.[3]

During Torrijos's rule, a number of journalists were imprisoned, including Leopoldo Aragón, who was tortured for a year before he was deported to Sweden.[4] In 1977, Aragón set himself on fire in front of the U.S. Embassy in Sweden to protest the signing of the Panama Canal Treaty. During the negotiations with the United States over the canal, Torrijos eased media controls somewhat. Yet in 1978, a new law mandating that all journalists obtain licenses was seen as a sign that media would remain restricted.[5]

In 1979, a group of Panamanians seeking to establish a high-quality independent newspaper asked the Inter American Press Association for "moral support," and in 1980, *La Prensa* began publishing.[6] In 1981, Torrijos was killed in a plane crash, and in 1983 General Manuel Noriega became head of the National Guard and the new leader of Panama. Though media were not free, there were journalists and news outlets that persisted in criticizing government, in particular *La Prensa*.[7] Consequently, journalists working for *La Prensa* were harassed and attacked, and in 1987, the government imposed strict censorship over all media.[8] In 1988, threatened by U.S. charges of drug smuggling and an attempted coup, Noriega declared a state of emergency, opposition newspapers were banned, and a number of radio stations were closed down.[9] In 1989, U.S. troops invaded Panama and ousted Noriega.

1990–2012: Imperfectly Free

In 1990, independent news outlets closed by Noriega's regime began to reemerge.[10] The restoration of media freedom was underway, but not immediate because many of the previous regime's laws restricting news outlets remained in place during the early 1990s.[11]

By 2010, Panama had a vibrant and independent news media, and although violence against journalists was rare, defamation laws remained in place.[12]

Media Today

Panamanian media remain imperfectly free. Though there is a wide range of privately owned news media, they are subject to pressures that sometimes encourage self-censorship. Though violence against journalists has been rare in recent years, in 2012, there was an increase in attacks on journalists.[13] The relationship between news media and President Ricardo Martinelli has become quite contentious, with critical journalists often facing retaliation in the form of defamation charges.[14]

Though Internet content is not restricted, the government has shown a willingness to limit access to new media. In February 2012, the Public Utilities Authority shut down mobile phone and Internet access in the provinces of Veraguas and Chiriquí for five days during protests by the Ngobe Bugle indigenous group.[15]

Notes

1. Rick J. Rockwell and Noreene Janus, *Media Power in Central America* (Urbana and Chicago: University of Illinois Press).
2. This is based on surveys conducted by Russell Fitzgibbon and Kenneth Johnson and presented in this study: Kim Quaile Hill and Patricia A. Hurley, "Freedom of the Press in Latin America: A Thirty-Year Survey," *Latin American Research Review*, 15 no. 2 (1980): 212–18.
3. Rockwell Janus, *Media Power in Central America*.
4. *Report of the Committee on Freedom of the Press and Information*, 1977 General Assembly (Miami, FL: Inter American Press Association, 1978).
5. *Report of the Committee on Freedom of the Press and Information*, 1978 General Assembly (Miami, FL: Inter American Press Association, 1979).
6. *Report of the Committee on Freedom of the Press and Information*, 1979 General Assembly (Miami, FL: Inter American Press Association, 1980), 6-a.
7. Sandra W. Meditz and Dennis M. Hanratty, *Panama: A Country Study* (Washington, DC: Library of Congress Federal Research Division, 1987). Available at http://lcweb2.loc.gov/frd/cs/cshome.html.
8. Ibid.
9. *World Press Freedom Review*, IPI Report (Zurich: International Press Institute, December 1989).
10. *World Press Freedom Review*, IPI Report (Zurich: International Press Institute, December 1990).
11. *Country Reports on Human Rights Practices for 1991* (Washington, DC: U.S. Department of State, 1992). Available at https://archive.org/stream/country reportson1991unit/countryreportson1991unit_djvu.txt.
12. *World Press Freedom Review: Focus on the Americas*, IPI Report (Vienna: International Press Institute, 2010).
13. *Freedom of the Press* (Washington, DC: Freedom House, 2013). Available at http://freedomhouse .org/report/freedom-press/2013/panama.
14. Ibid.
15. Ibid.

Papua New Guinea: 1975–2012

Papua New Guinea Year by Year

Year	Media	Government
1975	Free	Anocracy
1976	Free	Anocracy
1977	Free	Anocracy
1978	Free	Anocracy
1979	Free	Anocracy
1980	Free	Anocracy
1981	Free	Anocracy
1982	Free	Anocracy
1983	Free	Anocracy
1984	Free	Anocracy
1985	Free	Anocracy
1986	Free	Anocracy
1987	Free	Anocracy
1988	Free	Anocracy
1989	Free	Anocracy
1990	Free	Anocracy
1991	Free	Anocracy
1992	Free	Anocracy
1993	Free	Anocracy
1994	Free	Anocracy
1995	Free	Anocracy
1996	Free	Anocracy
1997	Free	Anocracy
1998	Free	Anocracy
1999	Free	Anocracy

MEDIA FREEDOM HISTORY IN A NUTSHELL

- Heavily influenced by Australia, media are extremely limited but free
- Papua New Guinea has two paid-for daily newspapers with a total average circulation of 53,000 (World Association of Newspaper's 2010 World Newspaper Trends)
- Because of low literacy rates, radio is the most important medium; in addition to the public radio network, some commercial stations are available
- Public and commercial television are available only in the provincial capitals
- As of 2012, about 2 percent of Papua New Guineans had Internet access (according to the International Telecommunication Union's 2012 ICT Indicators Database)

In Brief

Papua New Guinea has very little media. Outside the national or provincial capitals, media, or any substantive flows of information from the outside world, are simply unavailable. With terrain so rugged that the majority of the country's population was not even known to exist until spotted by aerial surveys in the 1950s, it remains a land of extremely isolated villages.

Chronology

1975–2012: Free

Although Papua New Guinean law provided for media freedom, there was very little media to speak of in the 1970s. The government owned the only radio station, which did at times include news coverage that was unflattering to the government.[1] Broadcasts from Australian radio stations were also accessible.

Year	Media	Government
2000	Free	Anocracy
2001	Free	Anocracy
2002	Free	Anocracy
2003	Free	Anocracy
2004	Free	Anocracy
2005	Free	Anocracy
2006	Free	Anocracy
2007	Free	Anocracy
2008	Free	Anocracy
2009	Free	Anocracy
2010	Free	Anocracy
2011	Free	Anocracy
2012	Free	Anocracy

Australia exerts a substantial influence over its former territorial holding. Media freedom is supported by Australia and accepted as part of the governance of the country, but that has little if any meaning outside the small capital cities.

Media Today

Media are limited but free, and there seems little evidence of significant change in that situation. In addition to public radio, Papua New Guinea has several commercial networks. There are some concerns that the independence of one of the two daily newspapers is compromised by its connection to the timber industry.[4] State-run and commercial television stations are available to limited parts of the country.

Notes

1. *Country Reports on Human Rights Practices for 1979* (Washington, DC: U.S. Department of State, 1980). Available at http://babel.hathitrust.org/cgi/pt?id=mdp.39015014188273;view=1up;seq=9.
2. *Country Reports on Human Rights Practices for 1994* (Washington, DC: U.S. Department of State, 1995). Available at http://dosfan.lib.uic.edu/ERC/democracy/1994_hrp_report/94hrp_report_eap/PapuaNewGuinea.html.
3. Ibid.
4. *Freedom of the Press* (Washington, DC: Freedom House, 2013). Available at http://www.freedomhouse.org/report/freedom-press/2013/papua-new-guinea.

In the late 1980s, a secessionist movement in Bougainville became violent, and as the conflict continued in the 1990s, the government limited journalists' access to that region.[2]

By the 1990s, Papua New Guinea had two privately owned daily newspapers—one of which was owned by a company connected to the timber industry.[3]

Paraguay: 1948–2012

Paraguay Year by Year

Year	Media	Government
1948	Not Free	Anocracy
1949	Not Free	Anocracy
1950	Not Free	Anocracy
1951	Not Free	Anocracy
1952	Not Free	Anocracy
1953	Not Free	Anocracy
1954	Not Free	Autocracy
1955	Not Free	Autocracy
1956	Not Free	Autocracy
1957	Not Free	Autocracy
1958	Not Free	Autocracy
1959	Not Free	Autocracy
1960	Not Free	Autocracy
1961	Not Free	Autocracy
1962	Not Free	Autocracy
1963	Not Free	Autocracy
1964	Not Free	Autocracy
1965	Not Free	Autocracy
1966	Not Free	Autocracy
1967	Not Free	Autocracy
1968	Not Free	Autocracy
1969	Not Free	Autocracy
1970	Not Free	Autocracy
1971	Not Free	Autocracy
1972	Not Free	Autocracy
1973	Not Free	Autocracy
1974	Not Free	Autocracy
1975	Not Free	Autocracy

> ### MEDIA FREEDOM HISTORY IN A NUTSHELL
>
> - With the exception of the 1990s and the first decade of the 2000s, news media have been restricted
> - As of 2009, Paraguay had six total paid-for daily newspapers with an average circulation per issue of 115,000, more than seventy radio stations and four television stations (World Association of Newspaper's 2010 World Newspaper Trends).
> - As of 2012, about 27 percent of Paraguayans had Internet access (International Telecommunication Union's 2012 ICT Indicators Database).

In Brief

For much of Paraguay's recent history, news media have been restricted. With the end of the Stroessner dictatorship, journalists became functionally free in the 1990s. In recent years however, media freedom has been compromised by punitive lawsuits from government officials and threats from organized crime in the border regions.

Chronology

1948–1989: Not Free

At the end of World War II, Paraguay plunged into civil war and civil liberties, including media freedom, were suspended. In 1954, General Alfredo Stroessner assumed the presidency. During these years, there was almost no opposition press, the official press served as a megaphone for the government and the commercial press and broadcast media were restricted.[1] Moreover, the Post Office confiscated foreign newspapers if they included nonofficial versions of events in Paraguay.[2]

Year	Media	Government
1976	Not Free	Autocracy
1977	Not Free	Autocracy
1978	Not Free	Autocracy
1979	Not Free	Autocracy
1980	Not Free	Autocracy
1981	Not Free	Autocracy
1982	Not Free	Autocracy
1983	Not Free	Autocracy
1984	Not Free	Autocracy
1985	Not Free	Autocracy
1986	Not Free	Autocracy
1987	Not Free	Autocracy
1988	Not Free	Autocracy
1989	Not Free	Anocracy
1990	Imperfectly Free	Anocracy
1991	Imperfectly Free	Anocracy
1992	Imperfectly Free	Democracy
1993	Imperfectly Free	Democracy
1994	Imperfectly Free	Democracy
1995	Imperfectly Free	Democracy
1996	Imperfectly Free	Democracy
1997	Imperfectly Free	Democracy
1998	Imperfectly Free	Democracy
1999	Imperfectly Free	Democracy
2000	Imperfectly Free	Democracy
2001	Imperfectly Free	Democracy
2002	Imperfectly Free	Democracy
2003	Imperfectly Free	Democracy
2004	Imperfectly Free	Democracy
2005	Imperfectly Free	Democracy
2006	Imperfectly Free	Democracy
2007	Imperfectly Free	Democracy
2008	Imperfectly Free	Democracy
2009	Imperfectly Free	Democracy
2010	Imperfectly Free	Democracy
2011	Imperfectly Free	Democracy
2012	Not Free	Democracy

1990–2011: Imperfectly Free

In 1989, the Stroessner dictatorship ended in a violent military coup. His successor, General Andrés Rodríguez, pledged to restore freedom of expression, including freedom of the press. Opposition media that had been closed down for years began to reopen.[3] Although news media functioned freely, attacks on journalists were a problem. Thus, as the country democratized, media became imperfectly free.

2012: Not Free

Conditions for news media continued to deteriorate and, in 2012, reached a point where it became extremely difficult for journalists to criticize government. Journalists who did report critically were subject to legal harassment as well as physical threats and attacks. Reporting was especially dangerous in border areas, in particular Paraguay's border with Brazil, because of organized criminal groups.

Media Today

Although the constitution calls for press freedom, there are also defamation laws that can be used to punish journalists, and the 2011 Telecommunications Law limits the broadcasting range of community radio stations and prohibits them from accepting advertising. Journalists also have limited access to information. The country has no freedom of information law, and in 2011, the Senate passed a resolution requiring authorization from the Senate President before any Senate documents can be released to the media.[4] While most newspapers and broadcast media are privately owned, the government does control Radio Nacional del Paraguay and TV Pública Paraguay.

Notes

1. *State of the Press Report*, XI Annual Meeting 1955 (Miami, FL: Inter American Press Association. 1956).
2. Ibid.
3. *World Press Freedom Review*, IPI Report (Zurich: International Press Institute, December, 1989).
4. *Freedom of the Press* (Washington, DC: Freedom House, 2012). Available at http://www.freedomhouse.org/report/freedom-press/freedom-press-2012.

Peru: 1948–2012

Peru Year by Year

Year	Media	Government
1948	Not Free	Autocracy
1949	Not Free	Autocracy
1950	Not Free	Anocracy
1951	Not Free	Anocracy
1952	Not Free	Anocracy
1953	Not Free	Anocracy
1954	Not Free	Anocracy
1955	Not Free	Anocracy
1956	Not Free	Anocracy
1957	Imperfectly Free	Anocracy
1958	Imperfectly Free	Anocracy
1959	Imperfectly Free	Anocracy
1960	Imperfectly Free	Anocracy
1961	Imperfectly Free	Anocracy
1962	Imperfectly Free	Autocracy
1963	Imperfectly Free	Anocracy
1964	Imperfectly Free	Anocracy
1965	Imperfectly Free	Anocracy
1966	Imperfectly Free	Anocracy
1967	Imperfectly Free	Anocracy
1968	Imperfectly Free	Autocracy
1969	Not Free	Autocracy
1970	Not Free	Autocracy
1971	Not Free	Autocracy
1972	Not Free	Autocracy
1973	Not Free	Autocracy
1974	Not Free	Autocracy
1975	Not Free	Autocracy

MEDIA FREEDOM HISTORY IN A NUTSHELL

- In spite of grim conditions, Peruvian journalists have been willing to report critically on government behavior, making this one of the most difficult media environments to evaluate
- Independent media express a variety of views, and radio is a particularly important news medium
- As of 2011, Peru had 101 total daily newspapers with an average circulation per issue of 1,659,000 (World Association of Newspaper's 2012 World Newspaper Trends)
- As of 2012, about 38 percent of Peruvians had Internet access (International Telecommunication Union's 2012 ICT Indicators Database)

In Brief

For most of the years since World War II, the conditions for news media in Peru have hovered around the border of imperfectly free and not free, making this one of the most difficult media environments to evaluate. This is to a large extent due to the apparent willingness of journalists to criticize government even when it is perilous to do so.

Chronology

1948–1956: Not Free

In the late 1940s, political tensions escalated between President José Luis Bustamante and the Congress that was dominated by the Alianza Popular Revolucionaria Americana (APRA) party—in part due to militant members of APRA's assassination of Francisco Grana Garland, the director of *La Prensa* newspaper.[1] In 1948, the military seized control of the country and General Manuel Odria took over the presidency. During

Year	Media	Government
1976	Not Free	Autocracy
1977	Not Free	Autocracy
1978	Not Free	Anocracy
1979	Not Free	Anocracy
1980	Not Free	Democracy
1981	Imperfectly Free	Democracy
1982	Imperfectly Free	Democracy
1983	Imperfectly Free	Democracy
1984	Imperfectly Free	Democracy
1985	Imperfectly Free	Democracy
1986	Imperfectly Free	Democracy
1987	Imperfectly Free	Democracy
1988	Imperfectly Free	Democracy
1989	Imperfectly Free	Democracy
1990	Imperfectly Free	Democracy
1991	Imperfectly Free	Democracy
1992	Imperfectly Free	Anocracy
1993	Imperfectly Free	Anocracy
1994	Imperfectly Free	Anocracy
1995	Imperfectly Free	Anocracy
1996	Imperfectly Free	Anocracy
1997	Not Free	Anocracy
1998	Not Free	Anocracy
1999	Not Free	Anocracy
2000	Not Free	Anocracy
2001	Imperfectly Free	Democracy
2002	Imperfectly Free	Democracy
2003	Imperfectly Free	Democracy
2004	Imperfectly Free	Democracy
2005	Imperfectly Free	Democracy
2006	Imperfectly Free	Democracy
2007	Imperfectly Free	Democracy
2008	Imperfectly Free	Democracy
2009	Imperfectly Free	Democracy
2010	Imperfectly Free	Democracy
2011	Imperfectly Free	Democracy
2012	Imperfectly Free	Democracy

this time, the State of Internal Security Decree allowed government to restrict news media, and those affiliated with APRA were closed.

1957–1968: Imperfectly Free

In the buildup to the 1956 elections, the Odria administration increased restrictions on the news media, but later that year Manuel Prado was elected president, and once he took office, the Interior Security Law that had been used against the press was repealed.[2] By 1957, newspapers that had been closed were reopened and journalists were reporting freely.

1969–1980: Not Free

In October 1968, General Velasco led a military takeover that ousted President Belaúnde. Within one month, Velasco's regime began to close down and take over newspapers.[3] During this period, several journalists were deported, others were imprisoned, some publications were confiscated, and the government took over the supply of newsprint.[4] Rather than promoting media freedom, the 1970 Freedom of the Press Statute was used "as an instrument of harassment" against newspapers that criticized the government and a mechanism to encourage self-censorship.[5] In 1974, the Expropriation Decree gave the government authority to take over newspapers with circulations greater than 20,000.[6]

1981–1996: Imperfectly Free

In 1980, former president Belaúnde was reelected and one of his administration's first actions was to begin restoring freedom of the news media. In October of 1980, a law was passed that revoked the Expropriation Decree and other laws that had been used to regulate and take over broadcast media.[7] The new law also created a compulsory Journalists' Collegium to oversee the profession that required that those affiliated have a university degree in journalism.[8] By 1982, media were functionally free, but journalists were sometimes caught in the crossfire between the government and the Sendero Luminoso (Shining Path) movement. In January of 1983, eight journalists and their guide were killed when they traveled to Uchuraccay (a village in the Andes) to investigate the killings of peasants. A commission concluded that the journalists were killed by villagers who thought they were from the Sendero

Luminoso, but the victims' families have long contested these findings and have repeatedly requested that the case be reopened.

In April of 1992, with the backing of the military, President Alberto Fujimori dissolved the legislative and judicial branches of the government, suspended the constitution, and imposed censorship on the media. "The coup began with the takeover of the media by armed soldiers. For two days, almost all Lima media were censored. In some cases, newspapers were published with blank spaces. Radio and television programs were cut."[9] Although the new government ceased much of this censorship in the weeks that followed the coup, attacks on journalists (sometimes by police and sometimes by members of the Sendero Luminoso) continued to be a problem. Following the coup, the state of the news media skirted the border between imperfectly free and not free. Conditions were poor. For the most part, journalists persisted in criticizing the government, but when they did they were usually punished.

1997–2000: Not Free

The environment for Peruvian journalists continued to deteriorate. In 1997, the government launched a campaign to silence the television network, Frecuencia Latina, which frequently aired programs that were critical of the government. This culminated in the government stripping the network's primary owner of his Peruvian citizenship and handing the network over to progovernment stockholders.[10] That same year, there were reports of journalists being threatened, arrested, kidnapped, and beaten.[11] Conditions remained grim through 2000. The Fujimori administration also bribed news media to gain favorable coverage. Nonetheless, some journalists persisted in reporting on government corruption, and this reporting eventually helped delegitimize Fujimori. Following a bribery scandal involving his intelligence adviser, Fujimori was dismissed by Congress and fled to Japan.

2001–2012: Imperfectly Free

With the election of President Alejandro Toledo in 2001, conditions began to improve

for news media. Journalists who had been behind bars for years were released from prison. Yet journalists were still subject to harassment, and libel charges were often used to intimidate journalists.[12]

Media Today

Peru has a wide range of privately owned print and broadcast media, as well as government-owned print and broadcast media. Corruption problems that emerged during the Fujimori years linger—some journalists can be bribed to provide favorable news coverage.[13] Politicians often punish critical journalists with lawsuits.

Notes

1. Rex A. Hudson, *Peru: A Country Study* (Washington, DC: Library of Congress Country Studies, 1992). Available at http://lcweb2.loc.gov/frd/cs/.
2. *State of the Press*, Annual Meeting 1956 (Miami, FL: Inter American Press Association, 1957).
3. *Freedom of the Press Committee Report*, Annual Meeting 1972 (Miami, FL: Inter American Press Association, 1973).
4. Ibid.
5. Ibid., 128.
6. *Report of the Committee on Freedom of the Press and Information*, General Assembly 1974 (Miami, FL: Inter American Press Association, 1975).
7. *Report of the Committee on Freedom of the Press and Information*, General Assembly 1980 (Miami, FL: Inter American Press Association, 1982).
8. Ibid.
9. *Peru*, 1992 General Assembly (Miami, FL: Inter American Press Association, 1992). Available at http://www.sipiapa.org/en/asambleas.
10. *Peru*, 1997 General Assembly (Miami, FL: Inter American Press Association, 1997). Available at http://www.sipiapa.org/en/asambleas.
11. Ibid.
12. *Freedom of the Press* (Washington, DC: Freedom House, 2003). Available at http://www.freedomhouse.org/report/freedom-press/freedom-press-2003.
13. *Freedom of the Press* (Washington, DC: Freedom House, 2013). Available at http://www.freedomhouse.org/report/freedom-press/freedom-press-2013.

Philippines: 1948–2012

Philippines Year by Year

Year	Media	Government
1948	Free	Anocracy
1949	Free	Anocracy
1950	Free	Anocracy
1951	Free	Anocracy
1952	Free	Anocracy
1953	Free	Anocracy
1954	Free	Anocracy
1955	Free	Anocracy
1956	Free	Anocracy
1957	Free	Anocracy
1958	Free	Anocracy
1959	Free	Anocracy
1960	Free	Anocracy
1961	Free	Anocracy
1962	Free	Anocracy
1963	Free	Anocracy
1964	Free	Anocracy
1965	Free	Anocracy
1966	Free	Anocracy
1967	Free	Anocracy
1968	Free	Anocracy
1969	Free	Anocracy
1970	Imperfectly Free	Anocracy
1971	Not Free	Anocracy
1972	Not Free	Autocracy
1973	Not Free	Autocracy
1974	Not Free	Autocracy

(Continued)

- Democratic institutions and a free media system were part of the transition from U.S. control to independence
- As part of the transition from elected leader to dictator, Ferdinand Marcos gradually quashed media freedom during the period from 1969 to 1972
- Media freedom was restored after the fall of the Marcos regime in 1986 and has been sustained since, despite several challenges
- In 2009, thirty-two journalists were among fifty-eight people killed in what has come to be called the Maguindanao massacre; as of early 2014, there were no convictions in connection with these killings
- As of 2012, the Philippines had twenty-eight total paid-for daily newspapers with an average circulation per issue of 3,800,000 (World Association of Newspaper's 2012 World Newspaper Trends)
- The Philippines has a mix of state-owned and privately owned broadcast media
- As of 2012, about 36 percent of Filipinos had Internet access (International Telecommunication Union's 2012 ICT Indicators Database)

In Brief

The history of media freedom in the Philippines is far simpler than it might first appear from the data. Free media had already been established prior to WWII as part of the U.S. commitment to an independent Philippines, and they were a central part of the postwar, independent government. Ferdinand Marcos quashed media freedom as he made the transition from elected president to dictator, and media freedom was restored after he was deposed. The United States has continued to exert significant influence. Today media are functionally free, but the Philippines has come under fire

(Continued)

Year	Media	Government
1975	Not Free	Autocracy
1976	Not Free	Autocracy
1977	Not Free	Autocracy
1978	Not Free	Autocracy
1979	Not Free	Autocracy
1980	Not Free	Autocracy
1981	Not Free	Autocracy
1982	Not Free	Autocracy
1983	Not Free	Autocracy
1984	Imperfectly Free	Autocracy
1985	Imperfectly Free	Autocracy
1986	Free	Anocracy
1987	Free	Democracy
1988	Free	Democracy
1989	Free	Democracy
1990	Free	Democracy
1991	Free	Democracy
1992	Free	Democracy
1993	Free	Democracy
1994	Free	Democracy
1995	Free	Democracy
1996	Free	Democracy
1997	Free	Democracy
1998	Free	Democracy
1999	Imperfectly Free	Democracy
2000	Imperfectly Free	Democracy
2001	Imperfectly Free	Democracy
2002	Free	Democracy
2003	Imperfectly Free	Democracy
2004	Imperfectly Free	Democracy
2005	Imperfectly Free	Democracy
2006	Imperfectly Free	Democracy
2007	Imperfectly Free	Democracy
2008	Imperfectly Free	Democracy
2009	Imperfectly Free	Democracy
2010	Imperfectly Free	Democracy
2011	Imperfectly Free	Democracy
2012	Imperfectly Free	Democracy

from press freedom organizations in recent years for facilitating a culture of impunity in which attacks on journalists often go unpunished.

Chronology

1948–1969: Free

Starting in 1935, the ten-year transition from a U.S. colonial holding to an independent democratic state was interrupted by WWII and the Japanese invasion. With the end of the war, the process was restarted and independence was granted in 1946, just a year later than originally planned. A robust and effective free media system and democratic institutions were central to the new Philippine government.

Charges of corruption and fraud tainted the 1969 reelection of Ferdinand Marcos, and at about the same time a guerilla campaign was launched by Muslim separatists in the south.

1970: Imperfectly Free

With mass protests in early 1970, government pressure and efforts to exert unofficial influence on media content became noticeable and steadily increased over the year. It is arguable that Marcos's domestically unpopular support for the U.S. Vietnam campaign provided his authoritarian maneuvers with at least tacit support from the Nixon administration.

1971–1983: Not Free

Violent opposition to Marcos's rule erupted, and continued escalation of government pressure and influence on media reached the point where the media could no longer function in a free and independent manner.

In 1972, martial law and the suspension of parliament marked the final shift from elected government to dictatorship. Strict censorship of the media was imposed. The 1973 constitution instituted by Marcos gave him absolute control of government, and with that established, direct control of media content and strict censorship laws were relaxed. However, the indirect controls exerted were as effective as direct control, and media remained fully controlled. In the late 1970s, the Carter administration's pressure for democratic reform of its allies was probably a factor in the process that led to the lifting of martial law and elections in 1981. These changes, however, were superficial and the dictatorship remained in full control of the government and media.

1984–1985: Imperfectly Free

The assassination of opposition leader Benigno Aquino in August 1983 added fuel to anti-Marcos forces, and by 1984, enough media outlets were defying governmental efforts at direct control, and they were sufficiently protected by opposition forces to create an effectively free press despite government efforts to restrict content.

1986–1998: Free

The "people power" revolution of 1986 finally restored media freedom in the Philippines. Despite efforts to control, suppress, and manipulate the vote in the 1986 election, few believed that Marcos actually defeated opposition candidate Corazon Aquino, the widow of Benigno. Marcos attempted to declare himself the winner, but massive protests and the loss of both external and internal support brought down the Marcos regime. Again the United States played a key role, with the offer of asylum from the Reagan administration, combined with clear indications of the withdrawal of support for Marcos, providing a mechanism for ending the regime without open civil war. Despite continued unrest, violence, and assassination attempts, media freedom was sustained.

1999–2001: Imperfectly Free

Attempts at enacting economic reforms by newly elected President Joseph Marcelo Estrada were followed by accusations of corruption and eventually led to an impeachment effort and political crisis. During this period, media freedom was challenged by efforts to influence and limit coverage, but these efforts fell short of control.

2002: Free

After the Supreme Court took the presidency from Estrada, the crisis decreased and the various efforts to influence the media eased considerably.

2003–2012: Imperfectly Free

The easing of pressures on the free media was short lived. Pressures and attempts to coerce the media returned in the lead up to the 2004 elections and have persisted in the unsettled political environment that has continued since then. In particular, the Philippines has gained a reputation for fostering a culture of impunity in which attacks against journalists often go unpunished. In particular, to date there have been no convictions in the 2009 Maguindanao massacre of 58 people including 32 journalists, and at the end of 2013, Human Rights Watch declared the case was in "judicial limbo," with 101 suspects in custody and 94 suspects still at large.[1]

Media Today

Media remain functionally free but are constantly challenged by efforts to restrict or control content. Libel remains a criminal offense, punishable by imprisonment and harsh fines. The Philippines is also one of the most dangerous countries for journalists. In 2012, the Committee to Protect Journalists ranked the Philippines third on its impunity index because at least fifty-five murders of journalists remained unsolved.[2] In 2013, nine journalists were killed, and in three cases the motive was connected to their work.[3]

The current state of the Philippine media reflects the difficult and still unsettled nature of the Philippine political environment. Secessionist movements have become a less prominent part of the political environment over the last few decades, but a significant electoral cleavage runs roughly along class lines, pitting the large but impoverished bulk of the population against the wealthy and powerful political, religious, and business elites.

Notes

1. Carlos Conde, "Dispatches: Four Years On, No Justice for Maguindanao Massacre Victims." *Dispatches: A Look at Human Rights in the News Today.* (New York: Human Rights Watch, November 21, 2013).

2. *Attacks on the Press 2012: Philippines* (Committee to Protect Journalists, 2013). Available at http://cpj.org/2013/02/attacks-on-the-press-in-2012-philippines.php.

3. *76 Journalists Killed in the Philippines Since 1992/Motive Confirmed* (Committee to Protect Journalists, 2013). Available at http://cpj.org/killed/asia/philippines/.

Poland: 1948–2012

Poland Year by Year

Year	Media	Government
1948	Not Free	Autocracy
1949	Not Free	Autocracy
1950	Not Free	Autocracy
1951	Not Free	Autocracy
1952	Not Free	Autocracy
1953	Not Free	Autocracy
1954	Not Free	Autocracy
1955	Not Free	Autocracy
1956	Not Free	Autocracy
1957	Not Free	Autocracy
1958	Not Free	Autocracy
1959	Not Free	Autocracy
1960	Not Free	Autocracy
1961	Not Free	Autocracy
1962	Not Free	Autocracy
1963	Not Free	Autocracy
1964	Not Free	Autocracy
1965	Not Free	Autocracy
1966	Not Free	Autocracy
1967	Not Free	Autocracy
1968	Not Free	Autocracy
1969	Not Free	Autocracy
1970	Not Free	Autocracy
1971	Not Free	Autocracy
1972	Not Free	Autocracy

MEDIA FREEDOM HISTORY IN A NUTSHELL

- Changes in the media began well before the fall of the Berlin Wall
- The media played an important role supporting labor union–led pushes for liberalization
- The transition from an indirectly controlled media system to a free media system was slow but steady
- Media are now free
- As of 2011, there were thirty-six daily newspapers, thirty-five of them were paid-for daily newspapers, with a total average circulation per issue of 2,820,180 (World Association of Newspaper's 2012 World Newspaper Trends)
- Poland has state-run television and radio stations, as well as numerous privately owned broadcast media
- As of 2012, about 65 percent of Poles had Internet access (International Telecommunication Union's 2012 ICT Indicators Database)

In Brief

A relatively flat and open expanse of land between the Carpathian Mountains and the Baltic Sea, Poland's history is largely defined by an unenviable geography that makes it the ideal military route between East and West. The result has been countless invasions and centuries of intermittent, partial, total, or indirect occupation by military powers. Through it all, a clear national identity has been sustained, and this history may in part explain why Poland was the instigator of the independence movements that ended in the collapse of the Soviet Bloc.

Chronology

1948–1997: Not Free

Soviet occupation during World War II and for several years after included a massive purge of

Year	Media	Government
1973	Not Free	Autocracy
1974	Not Free	Autocracy
1975	Not Free	Autocracy
1976	Not Free	Autocracy
1977	Not Free	Autocracy
1978	Not Free	Autocracy
1979	Not Free	Autocracy
1980	Not Free	Autocracy
1981	Not Free	Autocracy
1982	Not Free	Autocracy
1983	Not Free	Autocracy
1984	Not Free	Autocracy
1985	Not Free	Autocracy
1986	Not Free	Autocracy
1987	Not Free	Autocracy
1988	Not Free	Autocracy
1989	Not Free	Anocracy
1990	Not Free	Anocracy
1991	Not Free	Democracy
1992	Not Free	Democracy
1993	Not Free	Democracy
1994	Not Free	Democracy
1995	Not Free	Democracy
1996	Not Free	Democracy
1997	Not Free	Democracy
1998	Imperfectly Free	Democracy
1999	Imperfectly Free	Democracy
2000	Imperfectly Free	Democracy
2001	Imperfectly Free	Democracy
2002	Free	Democracy
2003	Free	Democracy
2004	Free	Democracy
2005	Free	Democracy
2006	Free	Democracy

Year	Media	Government
2007	Free	Democracy
2008	Free	Democracy
2009	Free	Democracy
2010	Free	Democracy
2011	Free	Democracy
2012	Free	Democracy

Polish leaders and the installation of a Communist political system, including the direct editorial control of the media.

Starting in the 1970s, the decade of strikes in the Gdansk shipyards are well known as the initiator of the dissolution of the Soviet Bloc and the end of Soviet domination of Eastern Europe. Yet the growth of independent but indirectly controlled media at the same time may have had more long-term significance. Polish ports and shipyards were critical economic resources for the Warsaw Pact nations, and this raised the potential cost of violent repression enough to create some space for both the strikes and the change in the media. The media were then ideally placed to take advantage of Perestroika and Glasnost and enable the swift transition to a democratic political system.

1998–2001: Imperfectly Free

While the early shift to indirectly controlled media may have played a critical role in Poland's ability to quickly transition to a democratic political regime, the growth of truly independent and free media was much slower than many of the former Soviet Bloc countries.[1] Commercialization began almost immediately after the fall of the Berlin Wall, but the extremely gradual loosening of government mechanisms for indirect control that followed can probably be attributed to two factors. First, the media had been firmly on the side of the anticommunist push, and with the quick establishment of a democratic government, media were seen as a key tool the regime could use to establish and sustain those liberal institutions. This fed into a second reason for the slow process of liberalization: a significant and widespread fear of a resurgence of communism from within Poland, which may or may not have been supported by external forces.[2]

2002–2012: Free

The liberalization of the media may have lagged behind the liberalization of politics, but it was as steady as it was gradual, and it continued well after the shift to an imperfect but functionally free and independent media. It is be difficult to identify a specific event or change that marks the point where this gradual process of privatization and shift to public service broadcasting carried media freedom up to a standard comparable to Western Europe, but toward the end of 2001, it became clear that the last of the serious compromises had been overcome.

Media Today

A competitive and diverse commercial media and public service mix that is roughly comparable to long-established free media environments in Western Europe.

Notes

1. *World Press Freedom Review*, IPI Report (Vienna: International Press Institute, 1998).
2. Ibid.

Portugal: 1948–2012

Portugal Year by Year

Year	Media	Government
1948	Not Free	Autocracy
1949	Not Free	Autocracy
1950	Not Free	Autocracy
1951	Not Free	Autocracy
1952	Not Free	Autocracy
1953	Not Free	Autocracy
1954	Not Free	Autocracy
1955	Not Free	Autocracy
1956	Not Free	Autocracy
1957	Not Free	Autocracy
1958	Not Free	Autocracy
1959	Not Free	Autocracy
1960	Not Free	Autocracy
1961	Not Free	Autocracy
1962	Not Free	Autocracy
1963	Not Free	Autocracy
1964	Not Free	Autocracy
1965	Not Free	Autocracy
1966	Not Free	Autocracy
1967	Not Free	Autocracy
1968	Not Free	Autocracy
1969	Not Free	Autocracy
1970	Not Free	Autocracy
1971	Not Free	Autocracy
1972	Not Free	Autocracy
1973	Not Free	Autocracy
1974	Not Free	Anocracy

(Continued)

MEDIA FREEDOM HISTORY IN A NUTSHELL

- Media freedom was not part of the burst of freedoms arising with end of Fascist rule
- Economic growth and efforts to integrate into European cooperative institutions eventually led to a relatively sudden transition to media freedom
- Massive economic challenges threaten media freedom
- As of 2011, Portugal had a total of eighteen daily newspapers; all eighteen were paid-for daily newspapers, with a total average circulation per issue of 572,980 (World Association of Newspaper's 2012 World Newspaper Trends)
- Portugal has both public and privately owned television stations, and hundreds of radio stations, including the Roman Catholic Church's very popular Rádio Renascença
- As of 2012, about 64 percent of Portuguese had Internet access (International Telecommunication Union's 2012 ICT Indicators Database).

In Brief

A casual familiarity with Portuguese history would create an expectation that free media would have emerged with the burst of liberalization following the leftist military coup that ended its long history of fascist rule. Yet it took nearly two decades before a functionally free media environment could be established.

Chronology

1948–1994: Not Free

A 1911 coup shifted the nature of authoritarian rule from monarchal to fascist, but it remained staunchly authoritarian, and the media were directly controlled, until a leftist coup in 1974.

(Continued)

Year	Media	Government
1975	Not Free	Anocracy
1976	Not Free	Democracy
1977	Not Free	Democracy
1978	Not Free	Democracy
1979	Not Free	Democracy
1980	Not Free	Democracy
1981	Not Free	Democracy
1982	Not Free	Democracy
1983	Not Free	Democracy
1984	Not Free	Democracy
1985	Not Free	Democracy
1986	Not Free	Democracy
1987	Not Free	Democracy
1988	Not Free	Democracy
1989	Not Free	Democracy
1990	Not Free	Democracy
1991	Not Free	Democracy
1992	Not Free	Democracy
1993	Not Free	Democracy
1994	Not Free	Democracy
1995	Free	Democracy
1996	Free	Democracy
1997	Free	Democracy
1998	Free	Democracy
1999	Free	Democracy
2000	Free	Democracy
2001	Free	Democracy
2002	Free	Democracy
2003	Free	Democracy
2004	Free	Democracy
2005	Free	Democracy
2006	Free	Democracy
2007	Free	Democracy
2008	Free	Democracy
2009	Free	Democracy
2010	Free	Democracy
2011	Free	Democracy
2012	Free	Democracy

The period following the coup is often referred to as an extreme of freedom, bordering on anarchy. Yet, while the media were released from direct government control, journalists were no freer than they had been before the coup. Economic collapse limited resources for the establishment of an independent media, and with no previous experience with free media in any form, there was little public demand. Further, the suppression of the media, particularly regarding investigation of corruption, was in the interest of the wealthy and powerful who plundered the country in the wake of the coup. The media outlets that were available were often owned or controlled by those opportunistic elites.

1995–2012: Free

The 1994 decision by the Lisbon High Court to uphold the news media's right to criticize Portuguese military commanders paved the way for the shift to free media.[1] Integration into Europe began in earnest in the mid-1980s, along with a period of tremendous economic growth, but it was not until the parliamentary elections of 1995 that the media landscape shifted rather abruptly to a relatively free media, driven by a commercial imperative.

Media Today

Massive deficit spending and high levels of corruption left Portugal in a particularly vulnerable position when the European economic crisis struck, and economic difficulties have hit Portuguese media particularly hard. Many analysts question the likelihood that free media can be sustained in such dire economic conditions. According to Freedom House, younger journalists are particularly vulnerable and likely to self-censor to keep their jobs.[2]

Notes

1. *World Press Freedom Review*, IPI Report (Vienna: International Press Institute, 1994).
2. *Freedom of the Press* (Washington, DC: Freedom House, 2013). Available at http://www.freedomhouse.org/reports.

Qatar: 1971–2012

Qatar Year by Year

Year	Media	Government
1971	Not Free	Autocracy
1972	Not Free	Autocracy
1973	Not Free	Autocracy
1974	Not Free	Autocracy
1975	Not Free	Autocracy
1976	Not Free	Autocracy
1977	Not Free	Autocracy
1978	Not Free	Autocracy
1979	Not Free	Autocracy
1980	Not Free	Autocracy
1981	Not Free	Autocracy
1982	Not Free	Autocracy
1983	Not Free	Autocracy
1984	Not Free	Autocracy
1985	Not Free	Autocracy
1986	Not Free	Autocracy
1987	Not Free	Autocracy
1988	Not Free	Autocracy
1989	Not Free	Autocracy
1990	Not Free	Autocracy
1991	Not Free	Autocracy
1992	Not Free	Autocracy
1993	Not Free	Autocracy
1994	Not Free	Autocracy

(Continued)

MEDIA FREEDOM HISTORY IN A NUTSHELL

- Media were, and for the most part still are, directly owned and run by the government
- A 1995 coup within the ruling family brought significant changes, and Al-Jazeera was founded in Qatar in 1996
- The second Iraq War brought back significant media restrictions
- The media environment appears to be heading toward greater restrictions
- As of 2012, Qatar had seven newspapers (according the World Newspaper Association's World Press Trends 2012 Report), which were owned either by the ruling family or their associates (Freedom House's Report on Freedom of the Press 2013)
- The government owns all broadcast media
- As of 2012, about 88 percent of Qataris had Internet access (International Telecommunication Union's 2012 ICT Indicators Database)

In Brief

Although the Qatari ruling family funds Al-Jazeera, within Qatar, media are restricted. With the exception of a brief period in the late 1990s, media have always been restricted.

Chronology

1971–1996: Not Free

Despite infighting within the ruling family, control of this small country remained closely held and media were directly owned and controlled by the government.

After a 1995 bloodless coup within the ruling family, the government announced it would no longer censor the press.[1] In 1996, the emir founded

(Continued)

Year	Media	Government
1995	Not Free	Autocracy
1996	Not Free	Autocracy
1997	Imperfectly Free	Autocracy
1998	Imperfectly Free	Autocracy
1999	Imperfectly Free	Autocracy
2000	Imperfectly Free	Autocracy
2001	Imperfectly Free	Autocracy
2002	Not Free	Autocracy
2003	Not Free	Autocracy
2004	Not Free	Autocracy
2005	Not Free	Autocracy
2006	Not Free	Autocracy
2007	Not Free	Autocracy
2008	Not Free	Autocracy
2009	Not Free	Autocracy
2010	Not Free	Autocracy
2011	Not Free	Autocracy
2012	Not Free	Autocracy

(and funded) Al-Jazeera satellite television. This marked a notable and rapid shift in the media environment in Qatar.

1997–2001: Imperfectly Free

The cessation of direct censorship and further relaxation of media restrictions led to an imperfectly free media environment by 1997.[2]

Al-Jazeera quickly gained a reputation for tackling controversial issues in a free and independent manner.

2002–2012: Not Free

The Second Iraq War brought the U.S. Central Command forward base to Qatar and with it wartime media restrictions. Though the government was no longer directly censoring media, it was clear that most journalists were practicing self-censorship.[3] Also in 2002, a journalist for *Qatar TV* was sentenced to death after being convicted of espionage (he was later pardoned).[4]

Media Today

Criticism of the ruling family, the government, and Islam is prohibited. This holds for domestic media as well as the Qatari-based network Al-Jazeera.[5] The government retains the right to censor all media, and online content is censored by the state-owned Internet service provider.[6]

Notes

1. *Country Reports on Human Rights Practices for 1995* (Washington, DC: U.S. Department of State, 1996). Available at http://dosfan.lib.uic.edu/ERC/democracy/1995_hrp_report/95hrp_report_nea/Qatar.html.
2. *World Press Freedom Review*, IPI Report (Vienna: International Press Institute, 2005).
3. *Freedom of the Press* (Washington, DC: Freedom House, 2003). Available at http://www.freedomhouse.org/report/freedom-press/2003/qatar.
4. *World Press Freedom Review*, IPI Report (Vienna: International Press Institute, 2002).
5. *Freedom of the Press* (Washington, DC: Freedom House, 2013). Available at http://www.freedomhouse.org/report/freedom-press/2013/qatar.
6. Ibid.

Romania: 1948–2012

Romania Year by Year

Year	Media	Government
1948	Not Free	Autocracy
1949	Not Free	Autocracy
1950	Not Free	Autocracy
1951	Not Free	Autocracy
1952	Not Free	Autocracy
1953	Not Free	Autocracy
1954	Not Free	Autocracy
1955	Not Free	Autocracy
1956	Not Free	Autocracy
1957	Not Free	Autocracy
1958	Not Free	Autocracy
1959	Not Free	Autocracy
1960	Not Free	Autocracy
1961	Not Free	Autocracy
1962	Not Free	Autocracy
1963	Not Free	Autocracy
1964	Not Free	Autocracy
1965	Not Free	Autocracy
1966	Not Free	Autocracy
1967	Not Free	Autocracy
1968	Not Free	Autocracy
1969	Not Free	Autocracy
1970	Not Free	Autocracy
1971	Not Free	Autocracy
1972	Not Free	Autocracy
1973	Not Free	Autocracy
1974	Not Free	Autocracy
1975	Not Free	Autocracy
1976	Not Free	Autocracy
1977	Not Free	Autocracy
1978	Not Free	Autocracy

(Continued)

MEDIA FREEDOM HISTORY IN A NUTSHELL

- Direct Soviet-style control of the media continued after the end of the Cold War
- Reforms appear to have been largely driven by the push to join the European Union
- While functionally free and able to criticize, the media are under increasing economic pressure that threatens to compromise their independence
- As of 2011, there were forty-six daily newspapers, forty-four were paid-for daily newspapers, with a total average circulation per issue of 766,000 (World Association of Newspaper's 2012 World Newspaper Trends).
- As of 2012, about 50 percent of Romanians had Internet access (International Telecommunication Union's 2012 ICT Indicators Database).

In Brief

Soviet domination defines most aspects of Romania's post-WWII political and media environment. Authoritarian leaders were the norm prior to the end of the war, whether behind the façade of the liberal democratic monarchy or as outright dictators. Yet even with that caveat, the country may be the most extreme example of Soviet intervention in domestic politics and external domination. Although the communist party was almost a non-entity prior to the end of the war, with Soviet assistance all noncommunist political elites were eliminated within just a few years and the Romanian Peoples Republic was declared in 1947. The democratic shift in the post–Cold War era was strongly supported by the West, but divisive ethnic disputes around the Roma have proven to be problematic.

Chronology

1948–1995: Not Free

This model Soviet satellite state asserted direct control over the media and allowed little if any

(Continued)

Year	Media	Government
1979	Not Free	Autocracy
1980	Not Free	Autocracy
1981	Not Free	Autocracy
1982	Not Free	Autocracy
1983	Not Free	Autocracy
1984	Not Free	Autocracy
1985	Not Free	Autocracy
1986	Not Free	Autocracy
1987	Not Free	Autocracy
1988	Not Free	Autocracy
1989	Not Free	Anocracy
1990	Not Free	Anocracy
1991	Not Free	Anocracy
1992	Not Free	Anocracy
1993	Not Free	Anocracy
1994	Not Free	Anocracy
1995	Not Free	Anocracy
1996	Imperfectly Free	Democracy
1997	Imperfectly Free	Democracy
1998	Imperfectly Free	Democracy
1999	Imperfectly Free	Democracy
2000	Imperfectly Free	Democracy
2001	Imperfectly Free	Democracy
2002	Imperfectly Free	Democracy
2003	Imperfectly Free	Democracy
2004	Imperfectly Free	Democracy
2005	Imperfectly Free	Democracy
2006	Imperfectly Free	Democracy
2007	Imperfectly Free	Democracy
2008	Imperfectly Free	Democracy
2009	Imperfectly Free	Democracy
2010	Imperfectly Free	Democracy
2011	Imperfectly Free	Democracy
2012	Imperfectly Free	Democracy

dissent. Even when the brutal televised execution of Nicolae Ceaușescu in 1989 brought the communist dictatorship to an end, there was little if any change in the media environment. There was no history of any form of independent media, and the impromptu government that followed Ceaușescu was not only dominated by former Communists, but it also practiced the same kinds of media controls. Elections in 1990 made little difference. Cautious market reforms were implemented, but

tolerance of expressions of dissent was limited or nonexistent, as was made evident when the government thanked miners who marched into town and violently disbursed a group of protesters. In 1991, Romania's constitution was amended to allow freedom of opinion, and one year later, private radio and television were authorized.[1] Elections in 1992 changed little.

The first substantial change in the media environment occurred when the governing coalition began disintegrating in late 1994.[2] As parties abandoned the coalition, the media outlets began splintering and government control shifted to indirect, with different outlets dominated or heavily influenced by different factions. Dissent, protest, or criticism of government, however, remained difficult. The year 1995 was also when Romania made its first official application for inclusion in the European Union. Liberalization of media was one of several reforms that would be necessary for a successful application.

1996–2012: Imperfectly Free

Most likely driven by the desire to gain acceptance in the European Union and reap the associated economic benefits, media liberalization proceeded quickly in the run-up to the 1996 elections, and debate in the media was a notable aspect of the elections.[3]

Media Today

Beset by economic difficulties, Romanian media have managed to sustain a functional level of freedom. Recent coverage of issues related to the Roma was critical of government actions, which included fencing Roma communities and restricting their ability to travel. This ability to criticize and bring such issues to light, even when doing so is unpopular, is a concrete example of free media. However, political and economic influence over media appears to be increasing as sources of revenue continue to fall.

Notes

1. *Romania*, Media Landscape Reports (Maastricht, The Netherlands: European Journalism Centre, 2013). Available at http://www.eurotopics.net/en/home/medienlandschaft/rumaenienmdn/.
2. *World Press Freedom Review*, IPI Report (Vienna: International Press Institute, 1994).
3. *World Press Freedom Review*, IPI Report (Vienna: International Press Institute, 1996).

Russia: 1948–2012

Russia Year by Year

Year	Media	Government
1948	Not Free	Autocracy
1949	Not Free	Autocracy
1950	Not Free	Autocracy
1951	Not Free	Autocracy
1952	Not Free	Autocracy
1953	Not Free	Autocracy
1954	Not Free	Autocracy
1955	Not Free	Autocracy
1956	Not Free	Autocracy
1957	Not Free	Autocracy
1958	Not Free	Autocracy
1959	Not Free	Autocracy
1960	Not Free	Autocracy
1961	Not Free	Autocracy
1962	Not Free	Autocracy
1963	Not Free	Autocracy
1964	Not Free	Autocracy
1965	Not Free	Autocracy
1966	Not Free	Autocracy
1967	Not Free	Autocracy
1968	Not Free	Autocracy
1969	Not Free	Autocracy
1970	Not Free	Autocracy
1971	Not Free	Autocracy
1972	Not Free	Autocracy
1973	Not Free	Autocracy
1974	Not Free	Autocracy

(Continued)

MEDIA FREEDOM HISTORY IN A NUTSHELL

- A model of bureaucratic authoritarian control during the Cold War
- The end of the Cold War brought a diversification of ownership and control, but professional practices were not significantly liberalized
- A sufficient diversity of contesting elites created a short period where media were effectively free enough to criticize government
- Consolidation of power also brought an end to any appearance of media freedom
- Centralization of authoritarian control appears to be increasing
- As of 2011, there were 546 daily newspapers, 495 were paid-for daily newspapers, with a total average circulation per issue of 9,058,714 (World Association of Newspaper's 2012 World Newspaper Trends)
- As of 2012, about 53 percent of Russians had Internet access (International Telecommunication Union's 2012 ICT Indicators Database)

In Brief

The Soviet Union was the prototype of the single-party communist dictatorship. It used the media as a propaganda tool, directly controlled by the Communist Party, and its methods were exported to Eastern Europe and to a lesser degree other satellite states. The end of the Cold War and splintering of the Soviet Union brought upheaval to the media, but authoritarianism was still the norm. Post–Cold War Russia provides an interesting case study for the divergence of the Van Belle definition of press freedom from other definitions of media independence. Because the diversity and appearance of independence of the media largely reflected devolution of authoritative control from a single party to the power

(Continued)

Year	Media	Government
1975	Not Free	Autocracy
1976	Not Free	Autocracy
1977	Not Free	Autocracy
1978	Not Free	Autocracy
1979	Not Free	Autocracy
1980	Not Free	Autocracy
1981	Not Free	Autocracy
1982	Not Free	Autocracy
1983	Not Free	Autocracy
1984	Not Free	Autocracy
1985	Not Free	Autocracy
1986	Not Free	Autocracy
1987	Not Free	Autocracy
1988	Not Free	Autocracy
1989	Not Free	Anocracy
1990	Not Free	Anocracy
1991	Not Free	Anocracy
1992	Not Free	Anocracy
1993	Not Free	Anocracy
1994	Not Free	Anocracy
1995	Imperfectly Free	Anocracy
1996	Imperfectly Free	Anocracy
1997	Not Free	Anocracy
1998	Not Free	Anocracy
1999	Not Free	Anocracy
2000	Not Free	Democracy
2001	Not Free	Democracy
2002	Not Free	Democracy
2003	Not Free	Democracy
2004	Not Free	Democracy
2005	Not Free	Democracy
2006	Not Free	Democracy
2007	Not Free	Anocracy
2008	Not Free	Anocracy
2009	Not Free	Anocracy
2010	Not Free	Anocracy
2011	Not Free	Anocracy
2012	Not Free	Anocracy

brokers that splintered from that party, the nature of the media outlets was not significantly liberalized and the consolidation of authoritative political control also consolidated control of the media.

Chronology

1948–1994: Not Free

There is little doubt that the Soviet media were directly and completely controlled by the Communist Party. Content of *Pravda* was seen as the direct communication from the Party and the country's leadership. It was monitored and intently analyzed for signals regarding Soviet policy and indications of internal party politics. The now defunct term of Kremlinology became something of a generic reference to combining such media analysis with the personal histories of Communist Party officials to divine the dynamics of authoritarian single-party politics.

In 1989, the end of the Cold War and the disintegration of the Soviet Union brought turmoil to the media. While there were a multitude of outlets, there was no history of independence and no experience with anything like a liberal, Western notion of journalism. Further, ownership and control of the media outlets was transferred to former party officials and former party operators of the media outlets.[1] While there were some immediate impressions of liberalization, the appearance of independence was almost certainly a reflection of different outlets moving to support different elites as they struggled for political position in the new regime and economic control of former state resources, corporations, and other assets. Even as the ownership and control of media outlets shifted, liberalization was limited.

1995–1996: Imperfectly Free

It is probably no accident that the peak of media freedom coincided with the peak of the political contestation in domestic politics. For a brief period, there was sufficient conflict between political, criminal, and newly emerging economic elites and sufficient diversity in the control, alignments, or the association of news outlets across these contesting elites to create a highly partisan but effectively free media. This period of functional press freedom may have been more illusory than real, because crackdowns and arrests repeatedly exposed the danger of criticizing government.

1997–2012: Not Free

The consolidation of political power that would eventually bring Vladimir Putin to various positions of control and eventual authoritarian dominance of the nominally democratic structures that were established in post-Soviet Russia also brought the brief experiment with media freedom to an end. As soon as it became difficult or dangerous for elites to oppose those consolidating power, the media outlets those elites controlled fell silent.[2]

Since the turn of the century, even the façade of independence has been dropped and media have become so constrained that they are all but completely controlled by the government and its proxies. While this analysis focuses on the news, the well-publicized arrest and imprisonment of the punk protest band, Pussy Riot, was emblematic of the extent to which it had become unsafe to criticize government. It also made apparent the extent to which the Putin government wished to and was able to control the media.

Media Today

Casual use of reference material on Russian media can inadvertently create the impression that the media are far more liberal than they are. Many measures emphasize the diversity of ownership and other factors that simply do not reflect the fact that the underlying mechanism is still authoritarian even if independent of government. Further, with the clear example of the political control of expression being forcefully extended into the realm of pop culture, there is little expectation that anyone can feel safe expressing dissent or otherwise criticize government or political leaders in any medium.

Notes

1. *World Press Freedom Review*, IPI Report (Zurich: International Press Institute, 1989).
2. *World Press Freedom Review*, IPI Report (Vienna: International Press Institute, 1997).

Rwanda: 1962–2012

Rwanda Year by Year

Year	Media	Government
1962	Not Free	Anocracy
1963	Not Free	Anocracy
1964	Not Free	Anocracy
1965	Not Free	Anocracy
1966	Not Free	Anocracy
1967	Not Free	Anocracy
1968	Not Free	Anocracy
1969	Not Free	Anocracy
1970	Not Free	Anocracy
1971	Not Free	Anocracy
1972	Not Free	Anocracy
1973	Not Free	Autocracy
1974	Not Free	Autocracy
1975	Not Free	Autocracy
1976	Not Free	Autocracy
1977	Not Free	Autocracy
1978	Not Free	Autocracy
1979	Not Free	Autocracy
1980	Not Free	Autocracy
1981	Not Free	Autocracy
1982	Not Free	Autocracy
1983	Not Free	Autocracy
1984	Not Free	Autocracy
1985	Not Free	Autocracy

MEDIA FREEDOM HISTORY IN A NUTSHELL

- The Rwandan government has always restricted the news media
- In the early 1990s, the government relaxed some of the restrictions and the number of privately owned news outlets increased, including extremist media
- The extremist media were used to mobilize the masses to take part in the 1994 killings of Tutsis and moderate Hutus
- As of 2012, there were about ten regularly published newspapers (Freedom House's Report on Freedom of the Press 2013)
- In 2012, the government owned six of Rwanda's twenty-five radio stations, and one of the country's three TV stations (Freedom House's Report on Freedom of the Press 2013)
- As of 2012, about 8 percent of Rwandans had Internet access (International Telecommunication Union's 2012 ICT Indicators Database)

In Brief

Plagued by ethnic violence, including the 1994 genocide in which as many as 1 million people were killed, Rwanda has never had free media. In the early 1990s, the government eased some restrictions on media in an effort to transition to a multiparty system, and while some independent media emerged, they were overshadowed by the extremist media that were used to mobilize the masses to participate in the killing. The Rwandan news media remain restricted, and a number of journalists have fled the country.

Year	Media	Government
1986	Not Free	Autocracy
1987	Not Free	Autocracy
1988	Not Free	Autocracy
1989	Not Free	Autocracy
1990	Not Free	Autocracy
1991	Not Free	Autocracy
1992	Not Free	Autocracy
1993	Not Free	Autocracy
1994	Not Free	Autocracy
1995	Not Free	Autocracy
1996	Not Free	Autocracy
1997	Not Free	Autocracy
1998	Not Free	Autocracy
1999	Not Free	Autocracy
2000	Not Free	Anocracy
2001	Not Free	Anocracy
2002	Not Free	Anocracy
2003	Not Free	Anocracy
2004	Not Free	Anocracy
2005	Not Free	Anocracy
2006	Not Free	Anocracy
2007	Not Free	Anocracy
2008	Not Free	Anocracy
2009	Not Free	Anocracy
2010	Not Free	Anocracy
2011	Not Free	Anocracy
2012	Not Free	Anocracy

Chronology

1962–2012: Not Free

Ethnic violence erupted in Rwanda a couple of years before the country gained independence from Belgium in 1962. The Tutsi minority had traditionally dominated the Hutu majority, but in 1959, the Hutus overthrew the Tutsi king and thousands of people were killed as the Hutus forced as many as 150,000 Tutsis into exile. In the 1960s, Rwanda had two state-owned newspapers and two that were published by the Catholic Church, but the main source of news for most Rwandans was the government-controlled *Radio Rwanda*, which began broadcasting in 1961.[1]

The Hutus remained in control of the country under President Gregoire Kayibanda, and the ethnic conflict continued and intensified in the early 1970s. Major General Juvenal Habyarimana seized control of the country in a coup in 1973 and ruled Rwanda as a one-party state. In the early 1990s facing increased military attacks from the Rwandan Patriotic Front (FPR), Habyarimana moved to establish a multiparty system and legalized opposition parties. This included some relaxing of media restrictions which led to a dramatic increase in privately-owned newspapers—from twelve in 1990 to more than sixty by the end of 1991.[2] In addition each opposition party was given twelve minutes of airtime on Radio Rwanda.[3] The independent newspapers and at times even the government newspapers began to criticize government policies.[4] To cope with this, the government adopted a press law that established a National Commission on the Press to oversee the news media and defamation of the president became punishable by imprisonment.[5] At least six journalists were arrested by the end of 1991.

The increase in privately owned newspapers also brought about an increase in extremist papers, in particular, the paper *Kangura* was used "to mobilize people around the president on the basis of an ethnic ideology excluding Tutsi."[6]

Although public television began broadcasting in 1992, it made little impact because so few people had television. Instead, most Rwandans continued to rely on radio to get their information, and in 1993, *Radio Television Libre des Mille Collines* (*RTLM*) was granted a license and started broadcasting. Its founders had close ties to government and included Ferdinand Nahimana, the former director of L'Office Rwandais d'Information (ORINFOR).[7]

In 1993, President Habyarimana signed the Arusha Accords, a power-sharing agreement with the Tutsis aimed at ending the conflict.

Following the 1993 assassination of neighboring Burundi's Hutu president, *RTLM* began airing programs that encouraged ethnic hatred of the Tutsis, and these broadcasts were supported by the extremist papers and eventually echoed on *Radio Rwanda*.[8]

On April 6, 1994, President Habyarimana and the Burundian president were killed when their plane was shot down. Shortly thereafter, *RTLM* began urging its listeners to kill the Tutsis. The killing continued for one hundred days, and it is estimated that as many as one million people were killed, most of them Tutsis and moderate Hutus. The International Press Institute reported that at least thirty-seven journalists were among those killed.[9]

Eventually, the FPR gained control of the country and Pasteur Bizimungu became president with Paul Kagame as vice president. The new government had little tolerance for media criticism, and journalists who challenged official views were harassed and threatened.[10]

In 2007, Reporters Without Borders declared that Rwandan President Paul Kagame was one of the world's "Predators of Press Freedom," and the International Press Institute reported that "Rwanda was one of the top five countries worldwide from which journalists flee into exile to escape death threats and violent attacks, as well as surveillance by security services."[11]

Media Today

In spite of constitutional provisions for media freedom, Rwandan media remain strictly restricted. There are a number of press offenses including public incitement to "divisionism" and defamation of government officials, both of which are punishable with up to five years of imprisonment.[12] Journalists have faced attacks and harassment, and many have fled the country.[13] In 2012, there were about ten regularly published newspapers.[14] The government owns six of the country's twenty-five radio stations and one of its three television stations. Although Internet access is limited, mobile phone penetration was at 52 percent in 2012.

Notes

1. Alexis, Monique and Ines Mpambara, *IMS Assessment Mission: The Rwanda Media Experience from the Genocide* (Copenhagen, Denmark: International Media Support, 2003).
2. *Country Reports on Human Rights Practices for 1991* (Washington, DC: US Department of State, 1992). Available at https://archive.org/stream/country reportson1990unit/countryreportson1990unit_ djvu.txt.
3. Ibid.
4. Ibid.
5. Alexis and Mpambara, *IMS Assessment Mission: The Rwanda Media Experience from the Genocide.*
6. Ibid., 14.
7. Ibid.
8. Ibid.
9. *World Press Freedom Review*, IPI Report (Vienna: International Press Institute, November/December 1995).
10. *Country Reports on Human Rights Practices for 1996* (Washington, DC: US Department of State, 1997). Available at http://www.state.gov/www/ global/human_rights/1996_hrp_report/rwanda .html.
11. *World Press Freedom Review*, IPI Report (Vienna: International Press Institute, 2007), 49.
12. *Freedom of the Press* (Washington, DC: Freedom House, 2013). Available at http://freedomhouse .org/report/freedom-press/2013/rwanda.
13. Ibid.
14. Ibid.

Samoa: 1962–2012

Samoa Year by Year

Year	Media	Government
1962	Imperfectly Free	Anocracy
1963	Imperfectly Free	Anocracy
1964	Imperfectly Free	Anocracy
1965	Imperfectly Free	Anocracy
1967	Imperfectly Free	Anocracy
1968	Imperfectly Free	Anocracy
1969	Imperfectly Free	Anocracy
1970	Imperfectly Free	Anocracy
1971	Imperfectly Free	Anocracy
1972	Imperfectly Free	Anocracy
1973	Imperfectly Free	Anocracy
1974	Imperfectly Free	Anocracy
1975	Imperfectly Free	Anocracy
1976	Imperfectly Free	Anocracy
1977	Imperfectly Free	Anocracy
1978	Imperfectly Free	Anocracy
1979	Imperfectly Free	Anocracy
1980	Imperfectly Free	Anocracy
1981	Imperfectly Free	Anocracy
1982	Imperfectly Free	Anocracy
1983	Imperfectly Free	Anocracy
1984	Imperfectly Free	Anocracy
1985	Imperfectly Free	Anocracy
1986	Imperfectly Free	Anocracy

(Continued)

MEDIA FREEDOM HISTORY IN A NUTSHELL

- Since independence, news media have been functionally free, with the exception of the late 1990s
- In the late 1990s, the government employed a variety of tactics to muzzle the news media and allowed officials to use public funds to cover legal costs of suing journalists and news outlets
- Samoa has several independent newspapers and a mix of private and government broadcast media
- As of 2012, about 13 percent of Samoans had Internet access (International Telecommunication Union's 2012 ICT Indicators Database)

In Brief

Formerly Western Samoa, Samoa is comprised of nine islands in the South Pacific. With the exception of the late 1990s, media have been imperfectly free.

Chronology

1962–1996: Imperfectly Free

Upon gaining independence from New Zealand in 1962, news media in Samoa were limited and imperfectly free. For example, the owner and editor of an independent newspaper faced libel charges and harassment by local authorities, but was for the most part able to report freely about government policies and actions.[1] The government was a modified parliamentary democracy that incorporated Polynesian cultural traditions and limited suffrage.[2]

By the 1970s, Samoa had a mix of government-owned and privately owned newspapers, but the government owned the only radio station.[3] Though Samoans were able to access television broadcasts

(Continued)

Year	Media	Government
1987	Imperfectly Free	Anocracy
1988	Imperfectly Free	Anocracy
1989	Imperfectly Free	Anocracy
1990	Imperfectly Free	Democracy
1991	Imperfectly Free	Democracy
1992	Imperfectly Free	Democracy
1993	Imperfectly Free	Democracy
1994	Imperfectly Free	Democracy
1995	Imperfectly Free	Democracy
1996	Imperfectly Free	Democracy
1997	Not Free	Democracy
1998	Not Free	Democracy
1999	Not Free	Democracy
2000	Imperfectly Free	Democracy
2001	Imperfectly Free	Democracy
2002	Imperfectly Free	Democracy
2003	Imperfectly Free	Democracy
2004	Imperfectly Free	Democracy
2005	Imperfectly Free	Democracy
2006	Imperfectly Free	Democracy
2007	Imperfectly Free	Democracy
2008	Imperfectly Free	Democracy
2009	Imperfectly Free	Democracy
2010	Imperfectly Free	Democracy
2011	Imperfectly Free	Democracy
2012	Imperfectly Free	Democracy

from American Samoa, the country did not have its own television station until 1993, and it was owned and operated by the government.

In 1990, Samoa adopted universal suffrage.

1997–1999: Not Free

Conditions for news media deteriorated in the late 1990s as the government banned opposition leaders from the government-controlled broadcast media and filed civil and criminal charges against the country's primary independent newspaper, the *Samoa Observer*, and its publisher.[4] Furthermore, the government determined that senior officials could use public money to cover legal fees if they sued the news media.[5] On several occasions news media received injunctions ordering them not to publish stories.[6] The publisher of the *Samoa Observer* was threatened and attacked, advertising was withdrawn, and the paper's printing press was burned down.[7] The only private radio station carrying news decided to stop doing so.[8]

2000–2012: Imperfectly Free

In 2000, conditions improved for news media as the Supreme Court ruled that the government's banning of opposition leaders from the state-owned broadcast media had violated their right to freedom of expression and ordered that they be given free access to the government media.[9]

Media Today

Samoan media remain functionally free. There are several independent newspapers and a mix of government-owned and privately owned broadcast media. Internet access remains limited.

Notes

1. R. F. Rankin, *Can the Developing Countries Compromise on a Free Press*, IPI Report (Zurich: International Press Institute, January 1966).
2. *Country Reports on Human Rights Practices for 1979* (Washington, DC: U.S. Department of State, 1980). Available at http://babel.hathitrust.org/cgi/pt?id=mdp.39015014188273.
3. Ibid.
4. *World Press Freedom Review*, IPI Report (Vienna: International Press Institute, December 1998).
5. Ibid.
6. *World Press Freedom Review*, IPI Report (Vienna: International Press Institute, December 1999).
7. Ibid.
8. Ibid.
9. *World Press Freedom Review*, IPI Report (Vienna: International Press Institute, 2000).

San Marino: 1992–2012

San Marino Year by Year

Year	Media	Government
1992	Free	Democracy
1993	Free	Democracy
1994	Free	Democracy
1995	Free	Democracy
1996	Free	Democracy
1997	Free	Democracy
1998	Free	Democracy
1999	Free	Democracy
2000	Free	Democracy
2001	Free	Democracy
2002	Free	Democracy
2003	Free	Democracy
2004	Free	Democracy
2005	Free	Democracy
2006	Free	Democracy
2007	Free	Democracy
2008	Free	Democracy
2009	Free	Democracy
2010	Free	Democracy
2011	Free	Democracy
2012	Free	Democracy

MEDIA FREEDOM HISTORY IN A NUTSHELL

- Reputedly the world's oldest republic, San Marino has had free media since it joined the UN in 1992 and probably had free media for many decades prior
- As of 2013, San Marino had several privately owned newspapers, privately owned radio, and state-run radio and television (Freedom House's Report on Freedom in the World 2013)
- Italian media are widely available
- As of 2012, about 51 percent of Sammarinese had Internet access (International Telecommunication Union's 2012 ICT Indicators Database)

In Brief

Believed to have been founded in 301 CE, San Marino is considered the world's oldest republic, has had free media since the 1990s, and probably had free media in previous decades as well. Information is scarce about media in this tiny country that is surrounded by Italy. San Marino joined the United Nations in 1992, which is where we start our chronology.

Chronology

1992–2012: Free

While there is little information about the Sammarinese media prior to the 1990s, they were probably free. In 1992, there was no government censorship and the Sammarinese had access to privately owned newspapers produced domestically and in neighboring Italy, as well as Italian broadcast media.[1] Access to media continued to improve, and by 2002, there were several domestically produced newspapers published by political parties, trade unions, and the government, and a private radio station in addition to the state-run broadcast media.[2]

Media Today

Sammarinese media remain free.

Notes

1. *Country Reports on Human Rights Practices for 1992* (Washington, DC: U.S. Department of State, 1993). Available at https://archive.org/details/countryreportson1992unit.
2. *Freedom of the Press* (Washington, DC: Freedom House, 2003). Available at http://www.freedomhouse.org/report/freedom-press/2003/san-marino.

São Tomé and Principe: 1975–2012

São Tomé and Principe Year by Year

Year	Media	Government
1975	Not Free	Autocracy
1976	Not Free	Autocracy
1977	Not Free	Autocracy
1978	Not Free	Autocracy
1979	Not Free	Autocracy
1980	Not Free	Autocracy
1981	Not Free	Autocracy
1982	Not Free	Autocracy
1983	Not Free	Autocracy
1984	Not Free	Autocracy
1985	Not Free	Autocracy
1986	Not Free	Autocracy
1987	Not Free	Autocracy
1988	Not Free	Autocracy
1989	Not Free	Autocracy
1990	Not Free	Autocracy
1991	Imperfectly Free	Democracy
1992	Imperfectly Free	Democracy
1993	Imperfectly Free	Democracy
1994	Imperfectly Free	Democracy
1995	Imperfectly Free	Democracy

(Continued)

MEDIA FREEDOM HISTORY IN A NUTSHELL

- The smallest country in Africa, São Tomé and Principe was a one-party state with controlled media until it democratized in the early 1990s and media became imperfectly free
- The government owns the only radio and television stations, but foreign broadcasts are available
- As of 2012, there were three privately owned newspapers and one government-owned newspaper (BBC News Country Profiles)
- As of 2012, about 22 percent of São Toméans had internet access (International Telecommunication Union's 2012 ICT Indicators Database)

In Brief

The smallest country in Africa, São Tomé and Principe is made up of two main islands that add up to 372 square miles. With a population of 186,817 in 2013,[1] it is a small media market. For the first decade and a half after independence, São Tomé and Principe was a one-party state with controlled media. In 1990, it democratized and media became imperfectly free. Today media are limited but functionally free.

Chronology

1975–1990: Not Free

Upon gaining independence from Portugal, São Tomé and Principe was a one-party state under the leadership of President Manuel Pinto da Costa, and the media were government controlled.[2]

(Continued)

Year	Media	Government
1996	Imperfectly Free	Democracy
1997	Imperfectly Free	Democracy
1998	Imperfectly Free	Democracy
1999	Imperfectly Free	Democracy
2000	Imperfectly Free	Democracy
2001	Imperfectly Free	Democracy
2002	Imperfectly Free	Democracy
2003	Imperfectly Free	Democracy
2004	Imperfectly Free	Democracy
2005	Imperfectly Free	Democracy
2006	Imperfectly Free	Democracy
2007	Imperfectly Free	Democracy
2008	Imperfectly Free	Democracy
2009	Imperfectly Free	Democracy
2010	Imperfectly Free	Democracy
2011	Imperfectly Free	Democracy
2012	Imperfectly Free	Democracy

1991–2012: Imperfectly Free

After a couple of attempted coups, São Tomé and Principe adopted a new constitution in 1990, transitioned to a multiparty system, and held its first democratic elections in 1991. The new constitution included provisions for media freedom, and the opposition was given access to the government-controlled broadcast media.[3] Moreover, in addition to the government-owned newspaper, which was published intermittently, independently published pamphlets emerged, and these were critical of the government.[4]

Media Today

The limited media are probably a function of market forces rather than politics. The government controls the country's only radio and television stations, but there are no laws prohibiting private stations and foreign broadcasts are accessible.[5] There are four newspapers, one state-owned and three privately owned.[6] There are also newsletters that often criticize the government, and members of the opposition party are given access to the broadcast media.[7]

Notes

1. *São Tomé and Principe* (Washington, DC: CIA World Factbook, 2013). Available at https://www.cia.gov/library/publications/the-world-factbook/geos/tp.html.
2. *Country Reports on Human Rights Practices for 1977* (Washington, DC: U.S. Department of State, 1978). Available at http://babel.hathitrust.org/cgi/pt?id=mdp.39015078705632.
3. *Country Reports on Human Rights Practices for 1991* (Washington, DC: U.S. Department of State, 1992). Available at https://archive.org/details/countryreportson1991unit.
4. Ibid.
5. *Freedom of the Press* (Washington, DC: Freedom House, 2013). Available at http://www.freedomhouse.org/report/freedom-world/2013/s%C3%A3o-tom%C3%A9-and-pr%C3%ADncipe.
6. *Sao Tome and Principe, BBC Country Profiles* (London, UK: British Broadcasting Company). Available at http://www.bbc.co.uk/news/world-africa-14093667.
7. Ibid.

Saudi Arabia: 1948–2012

Saudi Arabia Year by Year

Year	Media	Government
1948	Not Free	Autocracy
1949	Not Free	Autocracy
1950	Not Free	Autocracy
1951	Not Free	Autocracy
1952	Not Free	Autocracy
1953	Not Free	Autocracy
1954	Not Free	Autocracy
1955	Not Free	Autocracy
1956	Not Free	Autocracy
1957	Not Free	Autocracy
1958	Not Free	Autocracy
1959	Not Free	Autocracy
1960	Not Free	Autocracy
1961	Not Free	Autocracy
1962	Not Free	Autocracy
1963	Not Free	Autocracy
1964	Not Free	Autocracy
1965	Not Free	Autocracy
1966	Not Free	Autocracy
1967	Not Free	Autocracy
1968	Not Free	Autocracy
1969	Not Free	Autocracy
1970	Not Free	Autocracy
1971	Not Free	Autocracy
1972	Not Free	Autocracy
1973	Not Free	Autocracy

(Continued)

MEDIA FREEDOM HISTORY IN A NUTSHELL

- With one of the most autocratic and conservative governments in the world, all Saudi Arabian media are directly controlled or heavily censored
- As of 2012, Saudi Arabia had sixteen daily paid-for newspapers with an average total circulation per issue of 2,168,000 (World Association of Newspapers' World Press Trends)
- The government controls all domestic radio and television, but satellite television remains popular, though the satellite dishes are illegal
- The government monitors and filters internet content
- As of 2012, 54 percent of Saudis had Internet access (International Telecommunication Union's 2012 ICT Indicators Database)

In Brief

The royal family and the government directly own or strictly control all media.

Chronology

1948–2012: Not Free

Since Saudi Arabia was founded in 1932, media have been controlled. The 1964 Press Code gave the government the power to censor any content deemed offensive to or critical of the government, the ruling family, or Islam.[1]

Media Today

One of the most autocratic nations in the world, there is little to indicate any change in the strictly controlled media environment. The Ministry of

(Continued)

Year	Media	Government
1974	Not Free	Autocracy
1975	Not Free	Autocracy
1976	Not Free	Autocracy
1977	Not Free	Autocracy
1978	Not Free	Autocracy
1979	Not Free	Autocracy
1980	Not Free	Autocracy
1981	Not Free	Autocracy
1982	Not Free	Autocracy
1983	Not Free	Autocracy
1984	Not Free	Autocracy
1985	Not Free	Autocracy
1986	Not Free	Autocracy
1987	Not Free	Autocracy
1988	Not Free	Autocracy
1989	Not Free	Autocracy
1990	Not Free	Autocracy
1991	Not Free	Autocracy
1992	Not Free	Autocracy

Year	Media	Government
1993	Not Free	Autocracy
1994	Not Free	Autocracy
1995	Not Free	Autocracy
1996	Not Free	Autocracy
1997	Not Free	Autocracy
1998	Not Free	Autocracy
1999	Not Free	Autocracy
2000	Not Free	Autocracy
2001	Not Free	Autocracy
2002	Not Free	Autocracy
2003	Not Free	Autocracy
2004	Not Free	Autocracy
2005	Not Free	Autocracy
2006	Not Free	Autocracy
2007	Not Free	Autocracy
2008	Not Free	Autocracy
2009	Not Free	Autocracy
2010	Not Free	Autocracy
2011	Not Free	Autocracy
2012	Not Free	Autocracy

Culture and Information has the authority to close down any news outlet deemed to be in violation of the press law. In 2011, the government mandated that all bloggers and online newspapers obtain licenses from the Ministry of Culture and Information. The country's newspapers are privately owned, but the owners have close ties to the ruling family.[2] While more than half the population has Internet access, the government routinely monitors and blocks Internet content. The government controls all domestic broadcast media. Though it is against the law to have a satellite dish, satellite television remains popular.[3]

Notes

1. *World Press Freedom Review,* IPI Report (Vienna: International Press Institute, 2000).
2. *Freedom of the Press* (Washington, DC: Freedom House, 2013). Available at http://www.freedom house.org/report/freedom-press/2013/saudi-arabia.
3. Ibid.

Senegal: 1960–2012

Senegal Year by Year

Year	Not Free	Government
1960	Not Free	Anocracy
1961	Not Free	Anocracy
1962	Not Free	In Transition
1963	Not Free	Autocracy
1964	Not Free	Autocracy
1965	Not Free	Autocracy
1966	Not Free	Autocracy
1967	Not Free	Autocracy
1968	Not Free	Autocracy
1969	Not Free	Autocracy
1970	Not Free	Autocracy
1971	Not Free	Autocracy
1972	Not Free	Autocracy
1973	Not Free	Autocracy
1974	Not Free	Autocracy
1975	Not Free	Autocracy
1976	Not Free	Autocracy
1977	Not Free	Autocracy
1978	Not Free	Anocracy
1979	Not Free	Anocracy
1980	Not Free	Anocracy
1981	Imperfectly Free	Anocracy

(Continued)

In Brief

Media were restricted for the first two decades following independence as Senegal became a one-party state. In the mid-1970s, some political parties were permitted and the opposition media began to emerge. In 1981, when the restrictions on political parties were lifted, media became functionally free. Media today remain functionally free, but are somewhat restricted by laws which criminalize media offenses.

Chronology

1960–1980: Not Free

Senegal gained independence from France in 1960, and Leopold Senghor became president only to face an attempted coup in 1962 by then Prime Minister Mamadou Dia. Perhaps this early power struggle contributed to the government's desire to control of the media. In any case,

(Continued)

Year	Not Free	Government
1982	Imperfectly Free	Anocracy
1983	Imperfectly Free	Anocracy
1984	Imperfectly Free	Anocracy
1985	Imperfectly Free	Anocracy
1986	Imperfectly Free	Anocracy
1987	Imperfectly Free	Anocracy
1988	Imperfectly Free	Anocracy
1989	Imperfectly Free	Anocracy
1990	Imperfectly Free	Anocracy
1991	Imperfectly Free	Anocracy
1992	Imperfectly Free	Anocracy
1993	Imperfectly Free	Anocracy
1994	Imperfectly Free	Anocracy
1995	Imperfectly Free	Anocracy
1996	Imperfectly Free	Anocracy
1997	Imperfectly Free	Anocracy
1998	Imperfectly Free	Anocracy
1999	Imperfectly Free	Anocracy
2000	Imperfectly Free	Democracy
2001	Imperfectly Free	Democracy
2002	Imperfectly Free	Democracy
2003	Imperfectly Free	Democracy
2004	Imperfectly Free	Democracy
2005	Imperfectly Free	Democracy
2006	Imperfectly Free	Democracy
2007	Imperfectly Free	Democracy
2008	Imperfectly Free	Democracy
2009	Imperfectly Free	Democracy
2010	Imperfectly Free	Democracy
2011	Imperfectly Free	Democracy
2012	Imperfectly Free	Democracy

in the early 1960s, there were reports of newspapers being confiscated and at least one foreign correspondent was expelled.[1] Although the 1963 constitution provided for media freedom, the government did not respect this in practice. In 1966, Senegal officially became a one-party state and the opposition press disappeared.[2]

In the mid-1970s, President Senghor permitted some political parties and opposition newspapers reemerged.[3] Yet there was a backlash in the form of the 1977 penal code:

Alarmed by the rise of a highly critical national press, the government elaborated a tough press code that tightened the state's control over media and certification of journalists. It also stepped up its prosecution of Senegalese editors and journalists for libeling public figures in government or for spreading false rumors.[4]

Though the U.S. Department of State's report on Senegalese human rights concluded that the government "bent over backwards to avoid apply the law in any way that even appears to restrict press freedom,"[5] this new law likely had a chilling effect and promoted self-censorship.

1981–2012: Imperfectly Free

With the resignation of President Senghor in early 1981 and the move to an unlimited multi-party system, the conditions for news media improved and more newspapers began publishing.[6] Yet the government retained its monopoly over broadcast media.

In 1995, the Senegal gained its first private radio station.[7]

Media Today

Although they remain functionally free, Senegalese media continue to face a number of pressures. The 1977 penal code remains in effect and has been used by government to punish critical journalists.[8] Libel, defamation, and insult remain criminalized.[9] Although Senegal has a number of independent newspapers, these publications are not widely distributed beyond the capital.[10] Senegal has a mix of private and public radio stations, and because of high illiteracy, radio is the more accessible medium.[11] Senegal also has both commercial and public television stations. Internet access remains limited.

Notes

1. *The Toils of the Press*, IPI Report (Zurich: International Press Institute, September 1963 and November 1963).
2. Sheldon Gellar, *Democracy in Senegal: Tocquevillian Analytics in Africa* (New York: Palgrave MacMillan, 2005).
3. Ibid.
4. Ibid., 80.
5. *Country Reports on Human Rights Practices for 1979* (Washington, DC: U.S. Department of State, 1980). Available at http://babel.hathitrust.org/cgi/pt?id=mdp.39015014188273;view=1up;seq=9.
6. Gellar, *Democracy in Senegal: Tocquevillian Analytics in Africa*.
7. *World Press Freedom Review*, IPI Report (Vienna: International Press Institute, November/December 1995).
8. *Freedom of the Press* (Washington, DC: Freedom House, 2013). Available at http://www.freedomhouse.org/report/freedom-press/2013/senegal.
9. Ibid.
10. Ibid.
11. Ibid.

Serbia: 2006–2012

Serbia Year by Year

Year	Media	Government
2006	Imperfectly Free	Democracy
2007	Imperfectly Free	Democracy
2008	Imperfectly Free	Democracy
2009	Imperfectly Free	Democracy
2010	Imperfectly Free	Democracy
2011	Imperfectly Free	Democracy
2012	Imperfectly Free	Democracy

In Brief

The effort to integrate Serbia into Europe defines its recent history. This includes a commitment to establishing and developing free media. This effort, however, remains a work in progress.

Chronology

2006–2012: Imperfectly Free

Free media exist both legally and in practice, but the echoes of authoritarian media control are still apparent in the media environment.[1] The long history of leaders using of the media for propaganda purposes, stretching all of the way back through Serbia's inclusion in Yugoslavia and the Ottoman Empire, continues to influence the nature of coverage and the relationship between media, government, and the public. Nationalistic tone is common in coverage. Additionally, there is significant concern over inappropriate influence over news outlets, and the unwinding of harsh libel laws has stalled recently.

MEDIA FREEDOM HISTORY IN A NUTSHELL

- The push for integration into Europe has dominated Serbia's brief period of recognized independence
- Legally and in practice, the media are free, yet the long history of authoritarian use of the media for propaganda is still apparent
- As of 2011, there were thirteen daily newspapers, twelve of them were paid-for daily newspapers, with a total average circulation per issue of 1,202,000; Serbia had 157 television stations and 550 radio stations (World Association of Newspaper's 2012 World Newspaper Trends)
- As of 2012, about 48 percent of Serbians had Internet access (International Telecommunication Union's 2012 ICT Indicators Database)

Media Today

Media are functionally free, but political and social pressures that threaten a return to controlled media are only held in check by wider European support for liberalization and professionalization. Serbia's media environment is restrained by political pressures, corruption, regulatory setbacks, and economic difficulties.[2]

Notes

1. *Serbia*, Media Landscape Reports (Maastricht, The Netherlands: European Journalism Centre, 2013). Available at http://ejc.net/media_landscapes/Serbia.
2. *Freedom of the Press* (Washington, DC: Freedom House, 2013). Available at http://www.freedomhouse.org/report/freedom-press/2012/serbia.

Seychelles: 1976–2012

Seychelles Year by Year

Year	Media	Government
1976	Not Free	Anocracy
1977	Not Free	Autocracy
1978	Not Free	Autocracy
1979	Not Free	Autocracy
1980	Not Free	Autocracy
1981	Not Free	Autocracy
1982	Not Free	Autocracy
1983	Not Free	Autocracy
1984	Not Free	Autocracy
1985	Not Free	Autocracy
1986	Not Free	Autocracy
1987	Not Free	Autocracy
1988	Not Free	Autocracy
1989	Not Free	Autocracy
1990	Not Free	Autocracy
1991	Not Free	Autocracy
1992	Imperfectly Free	Anocracy
1993	Imperfectly Free	Anocracy
1994	Imperfectly Free	Anocracy
1995	Imperfectly Free	Anocracy
1996	Imperfectly Free	Anocracy

(Continued)

MEDIA FREEDOM HISTORY IN A NUTSHELL

- Shortly after independence, Seychelles became a one-party state with government-controlled media
- In the early 1990s, as the country transitioned to a multiparty democracy, the government eased media restrictions
- Media today are functionally free but constrained by libel laws
- As of 2012, there were three daily newspapers as well as several weekly newspapers (Freedom House's Freedom of the Press 2013)
- In 2012, the only broadcast media were state owned, but the government did grant two licenses for independent radio stations (Freedom House's Freedom of the Press 2013)
- As of 2012, about 47 percent of Seychellois had Internet access (International Telecommunication Union's 2012 ICT Indicators Database)

In Brief

An archipelago in the Indian Ocean, Seychelles became a one-party state shortly after gaining independence. The government kept media tightly restricted until the early 1990s, when the country transitioned to multiparty system. Since then, media have been functionally free but only just so. Given the small media market, there are a limited number of news outlets, and in 2012, the only broadcast media and one daily newspaper were state owned. Opposition newspapers are vulnerable to libel lawsuits but have persisted in criticizing the government.

(Continued)

Year	Media	Government
1997	Imperfectly Free	Anocracy
1998	Imperfectly Free	Anocracy
1999	Imperfectly Free	Anocracy
2000	Imperfectly Free	Anocracy
2001	Imperfectly Free	Anocracy
2002	Imperfectly Free	Anocracy
2003	Imperfectly Free	Anocracy
2004	Imperfectly Free	Anocracy
2005	Imperfectly Free	Anocracy
2006	Imperfectly Free	Anocracy
2007	Imperfectly Free	Anocracy
2008	Imperfectly Free	Anocracy
2009	Imperfectly Free	Anocracy
2010	Imperfectly Free	Anocracy
2011	Imperfectly Free	Anocracy
2012	Imperfectly Free	Anocracy

Chronology

1976–1991: Not Free

Immediately following independence from Britain in 1976, Seychelles was a multiparty democracy, but following a 1977 coup, France Rene took control of the country and turned it into a one-party state. During these years, the government owned and controlled the country's only radio station and its main newspaper, but some foreign news magazines were available. In 1979, a new law gave the government the authority to imprison up to three years:

any person who publishes, whether orally or in writing or otherwise, any statement, rumor or report which is likely to cause fear and alarm to the public or disturb the public peace or any person who with intent to bring the President into hatred, ridicule, or contempt who publishes any defamatory or insulting matter whether in writing, print, word of mouth or in any other manner.[1]

In 1983, Radio Television Seychelles launched the country's first television station, which like the radio station was run by the Ministry of Information.

At the end of 1991, President Rene announced the country would transition to a multiparty democracy.

1992–2012: Imperfectly Free

In 1992, Radio Television Seychelles became the Seychelles Broadcasting Corporation, and though these outlets were generally supportive of government, they also carried news that was at times critical of government.[2] While restrictive press laws remained in place, the government seemed to be a bit more tolerant of media criticism and a number of new newspapers began publishing, many of which had connections to opposition parties and were quite critical of government.[3] Foreign broadcasts and print media were also available. In 1993, President Rene was reelected, and he remained in power until he resigned in 2004. During his tenure, the independence of the Seychelles Broadcasting Corporation remained questionable. In 2002, the Court rejected a lawsuit that claimed the appointment of the president's wife and eight civil servants to the ten-member board compromised the corporation's independence.[4] Thus, the government maintained control over the Seychellois broadcast media and the country's only daily newspaper, and little attention was paid to the opposition media.[5] In the early 2000s, the only opposition media to receive any attention was the weekly *Regar*, which was frequently sued for libel.[6]

Media Today

Seychellois media remain functionally free but only barely so. The government retains control over the country's primary media sources and uses libel laws to restrict the opposition media. Critical journalists have been attacked, harassed, and sued for libel to the point where many resort to self-censorship.[7] Yet the opposition media do persist in watchdog reporting. While nearly half of Seychellois have Internet access, there are reports of the government monitoring Internet activity and blocking the sites connected to the opposition.[8]

Notes

1. *Country Reports on Human Rights Practices for 1980* (Washington, DC: U.S. Department of State, 1981), 222. Available at http://babel.hathitrust.org/cgi/pt?id=mdp.39015014143476;view=1up;seq=2.

2. *Country Reports on Human Rights Practices for 1993* (Washington, DC: US Department of State, 1993). Available at https://archive.org/details/countryreportson1992unit.

3. Ibid.

4. *Country Reports on Human Rights Practices for 2002* (Washington, DC: US Department of State, 2002). Available at http://www.state.gov/j/drl/rls/hrrpt/2001/af/8401.htm.

5. *Country Reports on Human Rights Practices for 2003* (Washington, DC: US Department of State, 2003). Available at http://www.state.gov/j/drl/rls/hrrpt/2002/18224.htm.

6. Ibid.

7. *Freedom of the Press* (Washington, DC: Freedom House, 2013). Available at http://www.freedomhouse.org/report/freedom-press/2013/seychelles.

8. Ibid.

Sierra Leone: 1961–2012

Sierra Leone Year by Year

Year	Media	Government
1961	Imperfectly Free	Democracy
1962	Imperfectly Free	Democracy
1963	Imperfectly Free	Democracy
1964	Imperfectly Free	Democracy
1965	Imperfectly Free	Democracy
1966	Imperfectly Free	Democracy
1967	Not Free	Autocracy
1968	Not Free	Anocracy
1969	Not Free	Anocracy
1970	Not Free	Anocracy
1971	Not Free	Autocracy
1972	Not Free	Autocracy
1973	Not Free	Autocracy
1974	Not Free	Autocracy
1975	Not Free	Autocracy
1976	Not Free	Autocracy
1977	Not Free	Autocracy
1978	Not Free	Autocracy
1979	Not Free	Autocracy
1980	Not Free	Autocracy
1981	Not Free	Autocracy
1982	Not Free	Autocracy
1983	Not Free	Autocracy
1984	Not Free	Autocracy

MEDIA FREEDOM HISTORY IN A NUTSHELL

- Immediately following independence, Sierra Leonean media were functionally free
- In 1967, a coup marked the end of democracy and media freedom
- From 1991 to 2002, as civil war ravaged the country and left more than 50,000 dead, Sierra Leone became one of the most dangerous countries in the world for journalists
- With the end of the war, media became functionally free but limited by a lack of professionalism and harsh libel laws
- As of 2012, there were fifty-eight newspapers, the majority were independent, many were connected to political parties, and most criticized the government (Freedom House's Freedom of the Press 2013)
- Sierra Leone has a mix of public and private broadcast media; there were forty radio and thirteen television stations in 2012 (Freedom House's Freedom of the Press 2013)
- As of 2012, less than 2 percent of Sierra Leoneans had Internet access (International Telecommunication Union's 2012 ICT Indicators Database)

In Brief

Upon independence Sierra Leone was a democracy with some media freedom, but following several coups and attempted coups, media were restricted and Sierra Leone became a one-party state. In 1991, civil war erupted and continued until 2002, leaving more than 50,000 dead and as many as 2 million displaced. Since the end of the war, media have been functionally free but constrained by a lack of professionalism, limited resources, and repressive libel laws.

Year	Media	Government
1985	Not Free	Autocracy
1986	Not Free	Autocracy
1987	Not Free	Autocracy
1988	Not Free	Autocracy
1989	Not Free	Autocracy
1990	Not Free	Autocracy
1991	Not Free	Autocracy
1992	Not Free	Autocracy
1993	Not Free	Autocracy
1994	Not Free	Autocracy
1995	Not Free	Autocracy
1996	Not Free	Anocracy
1997	Not Free	Anocracy
1998	Not Free	Anocracy
1999	Not Free	Anocracy
2000	Not Free	Anocracy
2001	Not Free	Anocracy
2002	Not Free	Anocracy
2003	Imperfectly Free	Anocracy
2004	Imperfectly Free	Anocracy
2005	Imperfectly Free	Anocracy
2006	Imperfectly Free	Anocracy
2007	Imperfectly Free	Democracy
2008	Imperfectly Free	Democracy
2009	Imperfectly Free	Democracy
2010	Imperfectly Free	Democracy
2011	Imperfectly Free	Democracy
2012	Imperfectly Free	Democracy

Chronology

1961–1966: Imperfectly Free

As a British colony, Sierra Leone had a long tradition of press freedom.[1] Thus, upon gaining independence in 1961, Sierra Leone was a democracy with newspapers that were functionally free but with limited reach.[2] Yet the government controlled radio, the country's most popular medium.[3] Founded in 1934, the Sierra Leone Broadcasting Service (SLBS) was government funded and part of the Ministry of Information. SLBS began offering limited television service in 1963.[4] The 1965 Public Order Act criminalized libel and allowed the government to punish those distributing offending news media as well as those responsible for the actual content with imprisonment of up to seven years.

1967–2002: Not Free

In 1967, a military coup brought about an end to democracy in Sierra Leone, and as various factions sought to consolidate their power, restrictions on media increased. Following another coup in 1968, Siaka Stevens emerged as the country's leader. Stevens had very little tolerance for any form of opposition, including opposition media. "Regime violence, though infrequent, was directed at opposition newspapers, and took the form of blowing up the presses or ordering drive-by shootings."[5]

In 1978, Sierra Leone officially became a one-party state, and when Stevens retired in 1985, Joseph Saidu Momoh became president.

In 1991, civil war broke out as the Revolutionary United Front led by Foday Sankoh began to take over parts of the country near the border with Liberia. That same year, Sierra Leone adopted a new constitution that called for a multiparty system and President Momoh said that media should be free but that journalists needed to act responsibly.[6] Yet in 1991, several journalists were arrested on libel charges and foreign reporters covering the conflict were compelled to run their reports by a government censor.[7]

Civil war and several coups led to increased political instability throughout the 1990s. More than 50,000 people were killed in the war, and by the end of the decade, Sierra Leone was identified as the most dangerous country in the world for journalists.[8] In 1999 alone at least ten journalists were killed.[9] That same year, the UN intervened, but the fighting continued until 2002.

2003–2012: Imperfectly Free

With the end of the civil war, conditions for news media improved to the point where media were functionally free, but journalists were for the most part untrained, and the lack of professionalism left the media with little credibility.[10] The government continued to use the 1965 Public Order Act to charge critical journalists with libel.[11] Although the fighting was over, attacks on journalists and government raids of news outlets continued to be a problem.[12]

Media Today

Sierra Leonean media remain functionally free but constrained by draconian libel laws. The biggest threat to media freedom appears to be a lack of professionalism. "The media do not provide sufficient and objective information that sets an agenda, speaks truth to power and holds leadership accountable."[13] The media are regulated by the Independent Media Commission, and although its members are government appointed, the IMC has for the most part acted independently.[14] Most of Sierra Leonean newspapers are privately owned, and many have ties to political parties. Sierra Leone has a mix of private and public broadcast media, including many community radio stations. As of 2012, less than 2 percent of the population had Internet access.

Notes

1. Fred I. Omu, "The Dilemma of Press Freedom in Colonial Africa: The West African Example," *Journal of African History*, 9, no. 2 (1968): 279–98.
2. Christopher Allen, "Sierra Leone Politics since Independence," *African Affairs*, 67, no. 269 (1968): 305–29.
3. Ibid.
4. Alan Wells, *World Broadcasting: A Comparative View* (Westport, CT: Greenwood Publishing Group, 1996).
5. Earl Conteh-Morgan and Mac Dixon-Fyle, *Sierra Leone at the End of the Twentieth Century: History, Politics, and Society* (New York: Peter Lang Publishing, 1999), 81.
6. *World Press Freedom Review*, IPI Report (Zurich: International Press Institute, 1991).
7. Ibid.
8. *World Press Freedom Review*, IPI Report (Vienna: International Press Institute, 2000).
9. Ibid.
10. *Media Sustainability Index—Africa* (Washington, DC: IREX, 2012). Available at http://www.irex.org/project/media-sustainability-index-msi-africa.
11. *Freedom of the Press* (Washington, DC: Freedom House, 2004). Available at http://www.freedomhouse.org/report/freedom-press/2004/sierra-leone.
12. *World Press Freedom Review*, IPI Report (Vienna: International Press Institute, 2005).
13. *Media Sustainability Index—Africa* (Washington, DC: IREX, 2012), 343.
14. *Freedom of the Press* (Washington, DC: Freedom House, 2013). Available at http://www.freedomhouse.org/report/freedom-press/2013/sierra-leone.

Singapore: 1965–2012

Singapore Year by Year

Year	Media	Government
1965	Not Free	Anocracy
1966	Not Free	Anocracy
1967	Not Free	Anocracy
1968	Not Free	Anocracy
1969	Not Free	Anocracy
1970	Not Free	Anocracy
1971	Not Free	Anocracy
1972	Not Free	Anocracy
1973	Not Free	Anocracy
1974	Not Free	Anocracy
1975	Not Free	Anocracy
1976	Not Free	Anocracy
1977	Not Free	Anocracy
1978	Not Free	Anocracy
1979	Not Free	Anocracy
1980	Not Free	Anocracy
1981	Not Free	Anocracy
1982	Not Free	Anocracy
1983	Not Free	Anocracy
1984	Not Free	Anocracy
1985	Not Free	Anocracy
1986	Not Free	Anocracy

(Continued)

In Brief

A former province of the Malaysian Federation, Singapore might be best described as an authoritarian democracy. With extensive social regulations that have extended all the way to banning the sale of chewing gum, it is unsurprising that the media are strictly regulated.

Chronology

1965–2012: Not Free

In some respects Singapore is democratic, with popular representation and multiparty elections, but in others it is quite autocratic, with the

(Continued)

Year	Media	Government
1987	Not Free	Anocracy
1988	Not Free	Anocracy
1989	Not Free	Anocracy
1990	Not Free	Anocracy
1991	Not Free	Anocracy
1992	Not Free	Anocracy
1993	Not Free	Anocracy
1994	Not Free	Anocracy
1995	Not Free	Anocracy
1996	Not Free	Anocracy
1997	Not Free	Anocracy
1998	Not Free	Anocracy
1999	Not Free	Anocracy
2000	Not Free	Anocracy
2001	Not Free	Anocracy
2002	Not Free	Anocracy
2003	Not Free	Anocracy
2004	Not Free	Anocracy
2005	Not Free	Anocracy
2006	Not Free	Anocracy
2007	Not Free	Anocracy
2008	Not Free	Anocracy
2009	Not Free	Anocracy
2010	Not Free	Anocracy
2011	Not Free	Anocracy
2012	Not Free	Anocracy

People's Action Party dominating those elections since 1968 and exerting control over many aspects of social and political life. From 1965 to the late 1990s, this included direct control of the news media.

While little changed regarding the government attitude toward social control and the laws related to media control, the combination of a free trade agreement with the United States and the technological advances driving Internet expansion forced a slight acquiescence to the reality of external media penetration. Thus in the early 2000s, some media were restricted rather than directly controlled. Also in the early 2000s, the government launched the Global Media City campaign aimed at making Singapore "Asia's leading media marketplace and financing hub—one where quality content is produced and digital media is developed."[1]

Media Today

Clean, wealthy, and with little street crime or other common urban ills, Singapore has been described as the trade of liberty for a comfortable urban life. Media are highly developed, but government has the authority to censor them and does so. All media outlets and Internet service providers are required to obtain annual licenses, and critical journalists risk being charged with defamation, sedition, libel, and other crimes.[2] As of 2012, about three-fourths of Singaporeans had Internet access, and there are some indications that the Internet may provide a venue for opposition.[3] Yet there appears to be broad acceptance of extensive government control of social behavior, and there is little if any sign of demand for media freedom.

Notes

1. *Singapore Media City: Gateway to the World* (Singapore: Media Development Authority, 2011), para 5. Available at http://www.smf.sg/singapore mediacity/pages/singaporemediafusion.aspx.
2. *Freedom of the Press* (Washington, DC: Freedom House, 2013). Available at http://www.freedom house.org/report/freedom-press/2013/singapore.
3. Ibid.

Slovakia: 1993–2012

Slovakia Year by Year

Year	Media	Government
1993	Not Free	Democracy
1994	Not Free	Democracy
1995	Not Free	Democracy
1996	Not Free	Democracy
1997	Not Free	Democracy
1998	Not Free	Democracy
1999	Not Free	Democracy
2000	Imperfectly Free	Democracy
2001	Imperfectly Free	Democracy
2002	Free	Democracy
2003	Free	Democracy
2004	Free	Democracy
2005	Free	Democracy
2006	Free	Democracy
2007	Free	Democracy
2008	Free	Democracy
2009	Free	Democracy
2010	Free	Democracy
2011	Free	Democracy
2012	Free	Democracy

In Brief

As part of Czechoslovakia, Slovakia was already part of one of the most liberal of the communist regimes and experienced a reasonably smooth, if slow, transition to a free media environment at the end of the Cold War.

MEDIA FREEDOM HISTORY IN A NUTSHELL

- Slovakian media made a gradual but steady transition to media freedom following the Cold War
- As of 2011, there were nine daily newspapers; all nine were paid-for daily newspapers, with a total average circulation per issue of 352,000 (World Association of Newspaper's 2012 World Newspaper Trends)
- Slovakia has both public and private television and radio stations
- As of 2012, about 80 percent of Slovakians had Internet access (International Telecommunication Union's 2012 ICT Indicators Database)

Chronology

1993–1999: Not Free

Unlike the Czech half of the former Czechoslovakia, the newly independent Slovakia's press was controlled. The best explanation for this divergence appears to be related to the largely rural nature of Slovakia. The bulk of media liberalization in post-communist Czechoslovakia occurred in Czech urban centers, which benefitted from the quick establishment of links to Western Europe. The media outlets in Slovakia were small, underdeveloped, underfunded, and conservative.

In 1999, portions of the Slovak election law that banned radio and television election campaigning in media other than the public-owned broadcast media were ruled unconstitutional by the Slovak Constitutional Court. The ruling was based on the public's constitutional right to information as well as the right to freedom of speech for broadcasters, providing a step toward free media.[1]

2000–2001: Imperfectly Free

With the geography of Slovakia providing far easier physical linkages and trade with the East, the diffusion of Western European influences into the country's social and political structure was slower, but it was steady, and a relatively quiet shift to functionally free media occurred at roughly the turn of the century. Economic challenges were a significant threat to continued development, but the push for inclusion in the European Union, including significant support from Europe, accelerated the development of free, professional, and independent media. To that end, laws aimed at improving media freedom were passed, including in 2000 the Act on Free Access to Information, which allowed anyone to request information from state agencies and receive an answer within ten days.[2]

2002–2012: Free

Inclusion in the European Union provided a bulwark against any remaining conservative forces that desired a more restricted media environment. A high level of professionalism has been sustained in the decade since inclusion in the EU.

Media Today

Media remain free and reasonably stable, and the support of European Union inclusion limits significant challenges to that basic state of affairs. There are, however, several concerns and challenges. Libel judgments have produced very large financial penalties for media outlets. Already a small market, Slovakia's media are further fragmented by the need to service a linguistically diverse national market, which poses challenges to economic sustainability. Financial challenges and the decreasing audience for public service broadcasting forced the government to merge Slovakia's public radio and television networks into one.[3]

Notes

1. *World Press Freedom Review*, IPI Report (Vienna: International Press Institute, 1999).
2. *Freedom of the Press* (Washington, DC: Freedom House, 2013). Available at http://www.freedom house.org/report/freedom-press/2012/slovakia.
3. Ibid.

Slovenia: 1992–2012

Slovenia Year by Year

Year	Media	Government
1992	Not Free	Democracy
1993	Not Free	Democracy
1994	Not Free	Democracy
1995	Imperfectly Free	Democracy
1996	Imperfectly Free	Democracy
1997	Imperfectly Free	Democracy
1998	Imperfectly Free	Democracy
1999	Imperfectly Free	Democracy
2000	Imperfectly Free	Democracy
2001	Imperfectly Free	Democracy
2002	Free	Democracy
2003	Free	Democracy
2004	Free	Democracy
2005	Free	Democracy
2006	Free	Democracy
2007	Free	Democracy
2008	Free	Democracy
2009	Free	Democracy
2010	Free	Democracy
2011	Free	Democracy
2012	Free	Democracy

In Brief

Slovenia is one of many countries claiming that ancient liberal traditions and politics in one of its medieval city-states inspired the writers of the U.S. constitution. The exit from Yugoslavia was comparatively bloodless, with only brief and small-scale armed skirmishes with Yugoslav federal troops. Once independence was established, the push toward integration into Europe included a commitment to media freedom.

MEDIA FREEDOM HISTORY IN A NUTSHELL

- Following its break from Yugoslavia, Slovenia made a comparatively smooth transition to a free media system
- In the 1990s, commercial broadcast media emerged to challenge the public broadcasters, but the public stations remain the most popular (Euro topics Media Landscape Reports)
- As of 2011, there were eight daily newspapers; seven were paid-for daily newspapers, with a total average circulation per issue of 333,000 (World Association of Newspaper's 2012 World Newspaper Trends)
- As of 2012, about 70 percent of Slovenians had Internet access (International Telecommunication Union's 2012 ICT Indicators Database)

Chronology

1992–1994: Not Free

Already the most liberal and prosperous province of Yugoslavia, Slovenia's departure from the socialist country was initiated by a public referendum and the election of a nonsocialist government. There appears to have been little if any domestic opposition to the swift establishment of a liberal democratic political system.

While the split from Yugoslavia was almost bloodless, there was still some fighting with Yugoslav federal troops and the country remained on a war footing for nearly three years.

During this period, government controls on the press, held over from the previous regime, remained largely in place. However, the development of a commercial press did begin during this time.

1995–2001: Imperfectly Free

Once independence from the remnants of Yugoslavia appeared to be secure, the development of a free media environment proceeded quickly and was supported by Europe. However, only state-supported broadcast media could legally reach a nationwide audience.[1]

2002–2012: Free

Steady development of the free media environment and professionalism of the media offer no clear-cut date for the shift to a clearly free media. By roughly 2002, it became clear that any pressures that might drive the media back toward greater government control had been effectively marginalized. The 2003, Access to Information of Public Character Act ensured free access to information.[2] Yet journalists continued to face pressures from defamation suits, and the Mass Media Act of 2006 included the "right to correction," which granted anyone slighted by news coverage the right to demand a correction, even if the reporting was accurate.[3]

Media Today

Firmly established relationships with the EU help support the already strong commitment to media freedom. The primary challenges are typical of a very small, linguistically distinct market. Most major media organizations are effectively owned or funded by the government, and all media outlets struggle to survive economically in a market of only two million.

Notes

1. *World Press Freedom Review*, IPI Report (Vienna: International Press Institute, 1995).
2. *Freedom of the Press* (Washington, DC: Freedom House, 2013). Available at http://www.freedomhouse.org/report/freedom-press/2012/slovenia.
3. *Freedom of the Press* (Washington, DC: Freedom House, 2013). Available at http://www.freedomhouse.org/reports.

Solomon Islands: 1978–2012

Solomon Islands Year by Year

Year	Media	Government
1978	Imperfectly Free	Democracy
1979	Imperfectly Free	Democracy
1980	Imperfectly Free	Democracy
1981	Imperfectly Free	Democracy
1982	Imperfectly Free	Democracy
1983	Imperfectly Free	Democracy
1984	Imperfectly Free	Democracy
1985	Imperfectly Free	Democracy
1986	Imperfectly Free	Democracy
1987	Imperfectly Free	Democracy
1988	Imperfectly Free	Democracy
1989	Imperfectly Free	Democracy
1990	Imperfectly Free	Democracy
1991	Imperfectly Free	Democracy
1992	Imperfectly Free	Democracy
1993	Imperfectly Free	Democracy
1994	Imperfectly Free	Democracy
1995	Imperfectly Free	Democracy
1996	Imperfectly Free	Democracy
1997	Imperfectly Free	Democracy
1998	Imperfectly Free	Democracy
1999	Imperfectly Free	Democracy
2000	Imperfectly Free	Interregnum
2001	Imperfectly Free	Interregnum
2002	Free	Interregnum
2003	Free	Foreign Intervention
2004	Free	Democracy
2005	Free	Democracy

(Continued)

In Brief

Self-governing from 1976 and independent from 1978, this former British colonial holding has long had limited but reasonably free media.

Chronology

1978–2001: Imperfectly Free

Media have been effectively but imperfectly free since well before independence, but with a small population scattered across a large number of small islands, there has been limited media. In 1978, independent and government newspapers were available, but the government controlled the radio station.[1] Government support was necessary for any degree of national provision of news, and this made the system imperfect but still functionally free.

In the mid-1990s, the government tried to prevent the government-funded Solomon Islands Broadcasting Corporation (SIBC) from covering

(Continued)

Year	Media	Government
2006	Free	Democracy
2007	Free	Democracy
2008	Free	Democracy
2009	Free	Democracy
2010	Free	Democracy
2011	Free	Democracy
2012	Free	Democracy

news about the conflict in neighboring Bougainville.[2] In 1996, the government pressured SIBC to have the general manager screen all news prior to broadcasting, and in 1997, the prime minister, who was also the broadcasting minister, ordered that SIBC stop broadcasting a phone-in talk show.[3] These practices came to a stop in 1998 when the new government appointed a respected journalist to head SIBC.[4] In June 1999, when ethnic conflict erupted, the government declared a state of emergency and prohibited the news media from providing information that might incite violence, promote racism, or lead to dissatisfaction with government.[5] The restrictions were lifted in October 1999.[6] In 2000, with help from Australia, a peace agreement was reached and conditions for news media improved.

2002–2012: Free

In spite of the peace treaty, the conflict continued, yet the media persisted in critical reporting and government officials' attempts to interfere proved largely unsuccessful.[7] In 2003, intervention by external powers, notably New Zealand and Australia, also brought external support for the media and some extension of media networks across the islands creating media that were largely free of government influence.

Media Today

Media remain quite limited and are largely supported by New Zealand aid; they are, however, free and able to criticize government and policy. Yet defamation remains a criminal offense. Because of high illiteracy, radio is the most accessible medium. In addition to the SIBC's public radio stations, commercial radio is also available. Television is now available through *One Television*. The country has one daily newspaper and several weeklies.

Notes

1. *Country Reports on Human Rights Practices for 1979* (Washington, DC: U.S. Department of State, 1980). Available at http://babel.hathitrust.org/cgi/pt?id=mdp.39015014188273;view=1up;seq=9.
2. *Country Reports on Human Rights Practices for 1994* (Washington, DC: U.S. Department of State, 1995). Available at http://dosfan.lib.uic.edu/ERC/democracy/1994_hrp_report/94hrp_report_eap/SolomonIslands.html.
3. *World Press Freedom Review*, IPI Report (Vienna: International Press Institute, December 1997).
4. *World Press Freedom Review*, IPI Report (Vienna: International Press Institute, December 1998).
5. *World Press Freedom Review*, IPI Report (Vienna: International Press Institute, 1999).
6. Ibid.
7. *World Press Freedom Review*, IPI Report (Vienna: International Press Institute, 2003).

Somalia: 1960–2012

Somalia Year by Year

Year	Media	Government
1960	Imperfectly Free	Democracy
1961	Imperfectly Free	Democracy
1962	Imperfectly Free	Democracy
1963	Imperfectly Free	Democracy
1964	Imperfectly Free	Democracy
1965	Imperfectly Free	Democracy
1966	Imperfectly Free	Democracy
1967	Imperfectly Free	Democracy
1968	Imperfectly Free	Democracy
1969	Imperfectly Free	Autocracy
1970	Not Free	Autocracy
1971	Not Free	Autocracy
1972	Not Free	Autocracy
1973	Not Free	Autocracy
1974	Not Free	Autocracy
1975	Not Free	Autocracy
1976	Not Free	Autocracy
1977	Not Free	Autocracy
1978	Not Free	Autocracy
1979	Not Free	Autocracy
1980	Not Free	Autocracy
1981	Not Free	Autocracy
1982	Not Free	Autocracy
1983	Not Free	Autocracy

(Continued)

MEDIA FREEDOM HISTORY IN A NUTSHELL

- Upon independence, Somalia was a democracy with media freedom
- Following the 1969 coup, Somalia became a one-party state with government-controlled media
- After the 1991 ouster of dictator Siad Barre, Somalia descended into chaos and media have not been free since
- Conditions for news media vary in south-central Somalia, the breakaway territory of Somaliland and the semi-autonomous region of Puntland, but media are restricted in all three areas
- Somalia has a number of privately owned radio stations in addition to the government-supported Radio Mogadishu (Freedom House's Report on Freedom of the Press 2013)
- Although Puntland did not have any newspapers publishing in 2012, the region did have state-affiliated and private radio stations, as well as private television stations (BBC News' Country Profiles)
- As of 2012, Somaliland had one government-owned newspaper and seven privately owned newspapers, as well as one government-owned television station and one private television station; the government maintained ownership of the region's only radio station (Freedom House's Report on Freedom of the World 2013)
- As of 2012, less than 2 percent of Somalis had Internet access (International Telecommunication Union's 2012 ICT Indicators Database)

In Brief

Created by the unification of British Somaliland and Italian Somaliland and granted independence in 1960, Somalia was initially a democracy with media freedom. Following the 1969 coup, Somalia became a one-party state ruled by Mohamed Siad Barre and the media were government controlled. After the overthrow of Barre

(Continued)

Year	Media	Government
1984	Not Free	Autocracy
1985	Not Free	Autocracy
1986	Not Free	Autocracy
1987	Not Free	Autocracy
1988	Not Free	Autocracy
1989	Not Free	Autocracy
1990	Not Free	Autocracy
1991	Not Free	Anocracy
1992	Not Free	Anocracy
1993	Not Free	Anocracy
1994	Not Free	Anocracy
1995	Not Free	Anocracy
1996	Not Free	Anocracy
1997	Not Free	Anocracy
1998	Not Free	Anocracy
1999	Not Free	Anocracy
2000	Not Free	Anocracy
2001	Not Free	Anocracy
2002	Not Free	Anocracy
2003	Not Free	Anocracy
2004	Not Free	Anocracy
2005	Not Free	Anocracy
2006	Not Free	Anocracy
2007	Not Free	Anocracy
2008	Not Free	Anocracy
2009	Not Free	Anocracy
2010	Not Free	Anocracy
2011	Not Free	Anocracy
2012	Not Free	Anocracy

in 1991, Somalia descended into chaos. The absence of an effective central government and fighting between warring clans and militias has created a perilous environment for journalists in south-central Somalia. In the breakaway territory of Somaliland and the semi-autonomous region of Puntland, journalists are also restricted.

Chronology

1960–1969: Imperfectly Free

Upon independence, Somalia was a democracy with media that were functionally free. "The independent press, while not permitted to say everything it wished, was given wide latitude in which to criticize the government. And the government press permitted in its pages letters which were quite critical of the government's performance."[1]

Following the assassination of President Ali Shermaarke in October 1969, the military staged a coup and Major General Mohamed Siad Barre emerged as the leader of the new government known as the Supreme Revolutionary Council (SRC).

1970–2012: Not Free

The SRC outlawed political parties, and the new Ministry of Information and National Guidance set up a censorship board and soon controlled all print and broadcast media.[2]

In 1991, Mohamed Siad Barre was ousted by opposing clans. That same year, clans in region of the country that was previously the British protectorate declared an independent Somaliland (though the international community did not recognize this). In spite of U.S. and UN attempts at intervention, Somalia descended into chaos and civil war with fighting between warlords from rival clans. Journalists covering the conflict were in grave danger. One of the worst incidences of violence against journalists occurred in 1993 when four journalists were stoned to death by a mob.[3] During these years, many attempts to establish a central government failed. The few news outlets that existed were tied to warlords, businesses, or militias.[4]

In 1998, the Puntland region declared itself an autonomous state of Somalia.

In 2004, Somalia's transitional government introduced a new press law that criminalized defamation of government officials and mandated registration of news outlets.[5] Although violence against journalists, corruption, and bribery remained problems, Somalia had a range of independent print and broadcast media, but most of these had close ties to the warring clans.[6] According to the International Press Institute, conditions for journalists were worse in Somaliland and Puntland.[7]

In 2006, the al-Shabaab militia formed and began fighting for control of Somalia.

From 2010 to 2012, nearly 260,000 Somalis died as famine spread throughout the country.

Media Today

Somalia remains one of the most dangerous countries for journalists. In 2012 and 2013, sixteen journalists were killed in connection with their work.[8] Although the conditions for news media vary between south-central Somalia, Somaliland, and Puntland, journalists in all these regions are restricted.

In south-central Somalia, it is lawlessness rather than laws that constrain news outlets, because fighting with al-Shabaab and other militias continues to create perilous conditions for journalists who are often caught in the middle. Militias have been known to seize control of broadcast media. Yet south-central Somalia continues to have a range of privately owned radio stations in addition to the government-supported Radio Mogadishu.[9]

In Somaliland, though the government has some tolerance for independent media, critical journalists face threats, harassment, and arrest.[10] In 2012 alone, eighty-one journalists were arrested and detained.[11] Somaliland has one government-owned newspaper and seven privately owned newspapers, one government-owned television station and one private television station, and one-government-owned radio station.[12]

In Puntland, security forces and militias threaten and attack critical journalists, usually with impunity, and news coverage of al-Shabaab is outlawed.[13] Although Puntland did not have any newspapers publishing in 2012, the region did have state-affiliated and private radio stations, as well as private television stations.[14]

Though online media are generally unrestricted, Internet access is extremely limited.

Notes

1. David D. Laitin, *Politics, Language, and Thought: The Somali Experience* (University of Chicago Press, 1977), 122.
2. Helen Chapin Metz, *Somalia: A Country Study* (Washington, DC: Library of Congress Federal Research Division, 1992). Available at http://lcweb2.loc.gov/frd/cs/cshome.html.
3. *World Press Freedom Review*, IPI Report (Vienna: International Press Institute, December 1993).
4. *Freedom of the Press* (Washington, DC: Freedom House, 2002). Available at http://www.freedomhouse.org/report/freedom-press/2002/somalia.
5. *World Press Freedom Review*, IPI Report (Vienna: International Press Institute, 2005).
6. Ibid.
7. Ibid.
8. *52 Journalists Killed in Somalia since 1992/Motive Confirmed* (Committee to Protect Journalists, 2013). Available at http://cpj.org/killed/africa/somalia/.
9. *Freedom of the Press* (Washington, DC: Freedom House, 2013). Available at http://www.freedomhouse.org/report/freedom-press/2013/somalia.
10. Ibid.
11. *Freedom of the Press* (Washington, DC: Freedom House, 2013). Available at http://www.freedomhouse.org/report/freedom-world/2013/somaliland.
12. Ibid.
13. *Freedom of the Press* (Washington, DC: Freedom House, 2013). Available at http://www.freedomhouse.org/report/freedom-press/2013/somalia.
14. *Puntland*, BBC Country Profiles (London, UK: British Broadcasting Company, 2012). Available at http://www.bbc.co.uk/news/world-africa-14114750.

South Africa: 1948–2012

South Africa Year by Year

Year	Media	Government
1948	Imperfectly Free	Anocracy
1949	Imperfectly Free	Anocracy
1950	Imperfectly Free	Anocracy
1951	Imperfectly Free	Anocracy
1952	Imperfectly Free	Anocracy
1953	Imperfectly Free	Anocracy
1954	Imperfectly Free	Anocracy
1955	Imperfectly Free	Anocracy
1956	Imperfectly Free	Anocracy
1957	Imperfectly Free	Anocracy
1958	Imperfectly Free	Anocracy
1959	Imperfectly Free	Anocracy
1960	Imperfectly Free	Anocracy
1961	Not Free	Anocracy
1962	Not Free	Anocracy
1963	Not Free	Anocracy
1964	Not Free	Anocracy
1965	Not Free	Anocracy
1966	Not Free	Anocracy
1967	Not Free	Anocracy
1968	Not Free	Anocracy
1969	Not Free	Anocracy
1970	Not Free	Anocracy
1971	Not Free	Anocracy
1972	Not Free	Anocracy
1973	Not Free	Anocracy
1974	Not Free	Anocracy
1975	Not Free	Anocracy

MEDIA FREEDOM HISTORY IN A NUTSHELL

- South African media were functionally free when the apartheid system was introduced in 1948
- As the government implemented apartheid, it instituted a number of policies aimed at controlling news media, and by the early 1960s, media were not free
- As apartheid laws were repealed in the early 1990s, the government eased its restrictions on news media, and by 1994, media were functionally free
- Media remain functionally free but somewhat restricted by policies and practices, some of which date back to the apartheid era
- As of 2012, there were twenty-one paid-for daily newspapers with a total average circulation per issue of 1,433,000 (World Association of Newspaper's 2012 World Newspaper Trends)
- The state-run South African Broadcasting Corporation (SABC) is the main source of radio and television news, but independent broadcast media are also available (Freedom House's Freedom of the Press 2013)
- As of 2012, about 41 percent of South Africans had Internet access (International Telecommunication Union's 2012 ICT Indicators Database)

In Brief

Starting in the late 1940s, South Africa's apartheid system slowly eroded media freedom as the government increasingly sought to control information. By the 1960s, media were not free, and this lack of freedom continued for more than three decades. In the early 1990s, as South Africa began to dismantle the apartheid system, restrictions on media were eased. Since 1994, media have been functionally free, though at times restricted by repressive policies and practices, including some holdovers from the apartheid years.

Year	Media	Government
1976	Not Free	Anocracy
1977	Not Free	Anocracy
1978	Not Free	Anocracy
1979	Not Free	Anocracy
1980	Not Free	Anocracy
1981	Not Free	Anocracy
1982	Not Free	Anocracy
1983	Not Free	Anocracy
1984	Not Free	Anocracy
1985	Not Free	Anocracy
1986	Not Free	Anocracy
1987	Not Free	Anocracy
1988	Not Free	Anocracy
1989	Not Free	Anocracy
1990	Not Free	Anocracy
1991	Not Free	Anocracy
1992	Not Free	Democracy
1993	Not Free	Democracy
1994	Imperfectly Free	Democracy
1995	Imperfectly Free	Democracy
1996	Imperfectly Free	Democracy
1997	Imperfectly Free	Democracy
1998	Imperfectly Free	Democracy
1999	Imperfectly Free	Democracy
2000	Imperfectly Free	Democracy
2001	Imperfectly Free	Democracy
2002	Free	Democracy
2003	Free	Democracy
2004	Free	Democracy
2005	Free	Democracy
2006	Free	Democracy
2007	Free	Democracy
2008	Free	Democracy
2009	Imperfectly Free	Democracy
2010	Imperfectly Free	Democracy
2011	Imperfectly Free	Democracy
2012	Imperfectly Free	Democracy

Chronology:

1948–1960: Imperfectly Free

In 1948, the National Party came into power and began to implement its apartheid policies, which established separate and unequal systems for the races, giving the whites complete control of the country and suppressing the blacks. Although the news media were initially imperfectly free, conditions deteriorated as apartheid took hold. In the mid-1950s, the Customs and Excise Act and the Official Secrets Act gave the government the authority to establish a Board of Censors.[1]

In 1960, police in Sharpeville gunned down 67 Africans who were protesting laws that required them to have passes. The killings led to a peaceful demonstration by as many as 30,000 people. As the unrest increased, the government continued to crackdown and eventually declared a state of emergency. Thus, by 1960, self-censorship was common and the government had the authority to use emergency powers to seize, confiscate, and ban publications deemed to be subversive.[2] As one South African newspaper executive reported to the International Press Institute, "There is ostensibly still a free press in South Africa. It is the same freedom as a baboon has chained to a pole."[3]

1961–1993: Not Free

By the early 1960s, conditions had deteriorated as the government continued to adopt a number of regulations aimed at limiting news coverage and increasing government control. The government maintained direct control over the country's only broadcast media through the South African Broadcasting Corporation (SABC).[4] Print media were restricted by the South African Press Council, which had the authority to fine editors who failed to comply with emergency regulations, which typically prohibited news coverage of political developments.[5]

Under emergency regulations in the 1980s, journalists were forbidden to report on banned organizations and people, and the media were prohibited from reporting events relating to "state security," such as protests and demonstrations. The public then had to rely on the government's Bureau of Information for official reports of political events. Some journalists were detained for violating emergency regulations without being charged, and newspapers were temporarily suspended. Some editors and reporters were prosecuted, and foreign journalists were expelled or refused entry visas.[6]

As unrest escalated in the late 1980s and international pressure increased, the South African government began to talk with the imprisoned leader of the African National Congress (ANC), Nelson Mandela, and in 1990, Mandela was released from prison and the ban on the ANC was lifted. At the same time, the government began to ease its restrictions on news media. In particular, in early 1990s, the Protection of Information Act was repealed, making it less risky for news media to criticize the government.[7]

1994–2001: Imperfectly Free

In 1994, as South Africa held its first democratic elections, conditions for news media improved to the point that they were functionally free. The SABC still had a monopoly on South African broadcast media but was no longer staffed by government appointees. In addition, the establishment of the Independent Broadcasting Authority paved the way for the development of privately owned broadcast media.

In the late 1990s the Truth and Reconciliation Commission investigated the role of the news media during Apartheid and concluded that "the racism that pervaded most of white society permeated the media industry."[8]

2002–2008: Free

By 2002, news media were functioning freely in spite of laws restricting media freedom. In particular, laws remained in effect that permitted government to compel journalists to reveal their sources. As the news media increasingly engaged in criticism of government, officials from the ANC-controlled government increasingly criticized journalists, accusing white journalists of racism and black journalists of disloyalty.[9]

2009–2012: Imperfectly Free

Although South African news media remained vibrant, by 2009, the relationship between the government and news media had become so contentious that media freedom was somewhat compromised.[10] Additionally, government attempts to control news media increased. A case in point, SABC, which still controlled the bulk of the country's broadcast media, appeared to favor the ANC and in 2009, the Parliament dissolved the SABC board following significant financial losses.[11] Yet the opposition did have a say in the appointment of the new board. Also in 2009, the Film and Publications Amendment Act was seen as potentially limiting media freedom; however, two years later, this measure was deemed unconstitutional.[12] In 2011, the government announced that its advertising budget would be spent on progovernment newspapers.[13]

Media Today

South African media remain functionally free but somewhat compromised by government efforts to minimize criticism. Although the constitution has provisions for media freedom, some restrictive laws, many of which are holdovers from the apartheid era, remain in place. There have been some reports of journalists being harassed, threatened, and attacked.[14]

South Africa has a wide range of independent newspapers. Although the state-run SABC continues to dominate the broadcast media, there are some privately owned radio and television stations.

Notes

1. Rita M. Byrnes, *South Africa: A Country Study* (Washington, DC: Library of Congress Federal Research Division, 1996). Available at http://lcweb2.loc.gov/frd/cs/cshome.html.
2. Gordon Young, *South Africa—A Press in Chains*, IPI Report (Zurich: International Press Institute, May 1960).
3. Ibid., 1.
4. Leonard Monteath Thompson, *History of South Africa* (New Haven, CT: Yale University Press, 2001).
5. Byrnes, *South Africa: A Country Study*.
6. Ibid., "Communications Media," para. 2.
7. Ibid.
8. *World Press Freedom Review*, IPI Report (Vienna: International Press Institute, December 1998), 53.
9. *Country Reports on Human Rights Practices for 2002* (Washington, DC: U.S. Department of State, 2003). Available at http://www.state.gov/j/drl/rls/hrrpt/2002/18227.htm.
10. *Freedom of the Press* (Washington, DC: Freedom House, 2010). Available at http://freedomhouse.org/report/freedom-press/2010/south-africa#.Us3Ft9JDtVk.
11. Ibid.
12. *Freedom of the Press* (Washington, DC: Freedom House, 2013). Available at http://freedomhouse.org/report/freedom-press/2013/south-africa.
13. Ibid.
14. Ibid.

South Korea: 1948–2012

South Korea Year by Year

Year	Media	Government
1948	Not Free	Anocracy
1949	Not Free	Anocracy
1950	Not Free	Anocracy
1951	Not Free	Anocracy
1952	Not Free	Anocracy
1953	Not Free	Anocracy
1954	Not Free	Anocracy
1955	Not Free	Anocracy
1956	Not Free	Anocracy
1957	Not Free	Anocracy
1958	Not Free	Anocracy
1959	Not Free	Anocracy
1960	Not Free	Democracy
1961	Not Free	Autocracy
1962	Not Free	Autocracy
1963	Not Free	Anocracy
1964	Not Free	Anocracy
1965	Not Free	Anocracy
1966	Not Free	Anocracy
1967	Not Free	Anocracy
1968	Not Free	Anocracy
1969	Not Free	Anocracy
1970	Not Free	Anocracy
1971	Not Free	Anocracy
1972	Not Free	Autocracy
1973	Not Free	Autocracy
1974	Not Free	Autocracy
1975	Not Free	Autocracy

(Continued)

MEDIA FREEDOM HISTORY IN A NUTSHELL

- After four decades of authoritarian rule and no media freedom, South Korea transitioned to democracy in the late 1980s, and media freedom followed in the early 1990s
- The 1948 National Security Law has recently been interpreted as prohibiting pro–North Korean content, and the government has attempted to censor such content online
- As of 2012, South Korea had 324 total paid-for daily newspapers with an average circulation per issue of 10,928,965 (World Association of Newspaper's 2012 World Newspaper Trends)
- South Korea has a mix of public and privately owned broadcast media
- As of 2012, about 84 percent of South Koreans had Internet access (International Telecommunication Union's 2012 ICT Indicator's Database)

In Brief

Any understanding of South Korea has to be contextualized by the fact that it has been at war with North Korea for nearly the entirety of its existence. While that is now commonly treated as an anachronistic technicality of the way the Korean War was concluded, it made South Korea a potential flash point in the Cold War, and North Korea has made it clear that they remain on a war footing even to this day. The end of the Cold War reduced the support for the North. As a result, its military capability has been eroding steadily for the past two decades, but there have been several minor military clashes since the Korean War. Still, provocations and threats from North Korea are the norm rather than the exception and South Korea is the one nation that is clearly within range of the North's ability to deliver nuclear weapons.

(Continued)

Year	Media	Government
1976	Not Free	Autocracy
1977	Not Free	Autocracy
1978	Not Free	Autocracy
1979	Not Free	Autocracy
1980	Not Free	Autocracy
1981	Not Free	Anocracy
1982	Not Free	Anocracy
1983	Not Free	Anocracy
1984	Not Free	Anocracy
1985	Not Free	Anocracy
1986	Not Free	Anocracy
1987	Not Free	In Transition
1988	Not Free	Democracy
1989	Not Free	Democracy
1990	Not Free	Democracy
1991	Not Free	Democracy
1992	Not Free	Democracy
1993	Imperfectly Free	Democracy
1994	Imperfectly Free	Democracy
1995	Imperfectly Free	Democracy
1996	Imperfectly Free	Democracy
1997	Imperfectly Free	Democracy
1998	Imperfectly Free	Democracy
1999	Imperfectly Free	Democracy
2000	Imperfectly Free	Democracy
2001	Imperfectly Free	Democracy
2002	Free	Democracy
2003	Free	Democracy
2004	Free	Democracy
2005	Free	Democracy
2006	Free	Democracy
2007	Free	Democracy
2008	Free	Democracy
2009	Free	Democracy
2010	Imperfectly Free	Democracy
2011	Imperfectly Free	Democracy
2012	Imperfectly Free	Democracy

After four decades of authoritarian rule, media freedom slowly established itself as part of the South Korean political and social environment, and even though there are still some vestiges of authoritarian influences, media are now functionally free.

Chronology

1948–1992: Not Free

While nominally presidential, the government of independent South Korea was in most respects a continuation of the U.S. military governance from the end of the Second World War, including restrictions on the media and state control of all broadcasting. Staunchly anticommunist and focused on reunification with the North, there were already signs that South Koreans did not support the government when the invasion by the North put it on a war footing in 1950.

Unrest followed the 1953 armistice that ended active fighting in the Korean War, yet autocratic rule, supported by massive aid from the United States, remained in place. Syngman Rhee's government was blatantly fraudulent in the rigging of elections and other manipulations of the nominally democratic governmental structures.

Student protests in 1960 led to the direct rule by the military, which installed a nominally democratic government in 1963. The newly installed Park Chunghee government focused on rapid industrialization, and it appeared that the resulting surge in economic growth would lead to democratization, but the increasing support for the opposition led to further authoritarian measures, and media remained not free.

In the early 1970s, support for the Park administration fell and an easing of Cold War tensions raised questions regarding the U.S. willingness to support undemocratic anticommunism. This led to increasing authoritarian measures including martial law and the revision of the constitution to effectively allow Park to retain the presidency for life. Political repression including arrests of opposition politicians was common.

Park was assassinated in 1979, and a period of unrest, coups, and dictatorial rule followed. By 1985, however, it was becoming clear that there was significant public sympathy for antiregime protestors and demand for a shift to democratic governance.

While opposition parties won the majority of seats in the 1985 elections, the government moved to protect authoritarian rule, and it was the massive antigovernment protests in 1987 that finally signaled the shift to democratic governance. Strategic errors by the opposition prevented them from winning the first direct election of the president, but the media began asserting some independence in coverage and defying rules controlling content. Despite being a participant in the coup that brought the military to power, President Roh Tae-woo began unwinding the legal foundations of authoritarian rule, including specific changes to the laws restricting the media. While media freedom was clearly expanded, government control over broadcasting remained in force and indirect influences limited criticism of the government.

1993–2001: Imperfectly Free

The election of the first civilian president in 1992 quickly led to further unwinding of authoritarian restrictions and a shift to an imperfect, professionally inexperienced, but functionally free media. Economic crises and scandal plagued the government. The International Press Association noted that although the media environment had "improved considerably" there were still a number of problems.[1]

2002–2009: Free

Elections in 2002 appeared to cement democratic rule and liberal freedoms. This included, for the first time, the effort to eliminate collusive and undemocratic ties between business and political elites. Yet former dissident and newly elected President Roh Moo-hyun had a contentious relationship with the conservative newspapers, and scandals plagued the government and allowed for pushback by industrial and military elites intent on retaining privilege.

2010–2012: Imperfectly Free

Media freedom was compromised by the very close relationships between political, industrial, and military elites, who appeared to be colluding on several fronts. Economic struggles and government efforts to prop up the South Korean industrial powers have only served to further strengthen these ties. In addition, there was an increase of government efforts to censor online news media.[2] Also, the global economic crisis left media outlets vulnerable to economic coercion.

Media Today

Media remain imperfectly, but functionally free. Ownership of media outlets tends to align them with the interests of industrial elites, and the ability to seriously challenge the collusion between industry, military, and government is questionable. In recent years, government has monitored online content and has made an effort to censor pro-North Korean content.[3]

Notes

1. *World Press Freedom Review*, IPI Report (Vienna: International Press Institute, December 1993), 57.
2. *Freedom of the Press* (Washington, DC: Freedom House, 2011). Available at http://freedomhouse.org/report/freedom-press/2011/south-korea.
3. *Freedom of the Press* (Washington, DC: Freedom House, 2013). Available at http://freedomhouse.org/report/freedom-press/2013/south-korea.

South Sudan: 2011–2012

South Sudan Year by Year

Year	Media	Government
2011	Imperfectly Free	Anocracy
2012	Imperfectly Free	Anocracy

In Brief

For years, Sudan was divided between a conservative Muslim North and a largely Christian South. Following more than two decades of civil war, in 2005, South Sudan became autonomous, and in 2011, it gained full independence.

Chronology

2011–2012: Imperfectly Free

South Sudan's constitution includes provisions for media freedom, and these were respected by government in practice. Yet there were reports of efforts to intimidate journalists and news organizations.[1]

Media Today

The failure of the government to pass a series of laws aimed at guaranteeing media freedom has raised concerns about the future of media in this

MEDIA FREEDOM HISTORY IN A NUTSHELL

- After years of civil war, South Sudan succeeded from Sudan in 2011 as part of 2005 peace agreement
- Although the constitution provides for media freedom, there are reports of government pressures on news media
- Given that this is a new country, there is little information regarding the number of media outlets and Internet penetration

new country. There were reports of journalists being intimidated, harassed, and attacked.[2] While there are a number of independent newspapers, radio is the most accessible medium, and there is a mix of state-run and private radio broadcasters. The government retains control over domestic television. To date there is no information regarding Internet access.

Notes

1. *Freedom of the Press* (Washington, DC: Freedom House, 2012). Available at http://www.freedom house.org/report/freedom-press/2012/south-sudan.
2. *Freedom of the Press* (Washington, DC: Freedom House, 2013). Available at http://www.freedom house.org/report/freedom-press/2013/south-sudan.

Spain: 1948–2012

Spain Year by Year

Year	Media	Government
1948	Not Free	Autocracy
1949	Not Free	Autocracy
1950	Not Free	Autocracy
1951	Not Free	Autocracy
1952	Not Free	Autocracy
1953	Not Free	Autocracy
1954	Not Free	Autocracy
1955	Not Free	Autocracy
1956	Not Free	Autocracy
1957	Not Free	Autocracy
1958	Not Free	Autocracy
1959	Not Free	Autocracy
1960	Not Free	Autocracy
1961	Not Free	Autocracy
1962	Not Free	Autocracy
1963	Not Free	Autocracy
1964	Not Free	Autocracy
1965	Not Free	Autocracy
1966	Not Free	Autocracy
1967	Not Free	Autocracy
1968	Not Free	Autocracy
1969	Not Free	Autocracy
1970	Not Free	Autocracy
1971	Not Free	Autocracy
1972	Not Free	Autocracy
1973	Not Free	Autocracy
1974	Not Free	Autocracy

(Continued)

MEDIA FREEDOM HISTORY IN A NUTSHELL

- After years of authoritarian rule, amendments to the constitution in 1978 allowed for freedom of opinion and of the press
- Spain has a mix of private and publicly owned print and broadcast media
- As of 2011, there were 125 daily newspapers; all were paid-for daily newspapers, with a total average circulation per issue of 3,092,000 (World Association of Newspaper's 2012 World Newspaper Trends)
- As of 2012, about 72 percent of Spaniards had Internet access (International Telecommunication Union's 2012 ICT Indicators Database)

In Brief

In the period from late 1975 through 1978, Spain made a remarkable transition from the rigidly controlled media environment of a right wing dictatorship, to a liberal free media marketplace of a European standard. Since 1978, the country's constitution has guaranteed freedom of speech and freedom of the press.[1]

Chronology

1948–1978: Not Free

The Cold War and Francisco Franco's credentials as a staunch anticommunist are the primary explanation for the seemingly anomalous acceptance of a right wing dictatorship in a major Western European country. Franco's dictatorship, often called fascist, included severe restrictions on the press, an active secret police, and the vigorous prosecution of any criticism of the regime. Liberalization of the ownership of some print media outlets began in the late 1960s, and even

(Continued)

Year	Media	Government
1975	Not Free	Anocracy
1976	Not Free	Anocracy
1977	Not Free	Anocracy
1978	Not Free	Democracy
1979	Imperfectly Free	Democracy
1980	Free	Democracy
1981	Free	Democracy
1982	Free	Democracy
1983	Free	Democracy
1984	Free	Democracy
1985	Free	Democracy
1986	Free	Democracy
1987	Free	Democracy
1988	Free	Democracy
1989	Free	Democracy
1990	Free	Democracy
1991	Free	Democracy
1992	Free	Democracy
1993	Free	Democracy
1994	Free	Democracy
1995	Free	Democracy
1996	Free	Democracy
1997	Free	Democracy
1998	Free	Democracy
1999	Free	Democracy
2000	Free	Democracy
2001	Free	Democracy
2002	Free	Democracy
2003	Free	Democracy
2004	Free	Democracy
2005	Free	Democracy
2006	Free	Democracy
2007	Free	Democracy
2008	Free	Democracy
2009	Free	Democracy
2010	Free	Democracy
2011	Free	Democracy
2012	Free	Democracy

though restrictions on content were only slightly relaxed, this broader base of direct control was crucial to the media's ability to take on a liberalizing role after Franco's death in 1974.

Little in the way of liberalization was expected when Don Juan Carlos de Borbón ascended to the Spanish throne. While the act legally initiated the establishment of a constitutional monarchy, and there was some degree of liberalization that accompanied the change, Juan Carlos had been handpicked by Franco. The new king's reign was expected to be a continuation of Franco's dictatorship, and it was generally expected to be brief. Both these expectations seemed to be confirmed when Juan Carlos retained Franco's ultra-conservative prime minister, Carlos Arias Navarro. The subsequent repression of protests and strikes further inflamed domestic unrest. During this time, the broadcast media remained strictly controlled, and were used largely for propaganda, but print media were allowed some degree of freedom even though the legal structure enabling control had not changed.

The appointment of a new prime minister in 1976 brought another Franco insider to the office, but Adolfo Suarez Gonzalez was also a pragmatist who was able to use the existing institutions and engage the entrenched right wing powerbases as part of the process of enacting reforms. A period of rapid democratization followed with free elections held in June 1977. Key to that rapid transition was the 1976 Law for Political Reform, which initiated sweeping changes in the legal framework surrounding the media. During this time, the media were explicitly used by the government as a means of educating the Spanish populace regarding democratic norms and expectations.

During the period from 1975 to 1977, print media had slowly developed the professional norms needed to function as free media, but they were still legally quite restricted even if left to act independently in practice. The year 1978 was a transitional period where the Law for Political Reform began unwinding many of the legal constraints on the media and the first steps toward liberalizing the broadcast media began.

1979: Imperfectly Free

As Spain moved rapidly toward the adoption of a new constitution, most of the significant challenges to media freedom faded.

1980–2012: Free

Significant development of liberal and professional norms continued, and by the mid-1990s, the Spanish media environment was comparable to the other free media markets in Europe. Spain joined the European Union in 1986, and since then it has seen sustained economic growth.[2] Private television was introduced in 1990.[3]

Media Today

Spain maintains a well-established and stable free media system that reflects the norms of Western Europe. Spain faces the same technical issues that confront the rest of the world's media with the expansion of the Internet. External media inflows and market fragmentation are concerns that are exacerbated by extended financial difficulties. However, unlike the situation faced by many European countries, where English language sources are displacing local language sources, there is a huge global audience for Spanish-language programming. Although Spain has come a long way, many newspapers are criticized for being too close to political parties. To some degree, Spain's substantial blogosphere neutralizes the partisan nature of outlets in other media.

Notes

1. *Spain*, Media Landscapes (Adenauerallee, Germany: Euro Topics Press Review, 2013). Available at http://www.eurotopics.net/en/home/medienlandschaft/spanienmdn/.
2. Ibid.
3. *Spain*, Media Landscape Reports (Maastricht, The Netherlands: European Journalism Centre, 2013). Available at http://ejc.net/media_landscapes/spain.

Sri Lanka: 1948–2012

Sri Lanka Year by Year

Year	Media	Government
1948	Not Free	Democracy
1949	Not Free	Democracy
1950	Not Free	Democracy
1951	Not Free	Democracy
1952	Not Free	Democracy
1953	Not Free	Democracy
1954	Not Free	Democracy
1955	Not Free	Democracy
1956	Not Free	Democracy
1957	Not Free	Democracy
1958	Not Free	Democracy
1959	Not Free	Democracy
1960	Not Free	Democracy
1961	Not Free	Democracy
1962	Not Free	Democracy
1963	Not Free	Democracy
1964	Not Free	Democracy
1965	Not Free	Democracy
1966	Not Free	Democracy
1967	Not Free	Democracy
1968	Not Free	Democracy
1969	Not Free	Democracy
1970	Not Free	Democracy
1971	Not Free	Democracy
1972	Not Free	Democracy
1973	Not Free	Democracy
1974	Not Free	Democracy
1975	Not Free	Democracy

MEDIA FREEDOM HISTORY IN A NUTSHELL

- Ethnic conflict, frequently violent, between Tamil and Sinhalese ethnic groups has dominated Sri Lanka
- Media freedom has briefly existed for short periods, but strict government control of media has been the norm
- As of 2012, there were seventeen paid-for daily newspapers with a total average circulation per issue of 590,000 (World Association of Newspaper's 2012 World Newspaper Trends)
- Sri Lanka has a mix of state-owned and privately owned broadcast media
- As of 2012, about 18 percent of Sri Lankans had Internet access (International Telecommunication Union's 2012 ICT Indicators Database)

In Brief

Independent Ceylon, called Sri Lanka after 1972, has been locked in a conflict between the Sinhalese and Tamil ethnic groups. While there have been brief periods of media freedom, these reflect times in which government restrictions were sufficiently weakened by the conflict to allow freedom to occur rather than government acceptance of media freedom as part of its democratic structures.

Chronology

1948–1990: Not Free

Independent Ceylon inherited a democratic political structure from the British, but unlike most of the other British Colonies that were granted independence in the wake of the Second World War, those democratic institutions did not include free media. This can largely be attributed

Year	Media	Government
1976	Not Free	Democracy
1977	Not Free	Democracy
1978	Not Free	Democracy
1979	Not Free	Democracy
1980	Not Free	Democracy
1981	Not Free	Democracy
1982	Not Free	Anocracy
1983	Not Free	Anocracy
1984	Not Free	Anocracy
1985	Not Free	Anocracy
1986	Not Free	Anocracy
1987	Not Free	Anocracy
1988	Not Free	Anocracy
1989	Not Free	Anocracy
1990	Not Free	Anocracy
1991	Imperfectly Free	Anocracy
1992	Imperfectly Free	Anocracy
1993	Imperfectly Free	Anocracy
1994	Imperfectly Free	Anocracy
1995	Not Free	Anocracy
1996	Not Free	Anocracy
1997	Not Free	Anocracy
1998	Not Free	Anocracy
1999	Not Free	Anocracy
2000	Not Free	Anocracy
2001	Not Free	Democracy
2002	Imperfectly Free	Democracy
2003	Imperfectly Free	Anocracy
2004	Imperfectly Free	Anocracy
2005	Imperfectly Free	Anocracy
2006	Not Free	Democracy
2007	Not Free	Democracy
2008	Not Free	Democracy
2009	Not Free	Democracy
2010	Not Free	Anocracy
2011	Not Free	Democracy
2012	Not Free	Anocracy

to the politics and conflict resulting from the disenfranchisement of the Tamil plantation workers who the British had brought in from Southern India. Media were strictly controlled in the interests of the Sinhalese effort to maintain control of the government, and those controls became even stricter as the ethnic conflict escalated. By 1982, the conflict was effectively a civil war, and in 1987, peace-keeping forces from India were brought in to try to stabilize the country.

The withdrawal of Indian Peacekeepers in 1990 effectively made it impossible for the Sri Lankan government to fully control the media in Tamil-controlled areas. This escalated as the central government's control was further challenged.

1991–1994: Imperfectly Free

By 1991, there was enough "counter media" in the Tamil-controlled areas, with enough of it available throughout the country to effectively nullify government efforts to control the media. Many newspapers did openly criticize the government, but the number of attacks against journalists also increased to the point that in 1992 several hundred journalists staged a demonstration in the capital.[1]

1995–2001: Not Free

The shift to open civil war and active military operations in the Tamil territory ended the quasi-freedom of the media. In 1995, the government required that all reports on the war be submitted to censors prior to publication.[2] During this time, there were also a number of police raids of news outlets.[3]

2002–2005: Imperfectly Free

A ceasefire ended government military operations in the Tamil-held areas, and the central government's step down from a war footing also brought some semblance of media freedom to the Sinhalese dominated areas of the country. The newly elected government repealed the Criminal Defamation Act that had been used to punish critical journalists.[4]

2006–2012 Not Free

The 2005 killing of the Sri Lankan Foreign Minister by a suspected Tamil assassin led to a state of emergency. This was followed by a resumption of open warfare in 2006 and an end to the fragile media freedom that had been established with the 2002 ceasefire. In spite of the hostile media environment, some journalists persisted in criticizing government behavior, but eventually violence against journalists had a chilling effect. In particular, the killing of Lasantha Wickrematunga in 2009 drew international condemnation. Wickrematunga was known for his critical reporting on the government, had received a number of death threats, and predicted his own killing in a posthumously published editorial.

Media Today

In 2009, the Tamils effectively lost the civil war as government troops took control of the last Tamil-controlled regions. Central government control has been fragile, and while there have been some democratic concessions toward the Tamil, majorities in the north and east, authoritarian restrictions, including press controls, remain in place, justified as antiterrorist measures.

Notes

1. *World Press Freedom Review*, IPI Report (Zurich: International Press Institute, December 1992).
2. *World Press Freedom Review*, IPI Report (Vienna: International Press Institute, November/December 1995).
3. Ibid.
4. *World Press Freedom Review*, IPI Report (Vienna: International Press Institute, 2002).

St. Kitts and Nevis: 1983–2012

St. Kitts and Nevis Year by Year

Year	Media	Government
1983	Free	Democracy
1984	Free	Democracy
1985	Free	Democracy
1986	Free	Democracy
1987	Free	Democracy
1988	Free	Democracy
1989	Free	Democracy
1990	Free	Democracy
1991	Free	Democracy
1992	Free	Democracy
1993	Free	Democracy
1994	Free	Democracy
1995	Free	Democracy
1996	Free	Democracy
1997	Free	Democracy
1998	Free	Democracy
1999	Free	Democracy
2000	Free	Democracy
2001	Free	Democracy
2002	Free	Democracy
2003	Free	Democracy
2004	Free	Democracy
2005	Free	Democracy
2006	Free	Democracy
2007	Free	Democracy
2008	Free	Democracy
2009	Free	Democracy
2010	Free	Democracy
2011	Free	Democracy
2012	Free	Democracy

MEDIA FREEDOM HISTORY IN A NUTSHELL

- Since independence, St. Kitts and Nevis has been a democracy with media freedom
- In 2013, there was one privately owned daily newspaper in addition to several weeklies with ties to political parties (BBC News Country Profiles)
- As of 2013, the government owned the only television station, but the country had a mix of state-owned and private radio stations (BBC News Country Profiles)
- As of 2012, more than 79 percent of Kittitians and Nevisians had Internet access (International Telecommunication Union's 2012 ICT Indicators Database)

In Brief

Since gaining independence, St. Kitts (also known as St. Christopher) and Nevis has been a democracy with free media.

Chronology

1983–2012: Free

Upon gaining independence from Britain in 1983, St. Kitts and Nevis was a democracy with media that were limited because of the market size, but free. The constitution included a provision that gave Nevis the right to secede in the future. The government owned the radio and television stations, and though these outlets did provide some coverage of opposing views, in the 1990s and early 2000s, there were complaints that government restricted coverage of the opposition.[1] Most political parties had their own newspapers, and there were also church-sponsored publications.[2]

By the 1990s, privately owned radio stations were broadcasting on the islands.

In 1998, the Nevisians narrowly voted down a referendum to secede.

Media Today

Media remain free but somewhat limited. The only television station is government owned, but privately owned radio stations compete with the government's radio station. In addition to the weekly newspapers published by the political parties, there is one privately owned daily newspaper. In recent years, corruption and drug-related crimes have plagued the country, but there is no evidence that these problems are threatening media freedom.[3] The government does not restrict Internet access or content, and in 2012, more than 79 percent of Kittitians and Nevisians had Internet access.

Notes

1. *Freedom of the Press* (Washington, DC: Freedom House, 1999). Available at http://www.freedom house.org/report/freedom-world/1999/st-kitts-and-nevis.
2. *Country Reports on Human Rights Practices for 1984* (Washington, DC: U.S. Department of State, 1985). Available at http://hdl.handle.net/2027/mdp.39015008874342.
3. *Freedom of the Press* (Washington, DC: Freedom House, 2013). Available at http://www.freedom house.org/report/freedom-world/2013/st-kitts-and-nevis.

St. Lucia: 1979–2012

St. Lucia Year by Year

Year	Media	Government
1979	Free	Democracy
1980	Free	Democracy
1981	Free	Democracy
1982	Free	Democracy
1983	Free	Democracy
1984	Free	Democracy
1985	Free	Democracy
1986	Free	Democracy
1987	Free	Democracy
1988	Free	Democracy
1989	Free	Democracy
1990	Free	Democracy
1991	Free	Democracy
1992	Free	Democracy
1993	Free	Democracy
1994	Free	Democracy
1995	Free	Democracy
1996	Free	Democracy
1997	Free	Democracy
1998	Free	Democracy
1999	Free	Democracy
2000	Free	Democracy
2001	Free	Democracy
2002	Free	Democracy
2003	Free	Democracy
2004	Free	Democracy
2005	Free	Democracy
2006	Free	Democracy
2007	Free	Democracy
2008	Free	Democracy
2009	Free	Democracy
2010	Free	Democracy
2011	Free	Democracy
2012	Free	Democracy

MEDIA FREEDOM HISTORY IN A NUTSHELL

- St. Lucia has a long history of media freedom
- In 2013, there were two newspapers publishing three times a week as well as several weeklies (BBC News Country Profiles)
- In addition to privately owned television and radio, there is one state-owned radio station (BBC News Country Profiles)
- As of 2012, about 49 percent of St. Lucians had Internet access (International Telecommunication Union's 2012 ICT Indicators Database)

In Brief

This Caribbean Island has had free media since before it gained independence in 1979.

Chronology

1979–2012: Free

Upon gaining independence from Britain in 1979, St. Lucia was a democracy with free media. St. Lucian media included three newspapers and a mix of private and government-owned broadcast media.[1]

Media in St. Lucia remained free of restrictive laws until 2003 when lawmakers passed a new criminal code which rendered the publication of false news and news endangering the public good criminal offenses punishable with imprisonment. Three years later, these measures were repealed.[2]

Media Today

St. Lucian media remain free. Most news outlets are privately owned. There are two newspapers that publish three times a week as well as several weekly newspapers. In addition to the privately owned television and radio stations, there is one state-owned radio station, Radio Saint Lucia.

Notes

1. *Country Reports on Human Rights Practices for 1979* (Washington, DC: U.S. Department of State, 1980). Available at http://babel.hathitrust.org/cgi/pt?id=mdp.39015014188273;view=1up;seq=9.
2. *Freedom of the Press* (Washington, DC: Freedom House, 2007). Available at http://www.freedom house.org/report/freedom-press/2007/st-lucia.

St. Vincent and the Grenadines: 1980–2012

St. Vincent and the Grenadines Year by Year

Year	Media	Government
1980	Free	Democracy
1981	Free	Democracy
1982	Free	Democracy
1983	Free	Democracy
1984	Free	Democracy
1985	Free	Democracy
1986	Free	Democracy
1987	Free	Democracy
1988	Free	Democracy
1989	Free	Democracy
1990	Free	Democracy
1991	Free	Democracy
1992	Free	Democracy
1993	Free	Democracy
1994	Free	Democracy
1995	Free	Democracy
1996	Free	Democracy
1997	Free	Democracy
1998	Free	Democracy
1999	Free	Democracy
2000	Free	Democracy
2001	Free	Democracy
2002	Free	Democracy
2003	Free	Democracy
2004	Free	Democracy
2005	Free	Democracy
2006	Free	Democracy
2007	Free	Democracy
2008	Free	Democracy
2009	Free	Democracy
2010	Free	Democracy
2011	Free	Democracy
2012	Free	Democracy

MEDIA FREEDOM HISTORY IN A NUTSHELL

- Since the country gained independence in 1979, the media have been free
- As of 2012, St. Vincent and the Grenadines had one daily newspaper and several weekly newspapers, all of which were privately owned (BBC News' Country Profiles)
- In 2012, the country had one public television station and a mix of private and public radio stations (BBC News' Country Profiles)
- As of 2012, about 48 percent of Vincentians had Internet access (International Telecommunication Union's 2012 ICT Indicators Database)

In Brief

Since gaining independence St. Vincent and the Grenadines has had free media.

Chronology

1980–2012: Free

Since St. Vincent and the Grenadines gained independence in 1979, news media have been free.

There are constitutional provisions for media freedom, and in practice these are generally respected. However, the country does have criminal defamation laws that carry harsh penalties, including up to five years in prison for seditious libel or *desacato* (contempt of authority). For the most part, news media can and do report critically on government policies. At times the government has pressured news media to provide more favorable coverage. For example, in 1984, the Minister of Information took an active role in the news coverage of the state-owned Radio 705. The staff was ordered to let the station manager make all decisions about coverage of the opposition parties. Specifically, "the minister instructed newsroom personnel how to write and present news, to discontinue editing government statements and releases and to ensure prominence and frequent broadcasting of official releases."[1]

Note

1. *Report of the Committee on Freedom of the Press and Information,* General Assembly 1987 (Miami: FL: Inter American Press Association, 1988), 6.

Sudan: 1956–2012

Sudan Year by Year

Year	Media	Government
1956	Imperfectly Free	Democracy
1957	Imperfectly Free	Democracy
1958	No Functioning Media During Conflict	Autocracy
1959	Not Free	Autocracy
1960	Not Free	Autocracy
1961	Not Free	Autocracy
1962	Not Free	Autocracy
1963	Not Free	Autocracy
1964	Not Free	In Transition
1965	Imperfectly Free	Democracy
1966	Imperfectly Free	Democracy
1967	Imperfectly Free	Democracy
1968	Imperfectly Free	Democracy
1969	Imperfectly Free	In Transition
1970	Imperfectly Free	In Transition
1971	Imperfectly Free	Autocracy
1972	Not Free	Autocracy
1973	Not Free	Autocracy
1974	Not Free	Autocracy
1975	Not Free	Autocracy
1976	Not Free	Autocracy
1977	Not Free	Autocracy
1978	Not Free	Autocracy
1979	Not Free	Autocracy

(Continued)

MEDIA FREEDOM HISTORY IN A NUTSHELL

- Although Sudan has been torn by almost constant civil war, media have occasionally been functionally free
- The recent split of the country may finally end the civil war, but there is little reason to believe that it will lead to enduring media freedom for either North or South Sudan
- Although media are constrained, Sudan has a number of outlets including close to twenty daily newspapers, state-run and commercial radio stations, and government-controlled television (Freedom House's Report on Freedom of the Press 2013)
- As of 2012, 21 percent of Sudanese had Internet access (International Telecommunication Union's 2012 ICT Indicators Database)

In Brief

Until recently, a country divided between a conservative Muslim north and a largely Christian south, Sudan has been torn by war and wracked by unrest. It has vacillated wildly between dictatorships, anarchy, and brief periods of democratic governance. Media have experienced brief periods of relative freedom but have never been able to establish any kind of robust business model or market presence.

Chronology

1956–1957: Imperfectly Free

Free media were part of the democratic political environment established by the British, who installed a government dominated by the Christian south. Media were technically free throughout the country, but in reality only a modest degree of freedom was possible and only in the south.

(Continued)

Year	Media	Government
1980	Not Free	Autocracy
1981	Not Free	Autocracy
1982	Not Free	Autocracy
1983	Not Free	Autocracy
1984	Not Free	Autocracy
1985	Imperfectly Free	In Transition
1986	Imperfectly Free	Democracy
1987	Imperfectly Free	Democracy
1988	Imperfectly Free	Democracy
1989	Not Free	Autocracy
1990	Not Free	Autocracy
1991	Not Free	Autocracy
1992	Not Free	Autocracy
1993	Not Free	Autocracy
1994	Not Free	Autocracy
1995	Not Free	Autocracy
1996	Not Free	Autocracy
1997	Not Free	Autocracy
1998	Not Free	Autocracy
1999	Not Free	Autocracy
2000	Not Free	Autocracy
2001	Not Free	Autocracy
2002	Not Free	Autocracy
2003	Not Free	Autocracy
2004	Not Free	Autocracy
2005	Not Free	Anocracy
2006	Not Free	Anocracy
2007	Not Free	Anocracy
2008	Not Free	Anocracy
2009	Not Free	Anocracy
2010	Not Free	Anocracy
2011	Not Free	Anocracy
2012	Not Free	Anocracy

1958: No Functioning Media

In 1958, a military coup led by General Abbud ousted the civilian government, and during the turmoil that followed it was impossible for media to function.

1959–1964: Not Free

The 1958 coup eventually settled into a military dictatorship under Abbud that directly controlled the media. Civil war between the north and the south began in 1962. In 1964, restoration of media freedom was one of the primary goals of the largely nonviolent October Revolution that started as a student uprising at Khartoum University, evolved into a general strike and eventually brought about an end to military rule.[1]

1965–1971: Imperfectly Free

The Islamic-led government that was put in place was too weak to control media in areas that supported the opposition. The result was de facto media freedom in much of the country, but there was little in the way of a media market and few media outlets of any significance.

1972–1984: Not Free

A peace agreement made the south a self-governing region, and both north and south moved quickly to control media and use them for propaganda purposes. Islamic law was imposed in 1983 and was immensely unpopular in the south. Civil war erupted, and fighting continued until 2002.

1985–1988: Imperfectly Free

Unrest led to a coup, and the council put in place by the military began an effort to democratize the government. Media freedom returned, but again, it was as much a matter of the government being too weak to control the media as it was a representation of an ideal or goal through policy. Media were limited. The government maintained control of radio and television and some print media, but independent newspapers began publishing.[2]

1989–2012: Not Free

The 1989 coup ended the democratization effort, and media were controlled. Across the country newspapers were closed down.[3] Human rights of any kind were all but nonexistent.

In the lead up to a peace deal, in 2001, the government addressed some of the worst of its human rights abuses and eased some controls on media.

The 2002 peace deal that ended the two decades of civil war also brought a return of direct control of the media. The degree to which the civil war actually ended is debatable, because the government continued to fight smaller armed groups.

Media Today

The agreement to split off an independent South Sudan from the rest of Sudan may finally provide some respite to this war-torn country. However, there is no indication that peace will bring media freedom, and history suggests exactly the opposite, with media freedom most often occurring when the government was unable to exert control. Under the 2009 press law, editors in chief are criminally liable for their newspaper's content and the government has broad powers to close down news outlets or restrict news media to preserve order and national security.[4] In 2012, there were reports of widespread prepublication censorship and frequent cases of journalists being harassed, arrested, attacked, and tortured.[5]

Freedom House reports that Sudan has a surprising number of news outlets given its hostile media environment. As of 2012, there were about twenty daily newspapers, a mix of state-run and private radio stations (though most private stations tended to focus on music and entertainment rather than news), and government-controlled television.[6]

Notes

1. Yusuf Fadl Hasan, "The Sudanese Revolution of October 1964," *Journal of Modern African Studies* 5, no. 4 (December 1967), 491-509.
2. *Country Reports on Human Rights Practices for 1985* (Washington, DC: U.S. Department of State, 1986). Available at http://babel.hathitrust.org/cgi/pt?id=mdp.39015011233270;view=1up;seq=7.
3. *World Press Freedom Review*, IPI Report (Zurich: International Press Institute, December 1989).
4. *Freedom of the Press* (Washington, DC: Freedom House, 2013). Available at http://www.freedomhouse.org/report/freedom-press/2013/sudan.
5. Ibid.
6. Ibid.

Suriname: 1975–2012

Suriname Year by Year

Year	Media	Government
1975	Imperfectly Free	Anocracy
1976	Imperfectly Free	Anocracy
1977	Imperfectly Free	Anocracy
1978	Imperfectly Free	Anocracy
1979	Imperfectly Free	Anocracy
1980	Not Free	Anocracy
1981	Not Free	Anocracy
1982	Not Free	Autocracy
1983	Not Free	Autocracy
1984	Not Free	Autocracy
1985	Not Free	Autocracy
1986	Not Free	Autocracy
1987	Not Free	Autocracy
1988	Not Free	Anocracy
1989	Imperfectly Free	Anocracy
1990	Imperfectly Free	Anocracy
1991	Imperfectly Free	Anocracy
1992	Imperfectly Free	Anocracy
1993	Imperfectly Free	Anocracy
1994	Imperfectly Free	Anocracy
1995	Imperfectly Free	Anocracy
1996	Imperfectly Free	Anocracy
1997	Imperfectly Free	Anocracy
1998	Imperfectly Free	Anocracy
1999	Imperfectly Free	Anocracy

MEDIA FREEDOM HISTORY IN A NUTSHELL

- Upon independence, Suriname was a multiparty democracy with free media
- Following the 1980 military coup, media were strictly censored
- In the late 1980s, Suriname began to democratize and controls on media were eased
- As of 2013, news media remained free, but the 2010 election of former dictator Desi Bouterse has raised concerns about the future of media freedom
- As of 2012, Suriname had two privately owned daily newspapers published in Dutch or English and two daily newspapers published in Mandarin (Freedom House's Report on Freedom of the Press 2013)
- Suriname has a mix of private and state-owned broadcast media
- As of 2012, about 35 percent of Surinamers had Internet access (International Telecommunication Union's 2012 ICT Indicators Database)

In Brief

An ethnically diverse population of Creoles and the descendants of African slaves and Indian and Javanese workers, the former Dutch colony of Suriname has a history of political instability. For the first five years following independence, Suriname was a multiparty democracy with media that could and did criticize the government. Following a military coup in 1980, media were censored. Suriname began to democratize in the late 1980s, and controls on media eased to the point where media were once again functionally free by 1989. Although Surinamese media remain vibrant and free, the 2010 election of former dictator Desi Bouterse has raised concerns about the future of media freedom and other human rights.

Year	Media	Government
2000	Imperfectly Free	Anocracy
2001	Imperfectly Free	Anocracy
2002	Free	Anocracy
2003	Free	Anocracy
2004	Free	Anocracy
2005	Free	Anocracy
2006	Free	Anocracy
2007	Free	Anocracy
2008	Free	Anocracy
2009	Free	Anocracy
2010	Free	Anocracy
2011	Free	Anocracy
2012	Free	Anocracy

Chronology

1975–1979: Imperfectly Free

Upon gaining independence from the Netherlands in 1975, Suriname was a multiparty democracy with media freedom. According the U.S. diplomats, "Criticism of the government is a popular pastime, opposition views get the fullest possible airing, and there have been no known cases of intimidation or other measures by the authorities against the media."[1]

1980–1988: Not Free

In 1980, the democratically elected government was overthrown in a military coup, and the new government imposed censorship on all domestic news media, and foreign correspondents were forced to submit their copy to military censors.[2]

In 1982, Lieutenant-Colonel Desire "Desi" Bouterse seized control of the country and established the Revolutionary People's Front. At the end of 1982, in what came to be known as the December murders, fifteen political dissidents, including five journalists, were detained and killed.[3] Additionally, the offices of an independent newspaper and two privately owned radio stations were destroyed by fire or bombs, and eventually all media that were not government controlled were closed down.[4] Political instability continued in the mid-1980s as the Surinamese Liberation Army (SLA) mobilized and began fighting.

1989–2001: Imperfectly Free

Following the 1988 election of President Ramsewak Shankar, Suriname returned to civilian rule and restrictions on news outlets eased to the point where media were imperfectly free. By this time privately owned media had reemerged and criticism of the government was once again possible.[5] Yet political instability continued in the early 1990s, as Bouterse rejected Shankar's peace accord with the SLA and then oversaw a coup that ousted Shankar. Although Bouterse continued to enjoy considerable influence in Suriname, the country did return to civilian rule in 1991 with the election of Ronald Venetiann, and in 1992, the government obtained a peace accord with the SLA. In the late 1990s, a Dutch court charged Bouterse with drug trafficking, tried him in absentia, and convicted him. Throughout these years media remained functionally free, though there were some threats from the political turmoil and journalists tended to self-censor.[6]

2002–2012: Free

By 2002, there were fewer reports of journalists facing harassment and threats, and conditions improved to the point that media were free.[7] In 2007, Bouterse and twenty-four codefendants were charged with the December murders, but the case was suspended in 2010 when Bouterse was elected president. In 2012, the Parliament voted to grant amnesty to Bouterse and his codefendants, and journalists covering these proceedings did face threats from the government.[8]

Media Today

Although there is some self-censorship, Surinamese media remain vibrant and include two daily newspapers and a mix of private and state-owned broadcast media.[9] Suriname also has an emerging media market in Mandarin that serves its increasing Chinese population.[10] While defamation remains a criminal offense punishable by up to seven years imprisonment, there have been no recent cases against journalists.[11] Given Bouterse's dictatorial past, it remains to be seen if he will continue to tolerate independent news media. Journalists have claimed that the government monitors their social media and email activity.[12]

Notes

1. *Country Reports on Human Rights Practices for 1979* (Washington, DC: U.S. Department of State, 1980), 404. Available at http://babel.hathitrust.org/cgi/pt?id=mdp.39015014188273;view=1up;seq=9.

2. *Report of the Committee on the Freedom of the Press and Information*, 1980 General Assembly (Miami: FL: Inter American Press Association, 1981).

3. *Country Reports on Human Rights Practices for 1982* (Washington, DC: U.S. Department of State, 1983). Available at http://babel.hathitrust.org/cgi/pt?id=mdp.39015014164753;view=1up;seq=2.

4. Ibid.

5. *Country Reports on Human Rights Practices for 1989* (Washington, DC: U.S. Department of State, 1990). Available at https://archive.org/details/countryreportson1989unit.

6. *World Press Freedom Report*, IPI Report (Vienna: International Press Institute, 2001).

7. *Country Reports on Human Rights Practices for 2002* (Washington, DC: U.S. Department of State, 2003). Available at http://www.state.gov/j/drl/rls/hrrpt/2002/18345.htm.

8. *Freedom of the Press* (Washington, DC: Freedom House, 2013). Available at http://www.freedomhouse.org/report/freedom-press/2013/suriname.

9. Ibid.

10. Ibid.

11. Ibid.

12. Ibid.

Swaziland: 1968–2012

Swaziland Year by Year

Year	Media	Government
1968	Not Free	Anocracy
1969	Not Free	Anocracy
1970	Not Free	Anocracy
1971	Not Free	Anocracy
1972	Not Free	Anocracy
1973	Not Free	Autocracy
1974	Not Free	Autocracy
1975	Not Free	Autocracy
1976	Not Free	Autocracy
1977	Not Free	Autocracy
1978	Not Free	Autocracy
1979	Not Free	Autocracy
1980	Not Free	Autocracy
1981	Not Free	Autocracy
1982	Not Free	Autocracy
1983	Not Free	Autocracy
1984	Not Free	Autocracy
1985	Not Free	Autocracy
1986	Not Free	Autocracy
1987	Not Free	Autocracy
1988	Not Free	Autocracy
1989	Not Free	Autocracy
1990	Not Free	Autocracy
1991	Not Free	Autocracy
1992	Not Free	Autocracy
1993	Not Free	Autocracy
1994	Not Free	Autocracy

(Continued)

MEDIA FREEDOM HISTORY IN A NUTSHELL

- One of the world's only remaining absolute monarchies, Swaziland has a long history of restricted media
- As of 2012, Swaziland had two newspapers and mix of state-run and private broadcast media, but the state-run radio was the primary source of news for most Swazis (Freedom House's 2013 Freedom of the Press Report)
- As of 2012, about 21 percent of Swazis had Internet access (International Telecommunication Union's 2012 ICT Indicators Database)

In Brief

In the lead up to a peace deal, in 2001, the government addressed some of the worst of its human rights abuses and eased some controls on media.

As one of the world's last absolute monarchies, Swaziland has a long history of restricted news media. Poverty, food shortages, and AIDS continue to take a toll on this country while the king and his wives live in luxury.

Chronology

1968–2012: Not Free

Upon gaining independence from Britain in 1968, Swaziland had a parliamentary system, but in 1973, with the support of the Parliament, King Sobhuza II suspended the constitution, which he deemed too "Western," banned political parties, and proceeded to rule by decree with the support of a system of tribal councils known as Tinkhundla. During these years, the government controlled and sometimes censored the news media and criticism of government policies had to go through the Tinkhundla system.[1]

(Continued)

Year	Media	Government
1995	Not Free	Autocracy
1996	Not Free	Autocracy
1997	Not Free	Autocracy
1998	Not Free	Autocracy
1999	Not Free	Autocracy
2000	Not Free	Autocracy
2001	Not Free	Autocracy
2002	Not Free	Autocracy
2003	Not Free	Autocracy
2004	Not Free	Autocracy
2005	Not Free	Autocracy
2006	Not Free	Autocracy
2007	Not Free	Autocracy
2008	Not Free	Autocracy
2009	Not Free	Autocracy
2010	Not Free	Autocracy
2011	Not Free	Autocracy
2012	Not Free	Autocracy

Additionally, Swaziland had a number of laws restricting press freedom including the Books and Newspaper Act of 1963 that required registration of all newspapers, the Proscribed Publications Act of 1968 that gave the government the right to ban publications for a variety of reasons including to protect public order and morality and national security, and other measures that criminalized defamation.[2]

In 1982, King Sobhuza II died and was eventually succeeded by his son King Mswati III. While most news outlets remained at least partially government owned, in the early 1980s, a privately owned newspaper began publishing. Yet self-censorship remained common, and criticism of the royal family was not tolerated.[3]

In the mid-1990s, following a series of general strikes, the government began to censor the state-owned broadcast media to prevent them from carrying stories about clashes between police and protesters.[4]

Amid a push for democratic reforms, King Mswati III approved a new constitution in 2006, and although this constitution guaranteed media freedom, a number of laws restricted media freedom remained in effect, including some that predated Swaziland's independence.[5] Thus, the new constitution had little effect in practice because the government continued to restrict news media. For example, in 2005, the king ordered the media to stop reporting on his spending following a report on his purchasing luxury vehicles for his wives, and in 2006, he mandated that newspapers obtain his permission before interviewing his wives.

Media Today

Swazi media remain vulnerable to both government censorship and self-censorship, and laws restricting media remain in place. Swaziland has two privately owned newspapers, both of which engage in critical reporting, but their circulation is limited to urban areas.[6] The government continues to control the country's primary source for news, which is radio. Although there is one private radio station, it focuses on religious programming.[7] Swaziland has a one private television station and one state-run television station. There have been some reports of government tracking social media and e-mail activity.[8]

Notes

1. *Country Reports on Human Rights Practices for 1977* (Washington, DC: U.S. Department of State, 1978). Available at http://babel.hathitrust.org/cgi/pt?id=mdp.39015078705632.
2. Richard Rooney, "The New Swaziland Constitution and Its Impact on Media Freedom,"*Global Media Journal Africa Edition* 2, no.1 (2008): 53–65.
3. *Country Reports on Human Rights Practices for 1982* (Washington, DC: U.S. Department of State, 1983). Available at http://babel.hathitrust.org/cgi/pt?id=mdp.39015014164753;view=1up;seq=2.
4. *World Press Freedom Review*, IPI Report (Vienna: International Press Institute, December 1996/January 1997).
5. Rooney, "The New Swaziland Constitution and Its Impact on Media Freedom."
6. *Freedom of the Press* (Washington, DC: Freedom House, 2013). Available at http://www.freedomhouse.org/report/freedom-press/2013/swaziland.
7. Ibid.
8. Ibid.

Sweden: 1948–2012

Sweden Year by Year

Year	Media	Government
1948	Free	Democracy
1949	Free	Democracy
1950	Free	Democracy
1951	Free	Democracy
1952	Free	Democracy
1953	Free	Democracy
1954	Free	Democracy
1955	Free	Democracy
1956	Free	Democracy
1957	Free	Democracy
1958	Free	Democracy
1959	Free	Democracy
1960	Free	Democracy
1961	Free	Democracy
1962	Free	Democracy
1963	Free	Democracy
1964	Free	Democracy
1965	Free	Democracy
1966	Free	Democracy
1967	Free	Democracy
1968	Free	Democracy
1969	Free	Democracy
1970	Free	Democracy
1971	Free	Democracy
1972	Free	Democracy
1973	Free	Democracy
1974	Free	Democracy

(Continued)

MEDIA FREEDOM HISTORY IN A NUTSHELL

- Sweden is an exemplar of media freedom with a significant public service media component
- As of 2011, there were 89 daily newspapers, 78 of them were paid-for daily newspapers, with a total average circulation per issue of 2,894,000 (World Association of Newspaper's 2012 World Newspaper Trends)
- Since the early 1990s, there has been an increase in the number of private broadcast media, but public broadcast media remain popular
- As of 2012, about 94 percent of Swedes had Internet access (International Telecommunication Union's 2012 ICT Indicators Database)

In Brief

In 1766, Sweden became one of the first countries to legally establish freedom of the press. Today the country is an exemplar of media freedom with a significant public service media component. In particular, public television remains strong in Sweden, but now faces competition from privately owned broadcast media.

Chronology

1948–2012: Free

There are no significant challenges to media freedom. In recent years, there have been some claims that Sweden's laws against hate speech encourage journalists to self-censor and thereby limit media freedom, but for the most part Swedish media are remarkably free.[1]

(Continued)

Year	Media	Government
1975	Free	Democracy
1976	Free	Democracy
1977	Free	Democracy
1978	Free	Democracy
1979	Free	Democracy
1980	Free	Democracy
1981	Free	Democracy
1982	Free	Democracy
1983	Free	Democracy
1984	Free	Democracy
1985	Free	Democracy
1986	Free	Democracy
1987	Free	Democracy
1988	Free	Democracy
1989	Free	Democracy
1990	Free	Democracy
1991	Free	Democracy
1992	Free	Democracy
1993	Free	Democracy

Year	Media	Government
1994	Free	Democracy
1995	Free	Democracy
1996	Free	Democracy
1997	Free	Democracy
1998	Free	Democracy
1999	Free	Democracy
2000	Free	Democracy
2001	Free	Democracy
2002	Free	Democracy
2003	Free	Democracy
2004	Free	Democracy
2005	Free	Democracy
2006	Free	Democracy
2007	Free	Democracy
2008	Free	Democracy
2009	Free	Democracy
2010	Free	Democracy
2011	Free	Democracy
2012	Free	Democracy

Media Today

With the largest population of all the Nordic countries and a relatively high level of wealth, the Swedish media market is probably robust enough to avoid the challenges facing smaller, linguistically distinct markets. Known as one of the most socialist of democracies, there is a strong and longstanding commitment to the support of public service broadcasting. With about 94 percent of the population enjoying Internet access, blogs are especially popular.

Note

1. Freedom of the Press (Washington, DC: Freedom House, 2013). Available at http://www.freedom house.org/reports.

Switzerland: 1948–2012

Switzerland Year by Year

Year	Media	Government
1948	Free	Democracy
1949	Free	Democracy
1950	Free	Democracy
1951	Free	Democracy
1952	Free	Democracy
1953	Free	Democracy
1954	Free	Democracy
1955	Free	Democracy
1956	Free	Democracy
1957	Free	Democracy
1958	Free	Democracy
1959	Free	Democracy
1960	Free	Democracy
1961	Free	Democracy
1962	Free	Democracy
1963	Free	Democracy
1964	Free	Democracy
1965	Free	Democracy
1966	Free	Democracy
1967	Free	Democracy
1968	Free	Democracy
1969	Free	Democracy
1970	Free	Democracy
1971	Free	Democracy
1972	Free	Democracy
1973	Free	Democracy
1974	Free	Democracy
1975	Free	Democracy
1976	Free	Democracy
1977	Free	Democracy

(Continued)

MEDIA FREEDOM HISTORY IN A NUTSHELL

- A small and linguistically diverse media market presents challenges
- A complex licensing and funding scheme supports much of the domestically produced media
- Switzerland is dominated by government supported public service broadcasting
- As of 2011, there were seventy-nine daily newspapers, seventy-five of them were paid-for daily newspapers, with a total average circulation per issue of 2,978,000 (World Association of Newspaper's 2012 World Newspaper Trends)
- As of 2012, about 85 percent of the Swiss had Internet access (International Telecommunication Union's 2012 ICT Indicators Database)

In Brief

Switzerland is one of the last remaining European countries that is not a member of the European Union. Long a bastion of neutrality and independence, media freedom is enshrined in the Swiss constitution and has been supported in practice by both the government and the public. There do not appear to be any significant threats to media freedom.[1]

Chronology

1948–2012: Free

Switzerland is, perhaps, the exemplar of public service broadcasting. Founded in 1931, the Swiss radio broadcasting corporation also operates the national television stations. Licensing fees are used to support programming to ensure that all four official languages (German, French, Italian and Romansh) and all the fiercely

(Continued)

Year	Media	Government
1978	Free	Democracy
1979	Free	Democracy
1980	Free	Democracy
1981	Free	Democracy
1982	Free	Democracy
1983	Free	Democracy
1984	Free	Democracy
1985	Free	Democracy
1986	Free	Democracy
1987	Free	Democracy
1988	Free	Democracy
1989	Free	Democracy
1990	Free	Democracy
1991	Free	Democracy
1992	Free	Democracy
1993	Free	Democracy
1994	Free	Democracy

Year	Media	Government
1995	Free	Democracy
1996	Free	Democracy
1997	Free	Democracy
1998	Free	Democracy
1999	Free	Democracy
2000	Free	Democracy
2001	Free	Democracy
2002	Free	Democracy
2003	Free	Democracy
2004	Free	Democracy
2005	Free	Democracy
2006	Free	Democracy
2007	Free	Democracy
2008	Free	Democracy
2009	Free	Democracy
2010	Free	Democracy
2011	Free	Democracy
2012	Free	Democracy

independent regions and locals receive media content of equal quality. There have been no significant challenges to media freedom in the post-war era, and the market is robust.

Media Today

Wealth and extremely high levels of literacy, news consumption, and civic engagement, along with a substantial government commitment to public service broadcasting have so far, buffered the Swiss media from many of the economic and technological challenges confronting the domestic media in other relatively small and linguistically diverse markets. Still, traditional news outlets face increasing competition from the Internet, and in particular, the blogosphere.

Note

1. *Switzerland,* Media Landscape Reports (Maastricht, The Netherlands: European Journalism Centre, 2013). Available at http://ejc.net/media_landscapes/switzerland.

Syria: 1948–2012

Syria Year by Year

Year	Media	Government
1948	Not Free	Anocracy
1949	Not Free	Autocracy
1950	Not Free	Anocracy
1951	Not Free	Autocracy
1952	Not Free	Autocracy
1953	Not Free	Autocracy
1954	Not Free	Democracy
1955	Not Free	Democracy
1956	Not Free	Democracy
1957	Not Free	Democracy
1958	Not Free	Foreign Interruption
1959	Not Free	Foreign Interruption
1960	Not Free	Foreign Interruption
1961	Not Free	Anocracy
1962	Not Free	Anocracy
1963	Not Free	Autocracy
1964	Not Free	Autocracy
1965	Not Free	Autocracy
1966	Not Free	Autocracy
1967	Not Free	Autocracy
1968	Not Free	Autocracy
1969	Not Free	Autocracy
1970	Not Free	Autocracy
1971	Not Free	Autocracy
1972	Not Free	Autocracy
1973	Not Free	Autocracy
1974	Not Free	Autocracy
1975	Not Free	Autocracy
1976	Not Free	Autocracy

(Continued)

MEDIA FREEDOM HISTORY IN A NUTSHELL

- Frequent coups and nearly constant domestic unrest have plagued independent Syria
- Media were indirectly controlled until the union with Egypt created the United Arab Republic (UAR)
- During the UAR period, media were transformed into a propaganda tool for the government and those mechanisms have remained in place since
- There is no indication that the civil war might lead to media freedom
- In 2013 alone, twenty-nine journalists were killed as they tried to cover the conflict, and at the end of the year, thirty journalists were missing in Syria and believed to have been kidnapped (Committee to Protect Journalists)
- As of 2010, Syria had nine paid-for daily newspapers with a total average circulation per issue of 385,000 (World Association of Newspapers World Press Trends 2012)
- As of 2012, about 24 percent of Syrians had Internet access (International Telecommunication Union's 2012 ICT Indicators Database)

In Brief

Authoritarian rule has been the norm, and media have never been free. Syria has been active in Middle-Eastern politics, participating in a short-lived union with Egypt, invading and occupying Lebanon, and fighting several wars against Israel. Significant domestic struggles and uprisings have also occurred, but through it all, authoritarian rule has been the norm and the media have been strictly controlled.

Chronology

1948–2012: Not Free

Frequent coups followed the end of the French mandate over Syria, and the power of the

(Continued)

Year	Media	Government
1977	Not Free	Autocracy
1978	Not Free	Autocracy
1979	Not Free	Autocracy
1980	Not Free	Autocracy
1981	Not Free	Autocracy
1982	Not Free	Autocracy
1983	Not Free	Autocracy
1984	Not Free	Autocracy
1985	Not Free	Autocracy
1986	Not Free	Autocracy
1987	Not Free	Autocracy
1988	Not Free	Autocracy
1989	Not Free	Autocracy
1990	Not Free	Autocracy
1991	Not Free	Autocracy
1992	Not Free	Autocracy
1993	Not Free	Autocracy
1994	Not Free	Autocracy
1995	Not Free	Autocracy
1996	Not Free	Autocracy
1997	Not Free	Autocracy
1998	Not Free	Autocracy
1999	Not Free	Autocracy
2000	Not Free	Autocracy
2001	Not Free	Autocracy
2002	Not Free	Autocracy
2003	Not Free	Autocracy
2004	Not Free	Autocracy
2005	Not Free	Autocracy
2006	Not Free	Autocracy
2007	Not Free	Autocracy
2008	Not Free	Autocracy
2009	Not Free	Autocracy
2010	Not Free	Autocracy
2011	Not Free	Autocracy
2012	Not Free	Autocracy

Arab Socialist Baath party grew. Strict control over the media was exercised, but it was largely indirect and included the use of violence, imprisonment, and legal harassment to prevent critical media content.

In 1958, Syria joined Egypt to form the United Arab Republic (UAR). Technically, the two countries became a single country, but domestically, they were independently governed. During this period, media controls in Syria gradually shifted to direct control and media became a propaganda tool of the government.

In 1961, army officers seized power and dissolved the union with Egypt. Direct media controls developed during the UAR period remained in place and largely unchanged despite coups in 1963, 1966, and 1970. Hafez al-Assad took power in 1970, founding the regime that is now controlled by his son, Bashar. Unrest was almost constant, and the domestic media were essentially a propaganda tool for the regime. The Ministry of Information censored both domestic and foreign print media and controlled broadcast media.[1]

In 2011, the government's brutal suppression of antigovernment demonstrations fueled the uprising, and eventually the country descended into civil war. That same year, the Assad regime issued a media law that on the one hand granted the media some freedoms, including the right to access to information, but on the other hand imposed restrictions, including prohibiting the publication of news deemed harmful to "national unity and national security."[2] As the conflict intensified, the government restricted coverage of it and arrested journalists on charges that they had threated national security.[3]

Media Today

Civil war has eliminated what little hope there might have been that media controls would be relaxed. Even if the Assad regime ends, there is no indication that possible successor regimes would embrace free media. New media outlets emerged as the Assad regime lost control of much of the country, but journalists trying to cover the conflict face a number of threats.[4] Both opposition media and state-run media have been attacked.[5] Online news outlets, bloggers, and activists using social media have been hacked, blocked, and in some cases physically attacked.[6] The Committee to Protect Journalists reported that Syria was the most deadly country for journalists in 2013 after confirming that twenty-nine journalists were killed covering the conflict in that year alone.[7] Moreover, at the end of 2013, thirty journalists were missing in Syria, prompting a group of international news organizations to call on the Syrian armed opposition to put a stop to the kidnapping of journalists.[8]

Notes

1. Thomas Collelo, *Syria: A Country Study* (Washington, DC: Library of Congress Federal Research Division, 1987). Available at http://lcweb2.loc.gov/frd/cs/cshome.html.

2. *Freedom of the Press* (Washington, DC: Freedom House, 2013). Available at http://www.freedomhouse.org/report/freedom-press/2013/syria.

3. Ibid.

4. Ibid.

5. Ibid.

6. Ibid.

7. Elana Beiser, *Syria, Iraq, Egypt Most Deadly Nations for Journalists* (Committee to Protect Journalists, 2013). Available at http://www.cpj.org/reports/2013/12/syria-iraq-egypt-most-deadly-nations-for-journalis.php.

8. Jason Stern, *Unprecedented Response to Kidnappings in Syria* (Committee to Protect Journalists, 2013). Available at http://cpj.org/blog/mideast/syria/.

Taiwan: 1949–2012

Taiwan Year by Year

Year	Media	Government
1949	Not Free	Autocracy
1950	Not Free	Autocracy
1951	Not Free	Autocracy
1952	Not Free	Autocracy
1953	Not Free	Autocracy
1954	Not Free	Autocracy
1955	Not Free	Autocracy
1956	Not Free	Autocracy
1957	Not Free	Autocracy
1958	Not Free	Autocracy
1959	Not Free	Autocracy
1960	Not Free	Autocracy
1961	Not Free	Autocracy
1962	Not Free	Autocracy
1963	Not Free	Autocracy
1964	Not Free	Autocracy
1965	Not Free	Autocracy
1966	Not Free	Autocracy
1967	Not Free	Autocracy
1968	Not Free	Autocracy
1969	Not Free	Autocracy
1970	Not Free	Autocracy
1971	Not Free	Autocracy
1972	Not Free	Autocracy
1973	Not Free	Autocracy
1974	Not Free	Autocracy
1975	Not Free	Autocracy
1976	Not Free	Autocracy

MEDIA FREEDOM HISTORY IN A NUTSHELL

- Chiang Kai-Shek ruled as a dictator until his death in 1975; during his tenure, media were limited and controlled
- Inheriting that dictatorship, Chiang Kai-Shek's son Chiang Ching-kuo initiated the process of liberalization and democratization, lifting martial law just before his death in 1988
- Liberalization continued after Chiang Ching-kuo's death with media becoming functionally free in 1991 and clearly free in the run up to the 2000 election
- Media have been called highly partisan, but they are well financed, independent, and robust
- As of 2012, Taiwan had more than 360 newspapers, more than 280 television channels, and numerous radio stations
- The Internet remains unrestricted, and in 2012 nearly 76 percent of people living in Taiwan had internet access (International Telecommunication Union's 2012 ICT Indicators Database)

In Brief

Under martial law until 1987, Taiwanese media were tightly controlled. A slow process of democratization followed, culminating in free media and fully democratic elections in 2000.

Chronology

1949–1990: Not Free

After losing the war for control of China to Mao Zedong and the communists, Chiang Kai-Shek moved the Nationalist Chinese capital to Taipei in 1949 and ruled as a dictator under martial law until his death in 1975. During these years, news media were controlled. The government ceased granting newspaper licenses in

Year	Media	Government
1977	Not Free	Autocracy
1978	Not Free	Autocracy
1979	Not Free	Autocracy
1980	Not Free	Autocracy
1981	Not Free	Autocracy
1982	Not Free	Autocracy
1983	Not Free	Autocracy
1984	Not Free	Autocracy
1985	Not Free	Autocracy
1986	Not Free	Autocracy
1987	Not Free	Anocracy
1988	Not Free	Anocracy
1989	Not Free	Anocracy
1990	Not Free	Anocracy
1991	Imperfectly Free	Anocracy
1992	Imperfectly Free	Democracy
1993	Imperfectly Free	Democracy
1994	Imperfectly Free	Democracy
1995	Imperfectly Free	Democracy
1996	Imperfectly Free	Democracy
1997	Imperfectly Free	Democracy
1998	Imperfectly Free	Democracy
1999	Free	Democracy
2000	Free	Democracy
2001	Free	Democracy
2002	Free	Democracy
2003	Free	Democracy
2004	Free	Democracy
2005	Free	Democracy
2006	Free	Democracy
2007	Free	Democracy
2008	Free	Democracy
2009	Free	Democracy
2010	Free	Democracy
2011	Free	Democracy
2012	Free	Democracy

1951, leaving the country with only thirty-one newspapers.[1] All daily newspapers were owned by the government or government officials, and domestic and foreign media were censored.[2]

Chiang Kai-Shek's son Chiang Ching-kuo took over control after his father's death and began a process of democratization, lifting martial law in 1987, shortly before his own death. In 1988, the ban on licensing new newspapers was lifted and the number of newspapers more than doubled.[3] The deregulation of the newspaper industry marked a shift from direct to indirect control of media content and the development of a news media industry.

1991–1998: Imperfectly Free

The progress toward a liberal political system was steady, and by the early 1990s, Taiwanese media were functioning freely. The International Press Institute reported that there were few restrictions on the press in 1991. "Even opinions concerning the Taiwan independent movement, a political taboo in the past, can often be read in the Taiwan press, although organized promotion of the movement is still forbidden by law."[4] In 1992, cable television, which had been operating illegally, was legalized.[5]

1999–2012: Free

As the lead up to the 2000 election intensified, the media operated freely and have continued to do so.

Media Today

Though highly partisan, the media remain free and operate with little or no governmental interference. There are laws intended to limit the possibility of provoking mainland China, such as the prohibition of agitating for independence, but these are largely ignored and unenforced. Defamation remains a criminal offense, punishable with up to two years imprisonment.[6] As of 2012, Taiwan had more than 360 newspapers, more than 280 television channels and numerous radio stations.[7]

Notes

1. *World Press Freedom Review*, IPI Report (Zurich: International Press Institute, December 1987).
2. *Country Reports on Human Rights Practices for 1983* (Washington, DC: U.S. Department of State,

1984). Available at http://babel.hathitrust.org/cgi/pt?id=mdp.39015014227832;view=1up;seq=1.

3. *World Press Freedom Review*, IPI Report (Zurich: International Press Institute, December 1988).

4. *World Press Freedom Review*, IPI Report (Zurich: International Press Institute, December 1991).

5. *World Press Freedom Review*, IPI Report (Zurich: International Press Institute, December 1992).

6. *Freedom of the Press* (Washington, DC: Freedom House, 2013). Available at http://www.freedomhouse.org/report/freedom-press/2013/taiwan.

7. Ibid.

Tajikistan: 1991–2012

Tajikistan Year by Year

Year	Media	Government
1991	Not Free	Anocracy
1992	Not Free	Autocracy
1993	Not Free	Autocracy
1994	Not Free	Autocracy
1995	Not Free	Autocracy
1996	Not Free	Autocracy
1997	Not Free	Anocracy
1998	Not Free	Anocracy
1999	Not Free	Anocracy
2000	Not Free	Anocracy
2001	Not Free	Anocracy
2002	Not Free	Anocracy
2003	Not Free	Anocracy
2004	Not Free	Anocracy
2005	Not Free	Anocracy
2006	Not Free	Anocracy
2007	Not Free	Anocracy
2008	Not Free	Anocracy
2009	Not Free	Anocracy
2010	Not Free	Anocracy
2011	Not Free	Anocracy
2012	Not Free	Anocracy

MEDIA FREEDOM HISTORY IN A NUTSHELL

- Media remain strictly controlled as authoritarian rule confronts civil unrest and civil war
- Government-run stations continue to dominate the market, although satellite television has begun to permeate the country (Freedom House's 2013 Freedom of the Press Report)
- As of 2012, Tajikistan had 350 registered print publications, only half of which were published with any regularity (Freedom House's 2013 Freedom of the Press Report)
- As of 2012, less than 15 percent of Tajikistanis had Internet access (International Telecommunication Union's 2012 ICT Indicators Database)

In Brief

One of the last of the former Soviet Republics to gain independence, Tajikistan immediately descended into civil war and then into the autocratic rule of Emomali Rahmon where the media were, and continue to be, tightly controlled.

Chronology

1991–2012: Not Free

Media were severely restricted, first by civil war and then by the autocratic dictatorship of Emomali Rahmon.

The year 2003 saw a few conciliatory moves toward liberalization, which allowed some media activity outside the direct control of the government. That same year, there were convictions in several cases involving killings of journalists, a move that media freedom advocates hoped signaled an end to a culture of impunity.[1] Yet the slight improvement in the media environment was likely in response to U.S. pressure and a gesture toward the sensibilities of the United States meant to facilitate cooperation and stimulate the flow of U.S. economic support into the country in the wake of the U.S. intervention in Afghanistan.

The façade of liberalization disappeared in 2005 when the arrest, failed extradition, kidnapping, and rearrest of opposition leader Mahmadruzi Iskandarov signaled the reassertion of authoritarian rule. That same year, opposition newspapers and two television stations were closed down, and popular Internet news sites were hacked.[2]

Media Today

With authoritarian rule constantly hovering on the brink of renewed civil war, the media are strictly controlled and there is no indication that the situation will change. Violence against journalists remains a problem, especially for those who criticize the government. Tajikistan has a mix of private and state-run broadcast media, but the state-run media have far greater reach.[3] Although the government reports the country has 350 registered print publications, only half publish with any regularity.[4] Although few Tajikistanis enjoy Internet access (less than 15 percent in 2012), the government has blocked news and social networking sites.[5]

Notes

1. *World Press Freedom Review*, IPI Report (Vienna: International Press Institute, 2003).
2. *World Press Freedom Review*, IPI Report (Vienna: International Press Institute, 2005).
3. *Freedom of the Press* (Washington, DC: Freedom House, 2013. Available at http://www.freedom house.org/report/freedom-press/2013/tajikistan.
4. Ibid.
5. Ibid.

Tanzania: 1961–2012

Tanzania Year by Year

Year	Media	Government
1961	Not Free	Autocracy
1962	Not Free	Autocracy
1963	Not Free	Autocracy
1964	Not Free	Autocracy
1965	Not Free	Autocracy
1966	Not Free	Autocracy
1967	Not Free	Autocracy
1968	Not Free	Autocracy
1969	Not Free	Autocracy
1970	Not Free	Autocracy
1971	Not Free	Autocracy
1972	Not Free	Autocracy
1973	Not Free	Autocracy
1974	Not Free	Autocracy
1975	Not Free	Autocracy
1976	Not Free	Autocracy
1977	Not Free	Autocracy
1978	Not Free	Autocracy
1979	Not Free	Autocracy
1980	Not Free	Autocracy
1981	Not Free	Autocracy
1982	Not Free	Autocracy
1983	Not Free	Autocracy
1984	Not Free	Autocracy

(Continued)

MEDIA FREEDOM HISTORY IN A NUTSHELL

- Shortly after gaining independence, Tanganyika merged with Zanzibar to form Tanzania
- For the first three decades, post-independence Tanzania was ruled by the Chama Cha Mapinduzi (CCM) party and media were restricted
- In the early 1990s, as Tanzania transitioned to a multiparty system, media became functionally free and have remained so, though the CCM party has remained dominate
- As of 2012, Tanzania had eighty-five radio stations and twenty-six television stations, but access to television is too expensive for most Tanzanians (Freedom House's 2013 Freedom of the Press Report)
- In 2012, Tanzania had several dozen daily and weekly newspapers, two of which were government owned (Freedom House's Report on Freedom of the Press Report 2013)
- As of 2012, about 13 percent of Tanzanians had Internet access (International Telecommunication Union's 2012 ICT Indicators Database)

In Brief

Following independence, Tanzania became a one-party state with restricted media. In the early 1990s, as Tanzania transitioned to a multi-party system, independent media emerged. Although the government has struggled to silence critical news outlets, media remain functionally free. Yet in the semi-autonomous archipelago of Zanzibar, journalists have always faced more restrictions.

Chronology

1961–1991: Not Free

Tanganyika gained independence from Britain in 1961, under the leadership of Prime

(Continued)

Year	Media	Government
1985	Not Free	Autocracy
1986	Not Free	Autocracy
1987	Not Free	Autocracy
1988	Not Free	Autocracy
1989	Not Free	Autocracy
1990	Not Free	Autocracy
1991	Not Free	Autocracy
1992	Imperfectly Free	Anocracy
1993	Imperfectly Free	Anocracy
1994	Imperfectly Free	Anocracy
1995	Imperfectly Free	Anocracy
1996	Imperfectly Free	Anocracy
1997	Imperfectly Free	Anocracy
1998	Imperfectly Free	Anocracy
1999	Imperfectly Free	Anocracy
2000	Imperfectly Free	Anocracy
2001	Imperfectly Free	Anocracy
2002	Imperfectly Free	Anocracy
2003	Imperfectly Free	Anocracy
2004	Imperfectly Free	Anocracy
2005	Imperfectly Free	Anocracy
2006	Imperfectly Free	Anocracy
2007	Imperfectly Free	Anocracy
2008	Imperfectly Free	Anocracy
2009	Imperfectly Free	Anocracy
2010	Imperfectly Free	Anocracy
2011	Imperfectly Free	Anocracy
2012	Imperfectly Free	Anocracy

Minister Julius Nyerere, and in 1964 merged with Zanzibar to form Tanzania. This union came after the Sultanate of Zanizibar, which had gained independence in 1963, was overthrown.

The government of Tanzania did not tolerate dissent. For example, in 1964, a British journalist was expelled from the country and two newspapers were banned after the government determined they had distorted the news.[1] In 1976, the Newspapers Act gave the government broad authority to order newspapers to cease publication "in the interest of peace and good order."[2] In 1977, Tanzania officially became a one-party state and the media remained restricted to reflecting the government's point of view.[3]

Throughout the 1980s, the government controlled the media, and while media at times obtained permission from the president's office to accuse senior officials of corruption and newspapers were able to publish letters to the editor complaining about specific government actions, criticism of major policy issues, the president, Cabinet members, and the government's socialist ideology was not tolerated.[4,5] With few exceptions, print and broadcast news outlets were owned by the mainland government, the Zanzibar government, or the ruling party.[6] In 1985, after leading the country for nearly two and a half decades, Nyerere resigned, but little changed for the media as the country remained under the control of the Chama Cha Mapinduzi (CCM) party.

1992–2012: Imperfectly Free

In 1992, in the wake of the government's announced plan to transition to a multiparty system and hold multiparty elections in 1995, a number of independent newspapers and magazines began publishing and the media environment improved.[7] In 1993, the government established the Tanzania Communications Regulatory Authority (TCRA), paving the way for the emergence of privately owned radio and television stations. Yet the two radio stations and two television stations that began broadcasting in 1994 did not provide political news coverage. Although the government had opened the door to independent news media, it was not prepared for the consequences. In 1994, the International Press Institute reported that "the emergence of a vibrant private press which exposed Government shortcomings, mismanagement and failure to tackle theft and corruption has angered the Ministry of Information and Broadcasting, prompting it to look at ways to prevent the publication of such stories."[8] But once the door to media freedom was opened, it was difficult for the government to close. The establishment of the Media Council of Tanzania (MCT) in 1995 was aimed at helping preserve media freedom through self-regulation.

Although Tanzania transitioned to a multi-party system, the CCM retained control as its candidate Benjamin Mkapa, a former editor for one of the state-owned newspapers, won the presidency in the 1995 elections. Thus, although opposition parties were permitted and media were functionally free, Tanzania remained in practice a one-party state because of the continued dominance of the CCM. Yet Tanzania continued to have functionally free media. In 2010, Reporters Without Borders noted that Tanzania remained "one of Africa's top 10 respecters of media freedom."[9]

Media Today

The Tanzanian media remain functionally free, though there are many laws that the government uses to encourage journalists to self-censor. Although there have been a number of calls for its repeal, the 1976 Newspapers Act remains in effect and the government continues to use it to ban critical newspapers. Similarly, the 1993 Broadcasting Services Act gives the TCRA the power to shut down broadcast media, and though the TCRA is supposed to function independently, the president appoints its leaders.[10] Yet Tanzania has a broad range of private and state-run print and broadcast media.

Journalists in Zanzibar face more challenges than their mainland counterparts. The semi-autonomous government of Zanzibar runs the archipelago's only daily newspaper and maintains control over most of the broadcast media.[11] Yet media from the mainland are for the most part available in Zanzibar.

Notes

1. *Toils of the Press*, IPI Reports (Zurich: International Press Institute, March 1964).
2. *The Newspapers Act* (Dar es Salaam: Tanzania Government Printer, 1976), 12. Available at http://polis.parliament.go.tz/PAMS/docs/3-1976.pdf.
3. *Country Reports on Human Rights Practices for 1980* (Washington, DC: U.S. Department of State, 1981). Available at http://babel.hathitrust.org/cgi/pt?id=mdp.39015014143476;view=1up;seq=2.
4. *World Press Freedom Review*, IPI Report (Zurich: International Press Institute, December 1988).
5. Ibid.
6. *Country Reports on Human Rights Practices for 1984* (Washington, DC: U.S. Department of State, 1985). Available at http://babel.hathitrust.org/cgi/pt?id=mdp.39015008874342;view=1up;seq=10.
7. *World Press Freedom Review*, IPI Report (Zurich: International Press Institute, December 1992).
8. *World Press Freedom Review*, IPI Report (Vienna: International Press Institute, December 1994).
9. *Tanzania* (Paris, France: Reporters Without Borders, 2010). Available at http://en.rsf.org/report-tanzania,252.html.
10. *Freedom of the Press* (Washington, DC: Freedom House, 2013). Available at http://www.freedomhouse.org/report/freedom-press/2013/tanzania.
11. Ibid.

Thailand: 1948–2012

Thailand Year by Year

Year	Media	Government
1948	Not Free	Anocracy
1949	Not Free	Anocracy
1950	Not Free	Anocracy
1951	Not Free	Anocracy
1952	Not Free	Autocracy
1953	Not Free	Autocracy
1954	Not Free	Autocracy
1955	Not Free	Anocracy
1956	Not Free	Anocracy
1957	Not Free	Anocracy
1958	Not Free	Autocracy
1959	Not Free	Autocracy
1960	Not Free	Autocracy
1961	Not Free	Autocracy
1962	Not Free	Autocracy
1963	Not Free	Autocracy
1964	Not Free	Autocracy
1965	Not Free	Autocracy
1966	Not Free	Autocracy
1967	Not Free	Autocracy
1968	Not Free	Anocracy
1969	Not Free	Anocracy
1970	Not Free	Anocracy
1971	Not Free	Autocracy
1972	Not Free	Autocracy
1973	Not Free	Anocracy
1974	Not Free	Anocracy
1975	Not Free	Anocracy

MEDIA FREEDOM HISTORY IN A NUTSHELL

- Military rule, occasionally under the guise of civilian leadership, was predominant until the mid-1990s
- Civilian rule has been unstable, but did manage to create a situation in which partisan presses were able to operate and create an imperfectly free media environment
- The military intervention against protestors in 2010 also eliminated enough of the partisan media to effectively bring media back under indirect government control
- As of 2012, Thailand had six television stations (all government-controlled), as well as satellite television and numerous radio stations (Freedom House's Report on Freedom of the Press Report 2013)
- As of 2012, Thailand had forty-six daily newspapers with a total average circulation per issue of 7,717,000 (World Association of Newspaper's 2012 World Newspaper Trends)
- As of 2012, about 27 percent of Thai had Internet access (International Telecommunication Union's 2012 ICT Indicators Database)

In Brief

As Thailand shifted between military rule and unstable civilian governments, media remained directly controlled or heavily restricted until the reaction to the Asian financial crisis led to the inclusion of opposition parties in government in 1998. Yet media freedom was imperfect, nonexistent in some parts of the country, and fragile. Eventually media restrictions returned in 2010.

Chronology

1948–1997: Not Free

The assassination of the king in 1946 was followed by a military coup in 1947, and the

Year	Media	Government
1976	Not Free	Autocracy
1977	Not Free	Anocracy
1978	Not Free	Anocracy
1979	Not Free	Anocracy
1980	Not Free	Anocracy
1981	Not Free	Anocracy
1982	Not Free	Anocracy
1983	Not Free	Anocracy
1984	Not Free	Anocracy
1985	Not Free	Anocracy
1986	Not Free	Anocracy
1987	Not Free	Anocracy
1988	Not Free	Anocracy
1989	Not Free	Anocracy
1990	Not Free	Anocracy
1991	Not Free	Anocracy
1992	Not Free	Democracy
1993	Not Free	Democracy
1994	Not Free	Democracy
1995	Not Free	Democracy
1996	Not Free	Democracy
1997	Not Free	Democracy
1998	Imperfectly Free	Democracy
1999	Imperfectly Free	Democracy
2000	Imperfectly Free	Democracy
2001	Imperfectly Free	Democracy
2002	Imperfectly Free	Democracy
2003	Imperfectly Free	Democracy
2004	Imperfectly Free	Democracy
2005	Imperfectly Free	Democracy
2006	Imperfectly Free	Anocracy
2007	Imperfectly Free	Anocracy
2008	Imperfectly Free	Anocracy
2009	Imperfectly Free	Anocracy
2010	Not Free	Anocracy
2011	Not Free	Anocracy
2012	Not Free	Anocracy

military ruled until 1973. The civilian government that took over from the military was ineffective and unstable, and the military took back power in 1976. Technically, civilian rule was restored in 1983, but both leaders before the 1991 military coup were generals. Though the different governments employed varying means and legal mechanisms, media were consistently and strictly controlled during this time.[12]

Protests followed the 1992 election of General Suchinda Kraprayoon to replace the nominally civilian leader, Anand Panyarachun, who had been installed by the military in 1991. Kraprayoon was forced to resign, leading to new elections late in 1992, which were won by the Democratic Party candidate, Chuan Leekpai. Direct control of the media was replaced by strict indirect controls. This allowed some development of a news media industry.

1998–2009: Imperfectly Free

The 1997 constitution provided "the most sweeping free press provisions in Asia," and these were somewhat respected in practice.[3] In desperate need of economic reforms to address the difficulties caused by the Asian financial crisis, Prime Minister Chuan Leekpai brought opposition parties into his government to push through the needed legislation. The inclusion of the opposition created a space where partisan media outlets could operate, creating an imperfect but functionally free media in most of but not all the country. Martial law returned to parts of the country in 2004, and Prime Minister Thaksin Shinawatra employed a number of tactics aimed at silencing the media including closing down radio and television programs and filing defamation lawsuits.[4] In 2006, the military staged a bloodless coup. In spite of the political unrest, in much of the country, and particularly in the capital, partisan newspapers still managed to operate, even during martial law. Yet at the end of the first decade of the 2000s, unrest and protests escalated.

2010–2012: Not Free

The "red shirt" protests brought Bangkok to a standstill, and when the military eventually stormed the protestors' makeshift barricades, they also shut down media outlets deemed sympathetic, ending the partisan but competitive and effectively free press environment. In particular, the government cracked down on online media and satellite television using the Computer Crime Act and the lèse-majesté laws, which render insulting the king or the royal family punishable by up to fifteen years imprisonment.[5] Although the government eased restrictions on the news media prior to the elections in 2011, by the end of that year the government was once again punishing critical journalists with the lèse-majesté laws and using a newly created agency to monitor online activity.[6]

Media Today

Unrest continues, protestors are still being confronted by troops, but peace efforts are being made. It is unclear when or if media freedom will be restored. The government maintains at least indirect control over broadcast media.[7] Most print media are privately owned. The government continues to monitor and censor the Internet.[8]

Notes

1. *Country Reports on Human Rights Practices for 1977* (Washington, DC: U.S. Department of State, 1978). Available at http://babel.hathitrust.org/cgi/pt?id=mdp.39015078705632;view=1up;seq=3.
2. Barbara Leitch LePoer, *Thailand: A Country Study* (Washington, DC: Library of Congress Federal Research Division, 1987). Available at http://lcweb2.loc.gov/frd/cs/cshome.html.
3. *World Press Freedom Review*, IPI Report (Vienna: International Press Institute, December 1998), 136.
4. *World Press Freedom Review*, IPI Report (Vienna: International Press Institute, 2005).
5. *Freedom of the Press* (Washington, DC: Freedom House, 2011). Available at http://www.freedomhouse.org/report/freedom-press/2011/thailand.
6. *Freedom of the Press* (Washington, DC: Freedom House, 2012). Available at http://www.freedomhouse.org/report/freedom-press/2012/thailand.
7. *Freedom of the Press* (Washington, DC: Freedom House, 2013). Available at http://www.freedomhouse.org/report/freedom-press/2013/thailand.
8. Ibid.

Timor-Leste (East Timor): 2002–2012

Timor-Leste Year by Year

Year	Media	Government
2002	Free	Democracy
2003	Free	Democracy
2004	Free	Democracy
2005	Imperfectly Free	Democracy
2006	Imperfectly Free	Democracy
2007	Imperfectly Free	Democracy
2008	Imperfectly Free	Democracy
2009	Imperfectly Free	Democracy
2010	Imperfectly Free	Democracy
2011	Imperfectly Free	Democracy
2012	Imperfectly Free	Democracy

MEDIA FREEDOM HISTORY IN A NUTSHELL

- As Timor-Leste gained independence in 2002, media were free in part because media freedom was perceived as critical to the country's development
- In 2005, unrest swept across the country and critical journalists were threatened by both government and opposition
- Since 2005, media have remained functionally free, but journalists do face occasional threats
- As of 2012, Timor-Leste had four daily newspapers (Freedom House, Freedom of the Press 2013)
- Timor-Leste's television and radio stations remained the primary sources for news. However, broadcasts were often interrupted because of poor signals. Many people had no access to television or radio (World Association of Newspaper's 2010 World Newspaper Trends)
- As of 2012, about 1 percent of Timorese had Internet access (International Telecommunication Union's 2012 ICT Indicators Database)

In Brief

After a long and brutal occupation, Timor-Leste gained independence in 2002. As part of this independence, Timorese media gained their freedom. In 2005, political unrest led to increased attacks on journalists, and since then, news media have fought to maintain media freedom. In recent years, the media environment has stabilized and media remain for the most part functionally free.

Chronology

2002–2004: Free

For nearly a quarter of a century, from 1975 to 1999, Timor-Leste was occupied by Indonesia. During these years as many as 100,000 to 250,000 people were killed and news media were restricted. In 1999, the United Nations and Australian-led peacekeeping intervened, and by 2002, when the UN recognized Timor-Leste as an independent state, media freedom was established. From independence, media freedom was perceived as crucial to the country's development and Timor-Leste received media assistance from the international community. The broadcast media were initially run by the United Nations and then handed over to the government, but there were also community radio stations, and print media were independently owned.[1] Although the country remained poor, in these first three years, its media were counted among the freest in Asia.[2]

2005–2012: Imperfectly Free

In 2005, concerns emerged about government respect for media freedom when a new penal code criminalizing defamation was approved by Prime Minister Mari Alkatiri.[3] Eventually though, President Xanana Gusmao refused to sign the measure. Yet, also in 2005, Alkatiri withdrew government advertising from the newspaper, *Suara Timor Lorosae*, and barred its reporters from government press conferences after the newspaper published stories about people dying of starvation.[4] The year 2006 was marked by civil unrest and increased attacks on journalists to such an extent that *Radio and Televisao Timor Lorosae* suspended broadcasting and at least two newspapers stopped publishing when their journalists were forced to flee for their lives.[5] The unrest subsided when Alkatiri resigned. Although political pressures on journalists decreased, journalists remained vulnerable. In 2009, Timor-Leste decriminalized defamation.

Media Today

News media remain imperfectly free. Although defamation is decriminalized, journalists who criticize government are sometimes attacked, arrested, or harassed.[6] Poverty and poor infrastructure have left many Timorese without media access. Radio remains the most accessible medium. Television is also popular, and Timor-Leste has one state-owned and one private station. Although Timor-Leste has four daily and four weekly newspapers, many people do not have access to these because of poverty and illiteracy.[7] Only about 1 percent of Timorese have Internet access; however, mobile phones are becoming more popular and perhaps offer the most potential for improving media access.[8]

Notes

1. *Freedom of the Press* (Washington, DC: Freedom House, 2004). Available at http://www.freedomhouse.org/report/freedom-press/2004/east-timor.
2. *World Press Freedom Review*, IPI Report (Vienna: International Press Institute, 2005).
3. Ibid.
4. Ibid.
5. *World Press Freedom Review*, IPI Report (Vienna: International Press Institute, 2006).
6. *Freedom of the Press* (Washington, DC: Freedom House, 2013). Available at http://www.freedomhouse.org/report/freedom-press/2013/east-timor.
7. Ibid.
8. Ibid.

Togo: 1960–2012

Togo Year by Year

Year	Media	Government
1960	Not Free	Autocracy
1961	Not Free	Autocracy
1962	Not Free	Autocracy
1963	Not Free	Autocracy
1964	Not Free	Autocracy
1965	Not Free	Autocracy
1966	Not Free	Autocracy
1967	Not Free	Autocracy
1968	Not Free	Autocracy
1969	Not Free	Autocracy
1970	Not Free	Autocracy
1971	Not Free	Autocracy
1972	Not Free	Autocracy
1973	Not Free	Autocracy
1974	Not Free	Autocracy
1975	Not Free	Autocracy
1976	Not Free	Autocracy
1977	Not Free	Autocracy
1978	Not Free	Autocracy
1979	Not Free	Autocracy
1980	Not Free	Autocracy
1981	Not Free	Autocracy
1982	Not Free	Autocracy
1983	Not Free	Autocracy

(Continued)

MEDIA FREEDOM HISTORY IN A NUTSHELL

- Since independence, Togo has been under authoritarian rule with restricted news media
- In the 1990s, the number of independent news outlets increased but the government-run media remained dominant
- Togo has a hostile media environment with a long history of violence against journalists
- As of 2012, Togo had approximately one hundred radio stations (mostly private), eight independently owned television stations, and two independent daily newspapers (Freedom House's Report on Freedom of the Press 2013)
- In every medium, state-run news media continue to have greater reach than privately owned media
- As of 2012, about 4 percent of Togolese had Internet access (International Telecommunication Union's 2012 ICT Indicators Database)

In Brief

Originally colonized by Germany, what is now Togo was taken over by France during World War I. Since gaining independence, Togo has been under authoritarian rule with restricted news media.

Chronology

1960–2012: Not Free

Upon gaining independence from France in 1960, Togo was led by Sylvanus Olympio, who quickly established a one-party state with government-controlled media.[1] Olympio was assassinated in a coup led by a group of former colonial soldiers who then installed Olympio's political rival and brother-in-law, Nicolas Grunitzky,

(Continued)

Year	Media	Government
1984	Not Free	Autocracy
1985	Not Free	Autocracy
1986	Not Free	Autocracy
1987	Not Free	Autocracy
1988	Not Free	Autocracy
1989	Not Free	Autocracy
1990	Not Free	Autocracy
1991	Not Free	In Transition
1992	Not Free	In Transition
1993	Not Free	Anocracy
1994	Not Free	Anocracy
1995	Not Free	Anocracy
1996	Not Free	Anocracy
1997	Not Free	Anocracy
1998	Not Free	Anocracy
1999	Not Free	Anocracy
2000	Not Free	Anocracy
2001	Not Free	Anocracy
2002	Not Free	Anocracy
2003	Not Free	Anocracy
2004	Not Free	Anocracy
2005	Not Free	Anocracy
2006	Not Free	Anocracy
2007	Not Free	Anocracy
2008	Not Free	Anocracy
2009	Not Free	Anocracy
2010	Not Free	Anocracy
2011	Not Free	Anocracy
2012	Not Free	Anocracy

led by Gnassingbé Eyadéma. Under President Eyadéma news media were strictly controlled.[2]

In the early 1990s, following strikes and demonstrations, Eyadéma agreed to transition to a multiparty system. The media were caught up in the power struggle as independent newspapers persisted in criticizing the government, and the International Press Institute reported an increase in threats and violence against journalists, "Security agents have threatened to murder journalists and editors who refuse to print what the Government sees fit to publish. Anyone who tries to analyse the political and economic situation in Togo can invite the wrath of security agents."[3] Several publications went underground.[4] In spite of this hostile climate, the independent news industry continued to expand throughout the 1990s.

Following the removal of a provision from the constitution that would have prohibited a third term, Eyadéma was reelected in 2003, prompting the European Union to suspend its aid. That same year, several domestic journalists were detained following critical reporting and foreign correspondents were barred from reporting after they failed to cover a conference on African elections.[5]

After ruling over Togo for nearly four decades, Eyadéma died in 2005, and the military appointed his son Faure Gnassingbé. This prompted international outrage, and Faure Gnassingbé resigned, only to win the presidency in elections held just months later. The news media's efforts to cover the elections were limited by severed phone lines, blocked Internet connections, and violent attacks.[6] Following the elections, the government shut down some radio stations and scrambled the signals of others.[7] There were also reports of opposition supporters attacking journalists and the offices for the state-run broadcast media.[8]

Media Today

In spite of constitutional provisions for media freedom, Togolese media remain restricted.

Although violence against journalists appears to have decreased in recent years, fear of violent reprisals has led many journalists to self-censor.[9] While journalists no longer face prison terms for defamation, they can still be fined. Togo has a wide range of independently owned

as president. Grunitzky's government employed indirect methods to restrict news media until he was deposed in 1967 in a bloodless military coup

print and broadcast media, yet the state-run media still enjoy larger audiences.[10] Given its long history of authoritarian rule and restricted news media, it seems unlikely that the media environment will improve without substantial political change. That said, the increased availability of independent news media may eventually facilitate some political change, especially if Internet access improves.

Notes

1. Dietmar Rothermund, *The Routledge Companion to Decolonization* (New York: Routledge, 2006).
2. *Country Reports on Human Rights Practices for 1977* (Washington, DC: US Department of State, 1978). Available at http://babel.hathitrust.org/cgi/pt?id=mdp.39015078705632;view=1up;seq=4.
3. *World Press Freedom Review*, IPI Report (Zurich: International Press Institute, December 1991), 29.
4. *World Press Freedom Review*, IPI Report (Zurich: International Press Institute, December 1992).
5. *World Press Freedom Review*, IPI Report (Vienna: International Press Institute, 2003).
6. *World Press Freedom Review*, IPI Report (Vienna: International Press Institute, 2005).
7. Ibid.
8. Ibid.
9. *Freedom of the Press* (Washington, DC: Freedom House, 2013). Available at http://www.freedomhouse.org/report/freedom-press/2013/togo.
10. Ibid.

Tonga: 1986–2012

Tonga Year by Year

Year	Media	Government
1986	Imperfectly Free	Anocracy
1987	Imperfectly Free	Anocracy
1988	Imperfectly Free	Anocracy
1989	Imperfectly Free	Anocracy
1990	Imperfectly Free	Anocracy
1991	Imperfectly Free	Anocracy
1992	Imperfectly Free	Anocracy
1993	Imperfectly Free	Anocracy
1994	Imperfectly Free	Anocracy
1995	Imperfectly Free	Anocracy
1996	Imperfectly Free	Anocracy
1997	Imperfectly Free	Anocracy
1998	Imperfectly Free	Anocracy
1999	Imperfectly Free	Anocracy
2000	Imperfectly Free	Anocracy
2001	Imperfectly Free	Anocracy
2002	Imperfectly Free	Anocracy
2003	Imperfectly Free	Anocracy
2004	Imperfectly Free	Anocracy
2005	Imperfectly Free	Anocracy
2006	Imperfectly Free	Anocracy
2007	Imperfectly Free	Anocracy
2008	Imperfectly Free	Anocracy
2009	Imperfectly Free	Anocracy
2010	Imperfectly Free	Anocracy
2011	Imperfectly Free	Anocracy
2012	Imperfectly Free	Anocracy

MEDIA FREEDOM HISTORY IN A NUTSHELL

- Although Tonga did not begin to democratize until 2010, media have been for the most part functionally free since the 1980s
- Tonga has a mix of independent and state-run print and broadcast media
- As of 2012, about 35 percent of Tongans had Internet access (International Telecommunication Union's 2012 ICT Indicators Database)

In Brief

Tonga, the last Polynesian monarchy, is a collection of 169 islands. Although this South Pacific country was a British protectorate for seven decades, it was never formerly colonized and has retained its indigenous governance. It became fully independent in 1970 under the rule of King Taufa'ahau Tupou IV. Given its small population (estimated at 106,322 in 2013[1]), Tonga is a small media market and there is very little information about its media system prior to the mid-1980s. For the most part, media have been limited but functionally free.

Chronology

1986–2012: Imperfectly Free

In 1986, the government owned the country's only radio station and the main newspaper, but privately owned news outlets were available.[2] In the early 1990s, the Pro-Democracy Movement was founded and began to push for democratic reforms, eventually introducing Tonga's first political party, the People's Party. By the mid-1990s, opposition views were covered regularly in Tonga's independently owned newspapers.[3] At times, the government did retaliate to critical reporting. In 1996, two journalists were imprisoned for thirty days for contempt of Parliament after the publication of a notice of impeachment against the Justice Minister.[4] That same year, following the publication of prodemocracy letters, two newspaper journalists were ordered to "be on good behavior" for a year to a year and a half after being found guilty of "angering a[s] civil servant."[5] In addition, New Zealand–based reporter Mike Field who had covered the Pro-Democracy Movement and the sale of Tongan passports was barred from traveling to Tonga in 1993.[6]

In 2001, Tongans were shocked by the news that the king's jester and financial adviser, former Bank of America employee Jesse Bogdonoff, had invested $26 million of the country's money (from passport sales) in a Nevada-based company that subsequently disappeared.[7]

At the turn of the century, criminal defamation lawsuits were commonly used in retaliation for critical reporting.[8] In 2003, the Parliament, at the direction of King Taufa'ahau Tupou IV, approved new laws that required all news outlets to be licensed and gave the government broad powers to restrict news media, including the authority to ban outlets deemed to violate "cultural traditions or the right to private life."[9] The government soon moved to ban the independent newspaper *Taimi o' Tonga*, and several other independent publications were denied licenses. Thousands of people protested the new measures, and in 2004, the Supreme Court struck them down.[10]

In 2005, thousands of Tongans took part in prodemocracy protests, and in 2006, following the death of King Taufa'ahau Tupou IV, the protests turned violent and much of Tonga's business district was destroyed. As the government declared a state of emergency, some news outlets were temporarily closed down.[11]

In late 2010, for the first time Tongans elected their members of parliament.

Media Today

Tongan media remain functionally free. As Tonga began to democratize in 2010, the media environment continued to improve. Yet journalists who criticize government often face fines from defamation and libel lawsuits. Tonga has a mix of state-run and private print and broadcast media.

Notes

1. *Tonga* (Washington, DC: CIA World Factbook, 2014). Available at https://www.cia.gov/library/publications/the-world-factbook/geos/tn.html.
2. *Country Reports on Human Rights Practices for 1986* (Washington, DC: U.S. Department of State, 1987). Available at http://babel.hathitrust.org/cgi/pt?id=mdp.39015013361749;view=1up;seq=1.
3. *Country Reports on Human Rights Practices for 1996* (Washington, DC: U.S. Department of State, 1997). Available at http://www.state.gov/www/global/human_rights/1996_hrp_report/tonga.html.
4. Ibid.
5. *World Press Freedom Review*, IPI Report (Vienna: International Press Institute, December 1996/January 1997), 96.
6. Ibid.
7. "The Money Is All Gone in Tonga, And the Jester's Role Was No Joke," *New York Times* October 7, 2001. Available at http://www.nytimes.com/2001/10/07/world/the-money-is-all-gone-in-tonga-and-the-jester-s-role-was-no-joke.html.
8. *World Press Freedom Review*, IPI Report (Vienna: International Press Institute, 2001).
9. *World Press Freedom Review*, IPI Report (Vienna: International Press Institute, 2003), 169.
10. *Freedom of the Press* (Washington, DC: Freedom House, 2005). Available at http://www.freedomhouse.org/report/freedom-press/2005/tonga.
11. *Freedom of the Press* (Washington, DC: Freedom House, 2008). Available at http://www.freedomhouse.org/report/freedom-press/2008/tonga.

Trinidad and Tobago: 1962–2012

Trinidad and Tobago Year by Year

Year	Media	Government
1962	Free	Democracy
1963	Free	Democracy
1964	Free	Democracy
1965	Free	Democracy
1966	Free	Democracy
1967	Free	Democracy
1968	Free	Democracy
1969	Free	Democracy
1970	Free	Democracy
1971	Free	Democracy
1972	Free	Democracy
1973	Free	Democracy
1974	Free	Democracy
1975	Free	Democracy
1976	Free	Democracy
1977	Free	Democracy
1978	Free	Democracy
1979	Free	Democracy
1980	Free	Democracy
1981	Free	Democracy
1982	Free	Democracy
1983	Free	Democracy
1984	Free	Democracy
1985	Free	Democracy
1986	Free	Democracy

MEDIA FREEDOM HISTORY IN A NUTSHELL

- News media in Trinidad and Tobago have remained functionally free since the country gained independence
- As of 2009, the country had a total of three daily newspapers with an average circulation per issue of 140,000, and a mix of state-owned and private radio and television stations (World Association of Newspaper's 2010 World Newspaper Trends)
- As of 2012, 60% of Trinidadians had internet access (International Telecommunication Union's 2012 ICT Indicators Database).

In Brief

News media in Trinidad and Tobago have remained functionally free since the country gained independence. At times the political tensions between the country's African and East Indian communities have led to a contentious relationship between media and government. There have been attempts to curtail media freedom, but these have been unsuccessful.

Chronology

1962–1995: Free

Since Trinidad and Tobago became independent in 1962, media have been free. There are constitutional provisions for media freedom; however, libel and defamation remain criminal offenses that carry harsh penalties. In particular, journalists convicted of seditious libel face prison terms of up to five years. Over the years, there have been some cases of restrictions on media freedom, but these appear to be isolated incidents rather than a general pattern. In 1980, the Trinidad press was "plagued with fires of unknown origin,"

Year	Media	Government
1987	Free	Democracy
1988	Free	Democracy
1989	Free	Democracy
1990	Free	Democracy
1991	Free	Democracy
1992	Free	Democracy
1993	Free	Democracy
1994	Free	Democracy
1995	Free	Democracy
1996	Imperfectly Free	Democracy
1997	Imperfectly Free	Democracy
1998	Imperfectly Free	Democracy
1999	Imperfectly Free	Democracy
2000	Imperfectly Free	Democracy
2001	Imperfectly Free	Democracy
2002	Free	Democracy
2003	Free	Democracy
2004	Free	Democracy
2005	Free	Democracy
2006	Free	Democracy
2007	Free	Democracy
2008	Free	Democracy
2009	Free	Democracy
2010	Free	Democracy
2011	Free	Democracy
2012	Free	Democracy

"green paper" calling for restrictions on press freedom. In 1998, hostilities increased to the extent that Basdeo Panday, the country's first prime minister of Indian descent, accused members of the primarily Afro-Trinidadian-owned media of racism, declared his administration to be "at war" with the media, launched an advertising boycott, and banned government officials and members of Parliament from speaking to reporters.[3] During the 2001 parliamentary election campaign, there were some reports of attacks on journalists, but the news media were able to report freely.[4]

2002–2012: Free

The tensions between news media and government eased when control of government shifted from Panday's United National Congress to the People's National Movement and Patrick Manning took over as prime minister. Yet Manning has criticized the news media and pointed to the need for a code of ethics.

Media Today

Trinidad has a mix of private and state-owned media. For the most part, journalists are able to report freely and news media are "vigorously pluralistic."[5]

Notes

1. *Report of the Committee on Freedom of the Press and Information*, General Assembly 1980 (Miami, FL: Inter American Press Association, 1982), A-18.
2. *Report of the Committee on Freedom of the Press and Information*, General Assembly 1988 (Miami, FL: Inter American Press Association, 1989).
3. *Caribbean*, General Assembly 1998 (Miami, FL: Inter American Press Association, 1998). Available at http://sipiapa.org/v4/archivo_de_asambleas.php?idioma=us.
4. *Freedom of the Press* (Washington, DC: Freedom House, 2002). Available at http://www.freedomhouse.org/report/freedom-press/2002/trinidad-and-tobago.
5. *Freedom of the Press* (Washington, DC: Freedom House, 2013). Available at http://www.freedomhouse.org/report/freedom-world/2013/trinidad-and-tobago.

including one that shutdown the *Trinidad Guardian* for several months.[1] In 1988, the company owning the *Sunday Punch* and the *Mirror* complained that the government had reduced its allocation of foreign currency for purchasing newsprint and banned its reporters from covering state functions and press conferences.[2]

1996–2001: Imperfectly Free

In 1996, the relationship between the government and the news media became contentious as the government threatened to consider a

Tunisia: 1956–2012

Tunisia Year by Year

Year	Media	Government
1956	Not Free	Autocracy
1957	Not Free	Autocracy
1958	Not Free	Autocracy
1959	Not Free	Autocracy
1960	Not Free	Autocracy
1961	Not Free	Autocracy
1962	Not Free	Autocracy
1963	Not Free	Autocracy
1964	Not Free	Autocracy
1965	Not Free	Autocracy
1966	Not Free	Autocracy
1967	Not Free	Autocracy
1968	Not Free	Autocracy
1969	Not Free	Autocracy
1970	Not Free	Autocracy
1971	Not Free	Autocracy
1972	Not Free	Autocracy
1973	Not Free	Autocracy
1974	Not Free	Autocracy
1975	Not Free	Autocracy
1976	Not Free	Autocracy
1977	Not Free	Autocracy
1978	Not Free	Autocracy
1979	Not Free	Autocracy
1980	Not Free	Autocracy

MEDIA FREEDOM HISTORY IN A NUTSHELL

- From 1956 to 2010, media were controlled
- The form of media control varied as a pragmatic response to domestic political conditions, but media were always controlled and strictly censored
- The Arab Spring brought media freedom to Tunisia in 2011, but the media environment is chaotic, and it is unclear if these freedoms can be sustained
- There is a mix of privately owned and state-owned newspapers and broadcast media
- As of 2012, 42 percent of Tunisians had Internet access (International Telecommunication Union's 2012 ICT Indicators Database)

In Brief

For more than five decades, the Tunisian government fluctuated between direct and indirect control of news media. These changing restrictions and the presence of independently owned news outlets made Tunisia's media environment seem freer than those of other countries in the region. Yet prior to 2011, the government had little to no tolerance for critical news coverage. The Tunisian protests, which began in late 2010 and started the wave of protests called the Arab Spring, transformed the Tunisian media environment. Since then, media have been functionally free, but whether this freedom will last remains uncertain.

Chronology

1956–2010: Not Free

Media were directly controlled at independence. The abolition of the monarchy and the shift to a republican form of government included

Year	Media	Government
1981	Not Free	Autocracy
1982	Not Free	Autocracy
1983	Not Free	Autocracy
1984	Not Free	Autocracy
1985	Not Free	Autocracy
1986	Not Free	Autocracy
1987	Not Free	Anocracy
1988	Not Free	Anocracy
1989	Not Free	Anocracy
1990	Not Free	Anocracy
1991	Not Free	Anocracy
1992	Not Free	Anocracy
1993	Not Free	Anocracy
1994	Not Free	Anocracy
1995	Not Free	Anocracy
1996	Not Free	Anocracy
1997	Not Free	Anocracy
1998	Not Free	Anocracy
1999	Not Free	Anocracy
2000	Not Free	Anocracy
2001	Not Free	Anocracy
2002	Not Free	Anocracy
2003	Not Free	Anocracy
2004	Not Free	Anocracy
2005	Not Free	Anocracy
2006	Not Free	Anocracy
2007	Not Free	Anocracy
2008	Not Free	Anocracy
2009	Not Free	Anocracy
2010	Not Free	Anocracy
2011	Imperfectly Free	In Transition
2012	Imperfectly Free	In Transition

a shift to indirect control of nominally independent media outlets. By 1959, independent media outlets represented a significant portion of the media environment, but Tunisia was a single-party state, and coverage that incited unrest or undermined governance was outlawed.

Starting in 1964, the government shifted to a socialist form and the ruling party took control of significant industrial and agricultural resources. Socialism collapsed in 1970, and socialized assets were returned to private ownership. Corruption plagued the reprivatization process, and in the mid-1970s, unrest prompted government to increase media restrictions to the point of enabling direct control by the ruling party.

By 1977, the government had returned to using indirect methods to control news media. In particular, the government controlled the distribution of newsprint.[1] Government repression of the general strike in 1978 did not include direct control of the media. Despite the establishment of an oil industry and increases in tourism, the beginning of economic distress was becoming apparent in emigration numbers in the late 1970s. The economy faltered in the early 1980s.

In 1983, riots followed the International Monetary Fund's mandated austerity measures that included an increase in the price of bread. To stifle the unrest, the government resumed direct control of media content.

In 1995, in response to rising Islamic fundamentalist movements, which used media to challenge the government, direct governmental control of the media was reestablished. There were also increased reports of harassment and attacks against journalists.[2] Over the course of the next decade, the nominal independence of media outlets was eroded to the point that a return to an indirectly controlled media environment became impractical.

2011–2012: Imperfectly Free

The Arab Spring had a profound effect on the Tunisian media environment. Perhaps in part because journalists and bloggers were empowered by the role they played in mobilizing the protests. In 2004, bloggers created Nawaat.org to document government corruption and unrest, and following WikiLeaks release of the diplomatic cables, the website TuniLeaks was established to highlight cables about Tunisian dictator

Ben Ali. These efforts contributed to a growing perception that Ben Ali was losing international support.[3] After Ben Ali fled the country in January 2011, official censorship ceased and a number of independent news outlets emerged.

Media Today

Media are experiencing greater freedoms than they have ever known, but the environment might best be described as chaotic. It is unclear if the newfound media freedom can be sustained. In 2012, there were some troubling signs. Freedom House reported that defamation charges and violence against journalists increased, and several reporters for state media were fired—apparently for political reasons.[4] The number and type of news outlets continues to change. Several that opened right after the revolution have closed down. There is a mix of privately owned and state-owned newspapers and broadcast media, and online media are increasingly popular.

Notes

1. *Country Reports on Human Rights Practices for 1977* (Washington, DC: U.S. Department of State, 1978). Available at http://babel.hathitrust.org/cgi/pt?id=mdp.39015078705632;view=1up;seq=3.
2. *World Press Freedom Review*, IPI Report (Vienna: International Press Institute, November/December 1995).
3. HeeMin Kim, Jenifer Whitten-Woodring, and Patrick James, "The Role of Media in the Repression-Protest Nexus: A Game Theoretic Model," *Journal of Conflict Resolution* (Online First: February 2014).
4. *Freedom of the Press* (Washington, DC: Freedom House, 2013). Available at http://www.freedomhouse.org/report/freedom-press/2013/tunisia.

Turkey: 1948–2012

Turkey Year by Year

Year	Media	Government
1948	Not Free	Democracy
1949	Not Free	Democracy
1950	Not Free	Democracy
1951	Not Free	Democracy
1952	Not Free	Democracy
1953	Not Free	Democracy
1954	Not Free	Anocracy
1955	Not Free	Anocracy
1956	Not Free	Anocracy
1957	Not Free	Anocracy
1958	Not Free	Anocracy
1959	Not Free	Anocracy
1960	Not Free	Democracy
1961	Not Free	Democracy
1962	Not Free	Democracy
1963	Not Free	Democracy
1964	Not Free	Democracy
1965	Not Free	Democracy
1966	Not Free	Democracy
1967	Not Free	Democracy
1968	Not Free	Democracy
1969	Not Free	Democracy
1970	Not Free	Democracy
1971	Not Free	Anocracy

(Continued)

MEDIA FREEDOM HISTORY IN A NUTSHELL

- Despite frequent and extended periods of democratic rule, media were restricted or directly controlled until 2002
- Reforms aimed at gaining EU membership included changes that created a free media environment
- While journalists are seldom killed or physically attacked, they are vulnerable to arrest and imprisonment; at the end of 2013, Turkey had more journalists imprisoned than any other country in the world
- In 2012, Turkey had more than 1,000 privately owned radio stations and hundreds of privately owned television channels in addition to the state-owned broadcast media (Freedom House's Report on Freedom of the Press 2013)
- As of 2012, Turkey had seventy-four paid-for daily newspapers with a total average circulation per issue of 4,748,000 (World Association of Newspapers World Press Trends 2012)
- In 2012, 45 percent of Turks had Internet access (International Telecommunication Union's 2012 ICT Indicators Database)

In Brief

Frequent and extended periods of democratic rule do not change the fact that Turkish media were heavily restricted until after the turn of the century. Media freedoms remain precarious as laws regarding religious participation in politics remain in place. These laws were previously used as one of the justifications for restricting media content.

Chronology

1948–2001: Not Free

From the first open elections in 1950, the media environment remained relatively consistent

(Continued)

Year	Media	Government
1972	Not Free	Anocracy
1973	Not Free	Democracy
1974	Not Free	Democracy
1975	Not Free	Democracy
1976	Not Free	Democracy
1977	Not Free	Democracy
1978	Not Free	Democracy
1979	Not Free	Democracy
1980	Not Free	Anocracy
1981	Not Free	Anocracy
1982	Not Free	Anocracy
1983	Not Free	Democracy
1984	Not Free	Democracy
1985	Not Free	Democracy
1986	Not Free	Democracy
1987	Not Free	Democracy
1988	Not Free	Democracy
1989	Not Free	Democracy
1990	Not Free	Democracy
1991	Not Free	Democracy
1992	Not Free	Democracy
1993	Not Free	Democracy
1994	Not Free	Democracy
1995	Not Free	Democracy
1996	Not Free	Democracy
1997	Not Free	Democracy
1998	Not Free	Democracy
1999	Not Free	Democracy
2000	Not Free	Democracy
2001	Not Free	Democracy
2002	Imperfectly Free	Democracy
2003	Imperfectly Free	Democracy

Year	Media	Government
2004	Imperfectly Free	Democracy
2005	Imperfectly Free	Democracy
2006	Imperfectly Free	Democracy
2007	Imperfectly Free	Democracy
2008	Imperfectly Free	Democracy
2009	Imperfectly Free	Democracy
2010	Imperfectly Free	Democracy
2011	Imperfectly Free	Democracy
2012	Imperfectly Free	Democracy

through a coup in 1960, the reestablishment of democratic rule in 1961, and the military-forced resignation of the prime minister in 1971. Many of the legal restrictions on media content related to the constitutional exclusion of religion from government, but criticism of the government or the media was punishable through a variety of statutes and self-censorship was extensive. The invasion and occupation of northern Cyprus led to trade embargoes and other sanctions. Unrest increased as the economy faltered.

In 1978, the government shifted into a crisis footing and direct media control as unrest continued to rise. A military coup led to the imposition of martial law in 1980. The Kurdish separatist movement began a guerilla campaign in the south in 1984.

In 1995, Turkey extended its military effort against the Kurds into the Kurdish region in the northern part of Iraq. The elimination of cross border sanctuaries led to a swift reduction in guerilla actions in Turkey and a relaxation of the crisis footing. Media restrictions in most of Turkey were significantly relaxed, but the Kurdish region in the south remained under martial law and was considered a war zone.

2002–2012: Imperfectly Free

Reforms focused on gaining EU membership included lifting several restrictions on media, creating a functionally free media environment.

Media Today

The constitutional buttresses meant to safeguard secular rule against Islamic forces include restrictions on the media, such as outlawing advocacy of Islamic law. However, the 2002 reforms eliminated most of the ways in which those restrictions were previously used to limit criticisms of government. Even so, the media environment in Turkey remains somewhat restricted. Though journalists are rarely killed or physically attacked, they are subject to arrest and imprisonment. At the end of 2013, forty journalists were behind bars in Turkey on charges connected to their work—the highest number of any country.[1] The Turkish government has a variety of laws it can use to punish journalists, including the antiterrorism law (which according to Freedom House makes it possible for any critical or investigative reporting to be construed as terrorism).[2] It is also against the law to characterize the deaths of about one and half million Armenians between 1915 to 1922 as genocide, and discussion of the division of Cyprus is also prohibited.[3] Broadcast media that violate these and other laws restricting media freedom can be sanctioned, and print media that do so can be closed down.[4] Government also has the authority to block websites deemed to be pornographic or obscene or insulting of Mustafa Kemal Atatürk, the founder of the Turkish Republic.[5] In spite of the limitations, Turkey has a wide range of print, broadcast, and online media that can and do criticize the government.

Notes

1. Elana Beiser, *Second Worst Year on Record for Jailed Journalists* (Committee to Protect Journalists, 2013). Available at https://www.cpj.org/reports/2013/12/second-worst-year-on-record-for-jailed-journalists.php.
2. *Freedom of the Press* (Washington, DC: Freedom House, 2013). Available at http://www.freedomhouse.org/report/freedom-press/2013/turkey.
3. Ibid.
4. Ibid.
5. Ibid.

Turkmenistan: 1991–2012

Turkmenistan Year by Year

Year	Media	Government
1991	Not Free	Autocracy
1992	Not Free	Autocracy
1993	Not Free	Autocracy
1994	Not Free	Autocracy
1995	Not Free	Autocracy
1996	Not Free	Autocracy
1997	Not Free	Autocracy
1998	Not Free	Autocracy
1999	Not Free	Autocracy
2000	Not Free	Autocracy
2001	Not Free	Autocracy
2002	Not Free	Autocracy
2003	Not Free	Autocracy
2004	Not Free	Autocracy
2005	Not Free	Autocracy
2006	Not Free	Autocracy
2007	Not Free	Autocracy
2008	Not Free	Autocracy
2009	Not Free	Autocracy
2010	Not Free	Autocracy
2011	Not Free	Autocracy
2012	Not Free	Autocracy

In Brief

Turkmenistan's President for Life, Saparmurat Niyazov, who renamed the months of the year after himself and other Turkmen heroes, strictly

controlled all media and had no tolerance for dissent. Nothing changed for the media when Niyazov died in 2006 and Gurbanguly Berdimuhamedow became president.

Chronology

1991–2012: Not Free

The exploitation of natural gas reserves gave President Niyazov the resources he needed to suppress the opposition and pursue outlandish projects such as the construction of a giant ice palace in the desert and to fund the direct, Soviet-style control of the media. The International Press Institute described the media as anything but free:

> Newspapers are encouraged to publish breathless eulogies of the President. Editors of registered newspapers have been removed if they fail to toe the line. Statues are erected in honour of the head of state and public buildings re-named. Opposition figures—including journalists—have been unable to operate.[1]

The death of Niyazov in 2006 brought no change to the media environment. The government continued to control all news media. Criticizing the government remained risky. In 2006, Radio Free Europe/Radio Liberty reporter Ogulsapar Muradova died in prison and evidence showed she had been beaten.[2]

Media Today

All national media—print, broadcast, and online—remain strictly controlled. The government has banned a number of foreign publications and continues to block access to many foreign websites that offer news and information.[3] Although satellite television is a popular news source, the government continues to try to limit access to that as well.[4] Criticizing the government remains a perilous business with harsh consequences. Two journalists who were arrested with Muradova in 2006 were released from prison in February of 2013 in very poor health after having served their seven-year sentences.[5]

Notes

1. *World Press Freedom Review*, IPI Report (Vienna: International Press Institute, December 1993), 64.
2. *Freedom of the Press* (Washington, DC: Freedom House, 2013). Available at http://www.freedom house.org/report/freedom-press/2013/turk menistan.
3. Ibid.
4. Ibid.
5. Ibid.

Tuvalu: 2000–2012

Year	Media	Government
2000	Imperfectly Free	Democracy
2001	Imperfectly Free	Democracy
2002	Imperfectly Free	Democracy
2003	Imperfectly Free	Democracy
2004	Imperfectly Free	Democracy
2005	Imperfectly Free	Democracy
2006	Imperfectly Free	Democracy
2007	Imperfectly Free	Democracy
2008	Imperfectly Free	Democracy
2009	Imperfectly Free	Democracy
2010	Imperfectly Free	Democracy
2011	Imperfectly Free	Democracy
2012	Imperfectly Free	Democracy

MEDIA FREEDOM HISTORY IN A NUTSHELL

- Tuvalu is one of the smallest countries in the world, and as such has very limited media
- The government controls the country's only radio station, but satellite television is available
- As of 2012, 35 percent of Tuvaluans had Internet access (International Telecommunication Union's 2012 ICT Indicators Database)

In Brief

Tuvalu, a collection of nine atolls in the South Pacific, is one of the tiniest countries in the world. Given its small population (estimated at 10,698 in 2013[1]), it has always had limited media, which are all government owned but for the most part functionally free.

Chronology

2000–2012: Imperfectly Free

Although Tuvalu gained independence from Britain in 1978, it was not admitted to the United Nations until 2000, which is where our chronology officially begins, but the media system has probably changed very little over the years. The Tuvalu Media Corporation Act of 1993 established the Tuvalu Media Corporation (TMC) to operate the country's only radio station. The government also published the *Tuvalu Echoes* newspaper, but publication was suspended from time to time due to a lack of resources. In the late 1990s, the TMC also operated a television station, which aired for three hours each week, but in 2001, the government stopped the broadcasts due to financial difficulties.[2] In the early 2000s, all copy for the radio station had to be approved by a government representative and there were reports of stories favoring the opposition being blocked.[3] In 2008, the TMC was decorporatized and became a government department, renamed the Tuvalu Media Department (TMD).[4]

Media Today

Tuvaluan media remain limited and imperfectly free. The lack of an independent press is more a function of the absence of a market for commercial media than the result of any government policy. The radio station remains a government department, and the government has been criticized for limiting political coverage.[5] Although the government has control over the domestic news content, the station also carries programming from the British Broadcasting Corporation. According to the Pacific Media Assistance Scheme, the TMD no longer publishes the *Tuvalu Echoes* newspaper but is producing a digital newsletter.[6] Satellite television is also available. Given Tuvalu's small population, it is unlikely that commercial media would be sustainable. Online media may eventually provide a better source for news and information, but Internet access remains limited and Internet connections are unreliable.[7]

Notes

1. *Tuvalu* (Washington, DC: CIA World Factbook, 2013). Available at: https://www.cia.gov/library/publications/the-world-factbook/geos/tv.html.

2. *Country Reports on Human Rights Practices for 2002* (Washington, DC: U.S. Department of State, 2003). Available at: http://www.state.gov/j/drl/rls/hrrpt/2002/18268.htm.

3. *Country Reports on Human Rights Practices for 2004* (Washington, DC: U.S. Department of State, 2005). Available at: http://www.state.gov/j/drl/rls/hrrpt/2004/41663.htm.

4. *Tuvalu: State of the Media & Communication Report* (Washington, DC: Pacific Media Assistance Scheme, 2013). Available at http://www.pacmas.org/wp-content/uploads/2013/10/06.-PACMAS_Tuvalu-Country-Report_FINAL.pdf.

5. *Freedom of the Press* (Washington, DC: Freedom House, 2013). Available at http://www.freedomhouse.org/report/freedom-world/2013/tuvalu.

6. *Tuvalu: State of the Media & Communication Report.*

7. Ibid.

Uganda: 1962–2012

Uganda Year by Year

Year	Media	Government
1962	Imperfectly Free	Democracy
1963	Imperfectly Free	Democracy
1964	Imperfectly Free	Democracy
1965	Imperfectly Free	Democracy
1966	Not Free	In Transition
1967	Not Free	Autocracy
1968	Not Free	Autocracy
1969	Not Free	Autocracy
1970	Not Free	Autocracy
1971	Not Free	Autocracy
1972	Not Free	Autocracy
1973	Not Free	Autocracy
1974	Not Free	Autocracy
1975	Not Free	Autocracy
1976	Not Free	Autocracy
1977	Not Free	Autocracy
1978	Not Free	Autocracy
1979	Imperfectly Free	Foreign Interruption
1980	Imperfectly Free	Autocracy
1981	Imperfectly Free	Autocracy
1982	Imperfectly Free	Autocracy
1983	Imperfectly Free	Autocracy
1984	Imperfectly Free	Autocracy
1985	Imperfectly Free	Interregnum
1986	Imperfectly Free	Autocracy

MEDIA FREEDOM HISTORY IN A NUTSHELL

- Upon independence, Uganda had functionally free media, but as Milton Obote sought to consolidate his power, media were restricted
- In the 1970s, as Idi Amin seized control of the country, media restrictions increased and a number of journalists were murdered
- Following the ouster of Amin in 1979, media again became functionally free
- Media have remained functionally free, though at times barely so, since Yoweri Museveni came to power in 1986
- In 2012, Uganda had more than 180 independent radio stations, more than two dozen newspapers (many with ties to political parties), one public network, and four privately owned television stations (Freedom House's Report on Freedom of the Press 2013)
- As of 2012, about 15 percent of Ugandans had Internet access (International Telecommunication Union's 2012I CT Indicators Database)

In Brief

Ugandan news media enjoyed a few years of limited media freedom until 1966 when Milton Obote seized control of the presidency and proceeded to rule under martial law. Although Idi Amin cited a lack of freedom of expression as one of the justifications for his 1971 coup, news media were controlled, a number of journalists were killed, and many more imprisoned under his regime. With the ouster of Amin in 1979, media again became functionally free, mostly because the governments that followed lacked the power to restrict the news media. The media were for the most part supportive of Yoweri Museveni when he took control of the country in 1986. Yet while Museveni is widely viewed internationally

Year	Media	Government
1987	Imperfectly Free	Autocracy
1988	Imperfectly Free	Autocracy
1989	Imperfectly Free	Autocracy
1990	Imperfectly Free	Autocracy
1991	Imperfectly Free	Autocracy
1992	Imperfectly Free	Autocracy
1993	Imperfectly Free	Anocracy
1994	Imperfectly Free	Anocracy
1995	Imperfectly Free	Anocracy
1996	Imperfectly Free	Anocracy
1997	Imperfectly Free	Anocracy
1998	Imperfectly Free	Anocracy
1999	Imperfectly Free	Anocracy
2000	Imperfectly Free	Anocracy
2001	Imperfectly Free	Anocracy
2002	Imperfectly Free	Anocracy
2003	Imperfectly Free	Anocracy
2004	Imperfectly Free	Anocracy
2005	Imperfectly Free	Anocracy
2006	Imperfectly Free	Anocracy
2007	Imperfectly Free	Anocracy
2008	Imperfectly Free	Anocracy
2009	Imperfectly Free	Anocracy
2010	Imperfectly Free	Anocracy
2011	Imperfectly Free	Anocracy
2012	Imperfectly Free	Anocracy

Publications Ordinance No. 33 established licensing fees that forced a number of small newspapers out of business.[1]

1966–1978: Not Free

Following an attempt to unseat him in 1966, Obote seized control of the country, suspended the constitution, and proceeded to rule the country under martial law. During this time, the government expelled several foreign journalists, banned at least one publication, and arrested critical journalists, yet the independent news media persisted in criticizing Obote and his administration.[2]

At the beginning of 1971, Obote was ousted in a coup led by Army Chief Idi Amin. Third on the list of Amin's eighteen points justifying the coup was the lack of freedom of political expression.[3] Yet Amin was quick to expel foreign journalists to minimize news coverage as he forced more than 60,000 Asians to leave the country.[4] And soon Ugandan journalists found their profession had become quite perilous as many were imprisoned and several were killed.[5]

In a showy and—with hindsight—menacing gesture, Amin donated a bull each to journalists at *Taifa Empya* and *Munno* newspapers because they had printed a statement during the former regime in which he had said he feared only God. It seemed like fun at the time, but within a year Amin was murdering those to whom the he had given the bulls: *Munno* editor Father Clement Kiggundo was burnt alive inside his car; news photographer Jimmy Parma was shot; *Munno* journalist John Serwaniko was found dead in his police cell; television journalist James Bwogi was murdered. Many more were jailed.[6]

1979–2012: Imperfectly Free

In 1979, Tanzanian troops joined forces with Ugandan National Liberation Army and ousted Idi Amin. There was a great deal of political uncertainty following Amin's departure because Uganda had three different failed governments in less than two years. During this power vacuum, a number of privately owned newspapers emerged, most of them with ties to political parties.[7] Although the media environment improved

as tolerating media freedom, critical journalists have faced defamation and sedition charges.

Chronology

1962–1965: Imperfectly Free

Upon gaining independence from Britain, Uganda was initially a democracy with functionally free media under Prime Minister Milton Obote. Yet in 1960, just prior to independence, the Newspaper

to the point where journalists were functionally free, this was largely because the interim governments did not have the power to silence the news media, but they did try. Critical journalists were arrested.[8] Obote returned to power in late 1980 and proceeded to ban several newspapers.[9] The media remained entangled in the political struggle. The news media were for the most part supportive when the National Resistance Army seized control of the country in 1986 and installed Yoweri Museveni as president.[10] While Museveni received international praise for respecting media freedom, in actuality, his government used sedition and defamation laws to punish critical journalists.[11] Yet media remained functionally free, though at times only barely so.

Media Today

Ugandan media remain functionally free, but critical journalists are often harassed to the point where self-censorship is a problem. Though journalists persist in criticizing government and government policies, they often face consequences for doing so, sometimes in the form of treason or criminal libel charges.[12] In 2013, police raided and temporarily shut down two newspapers and two radio stations after the newspapers published a letter alleging that there was a plot to assassinate opponents of a plan to have Museveni's son become president in 2013.[13]

Uganda has a wide range of news outlets, including more than 180 independent radio stations, more than two dozen newspapers, and one public television network as well as four privately owned television stations.[14]

Notes

1. George W. Lugalambi and Bernard Tabaire, *Overview of the State of Media Freedom in Uganda: A Research Report* (African Centre for Media Excellence, 2010). Available at http://www.acme-ug.org/index.php/an-overview-of-the-state-of-media-freedom-in-uganda/.
2. Ibid.
3. Ibid.
4. *Another Year of Lost Battles*, IPI Report (Zurich: International Press Institute, January 1973).
5. Lugalambi and Tabaire, *Overview of the State of Media Freedom in Uganda: A Research Report*.
6. Bernard Tabaire, "The Press and Political Repression in Uganda: Back to the Future," *Journal of Eastern African Studies* 1, no. 2 (2007): 193–211.
7. Ibid.
8. *World Press Freedom Review*, IPI Report (Zurich: International Press Institute, December 1979).
9. Tabaire, "The Press and Political Repression in Uganda: Back to the Future."
10. Lugalambi and Tabaire, *Overview of the State of Media Freedom in Uganda: A Research Report*.
11. Ibid.
12. *Freedom of the Press* (Washington, DC: Freedom House, 2013). Available at http://www.freedomhouse.org/report/freedom-press/2013/uganda.
13. *Police Raid News Outlets in Media Crackdown in Uganda* (Committee to Protect Journalists, 2013). Available at https://www.cpj.org/2013/05/police-raid-news-outlets-in-media-crackdown-in-uga.php.
14. *Freedom of the Press* (Washington, DC: Freedom House, 2013). Available at http://www.freedomhouse.org/report/freedom-press/2013/uganda.

Ukraine: 1991–2012

Ukraine Year by Year

Year	Media	Government
1991	Not Free	Democracy
1992	Not Free	Democracy
1993	Not Free	Anocracy
1994	Not Free	Democracy
1995	Imperfectly Free	Democracy
1996	Imperfectly Free	Democracy
1997	Not Free	Democracy
1998	Not Free	Democracy
1999	Not Free	Democracy
2000	Not Free	Democracy
2001	Not Free	Democracy
2002	Not Free	Democracy
2003	Not Free	Democracy
2004	Imperfectly Free	Democracy
2005	Imperfectly Free	Democracy
2006	Imperfectly Free	Democracy
2007	Imperfectly Free	Democracy
2008	Imperfectly Free	Democracy
2009	Imperfectly Free	Democracy
2010	Imperfectly Free	Democracy
2011	Imperfectly Free	Democracy
2012	Imperfectly Free	Democracy

In Brief

The Ukrainian media environment might best be described as contentiously precarious. Media

MEDIA FREEDOM HISTORY IN A NUTSHELL

- Attacks on journalists, whether from political elites or organized crime, have consistently threatened media freedom
- As of 2011, there were thirty-one daily newspapers; all were paid-for daily newspapers, with a total average circulation per issue of 2,516,680 (World Association of Newspaper's 2012 World Newspaper Trends)
- Private television dominates the media market; however, many media outlets rely on the support from private sponsors (British Broadcasting Company Country Reports)
- As of 2012, about 34 percent of Ukrainians had Internet access (International Telecommunication Union's 2012 ICT Indicators Database)

outlets are essentially tools used by elites in an authoritarian form of democratic competition. The hyper partisan system that has evolved may be a unique if imperfect form of media freedom. The Ukrainian media have consistently faced threats, either from the government or from organized crime.

Chronology

1991–1994: Not Free

Independence from the Soviet Union freed the media from direct government control. However, since media had always served what was effectively a propaganda role for the Soviet government, there was no experience with anything like a commercial or public service media model. As a result, the media were easily controlled and manipulated. During this period, the media system transformed into a patron-style partisan media system. Individual news outlets were quickly dominated by different political and economic elites who used the media as part of the struggle for political dominance.

1995–1996: Imperfectly Free

The diversity of political elites and the competition between them created a media system that was effectively free. Criticism of government and elites was evident. However, the system was volatile, prone to corruption, and the quality of news coverage was, by western standards, poor. Even though media were imperfectly free, journalists were consistently targeted by organized crime. In 1995, one journalist was killed in a bomb blast and another was wounded in an assassination attempt.[1]

1997–2003: Not Free

The combination of conservative push back against rapid liberalization and the consolidation of power among competing elites reduced the variety of media outlets such that the country effectively shifted to an indirectly controlled system dominated by the faction that controlled the government. Further, government interventions within the industry escalated at this time. Additionally, attacks on journalists rendered the country one of the most dangerous of the former Soviet republics in which to work as a reporter.[2]

2004–2012: Imperfectly Free

Immediate threats to the media's freedom eased as infighting disrupted the consolidation of political power in the ruling party. Demands for further liberalization and a disputed election result led to the Orange Revolution, which served to significantly reduce government interventions in the media industry. However, conservative threats to media freedom persisted, professionalism was rare, and stability remained elusive.

Media Today

In the Ukrainian media, there is little, if any, commitment to any kind of journalistic norms or professionalism. Media outlets are typically treated as the personal domain of owners or the tools of the wealthy and/or the influential people and groups who support them, including organized crime. Direct editorial control by owners, paid coverage that is indistinguishable from other coverage, bribery and other forms of coercion are common. Criticism of government does clearly occur, but in the absence of any movement toward journalism that is more independent of power factions, that will only remain a feature of the system that results from competition for control of government.[3] It cannot serve as a system that buttresses competition if a party or coalition should become predominant enough to use the leadership to stifle competition. Ukrainians traditionally trust media, and therefore, media outlets have tremendous power to shape public opinion.[3] In early 2014 media freedom was threatened by political upheaval, civil conflict and an emerging conflict between Russia and the Ukraine.

Notes

1. *World Press Freedom Review,* IPI Report (Vienna: International Press Institute, 1995).
2. *World Press Freedom Review,* IPI Report (Vienna: International Press Institute, 1997).
3. *Ukraine,* Media Landscape Reports (Maastricht, The Netherlands: European Journalism Centre, 2013). Available at http://ejc.net/media_landscapes/ukraine.

United Arab Emirates: 1971–2012

UAE Year by Year

Year	Media	Government
1971	Not Free	Autocracy
1972	Not Free	Autocracy
1973	Not Free	Autocracy
1974	Not Free	Autocracy
1975	Not Free	Autocracy
1976	Not Free	Autocracy
1977	Not Free	Autocracy
1978	Not Free	Autocracy
1979	Not Free	Autocracy
1980	Not Free	Autocracy
1981	Not Free	Autocracy
1982	Not Free	Autocracy
1983	Not Free	Autocracy
1984	Not Free	Autocracy
1985	Not Free	Autocracy
1986	Not Free	Autocracy
1987	Not Free	Autocracy
1988	Not Free	Autocracy
1989	Not Free	Autocracy
1990	Not Free	Autocracy
1991	Not Free	Autocracy
1992	Not Free	Autocracy
1993	Not Free	Autocracy
1994	Not Free	Autocracy

(Continued)

MEDIA FREEDOM HISTORY IN A NUTSHELL

- The UAE is an authoritarian oligarchy that uses strict media controls
- In recent years, methods of control have become less direct to accommodate increasing penetration from external media sources
- Dubai has become something of an enclave where foreign media sources are more easily accessed
- In 2012, there were multiple radio and television stations operating in the United Arab Emirates, most of which are owned by the government or those with close ties to the government (Freedom House's Report on Freedom of the Press 2013)
- As of 2012, there were approximately twelve newspapers published in Arabic and English (Freedom House's Report on Freedom of the Press 2013)
- As of 2012, about 85 percent of Emiratis had Internet access (International Telecommunication Union's 2012 ICT Indicators Database)

In Brief

Ruled by a council of representatives appointed by the leaders of the seven Emirates in the federation, the United Arab Emirates (UAE) represents an interesting case study in oligarchical political institutions. A great deal of tension has been created by the effort to find a compromise between an extremely conservative political elite and the push to become the region's global city and the winter home of Europe's wealthy. This tension is reflected in the media environment because the UAE has, on the one hand, one of the highest levels of Internet access in the region and, on the other hand, one of the more pervasive cases of government filtering of Internet content.

(Continued)

Year	Media	Government
1995	Not Free	Autocracy
1996	Not Free	Autocracy
1997	Not Free	Autocracy
1998	Not Free	Autocracy
1999	Not Free	Autocracy
2000	Not Free	Autocracy
2001	Not Free	Autocracy
2002	Not Free	Autocracy
2003	Not Free	Autocracy
2004	Not Free	Autocracy
2005	Not Free	Autocracy
2006	Not Free	Autocracy
2007	Not Free	Autocracy
2008	Not Free	Autocracy
2009	Not Free	Autocracy
2010	Not Free	Autocracy
2011	Not Free	Autocracy
2012	Not Free	Autocracy

Chronology

1971–2012: Not Free

The federation formed by the seven newly independent Emirates was ruled by Sheikh Sultan Bin-Muhammad al-Qasimi, who was supported by a council of representatives appointed by the rulers of each of the Emirates. Rule was authoritarian, and media were directly controlled. Although there were some privately owned newspapers, they did not criticize the government.[1]

In the late 1990s, the realities of advances in global communications technology, combined with increasing media access demands driven by a significant foreign presence in urban centers, particularly Dubai, made it impractical to enforce the myriad of laws and policies meant to keep foreign media sources out of the country. As Emiratis gained access to uncensored news on the Internet and satellite television, a policy shift moved practices toward more indirect methods of control, but domestic media were still dominated by the government. In 2000, there were hopes that media would become free as the Dubai Media City was established with the aim of creating a regional media hub.[2] Yet laws proscribing criticism of the ruling families and the government remained in place and journalists continued to practice self-censorship.[3] Additionally most newspapers relied on the government-run news agency for much of their content.[4] The government continued to have censors screen foreign newspapers and block access to websites with antigovernment or pornographic content.[5] In 2006, the Information and Privacy Cybercrime Law criminalized a number of Internet offenses.

Media Today

While external media sources are widely available and easily accessible in Dubai, much of the rest of the country is quite isolated from the outside world. Content of the domestic media is strictly controlled, and it is not possible to criticize government or local leaders. In 2012, government tolerance for criticism appeared to decrease as authorities arrested dozens of bloggers and activists.[6] It is against the law to use the Internet to disseminate information that goes against political or religious standards, threatens security or public order.[7] Although Internet penetration is high, with about 85 percent of Emiratis having access, the government limits access to a number of sites, including many with political content.[8]

Notes

1. *World Press Freedom Review*, IPI Report (Vienna: International Press Institute, December 1998).
2. *World Press Freedom Review*, IPI Report (Vienna: International Press Institute, 2001).
3. *World Press Freedom Review*, IPI Report (Vienna: International Press Institute, 2003).
4. Ibid.
5. *Freedom of the Press* (Washington, DC: Freedom House, 2004). Available at http://www.freedomhouse.org/report/freedom-press/2004/united-arab-emirates.
6. *Freedom of the Press* (Washington, DC: Freedom House, 2013). Available at http://www.freedomhouse.org/report/freedom-press/2013/united-arab-emirates.
7. Ibid.
8. Ibid.

United Kingdom: 1948–2012

United Kingdom Year by Year

Year	Media	Government
1948	Free	Democracy
1949	Free	Democracy
1950	Free	Democracy
1951	Free	Democracy
1952	Free	Democracy
1953	Free	Democracy
1954	Free	Democracy
1955	Free	Democracy
1956	Free	Democracy
1957	Free	Democracy
1958	Free	Democracy
1959	Free	Democracy
1960	Free	Democracy
1961	Free	Democracy
1962	Free	Democracy
1963	Free	Democracy
1964	Free	Democracy
1965	Free	Democracy
1966	Free	Democracy
1967	Free	Democracy
1968	Free	Democracy
1969	Free	Democracy
1970	Free	Democracy
1971	Free	Democracy

(Continued)

MEDIA FREEDOM HISTORY IN A NUTSHELL

- The United Kingdom has been a bastion of Press Freedom, and it is often chosen over the United States as a model of how a free press should function
- Newspapers are diverse and often strongly represent a political perspective in their coverage.
- As of 2011, there were 106 daily newspapers, 94 of them were paid-for daily newspapers, with a total average circulation per issue of 12,805,450 (World Association of Newspaper's 2012 World Newspaper Trends)
- The BBC is often used as a model for public service news broadcasting; the United Kingdom also has many privately owned broadcast media
- As of 2012, about 87 percent of people from the United Kingdom had Internet access (International Telecommunication Union's 2012 ICT Indicators Database)

In Brief

As one of the global exemplars for media freedom and one of its staunchest advocates, the United Kingdom also provides one of the best examples of the extremes of nuance that can be involved in academic and philosophical debates over media freedom. Issues that are raised or debated in relation to media freedom in the United Kingdom are generally about things that can only be considerations well after the fundamental commitment to media freedom is so well established that it is widely accepted as a human right that is above the domain of politics.

Chronology

1948–2012: Free

There is little to say about media freedom during the post–World War II era. There have

(Continued)

Year	Media	Government
1972	Free	Democracy
1973	Free	Democracy
1974	Free	Democracy
1975	Free	Democracy
1976	Free	Democracy
1977	Free	Democracy
1978	Free	Democracy
1979	Free	Democracy
1980	Free	Democracy
1981	Free	Democracy
1982	Free	Democracy
1983	Free	Democracy
1984	Free	Democracy
1985	Free	Democracy
1986	Free	Democracy
1987	Free	Democracy
1988	Free	Democracy
1989	Free	Democracy
1990	Free	Democracy
1991	Free	Democracy
1992	Free	Democracy
1993	Free	Democracy
1994	Free	Democracy
1995	Free	Democracy
1996	Free	Democracy
1997	Free	Democracy
1998	Free	Democracy
1999	Free	Democracy
2000	Free	Democracy
2001	Free	Democracy
2002	Free	Democracy
2003	Free	Democracy

Year	Media	Government
2004	Free	Democracy
2005	Free	Democracy
2006	Free	Democracy
2007	Free	Democracy
2008	Free	Democracy
2009	Free	Democracy
2010	Free	Democracy
2011	Free	Democracy
2012	Free	Democracy

been some very minor fluctuations with changing technology and changing political climates, but there has been no reason to question the fundamental freedom of media.

Media Today

One of the most prominent of current debates is a long-standing concern over rather strict libel laws and the potential they have to impinge on the watchdog function.[1] Many argue that recent celebrity sex abuse scandals would have been exposed decades earlier if not for the silencing effects of these laws. This debate is best considered in contrast to the United States where a nearly opposite situation exists and libel laws are so lax that there is almost no legal requirement for accurate or honest reporting.[1]

Press responsibility and codes of conduct have been salient because of privacy issues that arose regarding the publication of telephoto pictures of sunbathing royals and a scandal over the illegal hacking of a crime victim's phone. Key for analysts in the latter event is probably that the hacking was clearly illegal and treated as such by both the authorities and the public.

Note

1. *United Kingdom,* Media Landscape Reports (Maastricht, The Netherlands: European Journalism Centre, 2013). Available at http://ejc.net/media_landscapes/united-kingdom.

United States: 1948–2012

(Continued)

MEDIA FREEDOM HISTORY IN A NUTSHELL

- The First Amendment to the Constitution provides for media freedom and the government generally respects this
- Media critics have identified commercialization, concentration of ownership, and the tendency of journalists to rely on official sources as threats to media independence, yet U.S. media have the potential to criticize the government
- Although the United States has public broadcast media, the market is dominated by private broadcast and cable networks
- Both the number of newspapers and newspaper circulations have plummeted in recent years; in 2012, the United States had more than 1,400 daily newspapers with a total average circulation per issue of 45,729,000 (World Association of Newspapers' World Press Trends 2012 Report)
- As of 2012, about 81 percent of Americans had Internet access (International Telecommunication Union's 2012 ICT Indicators Database)

In Brief

Although the U.S. media are comparatively among the freest in the world, critics have identified a number of challenges to media independence including concentration of ownership, commercialization, and journalists' overreliance on official sources.

Chronology

1948–2012: Free

While the United States has a long history of media freedom, there have been many attempts by government to limit these freedoms, particularly in the name of national security and privacy

(Continued)

Year	Media	Government
1972	Free	Democracy
1973	Free	Democracy
1974	Free	Democracy
1975	Free	Democracy
1976	Free	Democracy
1977	Free	Democracy
1978	Free	Democracy
1979	Free	Democracy
1980	Free	Democracy
1981	Free	Democracy
1982	Free	Democracy
1983	Free	Democracy
1984	Free	Democracy
1985	Free	Democracy
1986	Free	Democracy
1987	Free	Democracy
1988	Free	Democracy
1989	Free	Democracy
1990	Free	Democracy
1991	Free	Democracy
1992	Free	Democracy
1993	Free	Democracy
1994	Free	Democracy
1995	Free	Democracy
1996	Free	Democracy
1997	Free	Democracy
1998	Free	Democracy
1999	Free	Democracy
2000	Free	Democracy
2001	Free	Democracy
2002	Free	Democracy
2003	Free	Democracy
2004	Free	Democracy

rights. Although the Inter American Press Association has consistently concluded that the United States had press freedom, it also documented a number of government infractions. In 1955, *Washington Post* Editor J. Russell Wiggins testified to a Senate subcommittee that the government had violated press freedom in a number of ways including withholding public information, engaging in prior restraint, attempting to intimidate news media, passing legislation requiring the Communist Party to register any printing equipment, and restricting through the postal system the shipping of any publications deemed subversive.[1]

Still, over the years there have been a number of cases in which the news media appeared to hold government accountable. For example, graphic news coverage of the Vietnam War was credited with turning public opinion against that conflict; however, studies have shown that the negative news coverage actually followed the shift in public opinion.[2] Also in the 1970s, the news media, led by *Washington Post* reporters Bob Woodward and Carl Bernstein, uncovered the Watergate scandal that eventually forced President Richard Nixon out of office. In the late 1990s, blogger Matt Drudge broke the story of President Clinton's relationship with White House intern Monica Lewinsky that led to Clinton's impeachment (he was acquitted).

In recent years, there have been challenges to media freedom. Since the 2001 terrorist attacks, both Republican and Democratic administrations have been accused of limiting journalists' access to information. Additionally, media have been criticized for failing to question official accounts of events, especially in the build-up to the war in Iraq.[3]

Media Today

U.S. media remain free. Yet organizations that monitor violations of media freedom have expressed concern over the thirty-five-year prison sentence handed down to Bradley (now Chelsea) Manning in connection with the release of classified information to Wikileaks, as well as the efforts to extradite and punish Wikileaks founder Julian Assange and former NSA contractor-turned-whistleblower Edward Snowden. In fact, Reporters Without Borders

Year	Media	Government
2005	Free	Democracy
2006	Free	Democracy
2007	Free	Democracy
2008	Free	Democracy
2009	Free	Democracy
2010	Free	Democracy
2011	Free	Democracy
2012	Free	Democracy

ranked the United States at 46 on its 2014 Press Freedom Index, placing it below South Africa, Trinidad and Tobago, Papua New Guinea, and Romania, and just above Haiti, Niger, and Italy.[4] Even so, news media in the United States for the most part remain free to criticize the government, though they do not always choose to do so.

Notes

1. *The State of the Press*, 1955 Annual Meeting (Miami, FL: Inter American Press Association, 1956).
2. For more on this see Daniel C. Hallin, *The "Uncensored War": The Media and Vietnam* (Berkeley: University of California Press, 1986).
3. For more on this see W. Lance Bennett, Regina G. Lawrence, and Steven Livingston, *When the Press Fails* (University of Chicago Press, 2007).
4. *World Press Freedom Index 2014* (Paris, France: Reporters Without Borders, 2014). Available at http://rsf.org/index2014/en-index2014.php.

Uruguay: 1948–2012

Uruguay Year by Year

Year	Media	Government
1948	Free	Anocracy
1949	Free	Anocracy
1950	Free	Anocracy
1951	Free	Anocracy
1952	Free	Democracy
1953	Free	Democracy
1954	Free	Democracy
1955	Free	Democracy
1956	Free	Democracy
1957	Free	Democracy
1958	Free	Democracy
1959	Free	Democracy
1960	Free	Democracy
1961	Free	Democracy
1962	Free	Democracy
1963	Free	Democracy
1964	Free	Democracy
1965	Free	Democracy
1966	Free	Democracy
1967	Free	Democracy
1968	Imperfectly Free	Democracy
1969	Imperfectly Free	Democracy
1970	Imperfectly Free	Democracy
1971	Imperfectly Free	Anocracy
1972	Imperfectly Free	Anocracy

In Brief

Historically, Uruguayan media have enjoyed more freedom than most media in Latin America. Yet they have also been vulnerable to lawsuits. With the exception of the 1973 to 1983 period, when Uruguay was under military control, Uruguayan media have been functionally free.

Chronology

1948–1967: Free

From the late 1940s to the mid-1950s, Uruguay—then known as the "Switzerland of South America"—experienced tremendous economic growth and improvement in the standard of living.[1] During this time, news media were free, though most newspapers were closely affiliated with political parties.[2] In the 1960s this period of prosperity came to an end and, like many industries, the Uruguayan news media

Year	Media	Government
1973	Not Free	Autocracy
1974	Not Free	Autocracy
1975	Not Free	Autocracy
1976	Not Free	Autocracy
1977	Not Free	Autocracy
1978	Not Free	Autocracy
1979	Not Free	Autocracy
1980	Not Free	Autocracy
1981	Not Free	Autocracy
1982	Not Free	Autocracy
1983	Not Free	Autocracy
1984	Imperfectly Free	Autocracy
1985	Free	Democracy
1986	Free	Democracy
1987	Free	Democracy
1988	Free	Democracy
1989	Free	Democracy
1990	Free	Democracy
1991	Free	Democracy
1992	Free	Democracy
1993	Free	Democracy
1994	Free	Democracy
1995	Free	Democracy
1996	Imperfectly Free	Democracy
1997	Imperfectly Free	Democracy
1998	Imperfectly Free	Democracy
1999	Imperfectly Free	Democracy
2000	Imperfectly Free	Democracy
2001	Imperfectly Free	Democracy
2002	Imperfectly Free	Democracy
2003	Imperfectly Free	Democracy
2004	Imperfectly Free	Democracy
2005	Imperfectly Free	Democracy
2006	Imperfectly Free	Democracy

experienced financial difficulties, including a strike in 1967 that left Montevideo without newspapers for three months.[3]

1968–1972: Imperfectly Free

By 1968, the economic decline fueled substantial social unrest. In addition, the Tupamaros, an urban guerrilla organization, began conducting a series of attacks, including kidnappings and bank robberies. Government efforts to stifle dissent also limited press freedom. Newspapers with articles deemed to be a threat to public order were confiscated or closed down.[4] Yet during this time, news media were able to report freely and critically about other national problems.[5]

1973–1983: Not Free

In June of 1973, President Bordaberry, with the support of the military, dissolved the General Assembly and restricted media freedom with a decree that prohibited newspaper and broadcast media from making any sort of reference to the decree or anything that might disturb public order.[6] Under this military regime, some privately owned newspapers continued to publish, but newspapers were frequently confiscated or closed down.

1984: Imperfectly Free

In late 1983 and early 1984, news media were heavily censored, but in February 1984, prior censorship of weekly newspapers was lifted.[7] As the November general elections approached, media freedom dramatically increased.

1985–1995: Free

As soon as he took office in March 1985, President Julio Maria Sanguinetti proposed a law that did away with many of the previous restrictions on media freedom.[8] Once again, news media in Uruguay were remarkably free compared to other media in the region.

1996–2008: Imperfectly Free

Pressures on media increased as government imposed new import duties on newsprint. Placement of government advertising in media outlets that were more favorable to government remained an issue. In addition, critical journalists continued to face libel and defamation lawsuits, as well as harassment and physical attacks.

Year	Media	Government
2007	Imperfectly Free	Democracy
2008	Imperfectly Free	Democracy
2009	Free	Democracy
2010	Free	Democracy
2011	Free	Democracy
2012	Free	Democracy

2009–2012: Free

In 2009, Uruguay decriminalized defamation and insult in news media regarding issues of public interest.[9] Yet insulting public officials or *desacato* remained criminal. The relationship between government and news media remained contentious, and politicians continued to target critical journalists with punitive lawsuits, but news media in Uruguay remained vibrant.

Media Today

News media in Uruguay are arguably the most free in South America. That said, journalists still face many pressures. In particular, journalists who criticize public officials can face defamation charges, and those who report on juvenile crimes, including murder, can be charged with violating the privacy of children.

Uruguay has a wide range of privately owned newspapers, television stations, and radio stations. There are also state-owned television and radio stations. Online media are not restricted and as of 2011, about 51 percent of the population had Internet access.

Notes

1. Rex A. Hudson and Sandra W. Meditz, *Uruguay: A Country Study* (Washington, DC: Library of Congress Country Studies, 1990). Available at http://lcweb2.loc.gov/frd/cs/cshome.html.
2. Ibid.
3. *Report by the Committee on Freedom of the Press*, Annual Meeting 1968 (Miami, FL: Inter American Press Association, 1969).
4. Ibid.
5. *Freedom of the Press Committee Report*, General Assembly 1972 (Miami, FL: Inter American Press Association, 1973).
6. *Report of the Committee on Freedom of the Press and Information*, General Assembly 1973 (Miami, FL: Inter American Press Association, 1974).
7. *Report of the Committee on Freedom of the Press and Information*, General Assembly 1984 (Miami, FL: Inter American Press Association, 1985).
8. *Report of the Committee on Freedom of the Press and Information*, Midyear Meeting 1985 (Miami, FL: Inter American Press Association, 1985).
9. *General Assembly 2009* (Miami, FL: Inter American Press Association, 2009). Available at http://www.sipiapa.org/en/asambleas-inform/as-2009-2-general-assembly-argentina/.

Uzbekistan: 1991–2012

Uzbekistan Year by Year

Year	Media	Government
1991	Not Free	Autocracy
1992	Not Free	Autocracy
1993	Not Free	Autocracy
1994	Not Free	Autocracy
1995	Not Free	Autocracy
1996	Not Free	Autocracy
1997	Not Free	Autocracy
1998	Not Free	Autocracy
1999	Not Free	Autocracy
2000	Not Free	Autocracy
2001	Not Free	Autocracy
2002	Not Free	Autocracy
2003	Not Free	Autocracy
2004	Not Free	Autocracy
2005	Not Free	Autocracy
2006	Not Free	Autocracy
2007	Not Free	Autocracy
2008	Not Free	Autocracy
2009	Not Free	Autocracy
2010	Not Free	Autocracy
2011	Not Free	Autocracy
2012	Not Free	Autocracy

In Brief

Since independence, Uzbekistani media have been controlled.

MEDIA FREEDOM HISTORY IN A NUTSHELL

- Soviet-style direct control of the media has been sustained since independence
- In 2012, the government reported there were thirty-five radio and fifty-three television stations operating in Uzbekistan (Freedom House's Report on Freedom of the Press Report 2013)
- As of 2012, the government reported Uzbekistan had 663 newspapers as well as almost 200 magazines (Freedom House's Report on Freedom of the Press Report 2013)
- As of 2012, about 37 percent of Uzbekistanis had Internet access (International Telecommunication Union's 2012 ICT Indicators Database)

Chronology

1991–2012: Not Free

Former Uzbek Communist Party leader Islam Karimov took over the leadership of the newly independent Uzbekistan and carried authoritarian rule forward. In the early 1990s, opposition parties were banned and their publications were closed down.[1] Domestic media were strictly controlled, and many foreign journalists were expelled.[2]

In 2005, news media were barred from covering the mass demonstrations that broke out in the city of Andijan. Thousands of people took to the streets in protest of the imprisonment of men accused of Islamic extremism. Radio stations were silenced, foreign television channels censored, online news media blocked, mobile phone service shut down, and journalists were barred from the city, as government troops opened fire on the demonstrators in a crackdown that, according to human rights organizations, left hundreds dead.[3]

Media Today

Media are directly controlled by government. According to the government, in 2012, there were 53 television stations, 35 radio stations, and more than 663 newspapers in Uzbekistan.[4] Most foreign journalists have been expelled from the country since the Andijan massacre. The government monitors Internet activity and blocks access to a number of websites, including many foreign news sites and social media networks.[5] The Committee to Protect Journalists has consistently placed Uzbekistan on its list of the world's worst jailers of journalists.[6]

Notes

1. *World Press Freedom Review,* IPI Report (Vienna: International Press Institute, December 1993).
2. Ibid.
3. *World Press Freedom Review,* IPI Report (Vienna: International Press Institute, 2005).
4. *Freedom of the Press* (Washington, DC: Freedom House, 2013). Available at http://www.freedom house.org/report/freedom-press/2013/uzbekistan.
5. Ibid.
6. Elana Beiser, *Second Worst Year on Record for Jailed Journalists* (Committee to Protect Journalists, 2013). Available at https://cpj.org/reports/2013/12/second-worst-year-on-record-for-jailed-journalists .php.

Vanuatu: 1980–2012

Vanuatu Year by Year

Year	Media	Government
1980	Imperfectly Free	Democracy
1981	Imperfectly Free	Democracy
1982	Imperfectly Free	Anocracy
1983	Imperfectly Free	Anocracy
1984	Imperfectly Free	Anocracy
1985	Imperfectly Free	Anocracy
1986	Imperfectly Free	Anocracy
1987	Imperfectly Free	Anocracy
1988	Not Free	Anocracy
1989	Not Free	Democracy
1990	Not Free	Democracy
1991	Not Free	Democracy
1992	Imperfectly Free	Democracy
1993	Imperfectly Free	Democracy
1994	Imperfectly Free	Democracy
1995	Imperfectly Free	Democracy
1996	Imperfectly Free	Democracy
1997	Imperfectly Free	Democracy
1998	Imperfectly Free	Democracy
1999	Imperfectly Free	Democracy
2000	Imperfectly Free	Democracy
2001	Imperfectly Free	Democracy
2002	Free	Democracy
2003	Free	Democracy

(Continued)

MEDIA FREEDOM HISTORY IN A NUTSHELL

- Upon independence the government owned the radio station and the only newspaper with national reach, but there were a few small newspapers owned by religious organizations and political parties
- In the late 1980s, political turmoil prompted government to restrict news media
- By the early 1990s, an independent press had begun to emerge and grow
- In 2012, there were several independent newspapers and at least one privately owned radio station in addition to the government-run weekly newspaper and broadcast media (Freedom House's Report on Freedom of the World 2013)
- As of 2012, 11 percent of Ni-Vanuatu had Internet access (International Telecommunication Union's 2012 ICT Indicators Database)

In Brief

A collection of more than eighty islands formerly known as New Hebrides, Vanuatu gained independence from Britain and France in 1980. With the exception of a few years in the late 1980s and early 1990s, Ni-Vanuatu media have been functionally free. Upon independence, virtually all media were government owned, but since the mid-1990s independent news outlets have become a vibrant source of news and information.

Chronology

1980–1987: Imperfectly Free

Vanuatu's independence began with a rough start as the new government almost immediately faced a secessionist rebellion on two islands. With military assistance from Papua New

(Continued)

Year	Media	Government
2004	Free	Democracy
2005	Free	Democracy
2006	Free	Democracy
2007	Free	Democracy
2008	Free	Democracy
2009	Free	Democracy
2010	Free	Democracy
2011	Free	Democracy
2012	Free	Democracy

Guinea, the rebellion was quickly put down. Although the constitution had provisions for media freedom, it also gave the government broad emergency powers to restrict news media.[1] While the government controlled the country's only national radio station and the only newspaper with a national circulation, there were also some newspapers published by religious organizations and political parties.[2]

1988–1991: Not Free

In 1988, a government minister was dismissed from Parliament after leading a violent protest against Prime Minister Walter Lini's land policies.[3] The political turmoil escalated when the president was arrested after he tried to abolish Parliament and establish an interim government.[4] In the aftermath of the protests, the media environment deteriorated as members of the opposition said they were denied access to the government-run radio and newspaper, which by this time were the only sources of news and information because the Ni-Vanuatu were not permitted to purchase satellite television.[5] Additionally, the government expelled an Australian journalist after deeming the reporter's coverage of the crisis was inaccurate. In 1990, at the request of Lini, the Parliament formed a constitutional committee to consider restricting freedom of speech.[6]

In 1991, journalists at the government-owned media pushed back against government censorship and persisted in providing some coverage of the opposition.[7] Although the government retaliated by forcing the manager of the radio station into retirement, eventually the High Court intervened and ordered the government to stop the censorship.[8] Following fighting within Prime Minister Lini's Vanua'aku Party and a no-confidence vote from Parliament, Lini was replaced.[9]

1992–2001: Imperfectly Free

In 1992, the number of news outlets increased when the independent newspaper *Vanuascope* began publishing and the government launched the country's first television station and a second radio station (both government-run). Members of the political opposition still had difficulties getting timely news coverage because publication or broadcasts of their statements were often delayed to allow the government time to prepare a response.[10] In 1993, the government threatened to take away the publishing license of *Vanuascope* when the newspaper failed to comply with the government's ban on the publication of statements made by former Prime Minister Lini and his supporters.[11] The government continued to have little tolerance for media criticism.[12] In 1994, *Vanuascope* stopped publishing due to financial problems, but the regional news agency PACNEWS relocated to Vanuatu and was sometimes critical of the government. Still PACNEWS was for the most part aimed at nondomestic audiences.[13] In 1995, the government once again threatened to revoke the license of an independent newspaper following critical reporting, and banned news coverage of the French nuclear testing on a remote atoll.[14] In the mid-1990s, Vanuatu filled the Ombudsman position called for in the constitution. Throughout the 1990s, shifts in political leadership failed to bring about much change in the media environment, but the emergence of some independent newspapers, the introduction of the Ombudsman, and the willingness of journalists for the state-run media to at times carry opposition views created a situation where media were imperfectly free, but only barely so. Journalists who engaged in watchdog reporting were often threatened and harassed.[15]

In 2001, investigative reporting by the independent *Vanuatu Trading Post* was credited with leading to the ouster of Prime Minister Barak Tame

Sope, but not before Sope had the newspaper's publisher deported.[16] The publisher was allowed to return within days and Sope was eventually convicted of abuse of office.

2002–2012: Free

Following the ouster of Sope, the media environment improved to the point that the news media were free. Although in 2002, the government maintained exclusive ownership of the country's broadcast media and one weekly newspaper, and there were several independent newspapers. Moreover, the government-run radio stations could and did provide reporting that criticized government policies. In 2008, Vanuatu gained its first independent radio station.

Media Today

Ni-Vanuatu media remain for the most part free. Although corruption remains a problem, the news media can and do criticize government. In addition to the government-run weekly newspaper and television and radio stations, Vanuatu had at least one private radio station in 2012 and several private newspapers.[17] There were no reports of government censoring the Internet, but as of 2012 only 11 percent of Ni-Vanuatu had Internet access.

Notes

1. *Country Reports on Human Rights Practices for 1981* (Washington, DC: U.S. Department of State, 1982). Available at http://babel.hathitrust.org/cgi/pt?id=mdp.39015039359891;view=1up;seq=5.

2. Ibid.

3. *Country Reports on Human Rights Practices for 1988* (Washington, DC: U.S. Department of State, 1989). Available at https://archive.org/details/countryreportson1988unit.

4. Ibid.

5. *Country Reports on Human Rights Practices for 1989* (Washington, DC: U.S. Department of State, 1990). Available at https://archive.org/details/countryreportson1989unit.

6. *Country Reports on Human Rights Practices for 1990* (Washington, DC: U.S. Department of State, 1991). Available at https://archive.org/details/countryreportson1990unit.

7. *Country Reports on Human Rights Practices for 1991* (Washington, DC: U.S. Department of State, 1992). Available at https://archive.org/stream/countryreportson1991unit.

8. Ibid.

9. Ibid.

10. *Country Reports on Human Rights Practices for 1992* (Washington, DC: U.S. Department of State, 1993). Available at https://archive.org/stream/countryreportson1992unit.

11. *Country Reports on Human Rights Practices for 1993* (Washington, DC: U.S. Department of State, 1994). Available at http://dosfan.lib.uic.edu/ERC/democracy/1993_hrp_report/93hrp_report_eap/Vanuatu.html.

12. Ibid.

13. *Country Reports on Human Rights Practices for 1994* (Washington, DC: U.S. Department of State, 1995). Available at http://dosfan.lib.uic.edu/ERC/democracy/1994_hrp_report/94hrp_report_eap/Vanuatu.html.

14. *World Press Freedom Review*, IPI Report (Vienna: International Press Institute, November/December 1995).

15. *World Press Freedom Review*, IPI Report (Vienna: International Press Institute, 1999).

16. *World Press Freedom Review*, IPI Report (Vienna: International Press Institute, 2001).

17. *Freedom of the Press* (Washington, DC: Freedom House, 2013). Available at http://www.freedomhouse.org/report/freedom-world/2013/vanuatu.

Venezuela: 1948–2012

Venezuela Year by Year

Year	Media	Government
1948	Imperfectly Free	Anocracy
1949	Not Free	Anocracy
1950	Not Free	Anocracy
1951	Not Free	Anocracy
1952	Not Free	Anocracy
1953	Not Free	Anocracy
1954	Not Free	Anocracy
1955	Not Free	Anocracy
1956	Not Free	Anocracy
1957	Not Free	Anocracy
1958	Imperfectly Free	Democracy
1959	Imperfectly Free	Democracy
1960	Imperfectly Free	Democracy
1961	Imperfectly Free	Democracy
1962	Imperfectly Free	Democracy
1963	Imperfectly Free	Democracy
1964	Imperfectly Free	Democracy
1965	Imperfectly Free	Democracy
1966	Imperfectly Free	Democracy
1967	Imperfectly Free	Democracy
1968	Imperfectly Free	Democracy
1969	Imperfectly Free	Democracy
1970	Imperfectly Free	Democracy
1971	Imperfectly Free	Democracy
1972	Imperfectly Free	Democracy
1973	Imperfectly Free	Democracy
1974	Imperfectly Free	Democracy
1975	Imperfectly Free	Democracy

MEDIA FREEDOM HISTORY IN A NUTSHELL

- Historically, Venezuelan media have been polarized and politicized, which has resulted in compromised media freedom
- Government control over news media is severe—as of 2013 the government operated six television stations and four radio stations, as well as a news agency and three newspapers (Freedom House's Freedom of the Press 2013 Report)
- As of 2009, Venezuela had 112 total daily newspapers, 109 of them are paid-for dailies with an average circulation of 1,948,000 (World Association of Newspaper's 2010 World Newspaper Trends)
- As of 2012, about 44 percent of Venezuelans had Internet access (International Telecommunication Union's 2012 ICT Indicators Database)

In Brief

Since its first newspaper, the *Gaceta de Caracas*, started publishing in 1808 and advocating for independence from Spain, Venezuelan news media have been politicized.[1] Historically, ownership of news media has been in the hands of a few families, and these include the family of 2013 opposition candidate Henrique Capriles Radonski. Thus, for much of recent history, the relationship between news media and government has been contentious, and this has often compromised media freedom.

Chronology

1948: Imperfectly Free

There was some political openness, including some media freedom, in post–World War II Venezuela, but this ended in November 1948

Year	Media	Government
1976	Imperfectly Free	Democracy
1977	Imperfectly Free	Democracy
1978	Imperfectly Free	Democracy
1979	Imperfectly Free	Democracy
1980	Imperfectly Free	Democracy
1981	Imperfectly Free	Democracy
1982	Imperfectly Free	Democracy
1983	Imperfectly Free	Democracy
1984	Imperfectly Free	Democracy
1985	Imperfectly Free	Democracy
1986	Imperfectly Free	Democracy
1987	Imperfectly Free	Democracy
1988	Imperfectly Free	Democracy
1989	Imperfectly Free	Democracy
1990	Imperfectly Free	Democracy
1991	Imperfectly Free	Democracy
1992	Not Free	Democracy
1993	Imperfectly Free	Democracy
1994	Imperfectly Free	Democracy
1995	Imperfectly Free	Democracy
1996	Imperfectly Free	Democracy
1997	Imperfectly Free	Democracy
1998	Imperfectly Free	Democracy
1999	Imperfectly Free	Democracy
2000	Imperfectly Free	Democracy
2001	Imperfectly Free	Democracy
2002	Not Free	Democracy
2003	Not Free	Democracy
2004	Not Free	Democracy
2005	Not Free	Democracy
2006	Not Free	Anocracy
2007	Not Free	Anocracy
2008	Not Free	Anocracy
2009	Not Free	Anocracy
2010	Not Free	Anocracy
2011	Not Free	Anocracy
2012	Not Free	Anocracy

when President Gallegos was overthrown in a military coup.[2]

1949–1957: Not Free

Following the 1948 coup, news media were strictly censored. During this period, some journalists were imprisoned without trial and others were forced into exile.[3]

1958–1991: Imperfectly Free

In January of 1958, following a bombing of the capital and a general strike, President Marcos Pérez Jiménez was forced to resign and fled to Miami (with much of Venezuela's treasury). The military junta restored media freedom to facilitate elections, which were held in December of 1958. Romulo Betancourt, who had been president from 1945 to 1948, was elected and took office in early 1959. During these years, newspapers associated with the Communist Party and the Movement of the Revolutionary Left were subject to confiscations and suspensions, and affiliated journalists were arrested and accused of inciting subversion. The year 1968 saw the restoration of the 1947 decree requiring approval from the Ministry of Defense for any news regarding that ministry.[4] Yet other news media were able to operate without censorship. In the early 1980s, a new law was enacted requiring all journalists to become members of the Colegio de Periodistas (Collegium of Journalism). Journalists who were not granted membership and persisted in practicing journalism could and sometimes were charged with "illegal exercise of journalism."[5]

1992: Not Free

In February 1992, an attempted coup led by Hugo Chávez prompted the government to institute prior censorship of news media. Though media leaders eventually convinced President Carlos Andrés Pérez to remove the censors, journalists continued to face attacks and threats. In November, a second coup attempt led to the declaration of a state of emergency and the suspension of civil liberties, including media freedom.

1993–2001: Imperfectly Free

In 1993, amid accusations of embezzlement and misuse of public funds, President Pérez was removed from office. Journalists who had fled the country to avoid politically motivated charges were pardoned.[6] Although journalists faced fewer restrictions and attacks, in 1994, Venezuelan lawmakers passed a bill that mandated the imprisonment of journalists who failed to join the Colegio de Periodistas. This law also required that journalists have a journalism degree from a university. In 1995, the Venezuelan Press Bloc filed a lawsuit with the Supreme Court to overturn the law, but the Supreme Court had yet to issue a ruling when it was replaced with the Supreme Tribunal of Justice under the 1999 Constitution. The Constitution, championed by newly elected President Hugo Chávez, contained contradictory clauses regarding media freedom. While Article 57 of this constitution guaranteed freedom of expression and prohibited censorship, Article 58 stated that "everyone has the right to timely, truthful and impartial information, without censorship, in accordance with the principles of this Constitution, as well as the right of reply and corrections when they are directly affected by inaccurate or offensive information."[7] The Communications Law of 2000 gave the president the authority to crack down on media groups and suspend broadcasting if it is in the country's interest to do so.

2002–2012: Not Free

As the relationship between the Chávez administration and media owners continued to deteriorate, journalists' freedom was compromised. Chávez was savagely critical of the news media, and media owners used their news outlets to portray government in an unflattering light. According to the Committee to Protect Journalists,

> journalists said they felt like cannon fodder in this struggle between Chávez and the media, who have become increasingly anti-Chávez. Some journalists charged that editors told them not to cover pro-Chávez events or rewrote copy to put the opposition in a better light.[8]

By 2003, private news media were supporting the opposition and public media were supporting Chávez in a media battle. Journalists and media owners who criticized Chávez faced lawsuits, threats, and attacks. In 2004, the Law of Social Responsibility in Radio and Television for the most part banned media from broadcasting images or descriptions of violence between 5 a.m. and 11 p.m. That same year, lawmakers increased the prison terms for *desacato* (insult) crimes.

Media Today

Restrictions on news media remain firmly in place in Venezuela. Media remain polarized and politicized such that most privately owned media are pro-opposition, and state-owned media serve as a megaphone for government. Critical news media face punitive lawsuits and are typically denied access to government events and information. Venezuela has a mix of private and state-owned media. As of 2011, about 40 percent of Venezuelans had Internet access.

Notes

1. Richard A. Haggarty, *Venezuela: A Country Study* (Washington, DC: Library of Congress Federal Research Division, 1990). Available at http://lcweb2.loc.gov/frd/cs/.
2. *State of the Press*, Annual Meeting 1955 (Miami, FL: Inter American Press Association, 1956).
3. *Report of the Committee on Freedom of the Press*, Annual Meeting 1957 (Miami, FL: Inter American Press Association, 1958).
4. *Report of the Committee on Freedom of the Press*, Annual Meeting 1963 (Miami, FL: Inter American Press Association, 1964).
5. *Report of the Committee on Freedom of the Press and Information*, General Assembly 1987 (Miami, FL: Inter American Press Association, 1987).
6. *General Assembly 1993* (Miami, FL: Inter American Press Association, 1993). Available at http://www.sipiapa.org/en/asambleas.
7. *Constitution of the Bolivarian Republic of Venezuela* (Seoul: Gobierno Bolivariano de Venezuela, 1999). Available at http://www.venezuelaemb.or.kr/english/ConstitutionoftheBolivarianingles.pdf.
8. Sauro Gonzalez Rodriguez, *Venezuela Special Report: Cannon Fodder* (Committee to Protect Journalists, 2002), para 9. Available at http://cpj.org/reports/2002/08/ven-aug02.php.

Vietnam: 1954–2012

North Vietnam Year by Year

Year	Media	Government
1954	Not Free	Autocracy
1955	Not Free	Autocracy
1956	Not Free	Autocracy
1957	Not Free	Autocracy
1958	Not Free	Autocracy
1959	Not Free	Autocracy
1960	Not Free	Autocracy
1961	Not Free	Autocracy
1962	Not Free	Autocracy
1963	Not Free	Autocracy
1964	Not Free	Autocracy
1965	Not Free	Autocracy
1966	Not Free	Autocracy
1967	Not Free	Autocracy
1968	Not Free	Autocracy
1969	Not Free	Autocracy
1970	Not Free	Autocracy
1971	Not Free	Autocracy
1972	Not Free	Autocracy
1973	Not Free	Autocracy
1974	Not Free	Autocracy
1975	Not Free	Autocracy

MEDIA FREEDOM HISTORY IN A NUTSHELL

- Upon independence, a militarized dictatorship in the South and single-party rule in the North both exerted strict control of the media
- Neither the war nor the unification changed the media environment—media remained controlled
- In the mid-1990s, some gestures toward liberalization and development of the media accompanied the normalization of relations with the United States
- Strict Communist Party control of the media continued in 2013
- As of 2010, Vietnam had fifty-five total paid-for daily newspapers with a total average circulation per issue of 4,000,000 (World Association of Newspaper's World Newspaper Trends 2012)
- As of 2012, about 40 percent of Vietnamese had Internet access (International Telecommunication Union's 2012 ICT Indicators Database)

In Brief

Divided in 1954 at the end of French rule, Vietnam was eventually reunified by the communist North in 1975. Media were controlled in the North, and in the whole of the country after 1975, by a single-party government. The media were no freer in the South, with a militarized authoritarian dictatorship, supported by the United States, controlling the press. Media today remain restricted, and there is little indication that this will change.

Chronology for North Vietnam

1954–1975: Not Free

The 1954 coordinated attack on Dien Bein Phu marked the effective communist control of

South Vietnam Year by Year

Year	Media	Government
1956	Not Free	Anocracy
1957	Not Free	Anocracy
1958	Not Free	Anocracy
1959	Not Free	Anocracy
1960	Not Free	Anocracy
1961	Not Free	Anocracy
1962	Not Free	Anocracy
1963	Not Free	Anocracy
1964	Not Free	Anocracy
1965	Not Free	Foreign Interruption
1966	Not Free	Foreign Interruption
1967	Not Free	Foreign Interruption
1968	Not Free	Foreign Interruption
1969	Not Free	Foreign Interruption
1970	Not Free	Foreign Interruption
1971	Not Free	Foreign Interruption
1972	Not Free	Foreign Interruption
1973	Not Free	Foreign Interruption
1974	Not Free	Foreign Interruption
1975	Not Free	Foreign Interruption

Vietnam Year by Year

Year	Media	Government
1976	Not Free	Autocracy
1977	Not Free	Autocracy
1978	Not Free	Autocracy
1979	Not Free	Autocracy
1980	Not Free	Autocracy
1981	Not Free	Autocracy
1982	Not Free	Autocracy
1983	Not Free	Autocracy
1984	Not Free	Autocracy

the North. Single-party rule included direct control of the media by the communist party. As the conflict intensified, the government also limited access to foreign media by refusing to grant visa to most correspondents.[1]

Chronology for South Vietnam

1956–1975: Not Free

Starting with a campaign against political dissidents in 1956, authoritarian rule included control of the media. The shift to a war footing as the conflict with the North escalated further justified media controls. As the United States entered the war in the mid-1960s, the International Press noted that restrictions on media intensified, "Censorship was imposed on the Press and radio. The Government suspended four Saigon dailies for 20 days on the grounds that they were trying to stir up public opinion and harm the national security. Six other newspapers were temporarily closed."[2]

Chronology for Vietnam

1976–2012: Not Free

As the North Vietnamese troops took over South Vietnam, the country was united as the Socialist Republic of Vietnam. Under communist rule, all media were government controlled.

In 1995, rapprochement with the United States culminated in the restoration of diplomatic ties. As the government sought to establish new and extended relationships with rising Asian economic powers, the push for economic development included a shift to indirect control of the media. Commitment to single-party rule, however, remained steadfast and prevented significant liberalization. Yet the International Press Institute noted some improvement in the media environment, "All the country's newspapers must have official sponsorship, and there is still a strong need not to bite the hand that feeds them. But the press does now cover stories on areas which were once taboo, such as corruption"[3]

Following the 2001 selection of Nong Duc Manh as the new leader of the Communist Party, 2002 began with a crackdown on publications that were operating without official approval, and in April, the Central Committee

Year	Media	Government
1985	Not Free	Autocracy
1986	Not Free	Autocracy
1987	Not Free	Autocracy
1988	Not Free	Autocracy
1989	Not Free	Autocracy
1990	Not Free	Autocracy
1991	Not Free	Autocracy
1992	Not Free	Autocracy
1993	Not Free	Autocracy
1994	Not Free	Autocracy
1995	Not Free	Autocracy
1996	Not Free	Autocracy
1997	Not Free	Autocracy
1998	Not Free	Autocracy
1999	Not Free	Autocracy
2000	Not Free	Autocracy
2001	Not Free	Autocracy
2002	Not Free	Autocracy
2003	Not Free	Autocracy
2004	Not Free	Autocracy
2005	Not Free	Autocracy
2006	Not Free	Autocracy
2007	Not Free	Autocracy
2008	Not Free	Autocracy
2009	Not Free	Autocracy
2010	Not Free	Autocracy
2011	Not Free	Autocracy
2012	Not Free	Autocracy

resolved to provide increased "leadership" over media.[4] In 2008, two prominent journalists were convicted for exposing a major corruption scandal, and democracy advocates were jailed in 2009.

Media Today

The government continues to control media and is increasingly censoring Internet content. Online dissent is also suppressed. At the end of 2013, at least eighteen journalists, many of them bloggers, were imprisoned in Vietnam.[5] Journalists who anger the government are often harassed, threatened, or attacked.[6] One promising sign in 2012 was a government decree to permit the establishment of foreign press agencies and to increase the number of visas granted to international journalists.[7]

Notes

1. Ernest Meyer, *IPI's Annual Review of Press Freedom*, IPI Report (Zurich: International Press Institute, January 1972).
2. *World Press Freedom Review*, IPI Report (Zurich: International Press Institute, January 1965), 10.
3. *World Press Freedom Review*, IPI Report (Vienna: International Press Institute, November/December 1995), 105.
4. *World Press Freedom Review*, IPI Report (Vienna: International Press Institute, 2002).
5. Elana Beiser, *Second Worst Year on Record for Jailed Journalists* (Committee to Protect Journalists, 2013). Available at https://cpj.org/reports/2013/12/second-worst-year-on-record-for-jailed-journalists.php.
6. *Freedom of the Press* (Washington, DC: Freedom House, 2013). Available at http://www.freedomhouse.org/report/freedom-press/2013/vietnam.
7. Ibid.

Yemen: 1948–2012

North Yemen Year by Year

Year	Media	Government
1948	No Media	Autocracy
1949	Not Free	Autocracy
1950	Not Free	Autocracy
1951	Not Free	Autocracy
1952	Not Free	Autocracy
1953	Not Free	Autocracy
1954	Not Free	Autocracy
1955	Not Free	Autocracy
1956	Not Free	Autocracy
1957	Not Free	Autocracy
1958	Not Free	Autocracy
1959	Not Free	Autocracy
1960	Not Free	Autocracy
1961	Not Free	Autocracy
1962	Not Free	Anocracy
1963	Not Free	Anocracy
1964	Not Free	Anocracy
1965	Not Free	Anocracy
1966	Not Free	Anocracy
1967	Not Free	Anocracy
1968	Not Free	Anocracy
1969	Not Free	Anocracy
1970	Not Free	Anocracy
1971	Not Free	Anocracy
1972	Not Free	Anocracy

MEDIA FREEDOM HISTORY IN A NUTSHELL

- A divided state that has seen almost constant violence between government and rebellious forces
- The point of conflict has shifted from a north-south divide to a government versus militant Islamist divide
- Government owns almost all media, but has vacillated between direct administrative controls and indirect controls enforced through terror tactics
- Illiteracy is rife, and broadcast media are the dominant forms
- As of 2012, Yemen had four daily newspapers (World Association of Newspapers World Press Trends 2012); newspaper circulation in Yemen was very low due to low literacy rates (Freedom House's 2013 Freedom of the Press Report)
- In 2012, there were four government-owned television stations, twelve government-owned radio stations, and two privately owned radio stations operating in Yemen (Freedom House's 2013 Freedom of the Press Report)
- In 2012, 17 percent of Yemenis had Internet access (International Telecommunication Union's 2012 ICT Indicators Database)

In Brief

In an unstable and divided state, Yemeni media have never been free. Illiteracy is widespread and broadcast media, most of which are controlled by the state, are the only source of news and information available to the vast majority of the population.

Chronology for North Yemen (The Arab Republic of Yemen)

1948–1989: Not Free

Independent since the fall of the Ottoman Empire, North Yemen was ignored or dismissed

Year	Media	Government
1973	Not Free	Anocracy
1974	Not Free	Anocracy
1975	Not Free	Anocracy
1976	Not Free	Anocracy
1977	Not Free	Autocracy
1978	Not Free	Autocracy
1979	Not Free	Autocracy
1980	Not Free	Autocracy
1981	Not Free	Autocracy
1982	Not Free	Autocracy
1983	Not Free	Autocracy
1984	Not Free	Autocracy
1985	Not Free	Autocracy
1986	Not Free	Autocracy
1987	Not Free	Autocracy
1988	Not Free	Anocracy
1989	Not Free	Anocracy

South Yemen Year by Year

Year	Media	Government
1967	Not Free	Anocracy
1968	Not Free	Anocracy
1969	Not Free	Anocracy
1970	Not Free	Autocracy
1971	Not Free	Autocracy
1972	Not Free	Autocracy
1973	Not Free	Autocracy
1974	Not Free	Autocracy
1975	Not Free	Autocracy
1976	Not Free	Autocracy
1977	Not Free	Autocracy
1978	Not Free	Autocracy
1979	Not Free	Autocracy

Year	Media	Government
1980	Not Free	Autocracy
1981	Not Free	Autocracy
1982	Not Free	Autocracy
1983	Not Free	Autocracy
1984	Not Free	Autocracy
1985	Not Free	Autocracy
1986	Not Free	Autocracy
1987	Not Free	Autocracy
1988	Not Free	Autocracy
1989	Not Free	Autocracy

Yemen Year by Year

Year	Media	Government
1990	Not Free	Anocracy
1991	Not Free	Anocracy
1992	Not Free	Anocracy
1993	Not Free	Anocracy
1994	Not Free	Anocracy
1995	Not Free	Anocracy
1996	Not Free	Anocracy
1997	Not Free	Anocracy
1998	Not Free	Anocracy
1999	Not Free	Anocracy
2000	Not Free	Anocracy
2001	Not Free	Anocracy
2002	Not Free	Anocracy
2003	Not Free	Anocracy
2004	Not Free	Anocracy
2005	Not Free	Anocracy
2006	Not Free	Anocracy
2007	Not Free	Anocracy
2008	Not Free	Anocracy
2009	Not Free	Anocracy
2010	Not Free	Anocracy
2011	Not Free	Anocracy
2012	Not Free	Anocracy

by the world, which considered the British colonial holding, along the southern coast, to represent Yemen. North Yemen entered the world stage when the army seized power in 1962 and set up the Yemen Arab Republic, initiating a civil war. Radio was the only medium available to most of the country, and stations were officially owned and controlled by the government, but in practice—with constant power struggles within government, influence being wielded by both Egypt and Saudi Arabia, and an inability to restrict content coming in from the south—control of content was exercised through threats and terror rather than direct administrative control.

In 1978, the appointment of Ali Abdallah Saleh as president represented a consolidation of power, and with that, the government moved to take direct editorial control of all media. Private broadcasting was illegal.

Chronology for South Yemen (Yemen People's Republic)

1967–1989: Not Free

A single-party communist state was formed out of the British colonial holding of Aden and the British protectorate of South Arabia. Media were directly controlled and used as a propaganda tool.

Chronology for Yemen

1990–2012: Not Free

With oil wealth enabling the north to capitalize on the near collapse of government in the south, the nearly constant war between the north and the south was finally brought to an end with the unification of the country under Saleh.

The move away from a wartime footing included a modest shift to more indirect means of controlling media, but there was no real decrease in control, just a shift in method allowing the south more leeway under a government dominated by the north. This peaked in April 1993 with the formation of a coalition government including ruling parties from both north and south. During this time, there were reports that the government sought to intimidate independent newspapers that were critical of its policies, and broadcast media remained controlled.[1] By August, the coalition had collapsed.

In 1994, both the north and south reasserted direct control over the media as they moved toward a split. Violence increased, military clashes returned, and civil war erupted when the south declared independence. Covering the conflict was perilous for journalists, and some were attacked by security forces.[2] Within two months, the south was crushed by northern forces.

By 1996, with the end of any significant threat of succession by the south, the government returned to an indirect method of control. Though the war was over, there was sporadic violence, but journalists who tried to cover it were themselves targeted, and the government did not tolerate any criticism.[3] With the U.S. invasion of Afghanistan, Yemen became an al-Qaeda stronghold and militant Islamic forces became a significant factor in domestic politics. Foreign Islamic scholars were expelled in 2002.

In 2004, violent clashes between government forces and Islamic militants brought a return of a wartime state of emergency and an end to what little independence the media had enjoyed. The government shut down some newspapers, imprisoned at least one journalist, and directly controlled all media as the country descended into chaotic bouts of violence.[4]

Media Today

The fight against Islamic militants has diverted domestic politics from the north-south divide, but that divide was the primary fulcrum that was used to force some media independence from the north-dominated government. Systematic violence against media outlets, restrictive laws, and self-censorship compliment the direct control of most broadcast media. Still there were some positive signs in 2012 as the parliament passed a freedom of information law.[5] Because of high illiteracy, radio is the most important medium, and Yemen now has a mix of privately owned and government-owned radio. All domestic television stations are government owned, though foreign broadcasts are available.[6] The government owns the country's Internet service providers and has at times limited access.[7]

YEMEN: 1948–2012 • 507

Notes

1. *World Press Freedom Review*, IPI Report (Vienna: International Press Institute, December 1993).
2. *World Press Freedom Review*, IPI Report (Vienna: International Press Institute, December 1994).
3. *World Press Freedom Review*, IPI Report (Vienna: International Press Institute, December 1996/January 1997).
4. *Freedom of the Press* (Washington, DC: Freedom House, 2005). Available at http://www.freedom house.org/report/freedom-press/2005/yemen.
5. *Freedom of the Press* (Washington, DC: Freedom House, 2013). Available at http://www.freedom house.org/report/freedom-press/2013/yemen.
6. Ibid.
7. Ibid.

Zambia: 1964–2012

Zambia Year by Year

Year	Media	Government
1964	Imperfectly Free	Anocracy
1965	Not Free	Anocracy
1966	Not Free	Anocracy
1967	Not Free	Anocracy
1968	Not Free	Anocracy
1969	Not Free	Anocracy
1970	Not Free	Anocracy
1971	Not Free	Anocracy
1972	Not Free	Autocracy
1973	Not Free	Autocracy
1974	Not Free	Autocracy
1975	Not Free	Autocracy
1976	Not Free	Autocracy
1977	Not Free	Autocracy
1978	Not Free	Autocracy
1979	Not Free	Autocracy
1980	Not Free	Autocracy
1981	Not Free	Autocracy
1982	Not Free	Autocracy
1983	Not Free	Autocracy
1984	Not Free	Autocracy
1985	Not Free	Autocracy
1986	Not Free	Autocracy
1987	Not Free	Autocracy
1988	Not Free	Autocracy
1989	Not Free	Autocracy

MEDIA FREEDOM HISTORY IN A NUTSHELL

- Just one year after independence, Zambian media became restricted as President Kaunda consolidated his power
- In the early 1990s, media became functionally free as Zambia transitioned to a multiparty system
- Following a failed coup in 1997, the government resumed media restrictions
- With the election of former opposition leader Michael Sata as president, Zambian media regained a minimal level of media freedom
- As of 2012, Zambia had three main daily newspapers, two of which are public and tend to favor the government (Freedom House's Report on Freedom of the Press 2013)
- Although public broadcast media still dominate the market, the number of private broadcast outlets is increasing; in 2012, there were four privately owned television stations as well as dozens of privately owned radio stations and the government granted a number of new licenses (Freedom House's Report on Freedom of the Press 2013)
- In 2012, approximately 13 percent of Zambians had Internet access (International Telecommunication Union's 2012 ICT Indicators Database)

In Brief

Formerly known as Northern Rhodesia, upon independence, Zambia initially had some media freedom, but within a year, media became restricted as President Kenneth Kaunda eradicated all opposition and Zambia eventually became a one-party state. In the early 1990s, Zambia transitioned to a multiparty system, and under the leadership of President Chiluba media became functionally free, but still faced substantial

Year	Media	Government
1990	Not Free	Autocracy
1991	Not Free	Democracy
1992	Imperfectly Free	Democracy
1993	Imperfectly Free	Democracy
1994	Imperfectly Free	Democracy
1995	Imperfectly Free	Democracy
1996	Imperfectly Free	Anocracy
1997	Not Free	Anocracy
1998	Not Free	Anocracy
1999	Not Free	Anocracy
2000	Not Free	Anocracy
2001	Not Free	Anocracy
2002	Not Free	Anocracy
2003	Not Free	Anocracy
2004	Not Free	Anocracy
2005	Not Free	Anocracy
2006	Not Free	Anocracy
2007	Not Free	Anocracy
2008	Not Free	Democracy
2009	Not Free	Democracy
2010	Not Free	Democracy
2011	Imperfectly Free	Democracy
2012	Imperfectly Free	Democracy

short-lived when President Kaunda sought to consolidate his power.

1965–1991: Not Free

In the mid-1960s, as President Kaunda proceeded to eradicate any and all opposition, media were restricted. An early sign of this was the deportation of a foreign journalist who had been working for the weekly newspaper *Zambia News*.[2] By 1972, when Kaunda outlawed all political parties except his United National Independence Party (UNIP), all news outlets were effectively controlled by the government.[3] While criticism of the Kaunda and his Humanism philosophy was not tolerated, news media were allowed to criticize government policies as long as they were "constructive."[4]

Following food riots in 1990, Zambia transitioned to a multiparty system in 1991 and independent newspapers began publishing. Subsequently, Frederick Chiluba defeated Kaunda in the 1991 elections.

1992–1996: Imperfectly Free

Although President Chiluba promised to respect media freedom, journalists continued to face challenges under his regime:

> President Chiluba rounded on the press, accusing them of taking advantage of the atmosphere of freedom by distorting, sensationalizing and libeling his Government. "We will give them (the media) time. They are excited. They will grow up and get tired when they realize that we are indifferent to their provocation," the President said.[5]

The Information Minister threatened reporters and banned some radio and television programs, but the bans were reversed, and eventually the Information Minister was fired.[6] Thus, while conditions for news media were far from ideal, they were much improved. During these years, journalists, especially those working for privately owned newspapers, could and did criticize government, yet they were often threatened and harassed for doing so.[7]

1997–2010: Not Free

Following a failed coup in 1997, the government became increasingly intolerant of media

restrictions. Following an attempted coup in 1997, the government tightened media restrictions, and media remained not free until 2011 when former opposition leader Michael Sata became president. Media today are just barely able to function freely as the Sata regime has been slow to make good on its promises to reform the policies and practices that restrict media.

Chronology

1964: Imperfectly Free

Upon gaining independence from Britain in 1964, Zambia had a mix of private and government-run media and journalists enjoyed some independence.[1] This independence was

criticism. Journalists for the state-run broadcasting network were accused of supporting the coup and were fired and several journalists working for independent news outlets were jailed.[8] Throughout the late 1990s and early 2000s, the government used threats, intimidation and criminal libel laws to silence and imprison critical journalists.[9]

2011–2012: Imperfectly free

With the 2011 election of opposition leader Michael Sata as president, the media environment improved to the point where media were functionally free. In particular, Sata's government promised that it would not interfere with the publicly owned media.[10]

Media Today

Although Zambian media remain imperfectly free, the Sata regime has for the most part yet to deliver on its promises to reform the policies and practices that restrict media freedom. Critical journalists still face criminal defamation and sedition charges as well as harassment and physical attacks from both the opposition and supporters of the ruling party.[11] Although the government promised to free the public media from government control, these news outlets rarely criticize the government.[12]

Because of poverty, radio remains the most popular medium. While the public broadcast media continue to dominate, the number of private broadcast media is growing. In 2012, there were four private television stations, a number of independently owned radio stations and community radio stations, and the government had issued licenses to additional private broadcasters.[13] Zambia has three main daily newspapers, two of which are public. Only about 13 percent of Zambians have Internet access.

Notes

1. Francis P. Kasoma, "Press Freedom in Zambia," in *Press Freedom and Communication in Africa*, ed. Festus Eribo and William Jong-Ebot (Trenton, NJ: African World Press, 1997), 136–56.
2. *Toils of the Press*, IPI Report (Zurich: International Press Institute, July/August 1965).
3. Ibid.
4. *Country Reports on Human Rights Practices for 1977* (Washington, DC: U.S. Department of State, 1978). Available at http://babel.hathitrust.org/cgi/pt?id=mdp.39015078705632;view=1up;seq=1.
5. *World Press Freedom Review*, IPI Report (Zurich: International Press Institute, December 1992), 44.
6. Ibid.
7. Kasoma, "Press Freedom in Zambia."
8. *World Press Freedom Review*, IPI Report (Vienna: International Press Institute, December 1997).
9. *Freedom of the Press* (Washington, DC: Freedom House, 2002). Available at http://www.freedomhouse.org/report/freedom-press/2002/zambia.
10. *Freedom of the Press* (Washington, DC: Freedom House, 2012). Available at http://www.freedomhouse.org/report/freedom-press/2012/zambia.
11. *Freedom of the Press* (Washington, DC: Freedom House, 2013). Available at http://www.freedomhouse.org/report/freedom-press/2013/zambia.
12. Ibid.
13. Ibid.

Zimbabwe: 1966–2012

Zimbabwe Year by Year

Year	Media	Government
1966	Not Free	Anocracy
1967	Not Free	Anocracy
1968	Not Free	Anocracy
1969	Not Free	Anocracy
1970	Not Free	Anocracy
1971	Not Free	Anocracy
1972	Not Free	Anocracy
1973	Not Free	Anocracy
1974	Not Free	Anocracy
1975	Not Free	Anocracy
1976	Not Free	Anocracy
1977	Not Free	Anocracy
1978	Not Free	Anocracy
1979	Not Free	Anocracy
1980	Not Free	Anocracy
1981	Not Free	Anocracy
1982	Not Free	Anocracy
1983	Not Free	Anocracy
1984	Not Free	Anocracy
1985	Not Free	Anocracy
1986	Not Free	Anocracy
1987	Not Free	Autocracy
1988	Not Free	Autocracy

(Continued)

MEDIA FREEDOM HISTORY IN A NUTSHELL

- When Prime Minister Ian Smith issued a unilateral declaration of independence under white-minority rule, he also implemented a system of censorship
- Guerrilla war and UN sanctions eventually pressured Smith into accepting a settlement, which led to the 1979 elections and the 1980 internationally recognized independence under Robert Mugabe, but media remained restricted
- In 2014, Mugabe remained in power and media remained restricted
- As of 2012, both of the primary daily newspapers in Zimbabwe were government controlled (Freedom House's Report on Freedom of the Press 2013)
- Although the government maintained control over most broadcast media, more than half the population is believed to have access to foreign broadcast media via satellite dishes (Freedom House's Report on Freedom of the Press 2013)
- As of 2012, about 17 percent of Zimbabweans had Internet access (International Telecommunication Union's 2012 ICT Indicators Database)

In Brief

Formerly Southern Rhodesia and then Rhodesia, Zimbabwe has always had restricted media first under a white supremacist government and then under Robert Mugabe who has ruled the country since it officially gained independence from Britain in 1980.

Chronology

1966–2012: Not Free

At the end of 1965, Prime Minister Ian Smith drew international condemnation when

(Continued)

Year	Media	Government
1989	Not Free	Autocracy
1990	Not Free	Autocracy
1991	Not Free	Autocracy
1992	Not Free	Autocracy
1993	Not Free	Autocracy
1994	Not Free	Autocracy
1995	Not Free	Autocracy
1996	Not Free	Autocracy
1997	Not Free	Autocracy
1998	Not Free	Autocracy
1999	Not Free	Anocracy
2000	Not Free	Anocracy
2001	Not Free	Anocracy
2002	Not Free	Anocracy
2003	Not Free	Anocracy
2004	Not Free	Anocracy
2005	Not Free	Anocracy
2006	Not Free	Anocracy
2007	Not Free	Anocracy
2008	Not Free	Anocracy
2009	Not Free	Anocracy
2010	Not Free	Anocracy
2011	Not Free	Anocracy
2012	Not Free	Anocracy

he issued a unilateral declaration of independence of what was then Rhodesia from Britain under white-minority rule. Smith's white supremacist policies included the application of media censorship, which journalist John Parker, the former president of the Rhodesian Guild of Journalists, saw as an effort not only to control the media but to also "denigrate the Rhodesian press in the eyes of the public."[1]

I believe that there was not one journalist in Rhodesia in whom something did not die when the censors walked into the newspaper offices as Mr. Smith finished speaking at 1:30 p.m. on November 11 last year. I also believe that there is not one among us who would not do his utmost to remove the censorship and so help to regain the professional pride which has been taken away from him.[2]

In the early 1970s, resistance to the white-minority rule intensified into a guerrilla war. During the war, censorship of privately owned newspapers continued and the government maintained control of all broadcast media.[3]

Eventually, the war, combined with UN sanctions, led to a settlement that paved the way to elections in 1979 and the internationally recognized independence in 1980 of Zimbabwe under the leadership of Robert Mugabe. Initially, there were hopes that Mugabe's government would allow media freedom, and some of the privately owned newspapers, in particular those with ties to the opposition, were able to criticize the government. Yet the government showed signs of seeking increased media control early on as it acquired a controlling interest in the country's primary newspapers to establish the Mass Media Trust.[4] Meanwhile, the government continued to control the broadcast media.[5] Then in the early 1980s, as government forces were accused of killing thousands of civilians in the country's southwestern region, the government was quick to restrict media freedom and criticism of Mugabe and other top officials was not tolerated.[6]

Government restrictions of news media continued throughout the 1980s and the 1990s. Then in 2002, government control became more direct as the Parliament passed the Access to Information and Protection of Privacy Act, which required all journalists (including foreign journalists) to register with the government-controlled Media and Information Commission and gave the government the authority to ban people from working as journalists.[7] In 2012, Mugabe remained in power, state media remained government controlled, and independent media remained highly restricted.

Media Today

Zimbabwean media remain restricted. Journalists for privately owned news outlets are prone to self-censor because those who offend the government are vulnerable to harassment, physical attacks, and imprisonment. State-run media are for the most part limited to providing government propaganda.[8]

Radio remains the most accessible medium, especially in rural areas. While the government-controlled Zimbabwe Broadcasting Corporation continues to control most of the country's broadcast media, two new radio stations began broadcasting in 2012.[9] Additionally, it is estimated that more than half the population has access to foreign broadcast media via satellite dishes.[10] The government maintains control over the country's two primary daily newspapers through the Mass Media Trust, but there are independently owned newspapers.[11] Though there were no confirmed reports of government censorship of the Internet in 2013, there were some claims that the government limited mass text messaging capabilities prior to the 2013 elections.[12]

Notes

1. John Parker, *When the Censors Walked In*, IPI Report (Zurich: International Press Institute, March 1966), 1.

2. Ibid., 1.

3. *Country Reports on Human Rights Practices for 1979* (Washington, DC: U.S. Department of State, 1980). Available at http://babel.hathitrust.org/cgi/pt?id=mdp.39015014188273;view=1up;seq=3.

4. *Country Reports on Human Rights Practices for 1983* (Washington, DC: U.S. Department of State, 1984). Available at http://babel.hathitrust.org/cgi/pt?id=mdp.39015014227832;view=1up;seq=11.

5. *Country Reports on Human Rights Practices for 1980* (Washington, DC: U.S. Department of State, 1981). Available at http://babel.hathitrust.org/cgi/pt?id=mdp.39015014143476;view=1up;seq=2.

6. *Country Reports on Human Rights Practices for 1983*.

7. *World Press Freedom Review*, IPI Report (Vienna: International Press Institute, 2002).

8. *Freedom of the Press* (Washington, DC: Freedom House, 2013). Available at http://www.freedomhouse.org/report/freedom-press/2013/zimbabwe.

9. Ibid.

10. Ibid.

11. Ibid.

12. *Freedom of the Press* (Washington, DC: Freedom House, 2013). Available at http://www.freedomhouse.org/report/freedom-net/2013/zimbabwe.

Chapter 5

Conclusion

Challenges to Media Freedom and Patterns in Its Evolution and Devolution

> The conception of it [press freedom] has always been fluctuating, never stable. It has been limited in one country by government action, in another by vested wealth, in another by political parties; elsewhere it has been controlled by the Church, in another country by the ascendant industry, in another by chauvinism, and everywhere by authority.
>
> —Lucy Maynard Salmon, 1923

This book provides an historical account of the evolution (and devolution) of media in 196 independent countries that were in existence at the end of 2013.[1] Although this chapter marks the end of this volume, it is really the opening chapter of a deeper inquiry into the causes and effects of media freedom. With these narratives contextualizing the empirical data on media freedom, it is now possible to examine the shifts in media freedom in a new light. We now have a bridge between the detailed information from historical accounts of individual cases and the sterile but consistent and comparable global data. This provides a better opportunity to identify which aspects of the political context are common to when these changes occurred. With this we can begin to identify patterns in media development and variations in relationships between news media and politics.

We began this book by challenging some of the assumptions regarding media freedom, most important, the assumption that free media will always serve as a fourth estate, actively working to keep government in check and thereby improving human rights and preventing corruption. These ideological assumptions have consistently constrained studies and explorations of the causes and effects of media freedom. They have also complicated the conceptualization and definition of media freedom. Are media free only if they fulfill their idealized role (which they often fail to do), or are they free if they have the capacity to do so? Most organizations that monitor media freedom actually focus on the limitations on media freedom, but by doing so they fail to incorporate the agency of reporters who often push back against restraints and persist in trying to hold government accountable. Such agency can be an indicator of an effectively free media system, but again, media freedom is separate from that agency. Here we define *media freedom* as a contextual condition where media have the ability to criticize government about issues that matter. This is a simple, clear, and historically adaptable threshold above which media are free and below which they are not. There are many commonalities in how such a condition is created, but as becomes clear in the country profiles, there are also different ways it can be achieved; and as long as criticism is possible, how that political, social, and economic condition is created is irrelevant. Once media freedom is achieved, it is up to journalists to decide what do to with it.

When Free Media Behave Badly

Advocates often overlook the potential downside of press freedom: Media that are free to serve as a fourth estate are also free to behave badly. Leaders who constrain media freedom often justify their actions by pointing to irresponsible media. As the case of antihomosexual media in Uganda illustrates, media that are free from government control and restrictions sometimes use their freedom in ways that are potentially harmful, particularly to groups that are already somewhat marginalized in society. Media can reflect and perhaps even magnify the intolerance of their audience. There may even be commercial incentives for them to do so. The human appetite for scandalous revelations is immense, and news outlets that cater to this craving make money. Additionally, information that lets people know that others share their political views and cultural prejudices both validates and reinforces these sentiments. A case in point is Uganda where media have been imperfectly free since the fall of Idi Amin in 1979. Ugandan society is largely conservative and Christian, and most people in Uganda have little tolerance for homosexuality. In fact, homosexual acts were already criminalized in 2010 when a Ugandan tabloid published the names, pictures, and addresses of one hundred people it claimed were homosexuals (for more on this see Chapter 1 Box 1.2 "When Media Are Free to Spread Hate"). Although a Ugandan High Court eventually ruled that news outlets should not publish the names of alleged homosexuals and the paper The Rolling Stone (no affiliation with the U.S. magazine of the same name) soon stopped publishing altogether, the article was linked to several attacks on homosexuals and killing of gay rights activist David Kato, whose picture had been featured on the tabloid's front cover.

This case garnered international attention. Yet in the end, domestic intolerance of gays and pressure from Ugandan politicians and Christian preachers to increase punishment for gays mattered more to President Yoweri Museveni than the international condemnation of Ugandan homophobia. In early 2014, he signed into law a bill that increased the penalties for homosexual acts, including life sentences for same-sex marriage and gay sex as well

as up to seven-year sentences for the promotion of homosexuality. Then, just one day after the signing, the Ugandan tabloid Red Pepper published the names of 200 people it claimed were the country's "Top Homos." Although UN Secretary-General Ban Ki-moon called for a repeal of the law and several countries threatened to withdraw aid, the publication of the names in the tabloid reflected the domestic support for the measure.

Recent events in Madagascar illustrate how media can be wielded as political weapons. Malagasy media had been functionally free for the better part of two decades in 2009 when they found themselves caught in a conflict between two media moguls-turned-politicians (for more on this, see the profile of Madagascar in Chapter 4). President Marc Ravalomanana and his challenger Andry Rajoelina, Mayor of Antananarivo, used their media outlets to criticize each other and incite mob attacks.[2] Both Madagascar's democracy and media freedom deteriorated as Ravalomanana was ousted and Rajoelina seized control in a coup.

Free media can also promote polarization in society. Consider the divisive effects of the contentious relationship between Nicaraguan President Daniel Ortega and the opposition press owned by the family of former President Violeta Barrios de Chamorro (for more on this, see the profile on Nicaragua in Chapter 4). Since Ortega returned to power in 2006, Nicaraguan society and the media have been divided into two camps—those who support Ortega and those who do not (led by the newspapers owned by the Chamorro family). It is unclear whether this polarization is driven by the media or the media are merely reflecting the societal division, but at the very least the media are serving to reinforce the divide.

Clearly, media freedom is not a panacea. Case studies and empirical analyses have identified mechanisms related to a free media environment that enable and encourage government accountability and leadership responsiveness to the needs and desires of the public. Enabling or even encouraging those things, however, does not always lead to the liberal ideals of tolerance, inclusiveness, justice, and human rights. The fact that media freedom does not guarantee the realization of these ideals highlights why it is so important to make the effort to separate the

Nicaragua's president and presidential candidate for the ruling Sandinista National Liberation Front, FSLN, Daniel Ortega, raises his election ink-stained thumb after casting his ballot in the general elections in Managua, Nicaragua, Sunday, November 6, 2011. First elected in 1984, Ortega regained power in 2006 and is expected to seek reelection in 2016, a move his critics say could be a prelude to a presidency for life.

Source: © Esteban Felix/ /AP/Corbis

pragmatics and measurement of media freedom from the idealism and undefined understandings of media freedom that are part of so many debates, studies, and analyses.

Challenges to Media Freedom

Similarly, clarifying definitions, measurement, and building this historical foundation should help better identify challenges to creating or sustaining a free media environment. Implicit in an ideal-driven analysis is a normatively negative predisposition in the discussion of threats or challenges to media freedom. However, it is unlikely that all threats to media freedom arise from something that has a normative dimension. Aside from political actions made by leaders and their challengers, there are other factors that can endanger the ability of news media to function independently. These include geography, population, conflict, poverty, and commercialization.

The Himalayan kingdom of Bhutan, isolated geographically as well as politically from the rest of the world for centuries, offered its citizens very limited news and information. Until the 1970s, when the government began offering short-wave radio broadcasts, the only news outlet was a government-produced newsletter. For years the government prevented citizens from accessing foreign broadcasts with a royal decree banning antennas. Although recent reforms have allowed some modernization,

including the emergence of independent media, it is difficult for news outlets to survive without government support.

Some countries simply do not have enough citizens to support independent news media. The limited availability of news outlets in Tuvalu, made up of nine atolls in the South Pacific with a population of about 10,700, is due to the lack of a market for commercial media rather than government policy. Efforts to corporatize the country's only radio station failed, and it is currently run as part of a government department. Although Micronesia's population of about 106,000 is substantially greater than that of Tuvalu, it is difficult for news outlets to reach all citizens in this collection of hundreds of islands and atolls scattered over one million square miles in the Central Pacific. While Micronesian media are free, they are limited. In these scenarios, access to online media, especially social media, could potentially provide news outlets and citizens with affordable avenues for sharing news and information.

Domestic conflict—from peaceful demonstrations to mass uprisings, from general strikes to armed resistance and coups—is almost always associated with restrictions on news media. Often the media are the first casualty in the struggle between government and opposition. This has certainly been the case in Fiji where the media environment has vacillated from being one of the freest in the South Pacific to being one of the more restricted in the region, because the country has experienced several coups largely due to the power struggle between indigenous Fijians and those descended of Indian immigrants. For the first decade and a half after independence, Fijian media were functionally free until 1987, when Colonel Sitweni Rabuka staged two coups aimed at returning the control of the country to indigenous Fijians. Both the country's daily newspapers were closed down for a week after the first coup, and following the second coup, the military took over all radio programming and exercised "oversight" of newspapers. These restrictions were lifted in 1989 as the political situation stabilized. Yet in 2000, journalists were again caught in the power struggle as rebel leader George Speight led an attempted coup. Media were once again functionally free in 2001 and remained so even after

The chief of former Fiji coup leader George Speight's village, Tui Naloto Ratu Sevanaia Tuinaloto (R), and village elder Maika Salababa (L) read about the fate of the town's most infamous son in the rebel stronghold of Naivicula, February 19, 2002. Speight was sentenced to death by hanging for high treason February 18, 2002, for his role in the overthrow of former prime minister Mahendra Chaudhry's government May 19, 2000. Fijian President Ratu Josefa Iloilo later in the day commuted the sentence to life imprisonment.

Source: AFP PHOTO/Torsten BLACKWOOD

the 2006 military coup until 2009, when the President repealed the constitution and imposed martial law. Thus, although countries do not typically shift back and forth between free and not free media environments, when they do, it is often because of conflict and nondemocratic regime transitions.

Poverty poses challenges to media freedom because it influences both the demand for news media and citizens' ability to access news media. The need for news and information is less pressing than the need for food and shelter, so people who lack basic necessities in life are unlikely to take the time to read a newspaper much less worry about who owns that newspaper (Maslow 1943). Similarly, people who cannot afford food are not going to invest in a radio, television, or computer. So they will not have access to most news media. It is telling that in many poorer countries the government will permit private ownership of newspapers but maintain tight control over radio stations, which are more accessible to the poor and illiterate. A case in point is India, which allows private ownership of newspapers, television stations, and some FM radio stations, but maintains government control over AM radio and only allows those stations to carry news.

While the threats of poverty are obvious, there are substantial threats to media freedom in developed countries as well. As evidenced in many studies of the U.S. media, commercialization and professionalization can both be argued to limit media freedom in developed democracies. Commercialization forces news organizations to prioritize news coverage that garners more advertising revenue, which can lead to an emphasis on news that sells—stories about celebrities, scandals, and crime rather than investigative journalism about the effects of government policies and corruption. Professionalization encourages journalists to follow a set of norms, which include ethical guidelines and also inculcate a preference for official sources. Both can be argued to impede or even prevent the criticism of government in the media.

Technology also has the capacity to threaten media freedom. As discussed in Chapter 3, throughout history, while technology has facilitated the flow of information, it has also been used to constrain that flow. This may seem counterintuitive given the potential of newer technologies like the Internet and smartphones to provide affordable and seemingly unlimited access to news and information. Yet the power of technology belongs to those who control it, and governments often have more capacity to control technology than citizens or news organizations. Recent evidence of this can be found in the

Demonstrators shout anti-government slogans as one of them carries a placard with a picture of Turkey's Prime Minister Tayyip Erdogan during a protest against internet censorship in Istanbul May 15, 2011. Thousands of people marched in central Istanbul to protest against the government's plan to filter the internet.

Source: REUTERS/Murad Sezer

Turkish government's imposition of Internet filtering, the Burmese government's shutdown of Internet and mobile phone service during the 2007 Saffron Revolution, and the shutdown of cell phone service by the Bay Area Rapid Transit Authority at stations near a planned Occupy protest in San Francisco, California, in 2011. Beyond the ability of government to control technology, technological developments sometimes threaten lower-tech media. Just as the availability of sound movies led to the demise of silent films, in countries where people can afford it, television has replaced radio as the most popular source of news, and now in many developed countries, new media—especially online news outlets—have decimated the newspaper industry. It remains to be seen, and it is beyond the scope of this book to ascertain, whether these changes wrought by technology will increase or decrease the actual quality of news and information. The concern is that in many developed countries newspaper reporters have led the news media in investigative reporting, and it is not yet clear whether new media will be able to fill this void.[3]

Patterns of Interest

What threatens media freedom and prevents its establishment? What enables its implementation and supports its continuation? Patterns are not explanations, but this project is meant to provide material to help bridge the gap between causal explanations and analyses and broader patterns across the world or over time. In writing the country profiles, we have noticed what appear to be some interesting patterns in the evolution of media freedom. The presence of these patterns offers opportunities to make predictions and helps us begin to identify the causes of media freedom. Of course, there are many exceptions to these patterns, so the list that follows is more of a starting point for future empirical studies than anything definitive, but it is still intriguing.

1. In countries that were colonized—from Sub Saharan Africa to the South Pacific, we often find the following pattern: Upon independence, the news media were imperfectly free, but soon became not free as the leader (often a leader of the independence movement) sought to consolidate his power. Cases where this has happened include Ghana, Mauritius, and Uganda.

2. In one-party states, monarchies and other nondemocracies, if economic problems led to political unrest, the leader often agreed to establish a multiparty system or make other democratic reforms to placate citizens. As part of the process, restrictions on news media were often reduced. Cases where this happened include Gabon in the early 1990s, Nepal in the 1980s and in 2006, and Bolivia in the early 1980s.

3. When a government minimally reduced media restrictions in an effort to create the illusion that media were free, journalists sometimes pushed the boundaries, and this sometimes led to media freedom. Cases where this has happened include Mexico and Burkina Faso.

4. When powerful and repressive dictators were overthrown or died and there was no clear successor, independent media tended to emerge, but critical journalists were vulnerable to attacks from both government and opposition. Cases where this has happened include Uganda after Idi Amin, Paraguay after Alfredo Stroessner, and Egypt after Hosni Mubarak.

5. When a country began to democratize and government permitted some media freedom, there was often a backlash effect as the government retaliated to media criticism of government and government policies by harassing, attacking, or suing journalists and news outlets. Cases where this has happened include Myanmar (Burma) in 2013, Malawi in 1995, and Timor-Leste in 2005.

6. Media freedom tends toward the bimodal. States tend to be clearly on the free side or clearly on the not free side, and instances of partial or near media freedom tend to be transitional or temporary. Mexico, however, provides an interesting exception to this pattern, because it spent decades right on the border between restricted and imperfectly free.

In the end, perhaps in reviewing these historic accounts of the evolution of media freedom and beginning to identify patterns, we can start the process of pinpointing the conditions that promote media freedom as well as the conditions that need to be in place for news media to function in their idealized role of holding government and businesses accountable, preventing corruption, and improving human rights.

Notes

1. We include Taiwan because it functions as an independent state even though it is not officially recognized as an independent state by the international community for political reasons. We do not include the Holy See (Vatican City) because, given its small population (estimated at 839 in 2013) and its location (within Italy), it does not function as an independent media market.

2. According to the Committee to Protect Journalists, Rajoelina's radio station directed mobs to the homes of Ravalomanana supporters, alleging that they had stolen the country's money (Committee to Protect Journalists 2009).

3. For more on this, see Jones (2009).

References and Further Readings

Committee to Protect Journalists. 2009. Attacks on the Press 2009: Madagascar.

Jones, Alex S. 2009. *Losing the News: The Future of the News that Feeds Democracy.* Oxford: Oxford University Press.

Maslow, A. H. 1943. "A Theory of Human Motivation." *Psychological Review* 50:370–96.

Appendix A

Media Freedom Region by Region

Africa

F=Free; IF=Imperfectly Free; NF=Not Free; NM=No Media

Africa 1948–1959

	1948	1949	1950	1951	1952	1953	1954	1955	1956	1957	1958	1959
Ethiopia	NF	NF	NF	NF	NF	NF	NF	NF	NF	NF	NF	NF
Ghana	—	—	—	—	—	—	—	—	—	IF	IF	IF
Guinea	—	—	—	—	—	—	—	—	—	—	NF	NF
Liberia	NF	NF	NF	NF	NF	NF	NF	NF	NF	NF	NF	NF
South Africa	IF	IF	IF	IF	IF	IF	IF	IF	IF	IF	IF	IF
Sudan	—	—	—	—	—	—	—	—	IF	IF	NM	NF

Africa 1960–1969

	1960	1961	1962	1963	1964	1965	1966	1967	1968	1969
Benin	NF	NF	NF	NF	NF	NF	NF	NF	NF	NF
Botswana	—	—	—	—	—	—	F	F	F	F
Burkina Faso	NF	NF	NF	NF	NF	NF	NF	NF	NF	NF
Burundi	—	—	NF	NF	NF	NF	NF	NF	NF	NF
Cameroon	NF	NF	NF	NF	NF	NF	NF	NF	NF	NF
Central African Republic	NF	NF	NF	NF	NF	NF	NF	NF	NF	NF
Chad	NF	NF	NF	NF	NF	NF	NF	NF	NF	NF
Congo, Democratic Republic of the	NF	NF	NF	NF	NF	NF	NF	NF	NF	NF
Congo, Republic of the	NM	NM	NM	NM	NM	NM	NM	NM	NM	NF

	1960	1961	1962	1963	1964	1965	1966	1967	1968	1969
Côte d'Ivoire	NF	NF	NF	NF	NF	NF	NF	NF	NF	NF
Equatorial Guinea	—	—	—	—	—	—	—	—	—	NF
Ethiopia	NF	NF	NF	NF	NF	NF	NF	NF	NF	NF
Gabon	—	NF	NF	NF	NF	NF	NF	NF	NF	NF
Gambia, The	—	—	—	—	—	F	F	F	F	F
Ghana	NF	NF	NF	NF	NF	NF	IF	IF	IF	IF
Guinea	NF	NF	NF	NF	NF	NF	NF	NF	NF	NF
Kenya	—	—	—	NF	NF	NF	NF	NF	NF	NF
Lesotho	—	—	—	—	—	—	NF	NF	NF	NF
Liberia	NF	NF	NF	NF	NF	NF	NF	NF	NF	NF
Madagascar	IF	IF	IF	IF	IF	IF	IF	IF	IF	IF
Malawi	—	—	—	—	NF	NF	NF	NF	NF	NF
Mali	NF	NF	NF	NF	NF	NF	NF	NF	NF	NF
Mauritania	NF	NF	NF	NF	NF	NF	NF	NF	NF	NF
Mauritius	—	—	—	—	—	—	—	—	IF	IF
Niger	—	NF	NF	NF	NF	NF	NF	NF	NF	NF
Nigeria	IF	IF	IF	IF	IF	IF	IF	IF	IF	IF
Rwanda	—	—	NF	NF	NF	NF	NF	NF	NF	NF
Senegal	NF	NF	NF	NF	NF	NF	NF	NF	NF	NF
Sierra Leone	—	IF	IF	IF	IF	IF	IF	NF	NF	NF
Somalia	IF	IF	IF	IF	IF	IF	IF	IF	IF	IF
South Africa	IF	NF	NF	NF	NF	NF	NF	NF	NF	NF
Sudan	NF	NF	NF	NF	NF	IF	IF	IF	IF	IF
Swaziland	—	—	—	—	—	—	—	—	NF	NF
Tanzania	—	NF	NF	NF	NF	NF	NF	NF	NF	NF
Togo	NF	NF	NF	NF	NF	NF	NF	NF	NF	NF
Uganda	—	—	IF	IF	IF	IF	NF	NF	NF	NF
Zambia	—	—	—	—	IF	NF	NF	NF	NF	NF
Zimbabwe	—	—	—	—	—	—	NF	NF	NF	NF

Africa 1970–1979

	1970	1971	1972	1973	1974	1975	1976	1977	1978	1979
Angola	—	—	—	—	—	NF	NF	NF	NF	NF
Benin	NF	NF	NF	NF	NF	NF	NF	NF	NF	NF
Botswana	F	F	F	F	F	F	F	F	F	F
Burkina Faso	NF	NF	NF	NF	NF	NF	NF	NF	IF	IF
Burundi	NF	NF	NF	NF	NF	NF	NF	NF	NF	NF
Cameroon	NF	NF	NF	NF	NF	NF	NF	NF	NF	NF
Cape Verde	—	—	—	—	—	NF	NF	NF	NF	NF
Central African Republic	NF	NF	NF	NF	NF	NF	NF	NF	NF	NF
Chad	NF	NF	NF	NF	NF	NF	NF	NF	NF	NF
Comoros	—	—	—	—	—	NF	NF	NF	NF	NF
Congo, Democratic Republic of the	NF	NF	NF	NF	NF	NF	NF	NF	NF	NF
Congo, Republic of the	NF	NF	NF	NF	NF	NF	NF	NF	NF	NF
Côte d'Ivoire	NF	NF	NF	NF	NF	NF	NF	NF	NF	NF
Djibouti	—	—	—	—	—	—	—	NF	NF	NF
Equatorial Guinea	NF	NF	NF	NF	NF	NF	NF	NF	NF	NF
Ethiopia	NF	NF	NF	NF	NF	NF	NF	NF	NF	NF
Gabon	NF	NF	NF	NF	NF	NF	NF	NF	NF	NF
Gambia, The	F	F	F	F	F	F	F	F	F	F
Ghana	IF	IF	NF	NF	NF	NF	NF	NF	NF	F
Guinea	NF	NF	NF	NF	NF	NF	NF	NF	NF	NF
Guinea-Bissau	—	—	—	—	NF	NF	NF	NF	NF	NF
Kenya	NF	NF	NF	NF	NF	NF	NF	NF	NF	NF
Lesotho	NF	NF	NF	NF	NF	NF	NF	NF	NF	NF
Liberia	NF	NF	IF	IF	IF	IF	IF	IF	IF	IF
Madagascar	IF	IF	IF	NF	NF	NF	NF	NF	NF	NF
Malawi	NF	NF	NF	NF	NF	NF	NF	NF	NF	NF
Mali	NF	NF	NF	NF	NF	NF	NF	NF	NF	NF
Mauritania	NF	NF	NF	NF	NF	NF	NF	NF	NF	NF
Mauritius	NF	NF	NF	NF	NF	NF	IF	IF	IF	IF
Mozambique	—	—	—	—	—	NF	NF	NF	NF	NF

	1970	1971	1972	1973	1974	1975	1976	1977	1978	1979
Niger	NF	NF	NF	NF	NF	NF	NF	NF	NF	NF
Nigeria	IF	IF	IF	IF	IF	IF	IF	IF	IF	NF
Rwanda	NF	NF	NF	NF	NF	NF	NF	NF	NF	NF
Senegal	NF	NF	NF	NF	NF	NF	NF	NF	NF	NF
Seychelles	—	—	—	—	—	—	NF	NF	NF	NF
Sierra Leone	NF	NF	NF	NF	NF	NF	NF	NF	NF	NF
Sao Tomé and Principe	—	—	—	—	—	NF	NF	NF	NF	NF
Somalia	NF	NF	NF	NF	NF	NF	NF	NF	NF	NF
South Africa	NF	NF	NF	NF	NF	NF	NF	NF	NF	NF
Sudan	IF	IF	NF	NF	NF	NF	NF	NF	NF	NF
Swaziland	NF	NF	NF	NF	NF	NF	NF	NF	NF	NF
Tanzania	NF	NF	NF	NF	NF	NF	NF	NF	NF	NF
Togo	NF	NF	NF	NF	NF	NF	NF	NF	NF	NF
Uganda	NF	NF	NF	NF	NF	NF	NF	NF	NF	IF
Zambia	NF	NF	NF	NF	NF	NF	NF	NF	NF	NF
Zimbabwe	NF	NF	NF	NF	NF	NF	NF	NF	NF	NF

Africa 1980–1989

	1980	1981	1982	1983	1984	1985	1986	1987	1988	1989
Angola	NF	NF	NF	NF	NF	NF	NF	NF	NF	NF
Benin	NF	NF	NF	NF	NF	NF	NF	NF	NF	NF
Botswana	F	F	F	F	F	F	F	F	F	F
Burkina Faso	IF	IF	NF	NF	NF	NF	NF	NF	NF	NF
Burundi	NF	NF	NF	NF	NF	NF	NF	NF	NF	NF
Cameroon	NF	NF	NF	NF	NF	NF	NF	NF	NF	NF
Cape Verde	NF	NF	NF	NF	NF	NF	NF	NF	NF	NF
Central African Republic	NF	NF	NF	NF	NF	NF	NF	NF	NF	NF
Chad	NF	NF	NF	NF	NF	NF	NF	NF	NF	NF
Comoros	NF	NF	NF	NF	NF	NF	NF	NF	NF	NF

	1980	1981	1982	1983	1984	1985	1986	1987	1988	1989
Congo, Democratic Republic of the	NF	NF	NF	NF	NF	NF	NF	NF	NF	NF
Congo, Republic of the	NF	NF	NF	NF	NF	NF	NF	NF	NF	NF
Côte d'Ivoire	NF	NF	NF	NF	NF	NF	NF	NF	NF	NF
Djibouti	NF	NF	NF	NF	NF	NF	NF	NF	NF	NF
Equatorial Guinea	NF	NF	NF	NF	NF	NF	NF	NF	NF	NF
Ethiopia	NF	NF	NF	NF	NF	NF	NF	NF	NF	NF
Gabon	NF	NF	NF	NF	NF	NF	NF	NF	NF	NF
Gambia, The	F	F	F	F	F	F	F	F	F	F
Ghana	F	F	NF	NF	NF	NF	NF	NF	NF	NF
Guinea	NF	NF	NF	NF	NF	NF	NF	NF	NF	NF
Guinea-Bissau	NF	NF	NF	NF	NF	NF	NF	NF	NF	NF
Kenya	NF	NF	NF	NF	NF	NF	NF	NF	NF	NF
Lesotho	NF	NF	NF	NF	NF	NF	NF	NF	NF	NF
Liberia	IF	IF	NF	NF	NF	NF	NF	NF	NF	NF
Madagascar	NF	NF	NF	NF	NF	NF	NF	NF	NF	NF
Malawi	NF	NF	NF	NF	NF	NF	NF	NF	NF	NF
Mali	NF	NF	NF	NF	NF	NF	NF	NF	NF	NF
Mauritania	NF	NF	NF	NF	NF	NF	NF	NF	NF	NF
Mauritius	IF	IF	IF	IF	IF	IF	IF	IF	IF	IF
Mozambique	NF	NF	NF	NF	NF	NF	NF	NF	NF	NF
Niger	NF	NF	NF	NF	NF	NF	NF	NF	NF	NF
Nigeria	NF	NF	NF	NF	NF	NF	NF	NF	NF	NF
Rwanda	NF	NF	NF	NF	NF	NF	NF	NF	NF	NF
Senegal	NF	IF	IF	IF	IF	IF	IF	IF	IF	IF
Seychelles	NF	NF	NF	NF	NF	NF	NF	NF	NF	NF
Sierra Leone	NF	NF	NF	NF	NF	NF	NF	NF	NF	NF
Sao Tomé and Principe	NF	NF	NF	NF	NF	NF	NF	NF	NF	NF
Somalia	NF	NF	NF	NF	NF	NF	NF	NF	NF	NF
South Africa	NF	NF	NF	NF	NF	NF	NF	NF	NF	NF
Sudan	NF	NF	NF	NF	NF	IF	IF	IF	IF	NF
Swaziland	NF	NF	NF	NF	NF	NF	NF	NF	NF	NF
Tanzania	NF	NF	NF	NF	NF	NF	NF	NF	NF	NF

	1980	1981	1982	1983	1984	1985	1986	1987	1988	1989
Togo	NF	NF	NF	NF	NF	NF	NF	NF	NF	NF
Uganda	IF	IF	IF	IF	IF	IF	IF	IF	IF	IF
Zambia	NF	NF	NF	NF	NF	NF	NF	NF	NF	NF
Zimbabwe	NF	NF	NF	NF	NF	NF	NF	NF	NF	NF

Africa 1990–2000

	1990	1991	1992	1993	1994	1995	1996	1997	1998	1999	2000
Angola	NF	NF	NF	NF	NF	NF	NF	NF	NF	NF	NF
Benin	NF	NF	NF	NF	NF	IF	IF	IF	IF	IF	IF
Botswana	F	F	F	IF	IF	IF	IF	IF	IF	IF	IF
Burkina Faso	NF	IF	IF	IF	IF	IF	IF	IF	IF	IF	IF
Burundi	NF	NF	NF	NF	NF	NF	NF	NF	NF	NF	NF
Cameroon	NF	NF	NF	NF	NF	NF	NF	NF	NF	NF	NF
Cape Verde	NF	IF	IF	IF	IF	IF	IF	IF	IF	IF	IF
Central African Republic	NF	NF	NF	IF	IF	IF	NF	NF	NF	NF	NF
Chad	IF	IF	IF	IF	IF	IF	IF	IF	NF	NF	NF
Comoros	NF	NF	NF	IF	IF	IF	IF	IF	IF	IF	IF
Congo, Democratic Republic of the	NF	NF	NF	NF	NF	NF	NF	NF	NF	NF	NF
Congo, Republic of the	NF	NF	NF	NF	IF	IF	IF	NF	NF	NF	NF
Côte d'Ivoire	NF	NF	NF	NF	NF	NF	NF	NF	NF	NF	NF
Djibouti	NF	NF	NF	NF	NF	IF	IF	IF	IF	NF	NF
Equatorial Guinea	NF	NF	NF	NF	NF	NF	NF	NF	NF	NF	NF
Eritrea	—	—	—	NF	NF	NF	NF	NF	NF	NF	NF
Ethiopia	NF	NF	NF	NF	NF	NF	NF	NF	NF	NF	NF
Gabon	NF	IF	IF	IF	IF	IF	IF	IF	NF	NF	NF
Gambia, The	F	F	F	F	F	NF	NF	NF	NF	NF	NF
Ghana	NF	NF	NF	IF	IF	IF	IF	IF	IF	IF	IF
Guinea	NF	NF	NF	NF	NF	NF	NF	NF	NF	NF	NF
Guinea-Bissau	NF	IF	IF	IF	IF	NF	NF	NF	NF	NF	NF

	1990	1991	1992	1993	1994	1995	1996	1997	1998	1999	2000
Kenya	NF	NF	NF	NF	IF	IF	IF	NF	NF	NF	NF
Lesotho	NF	NF	NF	IF	IF	IF	IF	IF	NF	IF	IF
Liberia	NF	NF	NF	NF	NF	NF	NF	NF	NF	NF	NF
Madagascar	IF	IF	IF	IF	IF	IF	IF	IF	IF	IF	IF
Malawi	NF	NF	NF	NF	NF	IF	NF	NF	NF	NF	NF
Mali	NF	NF	IF	IF	IF	F	F	F	F	F	F
Mauritania	NF	NF	NF	NF	NF	NF	NF	NF	NF	NF	NF
Mauritius	IF	IF	IF	IF	IF	IF	IF	IF	IF	IF	F
Mozambique	NF	NF	IF	IF	IF	IF	NF	NF	NF	IF	IF
Namibia	IF	IF	IF	IF	IF	IF	IF	IF	IF	IF	IF
Niger	IF	IF	IF	IF	IF	IF	IF	NF	NF	NF	NF
Nigeria	NF	NF	NF	NF	NF	NF	NF	NF	NF	NF	NF
Rwanda	NF	NF	NF	NF	NF	NF	NF	NF	NF	NF	NF
Senegal	IF	IF	IF	IF	IF	IF	IF	IF	IF	IF	IF
Seychelles	NF	NF	IF	IF	IF	IF	IF	IF	IF	IF	IF
Sierra Leone	NF	NF	NF	NF	NF	NF	NF	NF	NF	NF	NF
Sao Tomé and Principe	NF	IF	IF	IF	IF	IF	IF	IF	IF	IF	IF
Somalia	NF	NF	NF	NF	NF	NF	NF	NF	NF	NF	NF
South Africa	NF	NF	NF	NF	IF	IF	IF	IF	IF	IF	IF
Sudan	NF	NF	NF	NF	NF	NF	NF	NF	NF	NF	NF
Swaziland	NF	NF	NF	NF	NF	NF	NF	NF	NF	NF	NF
Tanzania	NF	NF	IF	IF	IF	IF	IF	IF	IF	IF	IF
Togo	NF	NF	NF	NF	NF	NF	NF	NF	NF	NF	NF
Uganda	IF	IF	IF	IF	IF	IF	IF	IF	IF	IF	IF
Zambia	NF	NF	IF	IF	IF	IF	IF	NF	NF	NF	NF
Zimbabwe	NF	NF	NF	NF	NF	NF	NF	NF	NF	NF	NF

Africa 2001–2012

	2001	2002	2003	2004	2005	2006	2007	2008	2009	2010	2011	2012
Angola	NF	NF	NF	NF	NF	NF	NF	NF	NF	NF	NF	NF
Benin	IF	F	F	F	F	F	IF	IF	IF	IF	IF	IF
Botswana	F	F	F	F	IF	IF	IF	IF	IF	IF	IF	IF
Burkina Faso	IF	IF	IF	IF	IF	IF	IF	IF	IF	IF	IF	IF
Burundi	NF	NF	NF	NF	NF	NF	NF	NF	NF	NF	NF	NF
Cameroon	NF	NF	NF	NF	NF	NF	NF	NF	NF	NF	NF	NF
Cape Verde	IF	IF	IF	IF	IF	F	F	F	F	F	F	F
Central African Republic	NF	NF	NF	NF	NF	IF	NF	NF	NF	NF	NF	NF
Chad	NF	NF	NF	NF	NF	NF	NF	NF	NF	NF	NF	NF
Comoros	IF	IF	IF	IF	IF	IF	IF	IF	IF	IF	IF	IF
Congo, Democratic Republic of the	NF	NF	NF	NF	NF	NF	NF	NF	NF	NF	NF	NF
Congo, Republic of the	IF	IF	IF	IF	IF	IF	IF	IF	IF	IF	IF	IF
Côte d'Ivoire	NF	NF	NF	NF	NF	NF	NF	NF	NF	NF	NF	NF
Djibouti	NF	NF	NF	NF	NF	NF	NF	NF	NF	NF	NF	NF
Equatorial Guinea	NF	NF	NF	NF	NF	NF	NF	NF	NF	NF	NF	NF
Eritrea	NF	NF	NF	NF	NF	NF	NF	NF	NF	NF	NF	NF
Ethiopia	NF	NF	NF	NF	NF	NF	NF	NF	NF	NF	NF	NF
Gabon	NF	NF	NF	NF	NF	NF	NF	NF	NF	NF	NF	NF
Gambia, The	NF	NF	NF	NF	NF	NF	NF	NF	NF	NF	NF	NF
Ghana	F	F	F	F	F	F	F	F	F	F	F	F
Guinea	NF	NF	NF	NF	NF	NF	NF	NF	NF	IF	NF	NF
Guinea-Bissau	NF	NF	NF	IF	IF	IF	IF	IF	IF	IF	IF	NF
Kenya	NF	NF	NF	NF	IF	IF	IF	IF	IF	IF	IF	IF
Lesotho	IF	IF	IF	IF	IF	IF	IF	IF	IF	IF	IF	IF
Liberia	NF	NF	NF	NF	NF	NF	NF	NF	NF	IF	IF	IF
Madagascar	IF	IF	IF	IF	IF	IF	IF	IF	NF	NF	NF	NF
Malawi	NF	NF	IF	IF	IF	IF	IF	IF	IF	IF	IF	IF
Mali	F	F	F	F	F	F	F	F	F	F	F	IF
Mauritania	NF	NF	NF	NF	NF	IF	IF	IF	IF	IF	IF	IF

	2001	2002	2003	2004	2005	2006	2007	2008	2009	2010	2011	2012
Mauritius	F	F	F	F	F	F	F	F	F	F	F	F
Mozambique	IF	IF	IF	IF	IF	IF	IF	IF	IF	IF	IF	IF
Namibia	IF	IF	IF	F	F	F	F	F	IF	IF	IF	IF
Niger	IF	IF	IF	IF	IF	IF	NF	NF	NF	IF	IF	IF
Nigeria	NF	IF	IF	IF	IF	IF	IF	IF	IF	IF	IF	IF
Rwanda	NF	NF	NF	NF	NF	NF	NF	NF	NF	NF	NF	NF
Sao Tomé and Principe	IF	IF	IF	IF	IF	IF	IF	IF	IF	IF	IF	IF
Senegal	IF	IF	IF	IF	IF	IF	IF	IF	IF	IF	IF	IF
Seychelles	IF	IF	IF	IF	IF	IF	IF	IF	IF	IF	IF	IF
Sierra Leone	NF	NF	IF	IF	IF	IF	IF	IF	IF	IF	IF	IF
Somalia	NF	NF	NF	NF	NF	NF	NF	NF	NF	NF	NF	NF
South Africa	IF	F	F	F	F	F	F	F	IF	IF	IF	IF
South Sudan	—	—	—	—	—	—	—	—	—	—	IF	IF
Sudan	NF	NF	NF	NF	NF	NF	NF	NF	NF	NF	NF	NF
Swaziland	NF	NF	NF	NF	NF	NF	NF	NF	NF	NF	NF	NF
Tanzania	IF	IF	IF	IF	IF	IF	IF	IF	IF	IF	IF	IF
Togo	NF	NF	NF	NF	NF	NF	NF	NF	NF	NF	NF	NF
Uganda	IF	IF	IF	IF	IF	IF	IF	IF	IF	IF	IF	IF
Zambia	NF	NF	NF	NF	NF	NF	NF	NF	NF	NF	IF	IF
Zimbabwe	NF	NF	NF	NF	NF	NF	NF	NF	NF	NF	NF	NF

Americas

F=Free; IF=Imperfectly Free; NF=Not Free; NM=No Media

Americas 1948–1959

	1948	1949	1950	1951	1952	1953	1954	1955	1956	1957	1958	1959
Argentina	NF	NF	NF	NF	NF	NF	NF	NF	F	F	F	F
Bolivia	NF	NF	NF	NF	NF	NF	NF	NF	NF	NF	NF	NF
Brazil	F	F	F	F	F	F	F	F	F	F	F	F
Canada	F	F	F	F	F	F	F	F	F	F	F	F
Chile	F	F	F	F	F	F	F	F	F	F	F	F

	1948	1949	1950	1951	1952	1953	1954	1955	1956	1957	1958	1959
Colombia	NF	NF	NF	NF	NF	NF	NF	NF	NF	NF	IF	IF
Costa Rica	F	F	F	F	F	F	F	F	F	F	F	F
Cuba	IF	IF	IF	IF	NF	NF	IF	IF	IF	NF	NF	NF
Dominican Republic	NF	NF	NF	NF	NF	NF	NF	NF	NF	NF	NF	NF
Ecuador	NF	NF	NF	NF	NF	NF	NF	NF	NF	F	F	F
El Salvador	NF	NF	IF	IF	IF	IF	IF	IF	IF	IF	IF	IF
Guatemala	IF	IF	IF	IF	IF	IF	IF	NF	NF	NF	NF	NF
Haiti	NF	NF	NF	NF	NF	NF	NF	NF	NF	NF	NF	NF
Honduras	NF	NF	IF	IF	IF	IF	IF	IF	IF	IF	IF	IF
Mexico	IF	IF	IF	IF	IF	IF	IF	IF	IF	IF	IF	IF
Nicaragua	NF	NF	NF	NF	NF	NF	NF	NF	NF	NF	NF	NF
Panama	IF	IF	IF	IF	IF	IF	IF	IF	IF	IF	IF	IF
Paraguay	NF	NF	NF	NF	NF	NF	NF	NF	NF	NF	NF	NF
Peru	NF	NF	NF	NF	NF	NF	NF	NF	NF	IF	IF	IF
United States	F	F	F	F	F	F	F	F	F	F	F	F
Uruguay	F	F	F	F	F	F	F	F	F	F	F	F
Venezuela	IF	NF	NF	NF	NF	NF	NF	NF	NF	NF	IF	IF

Americas 1960–1969

	1960	1961	1962	1963	1964	1965	1966	1967	1968	1969
Argentina	IF	IF	IF	IF	IF	IF	IF	IF	IF	NF
Barbados	—	—	—	—	—	—	—	F	F	F
Bolivia	NF	NF	NF	NF	NF	NF	NF	NF	NF	NF
Brazil	F	F	IF	IF	IF	IF	IF	IF	IF	NF
Canada	F	F	F	F	F	F	F	F	F	F
Chile	F	F	F	F	F	F	F	F	F	F
Colombia	IF	IF	IF	IF	IF	IF	IF	IF	IF	IF
Costa Rica	F	F	F	F	F	F	F	F	F	F
Cuba	NF	NF	NF	NF	NF	NF	NF	NF	NF	NF
Dominican Republic	NF	IF	IF	IF	IF	IF	IF	IF	IF	IF

	1960	1961	1962	1963	1964	1965	1966	1967	1968	1969
Ecuador	F	F	F	F	F	F	F	F	F	F
El Salvador	IF	IF	IF	IF	IF	IF	IF	IF	IF	IF
Guatemala	NF	NF	NF	NF	NF	NF	NF	NF	NF	NF
Guyana	—	—	—	—	—	—	—	NF	NF	NF
Haiti	NF	NF	NF	NF	NF	NF	NF	NF	NF	NF
Honduras	IF	IF	IF	NF	NF	NF	NF	IF	IF	IF
Jamaica	—	—	F	F	F	F	F	F	F	F
Mexico	IF	IF	IF	IF	IF	IF	IF	IF	IF	IF
Nicaragua	NF	NF	NF	NF	NF	NF	NF	NF	NF	NF
Panama	IF	IF	IF	IF	IF	IF	IF	IF	IF	NF
Paraguay	NF	NF	NF	NF	NF	NF	NF	NF	NF	NF
Peru	IF	IF	IF	IF	IF	IF	IF	IF	IF	NF
Trinidad and Tobago	—	—	F	F	F	F	F	F	F	F
United States	F	F	F	F	F	F	F	F	F	F
Uruguay	F	F	F	F	F	F	F	F	IF	IF
Venezuela	IF	IF	IF	IF	IF	IF	IF	IF	IF	IF

Americas 1970–1979

	1970	1971	1972	1973	1974	1975	1976	1977	1978	1979
Argentina	IF	IF	IF	IF	NF	NF	NF	NF	NF	NF
Bahamas	—	—	—	F	F	F	F	F	F	F
Barbados	F	F	F	F	F	F	F	F	F	F
Bolivia	NF	NF	NF	NF	NF	NF	NF	NF	NF	NF
Brazil	NF	NF	NF	NF	NF	NF	NF	NF	IF	IF
Canada	F	F	F	F	F	F	F	F	F	F
Chile	F	F	F	NF	NF	NF	NF	NF	NF	NF
Colombia	IF	IF	IF	IF	IF	IF	IF	IF	IF	IF
Costa Rica	F	F	F	F	F	F	F	F	F	F
Cuba	NF	NF	NF	NF	NF	NF	NF	NF	NF	NF
Dominica	—	—	—	—	—	—	—	—	—	F
Dominican Republic	IF	IF	IF	IF	IF	IF	IF	IF	F	F

	1970	1971	1972	1973	1974	1975	1976	1977	1978	1979
Ecuador	F	F	IF	IF	IF	IF	IF	IF	IF	IF
El Salvador	IF	IF	IF	IF	IF	IF	IF	IF	NF	NF
Grenada	—	—	—	—	NF	NF	NF	NF	NF	NF
Guatemala	NF	NF	NF	NF	NF	NF	NF	NF	NF	NF
Guyana	NF	NF	NF	NF	NF	NF	NF	NF	NF	NF
Haiti	NF	NF	NF	NF	NF	NF	NF	NF	NF	NF
Honduras	IF	IF	IF	NF	NF	NF	NF	NF	NF	NF
Jamaica	F	F	F	F	F	F	F	F	F	F
Mexico	IF	IF	IF	IF	IF	IF	IF	IF	IF	IF
Nicaragua	NF	NF	NF	NF	NF	NF	NF	NF	NF	NF
Panama	NF	NF	NF	NF	NF	NF	NF	NF	NF	NF
Paraguay	NF	NF	NF	NF	NF	NF	NF	NF	NF	NF
Peru	NF	NF	NF	NF	NF	NF	NF	NF	NF	NF
St. Lucia	—	—	—	—	—	—	—	—	—	F
Suriname	—	—	—	—	—	IF	IF	IF	IF	IF
Trinidad and Tobago	F	F	F	F	F	F	F	F	F	F
United States	F	F	F	F	F	F	F	F	F	F
Uruguay	IF	IF	IF	NF	NF	NF	NF	NF	NF	NF
Venezuela	IF	IF	IF	IF	IF	IF	IF	IF	IF	IF

Americas 1980–1989

	1980	1981	1982	1983	1984	1985	1986	1987	1988	1989
Antigua and Barbuda	—	—	IF	IF	IF	IF	IF	IF	IF	IF
Argentina	NF	NF	NF	NF	IF	IF	IF	IF	IF	IF
Bahamas	F	F	F	F	F	F	F	F	F	F
Barbados	F	F	F	F	F	F	F	F	F	F
Belize	—	IF	IF	IF	IF	IF	IF	IF	F	F
Bolivia	NF	NF	IF	IF	IF	IF	IF	IF	IF	IF
Brazil	IF	IF	IF	IF	IF	IF	IF	IF	IF	IF
Canada	F	F	F	F	F	F	F	F	F	F
Chile	NF	NF	NF	NF	NF	NF	NF	NF	NF	NF

	1980	1981	1982	1983	1984	1985	1986	1987	1988	1989
Colombia	IF	IF	IF	IF	IF	IF	IF	IF	IF	IF
Costa Rica	F	F	F	F	F	F	F	F	F	F
Cuba	NF	NF	NF	NF	NF	NF	NF	NF	NF	NF
Dominica	F	F	F	F	F	F	F	F	F	F
Dominican Republic	F	F	F	F	F	F	F	F	F	F
Ecuador	IF	IF	IF	IF	IF	IF	IF	IF	F	F
El Salvador	NF	NF	NF	NF	NF	NF	NF	NF	NF	NF
Grenada	NF	NF	NF	NF	NF	IF	IF	IF	IF	IF
Guatemala	NF	NF	NF	NF	NF	NF	NF	NF	NF	NF
Guyana	NF	NF	NF	NF	NF	NF	NF	NF	NF	NF
Haiti	NF	NF	NF	NF	NF	NF	NF	NF	NF	NF
Honduras	NF	NF	NF	NF	NF	NF	NF	NF	NF	NF
Jamaica	F	F	F	F	F	F	F	F	F	F
Mexico	IF	IF	IF	IF	IF	IF	IF	IF	IF	IF
Nicaragua	IF	IF	NF	NF	NF	NF	NF	NF	NF	NF
Panama	NF	NF	NF	NF	NF	NF	NF	NF	NF	NF
Paraguay	NF	NF	NF	NF	NF	NF	NF	NF	NF	NF
Peru	NF	IF	IF	IF	IF	IF	IF	IF	IF	IF
St. Kitts and Nevis	—	—	—	F	F	F	F	F	F	F
St. Lucia	F	F	F	F	F	F	F	F	F	F
St. Vincent and the Grenadines	F	F	F	F	F	F	F	F	F	F
Suriname	NF	NF	NF	NF	NF	NF	NF	NF	NF	IF
Trinidad and Tobago	F	F	F	F	F	F	F	F	F	F
United States	F	F	F	F	F	F	F	F	F	F
Uruguay	NF	NF	NF	NF	IF	F	F	F	F	F
Venezuela	IF	IF	IF	IF	IF	IF	IF	IF	IF	IF

Americas 1990–2000

	1990	1991	1992	1993	1994	1995	1996	1997	1998	1999	2000
Antigua and Barbuda	IF	IF	IF	IF	IF	IF	IF	IF	IF	IF	IF
Argentina	IF	IF	IF	IF	IF	IF	IF	IF	IF	IF	IF
Bahamas	F	F	F	F	F	F	F	F	F	F	F
Barbados	F	F	F	F	F	F	F	F	F	F	F
Belize	F	F	F	F	F	F	F	F	F	F	F
Bolivia	IF	IF	IF	IF	IF	IF	IF	IF	IF	IF	IF
Brazil	IF	IF	IF	IF	IF	IF	IF	IF	IF	IF	IF
Canada	F	F	F	F	F	F	F	F	F	F	F
Chile	IF	IF	IF	IF	IF	IF	IF	IF	IF	IF	IF
Colombia	IF	IF	IF	IF	IF	IF	IF	IF	IF	IF	NF
Costa Rica	F	F	F	F	F	F	F	F	F	F	F
Cuba	NF	NF	NF	NF	NF	NF	NF	NF	NF	NF	NF
Dominica	F	F	F	F	F	F	F	F	F	F	F
Dominican Republic	F	F	F	F	IF	IF	IF	F	F	F	F
Ecuador	F	F	F	F	F	F	F	F	F	F	F
El Salvador	NF	NF	NF	IF	IF	IF	IF	IF	IF	IF	IF
Grenada	IF	IF	IF	F	F	F	F	F	F	F	F
Guatemala	NF	NF	NF	NF	NF	NF	NF	NF	NF	IF	IF
Guyana	NF	NF	NF	NF	NF	IF	IF	IF	IF	IF	IF
Haiti	NF	NF	NF	NF	NF	IF	IF	IF	IF	IF	NF
Honduras	NF	NF	NF	NF	IF	IF	IF	IF	IF	IF	IF
Jamaica	F	F	F	F	F	F	IF	F	F	F	IF
Mexico	IF	IF	IF	IF	IF	IF	IF	IF	IF	IF	IF
Nicaragua	IF	IF	IF	IF	IF	IF	IF	IF	IF	IF	IF
Panama	IF	IF	IF	IF	IF	IF	IF	IF	IF	IF	IF
Paraguay	IF	IF	IF	IF	IF	IF	IF	IF	IF	IF	IF
Peru	IF	IF	IF	IF	IF	IF	IF	NF	NF	NF	NF
St. Kitts and Nevis	F	F	F	F	F	F	F	F	F	F	F
St. Lucia	F	F	F	F	F	F	F	F	F	F	F
St. Vincent and the Grenadines	F	F	F	F	F	F	F	F	F	F	F
Suriname	IF	IF	IF	IF	IF	IF	IF	IF	IF	IF	IF

	1990	1991	1992	1993	1994	1995	1996	1997	1998	1999	2000
Trinidad and Tobago	F	F	F	F	F	F	IF	IF	IF	IF	IF
United States	F	F	F	F	F	F	F	F	F	F	F
Uruguay	F	F	F	F	F	F	IF	IF	IF	IF	IF
Venezuela	IF	IF	NF	IF	IF	IF	IF	IF	IF	IF	IF

Americas 2001–2012

	2001	2002	2003	2004	2005	2006	2007	2008	2009	2010	2011	2012
Antigua and Barbuda	IF	IF	IF	IF	IF	IF	IF	IF	IF	IF	IF	IF
Argentina	IF	IF	IF	IF	IF	IF	IF	IF	IF	IF	IF	IF
Bahamas	F	F	F	F	F	F	F	F	F	F	F	F
Barbados	F	F	F	F	F	F	F	F	F	F	F	F
Belize	F	F	F	F	F	F	F	F	F	F	F	F
Bolivia	IF	F	IF	IF	IF	IF	IF	IF	IF	IF	IF	IF
Brazil	IF	IF	IF	IF	IF	IF	IF	IF	IF	IF	IF	IF
Canada	F	F	F	F	F	F	F	F	F	F	F	F
Chile	IF	F	F	F	F	F	F	F	F	F	F	F
Colombia	NF	NF	NF	NF	NF	IF	IF	IF	IF	IF	IF	IF
Costa Rica	F	F	F	F	F	F	F	F	F	F	F	F
Cuba	NF	NF	NF	NF	NF	NF	NF	NF	NF	NF	NF	NF
Dominica	F	F	F	F	F	F	F	F	F	F	F	F
Dominican Republic	F	IF	IF	IF	IF	IF	IF	IF	IF	IF	IF	IF
Ecuador	F	IF	IF	IF	IF	IF	IF	IF	IF	IF	IF	NF
El Salvador	IF	IF	IF	IF	IF	IF	IF	IF	IF	IF	IF	IF
Grenada	F	F	F	F	F	F	F	F	F	F	F	F
Guatemala	IF	IF	NF	IF	IF	IF	IF	IF	IF	IF	IF	IF
Guyana	IF	IF	IF	IF	IF	IF	IF	IF	IF	IF	IF	IF
Haiti	NF	NF	NF	NF	NF	IF	IF	IF	IF	IF	IF	IF
Honduras	IF	IF	IF	IF	IF	IF	IF	IF	NF	NF	NF	NF
Jamaica	IF	F	F	F	F	F	F	F	F	F	F	F
Mexico	IF	IF	IF	IF	IF	IF	IF	IF	IF	NF	NF	NF
Nicaragua	IF	IF	IF	IF	IF	IF	IF	IF	IF	IF	IF	IF

	2001	2002	2003	2004	2005	2006	2007	2008	2009	2010	2011	2012
Panama	IF	IF	IF	IF	IF	IF	IF	IF	IF	IF	IF	IF
Paraguay	IF	IF	IF	IF	IF	IF	IF	IF	IF	IF	IF	NF
Peru	IF	IF	IF	IF	IF	IF	IF	IF	IF	IF	IF	IF
St. Kitts and Nevis	F	F	F	F	F	F	F	F	F	F	F	F
St. Lucia	F	F	F	F	F	F	F	F	F	F	F	F
St. Vincent and the Grenadines	F	F	F	F	F	F	F	F	F	F	F	F
Suriname	IF	F	F	F	F	F	F	F	F	F	F	F
Trinidad and Tobago	IF	F	F	F	F	F	F	F	F	F	F	F
United States	F	F	F	F	F	F	F	F	F	F	F	F
Uruguay	IF	IF	IF	IF	IF	IF	IF	IF	F	F	F	F
Venezuela	IF	NF	NF	NF	NF	NF	NF	NF	NF	NF	NF	NF

East Asia and the Pacific

F=Free; IF=Imperfectly Free; NF=Not Free; NM=No Media

East Asia and the Pacific 1948–1959

	1948	1949	1950	1951	1952	1953	1954	1955	1956	1957	1958	1959
Australia	F	F	F	F	F	F	F	F	F	F	F	F
Cambodia	—	—	—	—	—	NF	NF	NF	NF	NF	NF	NF
China	IF	NF	NF	NF	NF	NF	NF	NF	NF	NF	NF	NF
Indonesia	—	—	NF	NF	NF	NF	NF	NF	NF	NF	NF	NF
Japan	—	—	—	—	F	F	F	F	F	F	F	F
Korea, Democratic People's Republic of (North Korea)	NF	NF	NF	NF	NF	NF	NF	NF	NF	NF	NF	NF
Korea, Republic of (South Korea)	NF	NF	NF	NF	NF	NF	NF	NF	NF	NF	NF	NF
Laos	—	—	—	—	—	—	NF	NF	NF	NF	NF	NF
Malaysia	—	—	—	—	—	—	—	—	—	IF	IF	IF
Mongolia	NF	NF	NF	NF	NF	NF	NF	NF	NF	NF	NF	NF

	1948	1949	1950	1951	1952	1953	1954	1955	1956	1957	1958	1959
Myanmar (Burma)	IF	IF	IF	IF	IF	IF	IF	IF	IF	IF	IF	IF
New Zealand	F	F	F	F	F	F	F	F	F	F	F	F
Philippines	F	F	F	F	F	F	F	F	F	F	F	F
Taiwan	—	NF	NF	NF	NF	NF	NF	NF	NF	NF	NF	NF
Thailand	NF	NF	NF	NF	NF	NF	NF	NF	NF	NF	NF	NF
Vietnam, North	—	—	—	—	—	—	NF	NF	NF	NF	NF	NF
Vietnam, South	—	—	—	—	—	—	—	—	NF	NF	NF	NF

East Asia and the Pacific 1960–1969

	1960	1961	1962	1963	1964	1965	1966	1967	1968	1969
Australia	F	F	F	F	F	F	F	F	F	F
Cambodia	NF	NF	NF	NF	NF	NF	NF	NF	NF	NF
China	NF	NF	NF	NF	NF	NF	NF	NF	NF	NF
Indonesia	NF	NF	NF	NF	NF	NF	NF	NF	NF	NF
Japan	F	F	F	F	F	F	F	F	F	F
Korea, Democratic People's Republic of (North Korea)	NF	NF	NF	NF	NF	NF	NF	NF	NF	NF
Korea, Republic of (South Korea)	NF	NF	NF	NF	NF	NF	NF	NF	NF	NF
Laos	NF	NF	NF	NF	NF	NF	NF	NF	NF	NF
Malaysia	IF	IF	IF	IF	IF	IF	IF	IF	IF	NF
Mongolia	NF	NF	NF	NF	NF	NF	NF	NF	NF	NF
Myanmar (Burma)	IF	IF	NF	NF	NF	NF	NF	NF	NF	NF
Nauru	—	—	—	—	—	—	—	—	F	F
New Zealand	F	F	F	F	F	F	F	F	F	F
Philippines	F	F	F	F	F	F	F	F	F	F
Samoa	—	—	IF	IF	IF	IF	IF	IF	IF	IF
Singapore	—	—	—	—	—	NF	NF	NF	NF	NF
Taiwan	NF	NF	NF	NF	NF	NF	NF	NF	NF	NF
Thailand	NF	NF	NF	NF	NF	NF	NF	NF	NF	NF
Vietnam, North	NF	NF	NF	NF	NF	NF	NF	NF	NF	NF
Vietnam, South	NF	NF	NF	NF	NF	NF	NF	NF	NF	NF

East Asia and the Pacific 1970–1979

	1970	1971	1972	1973	1974	1975	1976	1977	1978	1979
Australia	F	F	F	F	F	F	F	F	F	F
Cambodia	NF	NF	NF	NF	NF	NF	NF	NF	NF	NF
China	NF	NF	NF	NF	NF	NF	NF	NF	NF	NF
Fiji	IF	IF	IF	IF	IF	IF	IF	IF	IF	IF
Indonesia	NF	NF	NF	NF	NF	NF	NF	NF	NF	NF
Japan	F	F	F	F	F	F	F	F	F	F
Kiribati	—	—	—	—	—	—	—	—	—	IF
Korea, Democratic People's Republic of (North Korea)	NF	NF	NF	NF	NF	NF	NF	NF	NF	NF
Korea, Republic of (South Korea)	NF	NF	NF	NF	NF	NF	NF	NF	NF	NF
Laos	NF	NF	NF	NF	NF	NF	NF	NF	NF	NF
Malaysia	NF	NF	NF	NF	NF	NF	NF	NF	NF	NF
Mongolia	NF	NF	NF	NF	NF	NF	NF	NF	NF	NF
Myanmar (Burma)	NF	NF	NF	NF	NF	NF	NF	NF	NF	NF
Nauru	F	F	F	F	F	F	F	F	F	F
New Zealand	F	F	F	F	F	F	F	F	F	F
Papua New Guinea	—	—	—	—	—	F	F	F	F	F
Philippines	IF	NF	NF	NF	NF	NF	NF	NF	NF	NF
Samoa	IF	IF	IF	IF	IF	IF	IF	IF	IF	IF
Singapore	NF	NF	NF	NF	NF	NF	NF	NF	NF	NF
Solomon Islands	—	—	—	—	—	—	—	—	IF	IF
Taiwan	NF	NF	NF	NF	NF	NF	NF	NF	NF	NF
Thailand	NF	NF	NF	NF	NF	NF	NF	NF	NF	NF
Vietnam, North	NF	NF	NF	NF	NF	NF	—	—	—	—
Vietnam, South	NF	NF	NF	NF	NF	NF	—	—	—	—
Vietnam	—	—	—	—	—	—	NF	NF	NF	NF

East Asia and the Pacific 1980–1989

	1980	1981	1982	1983	1984	1985	1986	1987	1988	1989
Australia	F	F	F	F	F	F	F	F	F	F
Brunei	—	—	—	—	NF	NF	NF	NF	NF	NF
Cambodia	NF	NF	NF	NF	NF	NF	NF	NF	NF	NF
China	NF	NF	NF	NF	NF	NF	NF	NF	NF	NF
Fiji	IF	IF	IF	IF	IF	IF	IF	NF	NF	IF
Indonesia	NF	NF	NF	NF	NF	NF	NF	NF	NF	NF
Japan	F	F	F	F	F	F	F	F	F	F
Kiribati	IF	IF	IF	IF	IF	IF	IF	IF	IF	IF
Korea, Democratic People's Republic of (North Korea)	NF	NF	NF	NF	NF	NF	NF	NF	NF	NF
Korea, Republic of (South Korea)	NF	NF	NF	NF	NF	NF	NF	NF	NF	NF
Laos	NF	NF	NF	NF	NF	NF	NF	NF	NF	NF
Malaysia	NF	NF	NF	NF	NF	NF	NF	NF	NF	NF
Marshall Islands	—	—	—	—	—	—	F	F	F	F
Micronesia, Federated States of	—	—	—	—	—	—	F	F	F	F
Mongolia	NF	NF	NF	NF	NF	NF	NF	NF	NF	IF
Myanmar (Burma)	NF	NF	NF	NF	NF	NF	NF	NF	NF	NF
Nauru	F	F	F	F	F	F	F	F	F	F
New Zealand	F	F	F	F	F	F	F	F	F	F
Papua New Guinea	F	F	F	F	F	F	F	F	F	F
Philippines	NF	NF	NF	NF	IF	IF	F	F	F	F
Samoa	IF	IF	IF	IF	IF	IF	IF	IF	IF	IF
Singapore	NF	NF	NF	NF	NF	NF	NF	NF	NF	NF
Solomon Islands	IF	IF	IF	IF	IF	IF	IF	IF	IF	IF
Taiwan	NF	NF	NF	NF	NF	NF	NF	NF	NF	NF
Thailand	NF	NF	NF	NF	NF	NF	NF	NF	NF	NF
Tonga	—	—	—	—	—	—	IF	IF	IF	IF
Vanuatu	IF	IF	IF	IF	IF	IF	IF	IF	NF	NF
Vietnam	NF	NF	NF	NF	NF	NF	NF	NF	NF	NF

East Asia and the Pacific 1990–2000

	1990	1991	1992	1993	1994	1995	1996	1997	1998	1999	2000
Australia	F	F	F	F	F	F	F	F	F	F	F
Brunei	NF	NF	NF	NF	NF	NF	NF	NF	NF	NF	NF
Cambodia	NF	NF	IF	IF	NF	NF	NF	NF	NF	NF	NF
China	NF	NF	NF	NF	NF	NF	NF	NF	NF	NF	NF
Fiji	IF	IF	IF	IF	IF	IF	IF	IF	IF	IF	NF
Indonesia	NF	NF	NF	NF	NF	NF	NF	NF	IF	IF	IF
Japan	F	F	F	F	F	F	F	F	F	F	F
Kiribati	IF	IF	IF	IF	NF	NF	NF	NF	NF	NF	IF
Korea, Democratic People's Republic of (North Korea)	NF	NF	NF	NF	NF	NF	NF	NF	NF	NF	NF
Korea, Republic of (South Korea)	NF	NF	NF	IF	IF	IF	IF	IF	IF	IF	IF
Laos	NF	NF	NF	NF	NF	NF	NF	NF	NF	NF	NF
Malaysia	NF	NF	NF	NF	NF	NF	NF	NF	NF	NF	NF
Marshall Islands	F	F	F	F	F	F	F	F	F	F	F
Micronesia, Federated States of	F	F	F	F	F	F	F	F	F	F	F
Mongolia	IF	IF	IF	IF	IF	IF	IF	IF	IF	IF	IF
Myanmar (Burma)	NF	NF	NF	NF	NF	NF	NF	NF	NF	NF	NF
Nauru	F	F	F	F	F	F	F	F	F	F	F
New Zealand	F	F	F	F	F	F	F	F	F	F	F
Palau	—	—	—	—	IF	IF	IF	IF	IF	IF	IF
Papua New Guinea	F	F	F	F	F	F	F	F	F	F	F
Philippines	F	F	F	F	F	F	F	F	F	IF	IF
Samoa	IF	IF	IF	IF	IF	IF	IF	NF	NF	NF	IF
Singapore	NF	NF	NF	NF	NF	NF	NF	NF	NF	NF	NF
Solomon Islands	IF	IF	IF	IF	IF	IF	IF	IF	IF	IF	IF
Taiwan	NF	IF	IF	IF	IF	IF	IF	IF	IF	F	F
Thailand	NF	NF	NF	NF	NF	NF	NF	NF	IF	IF	IF
Tonga	IF	IF	IF	IF	IF	IF	IF	IF	IF	IF	IF
Tuvalu	—	—	—	—	—	—	—	—	—	—	IF
Vanuatu	NF	NF	IF	IF	IF	IF	IF	IF	IF	IF	IF
Vietnam	NF	NF	NF	NF	NF	NF	NF	NF	NF	NF	NF

East Asia and the Pacific 2001–2012

	2001	2002	2003	2004	2005	2006	2007	2008	2009	2010	2011	2012
Australia	F	F	F	F	F	F	F	F	F	F	F	F
Brunei	NF	NF	NF	NF	NF	NF	NF	NF	NF	NF	NF	NF
Cambodia	NF	NF	NF	NF	NF	IF	IF	NF	NF	NF	NF	NF
China	NF	NF	NF	NF	NF	NF	NF	NF	NF	NF	NF	NF
Fiji	IF	F	F	F	F	IF	IF	IF	NF	NF	NF	NF
Indonesia	IF	IF	IF	IF	IF	IF	IF	IF	IF	IF	IF	IF
Japan	F	F	F	F	F	F	F	F	F	F	F	F
Kiribati	IF	IF	IF	IF	IF	IF	IF	IF	IF	IF	IF	IF
Korea, Democratic People's Republic of (North Korea)	NF	NF	NF	NF	NF	NF	NF	NF	NF	NF	NF	NF
Korea, Republic of (South Korea)	IF	F	F	F	F	F	F	F	F	IF	IF	IF
Laos	NF	NF	NF	NF	NF	NF	NF	NF	NF	NF	NF	NF
Malaysia	NF	NF	NF	NF	NF	NF	NF	NF	NF	NF	NF	NF
Marshall Islands	F	F	F	F	F	F	F	F	F	F	F	F
Micronesia, Federated States of	F	F	F	F	F	F	F	F	F	F	F	F
Mongolia	IF	IF	IF	IF	IF	IF	IF	IF	IF	IF	IF	IF
Myanmar (Burma)	NF	NF	NF	NF	NF	NF	NF	NF	NF	NF	NF	NF
Nauru	F	F	F	F	F	F	F	F	F	F	F	F
New Zealand	F	F	F	F	F	F	F	F	F	F	F	F
Palau	IF	IF	IF	IF	IF	IF	IF	IF	IF	IF	IF	IF
Papua New Guinea	F	F	F	F	F	F	F	F	F	F	F	F
Philippines	IF	F	IF	IF	IF	IF	IF	IF	IF	IF	IF	IF
Samoa	IF	IF	IF	IF	IF	IF	IF	IF	IF	IF	IF	IF
Singapore	NF	NF	NF	NF	NF	NF	NF	NF	NF	NF	NF	NF
Solomon Islands	IF	F	F	F	F	F	F	F	F	F	F	F
Taiwan	F	F	F	F	F	F	F	F	F	F	F	F
Thailand	IF	IF	IF	IF	IF	IF	IF	IF	IF	NF	NF	NF
Timor-Leste	—	F	F	F	IF	IF	IF	IF	IF	IF	IF	IF
Tonga	IF	IF	IF	IF	IF	IF	IF	IF	IF	IF	IF	IF
Tuvalu	IF	IF	IF	IF	IF	IF	IF	IF	IF	IF	IF	IF
Vanuatu	IF	F	F	F	F	F	F	F	F	F	F	F
Vietnam	NF	NF	NF	NF	NF	NF	NF	NF	NF	NF	NF	NF

Europe and Eurasia

F=Free; IF=Imperfectly Free; NF=Not Free; NM=No Media

Europe and Eurasia 1948–1959

	1948	1949	1950	1951	1952	1953	1954	1955	1956	1957	1958	1959
Albania	NF	NF	NF	NF	NF	NF	NF	NF	NF	NF	NF	NF
Austria	F	F	F	F	F	F	F	F	F	F	F	F
Belgium	F	F	F	F	F	F	F	F	F	F	F	F
Bulgaria	NF	NF	NF	NF	NF	NF	NF	NF	NF	NF	NF	NF
Czechoslovakia	NF	NF	NF	NF	NF	NF	NF	NF	NF	NF	NF	NF
Denmark	F	F	F	F	F	F	F	F	F	F	F	F
Finland	IF	IF	IF	IF	IF	IF	IF	IF	IF	IF	IF	IF
France	F	F	F	F	F	F	F	F	F	F	F	F
Germany, East	NF	NF	NF	NF	NF	NF	NF	NF	NF	NF	NF	NF
Germany, West	NM	IF	IF	IF	IF	IF	IF	F	F	F	F	F
Greece	NF	NF	NF	NF	NF	NF	NF	NF	NF	NF	NF	NF
Hungary	NF	NF	NF	NF	NF	NF	NF	NF	NF	NF	NF	NF
Iceland	F	F	F	F	F	F	F	F	F	F	F	F
Ireland	F	F	F	F	F	F	F	F	F	F	F	F
Italy	F	F	F	F	F	F	F	F	F	F	F	F
Luxembourg	F	F	F	F	F	F	F	F	F	F	F	F
Netherlands	F	F	F	F	F	F	F	F	F	F	F	F
Norway	F	F	F	F	F	F	F	F	F	F	F	F
Poland	NF	NF	NF	NF	NF	NF	NF	NF	NF	NF	NF	NF
Portugal	NF	NF	NF	NF	NF	NF	NF	NF	NF	NF	NF	NF
Romania	NF	NF	NF	NF	NF	NF	NF	NF	NF	NF	NF	NF
Russia	NF	NF	NF	NF	NF	NF	NF	NF	NF	NF	NF	NF
Spain	NF	NF	NF	NF	NF	NF	NF	NF	NF	NF	NF	NF
Sweden	F	F	F	F	F	F	F	F	F	F	F	F
Switzerland	F	F	F	F	F	F	F	F	F	F	F	F
Turkey	NF	NF	NF	NF	NF	NF	NF	NF	NF	NF	NF	NF
United Kingdom	F	F	F	F	F	F	F	F	F	F	F	F

Europe and Eurasia 1960–1969

	1960	1961	1962	1963	1964	1965	1966	1967	1968	1969
Albania	NF	NF	NF	NF	NF	NF	NF	NF	NF	NF
Austria	F	F	F	F	F	F	F	F	F	F
Belgium	F	F	F	F	F	F	F	F	F	F
Bulgaria	NF	NF	NF	NF	NF	NF	NF	NF	NF	NF
Cyprus	NF	NF	NF	NF	NF	NF	NF	NF	NF	NF
Czechoslovakia	NF	NF	NF	NF	NF	NF	NF	NF	NF	NF
Denmark	F	F	F	F	F	F	F	F	F	F
Finland	IF	IF	IF	IF	IF	IF	IF	IF	IF	IF
France	F	F	F	F	F	F	F	F	F	F
Germany, East	NF	NF	NF	NF	NF	NF	NF	NF	NF	NF
Germany, West	F	F	F	F	F	F	F	F	F	F
Greece	NF	NF	NF	NF	NF	NF	NF	NF	NF	NF
Hungary	NF	NF	NF	NF	NF	NF	NF	NF	NF	NF
Iceland	F	F	F	F	F	F	F	F	F	F
Ireland	F	F	F	F	F	F	F	F	F	F
Italy	F	F	F	F	F	F	F	F	F	F
Luxembourg	F	F	F	F	F	F	F	F	F	F
Malta	—	—	—	—	—	F	F	F	F	F
Netherlands	F	F	F	F	F	F	F	F	F	F
Norway	F	F	F	F	F	F	F	F	F	F
Poland	NF	NF	NF	NF	NF	NF	NF	NF	NF	NF
Portugal	NF	NF	NF	NF	NF	NF	NF	NF	NF	NF
Romania	NF	NF	NF	NF	NF	NF	NF	NF	NF	NF
Russia	NF	NF	NF	NF	NF	NF	NF	NF	NF	NF
Spain	NF	NF	NF	NF	NF	NF	NF	NF	NF	NF
Sweden	F	F	F	F	F	F	F	F	F	F
Switzerland	F	F	F	F	F	F	F	F	F	F
Turkey	NF	NF	NF	NF	NF	NF	NF	NF	NF	NF
United Kingdom	F	F	F	F	F	F	F	F	F	F

Europe and Eurasia 1970–1979

	1970	1971	1972	1973	1974	1975	1976	1977	1978	1979
Albania	NF	NF	NF	NF	NF	NF	NF	NF	NF	NF
Austria	F	F	F	F	F	F	F	F	F	F
Belgium	F	F	F	F	F	F	F	F	F	F
Bulgaria	NF	NF	NF	NF	NF	NF	NF	NF	NF	NF
Cyprus	NF	NF	NF	NF	NF	NF	IF	F	F	F
Czechoslovakia	NF	NF	NF	NF	NF	NF	NF	NF	NF	NF
Denmark	F	F	F	F	F	F	F	F	F	F
Finland	IF	IF	IF	IF	IF	IF	IF	IF	IF	IF
France	F	F	F	F	F	F	F	F	F	F
Germany, East	NF	NF	NF	NF	NF	NF	NF	NF	NF	NF
Germany, West	F	F	F	F	F	F	F	F	F	F
Greece	NF	NF	NF	NF	NF	NF	NF	NF	NF	NF
Hungary	NF	NF	NF	NF	NF	NF	NF	NF	NF	NF
Iceland	F	F	F	F	F	F	F	F	F	F
Ireland	F	F	F	F	F	F	F	F	F	F
Italy	F	F	F	F	F	F	F	F	F	F
Luxembourg	F	F	F	F	F	F	F	F	F	F
Malta	F	F	F	F	F	F	F	F	F	F
Netherlands	F	F	F	F	F	F	F	F	F	F
Norway	F	F	F	F	F	F	F	F	F	F
Poland	NF	NF	NF	NF	NF	NF	NF	NF	NF	NF
Portugal	NF	NF	NF	NF	NF	NF	NF	NF	NF	NF
Romania	NF	NF	NF	NF	NF	NF	NF	NF	NF	NF
Russia	NF	NF	NF	NF	NF	NF	NF	NF	NF	NF
Spain	NF	NF	NF	NF	NF	NF	NF	NF	NF	IF
Sweden	F	F	F	F	F	F	F	F	F	F
Switzerland	F	F	F	F	F	F	F	F	F	F
Turkey	NF	NF	NF	NF	NF	NF	NF	NF	NF	NF
United Kingdom	F	F	F	F	F	F	F	F	F	F

Europe and Eurasia 1980–1989

	1980	1981	1982	1983	1984	1985	1986	1987	1988	1989
Albania	NF	NF	NF	NF	NF	NF	NF	NF	NF	NF
Austria	F	F	F	F	F	F	F	F	F	F
Belgium	F	F	F	F	F	F	F	F	F	F
Bulgaria	NF	NF	NF	NF	NF	NF	NF	NF	NF	NF
Cyprus	F	F	F	F	F	F	F	F	F	F
Czechoslovakia	NF	NF	NF	NF	NF	NF	NF	NF	NF	NF
Denmark	F	F	F	F	F	F	F	F	F	F
Finland	IF	IF	IF	IF	IF	IF	IF	IF	IF	IF
France	F	F	F	F	F	F	F	F	F	F
Germany, East	NF	NF	NF	NF	NF	NF	NF	NF	NF	NF
Germany, West	F	F	F	F	F	F	F	F	F	F
Greece	NF	NF	NF	NF	NF	NF	NF	NF	NF	NF
Hungary	NF	NF	NF	NF	NF	NF	NF	NF	NF	NF
Iceland	F	F	F	F	F	F	F	F	F	F
Ireland	F	F	F	F	F	F	F	F	F	F
Italy	F	F	F	F	F	F	F	F	F	F
Luxembourg	F	F	F	F	F	F	F	F	F	F
Malta	F	F	F	F	F	F	F	F	F	F
Netherlands	F	F	F	F	F	F	F	F	F	F
Norway	F	F	F	F	F	F	F	F	F	F
Poland	NF	NF	NF	NF	NF	NF	NF	NF	NF	NF
Portugal	NF	NF	NF	NF	NF	NF	NF	NF	NF	NF
Romania	NF	NF	NF	NF	NF	NF	NF	NF	NF	NF
Russia	NF	NF	NF	NF	NF	NF	NF	NF	NF	NF
Spain	F	F	F	F	F	F	F	F	F	F
Sweden	F	F	F	F	F	F	F	F	F	F
Switzerland	F	F	F	F	F	F	F	F	F	F
Turkey	NF	NF	NF	NF	NF	NF	NF	NF	NF	NF
United Kingdom	F	F	F	F	F	F	F	F	F	F

Europe and Eurasia 1990–2000

	1990	1991	1992	1993	1994	1995	1996	1997	1998	1999	2000
Albania	NF	NF	NF	NF	NF	NF	IF	IF	NF	NF	IF
Andorra	—	—	—	F	F	F	F	F	F	F	F
Armenia	—	NF	NF	NF	NF	NF	NF	NF	IF	IF	IF
Austria	F	F	F	F	F	F	F	F	F	F	F
Azerbaijan	—	NF	NF	NF	NF	NF	NF	NF	NF	NF	NF
Belarus	—	NF	NF	NF	NF	NF	NF	NF	NF	NF	NF
Belgium	F	F	F	F	F	F	F	F	F	F	F
Bosnia & Herzegovina	—	—	F	F	F	NF	NF	NF	IF	IF	IF
Bulgaria	NF	NF	NF	NF	NF	IF	IF	IF	IF	IF	IF
Croatia	—	—	—	F	F	NF	NF	NF	NF	NF	IF
Cyprus	F	F	F	F	F	F	F	F	F	F	F
Czechoslovakia	IF	IF	IF	—	—	—	—	—	—	—	—
Czech Republic	—	—	—	—	F	IF	IF	IF	IF	IF	IF
Denmark	F	F	F	F	F	F	F	F	F	F	F
Estonia	—	—	NF	NF	NF	F	F	F	F	F	F
Finland	IF	IF	IF	IF	IF	F	F	F	F	F	F
France	F	F	F	F	F	F	F	F	F	F	F
Georgia	—	NF	NF	NF	NF	IF	IF	IF	IF	IF	IF
Germany, East	NF	—	—	—	—	—	—	—	—	—	—
Germany, West	F	—	—	—	—	—	—	—	—	—	—
Germany (unified)	F	F	F	F	F	F	F	F	F	F	F
Greece	NF	NF	NF	NF	NF	NF	IF	IF	IF	IF	IF
Hungary	NF	NF	NF	NF	NF	IF	IF	IF	IF	IF	IF
Iceland	F	F	F	F	F	F	F	F	F	F	F
Ireland	F	F	F	F	F	F	F	F	F	F	F
Italy	F	F	F	F	F	F	F	F	F	F	F
Latvia	—	—	F	F	F	IF	IF	IF	IF	F	F
Liechtenstein	F	F	F	F	F	F	F	F	F	F	F
Lithuania	—	NF	NF	NF	NF	IF	IF	F	F	F	F
Luxembourg	F	F	F	F	F	F	F	F	F	F	F
Macedonia	—	—	—	—	NF	NF	NF	IF	IF	IF	IF
Malta	F	F	F	F	F	F	F	F	F	F	F
Moldova	—	—	NF	NF	NF	IF	IF	IF	NF	NF	NF
Monaco	—	—	—	IF	IF	IF	IF	IF	IF	IF	IF
Netherlands	F	F	F	F	F	F	F	F	F	F	F
Norway	F	F	F	F	F	F	F	F	F	F	F
Poland	NF	NF	NF	NF	NF	NF	NF	NF	IF	IF	IF
Portugal	NF	NF	NF	NF	NF	F	F	F	F	F	F
Romania	NF	NF	NF	NF	NF	NF	IF	IF	IF	IF	IF
Russia	NF	NF	NF	NF	NF	IF	IF	NF	NF	NF	NF
San Marino	—	—	—	F	F	F	F	F	F	F	F

	1990	1991	1992	1993	1994	1995	1996	1997	1998	1999	2000
Slovakia	—	—	—	NF	NF	NF	NF	NF	NF	NF	IF
Slovenia	—	—	NF	NF	NF	IF	IF	IF	IF	IF	IF
Spain	F	F	F	F	F	F	F	F	F	F	F
Sweden	F	F	F	F	F	F	F	F	F	F	F
Switzerland	F	F	F	F	F	F	F	F	F	F	F
Turkey	NF	NF	NF	NF	NF	NF	NF	NF	NF	NF	NF
Ukraine	—	NF	NF	NF	NF	IF	IF	NF	NF	NF	NF
United Kingdom	F	F	F	F	F	F	F	F	F	F	F

Europe and Eurasia 2001–2012

	2001	2002	2003	2004	2005	2006	2007	2008	2009	2010	2011	2012
Albania	IF	IF	IF	IF	IF	IF	IF	IF	IF	IF	IF	IF
Andorra	F	F	F	F	F	F	F	F	F	F	F	F
Armenia	IF	NF	NF	NF	NF	NF	NF	NF	NF	NF	NF	NF
Austria	F	F	F	F	F	F	F	F	F	F	F	F
Azerbaijan	NF	NF	NF	NF	NF	NF	NF	NF	NF	NF	NF	NF
Belarus	NF	NF	NF	NF	NF	NF	NF	NF	NF	NF	NF	NF
Belgium	F	F	F	F	F	F	F	F	F	F	F	F
Bosnia & Herzegovina	IF	IF	IF	IF	IF	IF	IF	IF	IF	IF	IF	IF
Bulgaria	IF	F	IF	IF	IF	IF	IF	IF	IF	IF	IF	IF
Croatia	IF	IF	IF	IF	IF	IF	IF	IF	IF	IF	IF	IF
Cyprus	F	F	F	F	F	F	F	F	F	F	F	F
Czech Republic	IF	F	F	F	F	F	F	F	F	F	F	F
Denmark	F	F	F	F	F	F	F	F	F	F	F	F
Estonia	F	F	F	F	F	F	F	F	F	F	F	F
Finland	F	F	F	F	F	F	F	F	F	F	F	F
France	F	F	F	F	F	F	F	F	F	F	F	F
Georgia	IF	IF	IF	IF	IF	IF	IF	IF	IF	IF	IF	IF
Germany	F	F	F	F	F	F	F	F	F	F	F	F
Greece	IF	F	F	F	F	F	F	F	F	F	F	IF
Hungary	IF	F	F	F	F	F	F	F	F	F	IF	IF
Iceland	F	F	F	F	F	F	F	F	F	F	F	F
Ireland	F	F	F	F	F	F	F	F	F	F	F	F
Italy	F	F	IF	IF	IF	F	F	IF	IF	IF	IF	IF
Kosovo	—	—	—	—	—	—	—	IF	IF	IF	IF	IF
Latvia	F	F	F	F	F	F	F	F	F	F	F	F
Liechtenstein	F	F	F	F	F	F	F	F	F	F	F	F
Lithuania	F	F	F	F	F	F	F	F	F	F	F	F
Luxembourg	F	F	F	F	F	F	F	F	F	F	F	F
Macedonia	IF	IF	IF	IF	IF	IF	IF	IF	IF	IF	IF	IF

Malta	F	F	F	F	F	F	F	F	F	F	F	F
Moldova	IF	IF	NF	NF	NF	NF	NF	NF	NF	IF	IF	IF
Monaco	IF	IF	IF	IF	IF	IF	IF	IF	IF	IF	IF	IF
Montenegro	—	—	—	—	—	IF	IF	IF	IF	IF	IF	IF
Netherlands	F	F	F	F	F	F	F	F	F	F	F	F
Norway	F	F	F	F	F	F	F	F	F	F	F	F
Poland	IF	F	F	F	F	F	F	F	F	F	F	F
Portugal	F	F	F	F	F	F	F	F	F	F	F	F
Romania	IF	IF	IF	IF	IF	IF	IF	IF	IF	IF	IF	IF
Russia	NF	NF	NF	NF	NF	NF	NF	NF	NF	NF	NF	NF
San Marino	F	F	F	F	F	F	F	F	F	F	F	F
Serbia	—	—	—	—	—	IF	IF	IF	IF	IF	IF	IF
Slovakia	IF	F	F	F	F	F	F	F	F	F	F	F
Slovenia	IF	F	F	F	F	F	F	F	F	F	F	F
Spain	F	F	F	F	F	F	F	F	F	F	F	F
Sweden	F	F	F	F	F	F	F	F	F	F	F	F
Switzerland	F	F	F	F	F	F	F	F	F	F	F	F
Turkey	NF	IF	IF	IF	IF	IF	IF	IF	IF	IF	IF	IF
Ukraine	NF	NF	NF	IF	IF	IF	IF	IF	IF	IF	IF	IF
United Kingdom	F	F	F	F	F	F	F	F	F	F	F	F

Near East

F=Free; IF=Imperfectly Free; NF=Not Free; NM=No Media

Near East 1948–1959

	1948	1949	1950	1951	1952	1953	1954	1955	1956	1957	1958	1959
Egypt	NF	NF	NF	NF	NF	NF	NF	NF	NF	NF	NF	NF
Iran	IF	IF	IF	IF	NF	NF	NF	NF	NF	NF	NF	NF
Iraq	NF	NF	NF	NF	NF	NF	NF	NF	NF	NF	NF	NF
Israel	F	F	F	F	F	F	F	F	F	F	F	F
Jordan	NF	NF	NF	NF	NF	NF	NF	NF	NF	NF	NF	NF
Lebanon	IF	IF	IF	IF	IF	IF	IF	IF	IF	IF	IF	IF
Libya	—	—	—	IF	IF	IF	IF	IF	IF	IF	IF	IF
Morocco	—	—	—	—	—	—	—	—	NF	NF	NF	NF
Oman	NF	NF	NF	NF	NF	NF	NF	NF	NF	NF	NF	NF

	1948	1949	1950	1951	1952	1953	1954	1955	1956	1957	1958	1959
Saudi Arabia	NF	NF	NF	NF	NF	NF	NF	NF	NF	NF	NF	NF
Syria	NF	NF	NF	NF	NF	NF	NF	NF	NF	NF	NF	NF
Tunisia	—	—	—	—	—	—	—	—	NF	NF	NF	NF
Yemen, North	NM	NF	NF	NF	NF	NF	NF	NF	NF	NF	NF	NF

Near East 1960–1969

	1960	1961	1962	1963	1964	1965	1966	1967	1968	1969
Algeria	—	—	NF	NF	NF	NF	NF	NF	NF	NF
Egypt	NF	NF	NF	NF	NF	NF	NF	NF	NF	NF
Iran	NF	NF	NF	NF	NF	NF	NF	NF	NF	NF
Iraq	NF	NF	NF	NF	NF	NF	NF	NF	NF	NF
Israel	F	F	F	F	F	F	F	F	F	F
Jordan	NF	NF	NF	NF	NF	NF	NF	NF	NF	NF
Kuwait	—	NF	NF	NF	NF	NF	NF	NF	NF	NF
Lebanon	IF	IF	IF	IF	IF	IF	IF	IF	IF	IF
Libya	IF	IF	IF	IF	IF	IF	IF	IF	IF	NF
Morocco	NF	NF	NF	NF	NF	NF	NF	NF	NF	NF
Oman	NF	NF	NF	NF	NF	NF	NF	NF	NF	NF
Saudi Arabia	NF	NF	NF	NF	NF	NF	NF	NF	NF	NF
Syria	NF	NF	NF	NF	NF	NF	NF	NF	NF	NF
Tunisia	NF	NF	NF	NF	NF	NF	NF	NF	NF	NF
Yemen, North	NF	NF	NF	NF	NF	NF	NF	NF	NF	NF
Yemen, South	—	—	—	—	—	—	—	NF	NF	NF

Near East 1970–1979

	1970	1971	1972	1973	1974	1975	1976	1977	1978	1979
Algeria	NF	NF	NF	NF	NF	NF	NF	NF	NF	NF
Bahrain	—	NF	NF	NF	NF	NF	NF	NF	NF	NF
Egypt	NF	NF	NF	NF	NF	NF	NF	NF	NF	NF
Iran	NF	NF	NF	NF	NF	NF	NF	NF	NF	NF
Iraq	NF	NF	NF	NF	NF	NF	NF	NF	NF	NF
Israel	F	F	F	F	F	F	F	F	F	F
Jordan	NF	NF	NF	NF	NF	NF	NF	NF	NF	NF
Kuwait	NF	NF	NF	NF	NF	NF	NF	NF	NF	NF
Lebanon	IF	IF	IF	IF	IF	IF	NF	NF	NF	NF
Libya	NF	NF	NF	NF	NF	NF	NF	NF	NF	NF
Morocco	NF	NF	NF	NF	NF	NF	NF	NF	NF	NF
Oman	NF	NF	NF	NF	NF	NF	NF	NF	NF	NF
Qatar	—	NF	NF	NF	NF	NF	NF	NF	NF	NF
Saudi Arabia	NF	NF	NF	NF	NF	NF	NF	NF	NF	NF
Syria	NF	NF	NF	NF	NF	NF	NF	NF	NF	NF
Tunisia	NF	NF	NF	NF	NF	NF	NF	NF	NF	NF
United Arab Emirates	—	NF	NF	NF	NF	NF	NF	NF	NF	NF
Yemen, North	NF	NF	NF	NF	NF	NF	NF	NF	NF	NF
Yemen, South	NF	NF	NF	NF	NF	NF	NF	NF	NF	NF

Near East 1980–1989

	1980	1981	1982	1983	1984	1985	1986	1987	1988	1989
Algeria	NF	NF	NF	NF	NF	NF	NF	NF	NF	NF
Bahrain	NF	NF	NF	NF	NF	NF	NF	NF	NF	NF
Egypt	NF	NF	NF	NF	NF	NF	NF	NF	NF	NF
Iran	NF	NF	NF	NF	NF	NF	NF	NF	NF	NF
Iraq	NF	NF	NF	NF	NF	NF	NF	NF	NF	NF
Israel	F	F	F	F	F	F	F	F	F	F
Jordan	NF	NF	NF	NF	NF	NF	NF	NF	NF	NF
Kuwait	NF	NF	NF	NF	NF	NF	NF	NF	NF	NF
Lebanon	NF	NF	NF	NF	NF	NF	NF	NF	NF	NF

	1980	1981	1982	1983	1984	1985	1986	1987	1988	1989
Libya	NF	NF	NF	NF	NF	NF	NF	NF	NF	NF
Morocco	NF	NF	NF	NF	NF	NF	NF	NF	NF	NF
Oman	NF	NF	NF	NF	NF	NF	NF	NF	NF	NF
Qatar	NF	NF	NF	NF	NF	NF	NF	NF	NF	NF
Saudi Arabia	NF	NF	NF	NF	NF	NF	NF	NF	NF	NF
Syria	NF	NF	NF	NF	NF	NF	NF	NF	NF	NF
Tunisia	NF	NF	NF	NF	NF	NF	NF	NF	NF	NF
United Arab Emirates	NF	NF	NF	NF	NF	NF	NF	NF	NF	NF
Yemen, North	NF	NF	NF	NF	NF	NF	NF	NF	NF	NF
Yemen, South	NF	NF	NF	NF	NF	NF	NF	NF	NF	NF

Near East 1990–2000

	1990	1991	1992	1993	1994	1995	1996	1997	1998	1999	2000
Algeria	NF	NF	NF	NF	NF	NF	NF	NF	NF	NF	NF
Bahrain	NF	NF	NF	NF	NF	NF	NF	NF	NF	NF	NF
Egypt	NF	NF	NF	NF	NF	NF	NF	NF	NF	NF	NF
Iran	NF	NF	NF	NF	NF	NF	NF	NF	NF	NF	NF
Iraq	NF	NF	NF	NF	NF	NF	NF	NF	NF	NF	NF
Israel	F	F	F	F	F	F	F	F	IF	IF	IF
Jordan	NF	NF	NF	NF	NF	NF	NF	NF	NF	NF	NF
Kuwait	NF	NF	NF	NF	NF	NF	NF	NF	NF	NF	NF
Lebanon	NF	NF	NF	NF	NF	NF	NF	NF	NF	IF	IF
Libya	NF	NF	NF	NF	NF	NF	NF	NF	NF	NF	NF
Morocco	NF	NF	NF	NF	NF	NF	NF	NF	NF	NF	NF
Oman	NF	NF	NF	NF	NF	NF	NF	NF	NF	NF	NF
Qatar	NF	NF	NF	NF	NF	NF	NF	IF	IF	IF	IF
Saudi Arabia	NF	NF	NF	NF	NF	NF	NF	NF	NF	NF	NF
Syria	NF	NF	NF	NF	NF	NF	NF	NF	NF	NF	NF
Tunisia	NF	NF	NF	NF	NF	NF	NF	NF	NF	NF	NF
United Arab Emirates	NF	NF	NF	NF	NF	NF	NF	NF	NF	NF	NF
Yemen (unified)	NF	NF	NF	NF	NF	NF	NF	NF	NF	NF	NF

Near East 2001–2012

	2001	2002	2003	2004	2005	2006	2007	2008	2009	2010	2011	2012
Algeria	NF	NF	NF	NF	NF	NF	NF	NF	NF	NF	NF	NF
Bahrain	NF	NF	NF	NF	NF	NF	NF	NF	NF	NF	NF	NF
Egypt	NF	NF	NF	NF	NF	NF	IF	IF	IF	NF	IF	NF
Iran	NF	NF	NF	NF	NF	NF	NF	NF	NF	NF	NF	NF
Iraq	NF	NF	NF	NF	NF	NF	NF	NF	NF	NF	NF	NF
Israel	IF	F	F	F	F	F	F	IF	F	F	F	IF
Jordan	NF	NF	NF	NF	NF	NF	NF	NF	NF	NF	NF	NF
Kuwait	NF	NF	NF	NF	NF	NF	NF	NF	NF	NF	NF	NF
Lebanon	NF	NF	NF	IF	IF	IF	IF	IF	IF	IF	IF	IF
Libya	NF	NF	NF	NF	NF	NF	NF	NF	NF	NF	IF	IF
Morocco	NF	IF	NF	NF	NF	NF	NF	NF	NF	NF	NF	NF
Oman	NF	NF	NF	NF	NF	NF	NF	NF	NF	NF	NF	NF
Qatar	IF	NF	NF	NF	NF	NF	NF	NF	NF	NF	NF	NF
Saudi Arabia	NF	NF	NF	NF	NF	NF	NF	NF	NF	NF	NF	NF
Syria	NF	NF	NF	NF	NF	NF	NF	NF	NF	NF	NF	NF
Tunisia	NF	NF	NF	NF	NF	NF	NF	NF	NF	NF	IF	IF
United Arab Emirates	NF	NF	NF	NF	NF	NF	NF	NF	NF	NF	NF	NF
Yemen	NF	NF	NF	NF	NF	NF	NF	NF	NF	NF	NF	NF

South and Central Asia

F=Free; IF=Imperfectly Free; NF=Not Free; NM=No Media

South and Central Asia 1948–1959

	1948	1949	1950	1951	1952	1953	1954	1955	1956	1957	1958	1959
Afghanistan	NF	NF	NF	NF	NF	NF	NF	NF	NF	NF	NF	NF
India	IF	IF	IF	IF	IF	IF	IF	IF	IF	IF	IF	IF
Nepal	NM	NM	NM	NM	NM	NM	NM	NM	NM	NM	NM	NM
Pakistan	NF	NF	NF	NF	NF	NF	NF	NF	NF	NF	NF	NF
Sri Lanka	NF	NF	NF	NF	NF	NF	NF	NF	NF	NF	NF	NF

South and Central Asia 1960-1969

	1960	1961	1962	1963	1964	1965	1966	1967	1968	1969
Afghanistan	NF	NF	NF	NF	NF	NF	NF	NF	NF	NF
India	IF	IF	IF	IF	IF	IF	IF	IF	IF	IF
Maldives	—	—	—	—	—	NF	NF	NF	NF	NF
Nepal	NF	NF	NF	NF	NF	NF	NF	NF	NF	NF
Pakistan	NF	NF	NF	NF	NF	NF	NF	NF	NF	NF
Sri Lanka	NF	NF	NF	NF	NF	NF	NF	NF	NF	NF

South and Central Asia 1970–1979

	1970	1971	1972	1973	1974	1975	1976	1977	1978	1979
Afghanistan	NF	NF	NF	NF	NF	NF	NF	NF	NF	NF
Bangladesh	—	—	NF	NF	NF	NF	NF	NF	NF	NF
Bhutan	—	NF	NF	NF	NF	NF	NF	NF	NF	NF
India	IF	IF	IF	IF	IF	NF	NF	NF	IF	IF
Maldives	NF	NF	NF	NF	NF	NF	NF	NF	NF	NF
Nepal	NF	NF	NF	NF	NF	NF	NF	NF	NF	NF
Pakistan	NF	NF	NF	NF	NF	NF	NF	NF	NF	NF
Sri Lanka	NF	NF	NF	NF	NF	NF	NF	NF	NF	NF

South and Central Asia 1980–1989

	1980	1981	1982	1983	1984	1985	1986	1987	1988	1989
Afghanistan	NF	NF	NF	NF	NF	NF	NF	NF	NF	NF
Bangladesh	NF	NF	NF	NF	NF	NF	NF	NF	NF	NF
Bhutan	NF	NF	NF	NF	NF	NF	NF	NF	NF	NF
India	IF	IF	IF	IF	IF	IF	IF	IF	IF	IF
Maldives	NF	NF	NF	NF	NF	NF	NF	NF	NF	NF
Nepal	IF	IF	IF	IF	IF	IF	IF	IF	IF	IF
Pakistan	NF	NF	NF	NF	NF	NF	NF	NF	NF	IF
Sri Lanka	NF	NF	NF	NF	NF	NF	NF	NF	NF	NF

South and Central Asia 1990–2000

	1990	1991	1992	1993	1994	1995	1996	1997	1998	1999	2000
Afghanistan	NF	NF	NF	NF	NF	NF	NF	NF	NF	NF	NF
Bangladesh	NF	NF	NF	NF	NF	NF	NF	NF	NF	NF	NF
Bhutan	NF	NF	NF	NF	NF	NF	NF	NF	NF	NF	NF
India	IF	IF	IF	IF	IF	IF	IF	IF	IF	IF	IF
Kazakhstan	—	NF	NF	NF	NF	NF	NF	NF	NF	NF	NF
Kyrgyzstan	—	IF	IF	IF	IF	NF	NF	NF	NF	NF	NF
Maldives	NF	NF	NF	NF	NF	NF	NF	NF	NF	NF	NF
Nepal	IF	IF	IF	NF	NF	NF	NF	NF	NF	NF	NF
Pakistan	IF	IF	IF	IF	IF	IF	NF	NF	NF	NF	IF
Sri Lanka	NF	IF	IF	IF	IF	NF	NF	NF	NF	NF	NF
Tajikistan	—	NF	NF	NF	NF	NF	NF	NF	NF	NF	NF
Turkmenistan	—	NF	NF	NF	NF	NF	NF	NF	NF	NF	NF
Uzbekistan	—	NF	NF	NF	NF	NF	NF	NF	NF	NF	NF

South and Central Asia 2001–2012

	2001	2002	2003	2004	2005	2006	2007	2008	2009	2010	2011	2012
Afghanistan	NF	NF	NF	NF	NF	NF	NF	NF	NF	NF	NF	NF
Bangladesh	NF	NF	NF	NF	NF	NF	NF	NF	IF	IF	IF	IF
Bhutan	NF	NF	NF	NF	NF	NF	NF	NF	IF	IF	IF	IF
India	IF	IF	IF	IF	IF	IF	IF	IF	IF	IF	IF	IF
Kazakhstan	NF	NF	NF	NF	NF	NF	NF	NF	NF	NF	NF	NF
Kyrgyzstan	NF	NF	NF	NF	NF	NF	NF	NF	NF	NF	NF	NF
Maldives	NF	NF	NF	NF	NF	NF	NF	IF	IF	IF	IF	IF
Nepal	NF	NF	NF	NF	NF	IF	IF	IF	IF	IF	IF	IF
Pakistan	IF	IF	IF	NF	NF	NF	NF	NF	NF	NF	NF	NF
Sri Lanka	NF	IF	IF	IF	IF	NF	NF	NF	NF	NF	NF	NF
Tajikistan	NF	NF	NF	NF	NF	NF	NF	NF	NF	NF	NF	NF
Turkmenistan	NF	NF	NF	NF	NF	NF	NF	NF	NF	NF	NF	NF
Uzbekistan	NF	NF	NF	NF	NF	NF	NF	NF	NF	NF	NF	NF

Appendix B

The Global Media Freedom Dataset: Data Gathering Methods, Guidelines for Using the Data, and Merging the Data with Freedom House Data

Where to Find the Data

The Global Media Freedom Data is available online at http://faculty.uml.edu/Jenifer_whitten-woodring.

Data Gathering Methods

As outlined in Chapter 2, the data were gathered using a multistage, multicoder sorting technique. At least two coders independently extracted raw data from historical documents, noted the significant detail in that data, and coded the country for every year of its inclusion in the database. In the majority of cases, the coders agreed on the code for a country-year, and neither noted any significant uncertainty in the code they assigned, which then completed the coding for that case. In the cases where the coders did not agree on the code or one of the coders indicated significant concerns about the code, the case was passed to a third coder who examined the evidence identified by each of the original coders. Most of the cases with discrepant coding were a result of one or sometimes both coders finding historical accounts that the other did not find, and simply combining the raw data resolved the discrepancy. A small number of cases involved conflicting information or other difficulties that required more extensive investigation by the third coder and sometimes a fourth. In those instances, the conclusions were vetted and discussed by a small group that included one or both of the principal investigators. In gathering the detailed historic information for this volume, we occasionally found the need to adjust our codes, but in most cases these changes were minor (usually between *free* and *imperfectly free*).

From 1948 to 2001, the media environments around the world are sorted into three basic categories.[1]

1—*Free*—countries where criticism of government and government officials is a common and normal part of the political dialogue in the mediated public sphere.

2—*Imperfectly Free*—countries where social, legal, or economic costs related to the criticism of government or government officials limits public criticism, but investigative journalism and criticism of major policy failings can and does occur.

3—*Not Free*—countries where it is not possible to safely criticize government or government officials.

In the dataset, additional codes are used for identifying states that for one reason or another cannot be effectively coded.

0—*No Media*—countries where there is no effective national media.

8—*Missing Data*—countries where political or social disruption makes it impossible to code for the year.

9—*Missing Data*—countries where media were known to exist, but there is insufficient historical material to effectively code the nature of the media environment.

999—*Missing Data*—countries that did not exist as independent political entities. Often occupied by foreign forces, annexed, or dissolved.

Guidelines for Using Data

Because both *free media* and *imperfectly free media* are able to function freely, the difference between these categories is much smaller than the difference between *imperfectly free media* and *not free media*. Simply put, *not free media* cannot function freely. Therefore, in studies where media freedom is an independent variable, where the effects of media freedom are what matters, we recommend using a dichotomous version of the variable where the categories of *free media* and *imperfectly free media* are collapsed into *functionally free media* versus *not free media*. In studies where media freedom is a dependent variable, where the causes of media freedom are what matters, we recommend using the trichotomous version of the variable (*free media, imperfectly free media*, and *not free media*) to explain these important variations. However, because the differences between these categories are not equal, it is important to use a model that accounts for this (ordered logistic regression or multinomial logistic regression are both possibilities).

Merging the Global Media Freedom Data With the Freedom House Data

We gathered data for all available countries from 1948 to 2001. We stopped at 2001, because this is the point where Freedom House adopted a far more detailed and transparent process of gathering its data for its Freedom of the Press reports. Freedom House's Freedom of the Press reports assign each country-year a code that theoretically ranges from 0 to 100, with 100 being the most restricted. Freedom House also categorizes each media environment as *Free* (for those with a score of 0 to 30), *Partly Free* (for those with a score of 31 to 60) or *Not Free* (for those with a

score of 61 to 100). While these categories for the most part correspond with our *Free, Imperfectly Free*, and *Not Free* categories, the borders between the Freedom House categories are less distinct than ours. In the Freedom House coding, the difference between countries with a score of 60 and 61 is slight, but with our dataset, the difference between countries that are *imperfectly free* and *not free* is the difference between being able to criticize the government and not being able to criticize the government. Consequently, in some cases the categories do not correspond, and this is usually the case where the Freedom House categories are closest to the scoring borders. In the country profiles in Chapter 4 and our updated dataset, we have used the Freedom House Freedom of the Press data as a guide, but have also relied on historic accounts and our own coding criteria. Thus, our dataset extends through 2012. For future updates, we advise using the Freedom House Freedom of the Press data and categorization as a guide but suggest careful consideration of countries that are on the borders. According to our coding guidelines, country-years in which the media are not free to criticize the government should be coded as *not free*, and country-years where the media are somewhat restricted but are for the most part able to criticize government should be coded as *imperfectly free*, and country-years where the media are clearly able to criticize government should be coded as *free*.

Note

1. In the original Van Belle definition and coding there was a fourth not free category for media that were completely controlled by government versus those that were indirectly controlled by government of a third party, but with the end of the cold war and the massive growth in information technology, distinguishing between state-operated news media and media that are controlled by other means has become something of a pointless exercise. Aside from North Korea, it is difficult to argue that any states have media run exclusively by the state as so many were during the cold war.

Index

media outlets, 357, 359
  Twenty Families, 357
Panday, Basdeo, 467
Panyarachun, Anand, 457
Papua New Guinea
  Internet access, 360
  media freedom, 360–361
  media outlets, 360, 361
  Vanuatu and, 495–496
Paraguay
  harassment of journalists, 363
  Internet access, 362
  media freedom, 362–363
  media outlets, 362, 363
Park Chunghee, 418
Parker, John, 512
Parma, Jimmy, 479
Patasse, Ange-Felix, 115
Patriotic Salvation Movement (MPS), Chad, 118
Pena Nieto, Enrique, 308
People's Republic of China. *See* China
Pérez, Carlos Andrés, 499
Pérez Jiménez, Marcos, 499
Perón, Juan Domingo, 52–53, 54
Peru
  corruption, 366
  deaths of journalists, 364, 365–366
  harassment of journalists, 365, 366
  Internet access, 364
  media freedom, 364–366
  media outlets, 364, 366
  Sendero Luminoso (Shining Path) movement, 365–366
Philippines
  corruption, 368, 369
  deaths of journalists, 369
  harassment of journalists, 369
  Internet access, 367
  libel laws, 369
  Marcos regime, 368–369
  media freedom, 367–369
  media outlets, 367
Picard, Robert G., 9
Pinochet Ugarte, Augusto, 119, 120
Pinto da Costa, Manuel, 389
Pol Pot, 106
Poland
  Internet access, 370
  media freedom, 26, 370–372
  media outlets, 370
  transition to democracy, 371
Polish-Lithuanian Commonwealth, 26
Polity IV Project, 37
Ponce Enríquez, Camilo, 161
Portugal
  colonies, 48
  corruption, 374

Internet access, 373
media freedom, 373–374
media outlets, 373
Postal services, 29
Poverty, 518
  See also Economic development levels
Prado, Manuel, 365
Preference falsification, 21, 24n13
La Prensa (Nicaragua), 339, 340
La Prensa (Panama), 359
Press freedom. *See* Media freedom
PRI. *See* Institutional Revolutionary Party
Print journalism
  cartoons, 4, 35, 151
  effects of online media, 519
  freedom, 2
  history, 2, 26, 27, 29–30
  See also Media; *and individual countries*
Prío Socarrás, Carlos, 142–143
Public ownership of broadcast media, 31, 34, 518
Public sphere role of media, 18, 20, 22
Public-service broadcasting, 31, 146, 337, 406, 441, 443–444
Puskas, Tivadar, 30
Pussy Riot, 381
Putin, Vladimir, 381

Qatar
  harassment of journalists, 376
  Internet access, 375
  media freedom, 375–376
  media outlets, 375–376
Quiroga Ramirez, Jorge, 85

Rabuka, Sitweni, 179, 517
Radio, technological development, 30–31
  See also Broadcast media; *and individual countries*
Radio France International, 133–134
Radio Free Europe, 150, 475
Radio Free Sarawak, Malaysia, 11
Radio Liberty, 73, 475
Radio Television Libre des Mille Collines (RTLM), 383, 384
Radio Television Seychelles, 398
Rahmon, Emomali, 451–452
Rajoelina, Andry, 286–287, 516
Ramkovski, Velija, 284
Ratsiraka, Didier, 286, 287
Ravalomanana, Marc, 286, 287, 516
Rawlings, Jerry, 196–197
Reagan, Ronald, 200
Red Pepper, 4
Rediffusion Ltd., 297
Regime types
  anocracies, 37
  autocracies, 37, 519

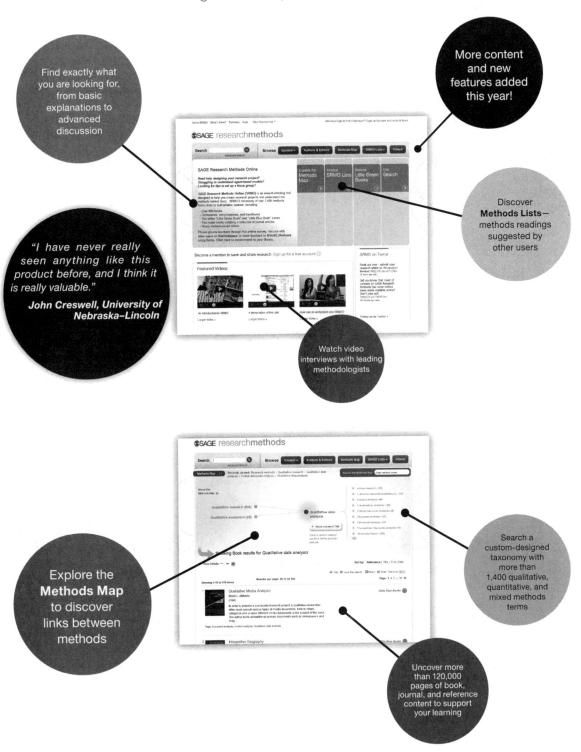